NINTH EDITION

Principles and Practices of Teaching Reading

Arthur W. Heilman

The Pennsylvania State University
Professor Emeritus

Timothy R. Blair

University of Central Florida

William H. Rupley

Texas A&M University

Merrill,
an imprint of Prentice Hall
Upper Saddle River, New Jersey   Columbus, Ohio

Library of Congress Cataloging-in-Publication Data

Heilman, Arthur W.
    Principles and practices of teaching reading / Arthur W. Heilman,
    Timothy R. Blair, William H. Rupley. —9th ed.
        p. cm.
    Includes bibliographical references and index.
        ISBN 0–13–267857–8 (alk. paper)
        1. Reading (Elementary)   I. Blair, Timothy R. II. Rupley,
    William H. III. Title.
    LB1573.H325   1998
    372.4—dc21   97–606
                                                    CIP

Cover photo: copyright David Young-Wolff/Photo Edit
Editor: Bradley J. Potthoff
Developmental Editor: Linda Scharp McElhiney
Production Editor: Alexandrina Benedicto Wolf
Photo Editor: Linda Gray
Design Coordinator: Julia Zonneveld Van Hook
Text Designer: John Edeen
Cover Designer: Brian Deep
Production Manager: Patricia A. Tonneman
Director of Marketing: Kevin Flanagan
Marketing Manager: Suzanne Stanton
Advertising/Marketing Coordinator: Julie Shough

This book was set in Meridien and Eras by The Clarinda Company and was printed and bound by R.R. Donnelley & Sons Company. The cover was printed by Phoenix Color Corp.

Photo credits: pp. 2, 21, 32, 58, 79, 146, 205, 238, 300, 372, 379, 410, 452, 461, 506, 513, 515, and 532 by Anthony Magnacca/Merrill; pp. 12, 67, 92, 99, and 362 by William H. Rupley; pp. 23, 38, 104, 114, 151, 282, 415, and 458 by Barbara Schwartz/Merrill; pp. 44, 49, 130, 149, 162, 219, 306, 388, 413, 422, 488, 501, and 453 by Anne Vega/Merrill; pp. 72, 248, 310, 498, and 526 by Scott Cunningham/Merrill; p. 202 by Linda Peterson/Merrill; p. 547 by KS Studios/Merrill; and p. 553 by Tom Watson/Merrill

Printed in the United States of America

10 9 8 7 6 5 4 3 2 1

ISBN: 0–13–267857–8

Prentice-Hall International (UK) Limited, *London*
Prentice-Hall of Australia Pty. Limited, *Sydney*
Prentice-Hall of Canada, Inc., *Toronto*
Prentice-Hall Hispanoamericana, S. A., *Mexico*
Prentice-Hall of India Private Limited, *New Delhi*
Prenctice-Hall of Japan, Inc., *Tokyo*
Simon & Schuster Asia Pte. Ltd., *Singapore*
Editora Prentice-Hall do Brasil, Ltda., *Rio de Janeiro*

To our wonderful wives, Jeanné and Agnes,

for their patience, continued understanding, and love

Preface

The ninth edition of *Principles and Practices of Teaching Reading* continues to emphasize the paramount importance of the classroom teacher and of providing a balanced literacy approach in today's elementary schools. The most sweeping changes coming from recent research are in the areas of effective teaching practices and of the reading comprehension process itself. Learning to read and reading to learn have never been of more importance in our society than today. In a recent State of the Union address, President Clinton highlighted the importance of learning to read and challenged all Americans to bind together to make sure that "every child can read independently and well by the end of third grade." As the President noted, "If a child can't read well by third grade, chances for later success are significantly diminished." The impetus for President Clinton's reading challenge was this statement from the office of Richard W. Wiley, U.S. Secretary of Education:

> Forty percent of all children are now reading below the basic level on national reading assessments. Children who cannot read early and read well are hampered at the very start of their education—and for the rest of their lives. This will be even more true as we move into the 21st century. To participate in America's high-skill workplaces, to cruise, much less use, the Internet, all children need to read better than ever before.

This edition of *Principles and Practices of Teaching Reading* reflects the importance of teaching children to read by presenting new topics and expanding other significant literacy topics for teachers-in-training. One of the hallmarks of this text is the continued presentation of multiple perspectives representing a comprehensive and balanced viewpoint in teaching children to become literate. As in previous editions, a variety of instructional activities for prospective teachers to examine and to use in their practicum and field experiences are also included. Throughout the text, practical examples, lesson plans, and classroom activities providing concrete ideas for instruction are presented.

■ New to This Edition

This edition includes three new sections in each chapter:

- ■ We recognize that many teacher education programs require their undergraduates to maintain a professional portfolio throughout their program. Two end-of-chapter sections have been added: **Field-Based Assignments** and **Portfolio Entries** focusing on the chapter content.

- Classroom teachers are often unfamiliar with particular strategies and techniques to use in teaching children with special needs to read. To address this problem, **Inclusion Strategies** have been added offering practical information, relevant to the chapter content, on modifying teaching strategies and presenting new strategies teachers can use when working with children with special needs in the regular classroom.

Major changes in this edition include:

- A major emphasis on a balanced literacy approach stressing the importance and necessity of combining research-based skills and strategies with fine literature;
- Complete coverage of the reading comprehension process, including the teaching of comprehension strategies;
- Expanded coverage of emergent literacy;
- Increased emphasis on the reading-writing connection in the language arts and content areas;
- A revised chapter on literature-based reading by Donna Norton, author of the classic textbook on children's literature, *Through the Eyes of a Child;*
- An updated chapter on teaching in a multicultural society;
- An updated appendix providing suggested games and activities for all reading skills and strategies;
- Updated flashback features, which provide a valuable historical perspective on teaching reading; and
- For the professors, a new Instructor's Manual that includes test questions, discussion questions, and blackline transparency masters.

■ Acknowledgments

We wish to thank our many students and fellow classroom teachers who have provided us with invaluable feedback on various parts of the book. We acknowledge the following for their insightful reviews: Susan J. Daniels, The University of Akron; Reta D. Hicks, Western Kentucky University; Peter Quinn, St. John's University; Mary S. Rogers, The University of Alabama; and William J. Valmont, University of Arizona.

The writing of this text has been a true team effort. We express our appreciation to the entire Merrill/Prentice Hall staff, especially Jeff Johnston, Brad Potthoff, Linda Scharp McElhiney, Alex Wolf, and copy editor Genevieve D'Arcy for their encouragement, expertise, and guidance throughout all the phases of the publishing process.

Brief Contents

PART **III**

Contents

PART **II**

Teaching Students to Become Strategic Readers   144

CHAPTER 5
Word Identification   146

PART

Principles and Practices of Teaching Reading

Aa Bb Cc Dd Ee Ff Gg Hh Ii Jj Kk Ll Mm N

Foundations of Literacy Instruction

Chapters

Overview

Children's growth and development in literacy depend on their having knowledgeable, caring, and thoughtful teachers; and helping students learn to read and write is an exciting, rewarding, and honorable responsibility. Thus, the first part of this text focuses on the overwhelming importance of the teacher in a successful literacy program, as well as specific characteristics of successful teachers, the nature of the reading process, guiding principles of a balanced literacy program, and language—the core from which effective literacy instruction emanates.

Integrating Principles of Teaching Reading

Individual principles of reading instruction, which will be presented in Chapter 1, will serve as fundamental guiding ideas throughout this text. The first four chapters will reinforce the following principles:

- Reading and writing are language processes.
- Reading and writing are interrelated and interactive processes, and literacy instruction should capitalize on this relationship.
- Instruction should lead children to understand that reading is a meaningful, active, and strategic process.
- The key to successful literacy instruction is the teacher.
- Teachers must recognize the enormous diversity among students, plan appropriate instruction for a wide range of individual differences in the classroom, and believe that all students can and will be successful in learning to read.

CHAPTER 1

Principles of
Reading Instruction

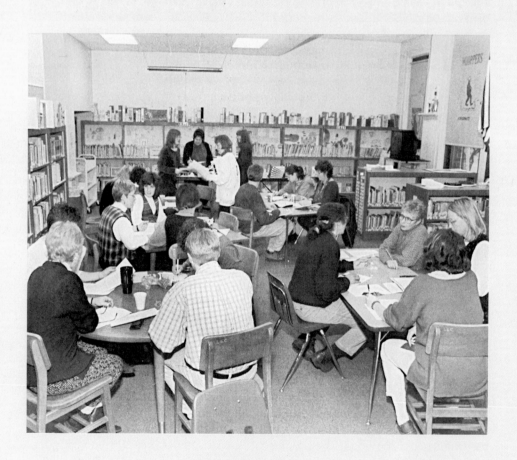

Chapter Outline

A Message to Teachers-in-training

The Reading Process

New Perspectives

What Constitutes a Balanced Literacy Program?

Principles of Reading Instruction

What Are the Stages of Reading Development?

For the Reader

As you prepare to become an effective teacher of reading, it is important that you understand your enormous influence on whether students will learn, the features of quality reading instruction, and the process of reading itself. Reading is a basic communication skill and a primary means of learning in our society. You most likely are a competent reader, one who gives little thought to how you read and how you get meaning from what you read.

Reading is a complex process. It depends on a variety of factors, such as the reader's experiential and conceptual background, word recognition strategies, reasoning ability, purpose for reading, environment, motivation, and text complexity. These features of reading influence our attempts to construct meaning from what we read. This chapter presents some basic aspects of the reading process and sets forth principles to help guide you at all grade levels of reading instruction.

Key Ideas

- Reading is interaction with language that has been coded into print.
- The result of reading is construction of meaning.
- Reading is a language process.
- Learning to read is a developmental process.
- Many methods can be used to teach reading effectively.
- Instruction must be tailored to the needs of each student.
- Teachers must strive for a balanced literacy program.

A Message to Teachers-in-Training

The ability to teach reading successfully has always been of paramount importance. This book is based on the premise that you will have a profound influence on how well your students learn to read. Teaching is a major challenge and a complex process. As you will learn throughout this text (especially in Chapter 2), research has helped us make tremendous advances in determining how effective reading teachers teach. As a teacher-in-training, you should be aware that how you promote **literacy,** the ability to read and write proficiently, in the classroom will have a profound effect on your students' lives. The ability to read—that uniquely human process that results from a multitude of factors—is truly a magical phenomenon. It can open the minds of children to new worlds, emotions, insights, and imaginative ideas; information of all types; and exciting, creative pursuits. It can also help them further their education and career opportunities and increase the quality of their lives through personal enjoyment. This is exactly why being a teacher of literacy is such a challenging, exciting, and rewarding experience.

Unfortunately, not all children experience the rewards and joys of literacy, and you will need to customize your instruction to suit students' varying strengths and weaknesses and to suit an intended instructional goal. If all reading instruction were the same for all students in each grade, teaching reading would be easy. One thing that makes teaching so rewarding and challenging, however, is the fact that children are different. They differ in a multitude of ways: in intelligence, background knowledge, language background, social awareness, thinking abilities, creativity, and interests, to name a few. Learning to read is a complex process that is affected by a host of factors, many of which are under your control and some of which are not. Your knowledge and expertise can help you make a difference in children's lives. You will have much influence in guiding children to develop their language abilities to the fullest; your involvement is both indispensable and a privilege. Historian Henry Adams articulated it best: "Teachers affect eternity; they never know where their influence will end."

The Reading Process

Do you sometimes "read" without thinking of or understanding some of the writer's message? We all have experiences in which we "read" material but are thinking of other things. You may still be able to "read" aloud from your high school French, Latin, or Spanish textbook, but can you understand or comprehend all of what you read? The true reading process is a dynamic one, requiring active, meaningful communication between the author and the reader. This text defines **reading** as the active process of constructing meaning from written text in relation to the experiences and knowledge of the reader.

The major goal of reading instruction is to foster in students the ability to interact with and to understand printed language. Reading is an internal, mental process that cannot be observed or studied directly. Many investigators relate reading to thinking and argue that the two are inseparable in understanding printed language. In a much-quoted study of reading comprehension, Thorndike (1917) defined *reading* as "thinking":

> The reading of a paragraph involves the same sort of organization and analysis as does thinking. It includes learning, reflection, judgment, analysis, synthesis, problem-solving behavior, selection, inference, organization, comparison of data, determination of relationships, and critical evaluation of what is read. It also includes attention, association, abstraction, generalization, comprehension, concentration, and deduction.

Reading once was thought to be a passive process: It was supposed to consist of a hierarchical list of word-identification and comprehension skills that, once mastered, would enable one to comprehend what one was reading. Instruction emphasized the identification and pronunciation of words, called **decoding** skills, because they were the most easily taught. Today, however, if teachers accept the idea that a major aspect of reading is comprehension, then they must put into proper perspective both major facets of reading: decoding words rapidly and accurately, and combining information from the text with existing knowledge to construct meaning. The following examples illustrate the importance of these two aspects as well as the basic features of reading; anyone who reads English will have no trouble with decoding or intonation:

> Some squares do not have four sides.

> Thomas Jefferson was a friend of tyranny.

Reading these sentences demands reader interaction, as does all written material. The reader must relate existing knowledge to the ideas that the text represents and use this knowledge to make sense of that text.

A person reading "Some squares do not have four sides" might react in any number of ways: "This is a misprint—it should say, 'All squares have four sides.' No, maybe that's not the kind of square that is meant; Reginald Philbut is a square, and he doesn't have four sides. No, that's not what it means. What is the author talking about? Well, no matter. I don't see how he can say that some squares do not have four sides. Maybe this is a trick statement. I had better read more to see if I can figure out what this statement means."

The last sentence illustrates how we use existing knowledge to make sense of what we read. The reader is using knowledge both about squares as geometric figures and about squares in a figurative sense (representing a conservative individual). In addition, the reader is employing a strategic approach by using such knowledge about text to realize that this may be a trick statement or that further reading may help explain the sentence. This reader is thus exercising the thinking abilities Thorndike described.

In the second example, a reader who knows little of Thomas Jefferson might reason, "Well, it's good to be apprised of this man's character. I'll be suspicious of everything he says or writes, particularly about government and people's rights." However, anyone who knows much about Jefferson might react by saying, "How ridiculous! Who is writing this stuff? Where was this book published? I had better

◀|||| F L A S H B A C K

One characteristic of American education is the commitment to the concept of universal education. Evidence of this commitment is seen in our compulsory school attendance laws. Massachusetts was the first state to enact a compulsory school attendance law in 1852. In the 1800s, only a small percentage of students completed high school.

From *Abraham Lincoln: The Boy, The Man* by Lloyd Ostendorf.
Springfield, IL: Hamann The Printer, Inc. 1962.

U P D A T E ||||▶

Today, 70 to 90% of students complete the 12th grade. Additionally, schools' populations are becoming increasingly culturally diverse. According to a recent report from the National Assessment of Educational Progress (NAEP) (1992), students are doing well in acquiring basic knowledge, but few students are learning to use this knowledge effectively in thinking and reasoning. Thus, teachers of reading today are being encouraged to promote comprehension of ideas requiring higher cognitive thinking. The authors of *Becoming a Nation of Readers* (Anderson, Hiebert, Scott, & Wilkinson, 1985) stated, "Discussions before reading and discussions and questioning after reading should motivate children's higher level thinking, with an emphasis on making connections with their prior knowledge of the topic" (p. 58).

These last sentences put the two essentials of reading—automatic decoding and comprehension—in proper perspective. Fluent reading demands rapid and accurate decoding of printed words, but mere decoding of words is not reading until it evokes the meaning or meanings that those words represent.

read more; this might be a misprint. Didn't Jefferson say, 'I have sworn eternal hostility to every form of tyranny over the mind of man'?"

New Perspectives

Just as the field of teacher effectiveness has seen advances, so too has our understanding of how children learn to read improved in the last two decades. This greater understanding of the reading process has emerged primarily from the field of cognitive psychology (Pearson & Stephens, 1994; Samuels & Kamil, 1984). While word identification is crucial, today's concept of the reading process stresses the process of meaning construction.

Two theoretical models, supported by an abundance of research, have helped shape our understanding of the reading process: the schema and interactive theories of reading. Harris and Hodges (1995) define schema theory as "a view that comprehension depends on integrating new knowledge with a network of prior knowledge (p. 227). **Schema theory** recognizes that reading involves many levels of analysis at the same time but at different levels. These levels include both text features (e.g., letters, word order, and word meaning) and the reader's background knowledge (e.g., content and hypotheses about meaning). A central component of this theory relates to the interrelated and interdependent relationship between text comprehension and the reader's background knowledge. Each student has schemata (plural of **schema**), which are background knowledge structures for various ideas, objects, or word meanings (see Chapter 6 for an illustrated discussion of schema theory). As students read, they use past experiences (schemata are activated) to interact with new information presented in the text. The integration of old information with new information results in improved or elaborated schemata (Tierney & Pearson, 1985). Thus, as readers process printed words, they construct meaning from them based both on the words and on background knowledge. This background knowledge, called **experiential and conceptual background,** is defined as a reader's experiences that are both concrete and abstract (knowledge), as well as the reader's reasoning abilities in using this knowledge. For example, in reading about how to grow vegetables, readers integrate knowledge about gardening and related experiences with new information. They process the text to formulate hypotheses that make sense in light of existing background knowledge.

Directly related to schema theory is the **interactive theory of reading,** which holds that reading is an active process in which, to comprehend text, students interact with a multitude of factors related to themselves, the text being read, and the context in which reading occurs. Figure 1.1 depicts the interactive nature of reading by grouping significant factors under the headings of Reader, Text, and Context. Central to the interactive theory (Rumelhart, 1985) is the reader's use of prior knowledge and various strategies to interact with text. In this sense, the reader is an active participant interacting with the text by applying specific strategies to construct meaning. The term *strategic reader* reflects the view that readers consciously apply strategies to enhance their understanding of ideas. (Chapters 2 and 7 discuss the schemata and interactive theories as well as specific comprehension strategies students can use to make sense out of what they are

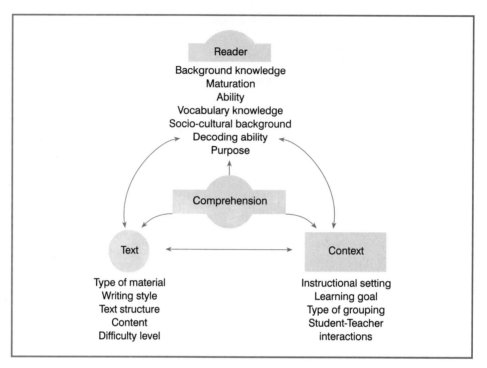

FIGURE 1.1
Interactive reading factors

reading.) Dole, Duffy, Roehler, and Pearson (1991) provide a concise summary of the latest thinking on the reading process:

> The cognitive views of reading present a different view of the reader. The traditional view assumes a passive reader who has mastered a large number of subskills and automatically and routinely applies them to all texts. The cognitive view assumes an active reader who constructs meaning through the integration of existing and new knowledge and the flexible use of strategies to foster, monitor, regulate, and maintain comprehension. The only thing that becomes automated in the newer view is the disposition to adopt strategies to the particular constraints in the act of comprehending a particular text. (p. 242)

What Constitutes a Balanced Literacy Program?

Before moving on to the stages of reading development, principles of teaching reading, and then specific reading approaches and strategies, it is helpful to have an overall view of a balanced literacy program in terms of its major content strands and major program areas. A **balanced literacy program** is one that uses a variety of teaching approaches, strategies, and materials to teach students what they need to know. Most literacy programs cover the following content strands: word recognition, word meaning, comprehension, reading study skills, in-

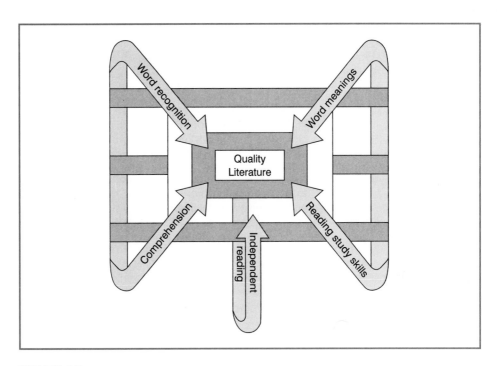

FIGURE 1.2
Major content strands of a balanced elementary school
literacy program

dependent or recreational reading, and literature. Each strand is fostered through instruction and an abundance of practice in meaningful text. The strands are analogous to braiding hair or weaving a basket, with each strand woven together in a continuum. The strands must be woven correctly to achieve the desired result. In most literacy programs today, such skills, strategies, and understandings are being developed increasingly through the reading of quality literature. (See Figure 1.2.)

It is also helpful to understand the major program areas of a complete, balanced literacy program. Regardless of grade level, the literacy curriculum includes experience in each of the following five program areas: developmental reading, application-transfer, independent or recreational reading, content reading, and functional reading.

Developmental reading involves sequential development of reading skills and strategies. Students also need interesting, varied practice with new material (application-transfer) if they are to master reading. In the recreational component, students apply their reading skills and strategies to a variety of literary forms to expand their interests and develop lifelong reading habits. The content reading component includes systematic instruction in reading study skills and comprehension strategies so that students are able to understand content material. Finally, the functional reading component includes experiences in which students apply their reading strategies in practical situations: For example, they receive instruction and practice in filling out job and loan applications, using telephone books, and reading magazines and newspapers. Figure 1.3 provides a view of the

COMPONENTS	PURPOSES	MATERIALS
Developmental reading	Systematic learning of word identification, word meanings, comprehension, content skills, and strategies. Development of proficient, strategic readers who comprehend written language.	Literature-based, basal-reader, language-experience, and content-area programs.
Application-transfer	Reading experiences designed to help students master skills and strategies taught in the main program component and to enhance the transfer of reading skills to other reading situations.	Various types of literature, high-interest/low-vocabulary readers, supplemental basal-reader programs, games, audiovisual aids, workbooks, teacher-made materials, newspapers, magazines, and content texts.
Recreational reading	Literary experiences to which students apply their reading abilities to expand their knowledge of a variety of subjects and become lifelong readers.	Various types of literature, paperback books, and book clubs.
Content reading	Specific learning of skills and strategies to use in content areas.	Various types of literature, encyclopedias, card catalogs, almanacs, atlases, maps, charts, graphs, tables, diagrams, and content texts.
Functional reading	Instruction in how to use reading to gain basic, practical information needed in everyday activities.	Telephone books, newspapers, catalogs, driver's manuals, job and loan applications, and magazines.

FIGURE 1.3
Program components of a balanced literacy program

major program areas of a balanced literacy curriculum, along with the purposes of each and materials used to implement their instructional goals.

Principles of Reading Instruction

Sound instructional principles tend to be learner oriented. They can be applied consistently to children who have noticeably different learning capacities, interests, and experiences. While learning to read is a complicated process, you already know many effective learning principles from your study of educational psychology. Learning to read depends on the same learning principles as do other cognitive skills, such as past experiential and conceptual backgrounds, purposes for learning, learner motivation, task difficulty, and instructional quality. You must integrate these principles with your specific knowledge of developing reading abilities.

Principles of teaching reading should evolve from the best knowledge available in general psychology, educational psychology, curriculum planning, studies in child growth and development, reading research, and from child guidance and psychological clinics. In formulating principles, it is necessary to consider all facets of human growth and development, including intellectual, physiological, psychological, and emotional aspects. As such, the principles discussed in this section can serve as guidelines for teacher behavior. You may question whether some of these principles are absolutely valid. Such questioning is healthy, especially if it stimulates the formulation of rational alternatives.

■ 1.   Reading and writing are language processes.

Teachers must understand the relationships between reading and writing and children's oral language. Children's oral language reflects their experiences with objects, ideas, relationships, and their interactions with their world. Much has been written about what children bring to school and the role of the school in building on each child's abilities. Teachers should help children transfer the language background that they bring to school directly to their reading and writing (Norton, 1993).

Recent studies have shown that experiences that promote success in reading occur long before a child begins formal schooling (Rudell & Rudell, 1994; Weiss & Hagen, 1988). For example, before starting school, many children can recognize letters of the alphabet, write their names, identify brand names, use books properly, and retell all or parts of favorite stories (Kontos, 1988). Many children also exhibit knowledge of written language and its purpose to communicate. They may scribble (write) letters and stories and read their compositions to others, make up spellings, and create letterlike forms (Martinez & Teale, 1987). In addition, children often demonstrate an understanding of stories and use stories to bring meaning to their play (Roskos, 1988). These behaviors indicate an understanding of language that can form the foundation for effective literacy instruction. Anderson et al. (1985) highlight the importance of oral language facility to the reading process:

> Reading instruction builds especially on oral language. If this foundation is weak, progress in reading will be slow and uncertain. Children must have at least a basic vocabulary, a reasonable range of knowledge about the world around them and the ability to talk about their knowledge. These abilities form the basis for comprehending text. (p. 30)

Unfortunately, teachers ignore many of the early signs of understanding language, and children's early experiences in literacy may mask the fact that they are engaged in a language process. Beginning reading and writing programs often ask children to focus on isolated parts of the literacy process.

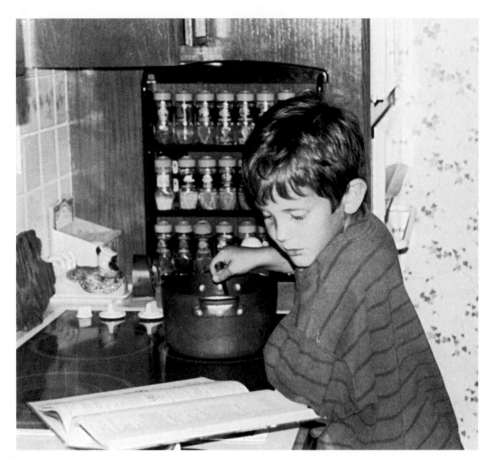

The meanings acquired from reading are closely
related to our experiential and conceptual
backgrounds.

Each child's learning background directly determines where and when to
begin reading instruction (see Chapter 4). Children who come to school from
homes full of rich literary experiences bring a wealth of language abilities and understandings with them (Lipson, 1988; Neuman & Roskos, 1993). They may already be reading with understanding and have strategies to help them identify
words. For such children, reading instruction should begin beyond basic decoding
instruction. Children who have had limited language and literacy experiences before entering school, however, should focus on the concepts that language serves
a communicative function and that print and oral language convey meaning (see
Chapter 13).

The relationship of oral language development is crucial to reading, as are the
other language processes. The language arts—listening, speaking, reading, and
writing—are the tools of communication. All of the language arts are interrelated;
growth in one reinforces and facilitates growth in the others. While it may be convenient to discuss the language arts separately, they are inextricably intertwined. A

primary method by which to promote all the language processes is through their integration in reading quality literacy selections (see principle 9).

Listening, the first language process to be developed, is the basis for oral language growth. Listening skills also are important in learning to read, especially in acquiring word-pronunciation or decoding skills and strategies. Likewise, the processes of reading and writing are interrelated and interdependent. The development of one enhances the other. While reading involves interacting with and making sense of written symbols, writing involves creating text that will communicate ideas to others. This relationship has been highlighted recently and given much emphasis in today's reading programs. To reflect its increased importance, principle 2 stresses this unique relationship.

Further evidence of the realization that reading cannot and should not be separated from the other language arts is the recent publication *Standards for the English Language Arts* (1996), a project of both the International Reading Association (IRA) and the National Council of Teachers of English (NCTE). This important document reflects a growing conception of literacy and presents standards defining what all students should know and be able to perform with respect to the language arts (see Figure 1.4). The goal and purpose of these standards, as set forth by the IRA/NCTE (1996), are as follows:

> [The] goal is to define, as clearly and specifically as possible, the current consensus among literacy teachers and researchers about what students should learn in the English language arts—reading, writing, listening, speaking, viewing, and visually representing. The ultimate purpose of these standards is to ensure that all students are offered the opportunities, the encouragement, and the vision to develop the language skills they need to pursue life's goals, including personal enrichment and participation as informed members of our society. (p. 1)

■ 2.   Literacy is a developmental process.

If teachers accept that reading and writing are the construction of meaning (comprehension), then there is no such thing as mastery of literacy ability; rather, it is a constantly evolving process. Individuals' experiential and conceptual backgrounds continue to grow. As one's background knowledge grows, so does one's ability to interact with text and acquire new information; therefore, literacy capabilities are constantly expanding. Reflecting the belief that reading is a developmental process whereby children move through various stages in an orderly and predictable manner, many authors have proposed that each child moves through various stages of reading development. While the stages are not entirely separate, they do provide teachers with an overall view of development and how their students' growth and their instruction fit into the big picture. Chall (1996) views reading development as a sequence of stages (see Figure 1.5). Stage 0 (preschool) focuses on learning to recognize and identify letters; Stage 1 (grade 1 and beginning of grade 2) emphasizes decoding or word-pronunciation abilities and comprehension of simple stories; Stage 2 (grades 2 and 3) centers on making decoding abilities automatic and increasing comprehension; and Stage 3 (grades 4–8) encourages comprehension in a variety of different texts, including content-area books and complex fiction.

**IRA/NCTE
STANDARDS FOR THE ENGLISH LANGUAGE ARTS**

The vision guiding these standards is that all students must have the opportunities and resources to develop the language skills they need to pursue life's goals and to participate fully as informed, productive members of society. These standards assume that literacy growth begins before children enter school as they experience and experiment with literacy activities—reading and writing, and associating spoken words with their graphic representations. Recognizing this fact, these standards encourage the development of curriculum and instruction that make productive use of the emerging literacy abilities that children bring to school. Furthermore, the standards provide ample room for the innovation and creativity essential to teaching and learning. They are not prescriptions for particular curriculum or instruction.

Although we present these standards as a list, we want to emphasize that they are not distinct and separable; they are, in fact, interrelated and should be considered as a whole.

1. Students read a wide range of print and nonprint texts to build an understanding of texts, of themselves, and of the cultures of the United States and the world; to acquire new information; to respond to the needs and demands of society and the workplace; and for personal fulfillment. Among these texts are fiction and nonfiction, classic and contemporary works.
2. Students read a wide range of literature from many periods in many genres to build an understanding of the many dimensions (e.g., philosophical, ethical, aesthetic) of human experience.
3. Students apply a wide range of strategies to comprehend, interpret, evaluate, and appreciate texts. They draw on their prior experience, their interactions with other readers and writers, their knowledge of word meaning and of other texts, their word

FIGURE 1.4
Standards for the English Language Arts
Source: From the International Reading Association and National Council of Teachers of English, 1996.

■ **3. Reading and writing are interrelated and interactive processes, and literacy instruction should capitalize on this relationship.**

Research (Greene, 1995) has highlighted the close relationship between reading and writing. Both are communicative processes that involve the interaction and understanding of ideas. Writing abilities improve with the development of various reading abilities, such as knowledge of how stories are constructed, the ability to use prior knowledge to create new meanings, decoding skills, and word meanings. Likewise, children's reading abilities benefit from those same skills used in identification strategies, and their understanding of textual features (e.g., sound-letter correspondence, sentence structure, context, graphics).

4. Students adjust their use of spoken, written, and visual language (e.g., conventions, style, vocabulary) to communicate effectively with a variety of audiences and for different purposes.

5. Students employ a wide range of strategies as they write and use different writing process elements appropriately to communicate with different audiences for a variety of purposes.

6. Students apply knowledge of language structure, language conventions (e.g., spelling and punctuation), media techniques, figurative language, and genre to create, critique, and discuss print and nonprint texts.

7. Students conduct research on issues and interests by generating ideas and questions, and by posing problems. They gather, evaluate, and synthesize data from a variety of sources (e.g., print and nonprint texts, artifacts, people) to communicate their discoveries in ways that suit their purpose and audience.

8. Students use a variety of technological and informational resources (e.g., libraries, databases, computer networks, video) to gather and synthesize information and to create and communicate knowledge.

9. Students develop an understanding of and respect for diversity in language use, patterns, and dialects across cultures, ethnic groups, geographic regions, and social roles.

10. Students whose first language is not English make use of their first language to develop competency in the English language arts and to develop understanding of content across the curriculum.

11. Students participate as knowledgeable, reflective, creative, and critical members of a variety of literacy communities.

12. Students use spoken, written, and visual language to accomplish their own purposes (e.g., for learning, enjoyment, persuasion, and the exchange of information).

the writing process, such as the abilities to revise one's thinking to delete or add important information, to predict and plan written ideas, and to summarize information.

■ **4.   Teachers must recognize the enormous diversity in students, plan appropriate instruction for the wide range of individual differences in the classroom, and believe that all students can and will be successful in literacy learning.**

In education, we have very few certainties, but one is that we are all different in a variety of ways. Capitalizing on those differences is what makes teaching so rewarding and satisfying—and at times so exasperating. With the increasing percentages of minority and exceptional children in school classrooms, we have seen a

1 STAGE DESIGNATION	2 GRADE RANGE (AGE)	3 MAJOR QUALITATIVE CHARACTERISTICS AND MASTERIES BY END OF STAGE	4 HOW ACQUIRED	5 RELATIONSHIP OF READING TO LISTENING
Stage 0: Prereading, "pseudo-reading"	Preschool (ages 6 months–6 years)	Child "pretends" to read, retells story when looking at pages of book previously read to him/her; names letters of alphabet; recognizes some signs; prints own name; plays with books, pencils, and paper.	Being read to by an adult (or older child) who responds to and warmly appreciates the child's interest in books and reading; being provided with books, paper, pencils, blocks, and letters.	Most can understand the children's picture books and stories read to them. They understand thousands of words they hear by age 6 but can read few if any of them.
Stage 1: Initial reading and decoding	Grade 1 & beginning grade 2 (ages 6 & 7)	Child learns relation between letters and sounds and between printed and spoken words; child is able to read simple text containing high-frequency words and phonically regular words; uses skill and insight to "sound out" new one-syllable words.	Direct instruction in letter-sound relations (phonics) and practice in their use. Reading of simple stories using words with phonic elements taught and words of high frequency. Being read to on a level above what child can read independently to develop more advanced language patterns, knowledge of new words, and ideas.	The level of difficulty of language read by the child is much below the language under-stood when heard. At the end of Stage 1, most children can understand up to 4,000 or more words when heard but can read only about 600.

FIGURE 1.5
Stages of reading development: An outline of the major qualitative characteristics and how they are acquired
Source: From Jeanne S. Chall, Stages of Reading Development, Second Edition (Fort Worth, TX: Harcourt Brace & Co., 1996) 85–86. Reprinted by permission.

1 STAGE DESIGNATION	2 GRADE RANGE (AGE)	3 MAJOR QUALITATIVE CHARACTERISTICS AND MASTERIES BY END OF STAGE	4 HOW ACQUIRED	5 RELATIONSHIP OF READING TO LISTENING
Stage 2: Confirmation and fluency	Grades 2 & 3 (ages 7 & 8)	Child reads simple, familiar stories and selections with increasing fluency. This is done by consolidating the basic decoding elements, sight vocabulary, and meaning context in the reading of familiar stories and selections.	Direct instruction in advanced decoding skills; wide reading (with instruction and independently) of familiar, interesting materials which help promote fluent reading. Being read to at levels above their own independent reading level to develop language, vocabulary, and concepts.	At the end of Stage 2, about 3,000 words can be read and understood and about 9,000 are known when heard. Listening is still more effective than reading.
Stage 3: Reading for learning the new Phase A Phase B	Grades 4–8 (ages 9–13) Intermediate, 4–6 Junior high school, 7–9	Reading is used to learn new ideas, to gain new knowledge, to experience new feelings, to learn new attitudes; generally from one viewpoint.	Reading and study of textbooks, reference works, trade books, newspapers, and magazines that contain new ideas and values, unfamiliar vocabulary and syntax; systematic study of words and reacting to the text through discussion, answering questions, writing, etc. Reading of increasingly more complex fiction, biography, nonfiction, and the like.	At beginning of Stage 3, listening comprehension of the same material is still more effective than reading comprehension. By the end of Stage 3, reading and listening are about equal; for those who read very well, reading may be more efficient.

greater emphasis on diversity (Olson & Platt, 1996). Today, more than ever before, our classrooms are multiracial, multicultural, and multiethnic. Many classrooms today each contain students representing more than a dozen languages and a great diversity of ethnic and racial backgrounds. Many students speak a dialect other than Standard English and many are learning English as a second language.

With the national movement in our schools toward inclusion and inclusive schooling, teachers also must provide for the needs of exceptional children in the regular classroom literacy program. Inclusion is predicated on the belief that all students, including those traditionally classified as mildly, moderately, and severely disabled, should be educated with their peers in neighborhood schools. Exceptional children often need different literacy instruction from that which is found in most classrooms (Sears, Carpenter, & Burnstein, 1994). Specialized services required to help these children meet their literacy needs are provided and coordinated in the classroom by the special education teacher and the regular classroom teacher. As a result of the inclusive movement, strategies for delivering instruction such as the consulting teacher model, collaborative consultation, computer instruction, and parents as teachers are among those now being recommended (David, 1991). To meet the needs of all students, literacy teachers need to recognize and appreciate student diversity, believe that all students can and will learn, and provide excellent, personalized instruction to all children (Allington, 1995).

■ 5. Instruction should lead children to understand that reading is a meaningful, active, and strategic process.

Reading is more than a mechanical process: It is a process of constructing meaning. Thus, beginning reading should go beyond mechanics with meaning inserted later in the learning continuum. The product of interacting with printed language should be comprehension. Reading involves **automaticity,** the ability to decode words with minimal effort, and a host of other text, reader, and contextual factors. Readers must be active; that is, they must use all available resources to construct meaning and make sense of the text. Reading involves the interaction of several factors, including textual factors, background knowledge, and the social setting in which reading occurs. In addition, the effective reader applies various reading strategies at the right time and in the right doses for understanding: The student becomes a strategic, or flexible, reader. Flexible readers choose from a variety of strategies to fulfill their purposes in comprehending text.

■ 6. Teachers must strive for a balanced literacy program to teach all students to read and write.

Because children are different in a multitude of ways, including the manner in which they become mature, strategic readers, teachers need to use a variety of approaches to successfully teach literacy. Speaking to this point, Spiegel (1994) states:

> Theorists and researchers may make pronouncements that a particular way is "the" way. But there is no one way to develop literacy, through a particular approach or through certain materials. And there never will be. The path through authors, texts, and contexts will vary for each reader. Therefore literacy teachers must strive to find the balance for each child. Fortunately many literacy educators understand this, and in spite of mandates from above or outside, modify the curriculum each day based on what their learners really need.

Effective teachers do not attempt to mold each child to a particular curriculum or approach. Students respond differently in a variety of areas, including responses to different types of instruction (direct and indirect); commercial and personalized, learner-centered programs; motivational strategies (intrinsic versus extrinsic); and instructional materials (published readers, literature books, computers, magazines, games, and so forth). Effective teachers teach children what they need to know by modifying and adjusting their curricula to meet their students' learning needs: "A balanced curriculum of the integrated language arts begins with an affirmation that different learners need different approaches to help them become proficient readers and writers" (Smith, 1996, p. 2) A balanced literacy approach that combines the best of all worlds is the most effective way to meet the needs of all the diverse learners in a classroom.

■ 7. Successful reading comprehension is dependent upon the provision of large amounts of classroom time for text reading and a multitude of opportunities for students to interact with their peers and teachers to talk about what they are reading.

Because reading is comprehending, an obvious and necessary ingredient for fostering students' comprehension abilities is the devotion of large amounts of classroom time to this end. Time must be allocated for text reading and effective instruction planned to develop active readers. In addition, students need to be encouraged to discuss what they have read with one another and with the teacher (Gambrell & Almasi, 1996; Fielding & Pearson, 1994), because reading comprehension is not only a cognitive process, but also a social one. Models of peer teaching and cooperative learning have proven to be effective in providing students with multiple ways to expand and refine their thinking through discussion (Meloth & Deering, 1994). Through peer and collaborative learning opportunities, students are provided the necessary means to process new ideas and to personally integrate new information. Palincsar and Brown (1984) believe that:

> understanding is more likely to occur when a child is required to explain, elaborate, or defend his position to others; the burden of explanation is often the push needed to make him or her evaluate, integrate, and elaborate knowledge in new ways. (p. 123)

■ 8. Teaching students to identify unknown words independently needs to be implemented through a balanced approach to decoding.

Developing independence in reading requires the acquisition of methods for identifying words, interaction with the text, and construction of meaning. It is essential that a balanced approach to reading be achieved using both a skill development program and a focus on fine literature. Whether using cues about analyzing spelling to help with pronunciation, looking at the structural parts of a word, or considering the context in which the word appears, one must develop facility in identifying (i.e., decoding) printed word forms. Fox (1996) speaks to the importance of providing a balanced instructional program in word identification, or decoding: "Overreliance on any one cue is inefficient, time-consuming and likely to result in poor comprehension. Good readers know this and hence balance syntactic context cues, semantic context cues, and code cues with the type of text they are reading, the reading environment, their own reasons for reading, and their own background knowledge" (p. 8). These cues are best taught and practiced in conjunction with sentences and/or whole texts, not in isolation. Students then learn to decode in the context of real reading, which involves the whole reading process. This principle is not in conflict with the principle that students must see reading as an active, meaning-making process. Research has shown the close relationship between decoding ability and total reading performance (Fox, 1996; Anderson et al., 1985). Once students can decode words at an automatic level, they can spend more time and energy on comprehension.

A recent trend in the literacy field is the acknowledgement of the importance of both teaching students to readily understand and apply sound-symbol relationships and using quality literary material as the main vehicle to teach students to read. Akamatsu (1995) advocates an integrated viewpoint regarding phonics and whole-language instruction: "The emphasis in phonics instruction has been shifted towards mastery of the reading skills which are relevant and meaningful to actual reading" (p. 13). In our experience, good teachers of literacy have always worked to strike a balance among and take the best of all theoretical stances in teaching their students what they need to know. This certainly applies to combining phonics instruction and the use of fine literature. The ability to pronounce and interpret written symbols is an integral component of the reading process; however, identifying words is not in itself reading but rather a means for developing reading efficiency. Achieving a balance of both phonics and holistic perspectives in teaching reading provides students with an integrated instructional program based on individual differences.

■ **9. The use of quality literature should be an integral part of literacy instruction throughout the entire school curriculum.**

The time has passed when literature was thought to be an add-on or separate entity reserved only for the recreational or independent reading program. Quality literature of all types should be an integral part of the daily language arts program and should be fused into content subjects (Langer, 1995; Buchoff, 1995). Entire works of quality literature or authentic texts can be the main vehicle for learning the language processes and achieving various instructional goals; learning basic vocabulary and how to decode knowledge; developing comprehension strategies, content reading skills and strategies, and inferential and critical-thinking abilities; and promoting a joy of reading.

**The effective literacy program integrates
the entire curriculum across all content areas
around reading, writing, listening,
and speaking activities.**

■ 10. Literacy instruction needs to be an integral component in all content areas.

Successful learning in content areas depends on students' application of reading study skills, comprehension strategies, and writing ability. A literacy program is not complete without adequate attention to content areas, and success in the regular literacy program does not automatically guarantee success in the content areas (Alvermann & Phelps, 1994). Many students experience difficulties in these areas that are further compounded when they are not taught to become independent learners. If we truly believe in the educational principle of independent learning, we must devote more time to teaching the skills and strategies needed in the content areas. For students to be independent learners, we must teach them how to pursue the ever-increasing amount of knowledge in nearly all fields. In other words, they must learn how to learn.

■ **11. Teachers need to foster students' abilities to reason and critically evaluate written ideas.**

Learning decoding and basic comprehension are important but not sufficient in today's world. Children also must understand how to interact with ideas beyond a basic level. Successful readers and writers can synthesize, analyze, and critically evaluate ideas to increase their knowledge (Gambrell & Almasi, 1996); however, critical thinking does not develop by chance. Teachers can use quality literature in a variety of ways as well as effective instructional strategies (e.g., using cooperative groups) to help children apply literacy skills to fulfill their own goals.

■ **12. Proper literacy instruction depends on the ongoing assessment of each student's reading strengths and weaknesses.**

The teacher's ability to assess students' needs lies at the heart of effective instruction. Effective reading teachers make instructional decisions based on assessment information. **Assessment** is defined as "the procedures used by teachers to identify students' strengths and weaknesses in planning and executing instruction to meet the students' needs." A key to correctly assessing students' progress in reading is to obtain information from multiple sources, both formal and informal. Kleitzien (1996) reported on the characteristics of nationally recognized elementary schools in the U.S. Department of Education's Blue Ribbon Schools recognition program. The schools that have been recognized utilize a variety of assessment tools ranging from teacher-made tests to basal program assessments to anecdotal records to portfolios to standardized tests. Teachers should ensure that the assessment process permeates all aspects of instruction, from making initial placement decisions to adjusting daily instruction based upon yesterday's lesson.

■ **13. Motivation contributes to the development of literacy and is fostered through meaningful instructional activities.**

Motivation is an important feature of both acquiring literacy and associating value with literacy (Gambrel, Palmer, Codling, & Mazzoni, 1996). Students who read and write both for school and for enjoyment become better readers and writers because the more students read and write, the better readers and writers they become. Classroom teachers have a direct influence on promoting motivation through their selection and implementation of instructional activities based on student need (Benton, Belk, & Holifield, 1994). Teachers who use strategies that promote high levels of student engagement and provide a wide range of meaningful literacy activities encourage the development of positive attitudes toward literacy. In sharing motivational strategies utilized by expert literacy teachers, Turner and Paris (1995) emphasize that classroom activities directly affect student motivation. They found that teachers who promote children's motivation for literacy do so "by molding literacy instruction to the needs, interests, and skills of their students" (p. 672).

■ 14.   Teachers must be able to create, manage, and maintain an environment conducive to learning.

Teaching children what they need to know while advancing their literacy abilities is a tall order. While classroom management is less important with a small group of students, you most likely will be responsible for a class of 20 to 30 students. Moreover, many school systems now organize the early grades into primary blocks, which group students from different age and grade levels. Studies on teaching reading have clearly shown that effective teachers are proficient in classroom organization and management (Emmer & Evertson, 1980). Proper planning, managing of group instruction, and monitoring of student progress can help teachers deal with a broad range of student abilities.

■ 15.   Teachers of literacy must forge partnerships with the home and community to promote reading growth.

Without a doubt, teachers alone cannot do a complete job of educating students. Teachers must have a cooperative relationship with parents and the community as a whole to have a successful literacy program. The role of school libraries can play a significant role in involving parents and students in literacy activities after regular school hours (Alvermann, DeGroff, Green, & Young, 1996). Parents—children's first teachers—are in a unique position to provide meaningful literacy experiences for their children (Edwards, 1991; Handel, 1992). In *Becoming a Nation of Readers* (Anderson et al., 1985), the National Institute of Education's Commission on Reading recommended two ways that parents can help their children:

- Parents should read to preschool children and informally teach them about reading and writing. Reading to children, discussing stories and experiences with them, and—with a light touch—helping them learn letters and words are practices that are consistently associated with eventual success in reading.
- Parents should support school-aged children's continued growth as readers. Parents of children who become successful readers monitor their children's progress in school, become involved in school programs, support homework, buy their children books or take them to libraries, encourage reading as a free-time activity, and place reasonable limits on such activities as TV viewing. (p. 117)

Parents can contribute a great deal to every stage of reading development. As teachers, we need to communicate with parents what we know about reading development, how we teach reading, and, specifically, how parents can help (Silvern & Silvern, 1990).

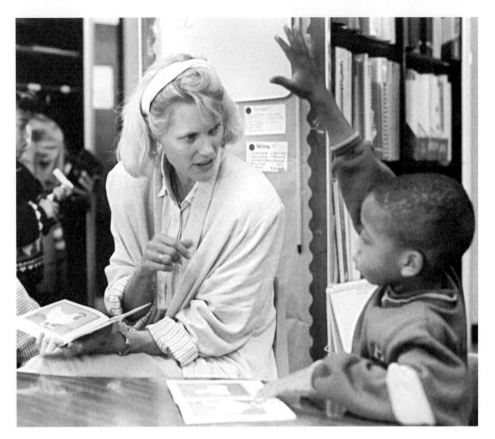

**The key to successful literacy instruction
is the teacher.**

■ 16. The key to successful literacy instruction
is the teacher.

Successful instruction and learning do not happen by accident. Observation of effective teachers and examination of current research make it clear that the classroom teacher has a tremendous influence on whether children are successful in learning to read. Results of research do not indicate that any particular literacy method or material is best for all children; rather, the teacher is one of the major variables that determine the effectiveness of reading instruction (Rupley & Blair, 1989; Rupley, Wise, & Logan, 1986). Numerous investigations have identified the instructional practices of effective reading teachers: ongoing assessment of students' literacy development, structure and direction of students' learning, provision of opportunities to practice and apply skills in meaningful contexts, and maintenance of a high level of student involvement in learning (Rupley & Blair, 1988).

Figure 1.6 summarizes the 16 principles of reading instruction.

1. Reading and writing are language processes.
2. Literacy is a developmental process.
3. Reading and writing are interrelated and interactive processes, and literacy instruction should capitalize on this relationship.
4. Teachers must recognize the enormous diversity in students, plan appropriate instruction for a wide range of individual differences in the classroom, and believe that all students can and will be successful in literacy learning.
5. Instruction should lead children to understand that reading is a meaningful, active, and strategic process.
6. Teachers must strive for a balanced literacy program to teach all students to read and write.
7. Successful reading comprehension is dependent upon the provision of large amounts of classroom time for text reading and a multitude of opportunities for students to interact with their peers and teachers to talk about what they are reading.
8. Teaching students to identify unknown words independently needs to be implemented through a balanced approach to decoding.
9. The use of quality literature should be an integral part of literacy instruction throughout the entire school curriculum.
10. Literacy instruction needs to be an integral component in all content areas.
11. Teachers need to foster students' abilities to reason and critically evaluate written ideas.
12. Proper literacy instruction depends on the ongoing assessment of each student's reading strengths and weaknesses.
13. Motivation contributes to the development of literacy and is fostered through meaningful instructional activities.
14. Teachers must be able to create, manage, and maintain an environment conducive to learning.
15. Teachers of literacy must forge partnerships with the home and community to promote reading growth.
16. The key to successful literacy instruction is the teacher.

FIGURE 1.6
Principles of reading instruction

What Are the Stages of Reading Development?

It is often said that reading programs never rise above the quality of instruction found within them. Teachers must understand students as learners and must view learning to read as a developmental process. Several reading authorities have offered considerable support for the developmental view of reading. Important reading behaviors identified by Clay (1979), Stanovich (1986), and Chall (1996) focus on well-developed decoding strategies and understanding of meaning.

Jeanne Chall's comprehensive reading development stages from preschool through grade 8 were discussed earlier in this chapter, in relation to the principle that literacy is a developmental process. Her proposed reading stages (shown in Figure 1.5) illustrate the major qualitative reading abilities, as well as the relationship of reading to listening comprehension. It is important to understand that these stages may overlap and are not fixed. That is, a first grader could be in Stage 3 and a sixth grader could be in Stage 1. The characteristics associated with each stage should be viewed as representative. They should serve as guidelines for understanding the curriculum and planning quality reading instruction.

☑ Summary

The ability to read is a uniquely human process that can open new worlds to children. Teaching students to read is an exciting, rewarding, and honorable responsibility. Effective teachers of reading are knowledgeable, skillful, exciting, and caring. This first chapter discussed the reading process, an overview of the reading curriculum, principles of teaching reading, and stages of reading development.

Reading is defined as "an active process of constructing meaning from written text in relation to the reader's experiences and knowledge." Reading is a complex process; our knowledge of it recently has been reshaped primarily by research on schema theory and by viewing reading as an interactive process. We now know that reading is an active, dynamic, and strategic process whereby readers use cues from themselves, the text, and the context in which the reading occurs to construct meaning.

An overview of a balanced literacy curriculum was presented. The major content strands of the elementary school curriculum for all grade levels—word recognition, word meaning, comprehension, reading study skills, independent or recreational reading, and literature—were covered. A balanced literacy program includes the program areas of developmental reading, application-transfer, independent or recreational reading, content reading, and functional reading.

To synthesize understanding of major concepts and provide a foundation for the rest of the text, principles for teaching reading were presented with brief explanations of each. Key elements of the principles include the importance of the teacher to student learning and the integration of reading development with the other language arts using quality literature. Finally, Chall's stages of reading development were presented with the qualitative characteristics of preschool through eighth grade.

☑ Your Point of View

Discussion Questions

1. In your opinion, which of the principles of teaching reading are the most important for improving the quality of reading instruction? Provide a rationale for your choices.

2. Refer to Chall's stages of reading development (Figure 1.5) and reread the category "How Acquired" for each stage. What features would a reading instructional program need in order to develop the reading abilities associated with each stage?

Take a Stand For or Against

1. A teacher's definition or concept of reading will, in the final analysis, have little impact on practices used in teaching students to read.
2. A child's problems in learning to read can usually be attributed to one factor.

Field-Based Assignments

1. In the classroom you are visiting, ask the teacher if you can shadow or work individually for a day with a child who is experiencing extreme difficulties in reading. Keep in mind that it is extremely beneficial to acquire sensitivity to a frustrated reader at any grade level. Be as helpful as you can with the student and informally ask some of the following questions:

> What are your favorite subjects in school?
>
> Do you like to read?
>
> How can I help you become a better reader? In what areas do you feel you need help?
>
> What kind of stories do you like to read?
>
> Do you have time to read at home? Do you read at home?

As you reflect on your time working with this student, ask yourself the following questions and share your perceptions with your peers:

> How did you feel about helping a problem reader?
>
> Did the student appear confident in completing activities during the day?
>
> What could you do to help this youngster improve?
>
> What sensitivities should a classroom teacher possess to meet the needs of children who are experiencing difficulties in reading?

2. Meeting the needs of children with a wide range of individual differences demands the very best from reading teachers. For instance, in a first-grade class, the teacher can expect the range of reading ability to span from readiness to the third- or fourth-grade level. In the third grade, the span can include first-through sixth-grade reading levels, and in the sixth grade, it can include second-grade through high school ability levels. Added to this factor, the many differences in the areas of emotional and social maturity, psychological well-being, personal interests, preferred learning styles, and language facility make teaching a tremendous challenge. Ask as many classroom teachers as you can the following question: "How do you handle the many differences among your

students in the teaching of reading?" Take notes and categorize your responses in the areas of teaching methods, grouping plans, and instructional materials. Compare your findings with those of your peers and create a master list of ways for teaching to meet individual needs. Remember, teachers of reading must realize that capitalizing on differences is an indispensable aspect of their profession. How successful one is in differentiating instruction will be seen in how much children progress in their reading and writing.

Accommodating student differences

Teaching Methods	Grouping Plans	Instructional Materials
_____	_____	_____
_____	_____	_____
_____	_____	_____
_____	_____	_____

Portfolio Entry

Because attitude guides practice, one of the first steps in becoming an effective reading teacher is to examine your own attitudes about reading. Taking into account what was discussed in this first chapter and your own reading habits, write a one-page entry entitled "Energetic reading." Include in your discussion answers to the following questions:

What do you think it means to be an energetic reader?

Are you an energetic reader?

What books have you read in the past two months?

Who are your favorite authors?

What magazines do you regularly read?

What do you think teachers can do to promote this quality of energetic reading?

What are some factors that can thwart the development of this desirable trait?

Bibliography

Akamatsu, N. (1995). A view of integrating phonics and whole language instruction. *Balanced Reading Instruction, Vol. II, 1,* 7–15.

Allington, R. L. (1995). Literacy lessons in the elementary schools: Yesterday, today, and tomorrow. In R. L. Allington & S. A. Walmsley (Eds.), *No quick fix: Rethinking literacy programs in America's schools* (pp. 1–15). New York: Teachers College Press and Newark, DE: International Reading Association.

Alvermann, D., DeGroff, L., Green, C., & Young, J. (1996). A dialogue about libraries and parents. *NRRC News: A Newsletter of the National Reading Research Center.* Athens, GA: NRRC, University of Georgia.

Alvermann, D. E., & Phelps, S. F. (1994). *Content reading and literacy: Succeeding in today's diverse classrooms.* Boston: Allyn & Bacon.

Anderson, P. C., Hiebert, E. H., Scott, J. A., & Wilkinson, I. A. G. (1985). *Becoming a nation of readers: The report of the Commission on Reading.* Washington, DC: The National Institute of Education.

Benton, G., Belk, J., & Holifield, S. (1994). Increased student motivation through paired reading. *Balanced Reading Instruction, 1,* 16–20.

Buchoff, R. (1995). Family stories. *The Reading Teacher, 49,* 230–233.

Chall, J. S. (1996). *Stages of reading development* (4th ed.). Fort Worth, TX: Harcourt Brace.

Clay, M. M. (1979). *The patterning of complex behavior.* Auckland, New Zealand: Heinemann Educational Books.

David, J. L. (1991). Synthesis of research on school-based management. *Educational Leadership, 46*(8), 45–53.

Dole, J. A., Duffy, G. G., Roehler, L. R., & Pearson, P. D. (1991). Moving from the old to the new: Research on reading comprehension instruction. *Review of Educational Research, 61*(2), 238–264.

Edwards, P. A. (1991). Fostering early literacy through parent coaching. In E. H. Hiebert (Ed.), *Literacy for a diverse society* (pp. 199–214). New York: Teachers College Press.

Emmer, E. T., & Evertson, C. M. (1980). Synthesis of research on classroom management. *Educational Leadership, 38,* 342–347.

Fielding, L. G., & Pearson, P. D. (1994). Reading comprehension: What works. *Educational Leadership, 5,* 62–67.

Fox, B. J. (1996). *Strategies for word identification.* Upper Saddle River, NJ: Prentice Hall.

Gambrell, L. B., & Almasi, J. F. (1996). *Fostering engaged reading.* Newark, DE: International Reading Association.

Gambrell, L. B., Palmer, B. M., Codling, R. M., & Mazzoni, S. A. (1996). Assessing motivation to read. *The Reading Teacher, 49,* 518–533.

Greene, B. G. (1995). Exploring the reading-writing relationship. *Reading Psychology, 16,* 261–268.

Handel, R. D. (1992). The partnership for family reading: Benefits for families and schools. *The Reading Teacher, 46,* 116–126.

Harris, T. L., & Hodges, R. E. (Eds.), (1995). *The literacy dictionary.* Newark, DE: International Reading Association.

Kleitzien, S. B. (1996). Reading programs in nationally recognized elementary schools. *Reading Research and Instruction, 35,* 260–274.

Kontos, S. (1988). Development and interrelationships of reading knowledge and skills during kindergarten and first grade. *Reading Research and Instruction, 2,* 14–28.

Langer, J. A. (1995). *Envisioning literature: Literary understanding and literature instruction.* New York: Teachers College Press and Newark, DE: International Reading Association.

Lipson, E. R. (1988). *The* New York Times *parents' guide to the best books for children.* New York: Times Books.

Martinez, M., & Teale, W. H. (1987). The ins and outs of kindergarten writing programs. *The Reading Teacher, 4,* 444–451.

Meloth, M. S., & Deering, P. D. (1994). Task talk and task awareness under different cooperative learning conditions. *American Educational Research Journal, 31,* 138–165.

National Assessment of Educational Progress. (1992). *Executive summary of the NAEP 1992 Reading Report Card for the Nation and the States* (ISBN 01-16-041942-5). Washington DC: U. S. Government Printing Office.

Neuman, S. B., & Roskos, K. (1993). *Language and literacy learning in the early years: An integrated approach.* Orlando: Harcourt Brace Jovanovich.

Norton, D. E. (1993). *The effective teaching of language arts* (4th ed.). Upper Saddle River, NJ: Merrill/Prentice Hall.

Olson, J. L., & Platt, J. M. (1996). *Teaching children and adolescents with special needs* (2nd ed.). Upper Saddle River, NJ: Prentice Hall.

Palincsar, A. S., & Brown, A. L. (1984). Reciprocal teaching of comprehension-fostering and comprehension-monitoring activities. *Cognition and Instruction, 1,* 117–175.

Pearson, P. D., & Stephens, D. (1994). Learning about literacy: A 30-year journey. In R. B. Rudell, M. R. Rudell, & H. Singer (Eds.), *Theoretical models and processes of reading* (4th ed., pp. 22–42). Newark, DE: International Reading Association.

Roskos, K. (1988). Literacy at work in play. *The Reading Teacher, 6,* 562–567.

Rudell, R. B., & Rudell, M. R. (1994). Language acquisition and literacy processes. In R. B. Rudell, M. R. Rudell, & H. Singer (Eds.), *Theoretical models and processes of reading* (4th ed., pp. 83–103). Newark, DE: International Reading Association.

Rumelhart, D. E. (1985). Toward an interactive model of reading. In R. B. Ruddell & H. Singer (Eds.), *Theoretical models and processes of reading.* Newark, DE: International Reading Association.

Rupley, W. H., & Blair, T. R. (1989). *Reading diagnosis and remediation: Classroom and clinic* (3rd ed.). Upper Saddle River, NJ: Merrill/Prentice Hall.

Rupley, W. H., & Blair, T. R. (1988). *Teaching reading: Diagnosis, direct instruction, and practice* (2nd ed.). Upper Saddle River, NJ: Merrill/Prentice Hall.

Rupley, W. H., Wise, B. S., & Logan, J. W. (1986). *Research in effective teaching: An overview of its development.* In J. V. Hoffman (Ed.), *Effective teaching of reading: Research and practice.* Newark, DE: International Reading Association.

Samuels, S. J., & Kamil, M. L. (1984). Models of the reading process. In P. D. Pearson (Ed.), *Handbook of reading research.* New York: Longman.

Sears, S., Carpenter, C., & Burnstein, N. (1994). Meaningful reading instruction for learners with special needs. *The Reading Teacher, 8,* 632–637.

Silvern, S. B., & Silvern, L. R. (1990). *Beginning literacy and your child.* Newark, DE: International Reading Association.

Smith, C. B. (1996). How to get information from your child's school. *The ERIC Parent Reader.* Bloomington, IN: ERIC/Family Literacy Center, Indiana University.

Spiegel, D. L. (1994). Finding the balance in literacy development for all children. *Balanced Reading Instruction, 1,* 6–11.

Standards for the English language arts. (1996). Urbana IL: National Council of Teachers of English and Newark, DE: International Reading Association.

Stanovich, K. E. (1986). Matthew effects in reading: Some consequences of individual differences in the acquisition of literacy. *Reading Research Quarterly, 21,* 360–406.

Thorndike, E. L. (1917). Reading as reasoning: A study of mistakes in paragraph reading. *Journal of Educational Research, 8,* 323–332.

Tierney, R., & Pearson, P. P. (1985). Learning to learn from text: A framework for improving classroom practice. In R. B. Ruddell & H. Singer (Eds.), *Theoretical models and processes of reading.* Newark, DE: International Reading Association.

Turner, J. C., & Paris, S. G. (1995). How literacy tasks influence children's motivation for literacy. *The Reading Teacher, 48,* 662–675.

Weiss, M. J., & Hagen, R. (1988). A key to literacy: Kindergartners' awareness of the functions of print. *The Reading Teacher, 6,* 574–579.

CHAPTER 2

Teacher Effectiveness in the Literacy Program

Chapter Outline

For the Reader

Teachers' tremendous influence upon learning has been documented and emphasized for years. Specific instructional behaviors that have the greatest impact on learning have not been at issue until relatively recently, however. General qualities, such as mental health and enthusiasm, are certainly important, but what specifically sets apart effective teachers of literacy from those who are less effective?

If you have had experience teaching, you realize the tremendous responsibilities that teachers have in the classroom. If you are preparing to become a teacher, the realities and complexities of working with 25 to 35 students in a teaching situation may (justifiably) seem overwhelming. Every day, teachers are responsible for covering certain material, ensuring learning, minimizing discipline problems, and maintaining a pleasant atmosphere for learning. You may ask, "What exactly does an effective teacher of literacy do?"

"Where should I place my efforts so that the classroom experience is rewarding and profitable for both me and my students?"

The overall objective of this text is to provide you with the essential knowledge, concepts, and skills of an effective teacher of literacy. This chapter synthesizes teacher characteristics that make a difference in teaching.

Key Ideas

- Studies of teacher effectiveness have pointed out a number of characteristics related to student learning of basic reading skills.
- The six areas of importance to competent reading instruction are (1) assessment, (2) interactive instruction, (3) opportunity to learn, (4) student attention to learning tasks, (5) teacher expectations, and (6) classroom management.
- A pattern of teaching practices is more likely to promote learning than is a single practice.
- The most pervasive conclusion of school and teacher effectiveness studies in the 1970s and 1980s was that teachers profoundly influence how much students learn.
- Guidelines for effective literacy instruction must be applied differently in each classroom and depend upon a host of variables, including students' needs, material content, grade level, and learning objectives.
- Teaching is a decision-making process, and the judgements teachers make are the keys to the success or failure of literacy programs.
- Effective teachers of literacy continually reshape teaching decisions, depending on each student's progress.

Studies of Teacher Effectiveness

It is generally accepted that the teacher plays a major role in determining the effectiveness of a literacy program. Recognition of this significant role is not new. Over the past 50 years, a number of major studies have demonstrated the importance of the teacher to student learning. Gates (1937) found that although mental age is correlated with beginning reading success, the type of teaching and the teacher's expertise and effectiveness are equally important. In her 3-year study, Jeanne Chall (1967) concluded that even more than the instructional materials, the teacher generally determines students' attitudes toward learning to read.

The importance of the teacher to student learning was apparent in a major investigation that compared different reading instructional methods at the first-grade level (Dykstra, 1967). The study noted wide differences in reading achievement among classes and school systems that were using similar instructional methods. The differences underscore the importance of the teacher's role in reading instruction.

Early studies on effective teaching yielded little specific information about exactly what teachers do in the classroom that makes them effective, however. Being a good, decent individual who is interested in students is clearly insufficient. As John Pescosolido (1980) stated, "Just being a 'nice' person doesn't a teacher of reading make, but a nice person doing some important things in terms of the reading process results in good teaching and good learning."

Recent Research

In early studies of reading teachers' effectiveness, researchers looked at what went on inside classrooms. They identified several factors (e.g., willingness to be flexible, skill in asking questions, and ability to personalize their teaching) that explained why students in some classrooms seemed to learn more than did students of similar ability in other classrooms. While this early research in teacher effectiveness did not go on to specify exact instructional guidelines, the studies generally associated the same characteristics with student learning of basic skills.

To avoid simplistic explanations of teacher effectiveness, it must be acknowledged that the majority of recent studies have been nonexperimental, thus prohibiting the conclusion that specific teacher behaviors actually cause student achievement. Until recently, the research has focused predominantly on word-identification skills and literal-comprehension skills as measured by standardized tests. Critical and creative reading skills, which are essential goals of education, have not received much attention. Thus, it is entirely possible that teacher behaviors that appear to promote basic reading skills also deter the development of other skills such as the ability to evaluate and to synthesize information. The material in this chapter therefore should be regarded as providing tentative guidelines.

We believe that it is reasonable to expect a teacher to benefit from knowing about practices of competent teachers. Before proceeding, however, another

◀||| F L A S H B A C K

Arthur I. Gates was one of the most influential scholars in the field of reading. His research and writing in the areas of vocabulary control, reading interests, spelling, diagnosis, remediation, reading readiness, and disabled children have influenced reading instruction and materials since the 1920s. Arthur I. Gates was truly a man ahead of his time. He pointed out in the 1930s that a key factor in determining students' success in beginning reading was the teacher. Professor Gates's contribution to reading was recognized by the International Reading Association in 1961, when he was awarded the Citation of Merit, and again in 1968, when he received the International Award.

Photo Courtesy of Teachers College, Columbia University.

U P D A T E |||▶

Teachers can expend their time and effort in a variety of ways when teaching reading. Research on teaching and on reading development in the past 25 years has helped us discern which efforts are helpful. These investigations have yielded principles of teaching that, when applied appropriately, enhance student learning and growth.

A more recent view of effectiveness builds on this research and emerges directly from new understandings of the reading process and how teachers can promote student understanding of text. This new view stresses teachers' abilities to tap students' prior knowledge of a subject, to interact with students in a variety of ways regarding the comprehension of ideas and when and how to use strategies to enhance understanding, and to provide practice with new skills and strategies using authentic reading situations rather than isolated exercises.

cautionary note is in order. Keep in mind that no teaching strategy or method works best for all students all of the time. Student factors, such as socioeconomic status, experiential background, language capabilities, grade level, and learning style, are also important to consider.

Characteristics of Effective Literacy Instruction

The areas that appear to be of primary importance in competent literacy instruction include the following:

> Assessing students' literacy strengths and weaknesses.
>
> Structuring literacy activities around an interactive instructional format.
>
> Providing students with opportunities to learn and apply skills and strategies in real-life literacy tasks.
>
> Ensuring that students attend to the learning tasks.
>
> Believing in one's teaching abilities and expecting students to be successful.
>
> Maintaining effective classroom control. (Blair, 1984)

■ Assessing Students' Reading

The ability to teach students what they need to know requires that teachers of literacy continually use a blend of formal and informal measures to identify students' strengths and weaknesses in interacting with text (Afflerbach & Kapinus, 1993). Without the teacher's pervasive concern for knowing and responding to students' needs, literacy instruction can be irrelevant and mindless drudgery for all concerned. This pervasive concern about assessment can be related to Chall's stages of reading development (see Chapter 1). Teachers should provide instruction that reflects the students' level of reading development.

Teachers' use of reading assessment and its effects on reading achievement have been part of many research investigations that span more than 30 years. Pescosolido (1962) appraised the effects of a variety of teacher factors on achievement and found that a major factor associated with high levels of reading achievement was the teacher's ability to judge accurately students' attitudes toward reading. Blair (1975) found that teachers who secured and used supplementary materials, provided differentiated instruction, kept records of student progress, and arranged conferences about student progress were effective in improving student reading skills. The results of this study also revealed significant differences in class-achievement scores for teachers who exerted more effort on the job. Finally, Rupley (1977) found that effective teachers of reading used more ongoing assessment than did less effective teachers.

More recently, assessment has been increasingly emphasized. External assessment of procedures, such as standardized tests, typically focuses on students' basic skills in reading and writing and provides little information for instructional decision making (Calfee & Heibert, 1991). Today's teachers of literacy realize that testing is only one small part of assessment and that literacy is the ability to use reading and writing as tools for learning, thinking, and problem solving (Brandt, 1989). In a recent survey of educators regarding the *National Assessment of Educational Progress* (NAEP) for reading, this view of literacy was reflected by teachers, researchers, and administrators associated with literacy instruction (Commeyras, Osborn, & Bruce, 1992). The respondents indicated that assessment should focus on the reading and writing processes, reading to inform, and reading to perform a task. Clearly, defining *literacy* as much more than basic skills has direct implications for effective instruction.

Effective teachers of literacy rely on a variety of assessment tools, including interviews, observations, samples of students' work, portfolios, and students' judgments of their own performance (Henk & Melnick, 1992). Such assessment procedures give teachers information about their students and help them make informed instructional decisions to maximize their teaching effectiveness.

Using assessment as an integral part of effective instruction involves several provisions. First, effective literacy teachers employ informal, ongoing assessment procedures rather than relying on infrequently administered standardized tests. Second, their procedures aim to determine appropriate instructional practices rather than simply students' grade-level placement. Third, effective teachers use ongoing assessment to evaluate student outcomes regularly in relation to actual classroom instruction. Effective teachers of literacy use a variety of assessment techniques to adjust instruction frequently so that students' chances of success in instructional tasks are increased.

The fact that effective teachers assess students' literacy more frequently using a variety of procedures (see Chapter 11) than do less effective teachers should be carefully analyzed. By itself, assessment has no beneficial effects. Therefore, one cannot expect students' literacy achievement to improve simply by increasing the frequency of assessment. Yet effective teachers of reading and writing expend considerable effort in developing and using ongoing assessment. It is how they incorporate this information into their instruction that probably determines students' reading achievement.

Another plausible explanation is that effective teachers select instructional strategies appropriate to the desired student outcomes in relation to the students' existing literacy capabilities. Instructional tasks that are too difficult for students limit their chances of successful learning. Teachers who pace their instruction by progressing in small, closely related steps to maximize students' success in literacy activities increase students' chances of success. Ongoing assessment that focuses on students' literacy strengths and weaknesses enables teachers to identify instructional procedures that increase success. A balance of high- and medium-success tasks, with greater emphasis on high-success tasks, results in students who achieve more at the end of the school year, retain more over the summer, and have a positive attitude toward school (Schneider, 1979).

Effective teachers of literacy, then, employ a variety of ongoing, informal assessment procedures to

- adjust instruction in terms of its impact on students' learning.
- identify instructional activities and tasks that maximize student success.

The key to interactive instruction is the active communication and interaction between teacher and student.

- select instructional strategies appropriate to desired literacy outcomes in relation to students' existing reading capabilities.
- pace reading instruction by progressing in small, related steps to maximize students' success rates.

■ Interactive Instruction

Effective teachers of reading teach students what they need to know. Although it seems simplistic and obvious, teachers of literacy "teach"; that is, students do not become independent learners through maturation alone. *Interactive instruction* means imparting new information to students through meaningful teacher-student interactions and teacher guidance of student learning. The key to interactive instruction is the active communication and interaction between teacher and student. An interactive style of teaching can be direct or indirect, well structured or less structured in nature. The type of learning to be accomplished determines the degree of directness or structure. The majority of learning objectives in teaching literacy can be classified as either skills or strategies. Both types of learning are important for success in literacy; however, they require different lesson-presentation methods. **Skills** involve lower-level cognitive processing, are specific in nature, and "are more or less automatic routines" (Dole, Duffy, Roehler, & Pearson, 1991). Examples of literacy skills include the various decoding methods used in phonics, structural analysis, and context analysis; specific comprehension skills such as recognizing sequential development, fact versus opinion, and a stated main idea; reading study skills such as using an index and interpreting a bar graph; and writing skills such as capitalization, punctuation, and spelling. **Strategies** require higher-level cognitive processing, are less specific in nature than skills and "emphasize intentional and deliberate plans under the control of the reader" (Dole et al., 1991). Examples of cognitive strategies applied to literacy include summarizing a story, reacting critically to what is read, and editing a piece of writing.

Each type of learning requires a different degree of directness and control by the teacher (see Figure 2.1). As shown, skill learning requires more control and direction by the teacher than does strategy learning, which requires less teacher directness and is more under the control of students. However, teaching is neither wholly direct nor indirect—on a continuum, a given teaching lesson is only more or less direct than another. Interactive teaching of both skills and strategies is important, and both types of lessons should be included in a teacher's repertoire.

Skill Learning.   Skill learning is particularly suitable to the **direct/explicit instruction** approach. Summarizing the literature on the teaching procedures for direct instruction, Rosenshine and Stevens (1986, 1995) delineated six instructional functions for teaching well-structured objectives (see Figure 2.2). Teachers who use these procedures consistently see higher-than-average achievement among their students.

At the heart of the direct/explicit instruction method are explicit explanations, modeling, and guided practice. Explicit explanations can include defining a reading skill, modeling or demonstrating its use in an actual reading situation, and thinking aloud with students about what the skill is and how it is used (i.e., showing how to apply it in context) (Blair & Rupley, 1988). Effective teachers provide varied, meaningful practice to ensure mastery and transfer of a skill to other

FIGURE 2.1
Skill versus strategy learning: Teacher directness and control

1. **Review**
   Review homework
   Review relevant previous learning
   Review prerequisite skills and knowledge for the lesson
2. **Presentation**
   State lesson goals or provide outline
   Present new material in small steps
   Model procedures
   Provide positive and negative examples
   Use clear language
   Check for student understanding
   Avoid digressions
3. **Guided Practice**
   Spend more time on guided practice
   High frequency of questions
   All students respond and receive feedback
   High success rate
   Continue practice until students are fluent
4. **Corrections and Feedback**
   Provide process feedback when answers are correct but hesitant
   Provide sustaining feedback, clues, or reteaching when answers are
      incorrect
   Reteach material when necessary
5. **Independent Practice**
   Students receive overview and/or help during initial steps
   Practice continues until students are automatic (where relevant)
   Teacher provides active supervision (where possible)
   Routines are used to provide help for slower students
6. **Weekly and Monthly Reviews**

FIGURE 2.2
Functions for teaching well-structured tasks
Source: From B. Rosenshine and R. Stevens (1995), Functions for Teaching
Well-structured Tasks. In B. Rosenshine, "Advances in Research in Education."
The Journal of Educational Research, May/June, Vol. 88, No. 5.

meaningful reading situations (Rupley & Blair, 1988). Directly controlled by the teacher, this practice is characterized by varying degrees of teacher-student interaction. In this process, the teacher acts as a mediator. Based on Vygotsky's theoretical work (1962), **mediated instruction** involves providing guidance to a student in learning a particular skill. During practice, the amount of guidance is great at the beginning; it then declines to little or none. Walker (1992) emphasizes both teacher guidance and continuous assessment of instruction in mediated instruction.

Guiding student learning is certainly not new; it has been an effective teaching strategy for years. The renewed interest today is the result of new research on the teaching-learning process and the social environment of the classroom.

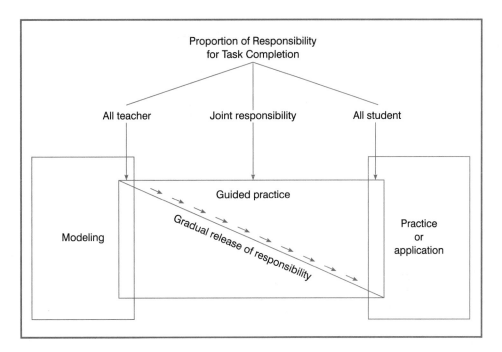

FIGURE 2.3
The gradual-release-of-responsibility model of instruction
Source: After Campione, 1981. Reprinted with permission from
P. D. Pearson and M. C. Gallagher, **The Instruction of Reading
Comprehension** (Urbana, IL: University of Illinois, Center for the Study
of Reading, October 1983), p. 732.

Figure 2.3 depicts this gradual shift of responsibility for the application of a reading skill from the teacher to the student.

Strategy Learning.   Teaching students strategies or strategic reading behaviors with which to interact with and comprehend text requires a different style of interactive teaching. Most strategies require higher-level thinking, as opposed to skills, which are more factual, or literal, and amenable to specific learning objectives. Strategies are behaviors a reader applies before, during, and after reading to construct and understand the author's message. Examples of strategies include the abilities to preview a selection, ask questions to understand and clarify ideas while reading, summarize a passage, and react critically to what was read. Referring again to Figure 2.1, it is important to note that teaching students strategies requires a different style of direct/explicit instruction from that used to teach skills. The emphasis is on helping students understand the "when" and "why" of utilizing various strategies. Teaching a strategy still requires teachers to explain, inform, model, or demonstrate what they want students to know, but it is not a strict step-by-step procedure under complete control of the teacher, as it is for skill instruction. Teaching cognitive strategies also follows the gradual shift of control and responsibility for the learning and application of a reading strategy from the teacher to the student (Figure 2.3). Rosenshine and Meister (1992, 1995) describe the teaching of cognitive strategies as including the following steps:

1. Present the new cognitive strategy.
2. Regulate difficulty during guided practice.
3. Provide varying contexts for student practice.
4. Provide feedback.
5. Increase student responsibility.
6. Provide independent practice. (p. 27)

Central to teaching strategies is the use of instructional procedures called **scaffolds** to aid students while they learn the strategy (see Chapter 6). A definition of *scaffolds* is provided by Rosenshine and Meister (1992, 1995):

> Scaffolds are forms of support provided by the teacher (or another student) to help students bridge the gap between their current abilities and the intended goal. . . . Instead of providing explicit steps, one supports, or scaffolds, the students as they learn the skill. (p. 26)

Scaffolds can be general aids such as modeling or demonstrating a strategy, or they can be specific aids used to teach a strategy. For example, in teaching the strategy of generating questions, a teacher may use the scaffold of teaching students to use reporters' questions *(Who? What? Where? When? Why?* and *How?)* as they think about what they read. In teaching any cognitive strategy, the teacher acts more as a facilitator than a director in helping students learn to interact critically with text.

The importance of giving analytical consideration to classroom structure and direct teaching as means for improving literacy teaching effectiveness seems clear. The literacy program should not be regimented and inflexible. Structure and direct instruction depend on the desired reading outcomes and the grade level. Analyzing how these variables influence students' reading and making changes when necessary enhance teacher effectiveness.

Effective teachers of literacy, then, utilize an interactive style of teaching to

- maximize student involvement in tasks or academic activities related specifically to lesson content and desired outcomes.
- control student behavior using task-related comments rather than criticizing or scolding.
- monitor and guide the direction of learning.
- vary the degree of structure in relation to desired behavioral objectives; less structure and less-direct instruction are employed for strategy or creative outcomes, and more structure and control are used for skill outcomes.
- utilize a pattern of instruction at the primary level that allows students to contact the teacher, work in small groups, and use a variety of materials.
- utilize a pattern of instruction at the intermediate level that allows for larger instructional groups, more discussion at higher cognitive levels, less teacher direction, and greater student-initiated learning.

■ Opportunity to Learn

Opportunity to learn refers to whether students have been taught the skills relevant to the areas for which they are assessed. Teachers who specify literacy behaviors to be achieved prior to teaching and who teach content relevant to these outcomes often have students who achieve at a higher reading level than do teachers who do not (Rupley, Wise, & Logan, 1986).

Opportunity to learn is a variable associated with direct instruction. Teachers could employ structure and direct instruction, but if the instruction does not relate to an assessed learning task or a valued outcome, then students have not had an opportunity to learn the product. For example, students who do well in learning isolated reading skills as a result of intensive instruction but who do poorly in actual reading may lack the opportunity to learn how to apply such skills in actual reading tasks. Allington reported that low-achieving readers receive different instructional emphases than high-achieving students (Allington 1983). Low-achieving students spent more time on worksheets rather than whole-text reading and on word recognition rather than comprehension activities.

A study of 1,828 fourth graders in Philadelphia (Vicino, 1979) indicates the importance of providing students with opportunities to apply their reading skills in actual reading tasks. In addition to daily whole-class or small-group reading instruction groups, the students spent a large portion of their class time reading silently. The result was more advanced reading skills. The importance of providing opportunities for students to apply their reading skills in real-life tasks is also apparent in a reading program developed by the Irwin School in Charlotte, North Carolina (Cohen & Irons, 1979). In addition to increasing the amount of students' engaged time, using ongoing assessment to plan instruction, and maintaining appropriate levels of structure and direct instruction, teachers focus on applying reading skills to comprehension tasks and literature-appreciation activities. Preliminary results indicated that the third, fourth, and fifth graders involved in the program were progressing at a rate of 3 months' growth for every 2 months of instruction.

Providing students with opportunities to apply their reading and writing skills in meaningful content areas appears to be extremely important; however, teachers must be sure to use materials that students can handle. The more time students spend on actual reading in which they can be highly successful, the more they probably will learn; while the more they are involved in actual reading tasks that limit success, the less likely they will be to enhance their learning.

Practice activities in reading are of the utmost importance. Such activities are best designed around three areas: (1) planning for practice, (2) delivering effective practice, and (3) evaluating the effectiveness of practice assignments.

When planning for practice, teachers should ask:

- Is the intended practice related to the students' needs?
- Is the level of the materials appropriate and interesting?
- Is the content of the practice within the students' experiential background?
- Are different ways of practice provided to meet students' needs and maintain their interest?

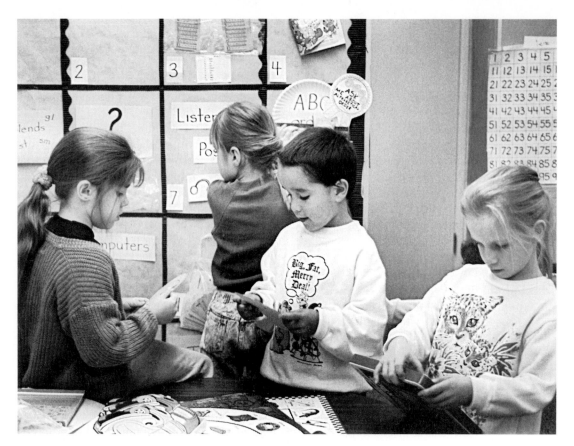

Students should gradually assume more control and responsibility for their own learning.

- Is the amount of practice appropriate for the instructional period?
- Are directions and examples provided to students to ensure understanding (i.e., are they clear)?
- Is it necessary to vary the type of practice in one class period (having students work on two or three different types of materials relating to one aspect of reading), or will one practice activity be sufficient?

When delivering practice, teachers should ask:

- Are several exercises completed with the students before they work on their own?
- How will the students' progress during practice sessions be monitored?
- Do individual students know how to get help if I am working with another student?
- What should students do if they finish an activity early?
- Do the students understand how the practice activity relates to reading in meaningful text?

When evaluating the effectiveness of practice assignments, teachers should ask:

- Did the practice accomplish its goal?
- What are the students' patterns of correct and incorrect responses?
- How will the results of this practice session modify the next practice activity? (Rupley & Blair, 1987)

Opportunity to learn is not equal to coverage of materials and topics. Opportunity to learn, ongoing assessment, structure, and direct instruction are related. The reading instruction that is offered must relate to assessment data, desired outcomes, instructional format, and application in actual reading tasks. Opportunity to learn should reflect the desired learning outcomes, not simply cover the content.

Effective teachers of reading, then, attend to students' opportunity to learn and apply skills in actual reading situations to

- ensure that instruction focuses on desired and valued reading outcomes.
- guard against isolated reading skills and strategies becoming ends in themselves rather than means to effective reading comprehension.
- provide for application of reading skills and strategies in silent reading tasks that ensure maximum student success.
- ensure that students understand how to apply their reading skills and strategies for reading enjoyment.

■ Attention to Learning Tasks

Students' attention to learning tasks and engagement in pertinent learning materials logically fall under the direct supervision of the teacher. The historic *Beginning Teacher Evaluation Study, Phase II* (McDonald, 1976) provided clear support for the importance of maintaining a reasonably high level of student involvement. Appropriate reading materials alone are not sufficient to maximize achievement. Effective teachers not only use appropriate materials but also attend to actively engaging students in learning from the materials. Simply requiring that all students complete similar learning tasks does not ensure maximum attention, because students approach various learning tasks with varying interest, capabilities, and understanding. Effective literacy teachers take these factors into account as they attempt to engage students in meaningful reading instruction.

Academic engaged time, or **time on task,** refers to the classroom time when students are actually attending to the work at hand. Classrooms in which students are actively engaged in learning for a large proportion of the time demonstrate higher achievement in reading and writing than do classrooms in which students are not so engaged. Engagement is the key; merely completing reading and writing activities is not synonomous with learning.

Researchers have modified the definition of *time on task* to include students' success rate while working productively. Fisher, Marliave, and Filby (1979) label this concept **academic learning time (ALT).** They define the term as "the amount of time a student spends engaged in an academic task he/she performs

The Importance of Additional Practice and Cooperative Learning Opportunities

The direct instruction approach works especially well for those reading skills and abilities that are specific in nature. This teaching approach is effective with all children. Still, each step in this approach should be modified to meet student needs and the topic at hand. An abundance of meaningful practice is necessary for all students in mastering the lesson objective in this approach. As you work with exceptional students in the regular classroom, it is helpful to know and be prepared to provide **additional** supervised and independent practice a few days after a lesson is finished. Many exceptional students will need a great deal of meaningful practice after the point at which you would normally judge that students have mastered the reading skill. This is not a reflection on your teaching but a reminder of the reality that different students need different amounts of practice.

Such practice needs to occur at an appropriate level of difficulty and be accomplished with a variety of materials. Additional practice can be supplied through supplemental textbooks, newspapers, magazines, commercial learning kits, literature books, teacher-made materials, games, computers, and various realia (real objects such as maps and word cards). Also, both teacher-supervised and independent practice can be accomplished in a variety of settings, especially in cooperative learning groups. Cooperative learning promotes more active learning, with students talking and working together rather than listening passively to the teacher. As with any type of cooperative grouping, this arrangement won't be successful without careful preparation and skillful application on your part. Requirements for cooperative grouping include the following:

1. Organizing students heterogeneously in small groups.
2. Explaining the lesson objective and the criteria for success for the entire group.
3. Reviewing the desired communication behaviors needed (e.g., listening to others, allowing everyone to participate, helping one another).
4. Monitoring the progress of each group and helping each group as students work on the assigned activities.
5. Evaluating the group's efforts and assigning a group grade for the entire activity.

with high success" (p. 52). A high success rate is considered to be above 80%. Allocated time, student engagement, and student success rate define academic learning time. Collectively, academic learning time occurs when a student has the time or opportunity to learn, is actively engaged with the task at hand, and is succeeding at the task.

Attention to learning and engagement in materials are important for learning in both directed and individual instruction. The key is active engagement in reading and writing instruction, not necessarily the total time allocated. Students may be passive or indifferent to instruction, even though a teacher devotes a large amount of instructional time to reading and writing. Alone, the number of minutes allocated for instruction does not affect level of reading achievement. However, with all other things being equal, the greater the time spent on instruction, the higher the achievement will be (Schneider, 1979).

Effective teachers of literacy, then, help maximize students' focus on learning tasks by

- allocating more time to reading instruction.
- keeping students actively engaged in learning during the instructional period.
- providing academic feedback to students about their work to increase attention to tasks and amount of engaged time.
- setting purposes for learning.
- presenting an overview of what is to be learned.
- using examples and illustrations to relate new learning to what has been presented previously and to help students understand how to apply what they are learning.
- monitoring students' involvement to ensure a high success rate.

Promoting Reading Comprehension.   Comprehension development has been the major focus in the literacy field since the mid-1970s. Our understanding of the reading process and the ways teachers can foster reading comprehension have greatly increased in the last 20 years (Watts & Cerra, 1996). The overall goal of reading instruction is the development of active readers who can both understand printed language and strategically monitor their own reading performance. All the best intentions and instruction are lost if students cannot comprehend successfully, are unable to regulate and monitor their reading, and do not choose to read for various purposes on their own. Central to this development of active, strategic readers is the important role of the classroom teacher. Only through the teacher's careful and expert planning, teaching, and guidance will students grow into mature, independent readers (Kincade, 1996). Pivotal to the development of reading comprehension are the instructional strategies used by the classroom teacher and the way in which instructional time is utilized during the day. Fielding and Pearson (1994) summarized the significant research on comprehension strategies that promote increased student learning. A consensus is building in the literacy field that a successful comprehension program includes the following components:

1. direct teaching of comprehension skills and strategies spanning different cognitive levels in both narrative and expository text
2. use of peer and cooperative learning in the classroom
3. provision of a multitude of opportunities for students to interact with their peers and teachers about what they are reading
4. allotment of large amounts of time for actual text reading (Fielding and Pearson, 1994)

The key point is how much classroom time is utilized for these areas. Unfortunately, past investigations paint a discouraging picture concerning the amount of time devoted to actual text reading in elementary classrooms. In *Becoming a Nation of Readers,* Anderson, Hiebert, Scott, & Wilkinson (1985) reported that students spend only a small amount of time in classrooms actually reading whole texts. Rosenshine (1979) reported that in some elementary classes, students spend 50 to 70% of their time completing seatwork assignments.

While there are no definitive data on the optimal time allocations to actual text reading, direct teaching, and discussion/interaction periods during reading class, Fielding and Pearson recommend that, "of the time set aside for reading instruction, students should have more time to read than the combined total allocated for learning about reading and talking or writing about what has been read" (p. 63). While common sense supports the importance of allocating sufficient classroom time to actual text reading and discussion of what has been read to promote reading comprehension, even more importantly, classroom research indicates the value of providing students with extensive practice with real reading. In a recent summary of some of the most important instructional advancements in the last 30 years, Rosenshine (1995) highlighted research in the following areas:

- cognitive processing (most notably, the importance of knowledge structure and developing student background knowledge)
- teacher-effectiveness literature (especially the need for direct teaching for well-structured skills)
- cognitive strategies (their importance and procedures for teaching them to students).

In all three areas, an important instructional implication for teachers is to provide an abundance of extensive practice through independent reading so that students develop and refine their knowledge structure, master specific skills, and develop the facility to use cognitive strategies. Aside from direct teaching, practice, practice, and more practice in real texts is needed to help students learn.

Thus, a major challenge for teachers is to monitor the amount of classroom time devoted to instruction, actual text reading, and writing or talking about what was read. Preliminary findings seem to indicate that classroom time may not be used as wisely as one might believe or wish. In an elementary school classroom-time study by Blair, Turner, and Schaudt (1995), the findings were the antithesis of the Fielding and Pearson recommendations referred to in the preceding paragraph. The Blair et al. study found that teachers only allocated a little over one third of classroom time to actual text reading (the rest of the time was devoted to instruction and discussion). With classroom time being such an important yet limited commodity and comprehension being the ultimate goal of literacy programs, it is crucial that teachers monitor how classroom time is spent.

■ Teacher Expectations

The most pervasive conclusion of school and teacher effectiveness studies in the 1970s and 1980s was that teachers of reading profoundly influence how much students learn. This influence stems from both classroom actions and belief systems. Effective literacy programs have teachers who believe in themselves and expect their students to succeed in learning. Simply put, students learn more if you hold high academic expectations for them. Thus, expectations for students may bias teachers' actions: If students perform according to what is expected of them, expectations can become self-fulfilling prophecies.

**Effective teachers monitor students' involvement
to ensure a high success rate.**

Having different expectations for different students is natural as long as the expectations reflect diagnostic data (such as achievement scores, specific strengths and weaknesses in comprehension, and motivational concerns) rather than socioeconomic status, gender, race, or ethnic background. Good and Brophy (1987) showed that students for whom teachers have low expectations may

receive less instruction.

be expected to do less work.

receive less frequent praise.

be called on less often.

receive less time to respond to questions.

be asked predominantly factual questions.

be seated farther from their teachers.

receive less eye contact.

be smiled at less often.

be criticized more frequently for incorrect responses.

receive less help.

It is fortunate that some students are not as affected by low teacher expectations as others are. However, it is important to realize the potential impact that expectations can have on students.

In addition to holding high, realistic expectations for students and communicating them, effective teachers have a strong sense of efficacy, or the expectation that their efforts will result in valued outcomes (Fuller, Wood, Rapoport, & Dornbush, 1982). In effect, teachers with a high sense of efficacy say, "I know I can teach these students!" These teachers believe in themselves and believe that investing substantial effort in their work will raise student achievement.

Being aware of the power of expectations and translating this awareness into sound instruction takes effort. That effort involves

- ensuring that reading instruction is based on diagnostic data.
- communicating goals and expectations to students.
- ensuring that all students participate in the reading lesson.
- classroom management.

■ Classroom Management

Directly related to student achievement in reading is the teacher's classroom management ability. Without the ability to manage complex interactions, a teacher's best intentions and instructional techniques are ineffective. Researchers have shown that teachers of high-achieving students in reading are good classroom managers (Emmer, 1987). Effective classroom management creates and maintains an atmosphere conducive for learning. Managerial skills include planning for instruction, developing routines to manage group interactions, devising monitoring procedures, and responding to off-task behavior (Blair, 1988). Chapter 12 covers classroom management in detail and discusses specific techniques and strategies for the teacher of reading and writing.

Effective teachers of reading, then, manage the classroom to

- ensure conditions that are conducive to student learning.
- plan meaningful reading activities.
- manage group instruction.
- monitor student progress throughout the reading period.
- respond appropriately to student misbehavior.

Decision Making in Reading Instruction

While the literature on effective teaching has yielded specific guidelines for teaching reading, the guidelines apply differently to each classroom depending upon a host of variables, including student needs, material content, grade level, and learning objectives. This realization underscores the notion of effective teachers of reading as decision makers: Teaching is a decision-making process, and teachers' judgments are the keys to the success or failure of reading programs.

To teach students what they need to know, teachers must base their decisions about planning and instruction on assessment information (as opposed to race, gender, socioeconomic status, ethnic background, or personal characteristics). Studies of teacher planning have reported that many teachers focus on instructional activities when making decisions (Stern & Shavelson, 1983). This contradicts the traditional thinking that teachers should focus on specific objectives in making decisions. A focus on activities should not be interpreted to exclude objectives in the planning process, however. Student characteristics should help shape reading and writing activities into meaningful experiences.

Figure 2.4 outlines the decision-making process for planning and actual teaching (interactive decision making). As shown, instructional implementation depends on decisions made both before and during teaching. Planning decisions center on the ability to modify and adapt the major reading activity to meet learning needs. Students' instructional levels, strengths, weaknesses, and personal qualities will factor into these decisions. The teacher's learning objectives (e.g.,

FIGURE 2.4
Interactive decision making

Diagnosis

Focus: Students' reading strengths and weaknesses

Features: Ongoing—combining both informal and standardized measures of reading outcomes related directly to instructional goals. Data are used to plan appropriate classroom structure and instruction.

Guiding questions:
- Are the students placed on their instructional level of reading materials (that is, not too difficult and not too easy)?
- Are you continually using informal observational techniques and diagnostic tests to detect strengths and weaknesses in word identification and comprehension?
- Is the instruction based on a diagnosis of student needs?
- Are you adjusting your instruction according to students' progress?

Direct Instruction

Focus: Instructional organization and process

Features: Stated purposes for learning in terms of academic skills. Direct instruction emphasizes the importance of the teacher in learning. It provides a focus on the product for identifying and conceptualizing instruction. Such instruction is differentiated by grade level and type of task.

Guiding questions:
- Do you vary the amount of structure in your class depending on student characteristics, grade level, and objectives?
- Do you allow for less structure when teaching more complex tasks (for example, do you solicit emotional responses to a story or judgments of the desirability or acceptability of a character's behaviors)?
- Do you devise more structured lessons when teaching basic reading skills (such as word identification and comprehension)?
- Do you give your students appropriate feedback?

Opportunity to Learn

Focus: Instruction aimed at measurable and desired reading outcomes; application of skills in actual reading tasks

Features: Matching the instruction to desired outcomes and teaching content relevant to these. Opportunity to learn maximizes students' understanding of the purposes for learning skills and of applying these skills to actual reading situations.

Guiding questions:
- Do you allow sufficient instructional time to teach what your students need to know?
- Do you allow time for your students to practice their reading skills in actual reading situations?
- Do you plan ways to monitor student practice of targeted reading skills?
- Are your students practicing their reading skills in materials that will ensure a high degree of success?

Attention to Learning Tasks

Focus: Maintaining a high level of student involvement in learning

Features: Maximizing students' involvement and attention to learning. Attention to the learning tasks looks at students' needs, based on diagnostic data. It involves students in instruction at a moderate level of difficulty, monitors their engagement in the instruction, and maximizes attention to learning by focusing on tasks related directly to desired outcomes.

Guiding questions:
- Do you clearly communicate the specific purposes of each lesson to your students?
- Do you plan your instruction to ensure a high percentage of academic engaged time?
- Do you design seatwork assignments to ensure student involvement?
- Do you use a reward system with students to reinforce specific positive behaviors?

Teacher Expectations

Focus: Believing one's students can learn and communicating this expectation to them

Features: Ensuring that instruction is based on diagnostic information. Teachers convince students that they will be successful in the classroom.

Guiding questions:
- Are your instructional decisions based on diagnostic data?
- Are all students involved in the reading class?
- Do you communicate to your students that they will be successful in your reading class?
- Are you exhibiting a positive attitude toward teaching and continually striving to learn and to grow?

Classroom Management

Focus: Creating, managing, and maintaining a classroom environment conducive to learning

Features: Preparation of materials and activities prior to actual teaching to prevent management difficulties. During instruction, successful managers grasp the total classroom situation, monitor students' work, and respond appropriately to student misbehavior.

Guiding questions:
- Do you prepare materials in advance and distribute them at appropriate times?
- Do you select and apply appropriate group management techniques to manage student misbehavior?
- Do you monitor student progress by responding quickly and appropriately to student responses to material?

FIGURE 2.5
Summary of effective teacher practices

basic word identification or critical thinking), teaching techniques (e.g., directed reading activity, language experience approach, direct instruction, or reciprocal teaching), and grouping or classroom organization will also influence decisions.

Planning instruction, however, does not mean the end of decision making. Effective teachers modify their instruction based on student responses: either mastery of material, which requires no modification, or difficulty, which requires further explanation or reteaching. The goal should be to progress at a speed that maintains student involvement and achieves instructional goals.

Figure 2.5 summarizes six areas of effective instruction. Attention to these areas should enable teachers to better determine and improve the effectiveness of their reading instruction.

☑ Summary

Time and time again, research has demonstrated the importance of the teacher in effective literacy instruction. Admittedly, we still have much to learn about what makes an effective teacher. However, a great deal of the available information warrants careful consideration. We know, for example, that teachers who include provisions for ongoing assessment, interactive instruction, opportunity to learn, attention to learning tasks, accurate expectations, and efficient classroom management are more effective than teachers who do not include provisions for these practices.

All teachers of literacy can benefit from knowing about the practices of competent teachers. Teacher-effectiveness research identifies some characteristics associated with effective teaching of literacy. Teachers of literacy should sort out and analyze these characteristics in terms of their own capabilities and classrooms.

☑ Your Point of View

Discussion Questions

1. What reasons account for the different characteristics of effective primary-grade teachers versus effective intermediate-grade teachers?
2. What are the implications of direct instruction for the teaching of critical-thinking skills?

Take a Stand For or Against

1. Opportunity to learn is the most powerful variable in education.
2. Small-group direct instruction is more beneficial than large-group direct instruction.

 ## Field-Based Assignments

1. Successful reading teachers work hard for their success and know where to put their time and effort to make a difference. As you are beginning to study what

effective reading teachers do, interview at least one classroom teacher in the school you are visiting to find out what he or she thinks constitutes effectiveness in teaching literacy at his or her grade level. Use the following questions as a guide in interviewing (add others if you wish) and share your results with your classmates and professor.

What do you think are the characteristics of effective reading teachers?

How do you plan for teaching an entire class in reading?

What types of assessments do you make on your students' literacy abilities?

What teaching methods do you use in teaching reading?

What do you think are the perennial problems of teaching in today's schools?

2. As discussed in this chapter, effective teaching and learning is context specific. This means that effective teaching behaviors need to be applied differently depending on the grade level taught, the instructional goal of the lesson, and the characteristics of your students. As you will recall, the degree of structure and control a teacher has in a lesson will vary depending upon the instructional goal. Different degrees of teacher control and structure are necessary for achieving different instructional goals. Make notes of the types of activities completed during the reading/language arts periods in the school you are visiting for 2 or 3 days and respond to the following questions:

In what types of activities did the teacher exercise the most control?

In what types of activities did the teacher exhibit less control?

What type of grouping was used for highly teacher-controlled activities as opposed to those activities that were less controlled and more open?

Looking back over the 2 or 3 days, do you think the control of the different learning activities varied in relation to the instructional goals? Did this seem to make a difference in terms of student learning?

Portfolio Entry

The statement, "It's the teacher who is the single-most significant factor in determining whether or not children will be successful in learning to read," is a popular pronouncement repeated by many educators. With this in mind, write a one-page response to one of the following in your teaching portfolio:

■ *Reflecting on your past teachers, do you remember having a teacher who particularly motivated you to read and learn on your own? If so, discuss the qualities of this person and the influence he or she had on your life.*

■ *"Good reading teachers are born teachers." Do you agree or disagree with this statement? Why?*

Bibliography

Anderson, R. C., Hiebert, E. H., Scott, J. A., & Wilkinson, I. A. G. (1985). *Becoming a nation of readers: The report of the Commission on Reading.* Washington, DC: The National Institute of Education.

Allington, R. L. (1983). The reading instruction provided readers of different reading abilities. *Elementary School Journal, 83,* 549–559.

Afflerbach, P., & Kapinus, B. (1993). Reading assessment: The balancing act. *The Reading Teacher, 47,* 62–64.

Blair, T. R. (1988). *Emerging patterns of teaching: From methods to field experiences.* Upper Saddle River, NJ: Merrill/Prentice Hall.

Blair, T. R. (1984). *What makes an effective reading program effective?* In R. Thompson (Ed.), *Reading research review* (273–281). Afton, MN; Burgess Publishing Co.

Blair, T. R. (1975). *Relationship of teacher effort and student achievement in reading.* Unpublished doctoral dissertation, University of Illinois, Urbana.

Blair, T. R., & Rupley, W. H. (1988). Practice and application in the teaching of reading. *The Reading Teacher, 41,* 536–539.

Blair, T. R., Turner, E. C., & Schaudt, B. A. (1995, October). *Classroom time allocation: Actual text reading and discussion time.* Paper presented at the College Reading Association Annual Conference, Clearwater, Fa.

Brandt, R. (1989). Strategies for teaching and learning strategies. *Educational Leadership, 46,* 2.

Calfee, R. & Hiebert, E. (1991). Classroom assessment of reading. In R. Barr, M. Kamil, P. Mosenthal, & P. D. Pearson (Eds.), *Handbook of reading research, Vol. II.* (pp. 28–309). New York: Longman.

Chall, J. S. (1967). *Learning to read: The great debate.* New York: McGraw-Hill Book Co.

Cohen, R. G., & Irons, B. R. (November 1979). Doubling up in reading. *The Allyn and Bacon Reading Newsletter, 7,* 4.

Commeyras, M., Osborn, J., & Bruce, B. (1992). The reactions of educators to the framework for the 1992 NAEP for reading. In C. K. Kinzer & D. Leu (Eds.), *Literacy research, theory, and practice: Views from many perspectives* (pp. 137–152). Chicago: National Reading Conference.

Dole, J. A., Duffy, G. G., Roehler, L. R., & Pearson, P. D. (1991). Moving from the old to the new: Research on reading comprehension instruction. *Review of Educational Research, 61,* 239–264.

Dykstra, R. (1967). *Continuation of the coordination center for first-grade reading instruction programs* (Final Report). Washington, DC: U.S. Department of Health, Education, and Welfare. Office of Education, Bureau of Research.

Emmer, E. T. (1987). Classroom management and discipline. In V. Richardson-Koehler (Ed.),

Educators' handbook: A research perspective (pp. 233–258). New York: Longman.

Fielding, L. G., & Pearson, P. D. (1994). Reading comprehension: What works. *Educational Leadership, 51,* 62–68.

Fisher, C., Marliave, R., & Filby, N. (1979). Improving teaching by increasing academic learning time. *Educational Leadership, 39,* 52–54.

Fuller, B., Wood, K., Rapoport, T., & Dornbush, S. (1982). The organizational content of individual efficacy. *Review of Educational Research, 52,* 7–30.

Gates, A. I. (1937). The necessary age for beginning reading. *Elementary School Journal, 37,* 497–508.

Good, T. L., & Brophy, J. E. (1987). *Looking in classrooms* (4th ed.). New York: Harper & Row.

Henk, W., & Melnick, S. (1992). The initial development of a scale to measure "perception of self as reader." In C. K. Kinzer & D. Leu (Eds.), *Literacy research, theory, and practice: Views from many perspectives* (pp. 111–118). Chicago: National Reading Conference.

Kincade, K. M. (1996). Improving reading comprehension through strategy instruction. *Reading Psychology, 17,* 273–81.

McDonald, F. J. (1976). *Summary report: Beginning teacher evaluation study: Phase II, 1973–74.* (Final Report: Vol. 1). Princeton, NJ: Educational Testing Service.

Pescosolido, J. D. (1962). *The identification and appraisal of certain major factors in the teaching of reading.* Unpublished doctoral dissertation, University of Connecticut, Storrs.

Pescosolido, J. D. (1980). Letter to author.

Rosenshine, B. (1995). Advances in research on instruction. *Journal of Educational Research, 88,* 262–268.

Rosenshine, B. (1979). Content time and direct instruction. In P. Peterson & H. Walberg (Eds.), *Research on teaching: Concepts, findings and implications* (pp. 28–56). Berkeley, CA: McCutchan.

Rosenshine, B., & Meister, C. (1995). Scaffolds for teaching higher-order cognitive strategies. In A. C. Ornstein (Ed.), *Teaching: Theory into practice.* Boston: Allyn & Bacon.

Rosenshine, B. V., & Meister, C. (1992). The use of scaffolds for teaching higher-level cognitive strategies. *Educational Leadership, 49,* 26–33.

Rosenshine, B. & Stevens, R. (1995). Functions for teaching well-structured tasks. *Journal of Educational Research, 88,* 262–268.

Rosenshine, B. V., & Stevens, R. (1986). Teaching functions. In M. C. Wittrock (Ed.), *Handbook of research on teaching* (3rd ed.) (pp. 376–391). Upper Saddle River, NJ: Prentice Hall.

Rupley, W. H. (1977). Stability of teacher effect on pupils' reading achievement gain over a two-year period and its relation to instructional emphases. In P. D. Pearson (Ed.), *Reading: Theory, research and practice* (pp. 69–72). Clemson, SC: National Reading Conference.

Rupley, W. H., & Blair, T. R. (1987). Assignment and supervision of reading seatwork: Looking in on 12 primary grade teachers. *The Reading Teacher, 40,* 391–393.

Rupley, W. H., & Blair, T. R. (1988). *Teaching reading: Diagnosis, direct instruction, and practice* (2nd ed.). Upper Saddle River, NJ: Merrill/Prentice Hall.

Rupley, W. H., Wise, B. S., & Logan, J. W. (1986). Research in effective teaching: An overview of its development. In J. V. Hoffman (Ed.), *Effective teaching of reading: Research and practice.* Newark, DE: International Reading Association.

Schneider, E. J. (Fall 1979). Researchers discover formula of success in student learning. *Educational R&D Report, 2,* 1–6.

Stern, P., & Shavelson, R. J. (1983). Reading teachers' judgments, plans, and decision making. *The Reading Teacher, 37,* 280–286.

Vicino, F. L. (Ed.). (1979). Philadelphia study pinpoints factors in improving reading achievement. *Pre Post Press, 5,* 1.

Vygotsky, L. (1962). *Thought and Language.* Cambridge, MA: M.I.T. Press.

Walker, B. J. (1992). *Diagnostic teaching of reading: Techniques for instruction and assessment* (2nd ed.). Upper Saddle River, NJ: Merrill/Prentice Hall.

Walmsley, S. A., & Allington, R. L. (1995). Redefining and reforming instructional support programs for at-risk students. In R. L. Allington & S. A. Walmsley (Eds.). *No quick fix: Rethinking literacy programs in America's elementary schools* (pp. 19–44). New York: Teachers College Press and Newark, DE: International Reading Association.

Watts, S. M. & Cerra, K. K. (1996). Can you teach reading comprehension with children's books? Fostering reader response and developing comprehension strategies. *Balanced Reading Instruction, III,* 1–7.

Language:
The Key to Literacy

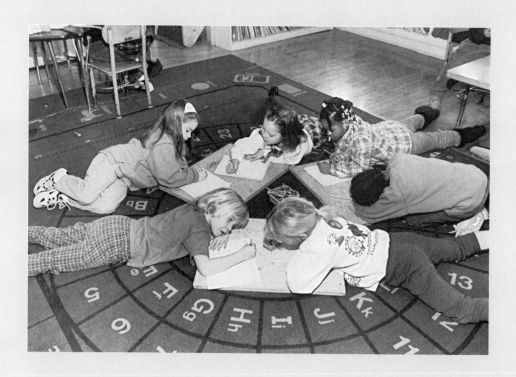

Chapter Outline

For the Reader

Language is a powerful means through which we learn, develop and expand our interests, communicate with others, and communicate with ourselves (Standards for the English Language Arts, 1996). Language continually shapes our views of the world and ourselves. Whether it is a child saying "cookie," a scientist explaining a new theory, an author writing a book, or a student reading a CD-ROM encyclopedia entry, the central purpose of language is communication of meaning. Reading is based on language, as are listening, speaking, and writing. Language cuts across every goal and function of the school. Everything that is taught in the school passes through a communication process before students learn it. Purposes for language use in the schools include (1) obtaining and communicating information through the use of a variety of text sources, (2) responding to creating and interpreting literary texts, (3) learning and reflecting, and (4) solving problems and thinking critically (Standards for the English Language Arts, 1996).

Key Ideas

■ Reading and writing are related to all language functions found in the elementary school curriculum.

■ Learning to read and write is related to, and built upon, past language experiences. Such experiences enable children to broaden and apply their knowledge of language systems and the functions of language.

■ Children's literacy development is enhanced through its use in meaningful and varied experiences with language. Literacy instruction should be a natural outgrowth of students' past language experiences.

■ Literacy learning is a developmental process related to continued language development that reflects an expansion of children's reading and writing experiences.

■ Different methods of teaching literacy may be justified, but a method should build logically and systematically on students' language capabilities.

The Interactive Features of Reading

Reading is a language process requiring the understanding of and the interaction with written language. Language provides a bridge that enables ideas, information, and data to pass between parent and child, teacher and student, and student and peer. Reading has a unique relationship with language. Because we acquire or refine most of our concepts and reasoning capabilities through the use of language, reading enables us to go beyond what we can see or manipulate. In a broad sense, reading frees both language and thinking from immediate experiences (Wells, 1981). There are, however, differences between spoken and written language. Spoken language is different in form from written language. As noted by Jeannette Veatch (1996), "One does not read spoken language easily. One reads written language as it was intended" (p. 513).

Recognizing Words

Written language involves the learner in solving two codes. One is accessing the text or print by understanding the relationship between the orthography (the writing system) and the phonemes (speech units represented by the writing system). This understanding permits the reader to recognize, decode, or approximate the pronunciation of words not recognized as whole words. Reading research has documented the importance of children understanding the relationship between letters and letter combinations and the sounds they represent (Rupley & Willson, in press); however, how best to facilitate this development in reading instruction is an ongoing debate. Children who are emerging readers and writers need to know the relationship between their own speech sounds and how these are represented in print. Some children find this difficult because they are not aware of how words and sounds in their speech are marked or that they are distinct units (Dickinson, Wolf, & Stotsky, 1993).

Constructing Meaning

Constructing meaning is the second important code. Readers interact with writers so that there is communication between the two. Writers of books, notes, lists, directions, and so forth are using language to communicate with a reader. Interaction between the text and reader depends on the reader's experiential and conceptual background, purposes for reading, and setting, as well as the text content. This interaction involves a strategic approach that requires knowledge of language structures, comprehension monitoring, and understanding meaning. Such interaction is language-related, but it goes beyond the reader's oral language background, because much of this interaction involves reading and writing experiences that support and extend all language capabilities.

Oral Language and Reading

The **oral language** capabilities of listening and speaking are related to the language processing capabilities of reading and writing **(literacy).** Several important relationships between oral language and literacy are that (1) oral language capabilities develop to a fairly high level of proficiency before written language capabilities develop, (2) oral and written language share the same vocabulary and grammar, (3) knowledge of oral language is used extensively by students in learning to read and write, and (4) oral language and literacy are keys to the development of more-complex cognitive capabilities (Raphael & Hiebert, 1996). Literacy builds a bridge of understanding between oral language capabilities and reading and writing.

One view of the relationship between oral and written language is that in the beginning stages of reading development, children depend on their oral language abilities for comprehension. That is, emerging readers' comprehension of print is linked closely to their spoken language capabilities and experiences with print. For example, a young child who frequently plays computer games will often learn to recognize words such as *exit, open,* and *close,* because of their importance in operating a computer and playing computer games. At this early stage of learning about words, called the *logographic* stage (Frith, 1985), children learn words as wholes. These words are often embedded in logos in print within children's environment, as the word *McDonald's* is embedded in golden arches. As children's reading becomes more automatic and proficient, their dependence on spoken language abilities in comprehending print generally disappears, and print is comprehended in terms of its structural and meaning features. This capability is reflected in stage 2 of Chall's (1996) reading stages, in which children begin to become more proficient in using letter-sound relationships in their reading. Samuels (1988) has attributed this increased proficiency to word recognition becoming more automatic; that is, it requires less attention to sounding out words and more attention to comprehension. Research findings have shown that children experience difficulty reading text that contains features and structures they have not yet acquired in their oral language. They also have problems with text that contains structures they are in the process of acquiring.

Research supports the idea that students undergo developmental shifts in the degree of importance of oral language in their comprehension of text. Young children often depend more on their oral language skills, while older students, who are more proficient in reading, depend more on their experience with reading and writing. Emergent readers who are learning about orthographic features and acquiring word-recognition skills are also developing an understanding of how print functions, the nature of stories, and other important components of literacy that will enhance their comprehension. As they build experience with print, emergent readers rely less upon the speech code representation and focus more on meaning.

This phenomenon suggests a reciprocal relationship between literacy and oral-language development. Students' language awareness depends heavily on their literacy experiences, which help them to understand language features, such as syntax and semantics, and to develop and expand their vocabularies. Direct experiences with reading and writing enhance and facilitate the development of language awareness, which enhances and facilitates literacy and reasoning development (Stahl, 1996). Language awareness, which includes knowledge about phonemes, words, sentences, story structure, and communication of meaning, evolves primarily through a variety of direct experiences with print in both reading and writing situations.

■ Reading Instruction That Builds on Oral Language

Reading for meaning is in many ways closer to children's previous experiences with language than is associating visual symbols with the sounds they typically represent. Prior to reading instruction, children have spent several years listening to and speaking meaningful language. Most children begin school with a speaking vocabulary of approximately 8,000 words and are capable of using language to express themselves. However, they use this language within familiar contextual settings and focus on communication with others. The process and the demands of literacy are based on **decontextualized language use,** which requires the development of language awareness. Decontextualized language has three characteristics that are more closely associated with written language than with oral language:

1. Information must be conveyed that is new to the hearer.
2. Background knowledge necessary for the hearer to interpret the message needs to be provided.
3. The information must be communicated through words and syntax, not by relying on intonation and extra-linguistic resources such as gestures. (Dickinson, Wolf, & Stotsky, 1993, p. 372)

■ Contextualized Language

Experiences with language in their environment begin to enhance children's development of decontextualized language skills. As children learn to recognize words by associating logos (e.g., Coke, Crest, McDonald's, Nike) with them, engage in pretend writing in their play, distinguish print from pictures, understand the features of books, and so forth, they begin to develop decontextualized language capabilities.

Because children learning to read and write rely heavily on their language backgrounds and their early experiences with literacy, they can experience difficulties when they are asked to do something that does not build on their existing capabilities. Failure to build on children's existing language capabilities may result in their failure to see that they are really involved in a language process. The materials and methods used for reading and writing instruction often divorce the act of reading from language involvement by emphasizing letter-sound relationships, the mechanics of writing, and other isolated skills that fail to stress the language-meaning features of print. Lack of balanced reading instruction may or may not be deliberate. Our concern is how the learner perceives what is going on. Phonics, for example, can provide motivation only for a limited time—it is not a self-sustaining activity. Only direct involvement in actual reading and writing will help children develop literacy capabilities that complement and extend their language development.

Teachers who are teaching and facilitating reading are aware of experiences and growth that children undergo before they enter school. Many children already have had language experiences that form a solid foundation for their

The Most Horible Night

By Billy Rupley

It's a horible
night, not
one light
in sight, and
you're traped
in the woods by
Ms.O. you take one big
breath, you think
that it's
death
and you try to escape
her grip, but
the bell rings
but your home work
walks in, how you
wish you could
fight but
your gun's not
in sight and you have no
weekend to look ford to.

FIGURE 3.1
An illustration of how children's experiences both in and out of school build the foundation for their writing development (Ms. O is the classroom's imaginary substitute teacher.)

experiences with reading. Children whose parents read to them often and who have been engaged in literacy experiences will begin to make connections between print and oral language, recognize some words as whole words, know the features of a book, relate pictures to text, develop emerging understanding about writing, and understand many other relationships between oral and written language. Children who have not had opportunities to engage in informal reading activities may not yet do so. Figure 3.1 provides an example of how language experiences outside of school and those in school contribute to children's writing.

As noted earlier, whether or not teachers build on children's oral language skills will influence the degree of their students' benefit from literacy activities. Students are not likely to be able to read language that is significantly different from their speaking and listening capabilities, nor are they likely to be able to write better than they can speak. Oral-language capabilities provide the foundation for literacy development at the beginning stages and at each stage that follows. Teachers of reading should view children's experiences both in and out of school as bound together with language and communication: All involve developing and extending concepts. Children build comprehension capabilities in reading and expression capabilities in writing on these concepts (Tompkins & Hoskisson, 1995).

Structure of Language

Language instruction has its own distinct terminology. Teachers of literacy will frequently encounter these terms in their readings about literacy instruction, as well as in many of the instructional materials and reading programs used to teach literacy.

■ Terms Associated with Phonology

Phoneme: the smallest unit of sound within a language. When the word *top* is pronounced, three phonemes are utilized: /t/, /o/, /p/.

Grapheme: a written symbol (letter or letter combination) used to represent a sound in a language. The word *top* has three graphemes representing three phonemes. The word *chop* has three graphemes representing three phonemes (*ch* is a consonant digraph representing one sound).

Grapheme-Phoneme Relationship: the sound(s) represented by a letter or a letter combination. Also referred to as *letter-sound correspondence*.

Phonics: different approaches and strategies designed to teach the orthographic (written) code of language and the relationships between spelling patterns and the speech sounds represented by the spelling patterns.

■ Terms Associated with Meaning Features of Language

Semantics: describes the meaning relationships among words. Semantic acquisition refers to how children acquire vocabulary and how they begin to acquire semantic systems that are based on simple vocabulary acquisition.

Morpheme: the smallest unit of meaningful language. Morphemes can be one of two types: free or bound. A free morpheme functions independently in larger language units. For example, *dog* is a free morpheme composed of three phonemes. A bound morpheme must be used with another morpheme. Bound morphemes include affixes and inflectional endings. If *s* is added to *dog* to form a plural, the *s* in *dogs* is a bound morpheme, and therefore the word *dogs* contains two morphemes.

■ Terms Associated with Structural Features of Language

Syntax: describes the patterns found within a language (the grammar of the language). Syntax includes the various patterns in which words can be strung together. It also includes the ways in which words function in different language patterns, as illustrated by the following example.

Light the fire. (verb)

She saw the **light.** (noun)

He danced **lightly** across the ring and threw a **light** punch. (adverb, adjective)

Research has supported the idea that children need to learn about the relationships between word spellings and pronunciations to become successful readers (Adams, 1990; Chall, 1996; Stahl, 1996). As one teaches these relationships, many of the language-development characteristics and features presented earlier in this chapter must be taken into consideration. However, reading instruction can overemphasize words as individual units. Overemphasizing words inhibits the development of abilities in using syntax and semantic features to arrive at meaning. Furthermore, it does not reflect the purpose of phonics, which is to develop automatic word recognition so children can devote their attention to comprehension. Understanding the importance of language in teaching literacy is essential to developing a quality instructional program.

Language Variations

Children acquire the language to which they are exposed—generally that of their parents, which reflects the parents' geographic region (Goldfield & Snow, 1993). Although most languages share some common features (e.g., syntactic, semantic, and phonetic features), variations occur even among speakers of a common language. Dialects, for example, differ from region to region. Another important variation influencing children's literacy acquisition occurs when they are learning to read and write in English but have a first language (e.g., Spanish, Vietnamese, or Navajo) other than English.

Culturally and Linguistically Diverse Learners

Culturally and linguistically diverse learners are children whose culture as well as language or dialect differ from those of the school. The number of linguistically diverse learners in American classrooms is growing.

Dialects, in a broad sense, are the ways that people speak in different parts of a country or in specific cultures. The components of a dialect are pronunciation, grammar, and vocabulary. Generally speaking, phonological divergences of dialects are differences in speech sounds within words; thus, a grapheme (written letter symbol) may represent different phonemes (speech sounds) in different dialects. Grammatical and syntactical divergences of dialects are differences in inflectional changes, verb forms, verb auxiliaries, and the structures of phrases and sentences.

Linguistically diverse (bilingual and non-English-speaking) students who lack competency in the language of the classroom do not enter the school setting from a linguistic void. These students have mastered a language and its systems of significant speech sounds, grammatical structures, and meaningful vocabulary.

Linguistically diverse children often face the expectation that they will read and comprehend English with competency as part of their school curriculum. Many factors, however, inhibit rapid acquisition of English as a second language, while others facilitate linguistically diverse students in becoming bilingual in their first language and in English. For example, linguistic components such as phonology, syntax, and semantics make learning English difficult. *Phonology* refers to the inventory of meaningful speech sounds used to form grammatical structures in a particular language system. Vietnamese children who are learning English as a second language, for example, have never heard in their native language the sounds /s/, /es/, /t/, and /d/ at the end of a word. Some languages follow a different syntax from that of English. Spanish, for example, contains no possessive forms of nouns (e.g., *my dad's car*), so children who are native Spanish speakers sometimes experience difficulties with such language structures in English. The semantics of other languages are also different. A Navajo speaker learning English would perceive the concept of the word *rough* as a series of many attributes, each having different labels depending on the texture of the object.

Reading development is linked to students' strengths and weaknesses in their oral language capabilities (listening and speaking). Many linguistically diverse students might experience greater success in literacy development if their primary language formed the basis for their learning. Children's primary language can provide a support system for learning English and can enhance the growth of their self-confidence.

For culturally and linguistically diverse learners, a lack of experience in curricular topics or themes can also inhibit reading development. Language expansion and concept development can contribute to such students' literacy development. A word, even when it is pronounced correctly, is nonsense to a student who attaches no meaning to that word. Providing opportunities for students to broaden and enrich both their language and informational backgrounds promotes their success in reading and writing.

The Reading and Writing Connection

The connection between reading and writing should be apparent, although each is often treated separately. As with listening, speaking, and reading, the purpose of writing is to communicate meaning. Students who understand that others can read their writing and that they can read the writing of others realize the communicative concept of reading and are likely to understand that reading is constructing meaning, not just sounding out words.

Researchers have found reading and writing to be interactive processes that share similar components (McCarthy & Raphael, 1992). Tierney and Pearson (1983) consider both reading and writing to be acts of composing. Writers compose meaning as they record their thoughts on paper; readers compose meaning as they process text. Reading and writing don't merely share the composition of meaning, however. Other researchers indicate that both readers and writers

Literacy instruction that provides meaning in rich and concrete contexts is likely to be most effective.

operate at several levels—using word-recognition strategies, using and understanding language structure, organizing ideas, applying background knowledge, and monitoring the composition-of-meaning process (Beck, 1985; Raphael & Englert, 1989). Generally, research has shown that children who are better readers tend to be better writers (Stahl, Pagnucco, & Suttles, 1996). The features that reading and writing share emphasize the importance of language in children's literacy development.

Meeting Students' Literacy Needs

Many factors influence student reading, such as knowledge of letter-sound relationships, knowledge of language functions and structure, and background knowledge of the text being read. Also, as students progress through school, their reading capabilities increase as they learn more about language through literacy activities and expand their experiential and conceptual knowledge. Writing development seems to follow a similar pattern. Students with superior language capabilities are often better able than students with less-developed abilities to organize their writing and to produce text that is more coherent and longer.

A classroom environment that nurtures language development is important for all students to experience growth in their literacy capabilities. For those exceptional students included in the classroom, modification of existing structure and language demands may be necessary. Children who do not have well-developed language skills can benefit from explicit language instruction. For example, young children in kindergarten or first grade who lag behind in their language development can often benefit from instruction that targets the lexicon (word meaning). The focus of such instruction would be on verbs, which are the key to grammar, and would include formal syntax training as an accompanying feature (Rice, 1996).

An additional feature that is appropriate for all children is a language environment within the classroom that invites children to engage in reasoning about language. Paired reading and writing can create situations in which students who are lagging behind their age-peers can work with younger children on reading and writing. Support is provided for each child, and each gets valuable practice and literacy opportunities. The result is a community of language users who have much to talk about and much to share through listening, reading, and writing.

■ Key Strategies Used by Readers and Writers

Some of the key strategies that successful readers and writers use have been summarized by Larry Lewin (1992). He points out that good readers and writers routinely and knowingly use the following strategies.

1. Prepare by

   - tapping their existing knowledge background for a topic before they read and write.
   - determining their purpose(s) for reading and writing.
   - predicting how what they are reading or what they are to write will turn out.
   - self-selecting topics they want to read about or write about.

2. Compose a first draft by

   - monitoring their own understanding of their text and the text of others.
   - monitoring their own reactions to text.
   - relating new information in their reading and writing to what they already know.

- expanding their vocabulary both during and after a first reading and a first draft of writing.
- knowing where to get help and assistance when either the reading or writing breaks down.
- distinguishing in their reading and writing the important from the less important ideas.

3. Repair by

- reconsidering the first meaning that they construct in their reading and writing.
- repairing their text to improve its meaning by rereading or rewriting.
- appreciating an author's craft and working to expand and enhance their own writing craft.

4. Share by

- communicating to others their reactions to their own and others' writing.
- applying their newly acquired information to future reading and writing tasks.

Students' experiential and conceptual backgrounds are important in both comprehending text when reading and composing comprehensive text when writing. Students write best about things of which they have background knowledge. Likewise, they read with best comprehension about things that are in their experiential and conceptual backgrounds. One of the most important features of reading and writing is that they both enhance children's language resources, particularly their oral language capabilities.

Several important observations (Stahl, Osborn, & Lehr, 1996) that support the integrated role that writing plays in the development of children's reading capabilities include the following:

1. Children often include in their writing the syntactic patterns, themes, and content of the materials they read.
2. Children learn through writing that the purpose of text is to be understood.
3. Children learn that different readers respond to the same text differently. They come to realize that meaning is a result of an interaction between the author and the reader.
4. Children realize that to write clearly and communicate well with readers, their writing must have an underlying organization and may require the use of other sources to maximize communication.
5. Children learn that reading is about thinking and reasoning. This is perhaps their most important understanding.

■ Interactive Features of Reading and Writing in Constructing Meaning

The connections between reading and writing suggest that teachers should integrate reading and writing throughout instructional programs. The key strategies noted in the previous section of this chapter are those that teachers can develop, nurture, and polish by combining reading and writing in the classroom to better develop children's literacy. Shanahan (1988) developed seven instructional principles based on the reading-writing relationship. Each of these principles, which are discussed in the following paragraphs, illustrates how to combine reading and writing in the classroom.

Teach Both Reading and Writing.   Although many individuals argue that reading and writing are similar in terms of the skills, strategies, and cognitive processes they involve, Shanahan (1988) does not consider them to be all that similar, suggesting that children need opportunities to be taught both. Students do not become writers only through reading instruction, nor do they become readers only through writing instruction. Students need both reading and writing opportunities so that each skill can enhance the development of the other.

Introduce Reading and Writing from the Earliest Grades.   Although Shanahan (1988) recommends early introduction, it is best to make reading and writing a pervasive part of the curriculum. Teachers who create literate environments in their classrooms don't treat literacy as a subject having a specific scheduled period. Language is an integral part of the learning environment, and reading and writing opportunities should abound throughout each day. Teachers should work to infuse reading and writing instruction in the study of literature and content-area subjects (Raphael & Hiebert, 1996). Writing and reading activities can vary in purpose, requirements, and audience for both literature texts and content-area texts. A valuable guide for helping teachers accomplish the infusion of literacy throughout the curriculum is presented in Table 3.1. The examples shown can be easily expanded and modified to meet the needs of individual children.

Reading typically is introduced early in children's formal education, but writing is often delayed until later. Sulzby and Barnhart (1992) argue that reading and writing should be taught in the first year of formal education because children begin school with much literacy learning already having occurred. Building on and nurturing this early literacy learning is what enables young children to develop conventional literacy. Early reading and writing behaviors, called *emergent literacy,* are discussed in Chapter 4.

Reflect the Developmental Nature of the Reading and Writing Relationship in Instruction.   Tierney (1992) suggests that reading and writing are developmental processes and that different abilities are dominant at different points in development. Shanahan (1988) notes that in the beginning stages of reading, spelling and word recognition are dominant. These findings coincide with Chall's (1996) research on stages of reading development and with Adams's (1990) analysis of beginning reading development. With more-capable readers, the connection between reading and writing focuses on comprehension, vocabulary, and organization. What students learn at different points in their reading and writing development can have important implications for instruction.

Reading and writing can be integrated at developmental stages by using writing activities that are appropriate for students' levels of reading and oral-language development. Teachers can use multiple types of materials in teaching

TABLE 3.1
Guidelines for infusing literacy throughout the curriculum

WRITING	PURPOSE	REQUIREMENTS	AUDIENCE
1. Weather and temperature charts	Compare conditions over a nine-month period.	Thermometer to take temperature. Observe clouds at same time of day. Accuracy.	Science class.
2. Personal letters	Exchange accounts of experiences with friend.	Interesting personal information. Informal writing level.	A friend who knows me.
3. Invitations	Inform and invite audience to a program, party, etc.	What, who, why, when, where. (Proofreading is important.)	Parents, neighbors, friends.
4. Puppet plays	Entertain.	Original story that entertains. Puppets.	Class, parents, other invited guests
5. Diaries	Record daily experiences and feelings.	Short notes on things important to me.	Me.
6. News stories	Inform about news, events, sports, etc.	Accuracy—who, what, when, where. Clear, brief reporting. (Editing and proofreading are important.)	Whole school. If city paper, large unknown audience that wants information.
7. Forms	Obtain social security card, driver's license. Send for information.	Accurate information, clear handwriting. (Proofreading is important.)	People who don't know me. Government.
8. Imaginative	Entertain, enjoy.	Fresh ideas, imagination, feelings.	Class. If published, a large, unknown audience.
9. Autobiographies	Tell others about myself. Compile class book.	Facts about myself, feelings, wishes. (Proofreading is important.)	Class and parents. If published, a large, unknown audience.
10. Book reports	Report author, title information, summary, and personal reactions.	Careful reading and writing for summary. (Proofreading is important.)	Class. If book review in a paper, people who might want to read the book.
11. Reports and projects in social studies, science, etc.	Share new facts and information.	Research from several sources, data, main ideas, and details. Accuracy of facts, best order for ideas. (Proofreading is important.)	Class. If journal or magazine article, people wanting that information.
12. Biographies	Report knowledge about well-known person.	Research from several sources. Comparisons of information. Accuracy. (Proofreading is important.)	Class. If published, a large, unknown audience.
13. Editorials	Persuade someone to my viewpoint.	Knowledge of ways to persuade and use facts. Rewriting to clearly persuade.	People who read the newspaper. Some will agree with the writer, some will disagree.
14. Minutes for meetings	Keep a record of what happened.	Accurate listening and reading.	Class, group, or organization.

SOURCE: From Donna Norton, *The Effective Teaching of Language Arts* (5th ed.) (pp. 466–467). Copyright 1997 by Merrill/Prentice-Hall Publishing Co. Reprinted with permission.

Teachers can use a variety of activities to stimulate students' writing.

students to read, write about, synthesize, evaluate, or analyze text. Writing activities that encourage children to use new words can reinforce vocabulary development. Such writing activities should focus on real-life experiences to ensure that students' language structure and text reflect their background knowledge. Writing activities can also replace or supplement many of the independent practice and application activities recommended in reading instructional materials.

Make the Reading and Writing Connection Explicit.   Teaching a particular reading or writing skill does not guarantee that it will transfer to actual applications. Students need direct instruction in reading and writing as well as close supervision by the teacher for learning to occur. They also need to understand when to use a skill or strategy. Lessons in reading and writing should therefore complement each other. In other words, when appropriate, what students learn in reading should be transferred for use in writing, and vice versa. Reading and writing instruction can be simultaneous, showing students the specific purpose of and the relationships between the two subjects. Students learn much about the nature and structure of writing through instruction in the grammar, process writing patterns, and expository writing patterns of stories and through other reading instruction that focuses on text processing. Learning these aspects of reading enables students to better use them in writing and thus develop more mature writing styles. Younger students often pattern their writing after books they have read or listened to. Schell (1993) points out a classic example of this: After reading *Brown Bear* by Bill Martin, children modeled the story language in their writing (Brown dog, brown dog, what do you see? I see a fat cat looking at me.). Literary aspects, such as characterization, irony, foreshadowing, dialogue, and sarcasm, that teachers focus on in their reading programs also are modeled for students to use in their own writing.

Emphasize Product and Process Knowledge in Instruction. Shanahan (1988) urges teachers to be aware of the differences between product knowledge and process knowledge. Product knowledge is substantive (vocabulary and word knowledge), while process knowledge is related to reasoning ability. The latter is concerned with strategies and procedures for solving problems and carrying out complex activities. Readers and writers both must monitor themselves to make sure the text makes sense and must use strategies to aid comprehension.

Reading and writing instruction that focuses on vocabulary knowledge and relates text to students' background knowledge can expand product knowledge. Most teachers do a good job of teaching in this area. The process aspect of reading and writing, however, requires a focus on the how and why. In process instruction, students discuss how they preview text, how they predict outcomes and events, how they come up with ideas about text they have read or stories they have written, how and why they choose to revise their thinking about text, and why they edit text. Awareness of the many processes that reading and writing share benefits both reading and writing acquisition and development.

Emphasize Communication. Reading and writing are communication processes; readers and writers are concerned with meaning. This text emphasizes that language is communication of meaning and that reading must be recognized as a language process. Highlighting the communication function of language capitalizes upon the essentials of language growth: people to talk to, read about, and write to, and things to read and write about that are meaningful to students.

Teach Reading and Writing in a Meaningful Context. The different functions of children's language (see Figure 3.2) can be used strategically for teaching reading and writing in a meaningful context. Teachers can explore and develop these functions by integrating reading and writing. They can have students write explanations of text, rewrite text, prepare lists, write directions, write and evaluate advertising aimed at encouraging consumer use, write and edit a class newspaper, write books and stories for other classes and students, keep minutes of group meetings, plan schedules, and so forth. The central point for teachers to consider is that students must have opportunities to integrate reading and writing in a variety of literacy experiences.

Instrumental Language—The teacher can:

1. Be accessible and responsive to children's requests, but teach independence by having children state their requests effectively.
2. Encourage the use of instrumental language with other children, helping them to expand their own language through providing help and direction to peers.
3. Analyze advertising, propaganda, etc., to help children become aware of how language can be used by people to get what they want.

Regulatory Language—The teacher can:

1. Create situations that let children be "in charge" of small and large groups.
2. Find instances in which regulatory language is used inappropriately to teach appropriate regulatory language or the alternative, instrumental language.
3. Attempt to use less regulatory language as a teacher.

Interactional Language—The teacher can:

1. Create situations that require children to share work areas or materials and talk about how they are to do it.
2. Find ways of having small group (especially pairs or trios) discussions in a variety of subject areas. Through these discussions, students not only learn the subject matter more thoroughly, they practice communication.
3. Let students work together to plan field trips, social events, and classroom and school projects.
4. Whenever possible, mix children of different ages, sexes, and races in work groups or discussion groups.
5. Have informal social times and, as a teacher, engage in some talk that is not "all business."

Personal Language—The teacher can:

1. Use personal language to give permission to children to share personal thoughts and opinions.
2. Be willing to listen and talk personally during transition times: for example, when children are coming in in the morning. Converse with children while on cafeteria or playground duty.
3. Provide some comfortable, attractive areas in the classroom where students can talk quietly.

FIGURE 3.2
Instructional strategies to promote language functions
Source: From G. S. Pinnell, "Ways to Look at the Functions of Children's Language." In B. Power and R. Hubbard (Eds.), **Language Development: A Reader for Teachers** (Upper Saddle River, NJ: Prentice Hall, Inc., 1996), pp. 152–153. Reprinted with permission of Gay Su Pinnell and Prentice Hall, Inc.

4. Encourage parents and family members to visit and participate in classrooms.
5. Read stories or books that prompt a very personal response from students.

Imaginative Language—The teacher can:

1. Create situations that naturally elicit spontaneous dramatic play; for example, house corner, dress up, blocks for younger children, and drama and role-playing for older children.
2. Read stories and books which feed the imagination and which are a stimulus for art, drama, and discussion.
3. Provide time for children to talk in groups and/or with partners before they begin their writing or imaginative topics.
4. Encourage "play" with language—the sounds of words and the images they convey.

Heuristic Language—The teacher can:

1. Structure classroom experiences so that interest and curiosity are aroused.
2. Create real problems for children to solve.
3. Put children in pairs or work groups for problem-solving activities.
4. Use heuristic language to stimulate such language in children. Saying "I wonder why" often prompts children to do the same. (This should, however, not be contrived; it should be an honest problem.)
5. Try projects which require study on the part of the entire class, including the teacher. Find some questions that no one knows the answer to.

Informative Language—The teacher can:

1. Plan activities which require children to observe carefully and objectively and then to summarize and draw conclusions from their observations (field trips are a good opportunity).
2. Require children to keep records of events over periods of time and then to look back at their records and draw conclusions; for example, keeping records on classroom pets.
3. Use questioning techniques to elicit more complex forms of information giving.
4. Instead of having tedious classroom reports, have children give their reports to small groups and encourage feedback and discussion of those reports.

FIGURE 3.2, continued

Considerations for a Language-rich Classroom Environment

■ Whole-language and Interactive Reading Instruction

Many of the teachers we have visited do an excellent job of creating a language- and literacy-rich classroom environment. What varies, however, is how they integrate this environment into their literacy program. Much of the variation reflects teachers' different philosophies about the best way to teach literacy.

Some teachers think that students learn best when reading and writing are naturally connected to oral language. This perspective or orientation is referred to as **whole language.** Whole language is not a method or program of reading instruction; rather, it is an orientation toward the development of literacy. Whole-language advocates believe that language acquisition (including reading and writing) is an essential part of an individual functioning within the environment. A whole-language approach assumes that (1) the function of language is making meaning, (2) writing is a language activity, so what is true for oral language is also true for written language, (3) cue systems of language (structural features) are present and interact in all instances of language, (4) language use occurs in real-life situations, and (5) real-life situations are crucial to the meaning aspect of language.

A teacher who has a true whole-language orientation would not use materials or activities (such as published reading materials) intended for teaching specific literacy skills and abilities (such as phenomenic awareness, vocabulary, and grammar of stories). Early proponents of whole language viewed subskill-practice activities as work substitutes that did not accurately reflect the acquisition and use of language (Goodman & Goodman, 1983). Today, a broader view of whole language includes the basic components—big books, shared reading, guided reading, and writing activities—used to practice necessary skills independently in meaningful contexts.

In talking with many teachers about a whole-language orientation toward literacy development, we have found that the term means different things to different teachers. Vacca and Rasinski (1992) noted similar variations in teachers' working definitions of *whole language:*

> In practice, teachers will vary in their working definitions [of whole language], usually placing emphasis on certain dimensions of their concepts of whole language. If, for example, you were to ask a room full of teachers to associate one or two words that come to mind quickly when thinking about whole language in their classrooms, their responses undoubtedly would vary. Some might use words that associate whole language with child-responsive environments for learning; others, with literature-based instruction; still others, with curriculum integration. (p. 6)

Teachers' perceptions and definitions of whole language vary because whole language is a philosophy rather than a clearly identified methodology or approach to reading instruction. Even though how teachers perceive whole language varies, however, their classroom environments exhibit many similar features. Any whole-language-oriented teacher's classroom would be rich in print.

The teacher would make little, if any, use of materials developed specifically to teach reading. The teacher would instead use literature, big books, shared reading, creative writing, and real-life print materials (e.g., real recipes for making cake, butter, or ice cream) (Edelsky, Altwerger, & Flores, 1991). In addition, in such classrooms the teacher would read aloud, vary organizational schemes, and interact with the students. The pervasive characteristic of a whole-language-oriented classroom is that it develops literacy from a real-life perspective. Students engage in communication of meaning for reading and writing and apply their skills in meaningful contexts.

As we have noted, *whole language* means various things to different teachers. We have talked with teachers who say they do some whole-language activities but focus more on text-processing skills. We have spoken with other teachers who use a literature-based reading program and believe that they are teaching reading from a whole-language perspective, even though they follow the recommendations in the teacher's guide for teaching reading.

We believe that there is not a single best way to teach reading. Instead of developing an orientation that is rigid, teachers need first to look at each student and ask themselves, "What does this child bring to the reading and writing situation? How can I capitalize upon the student's capabilities to maximize his or her reading and writing growth and development?" The whole-language concept has helped spur a reevaluation of how reading is taught: We now know that quality literacy instruction teaches skills for reading and writing and applies them in meaningful contexts.

There has beem a transformation in how whole language is perceived by teachers (Spiegel, 1996). Literacy instruction that is interactive and skills-based does not have to be rigid, repetitive, and scripted. Providing students opportunities to interact with print in a language-rich environment is essential, regardless of the teacher's beliefs about how best to teach reading. Therefore, teachers who are either interactive or whole-language oriented in their approach to reading instruction will often use the same instructional materials, employ a variety of reading situations, build on the language capabilities of their students, create a language-rich classroom, and so forth. Figure 3.3 presents some of the essential characteristics of a whole-language orientation, an interactive orientation, and the features shared by both.

■ Features of a Language-rich Environment

When considering how to create a language-rich environment in the classroom, a teacher should ensure two important qualities. One is a classroom environment that encourages and supports literacy development. The second is the incorporation of language-rich environmental features and activities into reading and writing instruction.

Sulzby and Barnhart (1992) describe what a literacy-rich environment generally is like:

> Materials are at children's reach and there is sufficient time during the day for children to interact with those materials. Reading and writing tend to become less visible as separate activities and become more deeply embedded in other aspects of classroom life. (p. 125)

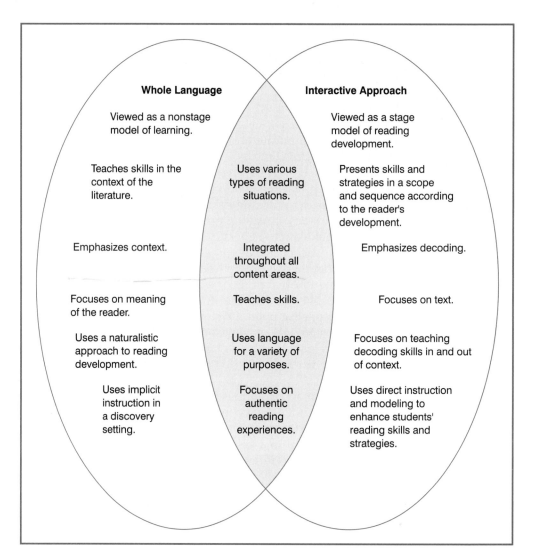

FIGURE 3.3
Characteristics of whole-language and interactive approaches to reading instruction
Source: Developed by W. D. Nichols, 1996.

Reading and writing are infused into the daily instructional activities and experiences of the children so that they become a natural and integral part of learning. Pinnell (1996) has conceptualized different ways for teachers to consider how children's language functions (see Figure 3.2). Knowledge of such functions can form the basis for using instructional strategies and materials to infuse literacy into children's classroom experiences. Language-rich classroom environments have features that encourage students to interact with language; that is, they have things to talk about, read about, and write about.

Any classroom arrangement that brings students together to talk and listen to one another can promote language development.

■ Classroom Centers

Centers to promote literacy development can be set up in the classroom. Such centers can focus on reading, writing, and oral language. A writing center could provide children with access to such things as a typewriter, a computer, pencils, pens, markers, lined and unlined paper, notepads, staplers, scissors, and other materials that encourage students to write and share their writing with others. To stimulate students' imagination and motivation to write, many teachers also include in their writing centers old magazines, pictures, artifacts, coupons, catalogs, stamp pads, and other objects they have collected.

A reading center is more than just a library with a collection of books. It is an area in the classroom that invites children to read. A large collection of reading materials could include books on a variety of topics and aimed at several different reading levels—including big books, read-along books, audiotaped books, rebus books, and picture books—along with catalogs, magazines, stories written by children in the class, newspapers, and travel brochures. A variety of reading materials for all grade levels is recommended for each classroom (our college students still get excited when they read children's books, as do many fifth and sixth graders). Furniture for the reading center can range from easy chairs to an old bathtub, as long as it is comfortable and inviting to students.

Centers to promote oral language (speaking and listening) are not as well defined as writing and reading centers; however, any classroom arrangement that brings students together to talk and listen to one another can promote oral-language development. Many of the suggestions presented in Figure 3.2 can be the focus of a permanent or temporary center in the classroom. For example, a drama center stocked with old clothes, hats, shoes, puppets, and other materials can be used to stimulate role-playing and dramatic play that result in spontaneous inter-action. A garden or plant center where students gather to watch and care for plants will create interest and stimulate their curiosity. This type of project can help students begin to better understand heuristic language as the teacher encourages them to interact with each other by asking questions that begin with "I wonder why."

How teachers use their activity centers to promote literacy depends on what functions the centers serve and how much direct instruction the teachers provide. Pinnell's instructional strategies to promote language functions (Figure 3.2) can serve as guidelines to help determine the functions and purposes of the centers and plan appropriate learning activities.

In addition to using centers to promote reading and writing development, teachers can display examples of students' writing; encourage them to write stories to take home; label objects in the classroom (e.g., This is the door. Here is our light switch.); write dictated lists and schedules; place notepads, paper, and writing tools in activity centers; establish pen pals for students; set up a classroom post office; write class newspapers; encourage diary and journal writing; and establish an interactive web site on the Internet.

■ Reading Activities and Instructional Opportunities in a Language-rich Environment

Incorporating a classroom's language-rich features into reading and writing in-struction capitalizes on the benefits of such an environment. Suggestions for inte-grating and promoting language development in literacy instruction appear throughout this book; expanded discussions are found in chapters dealing with emergent literacy, comprehension, meaning vocabulary, and instructional mate-rials and programs.

Reading aloud to students of all ages has several benefits and has been fre-quently cited (Adams, 1990) as a major factor contributing to reading and writing development. First, it can help students understand that the purpose of reading is to communicate meaning. Students often cry, laugh, and express other emotions when listening to stories read to them. Such reactions indicate that they compre-hend what they hear.

Second, reading aloud to students can foster a desire to read and can help students associate value with reading. Most students look forward to the teacher's reading aloud to them daily. Later, children may read many of the books and magazines from which the teacher reads.

Third, reading aloud to students can enable the teacher to take advantage of teaching moments. Teaching moments are situations that arise during a school day when the teacher can reinforce, reintroduce, or illustrate something that has been taught previously. For example, if a lesson about different meanings of words preceded reading aloud to children, and what is being read aloud has some multiple-meaning words, the teacher can point this out and illustrate the lesson concept with examples from the selection being read.

Students in the lower grades often benefit from hearing the same books read aloud to them several times. When these books are then made available for students to read independently, these frequently become the books they enjoy reading the most. In addition to reading books, students enjoy hearing poetry, limericks, and song lyrics. Students at all grade levels enjoy being read to, and teachers at all grade levels should be encouraged to make reading aloud part of their daily instruction.

Reading aloud to students gives them the opportunity to see the relationships among reading, writing, speaking, and listening. It is one way to enable them to connect, through the use of language, old learning with new learning. Encouraging students to discuss and ask questions about what is read aloud to them engages them in the reading and language relationship. Questions broaden their experiences and reinforce the concept that reading is a communication process. Therefore, questions that encourage children to express their feelings about their favorite parts of a story, the author's language, the characters, and possible upcoming events in the story are more beneficial than questions about literal information. Reading written materials aloud to students helps them acquire and develop language skills and creates an enjoyable experience for both teacher and students.

Shared reading is similar to reading aloud, except that in shared reading students see the text as the teacher reads aloud to them. Students are invited to read along and the focus is still on enjoyment of the story. Big books, which are large books with enlarged print and pictures that students in group settings can easily see, are frequently used in the early grades for shared reading. The language of most big books is repetitive and predictable, which helps the students to read along easily.

Although shared reading is typically associated with kindergarten and first grade, it can be used successfully at all grade levels. One benefit of shared reading is that it is a way to immerse students in language-rich activities regardless of their grade level or reading capabilities. An additional benefit is that shared reading can allow students to apply their reading skills in meaningful reading situations. For example, the teacher can point out beginning letters and letter combinations and encourage students to respond to the sounds represented, direct students' attention to common phonograms (e.g., *tion, at,* and *et*) found in words within the context of the story, ask students to predict what the next word might be within the syntax of the story, and ask students to predict what events might happen next in the story.

Paired reading is a modification of shared reading. In this version, one student reads aloud as another follows along. Students can take turns reading and following along as they read text. Paired reading is often employed with a less-capable reader following along as a more-capable reader reads the story aloud. This technique enables the students to support each other in their reading of text and provides valuable practice time for both students. The less-capable reader should also be given opportunities to read as the more-capable reader follows along. Paired reading is an enjoyable activity for older students who help

Reading teachers have long recognized reading aloud to children as a means to promote students' interest in reading. In years past, elementary school teachers, predominantly in the early grades, recognized that their students benefited greatly from listening to good literature. Some of the direct benefits of reading aloud to students that these teachers realized were gaining an appreciation of life's possibilities, helping to satisfy basic needs vicariously, nurturing young minds, motivating wide interests, and providing an escape into the world of fantasy and imagination.

The Country School by Winslow Homer, The St. Louis Art Museum.

Today, teachers view with even more importance the practice of reading aloud to children both in the early and the upper grades. Reading aloud is considered not just a worthwhile activity that is added on to the curriculum, but rather an integral component in the literacy program. By reading aloud to young students, the teacher is helping them develop important concepts about literacy such as that print communicates meaning and that stories follow a structure. Reading aloud to older students can provide such benefits as introducing them to classic literature, illustrating literary features, and motivating them to read recreationally.

younger students with their reading. For example, a fifth grader might do paired reading with a second grader.

Readers' theater and modifications of it are other ways that teachers can encourage students to work cooperatively and focus on oral language, listening, reading, and writing. Readers' theater is usually described in terms of children reading literature by performing the parts of characters. Students can perform stories, pieces of literature, picture books, plays, narrative poems, and other types of children's literature. Modifications can include children reading all or parts of a literary text and then turning it into a script to be acted out. Students collaborate with each other on the interpretation of their reading, what to act out, how to act it out, and how to bring everything together for a performance. Students benefit from working cooperatively, using creative writing and interpretation, and being motivated to read literature.

Independent reading is the cornerstone of successful reading instruction, because students need opportunities to practice and apply their reading skills to meaningful text. In independent reading, the teacher acts as facilitator and role model, providing students with a wide range of readily available reading material, encouraging them to read, and initiating informal discussions with them about their reading. Time should be set aside daily for students at all grade levels to read independently. Teachers should also read during this time to provide students with a model that demonstrates the value and enjoyment of reading. The practice and application of their reading capabilities make students better readers, expand their vocabularies, enhance their reasoning capabilities, and associate value with reading.

■ Writing Activities and Instructional Opportunities in a Language-rich Environment

A language-rich classroom environment gives students opportunities to participate in a variety of writing activities. Examples of such opportunities include displays throughout the classroom of writing by both teacher and students, notecards and notepads placed in activity areas (e.g., library, block center, drama center, and science center), story starters (beginnings that students devise based on their experiences and that the teacher uses to illustrate how stories are written), and discussions with students about what their attempts at writing (e.g., scribbles, invented spellings, letter strings, text for artwork, first drafts, and final drafts) mean to them.

Establishing a classroom to promote literacy development encourages students to engage in writing activities throughout the day. Implementing Atwell's (1987) beliefs about writing can serve teachers well in creating a language-rich environment for encouraging children to write:

Writers need regular chunks of time.

Writers need their own topics.

Writers need response.

Writers learn mechanics in context.

Children need to know adults who write.

Writers need to read.

Writing teachers need to take responsibility for the knowledge and teaching of writing. (pp. 17–18)

Teachers can integrate reading and writing at developmental stages by using writing activities appropriate to students' level of reading and oral-language development. Teachers can use multiple texts for students to read, write about, synthesize, evaluate, or analyze. Vocabulary can be reinforced through activities that encourage students to use the vocabulary words in their writing. Such writing activities should focus on real-life experiences to ensure that the language structure and text reflect the students' background knowledge. An excellent way to integrate reading and writing is encouraging students to each keep a reading log. A **reading log** (see Figure 3.4) involves short-term writing activities that can support student discussion or reflection about what they have read (Raphael & Hiebert, 1996). In addition, writing activities can replace or supplement many of the independent practice and application activities recommended in instructional reading materials.

Kenneth and Yetta Goodman (1983) suggest several reading and writing activities that focus on the practical functions of both. Activities such as making lists (e.g., of birthdays, attendance, or library books) can help students understand organizing, categorizing, and alphabetizing. Most students have some knowledge of list making because they see their parents and teachers doing it. Other practical activities similar to making lists include writing labels for items in the classroom, writing instructions for the care of plants and animals, and writing out job responsibilities. These activities are similar to the instructional strategies used to promote informative language presented in Figure 3.2.

Although students enjoy writing lists and similar tasks, such activities do not focus on the communicative features of printed language to the extent that diary and journal writing do. Diary writing is personal writing that students can easily read because it is based on their own experiences and concepts. Students can record classroom and personal events in their diaries. Figure 3.5 provides an example of a kindergartner's diary entry, written early in the school year, about a trip to Galveston, Texas (Rose Marie went on a ferry boat and on the ferry boat, she saw dolphins). Another approach is to keep a classroom diary for the whole class, with all members participating by dictating to the teacher their experiences with birthday parties, field trips, special occasions, and so forth.

Journal writing encourages students to share their feelings, noting important events in their lives. Such writing is intended for the teacher to read, and therefore students must communicate with a reader. In **response journals,** the teacher both reads and responds to the students' journals. The teacher's written responses provide students with a model of writing and reinforce the connection between reading and writing. Note and letter writing can be used to connect a writer with one or more readers. Classroom pen pals, teachers, parents, brothers, sisters, and other people familiar to students can be the audience to whom students write notes and letters. Because the writer and reader

PICTURES

Every time I read, I end up with some kind of picture in my head about the story. I can draw in my log and share my picture with the group. When I draw a picture, I need to write a little about why I drew it so that I can remember where the picture came from, what made me think about it, and why I wanted to draw it.

POINT OF VIEW

Sometimes as I read about a character I think that the author did not consider other points or ideas. In my log, I can write about a character's point of view that the author did not address.

WONDERFUL WORDS

Find some really wonderful words—words that are new to me, or crazy, descriptive, ones I might want to use in my own writing, ones that are confusing, or whatever. Write down the word or words and share them with my group. I'll write a short note about why I picked the word and the group number where I found the word so that I can find it again.

ME & THE BOOK

Sometimes what I read about a character or an event makes me think of things in my own life. I can write in my log and tell about what the character or the event or other ideas make me think about from my own life.

CHARACTER PROFILE

Think about a character I really liked (or really didn't like, or thought was interesting). The map can show what I think the character looked like, things the character did, how the character went with other characters, what made this character interesting, and anything else that I think is important!

BOOK/CHAPTER CRITIQUE

Sometimes when I'm reading, I think to myself. ``This is absolutely GREAT!!!'' Other times I think to myself, ``If I were the author, I sure would do this differently.'' I can write about things the author did really well, and things he or she might want to do better.

SEQUENCES

Sometimes events in the book might be important to remember the order they happened. I can make a sequence chart explaining why I thought it would be important to remember.

AUTHOR'S CRAFTS AND SPECIAL TRICKS

Sometimes authors use special words, paint pictures in my mind with words, make me wish I could write like they do, use funny language, write dialogue that is really good, and many other things. In my log, I can write examples of special things the author wrote in the story.

SPECIAL STORY PART

Mark the page number so I can remember where to find it. Write the first few words, then ``. . .'' and the last few words so I can remember what I want to share. Then write about why I thought it was interesting or special.

INTERPRETATION

When I read, I think about what the author is saying to me, what he or she hopes that I'll take away from the story. I can write down my interpretation in my reading log and share what I'm thinking with the rest of my group. I need to listen to others' interpretations to see if they have similar, the same, or different ideas.

FIGURE 3.4
An example of features of a reading log
Source: *From T. E. Raphael & E. H. Heibert,* **Creating an Integrated Approach to Literacy Instruction** *(New York: Holt, Rinehart, and Winston, Inc., 1996), p. 34.*

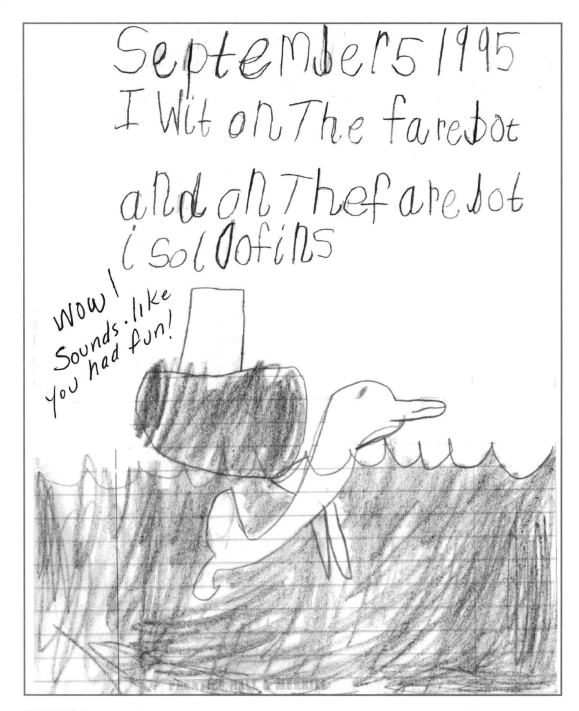

FIGURE 3.5
An example of a kindergartner's journal writing early in the school year

share many common experiences in this type of communication, the writer need not communicate as completely as in other types of writing for the reader to construct meaning.

Writing notes and letters to less-familiar people offers an opportunity to communicate with new audiences. Students can write notes and letters to their favorite authors, to national and community leaders, and to pen pals. The World Wide Web enables children today to correspond with people from all over the world. The responses that their letters generate provide students with further opportunities to understand the communicative features of literacy.

One of the important features of promoting numerous and varied opportunities for classroom writing is that the teacher demonstrates models of the writing process. Routman (1991) identified several ways that teachers can model writing. Many of these are presented and further discussed throughout this book; a few also are presented in the following list to illustrate how teachers can model the writing process for their students. A key feature of these modeling activities is that the teacher writes in front of the students and talks about the process involved in writing the message, story, outline, or whatever he or she is writing. Such think-aloud behavior helps students to reason about the act of writing as a means of communication.

- Many teachers write their daily schedules and classroom events on the chalkboard so that students know what will be occurring during the day. Rather than writing this information before students arrive, however, teachers can capitalize on this opportunity to model writing by doing so in front of students and talking with students about the process. For example, writing "Today is Bryan's birthday. He is 7 years old today." could announce the birthday of a classmate to students. The teacher could discuss with the class why certain words are capitalized, why certain punctuation is used, and so forth. It is best to write information in paragraph form rather than just listing events. The teacher can then ask questions that encourage students to figure out the structure of the writing as well as its conventions.

- Brainstorming about writing topics as a class enables the teacher to focus on students' interests and to model features of the writing process. Students can generate topics, which the teacher lists, and the teacher can demonstrate how to elaborate upon the topics and write a first draft. Students then can participate in topic elaboration as well as writing and revising the first draft. The teacher can use this first draft to again model for students how to revise and polish their writing. Whole-class and small-group rewriting and revising can help further model the writing process. Teachers can select examples of writing that students have generated together or can use examples of their own writing for modeling. The teacher can direct students to focus on word choice, descriptions, topic choice, and other features by questions such as "Is there another word that would work better here? I like the way this describes . . . How could you expand this section so the reader knows exactly what you mean?"

Modeling for students what is involved in the writing process—ranging from capitalization to communication of ideas—helps them better understand how writing functions. Many of the language functions presented in Figure 3.2 can form the basis for writing activities and help teachers focus on what to model for their students.

✓ Summary

Building on students' existing language capabilities is the key to effective literacy instruction. Reading is a language process related to all language functions in the elementary school curriculum. Students' language awareness depends on literacy experiences, which help them to understand language features such as syntax and semantics, develop and expand their vocabularies, and refine and extend their knowledge of text. Literacy builds a bridge of understanding between oral language and reading and writing. Reading, as a language process, frees the mind from direct experiences.

Oral-language capabilities contribute to students' literacy development. In the beginning stages of learning to read and write, their comprehension of print is linked closely to their spoken language. This important linkage should be reflected in instruction, which should be based on oral-language development. Culturally and linguistically diverse learners also need instruction that broadens and enriches both their language and informational backgrounds to encourage their success in literacy.

It is generally accepted that reading and writing are interrelated. Both reading and writing compose meaning, which involves interaction between an individual's experiential and conceptual backgrounds and the text. Although reading and writing are similar in many respects, each must be taught, and students need many varied opportunities to engage in reading and writing activities.

Literacy instruction must include a sense of involvement with language. A language-rich classroom environment is essential to promoting literacy growth. Such an environment does not treat reading and writing as separate subjects, but rather emphasizes them in all aspects of classroom life. A language-rich environment in the classroom should have two important components. First, it should encourage and support literacy development. Second, it should incorporate language-rich features and activities into reading and writing instruction.

✓ Your Point of View

Discussion Questions

1. How does student development in speaking, listening, and writing affect reading development?
2. Why is it important for teachers to understand the language and literacy needs of diverse learners?

Take a Stand For or Against

1. The processes of learning to speak and learning to read are basically the same.
2. A language-rich classroom environment allows the teacher simply to guide students' literacy acquisition, and little or no instruction is necessary.

Field-Based Assignments

1. Children's literacy capabilities vary within classrooms and in relation to literacy tasks. For example, a child writing in his or her journal may on one occasion write only one or two phrases or sentences and on another occasion write several sentences. In the school in which you are working, examine several journal entries of several different students. Note variations within and among the journals for such characteristics as (1) length, (2) spelling patterns, (3) topics, (4) creativity, (5) whether pictures are drawn to accompany writing, and (6) features of editing and revising. Interview some of the children about what they wrote, have them read their writing aloud to you, and discuss with them how they selected topics to write about.
2. The importance of a language-rich classroom environment was a focal point of this chapter. Visit several classrooms and note how language is represented in the classrooms. Some examples to look for include reading centers, written directions and examples, displays of children's writing, big books, classroom libraries, reading and writing materials, activity centers, and so forth.

Portfolio Entry

Using the information you gained from noting how language is promoted within various classrooms, list how you would utilize this information in your own classroom. You may wish to draw or use photographs of the language-promotion features of the classrooms you visited.

Bibliography

Adams, M. J. (1990). *Beginning to read: Thinking and learning about print.* Cambridge, MA: M.I.T. Press.

Atwell, N. (1987). *In the middle: Writing, reading, and learning with adolescents.* Portsmouth, NH: Heinemann.

Beck, I. L. (1985). Five problems with children's comprehension in the primary grades. In J. Osborn, P. T. Wilson, & R. C. Anderson (Eds.), *Reading education: Foundations for a literate America* (pp. 239–253). Lexington, MA: Lexington Books.

Chall, J. S. (1996). *Stages of reading development* (2nd ed.). New York: Harcourt Brace.

Dickinson, D., Wolf, M., & Stotsky, S. (1993). Words move: The interwoven development of oral and written language. In J. Berko & O. Gleason (Eds.), *The development of language* (3rd ed.) (pp. 369–420). Upper Saddle River, NJ: Merrill/Prentice Hall.

Edelsky, C., Altwerger, B., & Flores, B. (1991). *Whole language: What's the difference?* Portsmouth, NH: Heinemann Educational Books.

Frith, U. (1985). Beneath the surface of developmental dyslexia. In K. E. Patterson, K. C. Marshall, & M. Coltheart (Eds.), *Surface dyslexia: Neuropsychological and cognitive studies of phonological reading.* Hillsdale, NJ: Lawrence Erlbaum Associates.

Goldfield, B. A., & Snow, C. E. (1993). Individual differences in language acquisition. In J. Berko Gleason (Ed.), *The development of language* (3rd ed.) (pp. 299–324). Upper Saddle River, NJ: Merrill/Prentice Hall.

Goodman, K. S., & Goodman, Y. (1983). Reading and writing relationships: Pragmatic functions. *Language Arts, 60,* 590–599.

Lewin, L. (1992). Integrating reading and writing strategies using an alternating teacher-led/student-selected instructional pattern. *The Reading Teacher, 45,* 586–591.

McCarthy, S. J., & Raphael, T. E. (1992). Alternative research perspectives. In J. W. Irwin & M. A. Doyle (Eds.), *Reading/Writing connections: Learning from research* (pp. 2–30). Newark, DE: International Reading Association.

National Council of Teachers of English. (1996). *Standards for the English language arts.* Urbana, IL: Author.

Norton, D. E. (1997). *The effective teaching of language arts.* Upper Saddle River, NJ: Prentice Hall.

Pinnell, G. S. (1996). Ways to look at the functions of children's language. In B. M. Power & R. S. Hubbard (Eds.), *Language development: A reader for teachers* (pp. 146–154). Upper Saddle River, NJ: Prentice Hall.

Raphael, T. E., & Englert, C. S. (1989). Integrating reading and writing instruction. In P. Winograd, K. K. Wixson, & M. Y. Lipson (Eds.), *Improving basal reader instruction* (pp. 231–255). New York: Teachers College Press.

Raphael, T. E., & Hiebert, E. H. (1996). *Creating an integrated approach to literacy instruction.* New York: Holt, Rinehart, and Winston.

Rice, M. L. (1996). Children's language acquisition. In B. M. Power & R. S. Hubbard (Eds.), *Language development: A reader for teachers* (pp. 3–12). Upper Saddle River, NJ: Prentice Hall.

Routman, R. (1991). *Invitations: Changing as teachers and learners K–12.* Portsmouth, NH: Heinemann.

Rupley, W. H., & Willson, V. L. (in press). Content, domain, and word knowledge: Relationship to children's reading comprehension. *The Journal of Reading and Writing.*

Samuels, S. J. (1988). Decoding and automaticity: Helping poor readers become automatic at word recognition. *The Reading Teacher, 41,* 636–647.

Schell, L. (1993). Letter to the author.

Shanahan, T. (1988). The reading-writing relationship: Seven instructional principles. *The Reading Teacher, 45,* 636–647.

Stahl, S. A. (1996). Saying the "p" word: Nine guidelines for exemplary phonics instruction. In R. Robinson, M. McKenna, & J. Wedman (Eds.), *Issues and trends in literacy education* (pp. 52–61) Boston, MA: Allyn & Bacon.

Stahl, S. A., Osborn, J., & Lehr, F. (1996). Beginning to read: Thinking and learning about print Marilyn J. Adams: A summary. In R. Robinson, M. McKenna, & J. Wedman (Eds.), *Issues and trends in literacy education,* (pp. 176–185). Boston, MA: Allyn & Bacon.

Stahl, S. A., Pagnucco, J. R., and Suttles, C. W. (1996). First graders' reading and writing instruction in traditional and process-oriented classrooms. *The Journal of Educational Research, 89,* 131–144.

Sulzby, E., & Barnhart, J. (1992). The development of academic competence: All our children emerge as writers and readers. In J. W. Irwin & M. A. Doyle (Eds.), *Reading/writing connections: Learning from research* (pp. 120–144). Newark, DE: International Reading Association.

Tierney, R. J. (1992). Ongoing research and new directions. In J. W. Irwin & M. A. Doyle (Eds.), *Reading/writing connections: Learning from research* (pp 246–259). Newark, DE: International Reading Association.

Tierney, R., & Pearson, P. D. (1983). Toward a

composing model of reading. *Language Arts, 60,* 568–58.

Tompkins, G. E., & Hoskisson, K. (1995). *Language arts: Content and teaching strategies.* Upper Saddle River, NJ: Prentice Hall.

Vacca, R. T., & Rasinski, T. V. (1992). *Case studies in whole language.* New York: Harcourt Brace Jovanovich.

Veatch, J. (1996). From the vantage of retirement. *The Reading Teacher, 49,* 510–517.

Wells, G. (1981). Writing and the teaching of reading. *Language Arts, 60,* 600–606.

CHAPTER 4

Emergent Literacy

Chapter Outline

For the Reader

Long before children start school, reading and writing are a major part of their lives. Before the age of 6 months, children often are given alphabet blocks, books with print, picture books, mobiles with words and letters hanging from them, and so forth. Parents and older brothers or sisters interact with young children by reading books, pointing out signs, and playing "school." These early experiences with literacy form the foundation for later reading and writing development.

Can you recall your first experiences with literacy? You probably had a variety of literacy experiences prior to beginning school—children in our society generally do. You may have had books read to you. You probably saw adults making lists and writing messages. You encountered print in your everyday activities through trips to places such as McDonald's, Kmart, Sears, and Kroger. You could recognize the brand names of your favorite cereals, soft drinks, and toys. You may have also experienced print through educational television programs, such as **Sesame Street, Mr. Rogers' Neighborhood, Reading Rainbow,** and other programs with a rich reading and writing format. Furthermore, you may have begun at a young age to explore writing through scribbles, writing letters, and drawing, as well as asking others to write lists, stories, and titles for your art.

In addition to such direct experiences with print, children begin to develop an awareness of stories and story structure, and this is often reflected in their play and make-believe activities. Children's literacy experiences vary according to their home backgrounds and opportunities for language interaction with adults. These early experiences are the beginnings of reading and writing, which form the foundation for the lifelong process of learning to read and write (Teale & Sulzby, 1996).

Key Ideas

- Emergent literacy is a concept that applies to all young children.
- Children's early literacy experiences vary according to their home backgrounds and opportunities for language interaction with adults. These early experiences are the beginnings of reading and writing.
- Classrooms that are rich and varied in language opportunities contribute to and nurture children's emergent literacy development.
- Through exposure to print, children begin to establish concepts about print, experiment with its use, and develop understandings about what it means and how it functions.
- Parents reading aloud to their children contributes significantly to children's experiential and conceptual backgrounds for developing concepts about print, understanding relationships between oral and written language, and developing phonemic awareness.
- Experiences with environmental print help children understand both the forms and functions of print, develop a sight vocabulary, recognize letters and letter names, and develop knowledge of visual details.
- Children must understand the following about print before acquiring conventional literacy: (1) print is meaningful, (2) specific language is used to talk about language, and (3) letters and letter combinations represent speech sounds.
- Emerging and beginning literacy stages are broad and lay the foundation for ongoing literacy development in a developmentally appropriate way.
- In planning an emergent literacy and beginning reading program, teachers should capitalize upon what they know about effective teaching, children, learning, and language development.
- Teacher-directed instructional activities in the early literacy program should not be discrete, isolated skills lessons. They should be woven into literature-based instruction.
- Assessment in the literacy program helps teachers adjust their instruction to address students' literacy needs.

The Concept of Emergent Literacy

Working with young children, school, and teaching are delightful, dynamic, and captivating experiences for all of those involved. Early reading instruction is changing: It is becoming much more exciting, personal, and child-centered. Reading materials for teaching young children are abundant and creative. Literature-based reading instruction is popular, and instruction no longer is based only on commercially developed materials, such as basal readers. Teachers have more freedom of choice today about how they wish to structure their students' early literacy programs and what materials they use.

A concept that has contributed significantly to this more exciting teaching of reading and writing in kindergarten and first grade is emergent literacy. **Emergent literacy** has been defined in a variety of ways; however, features common to most definitions are that (1) emergent literacy is the reading and writing behaviors of children that occur before and develop into conventional literacy, and (2) emergent literacy is developmental (Sulzby & Barnhart, 1992). Teale (1987) considers the meaning of both *emergent* and *literacy* in his conceptualization. He notes that the term *literacy* is of major importance because it stresses both reading and writing rather than just reading development. Teale refers to *emergent* as a forward-looking term. It implies that children are developing in a positive manner in their literacy development.

Emergent literacy is a concept that can be applied to all children. As noted by Sulzby and Barnhart (1992):

> All children are becoming literate—all are emerging as writers and readers. It is clear that some children come from backgrounds in which they have been included in literacy events from birth forward as a matter of course. Other children have had few such experiences. In our research and that of other researchers we note that the kinds of [literacy] behaviors we describe . . . are shown by children from low- as well as middle- and high-income families and by children from all the ethnic and cultural backgrounds that have been studied. (pp. 122–123)

■ Characteristics of Emergent Literacy

Teale and Sulzby (1996) have painted a word portrait of young children as literacy learners. Important characteristics of their portrait include the following.

1. Almost all children in our society begin to exhibit understandings and learnings about reading and writing early in their lives. Most children, by the age of 2 or 3, can identify signs (e.g., McDonald's, Taco Bell), labels (e.g., favorite cereals, candy bars), and logos (e.g., Nike, Disney). Children are playing and using writing, and even though their writing attempts may look like scribbles, they reflect characteristics of the writing system (see Figure 4.1). Exactly when children's literacy learning begins is difficult to establish; what is clear is that it occurs long before they enter kindergarten or first grade.

2. Literacy learnings and understandings develop from direct experiences in which reading and writing are integral experiences directed toward the accomplishment of some goal. That is, the purpose is not to read something or to write something, but reading and writing are used to reach a goal. For example, children see others who are reading recipes to help them cook, television guides to determine what is on television, directions to help them assemble a toy or model, books for enjoyment or information, and so forth. Such experiences communicate to children that reading and writing are not ends in themselves, but a functional means to accomplish a variety of purposes.

3. The development of reading and writing in young children happen together and each is related to the other. Oral language development enhances literacy development and literacy development contributes to young children's continued oral language development. Children who are read to and given opportunities to experiment with writing grow in their understanding of how print functions. They increase their vocabulary, better understand story structure, and can recognize the difference between written and oral language.

4. Children's learning about literacy is best brought about by their active participation in multiple opportunities for reading and writing. A classroom environment that is rich in print and varied in providing students many different ways to engage in reading and writing will enhance young children's emergent literacy development.

■ Variations in Children's Literacy Experiences

Although all children are emerging in their reading and writing development, children will have had varying literacy experiences before beginning school. Reading materials in the home and the role of literacy in the home are two factors that directly influence children's literacy experiences. For example, children who have access to a variety of books, have parents who read aloud to them (or, in many instances, have older siblings who read aloud to them), see others write notes, make lists, and write letters, and who are exposed to print in their community are likely to exhibit understandings and behaviors of emergent literacy.

Contributing to variations in children's level of emergent literacy development are gender and school experiences. Teachers have always known that girls typically outpace boys in early literacy development. Beach and Robinson (1992) examined the knowledge and understanding of print that children brought to their first school experience and how these changed as a function of grade level and gender. The researchers administered several emergent literacy tasks to preschool through third-grade children. The results indicated the following.

1. Preschool children had some knowledge and understanding of written language when they came to school. For example, they recognized logos, realized that logos conveyed a message, and wrote using scribbles or letterlike forms. Many of the preschoolers could write at least the first letter of their names (see Figure 4.1) and respond to their own writing by telling what they had written.
2. Kindergarten children showed more knowledge about print and its meaning than did preschoolers. They were a little better in reading environmental print, and most of them knew that they read print in a book. All of them could write their names and were using many letters in their writing.
3. First graders attended more to the actual print than did pre-first-grade children. All of them knew that it is the print that is read in a story. Many of them knew the terminology used to talk about print (e.g., *words, letters, sounds*) and wrote stories using letters. Approximately two thirds of them were reading conventionally.
4. Finally, second- and third-grade children knew the concepts associated with print, used conventional and invented spellings in their writing, and were reading and rereading their writing in a conventional manner.

◀||| F L A S H B A C K

The concept of readiness for reading was greatly reinforced by the research conducted by Mabel V. Morphett and Carleton Washburne in the 1930s and 1940s. They concluded that children must attain a mental age of 6½ years before they are taught to read or even are ready for reading. As a result, reading instruction was delayed until children had reached this mental age. Teachers focused on "reading readiness" activities that were intended to prepare children for reading. However, many of the areas of instructional focus, such as eye-hand coordination and visual discrimination of shapes, were not related to reading acquisition.

Drawing by James H. Hubbard.

U P D A T E |||▶

Today, we realize that children have a wide range of literacy experiences prior to beginning school. They reflect their knowledge of literacy in their play and make-believe activities. They are often aware of print in their environment, they explore writing through scribbles, writing letters and lists, drawings, and titles for their artwork. They are often read to by their parents and are familiar with the features of books. These reading and writing behaviors that occur before and develop into conventional literacy are now the focus of early and beginning literacy acquisition.

Beach and Robinson (1992) also found differences between boys and girls in some of their emergent literacy behavior. Girls did better than boys on the tasks that were most like school literacy tasks (e.g., reading a book, noting errors in word and letter order) in first grade, but differences narrowed in second grade and disappeared in third grade. Girls also outperformed boys in writing and rereading their writing until second grade, when there was no difference. Boys scored higher when preschool and kindergarten boys and girls were compared on environmental print-in-context tasks. In other words, when given tasks from their everyday environment, pre-first-grade boys outperformed pre-first-grade girls. Pre-first-grade and first-grade girls excelled in written language that was more decontextualized from real life.

In summarizing the implications of their findings for classroom literacy instruction, Beach and Robinson noted the following:

> Both boys and girls should be provided with opportunities to interact with written language that requires both problem solving behaviors and lesson learning behaviors. Activities to foster problem solving behaviors would include reading and writing materials in play areas such as home centers or dramatic play areas such as hospital, restaurant, or post office centers as well as including functional print as part of everyday literacy routines. Activities to foster lesson learning behaviors would include structured literacy experiences around books, responses to books, language experience stories, the opportunity to read books independently or with friends, and the opportunity to not only observe an adult or literate "expert" write but also to experiment with writing and reading as well. (p. 16)

Early in their lives, children are exposed to environmental print. They see it in stores, on signs, on television, in restaurants, and in their homes. They are exposed in varying degrees to print in books, magazines, newspapers, and to adults who write lists, letters, notes, and other messages. Through this exposure to print, children begin to establish concepts about print, experiment with its use, and develop understandings about what it means and how it functions. The emerging literacy behaviors that children typically demonstrate in varying degrees are associated with their interactions with print (e.g., storybooks, writing opportunities, and art and play activities) and their environment. Through such experiences, children begin to develop concepts about print and what it means to read and write.

Acquiring Concepts About Print

The experiences that children have with print and the concepts that relate to these experiences contribute significantly to their emergent literacy. As discussed in earlier chapters, reading is an active process in which readers interact with a multitude of factors related to themselves, the text, and the context in which reading occurs to construct meaning. Meaning depends upon the reader's experiential and conceptual backgrounds. Knowledge that children's backgrounds

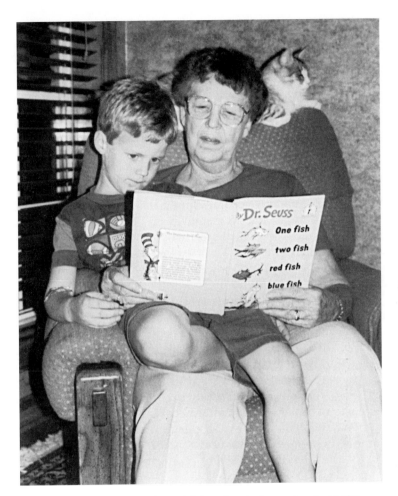

Through exposure to print, children begin to understand the concept of literacy.

develop through trips with their parents, playing with friends, watching television, and so forth forms a basis for language on which teachers can build meaningful literacy experiences.

As noted in *Becoming a Nation of Readers* (Anderson, Hiebert, Scott, & Wilkinson, 1985), how significant adults interact with children about their experiences influences children's understandings and knowledge. Interactions in which significant adults talk about their experiences with children helps children develop concepts and vocabulary. Although a background of experiences and oral language emerges from such interactions and helps establish a basis for success in reading, the abilities essential for reading rely more on written language experiences: parents and adults reading to children, children's experiences with environmental print, and children's art and play activities.

■ Parents Reading to Children

Reading experts have long recognized the value of parents reading to children. In the mid-1960s, scientific studies established support for the benefits of this practice in contributing to children's reading development. Since that time, additional support has accumulated. Anderson et al. (1985) identified reading to children as

> the single most important activity for building the knowledge required for eventual success in reading. . . . This is especially true during the preschool years. The benefits are greatest when the child is an active participant, engaging in discussions about stories, learning to identify letters and words, and talking about the meanings of words. (p. 23)

The value of parents' reading aloud to their children supports the language-development concepts and phonemic-awareness concepts of emergent literacy. Essentially, this activity contributes significantly to children's experiential and conceptual backgrounds for establishing ideas about print, understanding relationships between oral and written language, and developing phonemic awareness.

Reading aloud to children has many direct benefits that contribute to their emerging literacy. They may learn that print is read left to right, what a page is, where to begin reading on a page, that pages are read top to bottom, differences between pictures and print, what constitutes a word, and how oral language is represented in written form, among other things. Listing these benefits does not imply that parents and adults who read to children make a conscious effort to "teach" such concepts. Children acquire much of this understanding indirectly through parents' modeling and informal discussions. When parents ask questions such as "What do you think will happen next?" "How big do you think gigantic is?" and "Where does this story take place?" they are helping children develop concepts related to lifelong reading strategies and understandings. In addition, when parents make comments about the words and illustrations an author has used in a story, they are helping their children to understand the communicative aspects of print.

■ Environmental Print

Children acquire background knowledge for literacy through interaction with print in their environment. **Environmental print** is print in the environment that is encountered in meaningful settings. Examples of such print are labels and signs on objects (e.g., McDonald's restaurants, Coke and Pepsi cans, Kmart bags, and Crest toothpaste tubes), signs (e.g., *Stop, Yield,* and *Post Oak Mall*), and functional print (e.g., telephone books, newspapers, catalogs, TV guides, lists, and menus).

Experiences with environmental print help children understand both the forms and functions of print, build a sight vocabulary, recognize letters and letter names, and develop knowledge of visual details. Environmental print knowledge will vary in relation to children's opportunity to interact with it. For example, in some rural communities, children may not have eaten at a McDonald's, may never have shopped at WalMart, and may not have access to a public television station. This does not imply that these children have a deficit in environmental print experiences, it simply means that their experiences are different from those of many other children and must be accommodated in instruction.

Parents and adults who point out and talk about print in the child's environment are facilitating the development of print concepts. For example, parents facilitate the development of print concepts when they respond to questions such as "Is that McDonald's?" by saying, "Yes, look at the sign. It starts with a big golden *M* and says 'McDonald's.'" When parents point out the Dairy Queen sign and comment, "We are at Dairy Queen," they are helping to build their child's understanding of print and promoting the child's understanding of how print functions. Similar examples of parents and children interacting with environmental print are using the Yellow Pages together, talking about the pictures and text in menus, reading the newspaper comics, noting traffic signs, reading labels when shopping for food, and so forth. Such interactions help children realize that language in our society can direct, inform, and entertain us.

■ Art and Play Activities

Children's art and play activities are also important features related to their experiential and conceptual backgrounds for literacy development. Experiences with art, paper, and pencils are related to children's early reading and writing development. Drawings and scribbles are early forms of writing. Although these are not perceived as conventional writing, children use these forms to tell a story or represent an event.

For example, after going to see the circus, 3-year-old Rose Marie drew a series of pictures about her experience. She then asked her mother to write the words *balloons, clowns, elephants, lions,* and *cotton candy* under the appropriate pictures. Rose Marie then simulated reading by looking at each picture as she told a story to her mother. Rose Marie proudly announced, "I can read!" Later in the day, she was making wiggly lines beneath each of the circus pictures and said "I'm writing a story for Matthew," who is her 1-year-old brother. Rose Marie's pretend writing was linear, and she moved from left to right as she "wrote" her circus story. She also, as do many children, used some individual letters in her writing and put in some dots. When asked to read her story the next day, she was consistent in her rereading: It was almost identical to her reading of it on the day she wrote it.

When Matt, a 4-year-old, drew the picture shown in Figure 4.1, he proudly announced that it represented his mommy and daddy, then a short time later he returned to his parents saying, "I wrote a story. See, it says 'Mommy' and 'Daddy.'" Matt could easily differentiate the picture from what he had written and pointed to each word as he read it. Even days later, when he passed by his picture on the refrigerator, he would proudly say, "Mommy and Daddy and Matt," as he pointed to each of the words he had written. What is also notable about what Matt as a 4-year-old represented is a transfer of his understanding of the letter *M* in his name to the beginning letter in the word *Mommy.* Phonemically, he used invented spelling to represent the word *and* and represented knowledge of language structure in using the word *and.* In addition, he wrote in a left-to-right fashion, and he used

FIGURE 4.1
An example of a 4-year-old's incorporation of picture and print

predominantly upper case letters, which is a reflection of his interaction with print in his environment (Goodman, 1996).

Opportunities for young children to draw and experiment with paper and pencil establish background knowledge for later reading and writing tasks that are more instructional in nature. Children often request that their artwork be labeled or titled, that their names be written on it, and that a story about it be written.

Such requests show that they are beginning to acquire many of the print concepts associated with emerging literacy and are connecting oral language with literacy.

■ Print Concepts Associated with Decontextualized Language

Understanding how print functions in decontextualized language is central to acquiring literacy abilities that go beyond language in familiar contextual settings. Many of the literacy experiences children have before formal schooling determine how well they understand features of decontextualized language. Such experiences are related to storybook reading: for example, knowing that stories have structure, reading from left to right and top to bottom, and knowing the differences between print and pictures. These concepts about print often develop more slowly than others, but they are essential to acquiring conventional literacy capabilities.

■ Print Is Meaningful

Although most young children can tell the difference between print and pictures and can distinguish print from other graphic symbols, an essential understanding for continued literacy growth is the concept that print represents meaningful language. While some children understand the meaning features of print when they come to school, others do not see any connections among oral language, reading, and writing. Children will not benefit from literacy activities that do not reflect their speaking and listening capabilities. Teachers who provide opportunities for children to focus on the concepts that (1) print represents a message and (2) this message must be as sensible as spoken language will enhance the development of the concept that print is meaningful.

■ Language Used to Talk About and Teach Literacy

Adults often take for granted that young children understand what reading is, including the left-to-right progression of print, the meanings of basic language terms used in teaching literacy, the relationship of our writing system to features of oral language, and the basic **functions of written language,** which are to inform, to entertain, and to direct. For example, the term *word* is essential in most beginning reading instruction. The teacher may tell children that they will look at words, learn how to figure out words, spell words, think about words, write words, and so forth. Before beginning school, few children have been asked to think about written words and the language used to talk about written words. There is a major gap between understanding of language and understanding of the language we use to talk about language (e.g., *word, sentence, letters, paragraph*). Furthermore, children's concepts about print are developmental (Sulzby & Barnhart, 1992; Beach & Robinson, 1992). Children develop the concept of *word* over many varied and meaningful written language experiences. They are influenced by attention to environmental print, attention to visual details of print, phonemic awareness, and decoding ability.

Parents and others who read to children contribute significantly to their knowledge of the function of written language.

Emergence of concepts about print directly reflects early literacy experience in the child's environment. Parents and others who read to children and provide a literacy-based environment contribute significantly to knowledge of the function and form of written language. However, children's conceptual understanding of reading and writing instructional terminology and the functions of print are not simply the result of defining the terms and discussing the functions of print. Rather, a language-based literacy program emphasizing oral and written activities best helps children refine and apply their emerging abilities in these areas. Activities should expose children to print in the form of oral reading, environmental print, various arts forms (e.g., music and art), writing, shared-book experiences, meaningful language usage, and play activities.

■ Phonemic Awareness

Juel (1987) identified an issue that has direct implications for beginning reading programs. The issue is "whether phonemic awareness is a necessary precursor to successful acquisition or is merely a consequence of learning to read" (p. 240). Several recent studies (Adams, 1990; Juel, 1991; Willson & Rupley, 1995) support the importance of letter-sound awareness for success in early literacy.

I want a pocit nife and a
Nickelodeon pog maker.
I wand a new sega jinus and a
super soccer xp 55. I want a ant farm
and a miny trampileen. I want a
treder box and a moke kir grole hort
da ves modersicel.

FIGURE 4.2
A first grader's journal entry about what he wants for Christmas

As noted throughout this text, children must be able to recognize words and use their background knowledge to construct meaning. They can accomplish this in three major ways. First is visual memory (recognizing whole words), second is letter-sound correspondence (phonics), and third is context (semantics and syntax). Mature readers use all three of these, depending on the text they are reading. Beginning readers, however, need to develop automatic decoding skills (Chall, 1996; Stanovich, 1986; Stahl, 1996), which are facilitated by **phonemic awareness,** or understanding that words are made up of sounds.

Children acquire phonemic awareness through exposure to books that make language sing and something fun to play with. For example, nursery rhymes, Dr. Seuss books (e.g., *Hop on Pop, The Cat in the Hat,* and *Green Eggs and Ham*), toy books, "I can read" books, and interactive computer books are excellent sources for helping children develop phonemic awareness. Some children may acquire the ability to recognize letters by name before they develop phonemic awareness; however, phonemic awareness is necessary if they are to figure out the relationship between phonemes and words (Cunningham, 1996).

Two important areas related directly to phonemic awareness and literacy development are onsets and rimes, and invented spelling. Knowledge of syllables,

FIGURE 4.3
A 4-year-old's Easter card

which are the units of pronunciation in the English language, is enhanced when onsets and rimes are used for word recognition. (An *onset* is all the letters in a word before a vowel; a *rime* is the vowel and the letters that follow.) It appears that at the onset-rime level, children are better able to retain parts and wholes of words that assist them in word recognition (Moustafa, 1995). As illustrated in Figure 4.2, which depicts a first grader's journal entry about what he wants for Christmas, and Figure 4.3, which shows a 4-year-old's Easter card, invented spelling helps children practice and refine their understanding about symbol and sound relationships. Teachers have noted that children who use invented spelling often write more, use more complete thoughts, reflect more on their writing, and often say words aloud and listen to how the words sound as they represent these sounds with letters.

The issue regarding phonemic awareness appears to have been resolved: Phonemic awareness facilitates beginning reading development. The feature of phonemic awareness that promotes children's beginning reading development is the ability to understand that spoken words can be segmented into sounds. The concept of emergent literacy suggests that phonemic awareness further supports reading development as children interact more with print through reading and writing activities and develop word recognition capabilities.

Instructional Features of Early Literacy and Beginning Literacy Programs

There are general areas of the literacy curriculum that apply to various grade levels. These areas include developmental reading, application-transfer, independent or recreational reading, content reading, writing, and functional reading. Early and beginning literacy programs form a foundation for the literacy curriculum and include all of the significant components found at higher grade levels, such as word recognition, vocabulary, comprehension, study skills, independent reading, writing, literature, and so forth. As Schell (1992) noted, the early and beginning reading stage is not narrow, but rather is broad; for literacy to develop later, the early literacy instructional program should lay the foundation in a developmentally appropriate way. Children in a beginning literacy program have widely varying reading and writing abilities. As noted in Chall's stages (1996), Sulzby's research (1991), and Adams's (1990) summary of research on reading acquisition, some children enter kindergarten and first grade already reading and writing conventionally, while others may have limited understanding about and experiences with literacy. Instruction at the appropriate level is important for kindergarten and first grade teachers, because these levels lay the foundation for future literacy growth.

In planning an emergent literacy and beginning reading program, teachers should capitalize upon their knowledge of effective teaching, children, learning, and language development. To maximize the probability that children will learn to read and write, teachers should do the following:

- Design activities around a language arts base (listening, speaking, reading, and writing) to build on and extend the language backgrounds of children. A language-rich classroom provides the environment in which such activities flourish and nurtures children's literacy growth.
- Develop in children the concept that literacy is communication and that constructing meaning is essential.
- Teach and expand children's vocabularies through the use of both oral and written contexts.
- Provide children varied opportunities to read and to be involved with meaningful reading and writing activities, including reading literature, writing stories, participating in creative dramatics, and sharing books orally.

- In an integrated fashion, teach essential reading terminology (e.g., *word, letter, sound,* and *sentence*) and concepts (e.g., left-to-right progression, page, and letter names)
- Stimulate and support interest in reading by reading aloud a variety of stories that capture children's interest.
- Incorporate the arts (e.g., music and drama) as well as drawing, cutting, and pasting to increase motivation and foster language growth.
- Prepare activities to foster and teach listening skills associated with literacy.
- Set short-term goals based on assessment results that build on children's strengths and that they can readily achieve.
- Give children tasks that they understand and can complete with a high degree of success.
- Give responsibility to all children, not just those who are already confident.
- Select goals for your program according to children's needs, not according to what a commercially prepared program states.

Language-based Reading and Writing Instruction

Children who lack literacy-related experiences benefit from language-based initial literacy instruction. Such instruction includes numerous opportunities to experience and interact with print. For example, teachers should use a variety of writing activities, read books aloud, use shared reading, use story-telling, label objects in the room, and use read-along books. They also should make predictable books, big books, learning and play centers, catalogs, and magazines available to children. The appropriate beginning point is a language-rich classroom environment that helps children acquire and refine basic concepts that are emerging in their literacy knowledge.

The instructional activities discussed in the following sections can encourage, support, and extend students' learning in beginning reading. Many of the activities appropriate for early literacy instruction, such as oral reading, storytelling, journal writing, and language and learning centers, are important instructional components of emergent and beginning literacy instruction.

Play and Learning Centers

Teachers are an important part of classroom play and learning centers. Morrow and Rand (1991) found that adult guidance in using various materials during playtime in learning centers results in children participating in more literacy activities. In the Morrow and Rand study, adults guided students in the use of literacy materials by reminding them to perform tasks specific to the play area (e.g., fill out forms for prescriptions, fill out forms for patients, and read to pets in a veterinarian's office play area). Adults also modeled behaviors for children by participating in play with them. Results of the study indicate that the role of the teacher in using classroom play centers is extremely important in guiding and modeling literacy behavior that children can emulate. Morrow and Rand recommend that when selecting a setting for dramatic play areas, teachers choose those that relate to a theme being studied in the classroom that literacy materials can further enrich. They suggested the following themes and literacy materials for dramatic play areas:

- Fast-food restaurant, ice cream store, or bakery. Literacy materials could include menus, order pads, cash registers, specials of the day, recipes, and lists of flavors or products.
- A newspaper office with writing paper, telephones, computers, directories, maps, typewriters, and areas that focus on sports, travel, general news, and weather.
- A supermarket or local grocery story could include cans of food, cereal boxes, packaged foods, cash registers, shopping receipts, coupons, checkbooks, newspaper ads, and telephones.

Teachers can develop other play and learning centers focusing on situations familiar to all children, such as the local discount store, pet store, post office, and so forth. Teachers should make literacy props available in all of their play centers. Literacy props could include telephone books, cookbooks, food coupons, and grocery store ads in a kitchen play center; calendars, appointment books, signs, magazines, and assorted business forms in an office play center; and library book return cards, children's books, stamps and ink pads, bookmarks, and sign in/sign out sheets in a library play center.

■ Reading and Writing Centers

In addition to using thematic centers to support literacy activities, teachers should include reading centers and writing centers in their classrooms. Such centers can be for use by large groups, small groups, or individual students. Examples of how such centers can function (Labbo, Murray, & Phillips, 1996) include the following:

- **Rug-time center.** Students and teacher can meet to discuss a story they read together, plan a thematic unit, sing songs, share teacher- and student-authored stories, and so forth. A key feature of the rug-time center is that it can serve as a starting or jumping-off place for other center activities.
- **Computer writing center.** Children are offered a free choice to use the computer either individually or in collaboration to write stories, make lists, write letters, or write stories for pieces of art they made. The word-processing use of the computer writing center can be

enhanced by encouraging children to simply experiment with language and composition. Children who have difficulty writing by hand may be more expressive and experimental with language when using the computer. For example, Figure 4.4 shows a child's lengthy response, written on a computer, to a choral reading of "Five Little Monkeys Jumping on the Bed." She first drew the picture and then

One Child's Response to the Topic "Beds"

my bed Has mace mas on it my bed
Has 2 plos on is it is vare bec
sam tis my brair sies wath me in
my bed I Hav to dals won is namd
jenny and won is namd badea my mom
fasis cad bracfast for me

(My bed has Mickey Mouse on it. My bed has two pillows on it. It is very big. Sam is my brother sleep with me in my bed. I have two dolls. One is named Jenny and one is named Baby. My mom fixes good breakfast for me.)

FIGURE 4.4
A child's computer-typed response to a choral reading of "Five Little Monkeys Jumping on the Bed"
Source: From Labbo, D., Murray, B., & Phillips, S. (1996). Writing to Read: From Inheritance to Innovation and Invitation. **The Reading Teacher, 49,** p. 318.

wrote the story later at the computer writing center (Labbo et al., 1996).

■ **Computer center for skills practice and reinforcement.** Such a center can be based on the abundance of computer software available for the practice and reinforcement of reading and writing skills. In addition to commercial software, the World Wide Web has many sites that deal with reading and writing. For example, children can write letters to children in other states and countries, communicate with public and private agencies, and interact with children's authors and magazine publishers. The purpose of these computer activities is to provide opportunities for children to practice and apply their reading and writing skills to meaningful text and at a level appropriate to their individual needs.

■ **Listening library center.** This should be an inviting area furnished with pillows, carpet squares, and child-sized chairs in a corner or in the back of the classroom where children go to listen to tape-recorded books. Children can read the books and listen to the accompanying tape recording. Teachers can use commercially-prepared, adult-prepared, or older-student-prepared tapes.

■ **Art and making-things center.** Here, children can express themselves in ways that go beyond typing or writing in their journals. Such a center can extend and enrich children's understanding and reasoning about concepts and ideas. Children can illustrate events in stories that have been read to them or that they have written, they can infer ideas and characters through art, and they can compare and contrast their art with that of illustrators in the books they read.

■ Thematic Units for Writing and Reading Activities

For writing and reading to be an integral part of early literacy instruction, children need a wide range of experiences and activities to motivate them to read and write. Thematic units built around play centers can be expanded to thematic units that create an environment that promotes children's reading and writing.

Isom and Casteel (1991) described the success of two kindergarten teachers in promoting reading and writing by designing their yearly program around central themes. The teachers focused on the following three goals to build their literacy environment.

Create an Environment Around a Topic.   The teachers created a spectacular display for their topical unit to get children motivated. For example, the teachers made the outside of their classroom look like the front of a barn when they used a farm unit. They made their classroom into a jungle when the theme was jungles. For the jungle theme, paper vines, monkeys, a life-sized tiger, and a life-sized gorilla were used.

Provide for Language and Concept Development.   The teachers used oral reading, discussion, questioning, art projects, and individual inquiry to facilitate children's language and concept development. They used a variety of books, pictures, tapes, and models about the jungle.

Provide for Group and Individual Writing.   As a result of daily classroom discussions and activities, children produced group-dictated stories that were often followed by individually dictated stories and illustrations. Children also were stimulated to write at the classroom writing center, which contained blank books in the shape of the theme. They also dictated big-book stories and illustrated them. Children shared their writing with each other so much that their books became worn with use.

Some teachers build units to promote reading and writing development by using cereal boxes. The outsides of cereal boxes contain environmental print that appeals to all young children. Kettering and Graybill (1991) used the boxes to connect home and school in a way that demonstrated to children that reading is purposeful and relevant to everyday life. They used cereal boxes for developing literacy with graphs by having children place their favorite cereal boxes in columns on the floor and then asking questions about which cereal most students liked, how many more Fruit Loop boxes there were than Cheerios boxes, and of which cereal there were the fewest boxes. Later, they had the children make bar graphs that represented students' favorite cereals.

Cereal boxes were also used in a study of nutrition by having children graph the grains from which the cereals were made using columns for corn, oats, wheat, and rice. Stories such as *The Little Red Hen* were used to help children understand how grain is made into food. Other stories, such as *The Terrible Eater* and *What a Good Lunch*, were also employed in the unit on nutrition.

Writing activities included listing cereals by grain, writing ads for favorite cereals, designing new boxes, describing how to make breakfast, creating new cereals, and so forth. Children's writing was then combined into classroom books, displayed around the classroom, and shared with parents.

Writing and reading activities based around thematic units both create experiences for children to write about and motivate them to participate in reading and writing activities. Teachers can create a classroom environment in which writing and reading emerge as a consequence of students' interest and active participation.

■ Literature, Book, and Writing Activities

Early reading instruction can use children's literature in a variety of ways. Tape recorders can be used to tape children's books, and commercially taped books and stories also are available. Talking books that have been taped commercially can introduce youngsters to the content of children's literature or help them gain experiences with it. Books taped by the teacher should be read in a normal manner, with the children following along in the book as they listen to the recorded text. Without this instruction to follow along, children often simply listen to the stories, which defeats the purpose of taping the book: to help them connect what they hear with the print that represents language. Teacher-prepared tapes also are better for developing literature appreciation than commercially prepared tapes are. Children can help select the books to be taped if they are given brief overviews of the books.

Computer Software.   Computer software is also available for introducing and teaching literacy at the beginning reading level. New software programs are becoming available daily. A highly motivating feature of much of this software is that it is interactive. Children become actively involved in hearing, reading, and seeing the animation of the story. Some software allows children to select different events or endings for stories. Other software enables children to select animated characters and settings for stories that they write. Children can be introduced to the worlds of dinosaurs, underwater life, space travel, and other exciting places and events. They can see the pictorial representation of the print, they can hear the print read aloud, and they can see the print. We have been in kindergarten and first-grade classrooms in which children have drawn animals and events that they experienced through interactive computer software; these drawings are often labeled, written about, sequenced, talked about, and used as a focal point for language development.

Predictable Books.   A **predictable book** is one in which students can grasp easily what the author is going to say next. A basic feature of predictable books is much repetition of content and language. Generally, the pictures in predictable books closely match the text. Other basic characteristics of predictable books are strong rhythm and rhyme, repeated language patterns, logical sequence, supportive illustrations, and traditional story structure. These characteristics allow predictable books to be used in a variety of ways to support emergent literacy. Examples of support include identifying rhyming words, making sounds associated with animal characters, talking as the characters might talk, dramatizing how the characters might act, making picture dictionaries for items presented in the stories, creating murals and clay figures, identifying and classifying characters by similar and different traits, and writing different endings. Such activities with predictable books help create a language-based instructional program that enhances literacy development. The content and language repetition coupled with the pictures help children begin to feel and act like readers early in their reading development. Predictable books also help children to use prediction strategies as they read. This frees them from focusing on individual words as they read and allows them to devote their attention to meaning and making sense of the text. Procedures for using predictable books include the following:

- Discuss the book cover with the children by focusing on the illustrations, which may reflect the characters, the setting, and primary events. Point out and discuss the title: what a title is, how a title is related to the story, and what might be a good title for a book based on the cover illustrations. Praise the children for correct title predictions and point to each word in the title as it is read aloud. Ask the children to make predictions about the story and write these predictions down for later discussion.

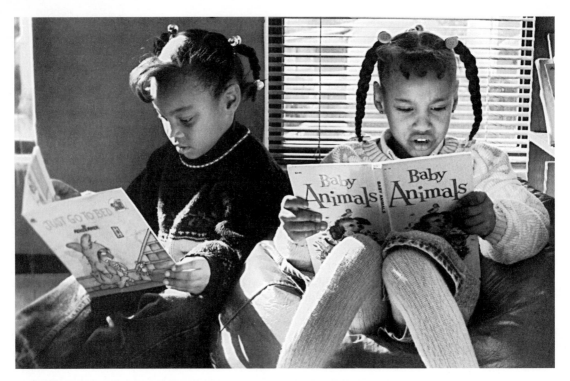

Teachers can create a classroom environment in which literacy emerges as a consequence of students' interest and active participation.

- Turn to the front inside page and point out the title, author, publisher, and dedication, if one is given. Direct the children to recall their predictions about the story and begin reading to them, pointing to each word as you read it.
- Read the entire story aloud. After you read the story, read the predictions that students made earlier about the story. Encourage individual children to share their interpretations of the story and relate them to their predictions.
- Stories can be reread as often as desired by the children. A variety of strategies can be used in rereading predictable books. Choral reading, in which all of the children read the story in unison as the teacher points to the words, can be used when children feel comfortable with the story. Echo reading, in which the teacher reads a part of the story, which the children repeat, echoing what was read, also can be used. After multiple readings of the same story, children often can be encouraged to begin reading along with the parts they know.

Once children begin to experience success with teacher direction, they can begin to read predictable books on their own. Teachers must be willing to accept approximations of story language and to support students' attempts to complete reading of predictable books. They also must provide ample opportunities for children to model and transfer their prediction strategies to other reading activities, such as shared and paired reading.

Wordless Picture Books.   The story in a wordless picture book is told by the sequence of detailed pictures. The story is often repetitive, and children "read" the story by interpreting the pictures.

Wordless picture books can be used to reinforce and extend concepts associated with emergent literacy. Dialogue balloons can be added for characters, and students can dictate to the teacher what the story characters may be saying; story text can be dictated and written strips attached to appropriate pages; and children can draw their own pictures to either change the ending or extend the story.

Writing is easily integrated into the use of wordless picture books because they provide children the opportunity to write or dictate their individual interpretations of a story. Their dictations can be written by the teacher, an older student, a parent volunteer, or a teacher's aide. Children's stories can be bound into big books, shape books, or regular-sized books to be read and reread by the students.

Big Books.   **Big books** have large pictures and print that children in group settings can easily see. The stories often use predictable, repetitive language and focus on content that is appealing to young children. Big books are used frequently in shared-reading settings, where the teacher is supportive because the children and the teacher read the story aloud together (Eldredge, Reutzel, & Hollingsworth, 1996). Because the language is repetitive, teachers can let children finish reading parts of sentences and phrases. Teachers point to the words as they read with feeling and expression. Using big books helps children to develop an appreciation for reading, make connections between print and oral language, understand directionality of print (reading left to right and top to bottom), and see relationships between graphemes and phonemes in meaningful context.

Introducing and using big books is an exciting and enjoyable experience for both the teacher and the children. The following procedures can be useful to teachers as they begin to use big books:

- Because big books are cumbersome to hold, it is recommended that the teacher use an easel to hold the book open. The use of an easel allows the teacher to point to important print features and pictures as the book is read aloud. A pointer is important to have when drawing children's attention to print and pictures because use of the hand often obscures part of the page. Writing materials (e.g., flip chart or chalkboard) should be handy to record children's responses.
- Children's involvement with big books is heightened when the teacher is enthusiastic about both the content of the books and the children's responses. Discussion can focus on the book's cover, title, inside cover page, and illustrations. Children can be asked to predict titles, events, sequence, and so forth. The predictions can then be written for later discussion as the book is read aloud by the teacher, chorally by the students, or with echo reading.

We have observed wide variation in the effective use of big books in kindergarten and first-grade classrooms. Some teachers working with children who have limited literacy experiences focus on helping them understand the features of books, such as the front and back, pages, left-to-right and top-to-bottom progression, title, author, and words. During shared reading, these teachers emphasize each of these features without interfering with appreciation and enjoyment of the story. They often have children come up and turn to their favorite page, indicate where the top of the page is, show where they would begin reading, and so forth. Big books are also placed in the reading center, where children can use them individually or with each other. We have often observed children playing "school" by using big books to read to two or three other children, modeling many of the things that their teacher emphasized during reading of the big book.

Teachers can purchase big books through commercial publishers or make their own. Many of the large, paperback picture books that can be purchased inexpensively at discount stores can be used to construct big books: Teachers buy two copies of the book, cut out and paste the pictures on tagboard, and write the story text beneath the appropriate pictures using large print. Books selected for use in making big books should reflect children's interests and background knowledge. Other ideas for making big books include using song lyrics, old calendars, and children's drawings.

Big books also can be made from cereal boxes and used either with a thematic unit on nutrition or in shared reading. Box fronts from children's favorite cereals can be glued to large sheets of tagboard, with large print used to write predictable text: "Trix, the cereal that the rabbit loves to munch." "Fruit Loops, the cereal where colors come in a bunch." and "Cheerios, the cereal that you can eat for lunch." Children can construct other types of big books by dictating group-experience stories about their favorite cereals.

Big books are available for subjects such as science and social studies. These books are excellent for introducing new concepts and vocabulary. Children can help the teacher create big books in content areas that relate to direct experiences they have had, both in and out of the classroom. Using shared experiences, children dictate to the teacher how they want their experiences to be represented in print. They can draw their own pictures to represent their experiences, or the teacher can help select appropriate illustrations, such as photographs or magazine pictures. Language-experience activities also can result in the construction of big books, shared experience charts, or individual student books. For example, one kindergarten class created a big book about the rabbit, mice, and gerbil that were kept as pets in the classroom. The children dictated information about the size of the animals, their living conditions, and the types of food they ate. The teacher recorded the children's dictations in large print and used photographs taken with an instant camera to illustrate the text. This activity preceded a visit by a veterinarian who specialized in exotic animals. After the veterinarian's visit, the children dictated additional information to add to their *Care and Feeding of Animals* big book. The children made a similar big book for a unit on farm animals.

Interactive Writing Activities.   Interactive writing has features that support and extend emergent reading capabilities acquired through the use of predictable books, wordless books, big books, and shared reading (see Figure 4.5). Interactive writing has two important features (Button, Johnson, & Furgerson, 1996). First, children are active in the writing process. That is, they are holding the pencil and doing the writing. Second, the teacher plays an active role through questioning and direct instruction to focus children's attention on the conventions of print (e.g., spacing, capital letters, punctuation).

Button et al. note that interactive writing is a valuable part of an emergent literacy program because

> it provides so many opportunities to teach directly about language conventions, sense of story, types of writing, and concepts about print. These teaching moments do not follow a specified sequence but evolve from the teacher's understanding of the students' needs. . . . Too often teachers feel they must choose between using holistic literacy experiences and teaching basic skills. In interactive writing sessions, teachers do both at the same time. (p. 454)

INTERACTIVE WRITING EXPECTATIONS AND GUIDELINES IN PRIMARY CLASSROOMS OVER A SCHOOL YEAR

Beginning of the year ⟶   Later in the year ⟶

Establish Routine	**Routine Established**
Negotiate simple text (a label)	Negotiate a more complex text
Construction of text may be completed in one day (news)	Construction of text continues over several days
Repeat orally word or line to be written	Count the words to be written before starting to write

The teacher will	*Students will*
Model hearing sounds in words	Hear dominant sounds in words
Model sound-symbol relationships	Represent sounds with symbols (letters)
Support letter recognition (using alphabet chart or chart listing class members' names)	Write letters without copy
Model and question for Concepts About Print (CAP): spacing, left-to-right directionality, top-to-bottom directionality, word-by-word matching during shared reading	Have control of core words
	Begin linking known words to unknown words
Link words to be written with names of children in the class	Leave spaces between words
	Use familiar chunks (*-ed, -ing*)
	Control word-by-word matching during shared reading
The teacher may	Punctuate sentences on the run
Write more of the text	Write text with little support
Write challenging parts of words/text	Make generalizations about print
Assist with letter formation	

FIGURE 4.5
Interactive writing expectations and guidelines in primary classrooms over a school year
Source: From K. Button, M. Johnson, & P. Furgerson. (1996). Interactive
Writing in a Primary Classroom. **The Reading Teacher, 49,** p. 450.

■ Poetry in the Literacy Program

Literature in the early reading program should include poetry, and the best way to introduce it is to read it aloud. Many other activities can further acquaint children with poetry, including writing, creative dramatics, art, reading, and language awareness activities.

Children enjoy listening to poetry that is predictable, and they will often join in reading it aloud with the teacher. For example, one child named Billy had a favorite poem about a frog; after the teacher read it to him several times, he took much delight in reading it to himself and to his friends. What made the poem so appealing to him was the repetition of the line "Hop, hop, hop," which made up about seven stanzas of the poem.

Poems can be read to children as they listen with their eyes closed to the melody of the poem. Children can be encouraged to form mental images of the contents and discuss their perceptions of the melody and mental images. By rereading the same poem with a different language melody each time, teachers can help children begin to appreciate and understand poetry's language features.

Teachers can use language activities to have children compose poems individually or in groups. An excellent poetry form for introducing such activities is the haiku. Colorful pictorial materials such as paintings, photographs, and drawings can stimulate children to form the word pictures for a haiku. A haiku is a 17-syllable pattern in three lines, with five syllables in the first and third lines and seven syllables in the second line. A picture of a dancing bear inspired one child, Donald, to dictate the following haiku to his teacher, who assisted him with identifying words to fit the haiku pattern. This assistance is important; the teacher can help children identify words by discussing features of the picture with them and offering word possibilities.

The brown dancing bear,
Dancing around in his cage,
Dancing on his toes.

Pictures that children draw can be used to stimulate poetry writing. One girl, Janet, drew a picture of some ghosts for a Halloween activity and dictated the following poem to her teacher.

Ghosts are floating in the air,
Floating, floating, floating.
Look out there's a monster
over there.

Other poetry-writing experiences can relate to music and art activities. For example, a kindergarten class composed the six lines of the following poem with guidance from their teacher.

Music, music in the air.
Music, music everywhere.
We went skipping,
sliding,
jumping,
running,
bouncing,
hopping,
dancing,
Round and round the room.

Poetry can be used to encourage students' reading and writing. In addition, children can learn concepts associated with phonemic awareness using the context of poems to focus on spelling patterns and the sounds represented. For example, a teacher could use the "Hop, hop, hop" part of the poem that so intrigued Billy to teach the sounds the letters *op* represent in words such as *stop, flop, mop,* and *pop.* Children could then use these words to generate more stanzas for the poem, replace words in the poem, and write new poems.

■ Reading Aloud and Telling Stories

We emphasize the importance of reading aloud to children to encourage all teachers to make it an integral part of their daily literacy program. Children need to understand early in their literacy development that the purpose of print is to communicate. Reading stories and other written materials that captivate their minds and stimulate their interest in reading helps youngsters conceptualize written language and the basic features of written text. Specifically, the daily oral sharing of books is important for emerging literacy development. Children learn basic concepts from this practice, including story language, expectations for story characters, and storytelling. In essence, they learn to talk like a book. Also, reading aloud to them expands their vocabularies and background knowledge and is an enjoyable experience.

Storytelling is another important practice that can help children understand the relationships between oral language and literacy. All children love to hear a well-told story. Sources that teachers can use for identifying stories to tell include family traditions or events, parts of favorite books that appeal to children, stories about traditional holidays or made-up holidays, and characters familiar to the children. Lundsteen (1989) recommends that teachers prepare for telling a story by (1) planning a brief introduction that relates the story to the children, (2) relating the story incidents in the intended sequence and being spontaneous, (3) making characters come alive by effective use of voice, gestures, and posture, (4) using interesting speech patterns to represent characters and mood, and (5) using verbal, mechanical, or musical sounds to accompany the telling of the story.

Teachers can use several variations in telling stories. They can tell the story and stop at appropriate places to ask children to predict what will happen next. They can also stop and ask children questions about their feelings or about why certain events might have happened in the story. Sometimes, interrupting a story diminishes youngsters' interest in it; on other occasions, however, discussions during a story heighten their interest. Teachers should monitor children's interest closely and adjust discussion during storytelling to maintain a high level of interest.

Another variation of storytelling is to have children illustrate a story that has just been told. This requires them to relate the story directly to their comprehension of language. Teachers can promote discussion of the pictures by the children and write their comments at the bottom of each of their picture pages. For example, Rose Marie, a kindergartner who lives close to Houston, Texas, drew a picture and wrote her reactions to a story told to her class about winter in Indiana (see Figure 4.6). Her teacher could use the drawing to discuss major story events, sequence, and character traits, and as a prompt if Rose Marie wishes to retell her story.

A third variation is to start a story and direct children to add to it. As each child makes a contribution, the teacher writes the response on a flip chart for everyone to see. This reinforces the relationship between oral and written language, and it also illustrates the concepts associated with literacy language such as words, letters, sentences, and communication of meaning. Interactive writing strategies can also be used as the children write their own contributions for discussion.

In still another variation of storytelling, children can dramatize stories told to them. This can be integrated into the concept of readers' theater, whereby children create a script for a book or part of a book. Students can write the script individually, in pairs, or in small groups. Once the script is written, the writers and other children can dramatize it. Dramatizing stories helps youngsters develop understanding of story parts. In preparing the script, children must translate the story parts into an integrated whole. Dramatization also reinforces the communicative function of print by helping the teacher better understand students' comprehension of stories that are told to them and read to them.

Direct/Explicit Instructional Activities

The majority of the activities presented so far place the teacher in the role of facilitator and promoter of literacy activities for children. However, some areas of early literacy programs do require direct/explicit instruction. Facilitating acquisition and development of listening capabilities, auditory discrimination, visual discrimination, phonics, comprehension, and vocabulary requires teacher-directed instruction. These are not taught as discrete, separate activities that resemble isolated skills lessons, but are woven into literature-based activities. Instruction in these areas still aims to develop capabilities within the context of meaningful text and language, but the teacher's role is more central in initiating, guiding, and directing students' learning.

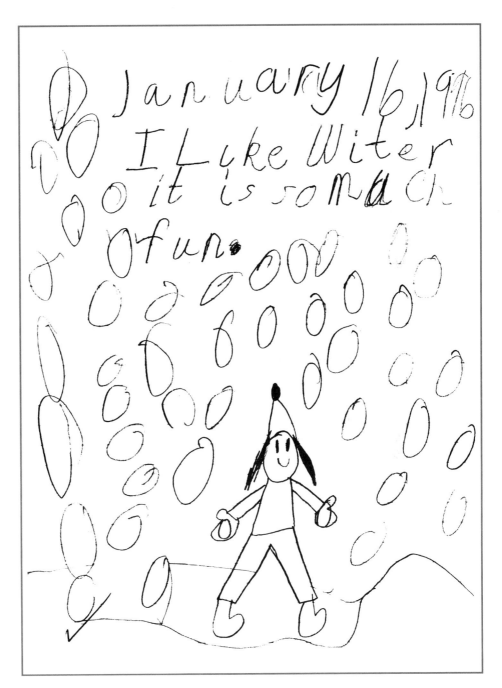

FIGURE 4.6
Rose Marie's representation of and written reaction to a story told
to her kindergarten class about winter in Indiana

■ Listening Capabilities

In developing listening skills, one deals with a much broader area than simple auditory discrimination of speech sounds. Listening is involved in all facets of the curriculum. Listening is required for following directions, developing and expanding concepts, maintaining discipline, planning curricular activities, and the like. Listening also is closely related to many literacy behaviors, such as developing auditory memory and processing language presented orally in stories and discussions. Therefore, what is required in the classroom is a variety of listening situations in which students can be engaged.

Children differ noticeably in their listening abilities. Some children come to school with poor listening habits, while others develop inadequate habits early in school. These deficits have a negative impact on classroom activities and deter learning. Listening involves more than just being physically present while someone is speaking. Providing a variety of experiences in listening is as important as providing experiences in literacy learning.

Providing students with direct listening instruction can make them better listeners. Children can be taught to focus on the speaker, predict while listening, form images of what they hear, think of questions, take notes, draw pictures, and select strategies appropriate to what the listening situation demands. Meaningful listening instruction can be developed around the following steps (Brent & Anderson, 1993):

- **Identify the needed skill or strategy.** Through observation, teachers can identify listening needs. They can help students to activate their background knowledge of what "good listening" is in relation to a specific activity. For example, if during sharing time, students appear not to be listening, the teacher can have them identify future ways to show that they are listening during sharing time. Additional listening strategies, such as blocking out distractions or taking one-word notes, might need to be added based on children's needs.
- **Teach the lesson.** Listening instruction is integrated into daily teaching activities. During shared reading, listening strategies can be integrated with the reading and discussing of the book. Teachers may choose to be more explicit in listening instruction and focus their lessons on individual listening strategies.
- **Supervise practice and debriefing.** At the ends of lessons, teachers can engage students in discussions about how they were effective listeners (e.g., how taking notes helped or how distractions were blocked out) and how strategies vary in relation to the purposes of listening. In addition, students may keep individual portfolio logs of how they use listening strategies and how they are becoming better listeners.
- **Review skills and strategies previously taught.** Listening strategies that have been taught need to be reviewed and extended into other listening situations. Teachers can help children use these strategies by alerting them before the strategies will be needed for a listening situation.
- **Select strategies for specific situations.** The ultimate goal of teaching listening skills is for students to analyze listening situations and adjust

their listening strategies automatically. This can be accomplished by encouraging students to predict what listening strategies they will need for different listening situations and by rewarding and reinforcing appropriate use of the strategies.

Many learning activities in school depend on listening—listening to stories, listening to the teacher, and listening to other students. Following are a few activities to involve children in listening to and interpreting language. They call upon the learner to attend to, process, retain, and respond to language stimuli.

Riddles.   Most youngsters are intrigued by riddles. They enjoy both telling and listening to riddles, and they often come up with many variations of the same riddle. Both factual and nonsense riddles are appropriate to use in developing children's listening capabilities. In addition, children often come away from an activity that uses riddles motivated to write their own riddles and sometimes even to construct a book of riddles. For example, one youngster named Sharon brought home her book of riddles, which consisted of seven pages. Each page was a variation of one riddle that her teacher had used to encourage listening: "Why did the hippopotamus cross the road?" (Answer: It was the chicken's day off.) Examples of riddles that Sharon had written include "Why did the cat cross the road?" "Why did the giraffe cross the road?" and "Why did the bug cross the road?" Of course, each riddle had the same answer: "It was the chicken's day off." The teacher had written this and several other riddles on the chalkboard; Sharon had copied the text and asked her teacher to help her write each of the different animal words. She also had drawn a picture for each variation of the riddle. Her parents knew that she must have been listening, because she also asked them several other riddles: "What chases the moon away every morning?" (the sun); "What goes away when you stand up?" (your lap); and "What holds up trains?" (train robbers). The classroom activity clearly had promoted careful listening by Sharon and had motivated her to create, write, and read her own riddles.

Teachers can write short, descriptive passages on the chalkboard—about objects, characters from a story, shared experiences, or events from stories—then direct students to listen carefully, read a passage to them, and ask them to draw a picture of what is being described. As the teacher reads the passage aloud, he or she should direct students to focus on the written text as well as the spoken words. Two examples of this kind of activity follow.

I wanted to catch a lot of fish.
I stuck my tail through a hole in the ice.
I didn't catch any fish.
I now have a short tail.
Who am I?

I grow outdoors.
In the summer I am full of leaves.
Sometimes I have baby birds living in me.
In the fall I am full of colors.
   What am I?

Not only does listening to these descriptions help children develop listening skills, but also, children can discuss what clues were the most important in helping them figure out what was being described.

Telling and Reading Stories. The activities described earlier for storytelling and reading aloud are also excellent ways to encourage listening in a meaningful context. Before telling or reading stories, the teacher can plant the ideas that good listening is the key to enjoyment of the story and that print is meaningful.

■ Visual Discrimination

By the time children come to school, they have had thousands of experiences in seeing and noting likenesses and differences. They are capable of fairly high-order visual discrimination, in many cases based on relatively small clues. **Visual discrimination** is the ability to see similarities and differences. For example, at the age of 3 years, most children can identify and claim their own tricycles from a group, even though they are not able to explain exactly how they do it.

Later, children can identify common trademarks on the basis of size, color, shape, and function. They can sort a group of objects by size and shape without much difficulty based on visual discrimination. They can identify and click on the correct icon when playing their favorite computer games.

Children's need for fine visual discrimination in reading is self-evident, because the symbols that they read are visual stimuli. Many words look alike, and a child who cannot differentiate among the various words in a passage cannot possibly understand that passage. The widely accepted definition of reading as "constructing meaning from printed symbols" slights the sensory skills that are essential to getting meaning.

We have found from working in many lower-grade classrooms that one of the most effective ways to help children develop the ability to visually differentiate letters and words is through wide exposure to meaningful text. Furthermore, as children begin to recognize whole words, they become better able to visually discriminate words that are spelled differently. Many times teachers must point out the features of words to facilitate development of visual discrimination. They can do this using meaningful text—big books, predictable books, library books, and children's writing, for example. An example of this practice was observed recently in a kindergarten classroom. Jason had checked out *The Whole Book of Wheels* from the school library. His teacher asked him which two words in the title start with the same letter. Jason did not respond. The teacher rephrased her question: "Show me the two words that start with the letter *W*." Jason immediately pointed to *Whole* and *Wheels*. This example illustrates the importance of integrating visual-discrimination activities into a literacy program rather than treating them separately as skill lessons that may not be meaningful for children.

■ Auditory Discrimination and Phonemic Awareness

The major objective of fostering **auditory discrimination** is to help children become conscious of speech sounds within words. This ability is also known as phonemic awareness. The importance of phonemic awareness was discussed in Chapter 3, where it was noted that it is an important precursor to acquiring conventional reading capabilities. Stahl (1996) points out that in learning to read, children need to view words in terms of the sounds they represent. By understanding that spoken words contain phonemes (sounds), children can learn the relationship between letters and the sounds they represent.

Many children come to school playing language games with rhyming words. Rhyming words are an excellent starting point for teaching and reinforcing phonemic awareness. However, for rhyming activities to be effective, teachers must ensure that children understand the concept of rhyming words. Examples of activities using rhyming words are presented next.

INSTRUCTIONAL ACTIVITIES

Rhyming Color Names.   Review some familiar color names with children (e.g., red, blue, green, orange, black, white, yellow, and brown). Write the color names on the chalkboard and direct students to listen carefully to the ending sounds in the two words you will pronounce. Ask students to think about which color word rhymes with (has the same ending sound as) the two words pronounced. Model one or two examples for them before calling on students to give a response.

> **Said** and **Fred** rhyme with? (red)
> **Down** and **frown** rhyme with? (brown)
> **Night** and **bright** rhyme with? (white)

Rhyming Lines and Jingles.   Jingles and rhyming lines can demonstrate intonation and rhyming elements. These involve longer language units that also provide experiences for auditory memory. The following example uses number words and asks children to discriminate the word that is stressed and complete the statement with a number word that rhymes with that word. Follow the same procedures used for the color-name activity.

> I saw a number on the door
> The number that I saw was _____. (four)
>
> The door led into a den
> The snakes I counted numbered _____. (ten)
>
> I left the room and I did see
> A boy who said his age was _____. (three)
>
> To keep this rhyming game alive
> We have to say the number _____. (five)

Many rhyming and jingle activities are similar to those that Griffith and Olson (1992) proposed for developing children's phonemic awareness. In addition to such activities, they recommend that teachers read books that play on language (e.g., those that use alliteration, repetition of vowel sounds within words, and rhymes), provide writing opportunities that allow children to use invented spellings, and draw boxes around sounds represented by letters in written words (e.g., [d] [u] [ck]).

■ Visual and Auditory Integration

Visual and auditory integration is combining visual and auditory capabilities with print. It usually occurs after children have learned to recognize letters and some words. A series of instructional activities can build on students' reading and writing experiences to help youngsters acquire these capabilities.

Once children have developed phonemic awareness and visual discrimination of letters and words, teachers can use words from big books, predictable books, children's writing, and environmental print to teach visual and auditory integration. The earlier example of Billy's fascination with the poem that repeated the phrase "Hop, hop, hop" in several stanzas suggests ways to teach auditory and visual integration.

- The word *hop* can be used to illustrate how the words *stop, pop, mop, flop,* and others require children to visually discriminate between the different beginning letters, hear the sounds represented, and integrate both to determine that *hop* and *pop* are different words.
- Using different endings can reinforce visual and auditory integration (*e.g., hop—hot* and *pop—pot*). Changing words and inserting them into text can prompt a discussion of changes in meaning and whether or not the language makes sense.

■ Phonics

Phonics is teaching reading in a manner that stresses symbol-sound relationships (Harris & Hodges, 1995). The focus here is on presenting some instructional guidelines that do not treat phonics as an isolated skill, but rather weave it into classroom literacy activities. Combining what is presented here with the variety of activities presented in Chapter 5 can help teachers develop a selection of activities that match their students' needs.

Literature and literacy activities that are happening in the classroom can provide materials for teaching phonics. These sources can furnish words to illustrate phonic generalization: The words are taken out of text and then placed back in the text to illustrate application of phonics in reading. This still allows for the systematic study of words in terms of their graphemic and phonemic features (letters and sounds typically represented); however, phonics is integrated into the literacy program, not isolated from it.

Stahl (1996) identified some guidelines for phonics instruction that can apply in literature-based classrooms and classrooms using a basal text as the core text:

- Phonics instruction builds on children's phonemic awareness. Stahl says, "Only by understanding that spoken words contain phonemes can one learn the relationships between letters and sounds" (p. 55).

- Phonics instruction is clear and direct. By using words familiar to students from their reading and writing activities, teachers can illustrate letter-sound relationships in a more meaningful fashion. It is recommended that teachers present a written word, such as *bear*, and stress that it starts with the letter *b* and represents the sound /b/. Or, teachers can present the letter *b*, then show words that begin with the sound that letter represents. Following these activities, children practice reading other words beginning with the letter *b*.
- Phonics is an integral part of the reading program, not a dominant feature of instruction. Teachers can use text that students have read or written to teach a high-utility phonic element (e.g., a beginning consonant digraph, such as *sh*). Written examples of words from the text can be applied to help in reading another text containing several examples of the phonic element.
- Phonics should focus on reading words, not learning rules. Children can be shown multiple examples of the application of a rule to illustrate a particular spelling pattern, but they should not be required to memorize or recite the rule.
- Phonics instruction may include the use of onsets and rimes. An **onset** is the part of a syllable before the vowel. A **rime** is the part of a syllable from the vowel onward. Approximately 500 words can be derived from the following rimes:

-ack	-ain	-ake	-all	-ame	-and
-ank	-ap	-ash	-at	-ate	-aw
-ay	-eat	-ell	-est	-ice	-ick
-ide	-ight	-ill	-in	-ine	-ing
-ink	-ip	-ir	-ock	-oke	-op
-or	-ore	-uck	-ug	-ump	-unk

Children can be taught to compare unknown words with known words and then ask themselves if their predictions or identifications of unknown words make sense in the story. Again, familiar literacy activities can supply words to highlight the use of onsets and rimes. For example, if students know the words *clap* and *duck*, then they can figure out the word *cluck* using their knowledge of onsets and rimes.

- Phonics instruction may include invented spelling practice. Although invented spelling is no substitute for direct phonics instruction, practice with invented spelling does improve children's awareness of phonemes and reinforces the meaning-making concepts of both reading and writing.
- Phonics instructions is intended to develop in children the ability to use independent word-recognition strategies, focusing on the internal structure of words. Phonics makes children aware of orthographic patterns in words and helps them use this knowledge to recognize words. The ability to recognize orthographic letter patterns makes children efficient in identifying words.

INCLUSION STRATEGIES

Meeting Students' Emergent Literacy Needs by Building Background Knowledge

Helping children increase their background knowledge is essential in promoting vocabulary development and comprehension of text. Children cannot understand things about which they have no prior knowledge, whether it be language structure, words that represent ideas, or the content of what they are reading. This inclusion strategies feature presents an example of how teachers can use visuals to better prepare children for literacy activities by expanding their background and vocabulary knowledge.

Visual materials are excellent ways to expand and refine concepts associated with children's background knowledge and literacy. For example, a picture of an eroded hillside is much more effective in fixing the concept of erosion than is a definition of the word.

The same picture can be used at different levels for teaching words and meanings. Imagine a picture available to almost every teacher: a downtown scene in an average-sized city. It shows a bus, a boy on a bicycle, various storefronts and offices, a police officer directing traffic, a fire hydrant, and a bank. Without going into more detail, we might build a hierarchy of concepts for children. The degree of teacher direction will vary according to students' existing capabilities.

"Point out the police officer."

"Where is the police officer standing?"

"Yes, he is really standing where two streets cross—what is that called?"

"That's an intersection." (The students' capabilities and interest will determine whether or not the teacher further explains the term **intersection.**)

"How many kinds of travel or transportation do we see?"

"Some people are walking."

"Some are riding in a bus. It is a city bus."

"How do we know that it is a city bus?"

Phonics instruction should develop automaticity in word recognition. Children who can automatically recognize words spend less time decoding the text and more time on comprehension. Automatic word recognition comes about through practice in reading words. This is the purpose of Chall's (1996) second stage of reading development, when children develop fluency in reading. Continuing to use meaningful literacy activities that allow children to apply their knowledge of phonics provides them with the practice needed to improve both their word-recognition capabilities and comprehension.

A classroom environment that supports children's acquisition of phonic knowledge will provide for application of phonic generalizations. Phonic charts that students and teacher develop cooperatively can be displayed for the students' reference when reading. Words that illustrate particular letter-sound

"There are lots of cars."

"Do you see any boats?"

"Why do you think there aren't any boats?"

The teacher points to a building with a symbol on it for the phone company and asks, "What is this building?"

"It must be the telephone office."

"How do we know that?"

"It has a sign for the phone company."

"What is this building?"

"McDonald's!"

"How do we know?"

"It has a McDonald's sign."

The teacher negotiates a discussion with the children about concepts related to background knowledge, vocabulary, and language. The picture we have visualized could be used in a variety of ways. Through its use the teacher can stress concepts and direct children to notice any of the following:

- Details
- Symbols standing for things
- Many different names for the same thing (e.g., **McDonald's, restaurant,** and **fast-food restaurant**)
- The same word having different meanings according to usage (e.g., **meter** for **parking meter, gas meter,** or **electric meter**)

The value of visuals is their wealth of detail and their ability to convey conceptual information in a concrete manner (e.g., seeing a picture of a longhorn steer). What children can see stays in their minds, so it can be referred to and recalled by children after a discussion has progressed to other things.

relationships on the charts can come from children's writing, predictable books, big books, and literature-based reading series. For example, teachers can develop large classroom charts such as the following using onsets and rimes.

	_____ ake
bake	shake
rake	lake
make	cake

Teachers can make such charts for individual students or for the whole class. Those used with individual students can be bound into a booklet that the child

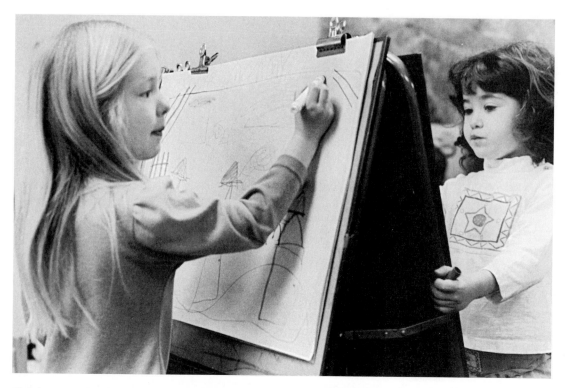

Children can begin to understand relationships among speaking, reading, and writing by creating stories from pictures.

refers to when reading and writing. Children can add their own words to those listed as they encounter words that fit the spelling pattern. The teacher also can add more words as they are found in children's reading and writing.

Another medium that can be used to develop children's phonic knowledge is big books. Children can make and add to their own phonic big books, which can be made available for the whole class to use. For example, after Mrs. Smalling's first grade went on a field trip to the zoo, each child selected an animal, drew a picture of it, and then drew pictures representing words that began with the same letter as the animal's name. One child, Shawn, drew pictures of a bear, a boat, a bottle, a box, a ball, Batman, and the Batmobile. Mrs. Smalling then printed the names of three of the objects beneath them and asked Shawn to print the beginning letter for the remaining objects. He printed the letter *b* and, with the teacher's help, then printed the rest of the words. Mrs. Smalling assembled all of the children's products into a big book that not only represented their trip to the zoo, but also served as a support for phonic knowledge and application.

We observed a first-grade teacher present part of a 60-minute video on the human body to her class. She used only that portion of the video (a section about the skeletal system) that was appropriate to her unit of instruction. Days later, when the class was studying insects, one of her students, Heather, asked where a ladybug's skeleton was. As the teacher began to explain the ectoskeleton of insects, she made many references to the video about the human skeletal system that the children had seen. Every child appeared to understand as they talked about the skeletal system of insects and humans.

■ Building Background Knowledge by Introducing New Storybooks to Children

Marie Clay (1991) sees much value in introducing new storybooks to young readers. Storybook introduction ensures that children have a "successful first reading early in the lesson before the teacher develops lesson activities" (p. 264). New storybooks also activate children's existing background knowledge and introduce new knowledge. Existing concepts are extended for both the storybook's content and its language (see Figure 4.7). The following steps are used to introduce new storybooks:

- The teacher uses illustrations to encourage students to respond to the storybook and relates the story to other stories they have read.
- The teacher gets students to discuss experiences related to the new story and then identifies areas that may confuse students. The teacher can then clear up these areas of confusion.
- The teacher sketches out the plot or the sequence of events up to the climax. The purpose is to create an overview of the story structure that will provide a framework for the children's anticipation of what will come later.
- The teacher stimulates children to relate personal experiences or other stories they have read to the theme or topic of the new story. Such a discussion identifies and clears up conceptual problems related to the plot.
- The teacher uses novel language features (e.g., an unusual name, unfamiliar syntax, or multiple-meaning words) in talking about the story. The discussion of the story deliberately focuses on these features.
- The teacher uses a particularly difficult or new sentence pattern two or three times and may have the students repeat it. This provides them with a language model (to help build background knowledge) that they can use in reading the text. Clay notes that this "is not memorizing the lines of the book but rather readying the mind and ear to grapple with novelty" (p. 267).

Assessing Emergent Literacy

Many commercially prepared tests are available for use in early literacy programs; however, many of these tests do not provide teachers with information they need to make informed decisions about their instruction. Furthermore, assessment results obtained from such tests often focus on comparing a child's

EXAMPLE 1: INTRODUCING A STUDENT TO *THE GREAT BIG ENORMOUS TURNIP*

Setting the topic, theme, and characters
Teacher: Let's look at our new book. This story is about a big turnip, isn't it? *The Great Big Enormous Turnip.*

Prompting constructive activity
Teacher: Let's see what happened. Here's a little old man and he's . . . (Pausing) What's he doing?
Child: He's telling it to grow.
Teacher: And then what's he trying to do?
Child: Pull it out.
Teacher: Pull it out! Can he pull it out?
Child: (Shakes his head.)
Teacher: No! Who does he ask to help him?
Child: The little old woman.

Increasing accessibility or presenting new knowledge
Teacher: (Turning the page) They're asking the granddaughter to help, aren't they?

Accepting a partially correct response
Teacher: Who do they ask next?
Child: The dog.
Teacher: The black dog, that's right.

Providing a model (of anticipating the outcome)
Teacher: And does it come up? Does it? I think it might. And they all . . . (turns the page). Oh, no, not yet! Who do they have to ask?

EXAMPLE 2: INTRODUCING A STUDENT TO *TRUG AND LEAF*

The teacher clearly thought this story might be difficult for this child to understand, but for some good reason she selected it at this stage of the child's progress.

Setting the topic, title, and characters
Teacher: I've got another book about Trug for you. It's about Trug and Leaf this time and poor Leaf is ill.

FIGURE 4.7
Examples of storybook introduction
Source: From Marie Clay, "Introducing a New Storybook to Young Children." **The Reading Teacher, 45** (December 1991), pp. 268–269. Reprinted with permission of the International Reading Association.

g. Name the characters pictured in stories? _____

h. Know how to recognize some words, such as store names (for example, McDonald's, Kmart, and Kroger), brand names (for example, of cereals, toys, and clothing), and his/her name? _____

Please list some of the words your child can recognize/read: _____

_____

i. Know the functions of lists, television guides, phone books, catalogs, and newspapers? _____

j. Scribble and tell you what he/she is writing? _____

k. Write letters in his/her scribbles? _____

l. Write some words, such as his/her name, family members' names, and common words (for example, *is, the,* and *and*)? _____

m. Know some of the letters of the alphabet by sight? _____

If so, which ones? _____

n. Know some of the sounds represented by letters? _____

o. Try to sound out words? _____

p. Know that words can rhyme and rhyme words? _____

5. Is your child already reading? If so, please list some of the books, magazines, and other materials that he/she reads. _____

_____

_____

_____

6. Please list any information about your child's reading and writing that would be of interest to his/her teacher. _____

_____

_____

_____

_____

_____

_____

FIGURE 4.8, *continued*

BROAD CATEGORIES	BRIEF EXPLANATION OF CATEGORIES
1. Attending to Pictures, Not Forming Stories	The child is "reading" by looking at the storybook's pictures. The child's speech is *just* about the picture in view; the child is not "weaving a story" across the pages. (Subcategories are "labelling and commenting" and "following the action.")
2. Attending to Pictures, Forming *ORAL* Stories	The child is "reading" by looking at the storybook's pictures. The child's speech weaves a story across the pages, but the wording and the intonation are like those of someone telling a story, either like a conversation about the pictures or like a fully recited story, in which the listener can see the pictures (and often *must* see them to understand the child's story). (Subcategories are "dialogic storytelling" and "monologic storytelling.")
3. Attending to Pictures, Reading and Storytelling Mixed	This category for the simplified version was originally the first subcategory of category 4. It fits between categories 2 and 4 and is easier to understand if it is treated separately. The child is "reading" by looking at the storybook's pictures. The child's speech fluctuates between sounding like a storyteller, with oral intonation, and sounding like a reader, with reading intonation. To fit this category, the majority of the reading attempt must show fluctuations between storytelling and reading.
4. Attending to Pictures, Forming *WRITTEN* Stories	The child is "reading" by looking at the storybook's pictures. The child's speech sounds as if the child is reading, both in the wording and intonation. The listener does not need to look at the pictures (or rarely does) in order to understand the story. If the listener closes his/her eyes, most of the time he or she would think the child is reading from print. (Subcategories are "reading similar to original story," and "reading verbatim like story.")
5. Attending to Print	There are four subcategories of attending to print. Only the final one is what is typically called "real reading." In the others the child is exploring the print by such strategies as refusing to read based on print-related reasons, or using only some of the aspects of print. (Subcategories are "refusing to read based on print awareness," "reading aspectually," "reading with strategies imbalanced," and "reading independently" or "conventional reading.")

FIGURE 4.9
Simplified version of the Sulzby storybook-reading classification scheme
Source: From Elizabeth Sulzby, "Assessment of Emergent Literacy: Storybook Reading." **The Reading Teacher, 44** (March 1991), p. 500. Reprinted with the permission of the International Reading Association.

and of initial conventional reading. It can be extended into the early conventional period by using other assessment strategies such as informal reading inventories and running records" (p. 499). She also notes that it has been found to be successful in assessing emergent reading and writing behaviors of children from middle- and low-income families of both Anglo and Hispanic backgrounds.

Results from the storybook-reading classification scheme can be used to plan appropriate reading and writing instruction. For example, if a child is attending to pictures and forming oral stories, the teacher can begin to provide more literacy activities that focus on reading and storylike language. Opportunities for the child to hear others read (e.g., the teacher's oral reading, taped books, paired reading, and shared reading) can be used to promote continued development of early literacy.

■ Language-based Assessment Techniques

In addition to the assessment strategies just noted, other language-based procedures can be used successfully to assess children's early literacy development. Coupled with observation of students' engagement in both formal and informal literacy opportunities—such as during instruction and during the time they spend at language-based centers—these other techniques can provide a wealth of assessment information. They include the following:

- Hand the child a book and observe how he or she holds it. Does the child turn the book so the cover is right-side up? Does the child turn the pages? Ask the child to point out or tell where the story begins, how to turn the pages, where to begin reading on a page, and what words, letters, and sentences are.
- Tell a short story and include parts that do not fit in with the story. Ask the child to tell you what is wrong with the story. A child who understands the concept that oral language must make sense will usually respond by indicating that he or she doesn't understand the story or that it is silly.
- Engage in discussions that help the child expand and refine his or her use of language. For example, if a child says "That's nice," the teacher can respond by saying, "You mean a gold watch is nice?" or "Why do you think my watch is nice?"
- Provide a sentence strip and ask the child to cut off a word, a letter, two words, the beginning word, the ending word, and so forth. This will give you some indication of the child's knowledge about ordinal and spatial features of print, such as word boundaries, as well as the child's understanding of beginning and ending words within the context of written sentences.
- Tell short, unfinished stories appropriate to the child's experiential and conceptual background and direct the child to complete the stories orally. Evaluate whether his or her endings relate to the beginnings of the stories. Also evaluate whether the child is attempting to provide endings that make sense.

- Present the child with a hypothetical situation in which a new student who doesn't know anything about reading and writing is coming into your classroom. Direct the child to share with you what he or she would tell this student about reading and writing.
- Provide the child with writing opportunities and note his or her attempts to communicate meaning. Note how the child uses invented spellings (e.g., *brthda* for *birthday* and *kresms* or *krms* for *Christmas*). The focus should be on attempts to construct meaning rather than sentence structure, correct spelling, grammar, and word usage.

■ Using Assessment Information

How teachers use information from their observations and informal assessments will depend on their instructional literacy program. As noted earlier, however, the purpose of assessment is to adjust instruction to address students' needs. Chall's stages of reading and Sulzby's storybook-reading classification scheme can provide help in interpreting assessment information and planning appropriate instruction. One way to use this assessment information is to consider how children's literacy capabilities are growing and changing. By looking at students' strengths, teachers can begin to consider the demands of subsequent learning and how these strengths can be used to meet the demands. For example, if a child in first grade has had limited experiences with print in the home and the environment, then the expectation that this child will succeed in conventional literacy activities will lead to failure. Instead, providing the child with abundant opportunities to engage in print activities associated with emergent literacy and offering literacy instruction that builds on these will prompt literacy growth.

☑ Summary

Emergent literacy is the reading and writing behaviors of children that precede and develop into conventional literacy. While all children experience emergent literacy, children's experiences before beginning school vary. Such variations may result from parents' reading aloud to them, opportunities to interact with environmental print, and experiences with art and play activities.

Before acquiring conventional literacy capabilities, children must (1) know that print represents a message and that this message must be as sensible as spoken language, (2) understand the concepts represented by the language used to talk about print, and (3) develop phonemic awareness, which is an awareness of sounds in spoken words. Children learn these concepts through a variety of written-language experiences, which suggests that a language-based literacy program best helps children refine and apply their emerging abilities in these three areas.

The literacy program in the early grades lays the foundation for later development. In planning an emergent and beginning reading program, teachers should take into account what they know about children, effective teaching, learning, and language development. The appropriate beginning point is a language-based classroom to help children acquire and refine basic concepts that are emerging in their literacy knowledge. Such an environment includes play and learning centers, thematic units for reading and writing, big books, predictable books, poetry, storytelling, and reading aloud.

Some areas of early literacy programs, however, do require direct/explicit instruction. Facilitating children's acquisition and development of listening capabilities, phonemic awareness, visual discrimination, background knowledge, vocabulary, and phonics requires teacher-directed instruction. These are not taught as discrete, separate activities that resemble isolated skills lessons, but rather are woven into the literature-based activities taking place in a language-rich classroom.

Assessment of children's early literacy experiences is important in an effective reading and writing program. Assessment should focus on the experiential and conceptual areas associated with success in beginning literacy: language development, concepts about print, the language of instruction, and phonemic awareness. Teachers can use several assessment techniques. Information from parents, observation, and classification schemes are informal procedures that focus on growth and change in children's literacy capabilities.

✔️ Your Point of View

Discussion Questions

1. Refer to the section Thematic Units for Writing and Reading Activities and discuss the important concepts that would bind together a unit on nutrition.
2. Assume that you have worked closely with a group of 6-year-olds who learned to read before entering school. Discuss the literacy capabilities you think they would possess and the types of instruction that would be appropriate for their continued literacy development.

Take a Stand For or Against

1. First graders don't need instruction in phonics because they will learn for themselves how to use letter-sound relationships to figure out unknown words.
2. Combining reading and writing instruction is too difficult to accomplish in the classroom, and if youngsters can read, they will also learn to write.

Field-Based Assignments

1. Big books, predictable books, toy books, shape books, read-along books, and computer books should be in abundance in kindergarten and first-grade classrooms. Visit a kindergarten and first-grade classroom in your school and examine the books and literacy materials used to support children's emergent literacy. Interview some of the children by asking them such questions as "Which is your favorite book?" "Why is that your favorite?" and "Can you tell me what it says on this page?" Either tape-record or write down the children's responses for sharing and discussion with your classmates.

2. Learning centers that promote the role of literacy are one important way to engage young children in meaningful reading and writing activities. Plan a learning center based on the features discussed in this chapter and set it up in your classroom. Observe how children interact in their use of language when playing in your center. Based on your observations of how children interact in your center, make appropriate modifications, adding more text materials, removing inappropriate materials, integrating writing to a greater extent and so forth.

Portfolio Entry

Using the assessment strategies recommended in this chapter, gather information about several children and record it in your portfolio. Alternative means for gathering information include interviewing students, photographing them in various literacy activities, and either attaching the outcomes of the activities with the photos or recording the children's comments about the activities. Reflect on what the information could mean for you in terms of your own emergent literacy instruction.

Bibliography

Adams, M. J. (1990). *Beginning to read: Thinking and learning about print*. Cambridge, MA: MIT Press.

Anderson, R. C., Hiebert, E. H., Scott, J. A., & Wilkinson, I. A. G. (1985). *Becoming a nation of readers: The report of the Commission on Reading*. Washington, DC: The National Institute of Education.

Beach, S. A., & Robinson, R. J. (1992). Gender and grade level differences in the development of concepts about print. *Reading Psychology, 12,* 309–328.

Brent, R., & Anderson, P. (1993). Developing children's classroom listening strategies. *The Reading Teacher, 47,* 122–126.

Button, K., Johnson, M. J., & Furgerson, P. (1996). Interactive writing in a primary classroom. *The Reading Teacher, 49,* 446–454.

Chall, J. S. (1996). *Stages of reading development* (2nd ed.). New York: McGraw-Hill Book Co.

Clay, M. M. (1991). Introducing a new storybook to young readers. *The Reading Teacher, 45,* 264–273.

Cunningham, P. M. (1996). What kind of phonics instruction will we have? In R. Robinson, M. McKenna, & J. Wedman (Eds.). *Issues and trends in literacy instruction* (pp. 76–90). Boston, MA: Allyn & Bacon.

Eldredge, J. L., Reutzel, D. R., & Hollingsworth, P. M. (1996). Comparing the effectiveness of two oral reading practices: Round-robin reading and the shared book experience. *Journal of Literacy Research, 28,* 201–225.

Goodman, K. S. (1996). Acquiring literacy is natural: Who skilled cock robin? In R. Robinson, M. McKenna, & J. Wedman (Eds.). *Issues and trends in literacy instruction* (pp. 65–70). Boston, MA: Allyn & Bacon.

Griffith, P. L., & Olson, M. W. (1992). Phonemic awareness helps beginning readers break the code. *The Reading Teacher, 45,* 516–525.

Harris, T. L., & Hodges, R. E. (1995). *The literacy dictionary: The vocabulary of reading and writing.* Newark, DE: The International Reading Association.

Isom, B. A., & Casteel, C. P. (1991). Creating a writing-rich environment in the preschool classroom. *The Reading Teacher, 44,* 520–521.

Juel, C. (1991). Beginning reading. In R. Barr, M. L. Kamil, P. B. Mosenthal, & P. D. Pearson (Eds.), *Handbook of reading research, (Vol. I)* (pp. 759–788). New York: Longman.

Juel, C. (1987). Support for the theory of phonemic awareness as a predictor in literacy acquisition. In J. Niles (Ed.), *Solving problems in literacy: Learners, teachers, and researchers* (pp. 239–243). Rochester, NY: National Reading Conference.

Kettering, L., & Graybill, N. (1991). Cereal boxes foster emergent literacy. *The Reading Teacher, 44,* 522–523.

Labbo, L. D., Murray, B. A., & Phillips, M. (1996). Writing to read: From inheritance to innovation and invitation. *The Reading Teacher, 49,* 314–323.

Lundsteen, S. W. (1989). *Language arts: A problem solving approach.* New York: Harper & Row.

Morrow, L. M., & Rand, M. K. (1991). Promoting literacy during play by designing early childhood classroom environments. *The Reading Teacher, 44,* 396–402.

Moustafa, M. (1995). Children's productive phonological recording. *Reading Research Quarterly, 30,* 464–476.

Schell, L. (1992). Letter to author.

Stahl, S. A. (1996). Saying the "p" word: Nine guidelines for exemplary phonics instruction. In R. Robinson, M. McKenna, & J. Wedman (Eds.). *Issues and trends in literacy instruction* (pp. 52–61). Boston, MA: Allyn & Bacon.

Stanovich, K. (1986). Matthew effects in reading: Some consequences of individual differences in the acquisition of literacy. *Reading Research Quarterly, 21,* 360–406.

Sulzby, E. (1991). Assessment of emergent literacy: Storybook reading. *The Reading Teacher, 44,* 498–500.

Sulzby, E., & Barnhart, J. (1992). The development of academic competence: All our children emerge as writers and readers. In J. W. Irwin & M. A. Doyle (Eds.), *Reading and writing connections: Learning from research* (pp. 120–144). Newark, DE: International Reading Association.

Teale, W. H. (1987). Emergent literacy: Reading and writing development in early childhood. In J. Readence & S. Baldwin (Eds.), *Research in literacy: Merging perspectives* (pp. 45–74). Rochester, NY: National Reading Conference.

Teale, W. H., & Sulzby, E. (1996). Emergent literacy: New perspectives. In R. Robinson, M. McKenna, & J. Wedman (Eds.), *Issues and trends in literacy instruction* (pp. 139–143). Boston, MA: Allyn & Bacon.

Willson, V. L., & Rupley, W. H. (1995). Structural components of single word recognition: Activation of orthographic, meaning, and phonological processors. *Reading Research and Instruction, 32,* 33–45.

PART **II**

Aa Bb Cc Dd Ee Ff Gg Hh Ii Jj Kk Ll Mm

Teaching Students to Become Strategic Readers

Chapters

o Pp Qq Rr Ss Tt Uu Vv Ww Xx Yy Zz

Overview

Just as a fine orchestra studies and practices interrelated parts of a performance with the ultimate goal of putting the parts together in splendid fashion, the teaching of literacy involves a host of interrelated understandings that must be studied and practiced and ultimately combined in an efficient and effective "performance." An effective literacy program stresses the instruction and application of the essential strategies, skills, and abilities that produce strategic readers and writers. The ability to interact successfully with text demands the simultaneous use of several tools in our language. Chapters in this part will focus on the role of word pronunciation and vocabulary growth and the development of strategies to comprehend written ideas.

Integrating Principles of Teaching Reading

The following principles, presented in Chapter 1, will be reinforced in this part:

- Literacy learning is a developmental process.
- Teaching students to identify unknown words independently needs to be developed through a balanced approach to decoding.
- Instruction should lead children to understand that reading is a meaningful, active, and strategic process.
- Successful reading comprehension is dependent upon providing large amounts of classroom time for text reading and a multitude of opportunities for students to interact with their peers and teachers about what they are reading.
- Teachers need to foster students' abilities to reason and critically evaluate written ideas.

Word Identification

Chapter Outline

For the Reader

The core of an effective literacy program is the instruction and application of skills and strategies that produce good readers. This assertion applies equally at all grade levels, with specific instruction dependent upon student learning needs. Regardless of the instructional materials utilized, research suggests that good literacy programs include emphasis on word identification, comprehension, writing, and reading study skills and strategies. Because learning to read is a long-term, developmental process, building a solid foundation in the essential reading abilities should be a goal of every education program. This chapter focuses on developing the various word-identification skills and strategies that skilled readers need.

Key Ideas

- Students need a variety of word-identification skills and strategies to arrive at the meaning of what they read.
- Basic sight vocabulary, phonics, structural analysis, and contextual analysis are word-identification skills and strategies that children should learn so that they can comprehend written language.
- Students must have opportunities to apply word-identification skills and strategies in meaningful authentic reading situations.
- Students need to develop flexibility in identifying words so that they can use all available cue systems to arrive at meaning.
- Each student needs to develop and continually expand a basic sight vocabulary.
- The major purpose of teaching word-identification skills and strategies is to provide tools for deriving meaning from reading.
- Word-identification skills and strategies are best taught through direct/explicit instruction.

Word-identification Strategies

Learning to read involves the interrelationship of two broad areas: word identification and comprehension. **Word identification** is the process of decoding written symbols. Research has indicated that good readers are superior in identifying words (Byrne, Freebody, & Gates, 1992). Comprehension involves understanding and interacting with the ideas expressed in text (or decoded text). Obviously, the ability to identify words is necessary for comprehension. To become proficient in identifying words, readers must employ a variety of strategies. Beginning readers must continually expand their sight vocabularies. A **sight vocabulary** is made up of words that are recognized instantly. Many of these words are not spelled the way they sound (e.g., *to, know,* and *they*); these irregular words are taught using the **whole-word approach. Phonics** instruction consists of teaching letter-sound relationships to provide an approximate pronunciation, whereby the sound elicits a meaningful association of the word meaning in the text. Instruction in **structural analysis** looks at visual patterns and meanings that change as a result of adding inflectional endings (e.g., *-s, -ed, ing,* and *-ly*), prefixes (e.g., *ex-* and *pre-*), and suffixes (e.g., *-ment* and *-ous*) and combining root words to form compounds (e.g., *sidewalk* and *playground*). Instruction in **contextual analysis** helps students figure out meanings of words by how they are used in the context of text.

Knowing words on sight, applying letter-sound relationships, recognizing word parts, and using context clues are important parts of decoding, that is, arriving at the pronunciation of a word, given the printed letter representations (Fox, 1996; Anderson, Hiebert, Scott, & Wilkinson, 1985). Equally important is an understanding of how to use all available word-identification cues simultaneously to comprehend written information. A number of studies support the idea that proficiency in using these cues for word identification is developmental (Fowler, 1992; Juel, 1991). Students who are learning to read rely predominantly on letter-sound relationships to identify words. More skilled and mature readers use larger units (e.g., word parts and whole words) and attend primarily to meaning because their word-identification strategies are automatic (Samuels, 1994). Children develop several language-cue systems simply through learning to communicate with oral language. The communicative function of spoken and written language is one cue system related to success in learning to read and write (Downing, 1979). Reading and writing also involve the student's awareness that words are strung together in meaningful units governed by structure and syntax. These features of language apply both to spoken and written text. The learner can transfer this knowledge of spoken language to master the reading process.

When fostering word-identification skills, remember the following:

- Students who receive planned and systematic instruction on word-identification skills and strategies are better able to use the alphabetic code than students who do not receive such instruction (Tunner & Hoover, 1993).
- Word-identification instruction is not reading; it is providing tools to help understand the meaning of written language. Instruction must

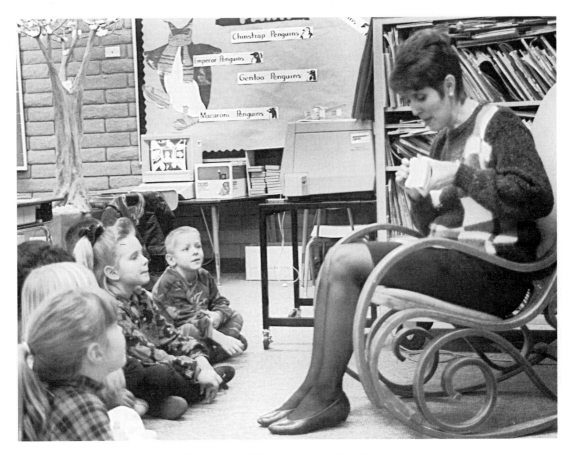

Students must develop flexibility in identifying words so that they can use all available cue systems to determine meaning.

provide opportunities for students to apply their word-identification skills in meaningful reading situations.

■ Students must develop flexibility in identifying words so that they can use all available cue systems to determine meaning. They need to develop independent and fluent mastery in the areas of whole-word recognition, phonics, structural analysis, and contextual analysis (Stahl, 1992) to focus on the meaning of what they read rather than just word pronunciation. The ability to decode a word with minimal effort is called *automaticity of word identification.*

■ Integration in Authentic Reading Situations

With automatic decoding of printed symbols a goal of reading instruction and a prerequisite for students to be able to devote a large percentage of their attention to processing meaning, an important consideration is how word-identification or decoding skills (i.e., whole-word recognition, phonics, structural analysis, and context) are taught and practiced in our schools. Chapters 2 and 6 discuss the direct/explicit instructional approach and its effectiveness in teaching reading skills. The actual teaching and guided practice of a particular skill precedes independent practice of it. Meaningful practice should be provided to ensure transfer of a new skill to a variety of situations. This stage—independent practice—signals a change in instructional practice. With our new understandings of the reading process, particularly its interactive nature, the emphasis for independent practice has switched from a reliance on isolated worksheets to integrating independent practice in more authentic reading situations. Hiebert (1994) defined authentic literacy tasks as "ones in which reading and writing serve a function for children, activities such as enjoying a book or communicating an idea in a composition" (p. 391). Workbooks and other types of practice materials (including games) are still used, but their use is supported through story content to ensure that students can apply the skill in recreational or independent reading.

Four Major Instructional Tasks

In mastering the reading process, four instructional tasks represent the major thrust of beginning reading instruction. These instructional tasks help students to do the following:

1. Understand that reading is a language process.
2. Develop and expand sight vocabulary.
3. Learn to associate visual symbols with speech sounds.
4. Realize that reading is always a meaning-making process and that printed word symbols represent language.

Some instructional materials and activities overlook or give undue emphasis to one or two tasks. Students can learn much of what is taught through such an instructional approach, but in doing so they run the risk of developing attitudes and habits harmful to the concept of reading. Beginning reading instruction that overemphasizes the mechanics and ignores comprehension is not meaningful.

Too much emphasis on word-identification skills can be detrimental. Students may develop a set of behaviors that neglects one or more aspects of the reading process. This may result in habits that handicap the reader in later development. For instance, a student may develop a habit of sounding out every word she encounters in reading. This means she will be sounding out the same word the 10th, 20th or even the 50th time she sees it in reading. She has learned that reading is sounding out words, and this becomes her goal in all reading situations. On the other hand, overemphasis on learning whole words rather than other word-identification techniques forces the student to make fine visual discriminations when minimal sounding techniques would have made the task much easier. Knowledge of whole words combined with context and minimal sounding clues are more efficient than using one technique alone.

The premise underlying this discussion is that major instructional tasks are inseparable parts of one total instructional process. Students should learn to use all of the cue systems in written language—whole-word recognition, phonics,

Students must have opportunities to apply word-identification skills and strategies in meaningful, authentic reading situations.

structure, and context—in learning to read. Thus, the major task of reading instruction is to blend these instructional components properly.

One thing that makes reading instruction complicated is that no blueprint spells out precisely where and how much instructional time and effort teachers should devote to each cue system. Second, no blueprint tells us which instructional techniques work best with individual learners. Understanding individual differences among learners offers the answers to these questions.

Sight Vocabulary

Students increase their sight vocabulary directly through instructional procedures, independent reading, and activities, and indirectly through television, road signs, bulletin boards, carton labels, and the like. Obviously, the most important source of learning is meaningful reading situations, such as those provided by charts, teacher-written stories, predictable books, big books, and easy-to-read trade books. A skill of such significance to the total reading process should be taught effectively. Following are several justifications for learning words as wholes:

- A child who knows a number of words as whole words can better understand, see, and hear similarities among these known words and new words. Having a large sight vocabulary is invaluable in helping identify other words.
- When words are recognized instantly, analysis is minimal. The reader can focus on reading for meaning.
- Numerous high-frequency words (e.g., *was, the,* and *those*) should be learned as units simply because students see them over and over in any reading situation and they contribute significantly to using syntax as a means of getting meaning from reading.

There is a difference between learning certain frequently used words and learning to rely extensively on one word-identification strategy in beginning reading, whether that strategy is whole words, phonic analysis, or context. The normal pattern of learning dictates that the student develop a sight vocabulary or learn some words as wholes through the whole-word approach.

The normal student's experience with reading results in a constantly growing stock of words recognized as wholes. The student establishes automatic stimulus-response patterns for dozens of frequently used words, such as *that, with, be, are, and, was, it, the, in, to, than, you, they, said, when,* and *can.* A number of these structure words and other frequently used words must be learned to the point at which recognizing them is automatic (Samuels, 1994).

The most popular list of high-frequency sight words is the 220-service-word Dolch list. Developed by Edward Dolch (1948) more than 40 years ago, this list includes a high percentage of irregularly spelled words found in beginning reading materials. Palmer (1986) recently tested whether the Dolch list applies to today's reading materials. Her findings agree with previous studies, which concluded that the Dolch list remains relevant. The Dolch words constituted 60 percent of the vocabulary in four of five basal series passages analyzed. Other common words in a student's sight vocabulary include words of personal interest, words in content areas, and words in reading and language arts books from preschool.

The whole-word approach focuses on learning words as wholes rather than through any form of analysis. Irregular words (i.e., those not spelled the way they sound) are best taught through this approach in meaningful context. The most common words taught by this approach include basic service words, words of personal interest to students, words that appear regularly in students' first readers, and content-area words, such as geographical, scientific, and mathematical terms. However, regular words (i.e., those spelled the way they sound) can also be learned through this approach. This is especially true when teaching new words as a way of building background knowledge before reading. As will be discussed later in the chapter, teaching new words as whole words in conjunction with teaching a story is a main avenue for word learning. The following is a step-by-step procedure detailing the teaching of a word through the whole-word approach.

- Present the word visually (e.g., on a posterboard or chalkboard) and pronounce the word.
- Pronounce the word for the student again, making sure the student is looking at the word at the time you say the word.
- Use the word in written context familiar to the student. Ask the student to make up a sentence containing the word and write the sentence on the board. Ask the student to discuss the meaning of the sentence.
- Present the word again visually and ask the student to pronounce it.
- Provide an abundance of meaningful practice in authentic reading situations (e.g., experience stories, big books, and writing).

A major avenue for teaching whole words is the Directed Reading Activity (DRA) for a story. A main component in a DRA is building vocabulary. Most vocabulary words are taught through the whole-word approach. The practice component of the whole-word approach is built into this instructional method through the ensuing story to be read and the variety of practice activities associated with most reading programs. The activities systematically present, integrate, and repeat new vocabulary words in a variety of authentic reading situations. If a teacher is using trade books for instruction without an accompanying teacher's guide, the teacher must select the key vocabulary to be taught and design appropriate independent practice. Words selected for emphasis should be those that contribute to understanding the story to enable students to recognize, understand, and use the words.

Teachers can include the teaching of whole words in the literacy program in innumerable ways, including the following:

- In conjunction with literature (narrative and expository)
- Language-experience stories
- Reading aloud using big books and predictable books
- Written activities including using the typewriter and computer, writing diaries and journals, and writing creative stories and poems
- Oral-language activities and games
- Development of scrapbooks
- Various games and puzzles
- Reading of newspapers and magazines
- Reading aloud to students
- Independent reading

Regardless of the means used to develop sight vocabulary, the application must be meaning-based, relating new vocabulary to prior knowledge and experience.

■ Names

One of the first printed words a child learns in his or her name. The practice of learning names in printed form provides the basis for teaching letter-sound relationships. Children also can begin to recognize names of common objects in the classroom that are labeled.

INSTRUCTIONAL ACTIVITIES

Reading Children's Names.   Tape each child's first name on the front of his or her desk. Use other words with it so that each name is within a meaningful context. Doing this will more likely result in processing print as it is related to comprehension.

Mary sits here.	Mike sits here.
Sarah sits here.	Sandy sits here.

Children learn the names of other children in meaningful context just as they learn the words in a sentence. Children also learn very quickly to recognize a number of names in printed form. Use chalkboard announcements involving students' names.

Hand out books	Water the plants
John and Helen	Jean and Billy

Labeling Objects.   Print naming words in short phrases on separate oaktag cards to make naming labels and attach them to objects in the room.

a door	a book	a plant

the chalkboard	the big table

Collect a number of pictures that depict objects or animals within the range of the children's experiential and conceptual backgrounds (photographs of the school and community are appropriate). Paste the pictures on cardboard and print the naming words in short phrases beneath them. Use these to generate language-experience stories.

a cat	a cow	a horse	a house

To add the kinesthetic mode to the words, duplicate a page of drawings and leave space for children to copy the names from models displayed on the chalktray. In the first experience, outline the printed words with dots. Have each child mark over the dots and "write" the words.

Later exercises may omit the dotted outlines. Have each child copy from the printed models on the chalktray, chalkboard, or bulletin board.

Writing Short Stories.   As children begin to recognize many words, provide many opportunities for them to apply this skill in context. Write short, meaningful sentences that relate directly to the names of the children and objects in the classroom. Children are more likely to succeed because the concepts represented are meaningful to them. Combine the sentences to construct a story.

<u>Our Class</u>

John and Helen hand out books.

Jean and Billy water the plants.

Mary, Mike, and Sarah sit at the big table.

A plant, a book, and a door are in the room.

Develop similar application activities for objects and animal names. Read a short phrase and direct students to select from a list the words that make sense in the sentence. Write the words in the spaces and call on students to read each sentence. If several choices make sense, ask about the meaning of each word selected.

On his farm there is _____ _____

In the woods lives _____ _____ .

Sandy went to the farm in _____ _____ .

At the farm she saw _____ _____

a cat   a cow   a bear   a horse   a car

Language-experience stories enhance sight vocabulary in meaningful context (Heilman, 1992). Stimulate students to dictate group-experience stories by posing questions that encourage them to use words introduced in teacher-directed instruction. For example, ask "What do we do at school? What is in our classroom? What do we know about a cat, a cow, and a horse?" to stimulate students to compose stories that make meaningful application of sight-word instruction. (See the Appendix for more practice activities and games.)

■ Picture Dictionaries

A picture dictionary is excellent for developing word meanings as well as a multitude of other skills, such as letter sounds and letter names.

INSTRUCTIONAL ACTIVITIES

Making a Picture Dictionary. Secure a number of small pictures from workbooks, magazines, and the like. Have one page devoted to each letter of the alphabet. Let the students paste pictures of animals whose names begin with each letter on the appropriate pages. Then print a picture-naming word beneath each picture. (Note the use of **a** or **some** with the words to focus attention on them.) A partial **M-m** page follows.

a man   some milk   a mule

a monkey   a mop   some meat

Using a Picture Dictionary. Use the picture dictionary in determining other words that make sense in the sentences and stories. For example, ask students to find two words in their picture dictionaries that have the long **a** sound. Use examples and illustrations to model for students how to use the dictionary to identify and select words for their writing activities.

■ Reporters' Questions

Instruction on and practice with reporter's questions *(Who? What? Where? When? Why?* and *How?)* help children learn some important terms used in reading instructions and in following directions. Each experience with these important words helps students learn them as sight words.

INSTRUCTIONAL ACTIVITY

Using Reporters' Questions. Write the words **who, what, where, when, why,** and **how** on the chalkboard. Say the words (making sure each student is thinking about the word as it is pronounced), and point to each word as you say it. Use the chalkboard, an overhead projector, or duplicated materials to present materials similar to the following.

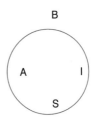

Direct students' attention to the written context for each of the materials. Encourage discussion and write their responses next to each question.

Circle A

How many dots?   There are four dots.

How did you learn this?   We counted them.

When did you count them?   Just now!

What color are the dots?   They are black.

Where is the circle?   Around the dots!

Why is the circle around   So we could ask how,

    the dots?   what, when, where, and

                      why questions.

Circle B

Where are the letters?

How many letters are there?

What are the letters?

What is around the letters?

Why is it around the letters?

■ Position Words

The importance of teaching the meanings of certain crucial terms used in reading helps avoid unnecessary instructional problems. Students must understand the position words *in, on, above, below, over, under,* and the like.

INSTRUCTIONAL ACTIVITY

Using Position Words.   Use a format similar to the following circle-square-table. Prepare cards on oaktag and put them on the chalktray or tape them on the chalkboard so all can see. Provide each participating student with three or four word cards. Each card should have the same position word printed on both sides. As children hold up the requested card, check for accuracy.

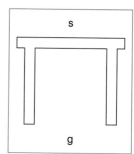

Read the following directions:

Hold up the word **in.** (pause) What letter is in the circle?

Hold up the word **over.** (pause) What letter is over the square?

Hold up the word **on.** (pause) What letter is on the table?

Continue using all of the word cards issued to the children. Each can be used more than once if desired—for example—**in** the circle, **in** the square, and **under** the circle, square, and table.

■ Words Often Confused

Students need varied and interesting practice on confusing words commonly found in their reading materials. This practice should help them recognize the words at sight.

INSTRUCTIONAL ACTIVITIES

Presenting Individual Words.   Use the chalkboard, an overhead projector, or duplicated materials consisting of words frequently confused in early reading. Present these words in pairs and direct students' attention to the differences in letter combinations. Following are several examples.

their	every	when	four	which
there	very	where	for	with

Presenting Words in Sentences.   Present words in meaningful context, underlining the frequently used words. Paying heed to the underlined words, read the sentences in unison with the class or a group. Focus discussion on the meaning features of the words.

Their house is over there.

Everyone said it was very cold.

When were they taken there?

These sell four for a dollar.

Which boy will go with you?

Using Words in Meaningful Context.   Prepare a short text that contains blank spaces. Write the two words that will complete the sense of the context. Ask students to write the correct word in each blank space. You may have to read the sentences aloud for many of the students. Discuss both the meaning features and graphic features of their word choices.

(to, two)   1. The _____ boys were going _____ the store.

(for, four)   2. These boxes sell _____ _____ a dollar.

(think, thank)   3. I _____ you should _____ him for it.

(very, every)   4. _____ teacher was _____ busy.

(you, your)   5. Have _____ had _____ dinner?

■ Scrambled Sentences

Practice in assembling scrambled sentences helps students acquire a basic sight vocabulary and a knowledge of terms used in reading instruction (such as *period* and *question mark*). Understanding basic sentence structure also aids in comprehension.

INSTRUCTIONAL ACTIVITY

Arranging Words into Sentences.   On separate cards, print individual words from sentences used previously on the chalkboard. Present them in scrambled order, then ask students to arrange the words in proper order. Follow each sentence with a card bearing the proper punctuation. This is one of many ways to repeat frequently used words.

■ Classification

Classifying words in a good way to introduce and practice sight vocabulary. It is also a beginning step toward successful comprehension. Classifying interesting and concrete terms can motivate students to succeed.

INSTRUCTIONAL ACTIVITIES

Classifying Words.   Write classification words on the board and underline them. Point to each word and read it. Ask students to repeat each word after you pronounce it. On oaktag or cardboard, print each of the other words to be used in the exercise. Hold up one card at a time and call on a student to pronounce the word and to tell under which heading the word belongs.

INCLUSION STRATEGIES

Kinesthetic-Tactile Reinforcement of Sight Words

All students learning the various word identification skills need additional practice to ensure mastery. Many exceptional students profit from a more multisensory approach to learning. Besides the many authentic tasks (e.g., applying a new skill in reading or writing a story), games, cooperative activities, computer software, commercial skills books, and various kits for practicing word-identification skills, teachers may develop a kinesthetic-tactile (movement-touching) technique or game for reinforcement as part of a lesson. This technique enables the reader to use four sensory modalities in the process of learning words. For example, you might obtain a cookie sheet and a small amount of white sand. After teaching certain vocabulary words through the whole-word approach, you can have a student spell the word in the sand as he or she is saying it. After the student prints the word in the sand, it can be retraced several times as it is pronounced. This provides a multisensory approach as the student uses the kinesthetic and tactile modes of learning in addition to the auditory-visual modes. The student sees the word (visual), hears the word (auditory), traces the word with a finger (kinesthetic), and feels the word as it is traced (tactile). As the teacher, you can easily shake the cookie sheet to smooth out the sand for the next student. A variation of this multisensory technique is to use cut-out letters made of sandpaper. Students can spell words and trace each word with an increased tactile sensory input.

animals	clothing	food	school
a dog	a hat	my milk	a book
a cat	the shoes	my cookies	a desk
a cow	a dress	my pie	the paper

As a variation, place a number of appropriate words in a box at the bottom of the page. Ask students to copy the words under the correct heading. They can work individually or in small groups. Focus discussion on why words were grouped together.

Using Classifications in Context.   Develop further categories. Have students complete short sentences by selecting the words that make sense in context. See the following for an example.

Animals	**Animal Sounds**	**Animal Homes**
a dog	moos	the farm
a cow	barks	the house
a cat	oinks	the woods
a bear	meows	

_____   _____ barks.

_____   _____ is the home of a cow.

A dog _____ .

On _____   _____ a cow moos.

A cat meows in _____   _____

Phonics

Purposes of Phonic Instruction

Phonic instruction consists of teaching letter-sound relationships so that the learner can identify new words in print. Because English is alphabetic in that written words represent a collection of speech sounds, phonic instruction is crucial in helping beginning readers understand how our language works (Adams, 1994; Juel, 1991; Samuels, 1994). Beginning readers inevitably encounter many words they do not recognize. By applying knowledge of letter-sound relationships in combination with available context clues and understanding that printed language must make sense, students can better comprehend what they read. Most likely, a written word that puzzles a student is one he or she has spoken or heard many times, so applying letter-sound relationships determines the pronunciation or yields an approximate pronunciation.

A purpose of phonic instruction is to teach the beginning reader that printed letters and letter combinations represent speech sounds heard in words. The sounds heard in words are quite different from sounds heard in isolation. In the sentence "The cat ran after the mice," the written word *cat* blends three phonemes just as they are in the oral word. But readers should not produce three syllables: *kuh-ah-tuh* (cat). Phonics instruction should teach the learner to blend the sounds that the printed letters represent when encountering a new word (Eeds-Kneip, 1979; Stahl, 1992). Blending permits a child to determine whether or not the word is in his or her speaking or listening vocabulary and whether it makes sense in context. Phonic instruction should teach the learner to use all available cue systems in combination with letter-sound relationships to identify words and comprehend written text, giving primary attention to word meanings and comprehension. Too much emphasis on using letter-sound relationships to identify isolated words will cause the learner to think these relationships constitute reading. Phonic instruction should stress that reading is a meaning-making process and provide extensive practice in authentic tasks.

Tasks in Phonics

Phonics involves a series of tasks taken together. Phonics teaching materials include a number of techniques common to all approaches. They may differ in the

Phonic instruction improves children's ability to identify words.

sequence in which skills are introduced, the emphasis on learning rules, the number of steps taught, and the degree of phonic instruction included in beginning reading. The major phonics tasks include the following:

- Discriminating speech sounds in words
- Using written letters to represent the speech sounds
- Using the sound represented by a letter or letters in a known word to unlock the pronunciation of unknown words in which these particular letters occur
- Identifying sounds of consonants in initial and final positions
- Blending consonants
- Identifying special consonant digraphs (such as *th, ch, she,* and *wh*)
- Discerning short and long vowel sounds.
- Distinguishing double vowels, vowel digraphs, and diphthongs
- Identifying vowels followed by *r*
- Identifying the effect of a final *e*
- Discerning the sounds of *y.*

All of the preceding tasks are not equally important in learning to read, and each should not receive the same amount of instructional time. They are simply the framework, because some include many specific elements.

A necessary prerequisite for and at the same time a powerful predictor of success in beginning reading is **phonemic awareness** (Ball & Blackman, 1991; Yopp, 1995). Richgels, Poremba, & McGee (1996) define this term and discuss its importance:

> Phonemic awareness is *conscious* attention to phonemes, which are the units of sound that speakers and listeners *unconsciously* combine and contrast to produce and perceive words in spoken language. For example, in English, the phonemes /d/, /i/, and /p/ are combined to make the word *dip,* and the /d/ and /t/ phonemes are contrasted when distinguishing the words *dip* and *tip.* Children must go beyond such unconscious use of phonemes when they learn to read and write. Conscious attention to phonemes is involved when they isolate sounds in words during invented spelling or use the sounds associated with letters to identify words and recognize word families. (p. 633)

Direct instruction lessons and activities that focus on phonemes, including adding and subtracting new sounds to words and analyzing words by sounds in meaningful and authentic materials, promote this ability.

The actual learning of phonics as it relates to reading usually begins early in the preschool years. The child learns the sound of a word like *mommy* and can easily differentiate it from similar-sounding words. He may have a pet kitty and a playmate Kathy. He can differentiate if asked "Where is Kathy?" even though the kitty is also present.

Phonic instruction begins when an adult talks with an infant, thus providing the child with a model. A child who associates sounds with objects and does not confuse words that are very similar—such as *mommy, money, monkey,* and *maybe*—is mastering auditory discrimination, which is important for phonic analysis in the reading process. The later tasks in learning phonics depend on mastery of this basic language function. Beginning reading instruction in the school should build on the child's previous language experiences. In reading, students must discriminate among written word symbols and learn that these symbols represent the speech sounds of words they speak and understand.

■ Phonic Instruction

While a variety of specific techniques can help students learn the relationships between letters and speech sounds, the main approach is the analytic (or implicit) approach. Regardless of the approach, however, teachers should remember that (1) an important goal of phonic instruction is the approximate, not exact, pronunciation of words, (2) letter-sound correspondences are best communicated through direct/explicit instruction, and (3) phonic instruction should include an abundance of practice in contextual reading situations.

The last two points highlight the importance of mastering automatic word-identification skills. Without direct instruction and meaningful practice to the point of overlearning and automaticity, students are less likely to understand and interact with the ideas in the text.

■ Teaching Methods

There are a multitude of teaching techniques in the area of phonics. Basically, instruction can be termed analytic or synthetic.

Analytic phonics teaches letter-sound relationship by referring to words already known to identify a particular phonic element. This approach begins by having students learn a certain number of words by the whole-word approach, after which they examine the relationships that exist among the phonic elements. Using this approach, there are two basic ways of teaching a skill lesson: *inductive,* in which the teacher begins by giving examples illustrating a generalization and guiding the children to a conclusion; and *deductive,* in which children are told the generalization and then asked for examples to verify it.

Examples of the inductive approach include the following:

- It is assumed that children know the words (e.g., *ball, bat,* and *bundle*) or the words are taught through the whole-word approach.
- The teacher asks the children what is alike about the words and leads the children to discover that the words contain the letter *b,* which represents the /b/ sound.
- Other words with the sound of /b/ are solicited.
- Words used are presented in written context.
- Practice exercises are given using the words in context.

Examples of the deductive approach include the following:

- The words (e.g., *ball, bat,* and *bundle*) are listed on the board. The words are in the children's listening-speaking vocabulary).
- The teacher tells the children that all the words begin with the letter *b* and represents the /b/ sound as in *big.*
- Other words are solicited with the sound of /b/.
- Words are presented in written context.
- Practice exercises are given using the words in context.

The inductive approach is generally preferred over the deductive approach, although this decision rests with the teacher, as some children respond better to the deductive method.

Synthetic phonics begins with direct instruction of phonic elements, beginning with letters of the alphabet, followed by syllables, then monosyllabic words through polysyllabic words, then phrases, and finally whole sentences. Once children learn the sounds represented by the letters, they blend the parts of the words together to form a known word. Synthetic phonics includes the following three variations of sound blending: (1) letter by letter *(b-a-t),* (2) the initial consonant is sounded and the rest of the word is added as a word family *(b-at)*, and (3) the initial consonant and vowel are sounded together and the final consonant is added *(ba-t)*.

The analytic approach to phonics is more widely used today. Keep in mind, however, that the difference between analytic and synthetic is one of initial emphasis (whole-word versus letter-sounds first). Emphasis must be evaluated in terms of successful teacher implementation of a particular method and learner preference. Auditory blending is a crucial skill in the analytic approach, as well as in the synthetic approach, because a youngster must be able to divide an unknown word into syllables or structural elements, attempt pronunciation of the smaller units, and, finally, blend the units together.

■ Direct/Explicit Teaching of Phonics

The most beneficial teaching method of phonics (whether you use an analytic or synthetic approach) is direct/explicit instruction. As stated in Chapter 2, skills are best taught and learned through the direct/explicit instructional approach. A teaching sequence that emphasizes direct/explicit instruction will ensure student mastery of phonic, structural, and contextual analysis skills and strategies. In direct/explicit instruction, the teacher gives direct, step-by-step explanations of a particular skill or strategy. Viewing this approach from an interactive viewpoint in the reading process, it also emphasizes the "when" and "why" of using various skills and strategies. Closely related to Rosenshine and Stevens's (1986) description in Chapter 2, another view of the process of direct/explicit instruction includes the following steps:

Stage one: planning

1. Area of needed reading instruction
2. Intended learning outcome
3. Past learning

Stage two: teaching

4. Building background
5. Teacher-directed instruction
6. Independent student practice
7. Ongoing diagnosis
8. Modifying instruction (Rupley & Blair, 1988)

In the planning stage, the teacher (1) selects the desired area of reading instruction appropriate to students' needs, (2) identifies specific learning outcomes and appropriate instructional features reflecting assessment information, and (3) determines areas of related past learning from assessment information. The first phase in teaching a skill or strategy is to review past learnings with students and to motivate them to participate in the lesson. The second phase is to explain formally, model, and/or demonstrate the goal of the lesson for students. Easy,

■ Area of Needed Reading Instruction

Understanding of the vowel diphthongs *oi* and *oy.*

■ Intended Learning Outcome

Given a series of words containing the vowel combinations *oi* and *oy,* students will be able to pronounce the words correctly.

■ Past Learning

Students know the vowel sounds (long and short).
Students know vowel principles.

■ Building Background

Review with students the vowel principle that helps them pronounce the words *heat* and *boat.* Remind students that when you discussed this principle, you reminded them that it did not hold true all of the time. Tell them that today they will learn two vowel combinations that do not follow the double vowel principle.

■ Teacher-directed Instruction

On the board write two lists of known words that contain the *oi* and *oy* vowel combination. For example:

oil	toy
soil	boy
boil	joy

Ask students to pronounce the words. Next ask: How many vowels are there in each word? What usually happens when there are two vowels together in a word? Do you hear the sound of the first vowel in *oil* and *toy?* Tell students that *oi* and *oy* are special vowel combinations that usually stand for the sound heard at the beginning of *oil.* Isolate the sound of *oi* for students. Solicit other words that have this sound. Lead students to the conclusion that *oi* and *oy* represent the vowel sound found in the word *oil.* Present a new list of real and nonsense words containing the vowel combinations *oi* and *oy.* Make sure they can pronounce the words correctly.

FIGURE 5.1
Direct/explicit instruction lesson
Source: Reprinted with the permission of Prentice-Hall Publishing Company from **Teaching Reading: Diagnosis, Direct Instruction, and Practice,** Second Edition, by William H. Rupley and Timothy R. Blair. Copyright © 1988 by Prentice-Hall.

concrete examples based on students' experiential backgrounds are most suitable for the actual instructional activities. This phase also includes teacher-directed or supervised practice of the particular skill or strategy. At this point, the teacher walks the students through an individual or group activity to make sure they all understand the skill or strategy and when and why they are to use it. In the next phase, independent practice, students are expected to complete an activity on

■ **Independent Student Practice**

Write the following words on the chalkboard and ask students to fill in the sentence blanks with the correct words. After they finish, read the sentences aloud to check mastery of *oi* and *oy* combinations.

soil	enjoy
boy	moisture
coin	toy
noise	poison

The plastic airplane was his favorite _____ .
The _____ is dry and needs to be watered.
The insects were killed with _____ .
That 1923 dime is a rare _____ .
I hope you will _____ the picnic.
The _____ in the air caused rain.
The _____ in the yellow shirt threw the ball.
The neighbors next door make a lot of _____ .

■ **Ongoing Diagnosis**

Read with each student individually during the silent reading section of a directed reading activity. Note the student's application of the vowel combination of *oy* and *oi* and decide if further direct instruction and/or practice is necessary.

■ **Modifying Instruction**

The independent student practice can be simplified by using pictures representing the words that students are to select to complete the sentences. Write the naming words beneath each picture to emphasize the written text that represents the pictures. Another modification is to write a choice of words beneath the blank and have students select the one that makes sense to complete the sentence. For example:

The plastic airplane was his favorite _____ .
toy   enjoy   soil

This can be made easier by giving the students only two words from which to select. The difficulty level can be increased by providing several choices that make sense in each sentence; have students identify all words that would meaningfully complete the sentences.

FIGURE 5.1, continued

their own to apply the skill and strategy in a real reading or authentic situation. Next, ongoing diagnosis focuses on assessing students' progress to ensure mastery of the intended goal. Last, in the modifying instruction phase, the teacher responds to his or her own monitoring of instruction and ongoing assessment procedures. Figure 5.1 provides an example of a direct/explicit instruction lesson on a word-identification skill.

■ Phonics in Proper Perspective

Throughout the history of reading instruction, phonics has occupied a variety of roles. While no one approach—whole-word or phonics—is used exclusively in learning to read, the pendulum swings back and forth between an emphasis on learning words as wholes or through sound-symbol relationships.

From the colonial days to 1840, letters and sounds were taught haphazardly. The year 1840 marked the publication of Josiah Bumstead's *My Little Primer,* a beginning reader based on the whole-word approach. Due in large part to Horace Mann's influence, the following years ushered in several other readers emphasizing the whole-word approach.

Rebecca Pollard's Synthetic Method, introduced about 1890 (Pollard, 1889), advocated reducing reading to a number of mechanical procedures, each of which focused on a unit smaller than a word. Reading became mechanistic and, when mastered, often produced individuals who were adept at working through a given word. The result among both teachers and students was that reading became equated with facility in calling words. Beginning around 1920 and continuing until 1950, phonics went out of favor again.

Rudolph Flesch's *Why Johnny Can't Read* was an influential book published in 1955. It advocated a return to intensive phonics. Since the mid-1950s, phonics has assumed a more dominant place in early literacy instruction.

Equally noteworthy was the publication of Jeanne Chall's 1967 classic, *Learning to Read: The Great Debate.* In this text, Chall underscored the importance of decoding in beginning reading. Since the publication of Chall's book, commercial programs in reading have emphasized decoding.

No other aspect of the literacy curriculum has received as much critical attention as phonic instruction. Each generation of reading teachers faces both old and new controversies about phonic instruction. Even today, unfortunately, many people believe that phonics is an enemy of reading for meaning. Individuals who oppose phonics argue that teaching students to read by focusing on letter-sound relationships interferes with comprehension. We, too, oppose phonics if it requires a student to sound out every word with the correct pronunciation of words becoming the primary goal of reading instruction.

The first objective of sounding out unknown words is to establish their identity, but this is not the end of the process. Words are identified to utilize their contribution to the meaning of the sentence. A student who sounds out a word without pursuing the meaning of the sentence is a casualty of either poor or inadequate instruction. The objective in using letter-sound relationships is to identify unknown words to read for meaning, not to identify words simply because they are there (Taylor & Nosbush, 1983).

As mentioned, several studies have found that students' word-identification skills progress developmentally. In the early stages, learners depend primarily on knowledge of letter-sound relations to identify words. Children who come to school knowing how to read usually possess basic phonic skills. Donald D. Durrell and Helen A. Murphy (1978), who have devoted more than 50 years of work to beginning reading instruction, state:

> The [letter names, writing letters, letter name sounds, and syntax matching] appear to be early stages of reading which all children acquire before they

◀IIII F L A S H B A C K

Horace Mann was responsible for the first educational reform related to reading in the nineteenth century. Mann was the secretary of the Massachusetts Board of Education in the mid 1830s. He was extremely critical of the prevailing ABC method of teaching reading. In a report to the board, Mann argued that using the alphabetic method to teach reading was presenting information to children that was totally unfamiliar to them. Mann's criticism had a major impact on the reading instruction practices used nationwide at this time. By the 1880s the alphabetic method had been abandoned in most of the progressive schools and replaced with the word method for teaching reading.

Library of Congress. Research Courtesy of James R.
Murray, Director, and Elio Gasperetti, Graphic Artist,
Educational Media Center, D.C. Public Schools,
Washington, D.C.

U P D A T E IIII▶

Today, a main goal of reading programs is automatic word identification. The goal is primarily achieved through teaching phonics and its content. Other strategies to promote automatic word identification include sight vocabulary learning through the whole-word approach, structural analysis, and contextual analysis. The importance of phonics was highlighted in the landmark book, *Becoming a Nation of Readers: The Report of the Commission on Reading* (1985). The authors of this important work summarized recent research on the reading process and the teaching of reading.

Though most children today are taught phonics, often this instruction is poorly conceived. Phonics is more likely to be useful when children hear the sounds associated with most letters both in isolation and in words, and when they are taught to blend the sounds of letters to identify words. Phonics instruction should be kept simple and it should be completed by the end of the second grade for most children.

become successful readers. Children who learn to read before coming to school invariably have these phonic skills; occasionally a child cannot write the letters, but the other abilities are always present. (p. 389)

Phonic instruction today is central to most reading programs. After reviewing classroom research on beginning reading and the effectiveness of phonics, the authors of the influential book *Becoming a Nation of Readers: The Report of the Commission on Reading* (1985) recommend phonics as an essential ingredient of beginning reading programs. Anderson, Hiebert, Scott, & Wilkinson state, "Thus the issue is no longer, as it was several decades ago, whether children should be taught phonics. The issues now are specific ones of just how it should be done" (p. 37). Their conclusions on the role of phonics follow:

> Phonics instruction improves children's ability to identify words. Useful phonics strategies include teaching children the sounds of letters in isolation and in words, and teaching them to blend the sounds of letters together to produce approximate pronunciations of words. Another strategy that may be useful is encouraging children to identify words by thinking of other words with similar spellings. Phonics instruction should go hand in hand with opportunities to identify words in meaningful sentences and stories. Phonics should be taught early and kept simple. (p. 57)

Stahl (1992) presented a balanced view of phonics instruction, emphasizing the necessity of all types of reading programs to include attention to the generalizations about the connections that exist between the spelling and pronunciation of a word. Noting the often-heard opposite extreme views on the use of phonics, he stated, "With these strong feelings, though, extreme views have been allowed to predominate, seemingly forcing out any middle position that allows for the importance of systematic attention to decoding in the context of a program stressing comprehension and interpretation of quality literature and expository text" (p. 618). He then discussed the following components of "exemplary phonics instruction," stating that "These components could be found in classrooms based on the shared reading of literature, as in a whole language philosophy, or in classrooms in which the basal reader is used as the core text" (p. 620).

Stahl believes that exemplary phonics instruction does the following:

1. Builds on a child's rich concepts about how print functions.
2. Builds on a foundation of phonemic awareness (awareness of sounds in spoken words).
3. Is clear and direct.
4. Is integrated into a total reading program.
5. Focuses on reading words, not learning rules.
6. May include onset and rime. (An onset is the part of the syllable before the vowel and a rime is the part from the vowel onward.)
7. May include invented spelling practice.
8. Develops independent word recognition strategies, focusing attention on the internal structure of words. (pp. 620–623)

Rather than taking extreme positions for or against phonic instruction, teachers must analyze how they will teach literacy. The optimum amount of phonic instruction for each student who is learning to read is not simply a matter of hours of instruction—it is the amount needed to make them independent readers. As in the case of all instruction, teachers hold the key to students' success in reading. Keep in mind that letter-sound analysis is most effective when used in combination with other skills.

The following instructional activities can be used to supplement a literacy program based on students' interaction with meaningful language. Reading and writing activities based on real-life experiences are invaluable.

Consonant Sounds.   Some instructional materials used in beginning literacy advocate that the teaching of the letter-sounds start with consonants because one of the most important clues to the sounds of vowels comes from consonants that follow vowels. A consonant-vowel-consonant pattern usually results in a short vowel sound, as in *cat, den,* and *can.* The same is true if the vowel is followed by two consonants (e.g., *cattle, dentist,* and *canvas*). Starting from the premise that children have learned to recognize a few words at sight—which for illustrative purposes we will assume include the words *be, back,* and *ball*—they are ready to associate the sound of /b/ in these words with the written symbol *b.*

INSTRUCTIONAL ACTIVITIES

Introducing Initial Consonants.   Print an uppercase **B** on the chalkboard and say, "Today we will learn all about the letter **B.** Next to the uppercase **B,** I will print a lowercase **b.** This uppercase **B** is also called a capital **B.** Now I am going to write some words that begin with lowercase **b.**"

Bb

Write **be, back,** and **ball** on the chalkboard. Point to each word and pronounce it. Stress the initial sound of **b** without distorting it. Direct students to look at each word as it is pronounced. Ask, "Who can give us another word that begins with the sound heard in the words?" Answer, "Yes, **bear, boat,** and **big.** We write **Bobby** with a capital **B** because it is somebody's name."

be

back

ball

bear

When a number of examples have been given, ask, "What sound do we hear at the beginning of each of these words?" Continue, "That's right, they all begin with the sound of *b—be, back, ball, bear, boat, big,* and *Bobby.*" Point to each word as it is pronounced. Note that in no instance were the children asked to sound the letter *b* in isolation.

boat

big

Bobby

Applying Initial Consonants.   To provide for immediate meaningful application of the sound represented by the letter *b* and ways that initial consonants combined with context can provide clues for word identification, write sentences such as the following on the board.

B_____ put the b_____ in the water.

We will b_____ coming b_____ to class after lunch.

Announce, "You all have done well telling me words that begin with the **b** sound. Look carefully at each word on the board as I say it. Each word begins with the letter **b** and the sound of **b.** I am going to read a sentence for you two times that has two words missing. The missing words begin with the letter **b** and the **b** sound." Point to the blanks and the letter **b.** "Listen and watch carefully as I read this sentence one time." Point to the first sentence and move your hand left to right under the words as you read each sentence to the children. "Now, I want each of you to listen and watch carefully as I read the sentence again. Tell me *which of the words from our list makes sense in the context." Point to the list and read aloud each word as you point. Read each sentence, asking a student for a word from the list that makes sense in each blank. Write each response in the appropriate blank.*

Engage all students in instruction by asking them if the word choices sound like something they would say. Ask if they could draw a picture of what is happening. Tell them why their choices are either correct (make sense) or incorrect.

Both of the preceding activities for teaching letter-sound association possess features of effective reading instruction. Specifically, these features include the following:

- Relating new learnings (letter-sound association) to past learnings (sight words).
- Asking literal-level questions such as, "Who can give other words beginning with the sound represented by *b?*" and "Does the sentence make sense?"
- Using direct instruction.
- Moving in small, related instructional steps.
- Providing for immediate application of skills in meaningful reading situations.
- Rewarding students' efforts and thinking, not just the correctness of responses.

In addition to the group work just described, you can begin to make the transition to student use and application by giving each child an opportunity to practice and apply the concept. Applications can be done in the group setting by using meaningful text that is similar to the earlier examples. Read the text several times as students follow along. Have them select and discuss their word choices for each blank. Monitor their performance closely to ensure that they are successful.

Most of these kinds of activities provide no opportunity to apply auditory discrimination skills in meaningful context and are intended to be supplementary. Application is extremely important, and the teacher must provide for it.

INSTRUCTIONAL ACTIVITIES

Identifying Objects. *In a row of pictures such as the following, ask each student to mark the objects whose names begin with the same sound as the name of the object in the picture on the extreme left.*

Matching Pictures and Words. *Show the picture of an object and follow it by four words, none of which names the picture but one or more of which begin with the same sound as the name of the pictured object. Ask students to draw a circle around the boxes or words that begin with the same sound. For example:*

| house | baby | cup | bath |

Show a picture of a familiar object along with the word represented by the object in the picture. The example shown here is a bell. Let the children see the letter **b** and hear the sound **b** represents. Then ask them to mark all the other words in a supplied list that begin with the same sound.

bell

be	play
lake	boat
book	

Identifying Sounds in Words.   Show a series of boxes, each containing three words. Pronounce one of the words and direct students to underline the word pronounced. They need not know all of the words as sight words, provided they are familiar with the initial sound of each. In the following example, you could pronounce the italicized words.

1	2	3	4	5
call	*tell*	hill	*may*	hat
bank	sell	fill	pay	show
play	fell	*bill*	say	*bat*

Matching Words.   In columns, present words, some of which begin with the same sound and the same letter. Ask students to draw a line from the word in column A to the word in column B that begins with the same sound. For example:

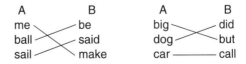

An important skill to learn is substituting known letter sounds in unknown words. Assume the children know the words *take* and *make*, then they encounter the unknown word *rake*. They should be able to combine the *r* sound that they know from words like *run, rain,* and *ride* with the sound of *ake* in *take*. By this process, they unlock the new word (Yopp, 1992).

In beginning reading, it is common to teach a number of monosyllabic words containing frequently used phonograms. Practically all workbooks use these word families to teach new words. Work on the substitution of initial consonants parallels early levels of most basal series. Moving through early levels, the child sees words such as *came, fame, same, name,* and *game* and words containing other common phonograms. Each of these words contains a familiar, often recurring, phonogram. Students should not receive isolated drills on these word endings. Nevertheless, students can understand a number of important words independently when they know some sight words containing commonly used letter combinations and can substitute initial letter sounds.

INSTRUCTIONAL ACTIVITIES

Using Pictures to Teach Letter-Sound Combinations.   Use pictures in teaching letter-sound substitutions. The pictures should present words that are part of students' experiential and conceptual backgrounds. In the following examples, some children may perceive the hen as a chicken. Direct students to name the picture, listen to the first sound in the picture name, and write the letter that represents this sound in the blank. Do the first two with them to make sure they understand what they are to do.

Applying Letter-sound Substitution Skills in Meaningful Sentence Context.   By applying such skills in context, students begin to understand that phonics is a tool for getting meaning. You can use sentences such as the following in a group setting to allow students to apply their skills. Such instruction builds on past learnings to enhance students' chances of success. Note that many of the words used for learning the sound represented by **b** are found in these sentences.

Bobby has a _____ pet _____ .

fat	cat
bat	hat
hat	mat

The _____ will be back at _____ o'clock.

pen	ten
men	hen
ten	pen

Bill took his _____ , _____ , and _____ to the baseball game.

hat	ball	cat
rat	fall	bat
fat	call	sat

Some teachers prefer to teach a particular consonant sound at the ends of words at the same time that they deal with it as an initial sound. Other teachers work through the initial sounds and then work on single consonant sounds at the ends of words. Either procedure teaches students to notice visually and aurally the final consonants in short words. They know words such as **men, log, pen, bold,** and **leg** and the sounds of letters, including **t.** They are then asked to substitute at the end of these words the sound presented by **t** to get **met, lot, pet, bolt,** and **let.**

Simple Consonant Blends.   To avoid confusion in dealing with many words that children will discover early in the literacy process, you must focus their attention on more than the initial consonant. Consonant blends fall into two classes: simple two-letter consonant blends, and a smaller group of three-letter blends.

The 24 two- and three-letter simple blends may be divided into three major groups on the basis of a common letter:

1. Those that begin with *s: sc, sk, sm, sn, sp, st, sw,* and *str*
2. Those that conclude with *l: bl, cl, fl, gl, pl, sl,* and *spl*
3. Those that conclude with *r: br, cr, dr, fr, gr, pr, tr, scr, spr,* and *str*

The preceding groups are not intended to suggest a particular order in which blends should be taught. A logical sequence would probably be determined by the vocabulary found in the instructional materials actually used in beginning reading.

Teachers and early readers differ according to when they deal with blends, which they teach/learn first, and how rapidly they cover the blends. Most materials suggest teaching initial blends before blends and special consonant sounds at the ends of words (as in *rest, nest, best, bark,* and *mark*). Although teaching consonant blends can take numerous approaches, the objectives of all methods are to lead the student to:

■ See the printed letters involved.
■ Understand that in every instance the letter sounds combine into a blended sound.
■ Discriminate auditorily among the sounds of individual letters and blends, as in *dug, rug, drug* and *sold, cold, scold.*

Any procedure for teaching initial consonant sounds can help teach each of the different consonant blends.

INSTRUCTIONAL ACTIVITIES

Identifying Blends in Object Names.   Secure a number of pictures of familiar objects whose names begin with a blend. Show the pictures one at a time and have students write or say the blended letters. (They are not to simply name the picture.) Examples are **skate, train,**

bridge, plate, grapes, sled, frog, clock, star, blanket, snake, store, plow, clown, swing, and **school.**

Adding Letters.   In step 1, list words on the chalkboard that begin with **p** to which **s** can be added as a first letter to form the blend **sp**. Pronounce these words with students.

In step 2, write the **sp**-blend word to the right of each original word. Have students note the visual pattern of **sp** at the beginning of each word. Guide them in pronouncing the two words in each pair in rapid succession and in noting the blended sound in the second word in each pair (such as **pot—spot, pin— spin,** and **pill—spill**).

Step 1	Step 2
pot	spot
pin	spin
pill	spill
peak	speak
pool	spool
poke	spoke
park	spark

Following is a variation of the previous activity. Instruct the students to add a letter such as **c, g, p** or **t** in front of each of the letter groups to pronounce a consonant blend. Circle the letters that blend.

_____ reat	_____ roud	_____ rain	_____ rop
_____ reek	_____ rail	_____ rice	_____ ruly
_____ rint	_____ reen	_____ row	_____ rize
_____ rip	_____ rack	_____ ree	_____ rand

Identifying Blends in Sentences.   Prepare and duplicate sentences containing a number of blends. Have students underline each blend. For example:

The black crow flew away from the tree.
Pretty bright flowers grew near the bridge.
What is the price of the green dress in the store window?
We will rest when we reach the coast about dusk.

Use Reading Clues in Teaching Initial Blends.   Instruct the students, "Write the blend that spells the word that fits the clue" Examples:

We use our __ __ ain to think.
Apples and pears are __ __ uits we eat.
We put our nose to a rose to __ __ ell it.
A __ __ amp is needed to mail a letter.

Consonant Digraphs.   A digraph is a combination of two letters that when pronounced result in one speech sound. This sound is not a simple blend of the two letters. Some digraphs have more than one sound (e.g., *ch* = *k* in *character, sh* in *chiffon,* and *ch* in *church*). The techniques used in teaching consonants and simple blends and the activities for teaching *ch* and *sh* that follow apply in teaching other digraphs.

INSTRUCTIONAL ACTIVITIES

Identifying Digraphs.   Place words beginning with **ch** on the board and direct students' attention to these initial letters. Pronounce each word, making sure students listen to the sound of **ch** in each word and look at the word at the same time you pronounce it. When pronouncing each word, emphasize but do not distort the **ch** sound.

Have students pronounce each word as you point to it. Point to words randomly to encourage maximum attention. Ask students to provide other words that begin with the **ch** sound heard in **chair, child,** and **chance.** Write these on the board beneath the original words.

chair

child

chance

chick

chill

chose

Contrasting Single Consonants and Digraphs.   Contrast single initial consonant sounds and initial digraph sounds in words. Write the words shown in column A on the chalkboard and pronounce these words with students. Next, write the words in column B, pointing out the visual pattern **sh** at the beginning of each word. Have students pronounce each pair of words (such as **hip—ship**) to contrast the differential initial sounds. Use the procedure outlined earlier with other words that begin with **s** or **sh**. As students contrast the initial sound in each pair of words, they note the visual pattern (**s—sh**) and hear the initial sounds these letters represent.

Use reading clues to introduce and teach initial digraphs. Read the clue and then ask students to spell the word by using one of the digraphs provided in parentheses. Discuss how the letters chosen determine the meaning of a word in context.

A	B
hip	ship
hop	shop
hot	shot
hark	shark
hare	share
harp	sharp
sell	shell
sort	short
sip	ship
save	shave
self	shelf
sock	shock

used in bread __ __eat (wh, ch)	not open __ __ut (th, sh)
find on seashore __ __ell (sh, th)	largest in ocean __ __ale (th, wh)
can sit on it __ __air (sh, ch)	not fat __ __in (wh, th)
never do it! __ __eat (th, ch)	sun can do it __ __ine (wh, sh)
use your head __ __ink (sh, th)	must be round __ __eel (wh, th)

Supplying Digraphs.   Read the clue, then ask students to spell the word by adding a digraph. Examples:

Part of your leg that rhymes with chin: __ __in

Doesn't cost much: __ __eap

At a later time, you may need to teach that *ch = k* as in *chorus, chemistry, chrome,* and *character,* and that *ch = sh* as in *chauffeur, chamois, chef,* and *Chicago.* Other frequently seen digraphs include *sh, wh, th, gh, ng,* and *ph.* The sounds of these letter combinations are as follows:

- *Sh* is the sound heard in *shoe, shop, shell, short, wish,* and *fish.*
- *Wh* sounds like *hw* in *when—hwen, wheel—hweel,* and *which—hwich.* When *wh* is followed by *o,* the *w* is silent as in *whole—hole, whose—hooz* and *whom—hoom.*
- *Th* has two sounds. When voiced, it sounds like *th* in *them, there, they,* and wi*th.* Voiceless, it sounds like *th* in *thin, three, throw,* and wid*th.*
- *Gh* can have the sound of *f* in lau*gh,* tou*gh,* and cou*gh.* It can be silent as in ni*gh*t, bou*gh,* ei*gh*t, and thou*gh*t.
- *Ng* sounds as in sa*ng,* wi*ng,* so*ng,* and ru*ng.*
- *Ph* usually sounds as *f* in *ph*one, ne*ph*ew, and gra*ph.*

Vowel Sounds.   Difficulties exist in teaching vowel phoneme-grapheme relationships because numerous vowel phonemes exist, but only a limited number of letters and letter combinations represent these phonemes. However, a majority of these difficulties are easily taken care of as students learn the various vowel generalizations and use this knowledge in their reading and writing. The teacher should provide guidance, and most students learn phonic analysis more quickly with guidance that leads to insights. Requiring rote memorization of a myriad of generalizations hinders some students' understanding of the relationships between the generalizations and their reading. Children may become so preoccupied with learning the generalizations that they miss the application. On the other hand, verbalizing a generalization often helps learning.

Short Vowel Sounds.   Techniques for teaching letter-sound relationships are unlimited. Each illustration presented deals with only one vowel-letter sound, because all of the other vowel sounds can be taught in the same manner, simply by changing the stimulus words. Practically any lesson can be presented using the chalkboard, an overhead projector, language-experience stories, recipes, big books, and so forth. The following activities illustrate the importance of teaching students to blend sounds represented by letters and letter combinations without distortion. Blending is an extremely important, yet often neglected, area in many reading programs (Anderson et al., 1985).

INSTRUCTIONAL ACTIVITIES

Visual and Auditory Association Illustrated Using Short e.   Select a few easy words that have been used previously and contain the vowel pattern being taught. Write these words in a column and pronounce each word with students. Have them note the vowel letter in the middle of the word and emphasize the sound it represents, for example, the **e** in **met, set,** and **pet.**

The following material may constitute different presentations on different days. Column A contains a pattern of CVC words, column B contains mixed patterns, and column C contains longer words. The sounds represented by these vowels in CVC words are highly regular. This allows you to structure learning around tasks in which students can experience success. Once students have learned such CVC pattern words, you can introduce the other CVC patterns that are less regular.

A	B	C
met	leg	desk
set	men	bell
pet	bed	dress
bet	pep	sled
let	wet	best
jet	hen	help

Experiencing great success with one pattern of CVC words should enable students to succeed with mixed patterns. Instruction can then focus on longer words. Thus, you build instruction in small, related steps.

For the following activity, instruct the students, "In the blank, write a word that makes sense in each sentence. Choose the word from the right-hand column."

I like to _____ a cat.	met
Bobby _____ me that he could ring the bell.	set
	let
Bill _____ me sail the ship.	bet
	pet

The _____ let me play in the big boat.	leg
	men
The cat fell off of the boat and got _____ .	bed
Bob took a nap in _____ .	hen
	wet

Bill had to _____ Bobby pull the _____ up the hill.	desk
	bell
They are _____ pals and like to play in the snow.	sled
Mary put her book on her _____ at school.	best
	help

Provide opportunities for application of each skill in meaningful context for each area of instruction. Use meaningful examples appropriate to children's needs and capabilities and build on previous learning.

INSTRUCTIONAL ACTIVITIES

Contrasting Short Vowel Sounds in Words.   In step 1, write a column of identical initial and final consonants, leaving a blank space for adding a vowel letter. In step 2, insert a vowel letter to complete the first word, and then in step 3, call on a student to name the word. Continue using a different vowel letter for each blank space. In step 4, when the column is complete, have students read the words in rapid succession to contrast the vowel sounds. In step 5, present the words in meaningful context, omitting the vowel letter. Call on each student to provide a vowel for the word that makes sense in the sentence.

Step 1   b__g

b__g

b__g

b__g

Step 2   (i)
(insert
vowel)   (e)

(u)

(a)

Step 3   big
(children
name   beg
word)
bug

bag

Step 4
(pronounce the
series of words
in rapid succession)

Step 5   Mark has a b__g pet.

Mark has a b__g for a pet.

Mark has a b__g b__g in a b__g

A dog will b__g for food.

Other stimulus patterns are b**u**d, b**a**d, and b**e**d; p**a**n, p**u**n, p**i**n, and p**e**n; p**a**t, p**e**t, p**i**t, and p**o**t; and h**u**t, h**i**t, h**o**t, and h**a**t.

Working with Final Phonograms.   Use pictures in teaching final phonograms. Have students name the picture, then blend the initial letter (shown beneath the picture) with each of the phonograms at the right of the picture. Focus students' attention first on naming the picture and then selecting the final phonogram. Finally, have the students write the correct letter pattern in the blank spaces to complete the word. If they experience difficulties, have them say each phonogram (such as /at/, /ot/, and /ut/) and then blend the initial letter (/c/) with each. Again, be sure that students can recognize each picture and name it. The pictures of the well and the cot may not be in all students' experiential and conceptual backgrounds.

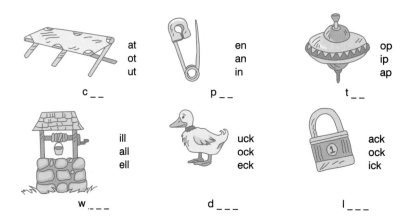

Long Vowel Sounds.   Generalizations covering vowel letter-sound relationships are numerous; however, many of these do not apply to a large number of letter patterns (Caldwell, Roth, & Turner, 1978). Therefore, separate teaching procedures are cited for two adjacent vowels (*ea, ai, ee,* and *oa* patterns) and final *e* words.

Two adjacent vowels representing a single sound are referred to as vowel di-graphs (f*ee*t, b*oa*t, s*ai*l, m*ea*n). One of the more widely quoted generalizations relates to vowel digraphs: "When two vowels come together the first vowel usually represents a long sound and the second is not sounded, or when two vowels come together, the first vowel does the talking, the second goes walking." Two-vowel combinations have about as many exceptions to this rule as instances in which it applies. For the specific vowel combinations of *ee, oa, ea,* and *ai,* it holds much more frequently.

INSTRUCTIONAL ACTIVITIES

Contrasting Single-Double Vowel Patterns.   Prepare lists of words in which column A has a single vowel (m**e**t) and column B is identical except for an added vowel (m**ea**t).

Ask students to read the first word under column A and listen for the short vowel sound. Then ask them to read the first word under column B, note the two-vowel pattern, and listen for the long vowel sound. As a final step, have them read each pair in rapid succession to note the contrasting vowel sound (such as m**e**t-m**ea**t and l**e**d- l**ea**d).

A	B	A	B	A	B
e	ea	a	ai	e	ee
met	meat	man	main	fed	feed
led	lead	lad	laid	met	meet
men	mean	pal	pail	pep	peep
bed	bead	ran	rain	bet	beet
stem	steam	bat	bait	wed	weed
set	seat	plan	plain	step	steep

Prepare similar word lists using the **o—oa, e—ea,** and **a—ai** patterns.

Provide opportunities for application by using sentences such as the following. Focus on selecting words that make sense in the sentence:

The _____ ate _____ for dinner.
　　　(man, main)　　　　(meat, met)

Bobby put the _____ in the _____ .
　　　　　　(bait, bat)　　　　　(pal, pail)

The _____ had to _____ on the _____ .
　　　(men, mean)　　　　(step, steep)　　　　(weed, wed)

INSTRUCTIONAL ACTIVITIES

The Effect of Final e.   Write a column of CVC words on the chalkboard, each of which contains the medial vowel a (step 1). As you pronounce these words, have students tell which vowel sound they hear in the word **(a).** Explain that you will change each word by adding the letter **e** at the end.

Print the words shown in step 2. As you pronounce these words, have students note the **a __ e** pattern and tell the vowel sound they hear in each of the words **(ā).**

Have students explain what vowel sound they hear in words with two vowels when one is a final **e.** Restate their explanations: "In many short words showing two vowels, a final **e** is not sounded while the first vowel has its long sound." Introduce the following word pairs for other final **e** series: **bit—bite, pin—pine, hid—hide, kit—kite, rid—ride, slid—slide, not—note, hop—hope, rod—rode,** and **rob—robe.**

Step 1	Step 2
can	cane
hat	hate
mad	made
pal	pale
rat	rate
plan	plane

Prepare an exercise for either chalkboard presentation or independent seatwork. List CVC words, some of which can be changed to another word by adding a final **e.** Have students read the stimulus word and determine if adding the letter **e** makes a known word. Make sure they ask themselves if the word they are making sounds like a word they have heard before. Make sure each child understands the task by completing some examples in a group. Name the word (if an oral exercise) or ask students to write the word in the space provided. For example, if the word can be changed into another word by adding a final **e,** write the new word on the line provided. If adding an **e** does not make a word, leave the line blank.

can _____	hid _____
rat _____	sob ____*____
top ____*____	mad _____
plan _____	bit _____
kit _____	not _____
hop _____	tap _____
cat ____*____	rob _____
cut _____	big* _____

*spaces left blank

Long Vowel Sounds at the End of Short Words.   Two generalizations cover single vowels at the end of words: "If a word has only one vowel that ends the word, the vowel sound usually is long" and "If a word has no other vowel and ends with *y,* the letter *y* serves as a vowel and is pronounced as long *i.*" These generalizations apply in a limited number of high-frequency words and can be taught at the chalkboard, using columns of words. Utilize activities similar to those discussed throughout the earlier sections.

be	by	try	go
me	my	sky	no
he	cry	fly	so
we	why	fry	ho
she	dry	shy	yo-yo

Vowels Affected by Particular Consonants.   The long and short vowel sounds are by far the most important vowel clues in helping determine the pronunciation of words. In addition, other vowel patterns should be explained, even though they may be of less importance in phonic analysis. When a vowel precedes *r,* the sound of that vowel is affected by the *r.* Usually a blend results, which is neither the long nor the short sound of the vowel (as in *car, curl, fir, for,* and *park*). When the vowel *a* is followed by *l* or *w,* the resulting sound is a blend (as in *yawn, tall, awful, talcum, awning,* and *ball*).

Although a number of words contain a vowel followed by *r,* it is debatable whether this particular letter-sound combination causes beginning readers much trouble. That is, if children master the long and short vowel relationships, they are not likely to experience serious trouble with vowels followed by *r.* Undoubtedly, many successful readers are unaware of the difference between the vowel sounds in the words *can* and *car.*

Diphthongs.   Diphthongs are two adjacent vowels, each of which is sounded, such as the *ou* in *house, oi* in *oil, oy* in *boy, ow* in *how* (but not the *ow* in *blow, grow,* or *throw,* where the sound is long *o*). Teaching diphthongs is probably not of major importance in the total phonics program. A number of words that are learned as sight words contain these sounds, and certain words can serve as keys to help students hear the sounds (such as *house, oil, boy,* and *how*).

Summary of Vowel Generalizations.   The following generalizations govern vowel pronunciation:

- A single vowel followed by a consonant in a word or syllable usually has the short sound (as in *can* or *cancel*).
- A single vowel that concludes a word or syllable usually has the long sound (as in *me, ti-ger,* and *lo-co-mo-tive*).
- In the vowel digraphs *oa, ea, ee, ai,* and *ay,* the first vowel is usually long and the second is silent (as in *coat, reap, head, wait,* and *play*). The digraphs *oo, au,* and *ew* form a single sound that is not the long sound of the first vowel (as in *food, good, haul,* and *few*).
- In words containing two vowels, one of which is final *e,* the final *e* is usually silent and the preceding vowel is long.
- Single vowels followed by *r* usually result in a blended sound (as in *fir, car, burn,* and *fur*). The vowel *a* followed by *l* or *w* usually results in a blended sound (as in *yawn, tall, claw,* and *awful*).
- The letter *y* at the end of words containing no other vowel has the letter sound of *i* (as in *my, try, sky,* and *shy*).
- Diphthongs are two-vowel combinations in which both vowels contribute to the speech sound (as in *house, boy,* and *cow*).

Structural Analysis

Structural-analysis instruction helps students identify words whose visual patterns change as a result of adding:

- Inflectional endings (such as *s, -ed, -ing,* and *-ly*).
- Prefixes (such as *pre-, ex-,* and *un-*).
- Suffixes (such as *-able, -ment,* and *-ness*).
- Root-to-root compounds (such as *sidewalk, playground,* and *basketball*).

Structural-analysis skills allow students to focus on larger units of letter patterns within known words (Rupley & Blair, 1988). Obviously, use of some of these techniques relies on previous learning. For instance, a child who uses structural analysis in unlocking words with inflectional endings must recognize the root word (such as *help*) as a familiar unit or be able to sound out the root word, solve the ending (such as *-ing*), and blend the two *(helping)*. Later, this type of analysis should not be necessary, because the student perceives the word *helping* as one familiar unit.

In applying structural-analysis skills to solve unknown words, children do better if they recognize parts of words that they have studied. Instruction thus should build on what students have already mastered in reading. By building on students' prior learning, you can increase their attention to new learning, increase their chances of success with new learning, and diagnose their progress from one learning outcome to the next.

An important concept in structural analysis is syllabication. A syllable is a vowel or group of letters containing a vowel that is pronounced as a unit. Students' ability to determine the basic units of pronunciation (that is, syllables) supports effective word learning. **Syllabication** is included under structural analysis because it is the division of a word into its basic units of pronunciation. Phonic generalizations are applied to letters only after this division.

Students usually learn a number of one-syllable root words before they try to understand polysyllabic words. As they encounter long words, they learn that most prefixes and suffixes and some inflectional endings constitute syllables. During early experience with high-frequency affixes, students break words into parts and then combine the parts into the whole, such as *re-read-ing, pre-heat-ed, bi-week-ly,* and *dis-appear-ance.* After many experiences, children reduce their reliance on this type of analysis and blend the parts into the whole more smoothly.

A series of pictures may help students develop the ability to combine syllables into words. The pictures presented should be familiar to students. They should either listen to the teacher's pronunciation of the picture's name or pronounce it themselves and indicate the number of syllables heard. Students may also clap out the number of syllables in words that the teacher pronounces.

A knowledge of vowel behavior within words is a major aid in breaking words into syllables, but the sounds of vowels and letter combinations are not as consistent as those of prefixes and suffixes. Nevertheless, many generalizations are useful. Although the following examples are not words, the letter combinations can be broken into syllables: *comration, ragmotex, obsebong,* and *fasnotel.* The likely syllabication is *com-ra-tion, rag-mo-tex, ob-se-bong,* and *fas-no-tel.* Most fluent readers would pronounce these nonsense words in substantially the same way. These readers probably would not recite rules to themselves before pronouncing these words, but they probably would be subconsciously influenced by rules they had learned.

INSTRUCTIONAL ACTIVITIES

Generalizing Two Consonants Between Vowels.   When you teach generalizations applicable to syllabication, provide a number of examples. Then lead students to see for themselves what happens. Out of this experience, they can develop rules. Starting with the question, "What usually happens when two consonants come between vowels?" place a number of words on the board. For example:

af ter	win dow	rab bit	let ter
gar den	can dy	din ner	sum mer
fas ter	pen cil	lit tle	cot ton

Work toward the generalization "When two consonants come between vowels, the syllable division comes between the consonants" or "One consonant goes with each vowel." Point out that this rule does not always hold, but that it is the best guess to make when trying to pronounce an unknown word. In the case of double consonants, there are few exceptions to the rule.

Generalizing One Consonant Between Vowels.   To teach what happens when one consonant comes between two vowels, place a list of known sight words on the board. For example:

be gin	fe ver	to tal	de cide
o ver	di rect	ti ger	me ter
fa tal	mo ment	pu pil	ho tel

■ Inflectional Endings

Inflectional endings include -s, -es, -ed, and -ing for verbs, -er and -est for adjectives and adverbs, and -ly for adverbs. Note that inflectional endings depend on context. Therefore, be sure to provide application exercises when you teach inflectional endings.

INSTRUCTIONAL ACTIVITIES

Adding -s, -ed, or -ing to Words.   Instruct students, "In the space provided, add **-s, -ed,** or **-ing** to the known word. Write each new word in the column, then read the words." Note that word endings are important features of syntax. Using one or two words with the new word being formed can heighten students' attention to syntax.

Known Word	-s	-ed	-ing
play	He _____	I _____	I am _____
look	He _____	I _____	She is _____
call	She _____	She _____	He is _____
flap	She	It _____	It is _____
wait	He	He _____	I am _____
rain	It	It _____	It is _____
work	She	I _____	They are _____

Adding -er, -est, or -ly to Words.   Instruct students, "In the space provided, add **-er, -est,** or **-ly** to the stimulus word. Then read each word."

Known Word	-er	-est	-ly
warm	_____	_____	_____
great	_____	_____	_____
high	_____	_____	_____
soft	_____	_____	_____
kind	_____	_____	_____

Using s Endings.   Present the known words **look, call, clap,** and **play,** and review them when **s** is added to the end. Do this on the chalkboard and direct students' attention to the written words.

A	B
I look	He looks
I call	He calls
I clap	She claps
I play	She plays

Direct them to look at sentences as you read each one aloud, pausing briefly when coming to a blank space, then reading the rest of the sentence. Using the words from list B, have the students orally give you a word that makes sense for each sentence. For example:

Bobby _____ in the yard.

The robin _____ his wings to fly.

The dog by the door _____ mean.

Bill _____ his dog to come in at night.

Choosing -er, -est, or -ly Endings. Write clues using words that can take **-er, -est,** or **-ly** inflectional endings. Provide blanks at the right of the clues for the new words formed. Instruct students, "Read the clue. In the blank to the right, write a new word, adding the proper inflectional ending to the underlined word. The new word must fit the clue." For example:

Ending: **-er, -est, ly**

Clue	**New Word**
1. sweeter than all others	_____
2. taller than all others	_____
3. in a quick manner	_____
4. works more hard than Bill	_____
5. in a quiet way	_____
6. with swift action	_____

Choosing s Endings. Provide application by using activities such as the following. Ask students to select the word that makes sense in each sentence.

play   1. He _____ ball with us.

plays   2. I _____ ball with him.

         3. They will _____ ball with us after school.

         4. She _____ a game with a bat and a ball.

work   1. Dad _____ at home on Saturday.

works   2. Mother _____ at school on Monday.

         3. Jan has to _____ at the game.

         4. The horse _____ on the farm.

Choosing -s, -er, -est, or -ly Endings.   Use sentences such as the following to provide further application of inflectional endings in meaningful context. Activities should build on what students have learned. Encourage them to think about whether their choices make sense in the sentences.

1. I like to _____ in the yard on _____ days.
   (play, plays)   (warm, warmer, warmest)

2. Today is the _____ day of the year.
   (warm, warmer, warmest)

3. This doll _____ like the _____ one in the store.
   (look, looks)   (soft, softest, softly)

Choosing Degrees of Comparison.   Use additional activities to point out how inflectional endings describe degrees of comparison. For example:

1. Mark is _____ than John. He is at the
   (high, higher, highest)

   _____ point on the ladder.
   (high, higher, highest)

2. This fur is the _____ fur of all.
   (soft, softer, softest)

3. Jane is a _____ person. She is _____ than
   (kind, kinder, kindest)   (kind, kinder, kindest)

   Fred, Bill, or Bob. She is the _____ person I know.
   (kind, kinder, kindest)

4. The _____ time I ever had was at the circus.
   (great, greater, greatest)

■ Prefixes and Suffixes

Prefixes are added at the beginnings of words to produce new words. Examples of prefixes include *pre-, ex-, un-, in-, dis-,* and *re-.* Suffixes are added at the ends of words to produce new words. Examples include *-able, -ment, -ness, -er, -or, -ful,* and *-ish.*

INSTRUCTIONAL ACTIVITIES

Adding Prefixes and Suffixes.   Using root words that take prefixes and suffixes, provide lists such as the following. Instruct the students, "In each blank space, add a prefix or suffix to make a word. For prefixes, use **in-, dis-,** or **re-.** For suffixes, use **-ment, -able,** or **-ness.**"

_____ agree	_____ disagree	_____ agree
_____ direct	_____ indirect	_____ direct
_____ fill	_____ refill	_____ fill

Choosing Suffixes.   Write clues using words that can take suffixes. Instruct students, "Read the clue. In the blank to the right, write a new word, adding the proper suffix to the underlined word. The new word must fit the clue." For example:

Suffixes: **-or, -less, -ful**

Clue	New Word
1. one who visits	_____
2. to be of help	_____
3. without end	_____
4. one who invents	_____
5. with hope	_____
6. without hope	_____
7. able to harm	_____
8. one who sails	_____

Suffixes: **able, -ness, -ish, -er**

Clue	New Word
9. something that looks like	_____
10. can be washed	_____
11. one who paints	_____
12. having a fever	_____
13. thinking only of oneself	_____
14. being idle	_____
15. can be adjusted	_____
16. can be fixed	_____
17. one who fixes	_____
18. looking green	_____
19. someone who sings	_____
20. something that you can sing	_____

Upon completion of the clue activities, have students use the new words formed from the clues in their own sentences or stories. Write some of these on the chalkboard and use them for class discussion. As a group, discuss the meaning of the stories or sentences. Example sentences for clues 1 through 3 follow.

Uncle Frank was a visitor at our house.

The apple is the sweetest of all the apples we picked.

Our teacher is very helpful.

The road was endless.

Choosing Prefixes and Suffixes. To help students apply their knowledge of prefixes and suffixes, use activities such as the following. Ask students to select the prefix or suffix to complete the underlined word so that the sentence makes sense.

1. I agree with Dan that we should buy a dog.

2. I ___agree___ with Dan that we should name the dog Spike.
   (in-, dis-, re-)

3. Dan and I are in ___disagree___ about the name for our dog.
   (-ment, -able, -ness)

4. I guess I am a ___disagree___ person.
   (-able, -ment, -ness)

1. Joe drank all of the water in the bottle.

2. He will ___fill___ the bottle with water.
   (re-, in-, dis-)

3. The bottle is ___fill___ .
   (re-, in-, dis-) (-ment, -able, -ness)

■ Compound Words

Compound words are formed by combining root words. Examples include *side-walk, playground,* and *basketball.*

INSTRUCTIONAL ACTIVITIES

Using the Same Word in a Number of Compound Words.   Write three compound words for each group of words. To maximize success, begin with two words to combine. Then, as students experience success, increase the number of combinations. For example:

air	plane	_____
book	case	_____
door	way	_____

air	plane		craft		port	
book	case		keeper		worm	
door	way		bell		mat	

Combining Words to Make Compounds.   Present lists of words that students can combine to form meaningful compound words. For example:

	A	B
shoe	_____	ball
sun	_____	light
basket	_____	maker

Choosing Compound Words.   Write three words in a row, only one of which is a compound. Tell students, "Each line contains one compound word. Underline the compound word and write it in the blank space at the end of the line." For example:

children	dancing	fireplace _____
someone	beaches	crawling _____
alike	mousetrap	puzzle _____
downpour	happily	permitted _____
autumn	mistake	handbag _____

Using Compounds in Sentences.   Write sentences, leaving a blank for students to fill in a compound word. Instruct them, "Complete each sentence by writing a compound word in the blank space." Provide practice in a group setting to make sure each student understands the task. For example:

A player can hit a home run in a game of _____ .

The teacher wrote on the _____ with a piece of chalk.

The front window in a car is the _____ .

The mail carrier puts mail in our _____ .

In addition to providing sentences, encourage students to suggest their own sentences that include compound words. If they have difficulty, provide them with a written list of compound words to use. Either write the sentences on the chalkboard or have students write them on a sheet of paper. Discuss each sentence and its meaning. Use the activity to write group-composed stories.

Contextual Analysis

Students can use contextual clues only when they can recognize or sound out most of the words in a sentence. Phonics is only one of many skills that can aid reading for meaning. For instance, when a student does not know the meaning of a word, arriving at its exact pronunciation through phonic analysis will not help. The following sentence contains an unknown symbol:

The man was attacked by a marbohem.

Everyone reading this page can sound out *mar-bo-hem,* but no one knows what attacked the man, since *marbohem* does not convey meaning to the reader. If other words are substituted for *marbohem,* some readers may still have trouble with the meaning, even though they can analyze the speech sounds in the words. For example:

The man was attacked by a pecarry.

The man was attacked by a freebooter.

The man was attacked by an iconoclast.

The man was attacked by a fusilier.

The man was attacked by a hypochondriac.

Contextual clues can help explain unknown words if the reader demands meaning. Using context plus a minimal amount of letter analysis of the beginning of the words is far better than context alone. This combination of clues is also better than intensively analyzing each word while ignoring the contextual setting of the unknown word.

In the following sentence the blank line represents an unknown word:

The boy waved good-bye as the train left the _____ .

Even with a blank line substituting, most readers have no problem supplying the correct word. The task is even simpler with the first letter supplied:

The boy waved good-bye as the train left the s _____ .

Other reading situations present more difficult problems, for example:

The girl waved good-bye to her _____ .

Here, a number of possible word choices make sense: *friend, mother, sister, teacher, brother, parents, family, playmate, aunt, cousin, uncle,* and so forth. Select any word that makes sense and insert only its first letter in the blank space. Note how that initial letter eliminates many of the words that were possibilities.

The importance of combining skills becomes more obvious in larger contexts. In the first version of the following story, it is possible to get the sense of the story even if one is not sure of the identity of a number of the missing words.

John and his cousin _____ started on their fishing trip. John

said, "I have my trusty _____ pole, a _____ full of lunch,

and a can of _____ ." After walking a long time, John said,

"Not far from here there is a _____ across the stream. We

can sit on the _____ and fish." When they started fishing,

John said, "I'm not going to _____ from this _____ until

I catch a _____ _____ ." Finally _____ said, "I am

tired of sitting on the _____ . I am going to take a walk along

the _____ ." _____ had walked only a short way when

he lost his _____ and fell into the stream. The water was not

very deep, and he waded out. "Hey," said John, "You're lucky.

You won't have to take a _____ when we get home."

This next version inserts the initial letter in each unknown word, which in all cases happens to be the letter *b*.

John and his cousin B_____ started out on their fishing trip.

John said, "I have my trusty b_____ pole, a b_____ full of

lunch, and a can of b_____ ." After walking a long time, John said, "Not far from here there is a b_____ across the stream.

We can sit on the b_____ and fish." When they started

fishing, John said, "I'm not going to b_____ from this b_____

until I catch a b_____ b_____ ." Finally said, "I am going to take a

walk along the b_____ ." B_____ had walked only a short

way when he lost his b_____ and fell into the stream. The

water was not very deep, and he waded out. "Hey," said John,

"You're lucky. You won't have to take a b_____ when we

get home."

(Words in order of their omission are **Bob, bamboo, bag, bait, bridge, budge, bridge, big bass, Bob, bridge, bank, Bob, balance,** and **bath.**)

Learning to read is very complicated. From the beginning, the learner who is attempting to identify unfamiliar words should look for and accept help from all available clues. The simultaneous use of all options helps simplify beginning reading. Occasionally, phonics is the only key to meaning that a student can utilize. More often than not, however, all of the word-identification skills—basic sight vocabulary, phonics, structural analysis, and contextual analysis—can be used together. Phonics should be used only when needed.

The two broad kinds of context clues are syntactic and semantic. The value of context clues lies not only in their ability to identify words by themselves but also in their ready application to whole-word learning, phonics, and structural analysis. As with the other decoding skills, students' ability to use context clues should be developed through both direct and informal instruction, with an abundance of practice in real reading situations. As we know, word learning is related to comprehension. Whether students are developing sight vocabularies or using phonics or structural analysis, they must have interesting, varied, and realistic practice with words in context. The use of context not only reflects the natural reading process, but also allows students to focus on meaning to aid them in determining whether the words make sense in context.

■ Syntactic Clues

The ordering of words in a sentence is syntax. Using an example presented earlier (The girl waved good-bye to her _____), knowledge of language helps us to determine that a person, place, or thing fits in the blank. This knowledge allows us to eliminate possibilities that do not make sense in this sentence.

When used in combination with phonics and structural analysis, **syntactic clues** enable students to figure out the meanings of unknown words. **Syntactic clues** include the following:

■ *Structure words.* Noun markers (such as *my, this,* and *any*), verb markers (such as *am, are,* and *is*), clause markers (such as *now, if,* and *before*), and question indicators (such as *why, who,* and *which*) signal what is coming next. For example:

He took *my* brother to the game.
He *is* going to the game.
My brother will go to the game *if* he is home.
Who is going to the game?

- *Phrases.* A phrase may describe or refine a word. For example:
  The boy *with the brown hair* is Mike.
  The game *between the Reds and the Cubs* is sold out.

- *Language grammar.* Meaning patterns in language can indicate where certain words fit.
  For example:
  He took my *brother* (noun) to the game.
  He *took* (verb) my brother to the game.
  He took my brother to the game in a big, *shiny* (adjective) car.

- *Appositives.* An appositive is a word or words that explain the previous word. For example:
  Jones, *the quarterback,* was injured on the first play.
  Jubilation, *great excitement,* filled the stadium when the home team won.

■ Semantic Clues

Semantics refers to the reader's knowledge of word meanings and the reader's conceptual and experiential backgrounds in relation to comprehending what is read. Although syntactic clues can help explain word meaning by allowing readers to limit their choices of meaning for unknown words, semantic clues provide them with more clues to word meaning.

If a related sentence or sentences either precede or follow a sentence, the additional contextual information can help indicate the meaning. Suppose that "The girl waved good-bye to her _____ " is followed by "He waved back and wiped tears from his eyes as the train began to move." In this example, the word *he* tells you that the unknown word refers to a male.

A reader who makes the connection between the male referent and the initial letter pattern or patterns of an unknown word and the sounds represented can even better determine meaning. In "The girl waved good-bye to her f_____ . He waved back and wiped tears from his eyes as the train began to move," the letter *f* further narrows down the possibilities.

Johnson and Pearson (1984) classified the major kinds of **semantic clues** available to readers. A modified listing of their categories follows. Again, recognize that for semantic clues to be used efficiently, the referent for the unknown word must be in the reader's experiential and conceptual backgrounds.

- *Definitions or explanations.* Difficult words that students encounter in their reading are often defined within the text. Words such as *is, are,* and *means* signal explanations.
  Herbivores are animals *that feed on green plants.*

■ *Synonyms and antonyms.* In addition to using the unknown word, writers often use synonyms or antonyms.

> The *robust* rabbit loved to visit the garden. He was so *fat* he could hardly squeeze through the fence.

■ *Figurative language.* Meanings of unknown words can be obtained from metaphors and similes used in relation to preceding and following text.

> It was raining *cats and dogs.* Several cars stalled in the flooded streets.

■ *Summary statements.* Based on connected story information, the meaning of an unknown word may become known.

> Mark used to be a *stellar* basketball player. He could make shots from anywhere on the court. The crowd always cheered when their star player was introduced.

■ Contextual-analysis Instruction

Ensuring application of word-identification skills in meaningful context allows students to develop an awareness of context for word meaning. Rather than repeating all of the earlier activities, following are a few examples.

Bobby put the b_____ in the water.

Bobby has a pet _____ .

We use our ___ ___ain (br) to think.

Clue: Used in bread: _____ eat.
  (ch, wh)

Mark wants to learn how to _____ .
  (sale, sail)

Bill has a ball and a bat. The bat and ball c_____ in a set.

Dad will paint Bill's n_____ on the bat and ball in green paint.

Oil comes from _____ wells.

The _____ time I ever had was at the circus.

If you can wash something, then it is _____ able.

Joe drank all of the water in the bottle. Joe will re_____ the bottle with

water. The bottle is _____ fill _____ .

A player hit a home run in the game of _____ .

The front window in a car is the _____ .

Dictionary Instruction

Using the dictionary is another important word-identification skill associated with reading instruction. The three major goals in dictionary instruction are (1) finding a particular word, (2) determining its pronunciation, and (3) selecting the correct meaning of the word in the context in which it is used.

Dictionary skills are often neglected, even though teachers acknowledge the value of these skills. This neglect may stem from a teacher's feeling of inadequacy about certain relatively difficult facets of dictionary use, such as diacritical markings or pronunciation keys. On the other hand, the teaching may fall short when dictionary skills are considered something extra rather than as an intrinsic part of literacy instruction.

Both teachers and pupils should use the dictionary as a source for word meanings, not as a form of rote drill or a penalty for making certain errors (Lehr, 1980). Certain knowledge is essential for successful use of the dictionary. This knowledge includes the following:

- Being aware of alphabetical order.
- Understanding that letters and combinations of letters have different sounds in different situations and that some letters are silent.
- Knowing that *y* at the end of most words is changed to *i* before adding *es* for plurals.
- Recognizing root words and the various inflected and derived forms of root words.
- Realizing that a word can have many different meanings.

Skill in using the dictionary paves the way for greater independence in reading because it does the following:

- Unlocks the sounds or pronunciations of words.
- Discloses new meanings of words that may be known in only one or a limited number of connotations.
- Confirms the spelling of a word when the reader can only approximate its correct spelling.
- Expands vocabulary through mastery of inflected and derived forms.

Teachers must refine and expand these skills as students move upward through the grades. The success that students feel and the utility they derive from dictionary usage can be most important factors in how they react to the dictionary as a tool for helping in all facets of communication. Students must realize that dictionary skills are needed throughout life; failure to master these skills can negatively influence their attitudes and learning development for many years to come.

Dictionary usage involves a number of developmental tasks. Educators generally agree on these tasks and the order in which they should be presented. The tasks include the following:

- Recognizing and differentiating letters.
- Associating letter names with letter symbols.

- Learning the letters of the alphabet in order.
- Arranging a number of words in alphabetical order by their initial letters.
- Extending the last skill to the second and third letters of words, eventually working through all letters of a word, if necessary.
- Developing facility in rapid, effective use of the dictionary, that is, knowing where letters (such as *h, p,* and *v*) fall in the dictionary, and opening the dictionary as near as possible to the word being studied.
- Developing the ability to use accent marks in arriving at word pronunciations.
- Learning to interpret the phonetic spellings used in the dictionary.
- Using the pronunciation key that appears on each double page of most dictionaries.
- Working out different pronunciations and meanings of words that are spelled alike.
- Determining which is the preferred pronunciation when several are given.
- Selecting the meaning that fits the context.
- Using the guide words found at the top of each page to tell at a glance if the page contains the word being sought.
- Using special sections of a dictionary intelligently (such as geographical terms and names, biographical data, and foreign words and phrases).

Although particular skills are characteristically taught at given grade levels, the individual student's skills should determine what is taught. Fortunately, dictionaries are available at all difficulty levels, from simple picture dictionaries to massive unabridged editions. The individual students' needs and abilities should dictate what type of dictionary to study.

☑ Summary

To become independent readers, students must learn to use a variety of word-identification skills and strategies. Sight vocabulary, phonics, structural analysis, and contextual analysis are the basic word-identification skills that enable readers to comprehend what they read. Competent and flexible readers do not rely heavily on any one skill; they use various clues in combination. In teaching word identification skills, remember the following principles:

- Students' language background should form the basis for word-identification instruction. Small, related instructional steps increase the likelihood that students will attend to the instruction and succeed. The teacher should closely monitor each student's progress.
- Instruction should build on what children know and are successful with.
- Opportunities to apply word-identification skills in meaningful contexts should be part of all word-identification instruction.
- Contextual analysis should be integrated with all other word-identification instruction. By combining sight vocabulary, phonics, and

structural analysis with context, children maximize their changes of determining meaning.

■ Word-identification skills can be taught in a number of ways. Any technique that proves successful for a child is justifiable, provided that it does not inhibit later growth and the instructional approach is reasonably economical in time and effort expended.

■ Students should not be taught to rely heavily on any one word-identification technique. Overemphasis on phonics causes children to sound out the same words hundreds of times and attempt to sound out words that do not lend themselves to letter-sound analysis, such as *once, knight, freight, some, one, eight, love, know, head, move, none, have,* and *laugh.*

■ Students require varying amounts of instruction while they are learning word-identification skills. Assessment that reveals what a child knows and does not know is essential for good instruction. In the final analysis, the optimum amount of word-identification instruction for each individual is the minimum that he or she needs to become an independent reader.

☑ Your Point of View

Discussion Questions

1. Early reading instruction inevitably causes children to develop a mindset relative to reading. What reading mindset might children develop when they receive no opportunities to apply word-identification skills in meaningful contexts?

2. Is it possible to teach children to rely too much on any word-identification technique? Does learning to read involve the simultaneous application of all word-identification skills? Is each a part of a unitary process called reading?

3. How do mature readers differ from beginning readers in their use of word-identification strategies?

4. What is the optimum amount of any type of word-identification instruction?

5. What role does ongoing assessment play in word-identification instruction?

Take a Stand For or Against

1. The spelling patterns found in the English language constitute a major obstacle in learning to read English.

2. Teaching sight words, letter-sound analysis, and contextual analysis at the same time inevitably leads to confusion.

3. Since a student must learn word-identification skills before becoming an independent reader, these skills should be taught before reading for meaning is stressed.

Field-based Assignments

1. Prepare a written lesson plan on a word identification skill and if possible teach the lesson to a small group of your peers or to actual children in the classroom you are visiting. Use the lesson format for direct/explicit instruction as described and illustrated in this chapter. Following the teaching of your lesson, respond to the following questions.

   > Did students understand the lesson objective?
   > Did students need additional explanation and practice?
   > Do I need to reteach a part of the lesson?
   > What did I learn today that would be of help in tomorrow's lesson?

2. Work individually with a student experiencing difficulties in decoding. Read a short story with the student, taking turns reading out loud. Note how the student decodes words as well as specific word-identification strengths and weaknesses. Prepare a short summary of your student's decoding abilities and list as many authentic practice opportunities or tasks to ensure mastery as you can (these practice activities would accompany your direct instruction lessons on the targeted areas). Use the following as a guide.

   > Reading level of material
   > Word-identification strengths
   > Specific areas needing improvement
   > Listing of possible authentic reading tasks or activities to ensure mastery

Portfolio Entry

Because of the widespread interest in both teaching students to decode words and using fine literature in the teaching of reading, a balanced literacy approach combining both emphases is being recommended by many experts. In your opinion, what are the possible negative effects of favoring one aspect over the other in the teaching of reading? Write a one-page reaction to this question.

Bibliography

Adams, M. J. (1994). Modeling the connections between word recognition and reading. In R. B. Rudell, M. R. Rudell, & H. Singer (Eds.), *Theoretical models and processes of reading* (4th ed., pp. 838–863). Newark, DE: International Reading Association.

Adams, M. J. (1990). *Beginning to read: Thinking and learning about print.* Cambridge, MA: MIT Press.

Anderson, R. C., Hiebert, E. H., Scott, J. A., & Wilkinson, I. A. G. (1985). *Becoming a nation of readers: The report of the Commission on Reading.* Washington, DC: National Institute of Education.

Ball, E. W., & Blachman, B. A. (1991). Does phoneme segmentation training in kindergarten make a difference in early word recognition and developmental spelling? *Reading Research Quarterly, 26,* 49–66.

Byrne, B., Freebody, P., & Gates, A. (1992). Longitudinal data on the relations of word-reading strategies to comprehension, reading time, and phonemic awareness. *Reading Research Quarterly, 27,* 141–151.

Dolch, E. W. (1948). *Problems in reading.* Champaign, IL: Garrard Press.

Downing, J. (October–December 1979). Linguistic awareness in learning to read. *Reading Today,* International Reading Association newsletter, p. 2.

Durrell, D. D., & Murphy, H. A. (1978). A prereading phonics inventory. *The Reading Teacher, 31,* 385–390.

Eeds-Kneip, M. (1979). The frenetic frantic phonic backlash. *Language Arts, 56,* 909–917.

Fowler, A. E. (1992). How early phonological development might set the stage for phoneme awareness. In S. Brady and D. Shankweiler (Eds.), *Phonological processes in literacy* (pp. 97–118). Hillside, NJ: Lawrence Erlbaum Associates.

Fox, B. J. (1996), *Strategies for word identification.* Upper Saddle River, NJ: Prentice Hall.

Harris, T. L., & Hodges, R. E. (1995). *The literacy dictionary.* Newark, DE: International Reading Association.

Heilman, A. W. (1992). *Phonics in proper perspective* (7th ed.). Upper Saddle River, NJ: Merrill/Prentice Hall.

Hiebert, E. H. (1994). Becoming literate through authentic tasks: Evidence and adaptations. In R. B. Rudell, M. R. Rudell, & H. Singer (Eds.), *Theoretical models and processes of reading* (4th ed. pp. 391–411). Newark, DE: International Reading Association.

Johnson, D. D., & Pearson, P. D. (1984). *Teaching reading vocabulary* (2nd ed.). New York: Holt, Rinehart & Winston.

Juel, C. (1991). *Beginning reading.* In R. Barr, M. L. Kamil, P. B. Mosenthal, & P. D. Pearson (Eds.), *Handbook of reading research* (Vol. II) (pp. 759–788). New York: Longman.

Lehr, F. (1980). ERIC/RCS: Content reading instruction in the elementary school. *The Reading Teacher, 33,* 888–891.

Palmer, B. C. (1986). Is the Dolch list of 220 sight words still relevant? *Reading Improvement, 23,* 227–230.

Pollard, R. S. (1889). *Pollard's synthetic method.* Chicago: Western Publishing House.

Richgels, D. J., Poremba, K. J., & McGee, L. M. (1996). Kindergartners talk about print: Phonemic awareness in meaningful contexts. *The Reading Teacher, 49,* 632–642.

Rupley, W. H., & Blair, T. R. (1988). *Teaching Reading: Diagnosis, direct instruction, and practice* (2nd ed.). Upper Saddle River, NJ: Merrill/Prentice Hall.

Rupley, W. H. L., & Blair, T. R. (1989). *Reading diagnosis and remediation: Classroom and clinic* (3rd ed.). Upper Saddle River, NJ: Merrill/Prentice Hall.

Samuels, S. J. (1994). Word recognition. In R. B. Rudell, M. R. Rudell, & H. Singer (Eds.), *Theoretical models and processes of reading* (4th ed., pp. 816–837). Newark, DE: International Reading Association.

Samuels, S. J. (1979). The method of repeated readings. *The Reading Teacher, 32,* 403–408.

Stahl, S. A. (1992). Saying the "p" word: Nine guidelines for exemplary phonics instruction. *The Reading Teacher, 45,* 618–625.

Taylor, B. M., & Nosbush, L. (1983). Oral reading for meaning: A technique for improving word identification skills. *The Reading Teacher, 39,* 234–237.

Tunmer, W. E. & Hoover, W. A. (1993). Phonological recoding skill and beginning reading. *Reading and Writing: An Interdisciplinary Journal, 5,* 161–179.

Yopp, H. K. (1995). A test for assessing phonemic awareness in young children. *The Reading Teacher, 49,* 20–29.

Yopp, H. K. (1992). Developing phonemic awareness in young children. *The Reading Teacher, 45,* 696–707.

6

Meaning Vocabulary

Chapter Outline

For the Reader

The meanings of words in written language are essential for comprehension. Meaning vocabulary can be thought of as hooks for background knowledge, concepts about the world, integration of new learning with what is known, and representation of abstract understandings. Thus, the broader our vocabularies, the better able we are to interact with and understand text.

As you read this book, you probably encounter words that are either new to you or different in meaning from those with which you are familiar. You may figure out the meanings of these words by using context or a dictionary, or by asking someone. Yet questions about how best to teach and expand vocabulary are varied and much depends on the capabilities and interests of your students.

The importance of vocabulary in reading has long been a major concern of researchers. Some researchers believe that vocabulary cannot be directly taught because students encounter so many new words in their reading (Nagy & Herman, 1996). Other researchers believe that vocabulary instruction helps foster vocabulary development (Beck, McKeown, & Omanson, 1990) and that direct instruction can improve reading performance.

This chapter recognizes both viewpoints. It advocates direct/explicit instruction, wide reading, and language-building activities to reinforce and extend students' meaning vocabularies.

Key Ideas

- Associating experiences and concepts with words contributes significantly to children's vocabulary development.
- Vocabulary is a major component contributing to reading comprehension.
- Vocabulary evolution comes about through a rich and varied exposure to words in all forms of language interaction.
- Effective vocabulary instruction helps students establish relationships between words and meaning in a personal manner.
- Providing varied opportunities to encounter and use new words is a key component in promoting vocabulary growth.
- Engaging students in active discussion of new words is critical to promoting vocabulary growth.
- Semantic-features analysis can help students understand relationships among words and associate their background knowledge with new words.

Vocabulary Knowledge and Reading

Reading has been presented throughout this book as an interactive process of constructing meaning. Meaning derived from reading depends upon the reader's word-recognition capabilities, purposes for reading, strategies for monitoring performance, and experiential and conceptual backgrounds. Vocabulary is a major factor contributing to reading comprehension (Anderson & Nagy, 1991; Stahl, Hare, Sinatra, & Gregory, 1991). The words that readers know represent the concepts and information available to help them make sense of what they read. Words and experiences are woven together to learn, to confirm, to reason, to experience, to enjoy, and to imagine. It is this interaction that makes vocabulary such a powerful part of reading and writing for meaning.

Role of Vocabulary in the Interactive View of Reading

Identifying words automatically and using background knowledge to construct meaning for the text are important features of the interactive view of reading. Readers can use recognition of whole words, application of phonic generalizations, knowledge of structural features, and knowledge of word order (syntax) but still not comprehend what they read unless they have meanings for the words and background for the concepts represented (Chall, 1996).

Language Development and Word Meanings

The groundwork of word-meaning development is the continuous development of language ability. Readers and writers share meanings. We acquire meanings for words through direct experiences with people, places, objects, and events that create and refine meaning vocabulary. Vocabulary is also acquired through vicarious experiences, including interactive technology, pictures, films, filmstrips, reading, and writing (Blachowicz & Fisher, 1996).

Increasing one's vocabulary is much more than learning names to associate with experiences. Students' **meaning vocabulary** closely reflects the breadth of their real-life and vicarious experiences. Without some knowledge of concepts that the words represent, students cannot construct meaning. Essentially, the author and the reader share and construct meaning through the meaning of the words that represent the language.

Vocabulary Growth

Knowing words can range from a simple level to a complex level. A form of simple-level word knowledge is definitional. **Definitional knowledge** is word knowledge based upon a definition, such as coming from a dictionary, thesaurus, glossary, word bank, or other individuals. Often, however, definitions do not help a reader understand the contribution of an unknown word to meaning. To comprehend, a reader needs some idea not only of a word's meaning, but also of the ways the meaning contributes to the concepts represented. The simple level of word knowledge may also be contextual. **Contextual knowledge** is word meaning derived from context, which can include a sentence, a passage, a discussion, or a picture (Watts, 1995). However, contextual clues have limitations, because using them requires some knowledge of the context and how the meaning of the words combine to facilitate author and reader interaction. As pointed out by Beck, McKeown, and Omanson (1990) in a review of vocabulary acquisition, "Simply put, knowing a word is not an all-or-nothing proposition: It is not the case that one either knows or does not know a word. Rather, knowledge of a word should be viewed in terms of the extent or degree of knowledge that people can possess" (p. 791). Knowing a word at a simple level helps readers construct some meaning for what they read. However, as new words are encountered more frequently in text, frameworks and relationships are established that contribute to refining, extending, changing, and adding to children's meaning vocabularies.

Both definitional and contextual features of vocabulary instruction can be part of an effective program, but in isolation, they have limited potential in increasing students' word knowledge. However, combining definitional and contextual approaches does help students develop a meaning vocabulary.

Knowing a word in its fullest sense goes beyond simply being able to define the word or get some gist of it from the context. Associating experiences and concepts with words contributes significantly to comprehension.

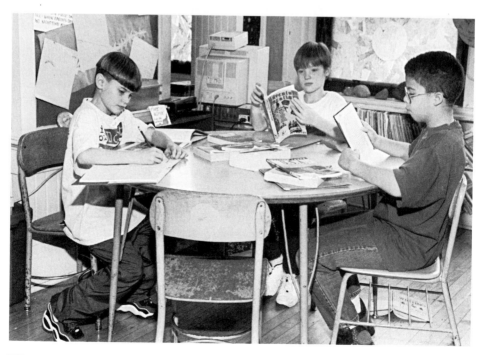

Wide reading and writing will provide students with many opportunities to learn new words.

■ Vocabulary and Concept Development

Readers' experiential and conceptual backgrounds are extremely important in vocabulary development. Background experiences enable readers to develop, expand, and refine the concepts that words represent. Vocabulary knowledge is developmental and is related to background experiences. Tennyson and Cocchiarella (1986) note two phases in the learning of concepts. The first phase is the formation of concepts in relation to attributes (which they refer to as prototypes), making connections with existing concepts. The second phase is using procedural knowledge, which is "the classification skills of generalizing to and discriminating between newly encountered instances of associated concepts" (p. 44). In phase 1, individuals may undergeneralize or overgeneralize as a result of their limited experiences with the concept. This is often evident in young children when, for example, they call all large animals in a pasture "cows" and all liquids for drinking "milk" or "juice." In phase 2, individuals can distinguish between cows and horses and among various liquids for drinking. Vocabulary expands when the student has numerous opportunities to encounter new words and examples that are representative of the word in rich contextual settings. Individuals do not use restricted definitions of words as they engage in literacy activities, but construct meaning in terms of word meanings for the concepts that represent their background knowledge.

Teacher-directed Vocabulary Instruction

Teaching vocabulary versus incidental learning of words through wide reading should not be viewed as competing philosophies. Some students may not benefit from incidental learning but do benefit from instruction that initially teaches word meaning in application to meaningful text (McKeown, 1993). Much of the criticism leveled at vocabulary teaching concerns practices in which students are not actively involved in the personal discussion of words, such as defining words using a dictionary and writing sentences for those words. Moreover, the numerous words that students learn through incidental activities call into question the effectiveness of teaching vocabulary. Any instructional practice must be called into question that fails to teach words so that students encounter the words in meaningful text and fails to immerse the students in vocabulary-rich activities. Teaching vocabulary within the context of real books and teaching words that are functionally important within a particular content area can promote vocabulary development (Zechmeister, Chrous, Cull, D'Anna, & Healy, 1995).

Vocabulary emphasis should include teacher-directed instruction and appropriate practice in specific skills along with broad reading opportunities and other language activities. Vocabulary instruction is most effective when it relates new words or derivations of words to existing vocabulary and background knowledge. For example, Mary is a first grader who thinks that all animals are pets. She will have a difficult time with the concepts of farm animals and zoo animals. Sending her to a dictionary, listing words on the chalkboard, or telling her would be ineffective in teaching the vocabulary words associated with milk cows, farm life, or

INCLUSION STRATEGIES

Expanding Children's Meaning Vocabularies

Vocabulary emphasis should include teacher-directed instruction and appropriate practice in specific skills along with the opportunity for wide reading, writing, and other language activities. We are not recommending that practice activities be unrelated to authentic reading and writing opportunities. Rather, some students—particularly those having difficulty in literacy learning—need to practice vocabulary. As noted earlier, context does not guarantee word learning, because students must be able to recognize enough of the words to construct meaning and to use context effectively as a clue to word meaning. Wide reading and writing will provide students with many opportunities to learn new words in contextual settings; however, direct teaching of vocabulary has a place.

Beck and McKeown (1991), Blachowicz and Lee (1991), and Blachowicz and Fisher (1996) recommend the following basic guidelines for teaching vocabulary.

1. Choose words for vocabulary instruction that come from contextual reading (literary and content texts) to be done in the classroom.
2. Use direct vocabulary instruction to take advantage of the many forms (such as mental pictures, kinesthetic associations, smells, and tastes) used to store word knowledge. These forms can assist children in using independent strategies for learning and retaining the meanings of words.
3. Build a conceptual base for word learning. Use analogies, language features, characteristics, sets (e.g., a horse is an animal), and relationships to known words (such as associating newspapers, magazines, and catalogs as information sources that can be read or looked at selectively) to trigger students' background knowledge of concepts and to relate new words to that which is known.
4. Provide many varied opportunities for students to engage in language-based activities (e.g., recreational reading, writing, field trips, interactive software, and creative dramatics). These should be the primary means of vocabulary learning. Teachers foster the learning of new words that are not taught directly by providing opportunities for students to use new words in the classroom in their speaking, listening, reading, and writing.
5. Generate learning of new words by helping students develop strategies associated with structural features of words (combining roots and adding prefixes and suffixes).

zoo animals. Imagine the possible comprehension problems Mary might experience when encountering such words as *Herford, hedgehog,* or *grizzly bear.*

■ Semantic Mapping

Semantic mapping incorporates many of the guidelines for vocabulary teaching and enables students to enlarge their vocabularies, understand relationships between existing and new concepts, perceive multiple meanings of words, and learn actively. Semantic mapping structures information categorically so that students can more readily see relationships between new words and concepts and their existing background knowledge.

Semantic mapping can be used for preteaching vital concepts and information for content area text before students read. Upon completion of the semantic map, the teacher discusses with the students how the new vocabulary words relate to words that they already know. Students thus understand better the content of the topic they will cover or the story they will read. Figure 6.1 presents an example of a semantic map for the topic of precipitation and illustrates how teaching certain words prior to reading can help students activate their background knowledge, relate existing knowledge to new concepts, and understand how new words and concepts are related. Teachers should invite class discussion by relating students' past reading and direct experiences to the semantic map. In discussing the semantic map, students must think about the relationships between the target word and their experiences.

The procedure for developing a semantic map for vocabulary instruction includes the following:

- Selecting a word that is central to a topic or story.
- Writing the central word on the chalkboard or a chart.
- Brainstorming words related to the central theme or topic and writing these words.
- Grouping the words into categories and labeling these categories.
- Noting additional words essential to the topic and placing these additional words in the appropriate categories.

■ Concept of Definition

A variation of semantic mapping is a procedure that Schwartz and Raphael (1985) devised to help students acquire a concept of definition. They recommend direct instruction considering three questions about a concept being studied: (1) What is it? (2) What is it like? and (3) What are some examples? The procedure is for students in grades 4 and above. Conducted over several instructional periods, its basic features include introduction and refinement of the strategy, further refinement, and writing a definition.

Introducing the Strategy.   Introduce students to the idea that they can develop a new strategy to aid them in the reading process. Focus on what they will learn, why it is important, and what they will be doing. Following the general introduction, introduce the word map (see Figure 6.2) and organize familiar information in terms of the three questions.

Modeling the Procedures.   Assist students in organizing the information by modeling for them using think-alouds. Then have students complete independent activities, mapping given words and a word of their choice. After mapping, have the students use the information to verbalize a definition with the class.

Refining the Strategy.   Following the introduction, give the students sentences that provide at least one class (What is it?), three properties (What is it like?), and three examples. Examine the sentences with the students and mark (check, circle,

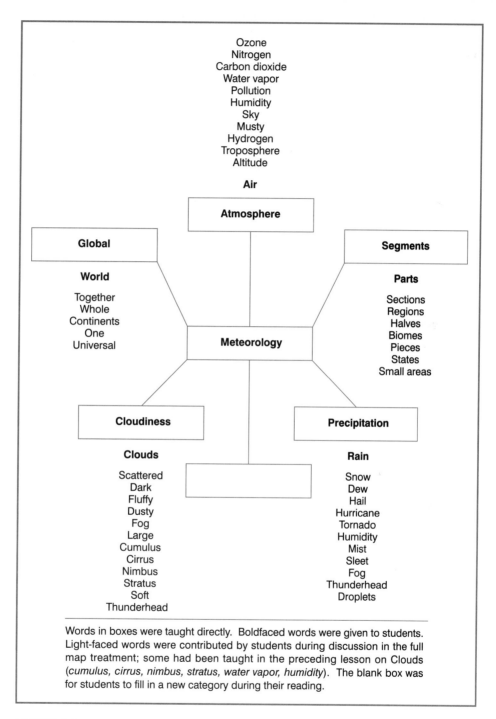

FIGURE 6.1

A completed semantic map for precipitation

Source: From S. A. Stahl and S. J. Vancil, "Discussion Is What Makes Semantic Maps Work in Vocabulary Instruction," **The Reading Teacher, 40** (Oct. 1986), p. 63. Reprinted with permission of Steven A. Stahl and Sandra Vancil and the International Reading Association.

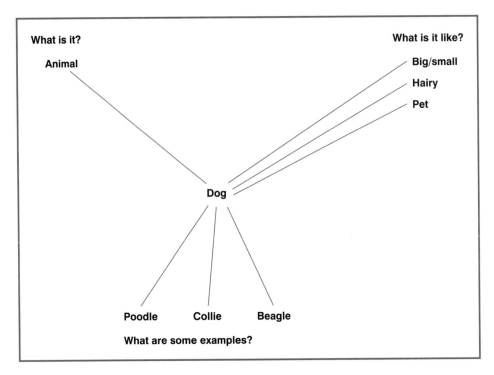

FIGURE 6.2
A concept-of-definition word map
Source: Adapted from R. M. Schwartz and T. E. Raphael, "Concept of Definition: A Key to Improving Students' Vocabulary," **The Reading Teacher, 39** (1985), p. 201.

or underline) the types of information necessary to map the information. Following this mapping, have students supply oral or written definitions for the given concepts. Assist them to realize that they need not always identify three properties or three examples; they may use fewer or more in understanding the word.

Further Refining the Concept.   Use context that is less complete and inspire students to use sources of word meanings (such as dictionaries, encyclopedias, and textbooks) to complete their word maps. Invite them to discuss the concepts, using their background knowledge and the other sources of information.

Writing a Definition.   Use all of the mapping components without using a map. This is an internalization. Ask the students to evaluate the completeness of given definitions. If definitions are incomplete, have the students write whatever additional information they feel is needed.

Providing students with direct instruction in vocabulary can lead to helping them acquire strategies for learning new words and understanding the relationships among words. This procedure aids teachers in affording students opportunities to discuss new concepts, and discussion appears to be a key in promoting active thinking about words.

■ Webbing

Webbing is similar to semantic mapping and word mapping. It graphically illustrates how to associate words meaningfully. Words or concepts selected for use in webbing can come from materials students have read, or webs can be used to introduce students to new concepts in both literary and content texts. Figure 6.3 presents a teacher-directed lesson using webbing to introduce first graders to a unit on machines that help us do our work. Students can be acquainted with the different kinds of machines they will read about through a teacher-directed discussion about home, highway, and office machines. Follow-up activities can also be done by referring back to the web and discussing how machines make work easier, writing stories about machines the students could invent, and constructing their own webs of association after reading the text. To ensure that students grasp the features and purposes of webbing, the teacher can use a web with an empty

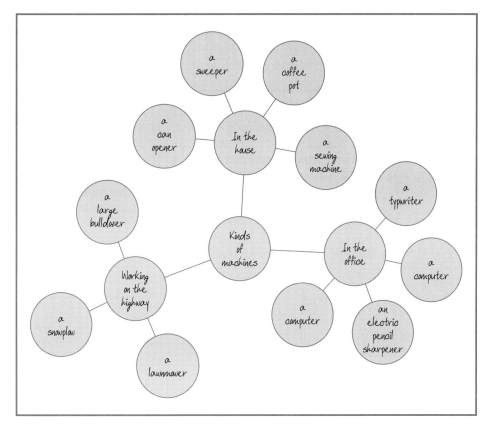

FIGURE 6.3
A teacher-directed lesson using webbing
Source: Reprinted with the permission of Prentice Hall Publishing Company from **Teaching Reading: Diagnosis, Direct Instruction, and Practice,** Second Edition, by William H. Rupley and Timothy R. Blair. Copyright © 1988 by Prentice Hall Publishing Company.

center. Students can begin to understand the relationship of words in the web by choosing and considering words that might complete the center word.

■ Semantic-features Analysis

Semantic-features analysis can help students understand relationships among words and relate their background knowledge to the new words. Figure 6.4 is an example. Semantic-features analysis is most appropriate for words related by class or common features.

To analyze, list several familiar words that are related (such as *books, newspapers, magazines, catalogs,* and *brochures*) on the chalkboard or a chart. Guide the students to discuss features associated with the words listed. As the students suggest features, write them across the top of the board or chart, creating a matrix that the students can complete in terms of present (+), absent (−), and sometimes (0). As the students broaden and define their concepts, the teacher adds words and features to the list and analyzes them. Semantic-features analysis can be used with narrative reading materials to analyze characters, settings, plots, and so forth. It is also effective in the content areas when introducing new topics, reviewing topics, and integrating topics across different content areas. The arrays can be developed and enlarged as students' knowledge backgrounds expand.

■ Teaching Relationships Among Words

To help students understand the relationships among given words, use words that differ in degree (such as *tiny, minute,* and *small*) and ask students to discuss them and generate other words that fit the examples. An assortment of procedures can teach relationships among words. A good source for choosing words for this activity is shared-literature study (Iwicki, 1992). By building connections between "old" vocabulary words and words found in their new books, students begin to understand relationships among words they encounter in reading. Students are not just asked to supply words that fit the example but rather to describe how the word fits in the stories they have read. For example, Matthew just finished

	Enjoyment	Information	Buying	Current Events	Sports
Books	+	+	0	−	0
Newspapers	+	+	+	+	+
Magazines	+	+	0	+	0
Catalogs	+	+	+	−	0
Brochures	+	+	0	+	0

Key: present (+), absent (−), sometimes (0).

FIGURE 6.4
A semantic-features analysis

reading *The Last Dinosaur* and used *enormous* to describe the size of the dinosaur. His teacher asked Matthew if he thought that Paul Bunyan could be described as enormous, too. Matthew responded by saying, "Yes. Because he was enormous and he was a giant, bigger than anyone else."

Such discussion and activities that relate new words and concepts to past readings and discuss them in relation to authentic text are helping to expand students' vocabularies meaningfully.

INSTRUCTIONAL ACTIVITIES

Understanding Relationships Among Words.   Give students several words that are related and ask them to identify others appropriate to the given words. The words supplied by the students can be similar or opposite in meaning and should be based on their reading of stories and books, as noted earlier.

Similar meanings can include:

big, huge, . . . (giant, grand, jumbo)
small, tiny, . . . (minute, wee, miniature)

Opposite meanings can include:

big, huge, . . . (small, tiny, minute)
Shout, yell, . . . (whisper, soft, quiet)

Combinations of meaning can include:

big, small, . . . (giant, little, enormous)
shout, whisper, . . . (yell, soft, quiet)

Ask students to provide context and write their context sentence for each of the words. After the students understand the relationships between the words, have them provide additional words that retain similar meaning in the sentences. The following example is based on a story the children had read that focused on the concepts associated with big and small:

In the story, **Our Little Wonder,** Rich and Robbie got a pet tiger kitten. It was so _____ that they could hold it in their hands. They thought about the mother tiger and wondered how such a little thing could grow up to be so _____ .

Students can supply words that relate to other stories they have read about size. For example, Donald might use the word **jumbo** to describe the mother cat, while Matthew might choose the word **giant** to describe her. Teachers can direct students to think about words that are the opposite of those supplied for either sentence. Words such as **minute, tiny, little,** and so forth could be used to complete the first sentence.

Develop additional activities around the concept of related words. For example, write the word **release** on the board. Ask the students to discuss words that are related in meaning and list them on the board. Then, ask students to discuss words that are different in meaning and list them. Have them discuss why they listed a word in a particular column. For example:

Related	**Different**
free	grasp
dismiss	hold
	clutch
	capture
	keep

Use sentences to illustrate the different meanings. Note the changes in meaning for the words substituted for **release.** Again encourage students to use their knowledge of stories they have read to construct sentences for the words and write the sentences on the board. Discuss with them how the meaning changes depending on which word is used in the sentence.

John decided to **free** the bird.

John decided to **grasp** the bird.

John decided to **capture** the bird.

John decided to **keep** the bird.

Compare related words for sentence comprehension. Invite the students to read sets of sentences and determine if they have similar meanings. Have them write **S** on the line to indicate that sentences communicate similar meanings, and have them write **D** to show that they have different meanings. Complete one or two examples with the students to make sure that they understand the task and will succeed at it.

_____ 1. Bill took his dog for a ride in the car.
_____   Bill took his dog for a ride in the park.

_____ 2. The park is not far from Bill's house.
_____   The park is close to Bill's house.

_____ 3. The park has an enormous field where Bill's dog can play.
_____   The park has a minute area where Bill's dog can play.

■ Word-association Vocabulary Instruction

Word-association vocabulary instruction enables students to learn the meanings of several connected words. Students can add new words to their existing vocabulary and understand relationships between the concepts that words represent.

This approach can be followed in teaching synonyms, antonyms, context clues, roots, prefixes, suffixes, and concept classifications (such as animals, size, actions, and story themes). Word-association strategy applies to all school subjects. Following are a few suggested activities to help promote meaningful vocabulary growth.

INSTRUCTIONAL ACTIVITIES

Associating Words with Known Concepts in Context.   Keep an accurate list of new words that students encounter and learn. Words that contain the same root, prefix, or suffix, and words in concept classifications can form the basis for expanding meaning vocabularies. Teach new words by relating them to similar words the students already know.

In content areas, such as mathematics, relate new words to known concepts in meaningful context, using examples in the students' background knowledge. For example, students connect concepts through reading and writing of connected vocabulary (see Figure 6.5).

In interest areas, such as basketball, connect new words to the concept in a meaningful context. For example, connect **court, score, second, scoreboard, bounce, shot, shoot, dribble, foul, rebound, time out,** and **rim.**

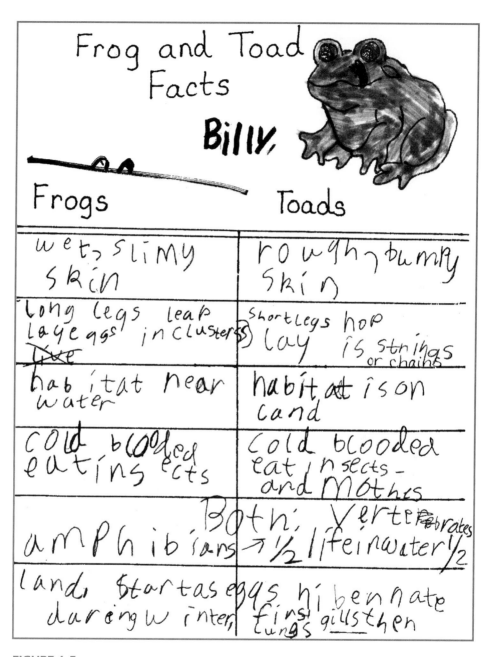

Frog and Toad Facts

Billy.

Frogs	Toads
wet, slimy skin	rough, bumpy skin
long legs leap lay eggs in clusters ~~live~~	short legs hop lay is strings or chains
habitat near water	habitat is on land
cold blooded eat insects	cold blooded eat insects and mothes
amphibians	Both: Vertebrates → ½ life in water ½
land, startas eggs during winter, fins	hibennate gills then lungs

FIGURE 6.5

Example of a student's connecting concepts through comparison and contrast or represented by vocabulary

Using Categories for Classification of Words.   Connect new words to words and concepts already known by the students for new word categories. For example, using **basketball,** illustrate word relationships with the same roots, prefixes, and suffixes.

Roots	Prefixes	Suffixes
basket**ball**	**re**bound	dribbl**ing,** dribbl**ed**
base**ball**	**re**take	jump**ing,** jump**ed**
foot**ball**	**re**make	scor**ing,** scor**ed**

Classify words that students know from their reading of literature and basal stories in terms of similar properties and introduce new words that relate to the known properties. For example, a thematic unit on farm life might use the following:

Animals	Farm Animals	Pets	Animal Sounds	Animal Sizes
pig	pig	—	pig—oink, grunt	enormous pig
cow	cow	—	cow—moo, low	huge cow
sheep	sheep	—	sheep—baa, bleat	large sheep
goat	goat	—	goat—baa, bleat	big goat
cat	cat	cat	cat—meow, hiss	small cat
dog	dog	dog	dog—bark, growl	tiny dog, little dog, great dog

INSTRUCTIONAL ACTIVITIES

Structural Analysis.   Generate instructional activities for the area of structural analysis. Teach affixes (prefixes, suffixes, and inflection endings) to help students relate the new to what they know. Using word families (derivations of known words, such as **depend—dependable, undependable, dependent,** and **independent**) can enhance understanding of the meaning relationships among derived words within a family and promote independent word learning.

Introduce prefixes and their effects on meaning by presenting sentences containing prefixes. Focus students' attention on what happens to the meaning of a known word when a specific prefix is used. Once the students understand the task, have them read the rest of a given story or use one that they have read and select the words that make sense in context. The following story illustrates the use of the prefix **un-:**

> Jason set off walking to town and on the way he met a kind man. The name of this kind man was Farmer John. Farmer John was kind to everyone, even Jack, who was never friendly or kind to anyone. Jason had never met anyone who was as unkind and unfriendly as Jack. Jason helped Farmer John load his wagon with hay. Jason and Farmer John took the wagon to town to sell the hay.

Farmer John's _____ friend went with them. Jason had
      (kind, unkind)

to walk beside the wagon. He thought that it was _____
                                  (fair, unfair)

that he had to walk and Farmer John and his _____
                                   (kind, unkind)

friend rode in the wagon. Jason knew that the _____
                                                (kind, unkind)

Jack would not help them _____ the wagon when they got to
                              (load, unload)
town.

When students express an interest in word building using roots, prefixes, and suffixes, construct activities to extend their understanding of word families and the effect that affixes have on word meaning. To build words, read the definition for a word that you already know (it is important that students have meaning for the base word). Then think about what you know about the prefixes and suffixes. Give short definitions to make new words. Do one or two examples with students to make sure that they will be able to do the task. For example:

depend: to rely on (clues: **in-, un-, -able, -ent**)

depend
_____: trustworthy, reliable

_____depend_____: not trustworthy, not reliable

_____depend_____ self-reliant, doing things oneself

depend
_____: relying on someone else, unable to do things oneself

agree: to consent to (clues: **dis-, -able, -ment**)

_____agree_____: a quarrel or argument

agree
_____: pleasing, pleasant

_____agree_____: not pleasing, unpleasant

agree
_____: a contract or an understanding

Provide opportunities for students to apply different prefixes in meaningful context. Progress from sentences to longer passages to ensure a high degree of success. Depending on students' needs, the teacher can introduce the activity with sentences and then proceed to using connected text from stories that the children have read.

Bob isn't able to go to the football game with me.
Bob is _____ to go to the football game with me.
       (able, unable)

The teacher said to read the story again.
The teacher said to _____ the story.
                        (read, reread)

Susan gave Billy a glass of milk. Billy drank all of it and asked for more.
Susan _____ his glass and said, "This is all of the milk."
       (filled, refilled)

Billy yelled, "It's _____ that Donald got three glasses of milk
                       (fair, unfair)
and I got just two."

Donald said, "It's _____ of you to yell at Susan."
                      (kind, unkind)

Susan _____ , "You are a(n) _____ person, Billy,
       (agreed, disagreed)   (kind, unkind)
when you yell at me."

■ Contextual Approaches

Often, a single sentence has inadequate context for students to use their prior knowledge to comprehend the meaning of a word. Consider the following sentence: *Fennecs were crouched behind several small bushes waiting for any type of prey to come along the path to the water hole.* Are fennecs people or animals?

Most likely, you must guess what a fennec is because the sentence does not provide enough information to allow you to use your background knowledge. If they know fennecs are animals, readers can use their knowledge of animals. If they know fennecs are wild animals, readers can use their knowledge of wild animals. Knowing that they are wild, fawn-colored animals with large ears may help readers form an even better understanding of fennecs. Furthermore, readers who are aware that fennecs are African foxes can use their knowledge of foxes to make sense of the sentence. Sufficient natural context is often essential in teaching word meaning.

Now consider this next sentence: *Randy's eyes became as large as silver dollars as the physician's assistant approached him with the sphygmomanometer.* The context helps to some degree to understand the context of the event (perhaps a doctor's office), that Randy is experiencing some kind of emotion (perhaps fear or excitement), and that the *sphygmomanometer* is a thing (perhaps an instrument). However, none of this context is helpful in getting the gist of the word or construction of meaning until one reads further: *She asked him to roll up his sleeve so she could take his blood pressure. Wrapping the wide band tightly around his upper arm, she commented "This new* sphygmomanometer *is so much more accurate in taking a patient's blood pressure than the old one we use to have."*

Skilled readers integrate information as they read to construct meaning. If context is not enough to explain an unknown word, skilled readers may use their knowledge of prefixes, suffixes, and root words to determine the meaning. They perform these operations so rapidly and automatically that they are not aware of them. If they cannot determine the meaning of a word, they may reason that it is not important to know the word and continue reading the text.

Knowledge of what skilled readers do when encountering unknown words has direct implications for teachers. In learning to use context, students must understand how their knowledge of content can help them determine meanings of unknown words. However, context does not always provide total understanding, and often it may mislead students.

■ Modeling Application/Contribution of Context to Word Meaning

Contextual analysis is best taught by guided practice in which the teacher models the procedure, uses familiar written examples, and provides scaffolding as children become proficient in using contextual analysis. **Modeling** means that the teacher thinks out loud, talking through the processes used in the application of structural analysis, thus providing instruction in strategies to use in real reading situations and supporting students' attempts to apply their knowledge through the use of scaffolds. Class discussions with students about how they derive word

**Discussions with students about how they derive word meanings
help them to develop strategies.**

meanings from context, and what they do if context does not work, help them
understand the strengths and limitations of the process.

An illustration of modeling the use of context clues follows. Assume that we
read a sentence containing an unknown word: "Jack was sure his _____
would let him go." This is the opening line of a story, and the author has yet to
unfold the plot or background. Many words might complete the idea when this is
all we know. Is Jack being held prisoner? The word could be *captors*. Is he thinking of getting permission? The word might be *mother, father, friends,* or *teacher*.

If we note something about the unknown word, we may get a valuable clue.
For instance, in "Jack was sure his p _____ would let him go," *mother, father,
teacher,* and *friends* can be eliminated because of the initial letter clue, but several
possibilities remain, such as *pal, playmates,* and *parents.*

When the sentence does not provide contextual clues, we can read further to
see if additional text provides the information. As we read on, we discover the context: "Mother and father both agreed that they would let Jack go to the game."
Thinking about the unknown word in the earlier sentence leads us to recognize it
as *parents,* because the later sentence refers to *mother* and *father,* who are parents.

Rarely does a sentence alone provide sufficient context to unlock the meaning of unknown words: For example, "Although their *sojourn* was brief, it was

enjoyable," "It was a *moot* point and the judge did not allow it," and "Most teachers today use an *eclectic* approach for teaching reading." If we consider the context supplied both before and after an unknown word, the meaning is more likely to be revealed.

Suppose a child is reading early in a passage the following: *"It's my _____ ," said Donald.* The child encounters a number of word-meaning possibilities that would make sense in context—my *idea, turn, opinion* or a possession such as *bike, bat, ball,* or *saxophone.* As the child considers the following context, the recognition of the unknown word falls into place. *The boys searched everywhere, but they did not find the lost puppy. "I hope Zach doesn't get hit by a car," said Billy. Donald was very worried. He had been thinking all afternoon about not closing the gate when he went to play ball. The puppy must have gotten out when he left the gate open. "It's my fault," said Donald. Then he told Billy about leaving the gate open.* Such examples can help students better use contextual analysis to get meaning from unknown words.

■ Different Meanings for the Same Word

Some words have more than one meaning. Such words are called **polysemous words.** In early language development, students master the concrete levels of understanding before the abstract. Students may know such words as *aid, blue, mine, broadcast,* and *fence,* and they can know several meanings for each word and still not be familiar with many others.

Students probably will have no difficulties with the following meanings for the word *air:*

My daddy puts **air** in the tires.

We hang our clothes outside to **air** them.

We breathe **air.**

The same students, however, may be confused by the following meanings:

Mrs. Jones is disliked because she puts on **airs.**

She was asked to **air** her view.

That was an **air** ball.

Students may understand what *blue* means in "The boy had a blue coat" but not be familiar with "The boy felt *blue* when his aunt left." They may understand "Grandfather rode the *horse*" but not "The coach warned the boys not to *horse* around," "That's a *horse* of a different color," or "The mayor accused the council of beating a dead *horse.*"

The relationships of words to each other and the subtle meanings that the same word conveys depend upon the context in which a word appears and the reader's background knowledge. Ample reading and language-based experiences broaden children's acquisition of meaning vocabularies.

INSTRUCTIONAL ACTIVITIES

Following are several activities for promoting students' interest in vocabulary development. While they all illustrate the importance of context in defining words, please note that context ranges from the highly concrete, such as labeling naming objects and pictures, to more abstract activities associated with guided writing activities.

Deriving Word Meanings Through Use in Context.   Learning meanings and multiple words for the same object can be fascinating and highly motivating for young children. Many primary-grade classrooms that we visit have words written in context and displayed throughout the classroom. For example, the door in one classroom was labeled in the following manner:

This is the **doorway** to our room.
This is the **entry** to our room.
This is the **entrance** to our room.
This is the **gateway** to our room.
This is the **portal** to our room.

Another classroom had a picture of a giant that reached from ceiling to floor. Listed alongside the giant were words in context, which the children had written. They obviously were intrigued by the word **enormous:**

This giant is **huge.**
This giant is as **huge** as a tree.
This giant is **jumbo.**
This giant is as **jumbo** as an elephant.
This giant is **enormous.**
This giant has **enormous** hands as big as a desk.
This giant has **enormous** ears as big as my kite.
This giant has **enormous** eyes as big as my head.

Other words and sentences written by the children to describe the giant included **immense, tremendous, massive,** and **stupendous.** The context of the picture and the sentence strips initially provided by the teacher were excellent stimuli for children to engage in a self-motivated study of words in context.

Different teachers help students realize that many words have several meanings according to how they are used. Many teachers we have observed illustrate this concept with simple words (such as **can, stick, run,** and **set**). As you ask for different usages, write the students' responses on the board or a chart. At the same time, attempt to fix the various meanings by using other words and concepts from stories the students have read and their experiential/conceptual backgrounds. For example:

I **can** spell my name. (**Can** means "able.")

Mother is going to **can** some peaches. (**Can** means "to preserve.")

Use some other examples for the word **can,** depending upon students' background knowledge:

Can it Joe. (**Can** means "stop talking.")
If you are late one more time, the boss will **can** you. (**Can** means "to dismiss from a job.")
Why don't you trade in that old tin **can** and get a new car? (**Can** means "a battered old car.")

After several group activities stressing different meanings, not simply different sentences, present written activities. Give students several words to illustrate different usages by using a word map.

This activity can provide information about students' background knowledge, writing capabilities, and ability to generalize word meanings. Furthermore, it is highly motivating; it can promote interest in expanding word knowledge through writing activities, as illustrated in Figure 6.6.

■ Homonyms

The relationships between homonyms are not so apparent as are those between words that are similar or opposite in meaning. **Homonyms** are words that sound exactly alike but are spelled differently. Many common homonyms look very much alike (such as *their—there, see—sea, hear—here,* and *course—coarse*), so young readers can have problems with both whole-word recognition and meanings.

INSTRUCTIONAL ACTIVITIES

Using Contextual Analysis with Homonyms. Context plays an important role for homonyms because it provides information for comprehension.

Use the Cloze-maze technique for instructional activities. Give students written sentences appropriate to their language backgrounds and ask them to identify the words that make sense in the sentences. For example:

The _____ made the grass shine in the sunlight.
    (do, dew)

Mother had to _____ the apples at the store.
        (way, weigh)

The softball team that _____ the game was from our town.
        (one, won)

I went down to the _____ to look for some fish.
     (sea, see)

Working with homonyms can be enjoyable and motivating for students. It can help them understand the influence that context has on word meaning. It also can help them use context to understand the contributions that words make to meaning. Once students have grasped the concept of homonyms, point out other examples in their reading of authentic text and focus discussion on how the context provides them with a strategy for determining the meaning of the word.

Language-based Approaches

Providing varied reading, writing, and language-based activities can contribute significantly to vocabulary development. Language-based activities help develop automaticity in word-recognition strategies using word knowledge and activate experiential and conceptual backgrounds to construct meaning.

Billy ⑮ Oct 7, 1994

The fish reminds me of
a barracuda swimming in the
Ocean. It reminds me of a
goldfish swimming quickly
in the salt water. It looks
like an upside down user.
It looks like a space ship
going up to outer space.
It smels like cheese on a
sandwich with mustard.
It smels like fresh pizza
when it's scarfed down.

It feels like a cement wall
that has already dried up.
It feels bumpy like tree
bark when it's picked off.
When dropped it sounds like
a domino falling from
the sky. The fish sounds
like ice hockey players
playing a game on the ice.
It tastes like dried up cheddar
cheese. It tastes like the fish
filled sea.

FIGURE 6.6
An example of an activity to encourage development of descriptive vocabulary

223

■ Independent Reading Programs

Teachers can use numerous techniques to promote independent reading. The essential point is to allocate time for students to read on their own. Ways to promote independent reading include bookselling sessions, class book fairs, reading aloud to students on a regular basis, creating a book corner in the classroom, using children's literature, and having free-reading sessions daily.

Providing students time to read independently is crucial to motivating them to read for pleasure. A particular time set aside each day for silent reading of self-selected materials by students and teacher is sustained silent reading (SSR), or uninterrupted sustained silent reading (USSR). This activity should stress enjoyment of reading materials, so students should not be required to report on this reading. SSR can stimulate students' independent reading, but just allowing time to read is not enough. Students need access to a variety of reading materials. The materials can include literature books, magazines, newspapers, and travel brochures. Some students may need help in locating interesting reading materials, and others may need direction in terms of their responsibilities during the reading period. Teacher guidance and assistance are extremely important in the beginning reading program.

In the beginning reading program, teachers can motivate independent reading in a variety of ways. One way is to use audiotape recorders to tape children's books. Students can help select the books to be taped if they are given a brief overview of each book before it is recorded. When taping, teachers should read relatively slowly to ensure that students can make the connection between what they hear and the print that represents the language.

Once a book has been taped, students can listen to it and follow along in the text at a listening center. The teacher should help students understand what they are to do and get them started. Without proper instruction, they may just listen to the stories.

Commercially taped books and stories as well as videocassettes (see Figure 6.7) are also readily available. Talking books and closed-caption videocassettes can introduce students to content or the experience of literature.

Predictable books help students begin to use prediction strategies as they read. This frees them from focusing on individual words. In predictable books, students can easily grasp what the author is going to say next. Such books contain much repetition of content and language structure.

Additional ways to encourage reading in the early grades include the use of big books, poetry, storytelling, reading aloud to students, learning and play centers, and creative dramatics. These techniques can help promote a language-rich classroom that motivates young students to engage in literacy. The poem shown in Figure 6.8 expresses one teacher's success in developing her students' interest in literacy through storytelling.

Broad reading is an integral part of the application phase of the reading program, and it is one of the basic characteristics of effective reading instruction. Opportunities for independent reading provide means for expanding vocabulary knowledge, refining and building experiential and conceptual backgrounds, and developing an interest in reading.

Video Descriptions

35. Abiyoyo

This book is a storysong retold and sung by its author, Pete Seeger. Based on a South African lullaby and folk story, a boy and his father come up with a plan to save the townspeople from a giant, Abiyoyo.

LeVar reveals some of the ways a story can be told with music. Features that are incorporated in this rhythmic episode include an upbeat music-video, a rap-video, a professional dance group, and computer animation accompanied by music.

FEATURE BOOK: *Abiyoyo*, a storysong by Pete Seeger.
REVIEW BOOKS: *Blackberry Ink*, poems by Eve Merriam; *Ayu and the Perfect Moon* by David Cox; *Peter and the Wolf*, adapted from the Musical Tale by Sergei Prokofiev.

72. The Adventures of Taxi Dog

A stray dog in New York City is adopted by a taxi driver, with whom he rides and shares adventures each day.

LeVar takes viewers to the city to see the many ways people "hail" taxi cabs, and then viewers discover how a canine companion helps Lisa, who is in a wheelchair.

FEATURE BOOK: *The Adventures of Taxi Dog* by Debra and Sal Barracca; *Las aventuras de Maxi, el perro taxista* (Spanish Version).
REVIEW BOOKS: *Taxi: A Book of City Words* by Betsy and Giulio Maestro; *I Want a Dog* by Dayal Kaur Khalsa; *The First Dog* by Jan Brett.

113. Alejandro's Gift ○

The "gift" Alejandro gives to various desert animals is that of water.

LeVar explores how important water is for all living things. He visits a California oasis and talks with a naturalist about the importance of this water source for the Cahuilla, a Native American tribe of the past, as well as for animals. Viewers visit Niagara Falls and find out how water power can provide electricity.

FEATURE BOOK: *Alejandro's Gift* by Richard E. Albert.
REVIEW BOOKS: *It Rained on the Desert Today* by Ken and Debby Buchanan; *The Desert Alphabet Book* by Jerry Pallotta; *Water, Water Everywhere* by Mark J. Rauzon and Cynthia Overbeck Bix.

27. Alistair in Outer Space

Alistair is on his way to return his books when he is captured in a spaceship by two creatures called Goots.

LeVar introduces viewers to the world through the use of the library and visits the Library of Congress where he checks out a book and then explores some of the more unusual areas including the map room, the film collection, and the rare book conservation section. An animated Conan The Librarian shows how to get a library card.

FEATURE BOOK: *Alistair in Outer Space* by Marilyn Sadler.
REVIEW BOOKS: *Check It Out! The Book About Libraries* by Gail Gibbons; *Commander Toad Series* by Jane Yolen; *Maps and Globes* by Jack Knowlton; *Mapas y globos terráqueos* (Spanish Version).

71. Alistair's Time Machine ◆

Alistair's entry in a science competition takes him to many places and time periods but unfortunately he can't prove this to the judges.

LeVar takes viewers to see creative student inventions, and shows some historic film clips of amusing projects that never made it.

FEATURE BOOK: *Alistair's Time Machine* by Marilyn Sadler.
REVIEW BOOKS: *Find Waldo Now* by Martin Handford; *¿Dónde está Waldo ahora?* (Spanish version); *The Many Lives of Benjamin Franklin* by Aliki; *What Does It Do? Inventions Then and Now* by Daniel Jacobs.

121. Always My Dad ★

Available Nov. 1, 1996

Always My Dad examines the wonderful, complex and multi-faceted relationships that make everyone's family unique. Written by Sharon Dennis Wyeth and illustrated by Raúl Colón, the story warmly explores a young girl's special relationship with her father, despite the fact that she does not see him frequently. LeVar drops in on a neighborhood "Family Day" picnic and pairs up with a young friend in a "Dad and Me" three-legged race.

FEATURE BOOK: *Always My Dad* by Sharon Dennis Wyeth.
REVIEW BOOKS: *Boundless Grace* by Mary Hoffman; *Taxi! Taxi!* by Cari Best; *The Perfect Spot* by Robert J. Blake.

91. Amazing Grace

Grace is a little girl who wants to be Peter Pan in the school play. She runs into obstacles, but refuses to give in despite the fact that she is black and a girl.

Breaking stereotypes in society and believing in yourself is the theme. Actress Whoopi Goldberg as well as other women share how they succeeded in nontraditional situations such as working as a boiler mechanic and playing hockey.

FEATURE BOOK: *Amazing Grace* by Mary Hoffman; *La Asombrosa Graciela* (Spanish Version).
REVIEW BOOKS: *Roses Sing On New Snow: A Delicious Tale* by Paul Yee; *Great Women In The Struggle* by Toyomi Igus, Beronica Freeman Ellis, Diane Patrick and Valerie Wilson Wesley; *Mirette On The High Wire* by Emily Arnold McCully.

26. Animal Cafe

Maxwell found the food on his shop shelves had vanished overnight, and his cash register was "stuffed full of money." This made him wonder what really happens during the middle of the night.

LeVar takes viewers to New York City, where they discover that while some people are drifting off to sleep, others are just beginning their day. Viewers meet some people who work the night shift—a disc jockey, fish market workers, a flower shop employee, bakery workers and workers in a diner. Then it's off to Texas for a scientist-guided tour of a bat cave and its nocturnal inhabitants.

FEATURE BOOK: *Animal Cafe* by John Stadler.
REVIEW BOOKS: *The Moon* by Robert Louis Stevenson; *The Dream Eater* by Christian Garrison; *Night Markets: Bringing Food To A City* by Joshua Horwitz.

4   ★ Premiere programs for 1996 and 1997.   ○ Science   ◆ Math

---

FIGURE 6.7

Examples of videocassettes of children's books that are available from the acclaimed **Reading Rainbow** children's program

Source: Reading Rainbow Video Catalog **(School Edition),** 1996–1997.

Literacy poem

The world of reading

Tammy Dornak

"Now sit down children, and get out your books."
They all looked at me with hesitant looks.
"It's not quite so bad as you all seem to think;
We're going on an adventure!"—and I gave them a wink.
"Oh, please, Miss Dornak, we all hate to read!
Can't we do science, maybe just plant a seed?"
I told them to listen and just close their eyes;
As the reading began, so did the surprise.

The students traveled to places way out of this world;
They traveled on waters that swallowed and swirled.
They fought with aliens from far away places.
They ran from huge animals with big scary faces.
They walked and they lived in the city that doesn't sleep.
They saved damsels in distress and even learned to weep.
They became great pilots and fought in a war;
They became the richest of rich and the poorest of poor.

I then closed my book, and their eyes opened wide.
They looked up and down and they looked side to side.
They were back in the classroom all snug in their seats.
As the bell rang, they left, and I heard one repeat,
"I never knew books could take you away;
I think I'll go home and read instead of out to play."
I'd succeeded because the children saw books could be fun;
Where someone had failed, I finally won!

When this poem was written, Dornak was a senior education major at Texas A & M University in College Station, Texas.

FIGURE 6.8
One teacher's view of developing an interest in literacy in her students
Source: From **The Reading Teacher, 46,** May 1993. Reprinted with the permission of the International Reading Association.

■ Poetry Writing

Writing activities can motivate students to become more actively engaged in learning new words and internalizing the meanings of words. Donna Norton (1996) has identified several ways that teachers can provide rich opportunities for students to use their developing vocabularies. Among the ways she suggests to expand vocabulary knowledge are poetry writing and individualized dictionaries.

Noah Webster's blue-backed *Speller* was one of the most widely used texts for beginning reading instruction between 1780 and the early 1800s. The *Speller* did not contain as much religious material for reading as earlier readers did and children could better relate to the reading content because of the inclusion of content that was appealing to them. Furthermore, the language and content were more appropriate to their background knowledge than that found in earlier reading instructional materials.

Spelling Book. 139

book, döve, full, use, can, chaise, gem, thin, thou,

No. 146.—CXLVI.

THE DOG.

This dog is the mastiff. He is active, strong, and used as a watch dog. He has a large head and pendent ears. He is not very apt to bite; but he will sometimes take down a man and hold him down. Three mastiffs once had a combat with a lion; and the lion was compelled to save himself by flight.

THE STAG.

The stag is the male of the red deer. He is a mild and harmless animal, bearing a noble attire of horns, which are shed and renewed every year. His form is light and elegant, and he runs with great rapidity. The female is called a hind; and the fawn or young deer, when his horns appear, is called a pricket or brocket.

Just as Noah Webster recognized in the 1700s, teachers today realize that children need wide and varied opportunities to read text with which they can associate their experiences to expand their concepts and vocabulary. Meaning vocabulary can be thought of as the hooks on which we hang ideas and construct meaning for our reading and writing. It is through our meaning vocabulary that we represent our world, both its concrete and its abstract features.

Writing poetry is an excellent means to encourage students to expand their vocabularies. Several different forms of poetry stress various types of vocabulary. For example, haiku can be used to expand students' meaning vocabularies. Teacher assistance is important in writing haikus; it enables the teacher to present a variety of words for the same poem.

The brown dancing bear,
Dancing around in his cage,
Dancing on his toes.

The teacher could help the student find other words for *dancing* and encourage her to think of her own. Words such as *gliding, prancing, swaying,* and *teetering* could replace *dancing.* The images that the different words convey can be discussed with the child, and she can illustrate them with pictures.

Another form of poetry that stresses descriptive words and action words is cinquains. Norton (1992) notes that students should first listen to or read numerous cinquains. Then the teacher should discuss the structure of cinquains and illustrate them for students. Following these activities, students can write their own poems. The structure of cinquains is as follows:

Line 1:   A single word for a title.

Line 2:   Two words to describe the title.

Line 3:   Three words to express action.

Line 4:   Four words to express feeling.

Line 5:   The title again, or a word like the title.

Norton recommends that teachers and students draw a diagram for the cinquain:

title
describe title
action, action, action
feeling about the title
title

Cinquains can be written in groups or by individual students and can be about characters from their reading to experiment with descriptive and action words. Norton presented the following examples of students' cinquains for books that they had read. After reading *The Story of Ferdinand,* a group of second graders wrote this cinquain:

Ferdinand
Happy, strong
Sitting, smelling, growing
Loves to smell flowers
Independent (p. 68)

A sixth-grade class wrote the following after reading *Johnny Tremain:*

Johnny
Brave, patriotic
Daring, delivering, riding
Made a strong commitment
Apprentice (p. 69)

Another form of poetry that encourages students to use contrasting words is diamante. The requirements for each line of diamante are as follows:

Line 1:   Noun

Line 2:   Two adjectives

Line 3:   Three participles

Line 4:   Four nouns or phrases

Line 5:   Three participles noting change

Line 6:   Two adjectives

Line 7:   Contrasting noun

Norton (1992) recommends that the diamante be illustrated to denote the structure and that the teacher discuss the structure, illustrate the terms, and read several written examples. Again, she urges the use of a written diagram to help students recall the form of the diamante:

noun
describing, describing
action, action, action
transition nouns or phrases
action, action, action
describing, describing
noun

A fourth-grade class produced the following diamante after reading *The Velveteen Rabbit:*

Toy
Stuffed, velveteen
Sitting, lying, riding
Love made him real
Walking, running, leaping
Real, furry
Rabbit (p. 70)

■ Writing: Journals, Diaries, and Response Journals

Additional writing forms that can promote and encourage the development of students' meaning vocabularies are journal writing, diary writing, and response-journal writing. Because journal writing is intended for the teacher to read, it provides an excellent opportunity for the teacher to use response-journal writing to further students' vocabulary. Students can select their own topics or teachers can provide students with ideas for journal writing. Topics and ideas can focus on characters, settings, events, and language features (words chosen by authors). Teachers can respond in writing and subtly introduce words that relate to what students have written.

For example, Matthew wrote in his journal, "I really liked reading *The Marble Cake Cat* because the cat kept looking for a home where he could be just a cat and Tommy liked him and treated him just the way a cat likes to be treated." Mrs. Hansen responded to Matthew's journal entry by writing, "Matthew, *The Marble Cake Cat* is one of my favorite books. He was really a unique cat, one of a kind, but all he wanted was to be treated like a cat. You and I liked the book and it sounds like it's one of your favorite books, too." The word *unique* appears throughout this book and is most likely a word that Matthew is beginning to associate meaning with. Mrs. Hansen took the opportunity to reinforce the meaning of the word and made a mental note to emphasize its use in her language interaction with Matthew.

■ Student-compiled Dictionaries

Teachers have long used student-compiled dictionaries to help children develop their meaning vocabularies. Dictionaries can vary from picture versions for emerging readers to content-area versions with graphs, examples, and written definitions for upper elementary students. These can take the form of paper-and-pencil versions to those developed on the computer. Lower-elementary-grade children can compile individual dictionaries for significant events in their lives that teachers can capitalize upon to further vocabulary growth.

For example, Billy's kindergarten teacher read a story to the class about a man who sells balloons. Billy drew a picture of his family as a "balloon family." He described his picture to his teacher in terms of the size of the balloons: "The biggest one is daddy. The littlest one is Matthew. The bigger one is mommy." His teacher wrote the words *littlest, biggest, and bigger* under the appropriate balloon family member. Billy added this page of artwork to his picture dictionary and was well on his way to understanding the graphic representation and meanings associated with the words *biggest, bigger,* and *littlest.*

Entries for individual dictionaries can come from stories that the children read, from discussion of topics in science, social studies, and math, from listening to stories read to them, and from field trips. The students can select their own words to include in the dictionaries or teachers can choose words that they believe are important to developing concepts.

INSTRUCTIONAL ACTIVITIES

Using a Semantic Map.   Following the completion of a semantic map, have the students write stories or plays to represent the concepts and words used in the map. Using the outline of semantic map shown in Figure 6.1, encourage students to write a story about traveling in snow, riding in an airplane, being a weather forecaster, or traveling across the United States. Discuss the words and concepts in the semantic map, and provide assistance as the students write their stories.

Using Word Maps.   Using a word map (see Figure 6.2), ask students to write several definitions for a given word or concept. Have them exchange definitions, then have each student try to identify the word that is defined. Use word maps as the framework for a story. Develop several related word maps (such as for dog, park, and games), and have the students integrate the concepts represented in the maps in a story that they write.

Using Webs.   Have the students use webs to organize and develop the stories and reports that they write. For example, if a student wants to write about a trip to the zoo, assist the student in developing a web of experiences to organize the information. If another student wants to write about space flight, help the student develop a web to organize this information. Figure 6.9 shows a story web that a third-grade student developed for a story about bats. Figure 6.10 is the story he wrote.

Using Semantic-features Analysis.   Basing writing activities around a semantic-features analysis, such as that shown in Figure 6.4, have the students write riddles such as the following and exchange them with each other:

> "You can find me almost everywhere. I am read for enjoyment, information, and current events. Who am I?"

> "I warm the earth, help plants grow, and help you start your day. Who am I?"

> "I have four legs, you can see me in a zoo, and I always have my trunk with me. Who am I?"

Have students use their analyses for content area subjects to help them organize and write reports.

Word Derivation.   Studying words of recent origin can motivate both word learning and writing. English is a living language, and as such it is always growing and changing. Introduce students to recently coined words. Then place the words in categories, using semantic maps, webs, and semantic-features analysis.

Following are some newly coined words. Have the students work in small teams, relying on their own knowledge and on materials available in the classroom and library.

rapper	desktop	in-line skates
SCUD missile	cellular telephone	ergonomics
fax	CD	Netscape

In the process of placing words in categories, students may discover that some categories are too broad, such as science or technology, because they cut across almost every heading. Have the students analyze words such as **ergonomics** for insights into the logic of coining new words.

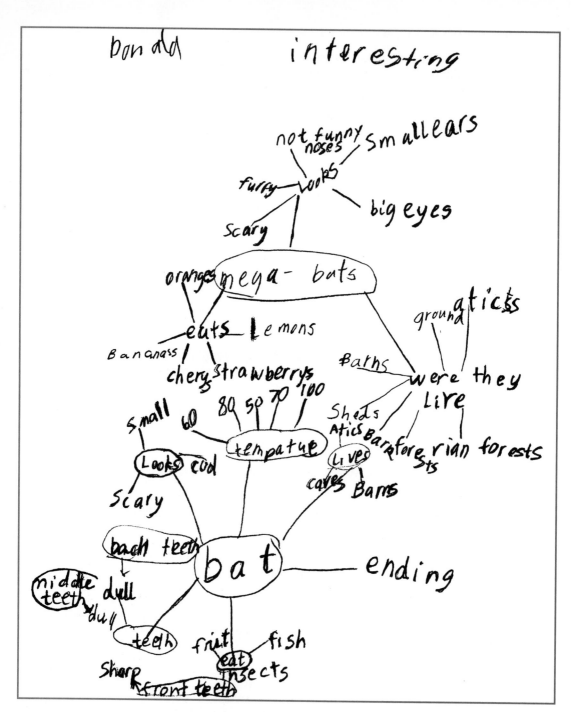

FIGURE 6.9
A story web about bats prepared by a third grader.

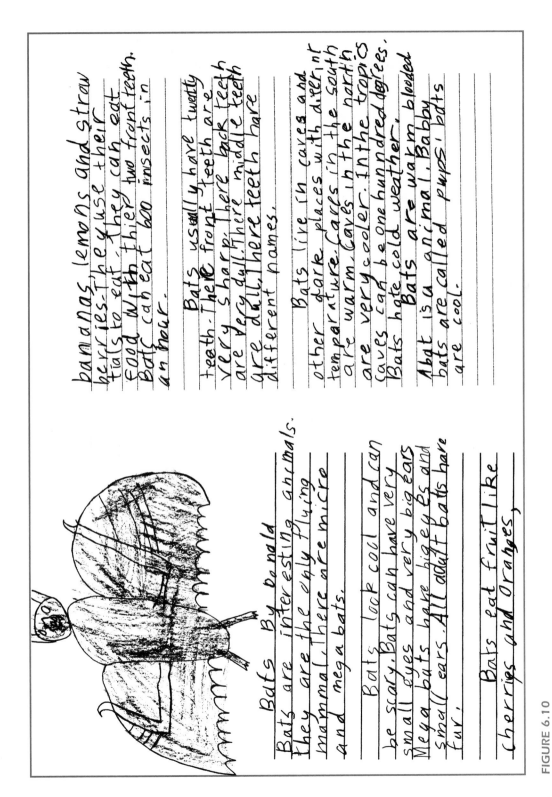

bananas, lemons and straw berries. They use their tials to eat. They can eat food with they two front teeth. Bats can eat 600 insects in an hour.

Bats usually have twenty teeth. There front teeth are very sharp. There back teeth are very dull. There middle teeth are dull. There teeth have different names.

Bats live in caves and other dark places with different temparature. Caves in the south are warm. Caves in the north are very cooler. In the tropics caves can be one hunndred degrees. Bats hate cold weather. Bats are warm blooded. A bat is a animal. Baby bats are called pups. bats are cool.

Bats By banald
Bats are interesting animals. they are the only flying mammal. there are micre and mega bats.

Bats look cool and can be scary. Bats can have very small eyes and very big ears. Mega buts have big eyes and small ears. All adult bats have fur.

Bats eat fruit like cherries and oranges,

FIGURE 6.10
The story about bats that was organized and written in relation to the story web the third grader prepared

Working on a unit devoted to new words in English leads to an understanding of how language works and develops. Motivation is high during such study, particularly among students who have become overdrilled on reading skills instruction. Many writing experiences can grow out of the study of newly coined words. For example, have students coin their own words and write definitions for them. Examples include the following:

rewhisperment	freezerator
uncar	peddlemobile
diseating	pickerupper

Not only can children write definitions, but they can also write stories using their coined words, draw pictures, write advertisements to sell a new product, and so forth. Students can keep their own dictionaries of newly coined words to share with classmates.

Using a language-based approach can encourage students to incorporate new words into their writing. Have the students develop word banks for the words they encounter in their oral language, reading, and writing. Words selected for their word banks have special meaning for the students. Words can be grouped in terms of activities (such as field trips, films, and guest speakers) and integrated into writing activities and reading activities.

☑ Summary

As students expand their experiential and conceptual backgrounds, they expand and refine their knowledge of words. Meaning vocabulary is a major factor in reading comprehension. The words that readers know represent the concepts and information that they have available to help them construct meaning for what they read. Readers who know a word in its fullest sense can associate experiences and concepts with the word. Students' vocabulary knowledge is developmental.

Researchers disagree about the effectiveness of direct vocabulary instruction. Some argue that students encounter far too many words in their reading for direct instruction to be beneficial and that wide reading and a variety of quality language activities promote vocabulary growth most effectively. Others believe that direct vocabulary instruction can increase vocabulary knowledge. This position supports teaching words that are usable, that generate the learning of other new words, and that are keys to understanding given text.

We support a position that recognizes both wide reading and teacher-directed vocabulary instruction to (1) relate new words to background knowledge, (2) provide opportunities to encounter and learn new words, and (3) focus on words that have utility in learning new concepts. Procedures for teaching vocabulary include semantic mapping, word mapping, webbing, and semantic-features analysis. To enhance vocabulary learning, engage students in discussions about the words they are learning from their reading of literary and content texts.

☑ Your Point of View

Discussion Questions

1. You have been given the responsibility to develop the concept "university or college life" for a group of incoming students. Develop a semantic map that would indicate what it is like to attend your university or college.

Share your semantic map with your classmates and discuss the concepts represented.

2. Assume that you are teaching the three states of matter (gas, solid, and liquid) to a group of fourth graders. Contrast having the students look up words such as *fluid, molten, solid, gaseous, evaporation,* and *condensation* and writing definitions that relate the students' existing knowledge to new words and concepts. Discuss some procedures for teaching new words and concepts that might be more effective than writing definitions and sentences for the new words.

Take a Stand For or Against

1. Teachers are wasting their time teaching new words to students.
2. Engaging students in discussions about new words promotes learning of these words.

Field-Based Assignments

1. As was noted in this chapter, semantic mapping incorporates many of the guidelines for vocabulary teaching and enables students to enlarge their vocabularies, understand relationships between existing and new concepts, perceive multiple meanings of words, and learn actively. Semantic mapping structures information categorically so that students can more readily see relationships between new words and concepts and their existing background knowledge.

   Identify a topic in a content area in which children with whom you are working have appropriate interest and background knowledge. Begin to develop a semantic map for the topic by following these guidelines:

   ■ Select a word that is central to a topic or story.
   ■ Write the central word on the chalkboard or a chart.
   ■ Brainstorm a list of words related to the central theme or topic and write these words.
   ■ Group the words into categories and label these categories.

   Focus your discussion on relating students' past reading and direct experiences to the semantic map. In examining the semantic map, students must think about the relationships between the target word and their experiences.

2. Identify one or two words in a dictionary that you think your students will not know the meaning of (such as *heinous, hiatus, sojourn, moot,* or *redoubtable*). Present a written dictionary definition and direct the students to give you a sentence using one of the words. Write each sentence on the chalkboard. Examine the limitations of using only a dictionary to understand new words by focusing on the students' use of the unknown words in their sentences.

Portfolio Entry

Collect some examples of students' webs and stories they have written in relation to the webs. Discuss with the students why they selected specific words to represent the concept or idea that is central to their web. For example, talking with the student who developed the web and story about bats in this chapter might lead you to ask questions such as, How did he know this information? What are descriptive words in comparison with action words? and What new words did he learn? Reflect on what the students share with you in terms of teaching meaning vocabulary in your own reading instructional program.

Bibliography

Anderson, R. C., & Nagy, W. (1991). Word meanings. In R. Barr, M. L. Kamil, P. B. Mosenthal, & P. D. Pearson (Eds.), *Handbook of reading research* (Vol. II) (pp. 690–724). New York: Longman.

Beck, I., McKeown, M., & Omanson, R. (1990). The effects and uses of diverse vocabulary instructional techniques. In M. McKeown & M. Curtis (Eds.), *The nature of vocabulary acquisition*. Hillsdale, NJ: Lawrence Erlbaum Associates.

Blachowicz, C., & Lee, J. J. (1991). Vocabulary development in the literacy classroom. *The Reading Teacher, 45,* 188–195.

Blachowicz, C., & Fisher, P. (1996). *Teaching vocabulary in all classrooms.* Upper Saddle River, NJ: Merrill/Prentice Hall.

Buchoff, R. (1996). Riddles: Fun with language across the curriculum. *The Reading Teacher, 49,* 666–668.

Chall, J. (1996). *Stages of reading development* (2nd ed.). New York, NY: Harcourt Brace.

Iwicki, A. L. (1992). Vocabulary connections. *The Reading Teacher, 45,* 736.

McKeown, M. G. (1993). Creating effective definitions for young word learners. *Reading Research Quarterly, 28,* 16–33.

Nagy, W., & Herman, P. (1996). Incidental vs. instructional approaches to increasing reading vocabulary. In R. Robinson, M. McKenna, & J. Wedman (Eds.), *Issues and trends in literacy education,* (pp. 257–268). Boston: Allyn & Bacon.

Norton, D. (1992). *The impact of literature-based reading.* Upper Saddle River, NJ: Merrill/Prentice Hall.

Norton, D. (1996). *The effective teaching of language arts.* Upper Saddle River, NJ: Merrill/Prentice Hall.

Schwartz, R. M., & Raphael, T. E. (1985). Concept of definition: A key to improving students' vocabulary. *The Reading Teacher, 39,* 198–205.

Tennyson, R., & Cocchiarella, M. (1986). An empirically based instructional design theory for teaching concepts. *Review of Educational Research, 56,* 40–71.

Watts, S. M. (1995). Vocabulary instruction during reading lessons in six classrooms. *Journal of Reading Behavior, 27,* 399–424.

Zechmeister, E. B., Chronis, A. M., Cull, W. L., D'Anna, C. A., & Healy, N. A. (1995). Growth of a functionally important lexicon. *Journal of Reading Behavior, 27,* 201–212.

Comprehension

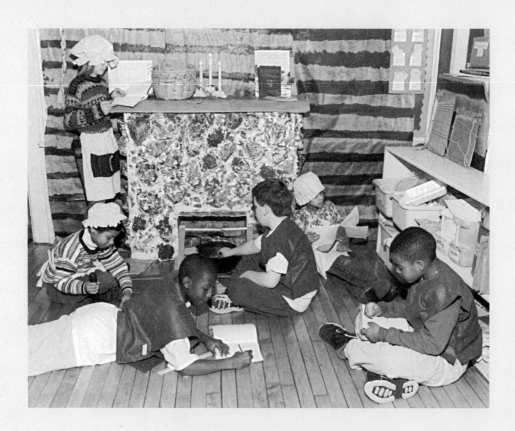

Chapter Outline

For the Reader

Can you recall having read something, thinking that you comprehended it, but being frustrated when asked to demonstrate your understanding on an exam? It was not that you didn't comprehend. Instead, your purpose for reading, your perception of important information, your level of understanding, or your background knowledge differed from the expectations of the person who wrote the exam. We have all read material that was beyond our background knowledge, and as a result, we just couldn't make sense of it.

The reading process is dynamic, requiring active, meaningful communication between the author and the reader. Reading without meaning is unsatisfying and inconsequential. As a teacher of reading, a paramount feature of your reading program should be to further students' comprehension abilities. This chapter examines the comprehension process and the factors that affect it. It recommends teaching strategies for improving comprehension. No other topic is more important in establishing a literate society.

Key Ideas

- Students' background knowledge of the content and the language functions of reading affect comprehension.
- Reading instruction should be comprehension based.
- Quality instruction can enhance and develop reading comprehension.
- Comprehension instruction based on a cognitive view focuses on teaching strategies that students can use as they read text; these strategies are adaptable to any text they read.
- Effective questioning and teacher response are crucial to promoting reading, comprehension, and understanding.
- Direct/explicit comprehension instruction emphasizes students' understanding the when and why of comprehension strategies.

- The curriculum of comprehension instruction should focus on teaching students strategies to help them determine importance, summarize information, draw inferences, generate their own questions, and monitor their understanding of what they read.
- Connecting reading and writing is a foremost feature of comprehension instruction that assists students in developing strategies for reading and interpreting text.
- Comprehension depends on a variety of factors, including background knowledge, text content, the context in which reading occurs, sociocultural background, purposes for reading, and the reader's motivation and strategies.

Conceptualizations of Reading Comprehension

Although we cannot observe comprehension directly, numerous research studies, theories, and models provide probable explanations about its components and development. Most of these explanations view reading comprehension as a number of interdependent skills and abilities.

Chapter 1 presented an interactive conceptualization of the reading process. The interactive view of reading has come about as a result of researchers and teachers reconceptualizing what reading comprehension is and focusing on cognitively based views of reading.

The Interactive View

The cognitively based view of reading comprehension emphasizes both the interactive nature of reading and the reader's role in constructing meaning (Dole, Brown, & Trathen, 1996). The interactive view recognizes the roles of both the reader and the written text in reading comprehension. It depends neither on only what the reader brings to the text nor on only what is written on the page. Essentially, readers simultaneously use many different areas of background knowledge as they read, ranging from print features (such as letters, word parts, and words) to facts to strategies (Rupley & Willson, 1996). The interactive view of reading considers the importance of both written text and background knowledge in comprehension of print. We believe it is most applicable to reading instruction. Tierney and Pearson's (1994) view of reading comprehension reflects much of the current understanding of the process:

> A reader's background knowledge, including purposes, has an overriding influence upon the reader's development of meaning, and reading comprehension involves the activation, focusing, maintaining, and refining of ideas toward developing interpretations that are plausible, interconnected, and complete. In addition, there is a sense in which the reader's comprehension involves two other facets: the reader knowing (either tacitly or consciously) that his or her interpretations for a text are plausible, interconnected, and completely make sense, and, ideally, the reader's evaluation of the transfer value of any acquired understanding. (p. 501)

We can view background knowledge as an individual's experiential and conceptual backgrounds for (1) written text (word recognition, concept of print, understanding of word order, and understanding of word meanings), as well as for (2) the content of what is being read and for (3) how text is organized (Alexander & Murphy, 1996). Background knowledge has been noted as being crucial to reading comprehension and is theorized to give text consistent with background knowledge a storage advantage over incidental information during reading and understanding of text (Symons & Pressley, 1993).

■ Schema Theory

A concept directly related to the interactive view of reading comprehension has had a major impact on both reading research and instruction since the mid-1970s. This concept is **schema theory,** which describes how knowledge is represented and how new knowledge is integrated with a network of prior knowledge (Harris & Hodges, 1995). Anderson (1994) described the essential features of schema theory in relation to reading:

> According to schema theory, reading involves more or less simultaneous analysis at many different levels. The levels include graphophonemic, morphemic, semantic, syntactic, pragmatic, and interpretive. This means that analysis does not proceed in a strict order from the visual information in letters to the overall interpretation of a text. (p. 473)

A powerful feature of schema theory is that it helps explain how new learning is integrated with an individual's existing knowledge. It explains how we learn, modify, and use information we acquire through our experiences.

A major concept of schema theory is that our experiences and knowledge are organized by meaning (as in a thesaurus) rather than by word (as in a dictionary). For example, we have **schemata** (plural of *schema*) for places (e.g., grocery store, home, and school), events (football game, political convention, and wedding), roles (parent, teacher, and student), emotions (love, hate, and fear), and language concepts (story, menu, and sentence structure).

Figure 7.1 illustrates the semantic features of schemata. It is a partial semantic network for *chair,* and it shows how *chair* is a schema as well as a member of other classes related to each other (functional furniture).

An adaptation of Taylor, Harris, and Pearson's (1995) description of this semantic network will help explain the nature of schemata. An important feature of this theory is that it refers to the attributes of a schema as slots. **Slots** (e.g., *seat,*

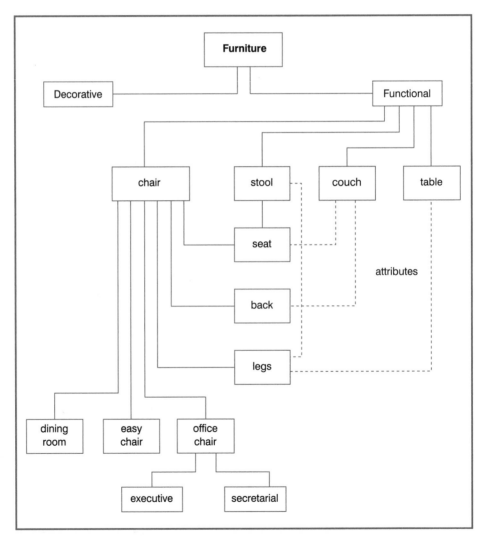

FIGURE 7.1
A partial representation of a schema for chair
Source: Reprinted with permission from B. Taylor, L. A. Harris, and P. D.
Pearson, **Reading Difficulties: Instruction and Assessment,**
Second Edition (New York: Random House, 1995), p. 13.

back, and *legs*) must be filled or recognized for an individual to activate a schema and recognize *chair.* The chair schema illustrates both an upward and downward organization. The upward organization shows the relationship of chair to functional furniture. The downward organization points out the different types or examples of chairs to fill a slot.

Schemata are considered to be abstract in nature. That is, they do not represent fixed concepts (e.g., specific events, objects, or emotions), but idealized concepts, which in fact may not even exist (Taylor, Harris, & Pearson, 1995). Anderson (1994) indicates differences between schemata for concepts versus for actions and events. Schemata for concepts and for actions and events differ mainly in the ways their slots are filled. Action and event schemata have episodic or sequential dimensions.

Figure 7.2 is a schema for an action—buying something. Slots for a *buy* schema may be selected. For example, the buyer and medium slots could be anyone from a small child with one dollar to a tycoon with millions of dollars. The possible slots for a *buy* scenario are episodes generally associated with buying

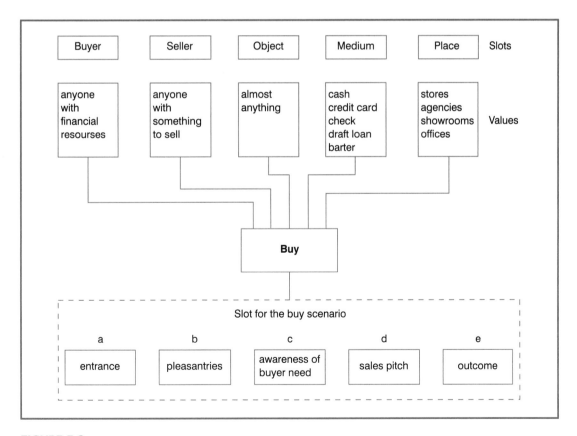

FIGURE 7.2
Partial representation of a possible buy schema
Source: Reprinted with permission from B. Taylor, L. A. Harris, and P. D. Pearson, **Reading Difficulties: Instruction and Assessment,** Second Edition (New York: Random House, 1995), p. 14.

something. How the slots in the buy schema are filled (a child with one dollar or a tycoon with millions) influences how the episodic slots are filled for the scenario. Taylor, Harris, and Pearson (1995) note:

> There is a great deal of cross-referencing among schemata. For example, if a buy schema is selected and the buyer is a criminal, then the separate schema for criminal is called up and added to the buy schema. The values (actors) that fill variable slots (roles) in one schema are themselves schemata in other parts of a person's semantically organized memory. (p. 13)

Schemata are considered to be incomplete; that is, empty slots are always waiting to be filled as a result of new experiences. Consider a group of first graders preparing to play a game of basketball. They meet on the basketball court and choose two teams. These children have only a partial schema for the game of basketball. When a teacher assists them in getting the game started by demonstrating a tip-off, a slot for their schema of basketball is filled. However, they fill additional empty slots (e.g., what constitutes a foul, how to keep score, and when to end a game) as they more fully develop a basketball schema.

In fact, readers may change, elaborate on, or discard a schema as they proceed through text. Readers comprehend by using existing knowledge, which can change when they encounter new information. Although changes in schemata happen slowly, they can be considered new learning. New learning may result from modifying an existing schema or from creating a new one (Rupley & Blair, 1988).

An important feature of schema selection (or constructing meaning from the text) is inference (Anderson, 1994). Inference also plays a major role in filling slots, and once a slot is filled, inference influences the filling of other slots.

How Schemata Influence Comprehension.   Schema theory helps to explain how readers use prior knowledge to comprehend and learn from text. Students' reading comprehension or lack of comprehension can be based on teachers' noting whether or not students are engaging their schemata before, during, and after reading. Rumelhart (1984) suggests several features of schemata that may influence comprehension:

- Students may not have the necessary schemata in relation to the content of the text. They may lack schemata for such topics as world politics, world economics, and farm life. As a result, students have no way to hypothesize about text content.
- Students may have appropriate schemata for text content but lack schemata for the language of the text; therefore, they cannot access schemata for understanding the content. For example, "The magistrate chastised the assembly of onlookers for the brouhaha that erupted when the verdict was rendered" is more easily understood when written as "The judge scolded the people in the courtroom for the disruption that took place when he gave his decision."
- Students may have well-developed schemata for the content and language, but the author may not have provided enough clues to suggest them. In such instances, students need assistance in filling in the gaps.

- Students may find their schemata activated and perceive meaning; however, their meaning may be different from that intended by the author. Students who often think that they know more than the author in their reading of text are most likely to demonstrate such comprehension.

How Social and Cultural Factors Affect Schemata.   Schema theory highlights the importance of readers' constructing meaning as they process text. In addition to helping to change the concept of reading comprehension to enhance instruction, schema theory has helped explain the effects of sociocultural variations on reading. Research conducted by Staffensen, Joag-Dev, and Anderson (1979) shows that readers from distinctly different cultures give differing interpretations of reading materials deemed culturally sensitive. Individuals who read materials related directly to their culture spend less time reading and recall more information.

Similar results were reported by Erwin (1991), who found that when elementary students were read a passage containing cultural information for which they had background knowledge, they could successfully answer questions without instruction. When hearing a story containing unfamiliar cultural information, however, they had extreme difficulty answering questions about the story. Even when the teacher added direct instruction to help the children build some knowledge of the different culture, they still had trouble both answering questions and discussing the content of what they read and studied.

An analysis of research (Anderson, 1994) supports the idea that reading material with identifiable cultural content directly influences an individual's comprehension. When the reader's culture and the text's cultural content are mismatched, the reader constructs different meaning. Linguistically and culturally diverse students may be unfairly evaluated if the teacher focuses on how closely their comprehension matches the text of what they are required to read. If the materials used for reading instruction contain culturally loaded content, students may not have the appropriate schemata to construct meaning that even approximates the author's intent.

Implications of Schema Theory.   Schema theory can help teachers develop better strategies to enhance reading comprehension. Several important considerations include the following:

- Make sure that the materials students are asked to read are within their experiential and conceptual backgrounds in terms of content and language.
- Help students activate their background knowledge prior to reading. Providing students with specific information to activate and build their background may be most beneficial when the goal of instruction is comprehension of a given text. Mapping strategies similar to those used in vocabulary instruction, discussions, student- and teacher-identified reading purposes, study guides, and prereading questions can help readers activate their prior knowledge relevant to the reading task.
- Help students develop background knowledge for materials that contain new information. Field trips, films, filmstrips, pictures, guest speakers, and

so forth can help students build background knowledge to construct meaning for new information. Discussing new vocabulary, exploring the relationships among new and known concepts, and directly experiencing new ideas help build background knowledge to which new information can be related. These activities are of major importance in the content areas of science and social studies, for which the suggestions in the teachers' manuals often are not extensive and the previous text read by the students is by itself insufficient to build background for text containing new information (McKeown, Beck, Sinatra, & Loxterman, 1992).

■ Demonstrate for students how to use strategies for constructing meaning. That is, if students are to understand information in what they read, model how to do this, using familiar materials. If they are to go beyond what is found in the materials, think aloud (model this) for them, relating the text to their background knowledge.

■ Monitor students' performance closely to determine whether they have an appropriate schema but fail to activate it or whether they lack a schema to construct meaning. This requires that teachers know their students well. Teachers must be sensitive to sociocultural factors that impede students' comprehension of the cultural aspects of reading matter.

In schema theory, readers build connections between old knowledge and new knowledge through repeated interactions with content. These interactions result in hypotheses that the readers confirm or reject in relation to the text and their background knowledge. Comprehension is the synthesis of these hypotheses that results in constructing meaning.

Metacognition. In addition to using background knowledge to construct meaning, readers must monitor their comprehension and know when the process is breaking down. This monitoring of comprehension is **metacognition.** Good readers are aware of how they construct meaning and can apply corrective strategies when they are not comprehending. Metacognition requires knowing how to achieve the goal that has not been accomplished and knowing when a goal has been reached. Readers therefore must have the ability to monitor their comprehension. Good readers know when they have achieved their purposes for reading, when they understand and do not understand what they are reading, and how to correct and regulate their comprehension of text.

Teachers should help students become aware of what they are doing and why they are doing it. In addition, teachers should model how to check, monitor, and test hypotheses. Metacognitive training makes students aware of what good readers do when reading for meaning. It enables them to employ strategies to monitor their own reading and focus on comprehension.

A cognitive view of reading comprehension based on an interactive model has direct implications for classroom reading-comprehension instruction. Decoding and comprehension are both essential elements of a literacy instructional program. Teaching strategies for constructing meaning from text, monitoring comprehension, and providing opportunities to apply metacognitive strategies to learning are major features of teaching literacy.

What to Teach

Early research in reading comprehension viewed it as a set of skills that students were to master. Learning each skill was assumed to result in a synthesis of skills: reading comprehension. Today, we realize that many factors influence comprehension and that a list of skills should not determine comprehension instruction. New views of reading comprehension recognize it as an interactive, cognitive process. Readers use their background knowledge, text information and cues, and the context in which they are reading to construct meaning. Comprehension instruction based on the cognitive view focuses on teaching strategies that students can use as they read text; these strategies should be adaptable to any text they read.

Dole and colleagues (1991a) identified what should be taught in a reading-comprehension curriculum that is based on teaching reading strategies. Their recommendations are presented in the following paragraphs.

Determining Importance

The majority of reading comprehension in school requires students to determine the author-dictated importance of what they read rather than what they as readers perceive to be important. How good readers do this has been investigated; the findings suggest that (1) good readers use their background knowledge to access and evaluate what they are reading, (2) good readers use their knowledge of the author's bias, goals, and intentions to sort out what is important from what is unimportant in what they are reading, and (3) good readers are knowledgeable about text structure, which helps them identify and organize important information in what they read. Dole and his colleagues (1991a) note, "In summary, the ability to separate the important from the unimportant leads to effective comprehension, and the ability to accomplish this task seems readily amenable to instruction" (p. 244).

Summarizing Information

Readers who can effectively summarize information can also sort through large pieces of text, distinguish important from unimportant ideas, and bring the ideas together so that the new text represents the original. The ability to summarize appears to be developmental (Rupley & Willson, in press). Young children can successfully summarize the plot of simple stories, but they appear to have more difficulty summarizing more complex tasks such as determining how story sections contribute to the story's theme.

Drawing Inferences

Inference provides the foundation for reading comprehension. Readers use inferences to fill in gaps, to relate their background knowledge to the text, and to make sense of what they read. A large amount of research supports teaching inference from the beginning of reading instruction.

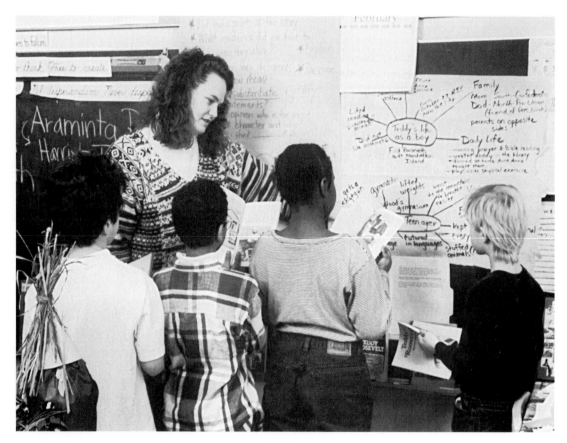

Quality instruction can enhance and develop reading comprehension.

■ Generating Questions

Students who learn and have opportunities to generate their own questions prior to reading have improved comprehension compared to students who answer teacher-asked questions. Young and Daines (1992) determined from their research with kindergarten through fifth-grade children that students are capable of asking predictive questions to set their own purposes for reading. Teachers must provide examples and structure on how to generate questions, however.

■ Monitoring Comprehension

As we noted earlier, comprehension monitoring (metacognition) is another important factor associated with good readers. "Comprehension monitoring and fix-it strategies appear to be important for developing expertise in reading comprehension. It is not only that good readers monitor; it is also that their monitoring appears to be the key to restoring lost comprehension" (Dole et al., 1991, p. 248).

Expert readers typically monitor their comprehension at an unconscious level as they continuously search for and construct meaning as they read.

Questioning Strategies to Promote Comprehension and Understanding

Teacher-identified questions are the most common method of comprehension instruction. Such questions are important for focusing students' learning on building understanding of a particular text content (Pearson & Fielding, 1991). Teachers must carefully identify questions that enable students to establish meaningful purpose for reading and to understand the text in an integrated fashion. Teacher-identified questions should help students attend to the important features of a story, not trivial information that may misdirect their thinking. In addition, teacher questions should help students relate their backgrounds to story content, develop strategies for interacting with text, and learn to understand written language.

Literal Questions

Both literal and inferential questions are important in teaching reading. **Literal questions** focus on explicitly stated information and require the reader to recall or recognize such information. Effective literal questions should help students to build comprehension of the total story (summarizing information). "What did John see in the woods?" is an important question if the fact that he found an unusual set of footprints leads him to spend a summer in the woods searching for a creature. However, a question such as "What is the dog's name?" is trivial if the answer does not contribute to students' understanding of the story.

Prereading questions, such as those often used in teacher-directed instruction, should encourage students to focus their attention on the text information related to the desired understanding. If the students are to know the content of what they read, then teacher-identified prereading literal-level questions are important.

Inferential Questions

Inferential questions require students to fill in information by using their background knowledge to deduce meaning as they read. A question such as "Why do you think so?" is an inferential question that should activate background knowledge appropriate for a story. "What do you think will happen?" can stimulate students to make predictions about story content before reading.

Asking both literal and inferential questions before reading a story can help students set purposes for reading, activate their background knowledge, and predict story information. Questions can come from the teacher, the students, or both. Again, it is important to remember that teacher-identified questions typically focus on knowledge of the text content.

Activating Students' Backgrounds. How questions are asked can either limit students' inquiry or expand it. For example, asking students, "Did you think about the story before you read?" does not promote activation of their background knowledge. However, asking, "What do you already know about this story and what do you think will happen?" will better assist students in understanding how they can use their background knowledge to understand what they read. The following comprehension-questioning strategy (Nessel, 1987) illustrates how teachers can engage students in better understanding of what they read and uses both teacher and student questions to activate students' experiential and conceptual backgrounds:

1. Identify one or two major turning points in the story.
2. Stop the reading at these points and ask, "What do you think will happen?" Encourage differences of opinion.
3. Have students give support for their predictions by asking, "Why do you think so?" or "What have you experienced that makes you think so?"
4. As students read further in the story, ask them to evaluate their original predictions in light of what they have read. Ask, "Do you still think that will happen or have you changed your mind?" Ask them to give reasons for retaining or changing their predictions. Ask, "Why do you want to keep (change) your prediction? What did you read that helped you decide?"
5. Design follow-up activities to encourage reflection on story content and language, to elicit creative responses (such as enacting, writing, and drawing), and to improve the students' ability to both make and justify predictions.

This strategy for teacher questioning focuses on the students' background for the story, not just their related experiences. It provides the students many opportunities to share information and to add to their existing knowledge base. Discussions also help students develop and refine their metacognitive abilities as they keep, change, and discard earlier predictions about a story. Students' predictions and supporting arguments provide insights into their ability to connect prior knowledge with story content to make sense of what they read.

■ Helping Students Develop Comprehension Strategies (Question-and-Answer Relationships)

Teaching question-and-answer relationships (QAR) facilitates students' story comprehension by providing them with a strategy for reading and answering questions (Raphael, 1984, 1986). Use of QAR with young students has been shown to be effective in helping them to determine whether a question can be answered with background knowledge alone or in combination with information in the text.

QAR identifies two basic sources of information for answering questions: in the book and in the reader's head (see Figure 7.3). Raphael (1986) notes that most students can make this distinction after discussions using a short text and

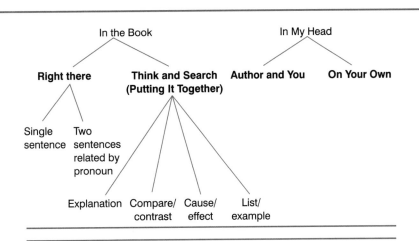

In the Book   In My Head

Right there   **Think and Search**   **Author and You**   **On Your Own**
                 (Putting It Together)

Single   Two
sentence   sentences
        related by
        pronoun

          Explanation   Compare/   Cause/   List/
                      contrast   effect   example

In the Book QARs

Right There
The answer is in the text, usually easy to find. The words used to make up the question and words used to answer the question are **Right There** in the same sentence.

**Think and Search
(Putting It Together)**
The answer is in the story, but you need to put together different story parts to find it. Words for the question and words for the answer are not found in the same sentence. They come from different parts of the text.

In My Head QARs

Author and You
The answer is *not* int he story. You need to think about what you allready know, what the author tells you in the text, and how it fits together.

On My Own
The answer is not in the story. You can even answer the question without reading the story. You need to use your own experience.

FIGURE 7.3
Relationships among the four types of question-and-answer relationships and ways to explain them
Source: From T. Raphael, "Teaching Question-Answer Relationships, Revisited," **The Reading Teacher, 39** (May 1986), pp. 517 and 519. Reprinted with permission of Taffy E. Raphael and the International Reading Association.

one or two related questions as examples. To introduce the relationships, present the sample text on an overhead projector or chart, read the text, and then ask the first question. This question should be one that has an answer in the book. As the students respond to the question, locate the information in the text rather than focusing on the accuracy of the responses.

The second question should require an "in-my-head" response. Focus on the source of the answer in addition to its appropriateness. Once students understand the differences between *in the book* and *in my head* (Raphael notes that this takes minutes for upper-grade students and several weeks for early primary students), focus on developing each type. You should try to expand only one of the categories at a time.

Developing the in-the-book category includes helping students to realize when the answer to a question is either (1) explicitly stated in the text in one or two sentences or (2) explicitly stated in the text but requires putting together information from several parts. Raphael suggest that teachers refer to the synthesis of explicit text as putting it together. This instruction stresses strategies for locating information.

Expand the think-and-search category (see Figure 7.3) when working with upper-elementary and middle-school students by including strategies for identifying information in terms of text structure. Knowledge of text structure can help students understand how text information is organized and how such knowledge helps them locate information to answer questions.

Once students are competent in the in-the-book QARs, expand the "in-my-head" component. The two categories for this component are (1) author and you, and (2) on my own. The primary distinction between these two is whether or not the student needs to read the text for a question to make sense. If the answer requires interaction of the text and the student's background, then the question is related to the author-and-you component. If the response to a question depends only on the student's background knowledge, then it is the on-my-own component. For example, if students are asked to answer a question such as, "Why did Sally run home and change her clothes?" it is important for them to know that Sally was playing in the sand pit even though her mother had told her never to play in such a dangerous area. This information—coupled with the reader's knowledge that by changing clothes Sally might be able to prevent her mother from knowing where she had been—provides an answer for the question. An on-your-own question might be "How do you feel when your mother punishes you for misbehaving?" which the reader can respond to without reading or understanding the story.

A valuable feature of QAR that we have observed is that teachers use it as a framework for their comprehension instruction. Teachers we have observed and worked with have used it to identify the types of questions that are most important for guiding students in the reading of a story. On-my-own questions are one means that they use to activate students' background knowledge and stimulate students to think about how it relates to a given story prior to reading. On-my-own and author-and-you questions help teachers extend and encourage student interaction with the text and promote their drawing inferences.

Enhancing Student Participation in Responding to Questions

Positive teacher comments to student discussions and responses such as, "You were thinking very well to come up with that idea," "Can you tell us more?" and "You are off to a good start" will encourage students to go beyond single-answer responses and become more reflective about what they read. In addition, restating questions that use prompts and cues will help maximize students' likelihood of responding successfully in discussions focused on what they have read. For example, after reading about leopard frogs in a science unit, a student is asked to respond to the question "Why do leopard frogs hibernate during the winter months?" If the student cannot respond, the teacher could use the following techniques:

- Rephrase the question—"Leopard frogs are reptiles. What have we learned about reptiles that causes them to hibernate in the winter?" (Student does not respond.)
- "Let me name some reptiles that hibernate that we have already read about— snakes, lizards, and turtles. Each of these reptiles hibernates in the winter just like the leopard frog. Why do these reptiles hibernate?" (Student does not respond.)
- During the hot months of summer, reptiles like to sun themselves in areas warmed by the sun. The body temperatures of reptiles depend on how warm it is around them. What happens in winter that would cause a leopard frog to hibernate?" (Student responds and elaborates on his response.)

The strategy of rephrasing questions built on background knowledge helps students to make cognitive connections between that which they have learned and how it relates to that which they are learning. In the example just provided, the teacher could have told the student why leopard frogs hibernate in the winter if the student had not built connections to prior knowledge. Telling the student why should be done in a friendly and knowledgeable manner, followed by asking the student to elaborate on the teacher's response. Teachers should avoid going to another student for a response because it often demeans the capabilities of the student who did not respond to the initial question.

■ Teacher Responses

Although the quality of questions is important, the teacher's responses to students' answers are equally important. To develop students' thinking and to improve the quality and quantity of class discussions, teachers should be aware of their reactions to student responses.

For example, allowing students enough time to organize information and think about a response to a question has many positive benefits. Waiting for approximately three to four seconds after asking a question, with no further comment can result in the following:

- The length of response increases.
- The number of unsolicited but appropriate responses increases.

- Failure to respond decreases.
- Confidence in responses increases.
- Student-to-student comparisons of information increases.
- Evidence-inference statements increase.
- The frequency of student questions increases.

The benefits of wait-time indicate that it is a powerful yet simple strategy to enhance students' interactions with questions posed by the teacher. Increasing wait-time benefits all students, shifts the responsibility for the dialogue to them, and encourages speculative and reasoning responses. Essentially, wait-time gives students the chance to activate their background knowledge and to relate their experiences to the questions asked. This is an important point for teachers to consider, especially when asking inferential questions.

Responding to Students.   Coupled with wait-time, responding effectively to students' answers and comments encourages them to make predictions, elaborate on the text content, and draw inferences. A teacher's response may involve asking questions that encourage students to clarify and expand their responses, redirecting students' thinking and strategy, or monitoring students' strategies to correct and provide alternatives. The teacher's response can also provide insights about how students derived an answer and can promote interaction among students about how an answer was derived. When students share their strategies with each other, it shifts the focus from getting a right answer to how the answer was derived.

Direct/Explicit Comprehension Instruction

Enabling students to interact with and construct meaning for text is the goal of literacy instruction. The concept of reading comprehension has been expanded to include background knowledge, text structure, flexible use of knowledge, reader habits, fluency, automatic word recognition, automatic word knowledge, and the orchestration of skills that support each other in a variety of ways. Such an expanded belief of comprehension should stimulate teachers to perceive themselves as people who assist students in developing understandings about text content, using strategies to understand the text, and learning how the process of reading functions.

■ Rethinking Direct/Explicit Instruction

Direct instruction once was thought of as the teacher directing and managing all aspects of students' learning, which included what they read, when they read it, and how they thought about it. An interactive view of literacy instruction often refers to direct instruction as explicit instruction. Explicit instruction emphasizes students' understanding the when and why of comprehension strategies. The importance of direct/explicit instruction was brought out in Smagorinsky and Smith's (1992) review of research addressing how best to facilitate students'

Story starting examples can include:

It was a cold, snowy morning in the mountains. Jim had lost all his camping gear and food to the grizzly bears last night. He prepared to turn back when suddenly he heard . . .

Jerry had one more lap of the car race to go. He was neck and neck with the other lead car. As they began the last lap of the race, Jerry . . .

■ Independent Student Practice

Hand out a story starter similar to the ones in the teacher-directed instructional activity. For example:

The hot July summer was making it hard to live in New York City. Several teenage youths were standing on the street corner near the jewelry store when suddenly . . .

Discuss the inferences that could be included in this story and list them on the chalkboard. Distribute an additional story starter and allow ample time for students to write an ending.

■ Ongoing Diagnosis

Teacher evaluation of the inferences made in students' written responses.
Discuss and share written responses to the story starter with the group. Students who are experiencing difficulty with this activity can be grouped together for additional instruction. Give them written passages and short stories and guide them in making inferences.

■ Modifying Instruction

The difficulty level for this activity can be easily varied. Easier tasks can focus on events that are extremely familiar to students: holidays, games, television programs, and so forth. More difficult tasks can be based on longer passages and more abstract concepts.

FIGURE 7.4, continued

used for instruction and practice application of comprehension strategies.

2. *Building background.* After determining what existing knowledge to activate, focus on how to do this in the lesson. Utilize students' existing schemata. Model, explain, and demonstrate the lesson objective; review examples for application in meaningful context; and provide purposes for learning by assisting students in asking questions and making predictions about the text and strategies they will use.

3. *Modeling, explaining, and demonstrating.* This component involves making sure students understand the tasks and how they are to apply their strategies to reading. Use materials familiar to the students and focus on explicit strategies and flexibility in the application of strategies.

4. *Practice in application of strategy.* Students can do this either independently or in small groups that the teacher monitors closely to provide appropriate scaffolding. Encourage students to monitor their own application of the comprehension task and relate its application to similar text and comprehension tasks. This will assist them in assuming more of the responsibility for their own learning.

5. *Ongoing assessment.* Based upon students' performance in both group and independent activities, assess their learning. Focus on their application of comprehension strategies in other comprehension tasks. Students' responses provide teachers with information about what students do and do not understand. This information is valuable in determining what instruction is needed to assure students' learning.

6. *Modifying instruction.* Based on ongoing learning assessment, the teacher modifies instruction. You may need to provide scaffolding for some students in the initial instruction of a comprehension strategy by simplifying the task. However, because an important feature of scaffolding is to enable students to perform comprehension tasks that are beyond their existing capabilities, some tasks may need to be extended and reinforced with more difficult activities, which in a sense stretch the students' capabilities and learning.

■ Using Direct/Explicit Instruction to Teach Strategic Reasoning

A direct/explicit instruction model (Baumann & Schmidt, 1986) for teaching reasoning strategies integrates three types of knowledge associated with strategic reasoning: (1) declarative knowledge, which is the strategy, (2) procedural knowledge, which is how the strategy is applied in reading, and (3) conditional knowledge, which is metacognitive awareness about why the strategy is important, and when or when not to use it. Four steps for direct/explicit reading-comprehension instruction incorporate these three types of knowledge:

1. *The what step.* Tell the students what comprehension strategy they will learn. Use familiar examples, definitions, illustrations, and descriptions to assist the students in conceptualizing what they are to learn. Building on students' background knowledge by using the familiar and that which they know helps them to understand the application of the new learning to existing cognitive capabilities.

2. *The why step.* Make sure that students associate value with their learning by understanding why the strategy will help them become better readers. Provide examples of and model the strategy using authentic text so that students can conceptualize its importance and connect their existing reading-for-meaning capabilities to the new learning.

3. *The direct/explicit instruction step.* Use direct/explicit instruction to ensure that students understand how the strategy helps construct meaning. Model, demonstrate, and discuss the strategy to facilitate their understanding of the procedures and steps associated with application of

the strategy. Use ongoing assessment of students' practice and application and provide appropriate scaffolding to maximize transfer of the strategy to other reading materials.

4. *The when-to-use-the-strategy step.* To help students realize when they should use a strategy, discuss and illustrate the conditions (such as the types of written text and purposes for reading) appropriate for using the strategy. This is the metacognitive feature of the instruction.

■ Determining What Is Important

Because determining what is important (the main ideas or central problems) is a major feature of comprehension instruction in elementary reading programs, teachers should use instructional procedures that promote this ability. Students benefit when teachers help them use their background knowledge to understand the story line of narrative text, recognize relationships among information presented in informational text, and apply reading strategies appropriate to the desired comprehension outcomes. This highlights the importance of enhancing students' comprehension by helping them determine what is important in what they read. Some basic guidelines for teaching students to determine what is important in text include the following:

1. *Build on students' background knowledge for both content and strategies for reading.* Use concrete examples from previous text the students have read to illustrate and model how they determined what was important in these texts. List students' responses for them to review and use as guides for reading new texts. A major feature of this guideline is that the teacher is never introducing totally new information or concepts, but always building on what the students already know.

2. *Organize the students' background and strategy knowledge.* Simply activating background and strategy knowledge is insufficient if these do not enhance understanding of the text content and what strategies work best in reading the text. Help students organize what they know that is directly applicable to what they are going to read and how they should best read it. For example, do they need to know genre, setting, main ideas, and so forth? Will they be looking for information that is right there, dispersed throughout the text, or combined with their knowledge and the author's knowledge (QAR)?

3. *Model the process for students.* Use examples within the students' background knowledge to model the strategies that best meet the desired purposes for reading and determining what is important. Two strategies for modeling (Pearson, Dole, Duffy, & Roehler, 1991) are (1) recall and compare ("This reminds me of . . .") and (2) predict and justify ("This will probably happen because of that."). For example, using familiar texts, help students recall and compare the three little pigs' wanting to build a house with Little Red Riding Hood's wanting to visit her grandmother. Assisting students in inferring from other events in such familiar stories enables them to understand that numerous

You probably read *Weekly Reader* or a similar type of school weekly news magazine when you were in elementary school. These news magazines have been an important feature of many teachers' reading programs for several years. Such news magazines provide students with opportunities to apply reading skills to reading materials dealing with timely topics and current events.

MY WEEKLY READER

Vol. I   SEPTEMBER 21, 1928   No. I

Two Poor Boys Who Made Good Are Now Running for the Highest Office in the World!

A QUAKER BOY

A LITTLE boy sat in Quaker meeting. He had been there an hour. He began wiggling and wiggling, and whispered to his father, "Dost thou think meeting will be over soon?" After

church, he was punished, for Quakers were very, very strict.

That was in Iowa, about fifty years ago. The boy was Herbert Hoover. Today we are talking of making him President. Herbert was born in a small cottage. Next to it was his father's blacksmith shop.

Issued weekly, from September to June, except Thanksgiving and Christmas weeks, by American Education Press, Inc., 40 South Third Street, Columbus, Ohio, and 1123 Broadway, New York, N. Y. Yearly subscription 75c a year. Special rates to schools.

Herbert went to Oklahoma to visit his Uncle Laban. His three were the only white children in town. All the rest were Indian boys and girls.

Such fun as he had playing with the Indian boys! They taught him how to build Indian fires; how to trap rabbits and squirrels, and how to catch fish.

When Herbert was nine, his mother took a very bad cold and died. The Hoover children were orphans now.

Herbert went to live on a nearby farm with his Uncle Allan. Here he fed the pigs, hoed the garden, and helped milk the cows. He went to the country school every day. Quakers were very strict about school, too. They thought that learning was next in importance to religion.

A LITTLE NEWSBOY

F IFTY-FIVE years ago, a baby boy was born in New York City. It was on the East Side, near the river, where

Special permission granted by *Weekly Reader*, published by Xerox Education Publications, © 1928, Xerox Corp.

Weekly Reader was and still is a popular type of reading material found in elementary classrooms. Along with various newspapers, magazines, catalogs, and quality literature, these materials represent the "real reading" component of a complete literacy program. This component emphasizes the application of literacy capabilities in meaningful reading situations. Several of the more recent magazines for elementary age children are *Time Magazine for Kids, Kids' Discover, Sports Illustrated for Kids,* and *Zillions: Consumer Reports for Kids.*

possibilities may exist, but they must make sense in the story. That is, they are credible in relation to important text events and information. For transfer and application, teacher guidance and scaffolding are important features of this step. Help students evaluate their story problems and redirect their thinking if necessary. You may have to use additional examples and illustrations within students' background knowledge.

4. *Use ongoing assessment and supporting transfer and application.* As students become more proficient in their application of their learning of text, concepts, and strategies, this learning can serve as a foundation for expanding their knowledge. Transfer to similar text may require maximum teacher scaffolding to help students build connections between their new learnings and similar text.

5. *Refine and expand students' strategies.* Students can equate what is important in text in numerous ways, such as by the category of problem, the variety of solutions, and multiple but related problems. Instruct vocabulary in relation to story problems. Concepts connected with vivid vocabulary can be used to classify characters (e.g., as *dauntless, intrepid, collaborative, domineering, spineless,* or *dependable*) and build relationships among character traits, problems, and solutions. Through examination of setting and its effect on story problems, continue to expand students' knowledge, concepts, and strategies.

■ Modifying Direct/Explicit Reading Instructional Activities

Many of the recommendations for teaching stories found in commercial reading series are based on directed reading activities (DRAs). The basic features of DRAs associated with commercial reading series are (1) introduction of identified vocabulary, (2) introduction of the story, (3) silent reading of the story, (4) questions about and discussion of the story, (5) skill activities with workbooks and worksheets, and (6) enrichment activities. Teachers may wish to modify this organization to meet the needs of their students. Modification can be accomplished in the following ways:

■ *Using enrichment activities before reading the story.* In one classroom we visited, the teacher used the enrichment activity about how shadows change in relation to the position of the light source before children read the story "Bear's Shadow" in their readers. Understanding why Bear did what he did to try to lose his shadow is a concept central to understanding the story. Using enrichment and extension activities prior to reading can activate students' background knowledge for the important information and concepts in the story they are going to read.

■ *Focusing on skill and strategy application both before and after reading.* Associating these specifically to a story before students read it and discussing examples of applying the skills and strategies after reading provide students with concrete examples for application. This enables students to apply the skills and strategies to the text rather than to isolated examples.

■ *Presenting and discussing comprehension questions before reading.* This enables students to use their background knowledge to predict content and establish purposes for reading.

■ *Classifying and discussing vocabulary after reading the story.* This often results in teachers' being better informed of students' acquisition of information and expansion of concepts related to vocabulary knowledge that is specific to a given piece of literature or a specific informational text.

Schmitt and Baumann (1986) also recommend modification of the DRA procedure to help students develop strategies for monitoring their comprehension. They argue in favor of metacognitive instruction, which can be incorporated into basal reader lessons with minimal modification. This modification can facilitate students' comprehension monitoring throughout the prereading, reading, and postreading phases of the directed reading activity.

Schmitt and Baumann recommend prereading strategies to activate students' background knowledge and to help students monitor their comprehension as they read. Teachers should model the following strategies:

1. *Activate background knowledge.* This recommendation is common to both typical and modified basal instruction. Students should use pictures, titles, and other text information to help them identify what they already know about the text.

2. *Make predictions about the content.* Students should make predictions about a story before analyzing the structure. Stimulate group discussion and record the predictions.

3. *Set purposes for reading.* Students should always read with purposes in mind. The predictions that the students make can serve as sources for meaningful reading purposes.

4. *Generate questions.* To be more actively engaged with the text as they read and to improve their comprehension, students should generate questions before they read. The questions should relate to the basic structural features of the story (such as setting, theme, plot, and resolution).

Guiding students through the silent reading of the text can enhance their comprehension-monitoring abilities. The following strategies are more detailed than the previous ones; however, they can easily be integrated with them:

1. *Summarize at various points.* Students should check for comprehension breakdowns by stopping their reading at various points. The features of story schema (see Story Schemata section) are points at which to use this strategy. For example, after a setting has been established, students should stop and check their understanding of it.

2. *Evaluate and make new predictions.* As students read the text, they should compare their prereading predictions with the new information they

encounter. They should understand that new information may cause them to change, discard, or create new predictions. Again, teachers should model this strategy and use familiar text to ensure students' understanding and application of the strategy.

3. *Relate new information to existing concepts and strategies.* Illustrate for students how to activate their background knowledge as they read the story. For example, if students are reading about animals sold at a fair, activate their animal background knowledge for animals that would be sold at a county fair.

As students become proficient in monitoring their comprehension, instruction can begin to focus on the following:

1. *Summarizing the total selection.* Through the use of group discussions and individual, written summaries, teach students to summarize story information.

2. *Reviewing the purposes set for the reading.* Assist students to build strategies by determining whether they satisfied the purposes they set for reading. Both group and individual written activities can help students perceive that the purposes they set directly influence the meanings they construct.

3. *Generating purpose-setting questions for the total selection.* Garner information about students' comprehension by encouraging them to ask questions about the whole selection. Questions about how the selection was structured and the strategies most appropriate for that structure can help students monitor their comprehension.

Teachers can easily modify the DRA to help students monitor their reading. The focus of such instruction is not on skills acquisition, but rather on development of strategies that give students responsibility for constructing meaning.

■ Anticipation Guides

Anticipation guides are intended to assist students in integrating new knowledge and concepts with their existing background knowledge. Generally, an anticipation guide incorporates a series of statements given to the students before reading a selection. The students agree or disagree with each statement and share their reasoning with each other. Anticipation guides are intended to stimulate students' thinking, inquisitiveness, and attention for the text that they will read. As a result of their reading the text, students will verify their beliefs, modify or refine their beliefs, and analyze their beliefs in light of new information. Figure 7.5 is an example of an anticipation guide for fifth graders studying colonization (Merkley, 1996/1997). As noted in the figure, students are provided with explicit statements about which they are to agree or disagree prior to reading the text.

AG for Fifth Graders Studying Early U.S. Colonization

Part A

Prereading directions: Carefully read statements 1–4. Under the "You" heading, put a check (✔) in the Agree column if you mostly agree. Put a check (✔) in the Disagree column if you mostly disagree. Be ready to explain why you checked as you did.

You

Agree   Disagree

1. The main reason people move to a new location is for better paying jobs.
2. Strangers to an area are welcomed by people already living in that area.
3. Available transportation is a major concern when choosing a new place to live.
4. If given enough time, a new location always turns out to be a better place to live than the old location.

(Group and/or class discussion)

Part B

Purpose for reading: Now read pages 117–121 about immigration to the New World from England in the 1600s. When you finish p. 121, mark under the "Colonist" heading how you think a colonist would respond to each statement. Be sure to have proof from the text, pp. 117–121, to support why you think the colonist would agree or disagree.

Colonist

Agree   Disagree

1. The main reason people move to a new location is for better paying jobs.
2. Strangers to an area are welcomed by people already living in that area.
3. Available transportation is a major concern when choosing a new place to live.
4. If given enough time, a new location always turns out to be a better place to live than the old location.

(Group and/or class discussion)

FIGURE 7.5

Example of an anticipation guide for a fifth-grade unit on U.S. colonization

Source: From D. Merkley, "Modified Anticipation Guides," **The Reading Teacher, 50** (December 1996/January 1997), pp. 365–368. Reprinted with permission of the International Reading Association.

Story Schemata

A **story schema** is a set of expectations about how stories are usually organized (Gordon & Braun, 1983). An internal organization of story knowledge enables readers to process print by retaining story information in memory until it makes sense and adding more information as they read. A reader's story schema also is important in recalling what is read.

Many reading researchers have investigated the concept of the story schema, and they have proposed several descriptions of it. Figure 7.6 is a direct/explicit instruction lesson for a possible story schema, including setting, initiating event, internal response, attempt, consequence, and reaction.

■ Setting

The story setting may contain both major and minor settings. Major settings include time, place, character, and state. Time may be either implied (e.g., "Sally looked out her window") or stated (e.g., "One clear and bright summer morning"). Time may also be represented by "Once upon a time" or "Long, long ago," both of which are characteristic of fables and fairy tales. Place, too, may be either implied (e.g., "Everyone sat down to breakfast") or stated (e.g., "Mark went to visit Aunt Jane's farm"). Major and minor characters are typically identified by name (e.g., Mark, Aunt Jane, or Frank), occupation (e.g., bellhop, police officer, or teacher), or relationships (e.g., friend, mother, or neighbor). State refers to what is occurring. Ongoing states found in different stories include a party at which children are playing games; wishes and superstitions; and fishing, camping, and hiking. Minor settings include the same elements as major settings and develop the story. For example, the major setting time may be summer, but a minor setting time may be one day. The major location may be Aunt Jane's farm, but a minor location may be an old barn on another farm. The major character may be Frank, the hired hand, but a minor character may be Aunt Jane. The ongoing state for the major setting may be new experiences on the farm, but a minor state may be new friendships.

■ Theme

Theme can be either the goal of the main character or the author's message. For example, Billy's wanting his friends to have a good time at his birthday party is a goal of the main character and is a story theme.

■ Plot

Story plot contains five subparts that together represent an episode. First, the starter event begins the episode. It may be an action by a character or an occurrence (e.g., Billy opening his birthday gifts). Second, the character has an inner response—feelings, thoughts, goals, or plans (e.g., Billy was disappointed when he didn't get a new bicycle for his birthday). Third, action is how the story

■ **Area of Needed Reading Instruction**

Ability to understand story parts.

■ **Intended Learning Outcome**

Students will be able to match sentences from a selected passage to appropriate story parts.

■ **Past Learning**

Students have an existing sight vocabulary and word-identification skills for reading a simple story.
Students understand story analysis and its importance in getting meaning from print.
Students understand that story analysis is related to reading comprehension.

■ **Building Background**

Review students' past experiences with the major categories of story analysis by providing a simple story on the chalkboard, listing each sentence next to its appropriate category, and guiding students through directed discussion of each category. Explain that the major categories of analyzing a story are setting, initiating event, internal response, attempt, consequence, and reaction. An analysis of the story "The Strange Tracks" might look like this:

Setting	Introduces character and provides background information	Once there was a man who lived on a mountain.
Initiating event	Begins the episode	One afternoon while climbing the mountain, he saw some huge, strangely shaped tracks in the snow.
Internal response	Decision	The man was curious and wanted to learn more about the tracks.
Attempt	A try at reaching a goal	He followed the tracks for two days. On the third day a heavy snow storm covered the tracks and made it impossible to search any farther.
Consequence	Outcome	The man discontinued his search and returned to his cabin on the mountain.

FIGURE 7.6

An example for teaching a story schema

Source: Reprinted with permission of Prentice-Hall Publishing Company from **Teaching Reading: Diagnosis, Direct Instruction, and Practice,** Second Edition by William H. Rupley and Timothy R. Blair. Copyright © 1988 by Macmillian/Prentice-Hall.

Reaction	Character's response	He realized that his attempt to find the source of the strange tracks was unsuccessful and that they would remain a mystery to him for a long time.

Use guided discussion to clarify each major category of story analysis using the written example on the chalkboard to facilitate understanding of setting, initiating event, internal response, attempt, consequence, and reaction. Use the story "The Strange Tracks" as a source to specify that *setting* includes introducing the character and providing background information, that *initiating event* refers to the first episode of the story, and so forth. Be certain that students clearly understand the terminology and can associate a meaningful relationship for each component with the story.

Remind students that if they understand story analysis they will better understand story meaning. Emphasize that story analysis is directly related to reading comprehension.

■ Teacher-Directed Instruction

Provide each student with a copy of a simple story. Write the same story on the chalkboard to use for reference in guided discussion. "The Foggy Night" is a simple story that contains the major components of setting, initiating event, internal response, attempt, consequence, and reaction:

The Foggy Night

An old woman lived in a lighthouse on the edge of the ocean shore. Late one night she noticed that a deep fog had set in and would make ocean travel dangerous for several nearby ships. She decided to turn the lighthouse lamp to its brightest wattage. So she climbed to the top of the lighthouse and turned the lamp switch to high. Now the ships could tell if they were too close to the shore. The old woman knew that she had fulfilled her mission and she was able to sleep soundly that night.

Instruct students to read the story silently. Guide them through a discussion of each story component by examining and categorizing each sentence. Use the chalkboard to list sentences and match components accordingly:

Setting	An old woman lived in a lighthouse on the edge of the ocean shore.
Initiating event	Late one night she noticed that a deep fog had set in and would make ocean travel dangerous for several nearby ships.

FIGURE 7.6, continued

Internal response	She decided to turn the lighthouse lamp to its brightest wattage.
Attempt	So she climbed to the top of the lighthouse and turned the lamp switch to high.
Consequence	Now the ships could tell if they were too close to the shore.
Reaction	The old woman knew that she had fulfilled her mission and was able to sleep soundly that night.

It is important that your students understand the meaning of the components used to analyze a story and that they can relate each component of story analysis to appropriate sentences. Again, emphasize the importance of story analysis to reading comprehension. Have the students notice that story components such as setting, initiating event, and so forth usually follow a sequential pattern. Ask students questions relating to story sequence: How would changing the sentence order of the story alter the meaning of the story? Would it make sense to list the old woman's reaction in the story analysis at the *beginning* of the story? Why or why not?

■ **Independent Student Practice**

Distribute a second handout for students to complete as seat work. Instruct students to match sentences from a simple story on the handout with their appropriate story components by using the correct letter that precedes each sentence as is done here:

Jasey the Cat

_____**A**_____ Setting
_____ Attempt
_____ Reaction
_____ Initiating event
_____ Consequence

(A) Once there was a cat named Jasey who lived on a farm. (B) One day Jasey was behind the barn hunting for field mice when he heard a rustling sound in a nearby bush. (C) He wanted to find out if the sound might be made by a mouse and so he decided to jump into the bush after it. (D) To his surprise and dismay the sound was coming from a skunk. (E) Jasey turned on his heels to run away but it was too late. The skunk sprayed Jasey from head to tail. (F) Jasey knew his trick didn't work and he had realized that the lingering odor on his fur would serve as a reminder never to jump into a bush unless first knowing what it holds.

Help students match the first component of the story with its appropriate sentence in order to assure their understanding of this activity. Refer students to the examples on the chalkboard to help them relate the meanings of the story components with the appropriate sentences.

FIGURE 7.6, continued

character plans to achieve his or her goal (e.g., Billy planned to work at odd jobs and save his money for a bicycle). Fourth, what happens is the outcome of the character's actions (e.g., Billy found only a few odd jobs and couldn't save enough money to buy a new bicycle). Fifth, reaction is a response to an outcome or earlier action (e.g., Billy decided to buy a used bicycle and fix it up). Episodes are tied together by relationships (e.g., Billy got a used bicycle and then began to fix it up or Billy spent all his money on a used bicycle and his parents gave him the money to fix it up).

■ Resolution

Resolution can be thought of as the main character achieving his or her goal or the moral of a story. For Billy and his bicycle, the resolution could be that he finally got a bicycle, which he was very proud of buying himself. A possible moral could be that a person who is willing to work hard for something can achieve his or her goal.

Figure 7.7 is a story written by a 4-year-old boy and clearly indicates that he has a concept of setting. His story begins with "Once upon a time." In addition, it is apparent that he has a well-established setting, theme, and plot in his story. However, he has limited use of resolution or bringing his story to a cohesive conclusion. Although the previous discussion of story structure represents the ideal,

---

Once upon a time there was a kid named Matt. He was walking through the woods. And then he saw a bunch of woodpeckers. And then he tried to catch one. And then he actually caught a baby. And then he saw the woodpecker crying. So and then the woodpecker actually lost his mommy. Then there was a kitten. And then they seemed like saying something to the bird and human. He saw a hole that a snake fits in. And well he seemed like he was going back and going into the woods. Then he saw a little girl named Suzanne. And then there was a kid named Donald. And standing with Donald, was a kid named Bobby, who was older than any of them. And he said: Why are you so far into the woods. We are going to pick berries and we just got to this place. The end.

FIGURE 7.7
This story illustrates children's knowledge of story grammar or schema and its emerging characteristics as their literacy capabilities grow

most children, such as this 4-year-old, recognize and incorporate story structure in their literary experiences. Knowledge of story structure may help students to utilize their inferential capabilities as they read and to construct meaning for story parts that are not well developed.

■ Guidelines for Teaching Story Schemata

Following are some basic guidelines for teaching story schemata.

1. Use well-formed stories to introduce both the structure and the terminology of story grammar. Demonstrate and model for students the features of story schemata using the stories as concrete examples. Connect the information to their experiential and conceptual background knowledge.

2. Initiate and illustrate reading purposes. Activate students' background knowledge in relation to the story content and concepts and to guide their thinking by referring to well-known examples.

3. Distinguish the story structure before identifying the content. Initially, examine and discuss the structural features to enable the students to perceive the permanence of the structure. Only the content of the stories changes.

4. When students are able to connect story structure with specific story content, ask story-specific questions. Questions should match the attributes of the story structure being dealt with. Comprehension of explicit story information should be the focus of the story. Following students' ability to note features of story structure with teacher-directed instruction, begin to focus more on inferential questions.

5. Introduce stories that don't adhere to ideal story structure to ensure that students realize that not all stories follow the same structure, which supports the earlier guideline for teacher-directed instruction, proceeding from the simple to the complex.

■ Story Frames

Story frames focus on the structure rather than the specific content of stories. They help direct students' attention to how the content fits the structure. Cudd and Roberts (1987) found story frames useful in teaching reading comprehension to first graders. Figure 7.8 presents the different types of story frames they developed for use with a basal reader. These educators note that developing story frames is not difficult and that in many instances, it is possible to change the basic frame (see example 1 of Figure 7.8) to fit appropriate stories. Therefore, this procedure can be used with longer pieces of text and whole books found in literature-based instruction.

1. Ask the following questions while reading the story.

   ■ Is there an identifiable problem? If there is, why is it a problem?
   ■ Are there important events that contribute to the solution of the problem? If there are, what is the sequence?

FIGURE 7.8
**Story frames that can be developed for the types of stories
students read**
Source: From E. T. Cudd and L. L. Roberts, "Using Story Frames to
Develop Reading Comprehension in a 1st Grade Classroom," **The
Reading Teacher, 41** (October 1987), pp. 75–79. Reprinted with
permission of Evelyn T. Cudd and the International Reading Association.

EXAMPLE 2

Basic frame with no sequence of events

Title <u>The New Pet</u>

The problem in this story was <u>Chen wanted a puppy.</u>

This was a problem because <u>his apartment was too</u>

<u>small for a dog.</u>

The problem was finally solved when <u>his mother gets</u>

<u>him a kitten.</u>

In the end, <u>Chen played with the kitten.</u>

EXAMPLE 3

Story specific basic frame

Title <u>The Sad Mule</u>

In this story a <u>mule</u> had a problem. His problem was <u>he was</u>

<u>too old to work.</u>

This was a problem for him because <u>the farmer was</u>

<u>going to sell him.</u>

Then one day a <u>hen</u> had a good idea. She <u>told the</u>

<u>farmer's children to ride on the mule's back.</u>

This solved the mule's problem because <u>the children had fun</u>

<u>and they wanted to keep the mule.</u>

In the end, <u>the farmer said yes and they were</u>

<u>happy.</u>

FIGURE 7.8, continued

EXAMPLE 4

Short summary frame

Title _Two Cats_

A country cat came to the _city_ to see _his brother_. But he didn't like _the cars_, and he didn't like _the noise._. Then the city cat went to _the country._ The city cat like _the soft grass_, and he liked _the old barn._ But he didn't like _the big dogs._ He ran back to _the city_ and stayed there.

EXAMPLE 5

Short frame with key sequence words

Title _Mike's House_

A little boy made a _playhouse_ out of a box

First, he _made windows_ on the sides.

Next, he _made a door_ on the front.

Then, he _put a rug_ on the floor.

Finally, he _put a sign_ on the door.

The sign said _Mike's House._

FIGURE 7.8, *continued*

EXAMPLE 6

Main episode frame

Title _Red Tail Learns a Lesson_

The problem in this story begins because _a greedy squirrel_
doesn't want to share his acorns.

The other animals warn Red Tail that _someday he might_
need their help.

After this, _a big storm comes and knocks_
Red Tail's house down.

Then, all of the acorns _are gone_ because _the tree_
fell in the river.

Finally, _the other animals share with_
Red Tail.

Red Tail's problem is solved when he learns _that it is better to share._

In the end _Red Tail and his friends sit down_
and eat.

FIGURE 7.8, continued

- How is the problem solved? or What is the solution to the problem?

2. After reading the story and answering the questions, determine whether the basic frame will work. If the basic frame does not fit the story, then add or delete the appropriate parts (see examples 2 and 3).

Based on their experiences in using these story frames, Cudd and Roberts (1987) recommend the following instructional procedures.

1. Begin instruction by drawing attention to the structural features in stories (such as setting, theme, plot, or resolution). Print the features on cards to help draw attention to the element being discussed.

2. Once students begin to understand the basic structural features, have them complete short summary frames (see example 4). Use stories that have an identifiable sequence (e.g., *first, second, then*, and *next*) to help students understand key sequence frames (see example 5). Begin the teaching of story frames with half-page frames, which are not as intimidating as full pages and can be completed in less time.

3. Introduce the frames, establishing meaningful purposes for them, to help students understand their function. Remind students not to worry about correct spelling. Also inform them that the purpose of the activity is to understand the story.

4. As students become more capable in completing story frames, use more complex stories and organize the frame around the main episode (see example 6). Provide concrete examples and supervise completion of the more complex frames so that students can apply the techniques independently.

Through the use of story frames, students begin to use their knowledge of story structure to organize and learn story information. Students exhibit more interaction with each other as they ask each other questions that deal with story structure. They even ask more probing and significant questions about stories. Perhaps one of the most important advantages is that students appear to perceive stories as wholes, made up of important and recurring parts.

Understanding basic story structure appears to have a significant impact on students' concepts of what reading means. Students begin to view reading as an interactive process and to understand that constructing meaning is the primary purpose for reading (as opposed to identifying words or reading to remember a number of details).

Visual Displays of Texts

Visual displays of story information can be used to teach reading-comprehension strategies and assist students in understanding text content. Webbing is a visual display that can help demonstrate the features of story structure and help students understand the relationships among text elements (e.g., characters, plot,

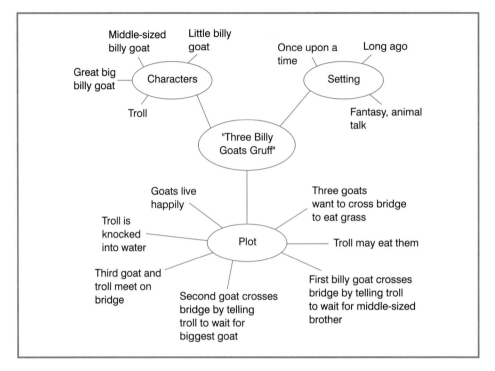

FIGURE 7.9
An example of a story web that represents characters and plot development in chronological order
Source: Reprinted with the permission of Prentice-Hall Publishing Company from **The Effective Teaching of Language Arts,** Fourth Edition by Donna E. Norton. Copyright © 1997 by Merrill/Prentice-Hall.

setting, and reaction) Norton (1997) concluded from the results of a 3-year study with literature webbing that it is one of the most effective ways to teach the important characteristics of a story. Figure 7.9 presents an example of a web for "Three Billy Goats Gruff."

■ Discussion Webs

The discussion web incorporates all of the language arts—listening, speaking, reading, and writing. It can be used as either a prereading or prewriting activity and as a postreading activity. In addition, the discussion web promotes the use of cooperative learning groups. Figure 7.10 is an example of a discussion web based on "Jack and the Beanstalk."

Teachers and students go through five steps in completing a discussion web (Alvermann, 1991):

1. Prepare students to read the selection by activating their background knowledge, establishing purposes for reading, and discussing new vocabulary and concepts.

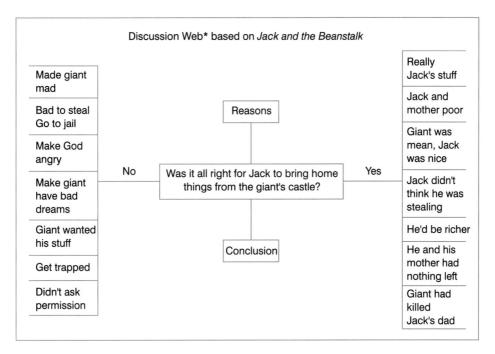

Discussion Web* based on *Jack and the Beanstalk*

| Made giant mad |
| Bad to steal Go to jail |
| Make God angry |
| Make giant have bad dreams |
| Giant wanted his stuff |
| Get trapped |
| Didn't ask permission |

Reasons

No — Was it all right for Jack to bring home things from the giant's castle? — Yes

Conclusion

| Really Jack's stuff |
| Jack and mother poor |
| Giant was mean, Jack was nice |
| Jack didn't think he was stealing |
| He'd be richer |
| He and his mother had nothing left |
| Giant had killed Jack's dad |

FIGURE 7.10
A discussion web based on "Jack and the Beanstalk"
Source: From D. Alvermann, "The Discussion Web: A Graphic Aid for Learning Across the Curriculum," **The Reading Teacher,** 45 (1991), p. 95.

2. Upon completion of their reading, introduce the discussion web with a question ("Was it all right for Jack to bring home things from the giant's castle?"). Students work in pairs and discuss the pros and cons associated with the question by writing key words in the no and yes columns. Although students need not write a response for each line in the columns, they should be encouraged to give an equal number of responses.

3. After students have had sufficient time to write their responses, they are paired with another set of partners, and the four students compare their responses. The focus of this step is for the group to reach a consensus; however, individuals may disagree with the conclusion.

4. When each group of four students has reached a conclusion, the teacher or group appoints a group spokesperson. Each group then has approximately 3 minutes to discuss which of all the reasons given most supports the group's conclusion. Each group should select only one reason to ensure that all spokespersons will have at least one new reason to present. Spokespersons report for each group as part of a whole-class discussion.

5. Individual students write answers to the discussion web question, including their own ideas as well as those expressed by other students. These individual responses are displayed in the classroom so other students can read them.

Elementary teachers can use the discussion web with a variety of students and content areas. It can serve as an alternative to end-of-story questions found in reading series and is appropriate for small groups as well as the whole class. Use of the discussion web has resulted in many students frequently constructing their own questions for the web.

Reciprocal Teaching

A strategy to help students establish purposes for reading and increase their inter-actions with the teacher and each other is called reciprocal teaching (Brown 1988). Reciprocal teaching has two major features: (1) instruction and rehearsal of questioning, summarizing, predicting, and clarifying, and (2) use of scaffolding dialogue from both the teacher and the students as a means for learning ques-tioning, summarizing, predicting, and clarifying (Rosenshine & Meister, 1994). Reciprocal teaching has been used primarily for teaching in the content areas, but it can be used to teach the structure of narrative text as well (Palincsar & Brown, 1988).

Essentially, with this strategy the teacher and students take turns in assum-ing the teacher's role. The goal of reciprocal teaching is gradually transferring to the student the responsibility for thinking while reading. Briefly, the procedure involves four basic steps: (1) predicting, which requires students to activate their background knowledge to predict what they will find in a given text; (2) ques-tioning, in which students learn to determine what a good question is, how to ask questions, and how to read to answer questions; (3) summarizing, or identifying the important content in a passage; and (4) clarifying, which requires students to address reasons that text might be difficult to understand (such as vocabulary, new concepts, and author style).

Reciprocal teaching with narrative text should focus on the features of story schemata, purposes for reading, and comprehension. Predicting should consider the resolution. Questioning should identify important information with which to establish purposes for reading. Summarizing should deal with plot. Finally, clari-fying should identify which strategies to employ to construct meaning. The pur-pose of associating the interactive procedure with story schemata is to teach an-other strategy to construct meaning. In introducing and developing the concepts associated with story schemata, model the strategy and demonstrate with familiar examples.

Oral Language, Readers' Theater, and Visual Arts

Students can demonstrate understanding of what they read using drama, readers' theater, oral-language activities, visual arts, and writing. These methods can also be used as means for instruction. Throughout this chapter and other chapters in this book, we have discussed the importance of oral language in literacy develop-ment. Furthermore, in our presentation of modeling, one of the essential features was encouraging students to talk aloud about the strategies they used to construct meaning for text.

Oral-language Interactions

Opportunities for oral-language interaction in the classroom need to be realistic and not based on situations contrived by the teacher. One example of a good opportunity is the discussion web, which gives students an opportunity to interact and learn from each other. Such interaction facilitates comprehension, understanding of text, and the recognition that individuals can have differing interpretations of text.

Additional ways to stimulate oral interaction among students are to group them together to complete projects (e.g., in science and social studies), share their reactions to books they have read, discuss features of language in books they have read (e.g., most interesting parts, most exciting parts, and confusing parts), and work cooperatively in writing activities (e.g., plays, poems, stories, and articles). Such activities can be used effectively at all grade levels and can encourage students to talk about and share what they are learning with others.

Readers' Theater

Readers' theater does not depend on students' action to convey meaning, but involves using the voices and emphasizing the meaning-bearing cadences of language to make the print come alive (Hoyt, 1992). Teachers can use either published scripts or the students' reading selections for readers' theater. However, using students' reading selections shifts the focus to their responses to literature and integrates features of story schemata, writing, and classroom discussion. Integrating such features reinforces and provides an opportunity to apply past learning.

Teachers can use several variations with readers' theater. They can have only one student at a time reading the part of each character, have several students take turns reading the same part and discuss the variations in their readings, use choral reading of parts, or read parts together in small groups. Hoyt (1992) argues that reading parts chorally or together in small groups gives all students a role, which encourages repeated reading for fluency.

Modeling and scaffolding are important components of readers' theater. The teacher can model reading the various parts with feeling and illustrate how variations in language communicate meaning. Teachers can use think-alouds to model how they decided to read certain parts with anger, excitement, disappointment, and so forth. Scaffolding is important to ensure that students who have difficulty have background knowledge to relate to the story content and characters. Repeatedly practicing the story with teacher assistance can help students become more confident in presenting the story to an audience.

Visual Arts

Visual arts such as drawing and painting offer students a way to express their understanding of text that doesn't require oral or written language expression. A pictorial representation of a story requires students to use both the affective and

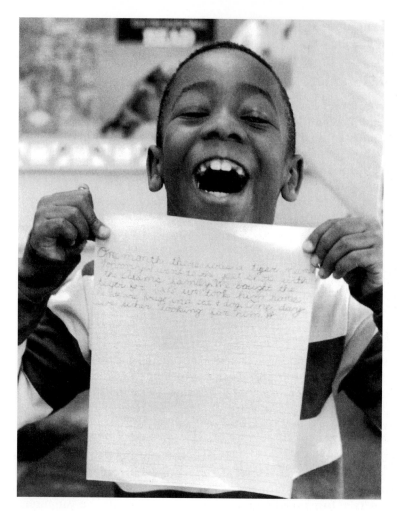

Integrating reading and writing enhances students' reading comprehension.

cognitive domains; they must think about the story as a whole in selecting what to represent visually. Although a visual representation may seem like a simple task, Hoyt (1992) notes that it requires a lot of evaluation, analysis, and summarization. Figure 7.11 is a student's visual representation of a language experience story, illustrated with computer clip art.

Hoyt (1992) recommends a visual arts activity, called sketch to stretch, that teachers can use to facilitate students' comprehension. After students have read some text (story, poem, or nonfiction), they have a limited time to create a sketch about what they learned, what they were thinking, what they liked, and so forth. The teacher also creates a sketch on the chalkboard, easel, or overhead projector. The time limit encourages students to create a general impression of the text rather than many details. The sketches serve as a focal point for discussion as

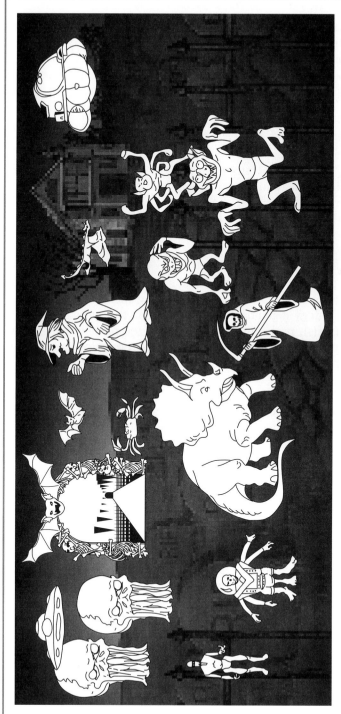

Once upon a time there was a kid named Matt. No one ever wanted to go to his special haunted house because it was very, very, very scary haunted. The kid started trick or treating. He first went to that very, very, scary haunted house because he thought it looked like very scary most decorated. So then he went there and he got really kind of scared because the mosters looked like they were moving. After that he started walking up it and they looked they were moving across and trying to block his way. Then, well he got to this kind of monster that had six hands and two legs. THE END.

FIGURE 7.11
Example of integrating computer visual arts with literacy experiences

students clarify, reflect, and consider relationships before verbally discussing their learning.

Visual arts activities should not take the place of actual time spent in reading and writing; however, they can provide teachers with alternative means for assessing and teaching reading comprehension. As stated by Hoyt (1992), Visual arts "can be a powerful vehicle for learning that deserves a place in the reading program" (p. 584).

The Reading and Writing Connection

Many of the instructional strategies discussed in this chapter can serve to integrate reading and writing and to enhance reading comprehension. Several additional strategies follow. The use of these strategies can help students develop and refine both their reading and writing capabilities.

Probable Passages

The probable-passages strategy developed by Wood (1984) can illustrate the similarities between processes used in constructing meaning for both reading and writing. This strategy depends on a story schema that uses the story features of setting, character(s), problem(s), solution(s) to the problem(s), and ending. The steps in developing a probable passage include preparation, prereading, reading, and postreading.

Preparation.   Analyze the story selection to identify the significant concepts and vocabulary. Present these words visually along with the story features (the features may need modification to correspond to the structure of the story to be read). Present an incomplete story frame on the chalkboard to use both before and after reading. In this incomplete story frame, incorporate the story features (e.g., "This story takes place in ———— and has a character who wants ———— .").

Prereading.   Read the list of significant concepts and vocabulary and direct students to construct a story line mentally. After the students have mentally developed a story line, have them determine where to place each of the key words in the story frame. They should realize that some words may fit in more than one feature and that they can use words from their background knowledge that are logical choices. Have the students justify their responses, requiring them to verbalize their versions of the probable passage.

Upon completion and discussion of the story features, have students use this information to develop a probable passage. Write in the information for the story frame and guide students' responses by asking such questions as "How can we make that idea fit here?" "Can we reword this sentence to better communicate an idea?" and "Can we shorten this and still make it say the same thing?"

Reading.   Upon completion and discussion of the story frame, have the students either read or listen to the story.

Postreading.   Have students modify the story frame after reading to represent the actual story events more accurately.

The probable-passages strategy integrates reading and writing. It also activates students' background knowledge prior to reading. It provides a structure for students to use in making predictions, reinforces the features of story schemata, and engages all students in writing text both before and after reading.

■ Reporting About Books

Use a story schema to assist students in summarizing and reporting on books they read. Olson (1984) developed the following general guidelines to help students summarize and write about books:

1. Use a story map for a familiar story to help students understand that stories have common features such as settings, main characters, events, problems, and goals.

2. Present the features of a story schema and use familiar stories to illustrate each feature. Use the features to specify questions that will guide the discussion of story features. To direct students to apply a story schema to these familiar stories, ask such questions as the following:

   ■ Where does the story take place?
   ■ Who is the major character?
   ■ What major things happen to the main character?
   ■ What does the main character want to do?
   ■ What happened to the main character at the end of the story?

3. After the students understand how to use the questions to guide their reading and summarizing of stories, assist them in identifying a book to read.

4. To help students in writing their book reports, have them list the main characters and events and the relationships among them. Use a story map to accomplish this or have students write responses to a series of questions. Encourage them to identify their own questions as well.

5. After students have either completed the story map or written their responses to the questions, have them write a summary of the book.

This strategy to assist students in writing book reports gives them opportunities to practice and develop an understanding of story structure. It also begins to develop an understanding that reading and writing share many common features.

■ Thinking and Writing About What Students Read

The importance of questioning and reading comprehension were discussed earlier in this chapter. Teacher- and student-identified questions were both cited as means to promote active engagement with text and purposes for reading. Questions also can be an integral part of a literacy program that encourages students to think about what they are reading. Teachers are often caught in a dilemma when making the transition from reading instruction based solely on a basal

Comparison and contrast card 1

Choose two characters from one story. Do the characters look alike? How are they alike? How are they different? What problems do the two characters have that are the same? How are the feelings of the characters different?

Comparison and contrast card 2

Choose two stories. Were the places alike? How were the stories the same? How were they different? How were the story endings different? Which story did you like better? Why? Which character did you like better? Why?

Opinions

What did you like about the main character? What did the character do that made you like him or her? What did you think about the ending? Was anything surprising to you in the story? What was it? Why were you surprised?

Inference

Look at the pictures and at the title. What do you know about the story before you begin to read it? Read the story. Think about the ending. If the story had continued, what might have happened? Why?

Drawing conclusions

Draw a picture of your favorite character. Tell as much as you can about what kind of person your character is. Tell things he or she did in the story. Is this a nice person? Why or why not? Would you like to have this person for a friend? Why or why not?

Characters

As you read a story you learn about the characters by what they say and do. Choose a character from your story. What kind of person is your character? Do you like him or her? Why? How would they act if you were with him or her?

FIGURE 7.12
Examples of question card
Source: From S. R. Angeletti, "Encouraging Students to Think About What They Read." **The Reading Teacher,** 45 (1992), pp. 295–296.

reader series to a literature-based reading program. Angeletti (1992) shares her experiences in making such a transition and how she used question cards to help her students think about and respond to what they read in their own books. One of the major features of her instruction was encouraging students to write about the books they were reading by writing questions on cards to stimulate higher-order thinking. The basic elements of her instruction follow:

1. Question cards were used to encourage students to state opinions (see Figure 7.12). The teacher modeled the cards' use during oral reading of the book to students. Students asked questions of the teacher, who modeled the role of the reader.
2. Practice opportunities were provided for the whole class as students asked the questions of readers who wanted to share the book they were

Author's style

Every writer has his or her own style of writing. When we learn the author's style, we know what to expect from that writer. We often know whether books written by a particular author will be easy picture books or chapter books. We know what kind of characters are typical of the writer—animals that talk, or people like us. We might know whether there will be a happy ending. We know whether we would enjoy reading another book by the same author. Choose an author whose style you know and tell what you know about the author's style of writing. Give examples from books you have read by that author.

Author's purpose

Sometimes authors write a story to teach you something. Sometimes they tell a story about something that happened to them. Sometimes they just want to entertain you. Or, they may have another reason for writing. Tell in one sentence why the author wrote the story you read. Then tell how you knew the author's reason for writing the story.

Type of literature

Tell what kind of book you are reading. Look for clues that let you know. If it is fantasy fiction, for example, there may be animals that talk, or magic things may happen. If it is realistic fiction, there may be real people in the story, and the story could have happened, but the author made it up, perhaps using ideas from his or her own life. If you find rhyming words, short lines, and writing that makes every word count, you are reading poetry. Or you may be reading facts from a book like an encyclopedia. If so, the book is factual. Think about what section of the library you would go to in order to find the book. Then put your book into one group and tell what clues let you know which type of book it is.

FIGURE 7.12, continued

reading. Angeletti recommends that the teacher provide guided practice opportunities for a long period to ensure that all students will succeed in the next steps.

3. Small-group practice was used with student-formed groups of two to five students. The groups used the cards as questioning guides. Through practice students became aware of books other students were reading, talked with each other about their books, and planned for other books they would read and talk about together.

4. Students' written responses to the question cards became a major focus of the instruction. Angeletti (1992) noted that students' writing moved from simple retelling to elaboration about what they read that included inferences, conclusions, and characters' motives.

The program was extremely successful with first, second, and fifth graders. Writing revealed that students at all ability levels learned to choose their own questions and write responses that reflected understanding and appreciation of the books they had read. Students were in control of their own learning as a result of the modeling and scaffolding that the teacher provided in the early stages of instruction.

■ Developing the Reader-Writer Relationship

Other procedures can make students aware of the reader-writer relationship in constructing meaning. Following are several examples that emphasize the reading-writing connection in comprehension (also see Figure 7.13).

- Have students rewrite stories and text to be appropriate for students at a lower grade level.
- To establish real purposes for writing, have students write to authors, companies, classmates, and so forth. Let them interact in small groups to evaluate the communication features of their writing. When their writing is not clear, ask such questions as the following:

  What do you want the reader to know or do?

  How can this say the same thing in a shorter manner?

  What did you mean to say here?

  Who do you want to be able to read this?

  Can you come up with a way to help me better understand what you want to say?

- Give students objects or puzzles and direct them to write directions or descriptions for these. Have them exchange the written directions or descriptions with other students who attempt to draw the object or puzzle.
- Provide stories that have no endings. Have students read the stories and write appropriate endings for them.
- Point out and illustrate examples of literary elements, such as foreshadowing, flashbacks, anticlimax, and so forth. Have students write examples of each and exchange them with each other for sharing.
- Give students examples of poorly formed stories to revise and rewrite in small groups. Have them discuss why they revised certain parts.

The preceding are just a few ways to connect reading and writing and to enhance reading comprehension. The key common element of these activities is their emphasis on communicating meaning.

Comprehension Activities

Figure 7.13 provides activities that are intended to help reinforce comprehension skills and strategies. Note that these activities are only supplemental and that di-

SEQUENCE OF EVENTS

A. Ask students to bring in their favorite comic strips from the newspaper. Collect these for several days. Cut the comic strips into individual frames and place in envelopes. Give these to students and allow them to arrange the pieces to tell a story. Variations of this can integrate reading and writing: (1) delete a frame and have students infer what is missing and write a description for it, (2) delete the ending frame and have students infer and write an ending for the strip, and (3) remove some of the balloons of dialogue and have students infer appropriate dialogue.

B. Prepare short stories in which the sentences are out of order. Students are to rearrange the sentences in an order that makes sense.

Example: (1) The strange man walked to the door and knocked.
          (2) He was invited into the house.
          (3) The small dog barked when he heard the sound at the door.
          (4) The lady walked to the door and opened it.
          (5) The man hummed to himself as he waited for the door to open.

Variations of this can be used for students to predict what happens next, write an ending, and construct sequence maps.

STORY DETAIL

A. Mount a detailed picture on a piece of cardboard. In an accompanying envelope, provide students with three-by-five cards on which individual paragraphs about the picture have been typed and numbered. Students are to read the paragraphs and determine which one provides such things as the (1) most detailed description, (2) enough information for someone who knows a lot about what the picture represents, (3) not enough information to understand the picture, and so forth. This activity can help students realize the importance of their background knowledge in relation to reading for details.

B. Provide students with a series of paragraphs in each of which a nonsense phrase or two has been inserted. Students read each paragraph and detect the absurd phrase, which can help identify students who are too reader-based in their reading. Students can replace the nonsense phrase with one that makes sense for the content of the paragraph, which requires them to activate their own background knowledge in relation to the meaning of the text.

C. Have students read several paragraphs each describing a different character. Have students select the character they like best and list the words from both the text and their own experiences that describe the character. Students can read their list to the class to see if classmates can identify the character. Encourage students to discuss why they used certain words to describe the character(s).

CAUSE OR EFFECT

A. Prepare or select several paragraphs which describe several events that result in the occurrence of a final event. Ask the students to determine what happened to cause the final event. (This is an excellent introductory activity for story schema, and instruction can progress to longer paragraphs and stories.)

FIGURE 7.13
Suggested activities for reinforcing and applying comprehension strategies and skills
Source: From Edward C. Turner, "Improving Comprehension Practice and Application Activities" (University of Florida, Gainesville), by permission of the author.

Example: Charlie left for work late one morning because the alarm clock didn't ring. Being late caused him to hurry and he slipped on the sidewalk and twisted his ankle. At work he spilled his coffee on some very important papers and the boss was angry. Charlie was caught in the rain and his new shirt faded on his pants. When Charlie got home he kicked the cat.

Question: What happened that made Charlie kick the cat? Encourage students to discuss and elaborate upon their answers for the question. As students respond, their ideas can be charted on a story map or story frame, which can be used to introduce the concept of story structure.

B. Select or prepare several short paragraphs in which there is a final act. Ask the students to explain and discuss why the act occurred.

Example: Jack slipped out of the house and ran to his favorite climbing tree. As he neared the top, a branch broke and he fell to the ground.

Question: What happened to make Jack fall?

This activity can help students realize how to identify important literal text information in relation to an outcome. Ask the question or questions before students read to direct their attention to important text information.

C. Find or make up several reasoning statements for the students and have them give the answers. Discuss with the students how they reached a conclusion and any statements about which they disagree. Encourage them to discuss what would have to change in the given statements to make their answers not be true.

Example: If there are clouds in the sky it may rain;
If there are not clouds in the sky it will not rain.
It is raining;
therefore, there are clouds in the sky.

A variation of this is to have students develop their own reasoning statements and exchange them with classmates who construct an answer.

INFERENCE

A. Proverbs can be identified for which students determine the different meanings that can be inferred. The fact that proverbs are brief and to the point permits different interpretations, which relate directly to individuals' background knowledge.

Examples: Don't put off till tomorrow what you can do today.
A journey of a thousand miles begins with a single step.
He who hesitates is lost.
Procrastination is the thief of time.
Without starting you will arrive nowhere.
He who is not ready today, will be less so tomorrow.
Make hay while the sun shines.

Getting students to speculate about meaning can also be introduced and practiced with other smaller language units: quotations, nonfactual statements, and analogies.

Examples: It is the good reader that makes a good book.
Character is what you are when no one is watching.
You must have a good memory to be a successful liar.
People are lonely because they build walls instead of bridges.

FIGURE 7.13, *continued*

Students can discuss and interact about the various interpretations for such quotations.

Examples: Good people are more miserable than other people.

Students can discuss why they agree or disagree with such a statement. They can write their own nonfactual types of statements and present them to the class for discussion.

Examples: Shoe is to foot as glove is to _____ .

Glove is to hand as shoe is to _____ .

_____ is to foot as _____ is to hand.

Students can discuss their choices for completing the analogies, and the teacher can emphasize that differences are due to the inferences students make in relation to their background knowledge.

These activities with smaller units of language are not intended to replace the reading of text; their primary purpose is to introduce a concept or strategy (reflecting the instructional guideline that instruction proceed from simple to complex). As students discuss and provide reasons for their inferences, insights into reading are developed. Soon the students begin to see that in the final analysis these words take on the meaning that each reader gives them.

B. Begin reading a story to the class but stop before completing it. Provide students with several possible endings and discuss why each ending would or would not be an appropriate ending for the story.

C. Select or prepare several paragraphs for students. For each paragraph, provide three or four questions which are not answered directly in the text. Before reading the paragraphs provide students with brief information about the content and have them predict what it is about, what happens, where it takes place, and so forth. Record their predictions on the board and have them read the paragraphs. After reading a paragraph ask the questions you prepared and discuss students' predictions with their responses to the questions.

Example: Henry flinched as he touched his swollen eye. He was mad at himself for not being more careful yesterday during the team's first game. The first game of the season, and Henry stepped right in front of the first pitch.
(a) What happened to Henry?
(b) What game was he playing?
(c) What do you think happened after he got hit?

INFERRING CONCLUSIONS

A. Give each student a slip of paper on which is written a job title and the characteristics of that job. Each describes to the class the characteristics of that job.

Example: I get up early. I wear overalls. I drive a tractor. I milk cows.
Job: A farmer.

Guide students to discuss the key features of the description that were most important in identifying the job. Have them explain why some features are more important than others.

B. Have students participate in a class activity involving riddles. In these riddles only a few facts are given and students must ask yes or no questions to obtain information to infer an answer for the riddle.

Example: There lying in an open field with a pack on his back. The question is, What can you determine about this situation?

FIGURE 7.13, continued

INFERRING MAIN IDEA

A. Have students write short news articles about world, local, or class events and then select titles for the articles which would be appropriate for newspaper headlines. Students read their headlines to the class and the class predicts what the article is about. The author of the headline and article can provide feedback (warm or cold) about students' predictions of main idea.

B. Provide students with short stories and articles. Students read the text and then represent the important information with a summary drawing. The drawings are presented to the class and the students compare and contrast the drawings and discuss why there are variations. Discussion should focus on the fact that students used different background knowledge in reading and representing story information. Have students explain why they did or did not include certain information in their pictures.

MOOD

A. Provide students with large pieces of drawing paper and make available crayons. Play an instrumental record for three to five minutes while students listen. Turn off the record player and direct students to draw anything they feel like. At the end of an appropriate time, ask students to write how they feel on the back of their drawings. As students share their drawings with the class, the class tries to determine how the artist was feeling.

FACT AND OPINION

A. Students collect and bring to class several advertisements from magazines and newspapers. In small groups have students select advertisements to discuss with the class. Analyze the advertisements to determine their validity.

B. After discussing with students the kinds of articles found in newspapers, have them bring to class two or three of each type discussed. Have students distinguish between articles that describe actual events and those that are the writer's ideas.

   Example: Report on a local bank robbery versus editorial about litterbugs.

C. Show students a short film or part of a film in which an incident takes place (an automobile accident, bank robbery, scene in a supermarket, etc.) Ask students to write about what they have seen. Discuss what they have written and then replay the film looking for things they have written about. Compare their descriptions with what actually happens in the film.

AUTHOR PURPOSE

A. Provide students with several types of books and articles (comics, cookbooks, science texts, fiction, history). Have them classify the books and articles as to why they were written.

B. Divide students into several small groups. Working together, each group prepares a short story to be read to the class. After hearing the story, members of the class try to determine the reason why the group wrote the story.

C. Provide students with several sets of paragraphs. In each set there are two paragraphs with the same main theme. One of the paragraphs in the set is written so as to provide the reader with factual information about the theme and the other tells a humorous story about the theme. Have the students read the paragraphs in each set and tell why each was written.

   Example: The theme might be raccoons. One paragraph gives facts about the raccoon and the other tells of humorous incidents when a raccoon gets into a camper's tent.

FIGURE 7.13, continued

rect/explicit instruction using the features of teaching comprehension strategies is recommended.

☑ Summary

Teachers must provide varied opportunities for students to learn comprehension strategies and to apply these strategies in familiar and meaningful reading materials. For any instructional activity to teach reading comprehension, teachers must follow some important guidelines. Pearson and Fielding (1991) offer some essential guidelines for teachers:

1. The strategy must be instructionally relevant.
2. Instruction should proceed from simple to complex.
3. An analysis of instruction and transfer tasks should provide evidence of where breakdowns occur.
4. Direct/explicit instruction should explain when and how to use the strategies.
5. The teacher should use modeling, scaffolding, and feedback during class discussions and during or following independent work.
6. A variety of passages and authentic text should be used to facilitate students' assuming responsibility for application to new situations.
7. Monitoring procedures should be inherent parts of comprehension instruction.

The guidelines for comprehension instruction reflect what research has told us about quality reading instruction and development of reading strategies. These guidelines can be adapted to fit most instructional programs, including both basal and literature-based programs.

Instructional strategies can help students develop processes for comprehension. Teachers should combine these strategies, which include direct/explicit instruction, metacognition, story structure, questioning, activation of students' schemata, purposes for reading, and wide and varied opportunities to read books and authentic texts.

☑ Your Point of View

Discussion Questions

1. Why do you think that it is more effective to teach students reading strategies for comprehension than reading-comprehension skills?
2. Assume that you are going to introduce a unit on the water cycle to a group of third-grade students. What background knowledge might you want to activate before the students read an opening introduction on the water cycle?

Take a Stand For or Against

1. Reading comprehension cannot be taught.
2. Integrating reading and writing has only a minimal effect on students' reading comprehension because reading and writing are different processes.

Field-Based Assignments

1. Collect several samples of children's writing and analyze their writing in terms of story schemata or story grammar. Look for features that may vary such as setting, theme, resolution, and so forth. Discuss with the students variations in features of their writing, for example, why they may have a more elaborate theme for one piece of writing than another, or why the characters are described in more detail in one piece of writing versus another piece, or why one piece has clear and logical resolution in comparison with another piece of writing that doesn't.
2. Select two of the comprehension activities presented in this chapter and use them for instructing a small group of youngsters. Apply the guidelines for teacher-directed/explicit instruction in teaching the activities.

Portfolio Entry

Collect various samples of students' comprehension such as answers to questions, writing responses, and discussion performance about stories read. Reflect on how these samples provide you with different insights and understandings about students' comprehension of what they read.

Bibliography

Alexander, P. A., & Murphey, P. K. (1996). The research base for APA's learner-centered psychological principles. In N. Lambert & B. McCombs (Eds.), *Issues in school reform: A sampler of psychological perspectives on learner-centered schools* (in press).

Alvermann, D. E. (1991). The discussion web: A graphic aid for learning across the curriculum. *The Reading Teacher, 45,* 92–99.

Anderson, R. C. (1985). Role of the reader's schema in comprehension, learning, and memory. In R. Ruddell, M. Ruddell, & H. Singer (Eds.), *Theoretical models and processes of reading* (4th ed.) (pp. 469–482). Newark, DE: International Reading Association.

Angeletti, S. R. (1992). Encouraging students to think about what they read. *The Reading Teacher, 45,* 288–297.

Baumann, J. F., & Schmitt, M. C. (1986). The what, why, how, and when of comprehension instruction. *The Reading Teacher, 39,* 640–647.

Brown, A. L. (1988). *Interactive learning environments.* Paper presented at University of Illinois Conference on Reading Comprehension, Urbana, IL.

Cudd, E. T., & Roberts, L. L. (1987). Using story frames to develop reading comprehension in a 1st grade classroom. *The Reading Teacher, 41,* 75–79.

Dole, J. A., Brown, K. J., & Trathen, W. (1996). The effects of strategy instruction on the comprehension performance of at-risk students. *Reading Research Quarterly, 31,* 62–85.

Dole, J. A., Duffy, G. G., Roehler, L. R., & Pearson, P. D. (1991a). Moving from the old to the new: Research on reading comprehension instruction. *Review of Educational Research, 61,* 239–264.

Dole, J. A., Valencia, S. W., Greer, E. A., & Wardrop, J. L. (1991b). Effects of two types of prereading instruction on the comprehension of narrative and expository text. *Reading Research Quarterly, 26,* 142–159.

Duffy, G. G., & Roehler, L. R. (1991). Teachers' instructional actions. In R. Barr, M. Kamil, P. Mosenthal, & P. Pearson (Eds.), *Handbook of reading research (Vol. II)* (pp. 861–884). White Plains, NY: Longman.

Erwin, B. (1991). The relationship between background experience and students' comprehension: A cross cultural study. *Reading Psychology, 12,* 43–62.

Gordon, C. J., & Braun, C. (1983). Using story schema as an aid to reading and writing. *The Reading Teacher, 2,* 116–121.

Harris, T. L., & Hodges, R. E. (1995). *The literacy dictionary: The vocabulary of reading and writing.* Newark, DL: International Reading Association.

Herrmann, B. A. (1992). Teaching and assessing strategic reasoning: Dealing with the dilemmas. *The Reading Teacher, 45,* 428–437.

Hoyt, L. (1992). Many ways of knowing: Using drama, oral interactions, and the visual arts to enhance reading comprehension. *The Reading Teacher, 45,* 580–585.

McKeown, M. G., Beck, I. L., Sinatra, G. M., & Loxterman, J. A. (1992). The contribution of prior knowledge and coherent text to comprehension. *Reading Research Quarterly, 27,* 78–93.

Merkley, D. (1997). Modified Anticipation Guides. *The Reading Teacher, 50,* 365–368.

Norton, D. E. (1994). *Through the eyes of a child* (4th ed.). Upper Saddle River, NJ: Merrill/Prentice Hall.

Norton, D. E. (1996). *The effective teaching of language arts* (5th ed.). Upper Saddle River, NJ: Merrill/Prentice Hall.

Olson, M. W. (1984). A dash of story grammar and . . . Presto! A book report. *The Reading Teacher, 37,* 458–461.

Pearson, P. D., & Fielding, L. (1991). Comprehension instruction. In R. Barr, M. Kamil, P. Mosenthal, & P. Pearson (Eds.), *Handbook of reading research (Vol. II)* (pp. 815–860). White Plains, NY: Longman.

Raphael, T. (1984). Teaching learners about sources of information for answering comprehension questions. *Journal of Reading, 28,* 303–311.

Raphael, T., (1986). Teaching question-answer relationships, revisited. *The Reading Teacher, 39,* 516–522.

Reynolds, R., Taylor, M., Steffenson, M. A., Shirey, L. L., & Anderson, R. C. (1981). *Cultural schemata and reading comprehension.* Urbana, IL: University of Illinois, Center for the Study of Reading, Technical Report No. 201.

Rosenshine, B., & Meister, C. (1994). Reciprocal Teaching: A Review of the Research. *Review of Educational Research, 64,* 479–530.

Rumelhart, D. E. (1984). Understanding understanding. In J. Flood (Ed.), *Understanding reading comprehension* (pp. 86–94). Newark, DE: International Reading Association.

Rupley, W. H., & Willson, V. L. (1996). Content domain and word knowledge: Relationship to comprehension of narrative and expository text. *Reading and Writing: An Interdisciplinary Journal, 8,* 419–432.

Rupley, W. H., & Willson, V. L. (in press). The relationship of reading comprehension to components of word recognition: Support for developmental shifts. *Journal of Research and Development in Education.*

Rupley, W. H., & Blair, T. R. (1988). *Teaching reading: Diagnosis, direct instruction, and practice.* (2nd ed.), Upper Saddle River, NJ: Merrill/Prentice Hall.

Schmidt, M. C., & Baumann, J. F. (1986). How to incorporate comprehension monitoring strategies into basal reader instruction. *The Reading Teacher, 40,* 28–31.

Smagorinsky, P., & Smith, M. W. (1992). The nature of knowledge in composition and literacy understanding: The question of specificity. *Review of Educational Research, 62,* 279–306.

Steffensen, M. S., Joag-Dev, C., & Anderson, R. C. (1979). A cross-cultural perspective on reading comprehension. *Reading Research Quarterly, 15,* 10–29.

Taylor, B., Harris, L. A., & Pearson, P. D. (1995). *Reading difficulties: Instruction and assessment.* (2nd ed.). New York: Random House.

Tierney, R., & Pearson, P. D. (1985). Learning to learn from text: A framework for improving classroom practices. In R. Ruddell, M. Ruddell, & H. Singer (Eds.), *Theoretical models and processes of reading* (4th ed.) (pp. 496–513). Newark, DE: International Reading Association.

Young, T. A., & Daines, D. (1992). Students' predictive questions and teachers' prequestions about expository text in grades K-5. *Reading Psychology, 13,* 291–308.

PART III

Aa Bb Cc Dd Ee Ff Gg Hh Ii Jj Kk Ll Mm

Developing Literacy and Teaching Reading

Chapters

o Pp Qq Rr Ss Tt Uu Vv Ww Xx Yy Zz

Overview

Designing and implementing appropriate literacy opportunities based on students' needs is a tall order for classroom teachers. If all literacy instruction could be the same for all students in each grade, teaching would be easy. The complexity of teaching reading becomes obvious to teachers when they try to differentiate their instruction according to student needs. This part of the text focuses on topics essential for successful elementary school literacy programs. The chapters in this part cover various instructional approaches, procedures, and materials for teaching reading; content-area reading; assessment of students' literacy abilities; classroom management and organization; and the provision of appropriate literacy instruction for children with diverse abilities. Our growing understanding of literacy development and of effective teaching have increased our appreciation of the subtleties and complexities in the learning process. The content in these chapters will furnish important information to help you provide a comprehensive and balanced literacy approach for your students.

Integrating Principles of Teaching Reading

The following principles, presented in earlier chapters, will be reinforced in this part:

- Reading and writing are interrelated and interactive developmental processes, and literacy instruction should capitalize on this relationship.

- Teachers must recognize the enormous diversity in students, plan appropriate instruction for a wide range of individual differences in the classroom, and believe all students can and will be successful in literacy learning.
- Instruction should lead children to understand that reading is a meaningful, active, and strategic process.
- Successful reading comprehension is dependent upon providing large amounts of classroom time for text reading and multiple opportunities for students to interact with their peers and teachers about what they are reading.
- Teachers must strive for a balanced literacy program to teach all students to read and write.
- The use of quality literature should be an integral part of literacy instruction throughout the entire school curriculum.
- Literacy instruction needs to be an integral component in all content areas.
- Teachers need to foster students' abilities to reason and critically evaluate written ideas.
- Proper literacy instruction depends on the ongoing assessment of each student's reading strengths and weaknesses.
- Motivation contributes to the development of literacy and is fostered through meaningful instructional activities.
- Teachers must be able to create, manage, and maintain an environment conducive to learning, and must forge partnerships with the home and community to promote reading growth.
- The key to successful literacy instruction is the teacher.

CHAPTER 8

Instructional Procedures
for Teaching Literacy

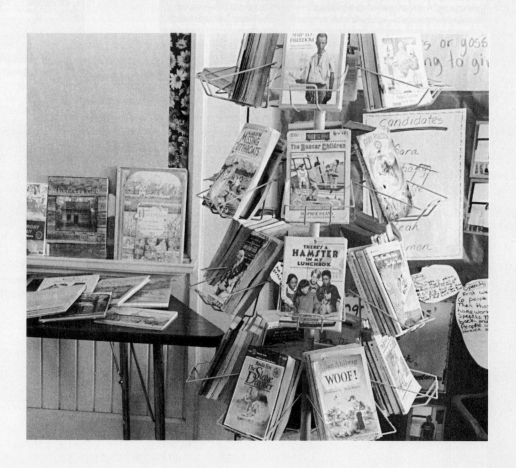

Chapter Outline

For the Reader

Because children are different in a multitude of ways, there has never been and never will be one single literacy approach that succeeds equally with all children. Effective teachers know there are many possible ways to teach reading successfully and strive to combine the best of different approaches to match their instruction to meet their student's learning needs. Effective teachers ask themselves the question "How can I use the best of various approaches to help my students become strategic readers?" Chapter 4 discussed emergent literacy and implementation of the whole-language philosophy. This chapter continues the discussion of how students learn literacy. Basal reader materials are popular and are fully explained in this chapter. Supplemental materials and instructional procedures for teaching literacy also are presented in this chapter as well as in Chapters 6, 7, and 13.

Key Ideas

- The successful use of materials and instructional procedures depends on the classroom teacher.
- Effective teachers use a combination of reading approaches to provide a balanced program to meet the needs of their students.
- Quality literature and real-life literacy experiences should be incorporated into the literacy program at all levels.

Literacy Instruction

A discussion of teaching literacy inevitably turns to how teachers teach. The materials and instructional procedures used to teach literacy have been the subjects of a large number of research studies, debates, and discussion. Unfortunately, research comparing reading materials and instruction has been inconclusive. No single approach to teaching literacy works best for all students. In a sense, no set of materials or instructional procedures is foolproof. By knowing when to modify or use different materials and instructional procedures to address students' needs, the teacher is the major factor in determining the success of a literacy program.

The following materials and instructional procedures for teaching literacy are discussed in this text: (1) basal readers, (2) literature-based programs, (3) the whole-language philosophy, and (4) individualized reading. Different materials and instructional procedures for teaching literacy are based on different philosophies regarding how children learn and different interpretations of literacy processes. However, all philosophies overlap each other to a certain degree, borrowing various procedures, strategies, and materials. Because of its unique relationship to the area of emergent literacy, the whole-language philosophy and its implementation were discussed in Chapter 4. Basal readers and literature-based procedures are by far the most popular materials used in U.S. schools. This chapter focuses on the basal reader in detail. Chapter 9 is devoted entirely to literature-based instruction, and Chapter 12 presents individualized reading. While each of these four is discussed separately, it must be emphasized that this treatment is for the sake of presentation. Effective reading teachers integrate features associated with different philosophies and materials to match the needs of their students.

Teachers also can use numerous beneficial supplemental materials and instructional procedures to teach literacy (Thompson, 1991). These procedures are supplemental in the sense that they are usually used in conjunction with other materials and procedures. Two widespread supplemental reading approaches are the language-experience approach and computer approaches. The language-experience approach and computers are discussed in this chapter because of their close relationship to and use with basal reader materials. Figure 8.1 lists some of the major features and assumptions associated with materials and instructional procedures for teaching literacy.

Basal Readers

Elementary schools rely heavily on basal reader programs. As stated in *Becoming a Nation of Readers* (Anderson, Hiebert, Scott, & Wilkinson, 1985), "The observation that basal programs 'drive' reading instruction is not to be taken lightly. These programs strongly influence how reading is taught in American schools and what students read" (p. 35). Effective teachers make good use of reading materials, especially the basal reader.

MATERIALS/INSTRUCTIONAL PROCEDURES	ASSUMPTIONS AND CHARACTERISTICS
1. Basal reader materials	■ Students learn best with an eclectic method.
	■ Includes provisions for teaching word identification, word meanings, comprehension, study skills, and literature appreciation.
2. Literature-based reading materials	■ Students learn best with literature as the main vehicle for reading instruction.
	■ Integrates reading skills with literature selections.
3. Whole-language philosophy	■ Instruction focuses on developing both writing and reading in a natural way.
	■ Emphasizes whole-text writing and reading.
4. Individualized reading	■ Students learn best when they select their own books to read, pace themselves in reading a book or learning a skill, and receive specific skill or strategy instruction based on individual need.
	■ Emphasizes interest in reading and motivation to read on one's own with a variety of materials.
5. Language experience	■ Students learn best through reading materials based on their own language and experiences.
6. Computer	■ Based on operant conditioning principles, students will respond favorably to step-by-step sequential presentation of information.

FIGURE 8.1
Assumptions and characteristics of materials and procedures
for teaching literacy

■ Design and Content

Each basal reader program differs in its rationale, sequence of skills and strategies, story content, instructional recommendations, and supplemental materials. However, most basals set meaning as the paramount goal from the outset. Also, as mentioned in Chapter 1, most basals cover the major content strands of the elementary school reading curriculum—decoding, comprehension, word meanings, reading-study skills, literature, and independent reading—in their own particular way.

Through a series of books of increasing difficulty (a separate book for each level), **basal readers** are designed to bring children to a high degree of reading proficiency. Each level functions as a prerequisite for success at the next level. The focus of basal programs is to develop the reader's competence in vocabulary, word identification, word meanings, comprehension, and study skills through fine literature.

Literature Works by Silver Burdett Ginn is a basal reader series for grades K–6. This is a literature-driven program that provides an integrated approach to reading and language arts. This basal reader program covers all the major content strands in the elementary school curriculum and the major program areas of a complete reading program, as outlined in Chapter 1. All instruction and classroom activities focus on children's literature (both fiction and nonfiction) and are organized around themes geared directly to students' interests. In addition to the student anthologies entitled "Collections" for grades 1–6 and their corresponding teacher's editions, there are "Theme Trade Books" for grades 1–6 that further understanding of each theme, "Readables" for grades K–12 that are 123 short, high-interest books, "Read Aloud Big Books" for grades 1–2, "Big and Little Shared Books" for grades K–1, and "Theme Magazines" for grades 3–6 that present literature in a new format to motivate reluctant readers. Practice materials in the program include additional support in phonics and comprehension skills and strategies; vocabulary; spelling instruction; language arts; English language support activities; and a vast array of technology resources including a CD-ROM library of 17 interactive storybooks; a CD-ROM program for phonics, structural analysis, and vocabulary; story tapes; and videotapes. Each basal has its own assessment program, and *Literature Works* has a multitude of assessment tools including portfolios and tools for process-oriented reading and language arts skills, phonics, writing, and initial placement assessment, in addition to an Informal Reading Inventory (IRI) and kindergarten assessment.

To promote strategic reading through fine literature, the teacher's edition provides a lesson plan for each story that models our understanding of the constructive nature of reading, involving prereading, during-reading and postreading development. The teaching of each story in this basal program is presented in a three-step process involving "Reading and Responding," "Literature-based Instruction," and "Integrated Curriculum." Figure 8.2, which is found in pages 312–313, summarizes this lesson plan format and its procedures. It is important to remember that the main vehicle to teach students to read is the individual story (this is true for whatever literacy approach you may use). The effective implementation of teaching a story is dependent upon the teacher's expertise in helping students interact with text in a meaningful way. The directed reading lesson is described in detail in Figure 8.2, and we encourage you to study this figure as an illustration of this important process.

All basal programs include a tremendous number of materials for both teacher and students. For teachers, programs may include the following:

- a teacher's edition for each level, giving detailed lesson plans for each story in the student's book; a complete listing of strategies and skills for developing reading, writing, listening, and speaking processes at each level; and assessment procedures
- detailed descriptions of supplemental literary libraries and recommendations for literacy development in various content areas
- various instructional supplements for application of strategies and skills

- prepared pictures of characters, teaching charts, posters, transparencies, and word cards for specific stories
- various films, filmstrips, recordings, videos, videodiscs, audiocasettes, compact discs, and CD-ROM storybooks and practice activities
- teacher's editions of student workbooks
- a management system, including an informal reading inventory or placement test, criterion-referenced pretests and posttests for each level, phonic inventories, alternative assessments for both reading and writing, portfolio assessment, and various record-keeping devices

For students, basal programs may include the following:

- a student book for each level
- a workbook for each level
- literature libraries including high-interest/low-vocabulary paperback books
- readiness posters and big books
- writing portfolios
- computer software programs
- supplemental games and activities to practice the skills and strategies being taught

Advantages of Basal Series

Although the abundance of materials in basal programs can be overwhelming, the crucial point to remember is that they do not guarantee an exciting and worthwhile program. An effective teacher of reading must orchestrate the materials based on learner needs. Some of the advantages of using a basal series include the following:

- Basal readers contain an anthology of different genres of literature.
- Books are sequenced in increasing difficulty to provide systematic instruction from the emergent literacy phase through the upper elementary grades.
- Graded materials permit teacher flexibility in dealing with individual differences.
- Teacher guides are available for each book or level. These provide suggestions for a step-by-step teaching program.
- If used properly, basal reader series deal with all phases of the reading program, guarding against overemphasis of some aspects and neglect of others.
- Basal series introduce practice of new skills and strategies in a logical sequence.
- Review is provided.
- Vocabulary is controlled to prevent frustration for beginning readers.
- Prepared materials allow teachers to save time.
- Formal and informal assessments that the series provides reflect the materials that teachers will use.

Quality literature should be an integral part of the literacy program.

■ Basal programs provide an overall management system for coordinating the elementary school reading program.

Wiggins (1994) cites further advantages of basal programs:

First, most classroom teachers are comfortable with the basal reader format. . . . Second, a basal program provides consistency as students move from one grade level to the next. . . . Third, a basal reading series provides specific activities designed to teach, reteach, and reinforce the requisite skills and strategies, as well as a consistent and concrete means by which to monitor the success of instruction. (p. 453)

■ Today's Newer Basals

The last two decades have seen dramatic changes in how we view and teach the reading process in the classroom. With the rise in interest in the study of comprehension, a shift in attention to how we process and retrieve information with corresponding comprehension strategies has taken center stage. This is in contrast to teaching techniques focusing on the isolated instruction of both word identification and comprehension skills. A second change has occurred with more serious attempts at the merging of the teaching of reading with the other language arts, especially the renewed close relationship between reading and writing. A third major change has been the growing emphasis on fine literature in all literacy approaches. Inclusion of this essential element has spurred a more holistic, integrated approach to the teaching of the language processes.

Have the newer basal programs changed to reflect these dramatic shifts in the teaching of literacy? After years of being criticized for not changing significant aspects of their programs, recent research by the National Reading Research Center (McCarthey & Hoffman, 1995) concluded that the newer basals are indeed different from the old ones, reflecting major changes in the literacy field. The researchers examined both the old and new student texts and teacher's manuals of five current basal programs at the first grade level. The researchers' conclusions follow:

> In summary, our analysis suggests that at the first-grade level the new pupil texts were different from the old: They offered reduced vocabulary control, minimal adaptations, more diversity of genre, more engaging literary quality, more predictable text, and increased decoding demands.
>
> The newer teacher's editions were different from the old in underlying instructional design, replacing a directed reading model with a shared reading model. Vocabulary was introduced more in the context of the stories in the new teacher's editions; fewer comprehension questions were offered, with a greater attempt to include more higher-level questions. The high degree of focus on skills and isolated skills instruction had decreased from the old to the new. Although skills were still prevalent, they tended to be slightly more integrated. Assessment tools had been broadened considerably from a testing-only mentality to a portfolio approach. The tone of the manuals was less prescriptive than the old, moving in the direction of a "teacher-as decision-maker" model. (p. 73)

Most basals today feature the following characteristics:

- Integrated language arts are emphasized not only during reading instruction but also in the content areas.
- Quality literature is viewed as the driving force in the elementary school reading program, with thematic units designed to facilitate student learning and appreciation.
- Reading and writing are linked specifically as mutually supportive processes.
- Appealing, high-quality literature is carefully selected for both the regular basal readers and supplemental libraries.
- Quality literature is emphasized for independent or recreational reading.
- Multicultural focus is increased.
- Lesson recommendations reflect the idea that reading is an interactive, constructive, and strategic process. Lessons give explicit attention to teaching decoding skills and strategies and comprehension strategies. Instruction includes use of authentic literature and prior knowledge in story preparation. Thinking and problem-solving abilities are taught through literature.
- Cooperative and partner grouping is encouraged.
- Assessment is viewed as ongoing and is linked directly to instruction using a variety of informal and formal measures.
- A real partnership is fostered between the school's elementary reading program and the home.

Economy of teacher time is a major factor in the widespread use of basal series. No teacher would ever have the time to match the meticulous planning that goes into a good basal series. Prepared materials leave teachers more time to develop supplementary exercises as needed. Teachers still must prepare these exercises for certain students, because the basal program cannot meet all individual needs; however, preparing supplementary lessons for a few is easier than building the entire program.

■ Teacher's Editions

One of the advantages of using a good basal series is the teacher's edition. These editions contain a variety of instructional procedures, lesson plans, and rationales for using certain materials and instructional procedures. Beginning teachers can benefit from becoming familiar with the rationales and concrete suggestions that basal readers contain. Experienced teachers might find the detail of these manuals a bit tedious, but they know that they can take what is offered and adapt it in light of their own experience and their students' learning needs. A teacher's edition is beneficial only if teachers use it properly, however. Teachers should not be awed by these impressive volumes, nor should they follow them word for word—that is not teaching. Teachers should know their students' learning needs better than any teacher's guide. Remember, basal materials work best for a knowledgeable, flexible teacher. Use the suggestions when they match your students' learning needs, and supplement and adapt suggestions at all other times. Teachers should view manuals as a compilation of suggestions that they can use, modify, or discard (Durkin, 1993).

■ Workbooks

Basal reader series generally contain workbook supplements. The educational value of using workbooks has been debated for years. It is true that workbook exercises can deteriorate into nothing more than busy work, yet, with proper, teacher-directed instruction, students can use workbooks for meaningful practice.

Properly used, workbooks can have considerable educational value. Because they deal with a wide variety of skills, some exercises will likely provide needed and meaningful practice in essential literacy skill areas. Workbooks also can serve as ongoing diagnostic instruments, because they identify individuals who do not understand a particular reading strategy or skill. A study of miscues will show the alert teacher where to provide further instruction. Workbook exercises are brief—usually one page—which makes them especially appealing to students with short attention spans.

Workbooks, like all other instructional media, are neither all good nor all bad. How the teacher uses workbooks determines whether they contribute to a quality instructional program. Osborn (1984) identified important guidelines for workbook tasks. Carefully consider these guidelines for using workbooks and worksheets that accompany basal reading series:

- ■ Workbook activities should match the instruction and learning taking place in the unit or lesson.

- Some workbook tasks should provide systematic, cumulative, and meaningful review of what students have been taught.
- Workbooks should match the most important learning taking place in the reading program. Activities of lesser importance should be voluntary.
- Workbooks should provide relevant tasks for students in need of extra practice.
- Both the vocabulary and concept features of workbook tasks should be within students' experiential and conceptual backgrounds and should relate to the rest of the program.
- The language features of a workbook page should be consistent with those in the instructional lesson and the rest of the workbook.
- Instructions for completion of a workbook activity should be clear and easy to follow. Teachers should direct one or two practice examples to ensure that students understand the tasks.
- Page layout should combine attractiveness and utility.
- Content should be sufficient to ensure that students are learning and not just being exposed to something.
- Discrimination activities should follow a sufficient number of tasks to provide practice in the components of the discriminations.
- Content of workbook activities should be accurate and precise to ensure that it presents neither incorrect information nor incorrect generalizations.
- Some workbook tasks should be fun.
- The manner in which students respond should be consistent from workbook task to workbook task.
- Response modes should match normal reading and writing as closely as possible.
- Cute and nonfunctional workbook activities, which may be time consuming (i.e., busy work), should be avoided.
- Workbook assignments should include teacher discussions about their purposes and their relationships to reading.

■ Directed Reading Activities

An integral part of the teacher's edition of a basal reader is a systematic description of how to teach a reading and/or writing lesson. The ultimate purpose of each lesson in a basal reader is to teach the strategies needed to read and write independently, comprehending and learning from both. Thus, each lesson is a vehicle for increasing youngsters' literacy abilities. The following set of suggested procedures is commonly referred to as a **directed reading activity** (DRA). The DRA provides a framework for systematic and sequential growth of reading and language abilities. Although each basal series has its own concept of the DRA, most contain the following components:

- readiness, including prior knowledge, previewing, key vocabulary and concepts, purpose-setting questions (either teacher set or student set, or both), and student predictions about the content of the selection

Prereading experiences with live objects are excellent motivators in preparing to read a story.

- silent reading
- comprehension development
- purposeful oral reading
- skill and strategy development, including word identification or decoding, comprehension, study, and vocabulary
- enrichment, including creative assignments related to the story

Similar in nature to the DRA is the **directed reading-thinking activity** (DRTA) (Stauffer, 1975). The three overall stages of the DRTA are readiness, active reading, and reaction to the story. This instructional procedure focuses on reading as a thinking process. Students are encouraged to predict; form a purpose for reading; read to verify, reject, or modify that purpose; then continue that process.

There is no set way to teach a reading lesson. Modern basal reader programs follow a similar instructional format to directed-reading and directed reading-thinking activities focusing on teaching strategies before, during, and after reading. Teacher's manual recommendations may be modified, expanded, deleted, or reordered according to students' existing abilities. Reflecting our growing knowledge of the interactive and constructive nature of reading comprehension, newer basals are improving upon the traditional DRA or DRTA format by arranging directed reading lessons into a three-step process. As shown in Figures 8.2 and 8.3, the new Silver Burdett Ginn directed reading lesson uses a three-step process including "Reading and Responding," "Literature-based Instruction," and "Integrated Curriculum." Our summary view of the steps in teaching a story are step 1, "Prereading," step 2, "Postreading Comprehension Discussion," and step 3, "Instruction and Follow-up Activities." The components of each step are as follows:

Prereading

Building background knowledge

Developing interest in the story and motivation to read by relating the story

Developing new vocabulary and concepts

Predicting what will happen

Setting purposes to read the story

Postreading comprehension discussion

Answering purpose-setting questions

Discussing outcomes of prereading

Summarizing the story, making connections between new and old understandings

Answering questions on different cognitive levels to develop an understanding of the story

Reflecting on the ideas presented with classmates and teacher

Rereading portions of the story orally, having a specific purpose in mind

Instruction and follow-up activities

Teaching direct instruction lessons on specific comprehension and decoding skills and strategies related to the story

Practicing new vocabulary, comprehension, and decoding abilities in a variety of formats and grouping plans

Combining reading and writing on topics related to the story

Developing other language arts abilities such as spelling and grammar

Completing creative literature activities related to the story

Developing skills and strategies to be utilized in content or cross-curricular areas

The teacher acts as the key to an effective DRA by selecting activities appropriate to students' needs. No teacher's manual can make reading meaningful and enjoyable. A thinking teacher who views the lesson plans in a manual as guides and not mandates is more likely to provide effective reading instruction.

Each lesson is divided into three parts:
1. **Reading and Responding**
2. **Literature-Based Instruction**
3. **Integrated Curriculum**

Reading and Responding

PART 1

In **Reading and Responding** a variety of activities elicit your students' prior knowledge and ensure their understanding of key vocabulary, concepts, skills, and strategies:

- **Building Background** focuses on engaging students' interest and ensuring their comprehension. The background information helps you focus on important selection-related concepts and introduces relevant cross-curricular connections.

- **Developing Vocabulary** provides opportunities for learning key vocabulary and concepts, as well as a Spelling and Phonics Preview for each theme at Grades 1-3.

- Highlighted **Reading Strategy** boxes reinforce strategic reading. They appear at key points in the selection pages of the Teacher's Guide.

- A **Meeting Individual Needs** section on each selection support page provides ideas for Comprehension Support, English Language Support, Challenge activities, and support for Spanish-speaking Students.

In **Reading and Responding** "point-of-use" notes help you immediately locate:

- Literature-based reading, language, and literature skills

- Support for fostering an appreciation of cultural and linguistic diversity

- Making connections across selections and to the themes.

Reader Response Groups

Have students form groups and discuss the pictures in their personal journals. Spark discussion with the following prompts.

- Why do you like the animal you drew?
- Why should the animal be saved?
- In w... ...animal be helped?

Personal Response

Have students record their responses to the animals in the article in their personal journals. They may want to respond to these questions.

- How does the article make you feel about endangered and extinct animals?
- Which animal(s) do you want to help the most?
- Which is the best home for endangered animals—a zoo, a sanctuary, or the wild?

Have the students express themselves visually as well as verbally. Suggest that they draw one of the endangered animals in the habitat in which it belongs. They can paste their drawing into their personal journal.

Responding provides a variety of ways to encourage students to respond to the literature through listening, speaking, and writing activities.

- Personal Responses

- Reader Response groups

- Creative and Critical Responses

There are also suggestions for encouraging students to make connections to the theme and across selections.

M17

FIGURE 8.2
Three-step process for a directed reading lesson from Literature Works, Silver Burdett Ginn
Source: From "The Lesson," **Teacher's Guide for Grade 4, vol. 1, Literature Works,** (1996), pp. M17–M18. Reprinted with permission of Silver Burdett Ginn.

Literature-Based Instruction

Literature-Based Instruction teaches students critical comprehension, literature, word study (phonics, structural analysis, vocabulary), and study skills. It includes:

- Skills and strategies that increase understanding of the selection

- Guided practice and independent applications

- Reteaching opportunities at "point-of-use"

- Activities and technology resources at Grades K-2, such as the Story Tapes (audio recordings of the selections) and Word Power (interactive CD-ROM computer program)

 Integrated Curriculum

Literature Works provides a thoroughly integrated approach to teaching the language arts. In addition, it offers numerous opportunities to make connections to the content areas. Its integrated approach includes:

- **Workshops** in writing, grammar, usage, mechanics, listening, speaking, and viewing. These workshops tie language arts instruction to the literature and build toward the theme Writing Process activity. Writing modes taught are narrative, expository, persuasive, and descriptive writing.

- **Spelling lessons** directly tied to phonics and structural analysis learning. A separate practice book, *Spelling Source: An Integrated Approach to Spelling* is also provided.

- **Cross-curricular Connections** to standard grade-level curricular goals in Mathematics, Science, Social Studies, as well as Art, Drama, Health, and Music.

M18

FIGURE 8.2, continued

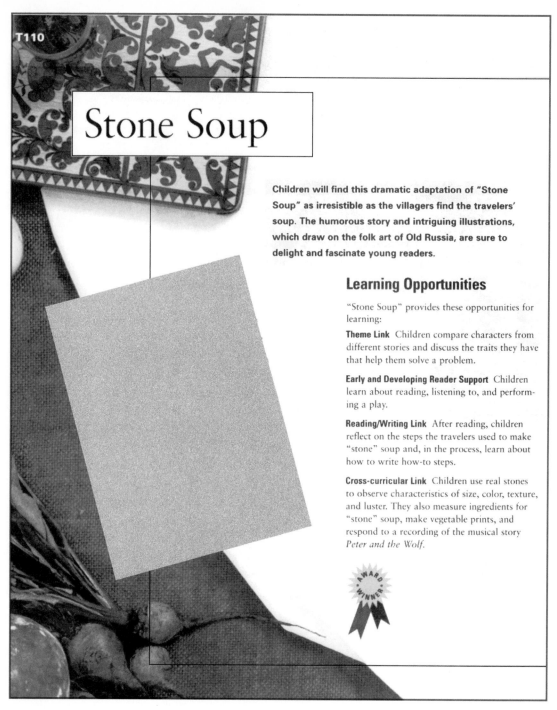

Stone Soup

Children will find this dramatic adaptation of "Stone Soup" as irresistible as the villagers find the travelers' soup. The humorous story and intriguing illustrations, which draw on the folk art of Old Russia, are sure to delight and fascinate young readers.

Learning Opportunities

"Stone Soup" provides these opportunities for learning:

Theme Link Children compare characters from different stories and discuss the traits they have that help them solve a problem.

Early and Developing Reader Support Children learn about reading, listening to, and performing a play.

Reading/Writing Link After reading, children reflect on the steps the travelers used to make "stone" soup and, in the process, learn about how to write how-to steps.

Cross-curricular Link Children use real stones to observe characteristics of size, color, texture, and luster. They also measure ingredients for "stone" soup, make vegetable prints, and respond to a recording of the musical story *Peter and the Wolf*.

FIGURE 8.3
**Directed reading lesson for "Stone Soup" from Literature Works,
Silver Burdett Ginn**
Source: From "Stone Soup," **Teacher's Guide for Tell Me a Story,
Literature Works Program 1996–1997,** pp. T110–139. Reprinted
with permission of Silver Burdett & Ginn.

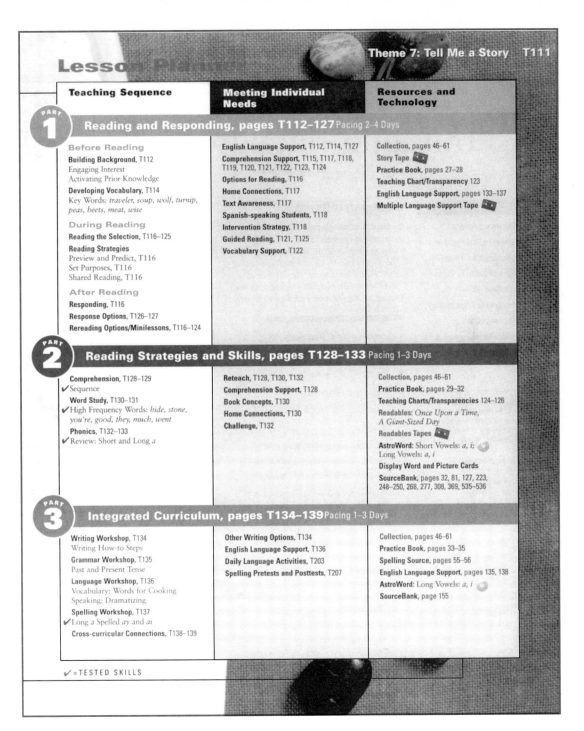

Lesson Plan

Teaching Sequence	Meeting Individual Needs	Resources and Technology

PART 1 — Reading and Responding, pages T112–127 Pacing 2–4 Days

Teaching Sequence	Meeting Individual Needs	Resources and Technology
Before Reading **Building Background**, T112 Engaging Interest Activating Prior Knowledge **Developing Vocabulary**, T114 Key Words: *traveler, soup, wolf, turnip, peas, beets, meat, wise* **During Reading** **Reading the Selection**, T116–125 **Reading Strategies** Preview and Predict, T116 Set Purposes, T116 Shared Reading, T116 **After Reading** **Responding**, T116 **Response Options**, T126–127 **Rereading Options/Minilessons**, T116–124	English Language Support, T112, T114, T127 Comprehension Support, T115, T117, T118, T119, T120, T121, T122, T123, T124 Options for Reading, T116 Home Connections, T117 Text Awareness, T117 Spanish-speaking Students, T118 Intervention Strategy, T118 Guided Reading, T121, T125 Vocabulary Support, T122	Collection, pages 46–61 Story Tape Practice Book, pages 27–28 Teaching Chart/Transparency 123 English Language Support, pages 133–137 Multiple Language Support Tape

PART 2 — Reading Strategies and Skills, pages T128–133 Pacing 1–3 Days

Teaching Sequence	Meeting Individual Needs	Resources and Technology
Comprehension, T128–129 ✓ Sequence **Word Study**, T130–131 ✓ High Frequency Words: *hide, stone, you're, good, they, much, went* **Phonics**, T132–133 ✓ Review: Short and Long *a*	Reteach, T128, T130, T132 Comprehension Support, T128 Book Concepts, T130 Home Connections, T130 Challenge, T132	Collection, pages 46–61 Practice Book, pages 29–32 Teaching Charts/Transparencies 124–126 Readables: *Once Upon a Time, A Giant-Sized Day* Readables Tapes AstroWord: Short Vowels: *a, i;* Long Vowels: *a, i* Display Word and Picture Cards SourceBank, pages 32, 81, 127, 223, 248–250, 268, 277, 308, 369, 535–536

PART 3 — Integrated Curriculum, pages T134–139 Pacing 1–3 Days

Teaching Sequence	Meeting Individual Needs	Resources and Technology
Writing Workshop, T134 Writing How-to Steps **Grammar Workshop**, T135 Past and Present Tense **Language Workshop**, T136 Vocabulary: Words for Cooking Speaking: Dramatizing **Spelling Workshop**, T137 ✓ Long *a* Spelled *ay* and *ai* **Cross-curricular Connections**, T138–139	Other Writing Options, T134 English Language Support, T136 Daily Language Activities, T203 Spelling Pretests and Posttests, T207	Collection, pages 46–61 Practice Book, pages 33–35 Spelling Source, pages 55–56 English Language Support, pages 135, 138 AstroWord: Long Vowels: *a, i* SourceBank, page 155

✓ = TESTED SKILLS

FIGURE 8.3, continued

Building Background

 SELECTION SUMMARY

Three travelers enter a Russian village, hoping for food and a place to sleep. But the villagers hide their scarce supplies. When the clever travelers set about making "stone soup," however, the villagers add meat and vegetables.

ESL **English Language Support** The following materials are available for children who need additional help in preparing to read the selection:
• English Language Support, pp. 133, 134, and 136
• Multiple Language Support Tapes for *Stone Soup*

Engaging Interest

Begin with a Role-play Ask children to pretend that three tired, hungry travelers have come to town. Ask: *What food would you offer the travelers?* Record responses on a chart, eliciting the word *soup*. Then have three volunteers dramatize entering town and asking for food and a place to sleep.

Food for the Travelers

Tia	peanut butter
Jorge	bananas
Alan	spaghetti
Lisa	hot soup

Traveler 1: *I would like some food.*
Traveler 2: *May I have a place to sleep?*
Traveler 3: *Where can I eat dinner?*

Encourage children to respond to the "travelers," using their ideas from the chart.

Activating Prior Knowledge

Discuss Soup Tell children that they will be reading a play about three travelers who come to a Russian village and make stone soup. Engage children in a discussion about different ways that people prepare soup—buying it in a can at the store or making it from scratch by cooking vegetables, and often meat, in liquid.

Encourage children to name some soups they like. Write these in a column on chart paper. Children can write their names on index cards and then place them in the row that names their favorite soup.

Our Favorite Soups

Alphabet	Tia	Len	Maria	Down
Chicken	Carol	Danny	Lee	
Vegetable	Bob	Erica		
Wonton	Arun	Kim	Ray	Addy

For Your Information

Russia, the country where this version of "Stone Soup" takes place, is the world's largest country, about twice the size of the United States. At the time of the play, most Russians lived in small villages. Villages were far apart, and a visit from travelers was a rare event. Villagers provided everything for themselves. They built their houses, hunted and fished, grew vegetables, baked bread, and made clothing.

The "stone soup" in this folk tale resembles borscht, a traditional soup made with beets, which comes from Russia. There are many ways to make borscht. Some use only vegetables; others, like the soup in the play, use vegetables and meat. In hot weather, borscht is often served cold with a spoonful of sour cream on top.

FIGURE 8.3, continued

─┤ **Building Background continued** ├─

Developing Vocabulary

Discuss the Word *Traveler* Write *traveler* on the board. Ask: *What would it be like to travel to a strange town? How might a traveler find food or a place to stay?*

Introduce Food Words Draw a soup pot on the chalkboard. Then ask children to name some foods used to make soup. You can record ideas in a word web, adding *peas, meat, turnip,* and *beets,* if children don't mention them.

Discuss the Word *Wolf* Have children find the entry for *wolf* in their Collection glossary (page 223). Point out that wolves are related to dogs. At the time of "Stone Soup," wolves often lived near villages like the one in the story, and people were afraid of them.

Discuss the Word *Wise* Write *wise* on the board. Ask: *Why is it wise to wear boots in the snow? Why is it wise to brush your teeth before bedtime?* Then have children tell things they do that are wise.

Hands-on Activity Children can work together to create an "I'm Wise to Eat Vegetables" chart, using cutouts from grocery circulars and food magazines.

Children can think about healthy foods as they create a vegetable chart.

Meeting Individual Needs

 English Language Support

Building Fluency For second language speakers in your class, you might bring in pictures of the key food words from "Stone Soup" and help them connect familiar words to the English equivalent.

English	Spanish	Chinese	Russian
soup	la sopa	tang	soup
turnip	el nabo	luobo	ryepa
beets	las remolachas	hong luobo	svyokla
peas	los guisantes	rou	gorokhi
meat	la carne	zai jian	myasa

FIGURE 8.3, *continued*

Display Teaching Chart 123 Tell children that you want them to use the words you have been talking about to make soup for the travelers.

- Point to each word at the top of the teaching chart and have children read it aloud.
- Invite volunteers to complete each sentence by choosing the word that goes with each picture.

For further practice, children can work in pairs to use the key words in a recipe for stew, following the "Add _____" pattern from the chart.

Previewing

Use Words in Sentences You may want to teach the high frequency words by writing the words on the board, reading each word, and having children repeat them after you. Then children can write the words in sentences. You can also teach high frequency words by using the lesson on pages T130–131 after reading the selection.

Spelling Words Words with long *a* spelled *ay* and *ai* are taught in the Spelling Workshop minilesson on page T137. The pretest and posttest for these words can be found on page T207 of the Theme Resources section.

Phonics The sounds and patterns of long and short *a* are reviewed on pages T132–133.

Spelling Words

may*   wait
day*   pain
say   sail

My Own Words

* Word appears in the story.

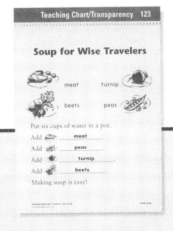

Teaching Chart/Transparency 123

Soup for Wise Travelers

meat   turnip

beets   peas

Put six cups of water in a pot.

Add ___ __meat__
Add ___ __peas__
Add ___ __turnip__
Add ___ __beets__

Making soup is easy!

Practice Book 27

Theme 7 Stone Soup

Name _____

The Travelers

beets soup peas
travelers turnip
wise meat

Read the words in the box. Read the story. Write the words from the box to complete the sentences.

One day three hungry __travelers__ met in the woods. The travelers decided to make a big pot of __soup__. The first traveler had green __peas__. The second traveler put in a __turnip__. The third traveler added red __beets__ and __meat__. The soup was good and they enjoyed the meal. The travelers were __wise__ to use their food for soup.

Optional Independent Practice

FIGURE 8.3, continued

Reading the Selection

Rereading Options

After a first reading, you may want to use the Rereading Minilessons on pages T118-125:

- **Reading**
- **Phonics and Vocabulary**
- **Language Arts**
- **Appreciating Cultural Diversity and Multilingualism**

Meeting Individual Needs

Introduce the Selection

Introduce the Play Have children turn to page 47 of the Collection. Tell children that "Stone Soup" is a folk tale, a very old story that has been retold many times. Explain that this version is told as a play that takes place in a Russian village long ago.

Preview and Predict Ask children to look at the pictures on pages 49–51 and ask:

- Why do you think the people of the village are hiding their food?
- What do you think will happen to the travelers?
- What do you think goes into stone soup?

Record children's predictions on a chart and revisit them after reading.

> **Ann:** The people of the village are afraid the travelers will take their food.
>
> **Tommy:** The travelers will stay in the village for good.
>
> **Juan:** Stone soup is made from magic stones.

Set Purposes

Set Purposes Children can read to find out what stone soup is or use their predictions to set a purpose for reading.

Shared Reading

Discuss How to Read a Play After you have read the play for the first time, tell children that you will all read it together. You may also want to have a volunteer help you demonstrate how to read a play script aloud. Assign roles, and tell children to look for the name of their character in dark type. Be sure they understand that they read aloud only the words that follow their character's name.

Responding

Personal Response Children can discuss or write about something they liked or didn't like about the play.

You might also ask children why they think the villagers said, "Thank you! Thank you!" at the end of the play.

FIGURE 8.3, continued

OPTIONS FOR REREADING

You can help children become familiar with the text and build reading fluency through the following rereading options.

Reading for Appreciation

Have Children Do a Dramatic Reading Groups of children can take turns doing a dramatic reading of "Stone Soup" for the rest of the class or for another classroom. Give children time to practice their lines. Encourage them to think about how their characters look and feel and how they would say their words. They might also create simple props for their characters.

Reading for Theme Content

Develop Children's Understanding of Character You might point out that in "Stone Soup" the travelers use cleverness to trick the people of the village and get food. Remind children that Fox also used cleverness in *Moon Rope* to get something he wanted: to persuade Mole to travel to the moon with him. Then invite children to think of characters in other tales and stories they have read and to discuss character traits that helped them solve a problem. List their ideas on a chart.

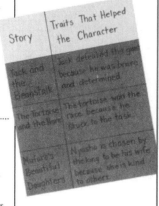

Reading to Support Skill Instruction

Construct Meaning Encourage children to consider what it might be like to have little or no food. Why do they think the villagers hid their food at first? How do children think the travelers felt when the villagers said they had no food? Why do they think the villagers changed their minds? Children can also work together to retell the story in sequence.

Develop Fluency Children can practice reading aloud with partners to develop their ability to read spoken language with expression.

(See instructional notes on pages T118–125.)

 Home Connections

Extending Meaning Encourage children to retell the story of "Stone Soup" at home. Family members might pick up other versions of the tale from the library, read them with their children, and discuss similarities and differences among the stories.

Comprehension Support

Visual Activity Discuss picture details that show that the setting of the play is "long ago and far away." Encourage children to focus on the characters' clothing. Invite them to tell how these clothes are different from what people wear today. Have children compare the houses in the pictures with houses or apartments in their own neighborhoods.

Text Awareness

Following Play Formats Make sure that children understand the markings common to plays: the boldface type highlighting characters' names before their speeches, the colon following characters' names, and the stage directions in parentheses, showing characters' actions.

FIGURE 8.3, continued

AUTHOR & ILLUSTRATOR

Marjorie and Mitchell Sharmat, two award-winning authors, often collaborate. Before their careers in children's book publishing, Mr. Sharmat was a businessman and Mrs. Sharmat a librarian. Mr. Sharmat feels that the appeal of his books comes from their humor and their ability to reflect how children feel.

Esther Baran's main interests are folk tales and natural imagery. Her folk-tale etchings include fabric patterns and ornamentation from the ethnic group from which the tale originated.

Stone Soup, pages 46–47

The authors and illustrator are introduced.

The front cover of the book is shown.

Meeting Individual Needs

Comprehension Support

 Story Tape Children who need additional support can listen to the selection on the Story Tape for this theme while following along in their books. You may also want the whole class to listen to the tape so that they can hear a performance of the play.

Spanish-speaking Students

Building Meaning In Spanish, the word *el pueblo* means "a small town or village." Write the words *el pueblo* and *village* on the board. Help children to understand that these two words mean about the same thing. Invite children to talk about things they might see in a small town.

Intervention Strategy

Strategic Reading Remind children that if the text they are reading doesn't make sense, they can start a section of the story again and reread. When reading a play, going back to reread a character's speech, after figuring out what each individual word is, sometimes clears up confusion.

FIGURE 8.3, continued

Stone Soup, pages 48–49

Literature: Genre
Play

To introduce elements common to plays, you can:

- discuss and read the list of characters on page 48. Explain that the pictures show the characters who appear in the play.
- point to the word *Narrator* on page 49. Explain that the dark print tells who is speaking and that the words that follow *Narrator* are the words the narrator speaks.
- ask children to identify the other speakers on page 49.

The characters, narrator, and setting are introduced.

Three hungry travelers are walking home.

Comprehension Support

Building Meaning After reading the names of the characters, explain that the narrator is the storyteller who tells readers what is happening in the play. The narrator's words explain things to the audience that the characters don't say. All of the other characters talk to each other, but the narrator talks only to the audience.

Comprehension Support

Building Meaning Use a Venn diagram to help children see similarities and differences between plays and stories.

Play	Both	Story
character list	plot	no character list
names before characters' words	setting character	paragraphs

FIGURE 8.3, continued

REREADING OPTION

Stone Soup, pages 50–51

Comprehension
Sequence

Tell children that stories and plays have a sequence—or order—that shows what happens first, what happens next, and what happens last. Use a think aloud to model how the Narrator's lines help to track this sequence.

Think Aloud
As I read, I notice the information the Narrator gives. First, the Narrator says that the three travelers have walked for many miles. Then the Narrator says that the three travelers entered the village late in the day. I think the Narrator will help us to keep track of important events.

Further Instruction:
Sequence, pages T128–129
✔ TESTED SKILL

The travelers come to a village. The villagers, who have little food themselves, see that the travelers are hungry and tired.

The villagers decide to hide their food and tell the travelers that a wolf ate all their food.

Meeting Individual Needs

Comprehension Support

Monitoring Reading Begin a chart like the one shown. Pause at intervals in the play, and have children help you complete a new box that tells what has happened in the play up to that point. When the sequence chart is completed, point out to children that such a chart can help them remember the order of events in a play or a story.

| Three travelers who want food and sleep enter town. | → | Village people hide their food from the three travelers. |

FIGURE 8.3, continued

324

Stone Soup, pages 52–53

Reading/Writing Link
Writing How-to Steps

On page 53, the travelers begin giving directions for making stone soup. Encourage children to pay attention to the different steps for making stone soup, beginning with finding a pot.

Further Instruction:
Writing Workshop, page T134

The travelers are told that there is no food but there is water. They want to make stone soup out of the water.

The villagers are unfamiliar with stone soup. One of the travelers requests a pot of water and three flat stones.

GUIDED READING

Comprehension/Critical Thinking
For Collection pages 50–51

Comprehension Check
1. Why did the village people hide all their food instead of sharing it with the travelers? *(They had very little food for themselves.)*

Critical Thinking
2. Instead of hiding their food, what could the people have done? *(Possible answers: share the small amount of food they had; tell the travelers the truth—that they didn't have much food to share.)*

Comprehension Support

Connect to Personal Experience Invite children to write about a time when they shared their toys, food, or other things with someone in school or at home. Ask: *What did you share? How did sharing make you feel? How does sharing with others show that you care for them?* Ask children to illustrate their work. Display their writing and artwork.

FIGURE 8.3, continued

LESSON REREADING OPTION

Stone Soup, pages 54–55

Appreciating Cultural Diversity

Awareness and Understanding

Explain that folk tales provide glimpses into the lives and concerns of people from different times and places. "Stone Soup" provides a look at village life in Russia many years ago, at a time when people didn't always have much food. Point out details in the illustrations that reflect village life in Russia long ago, such as the clothing and the houses.

The travelers build a fire and cook the stone soup.

One of the travelers decides that the soup would be better with green beans and a turnip. A woman says that the wolf did not eat all her beans and goes home to get some for the soup.

Meeting Individual Needs

Vocabulary Support

Contractions Point out the contractions *you're, didn't, I'll,* and *what's.* Remind children that a contraction is two words shortened to make one word. An apostrophe stands for the missing letters. Help children use context clues to figure out which two words have been shortened to form each contraction on page 55.

Contraction	Words
you're	you are
didn't	did not
I'll	I will
what's	what is

Comprehension Support

Connect to Personal Experience Ask children whether they ever say "M-m-m" after they get a treat. Ask: *What other words do you use that mean "something tastes great"?* Write children's responses on the chalkboard and read them aloud.

FIGURE 8.3, continued

Stone Soup, pages 56–57

Another woman goes home to get a turnip. Both the beans and turnip are put in the soup.

One of the travelers comments that the soup needs peas and beets. A man brings some from his home and puts them in the soup.

LESSON REREADING OPTION

Appreciating Multilingualism

Connections Across Languages

Point out that many languages use simple sounds such as *m-m-m, sh-h-h, ah-h-h,* and *ah-ha* to express feelings. Ask second language speakers to volunteer examples from their languages.

LESSON REREADING OPTION

Study Skills

Review: Following Directions

To check children's understanding of how to follow directions, have a volunteer take the role of a traveler and give the directions for making stone soup to other volunteers. The children can follow the directions by pantomiming making the soup.

Comprehension Support

Connections Across Literature Children might enjoy reading and comparing folk tales from different cultures that teach valuable lessons. Encourage children to look at library books as well as Big Books, theme trade books, and stories in the Collection.

Story	Main Characters	Connections to Life
Stone Soup	people of the village	It's best to be kind and share with others. Everyone wins.
Tricky Tortoise	Tortoise, Elephant	Those who are younger or smaller can sometimes overcome a bully by using their wits.
Nine-in-One Grr! Grr!	Tiger, Shao, Bird	Using one's head and making a plan can prevent a disaster.

FIGURE 8.3, continued

327

REREADING OPTION

Phonics/Spelling
Short and Long *a*

The words *make*, *land*, and *can* on pages 58–59 provide an opportunity to review long and short *a*.

- Frame each word and say it, emphasizing the vowel sound.
- Invite children to tell whether they hear the same vowel sound as in *cake*. If not, ask if they hear the same vowel sound as in *can*.
- Remind them that long *a* always sounds like the letter name.

Further Instruction:
Short and Long *a*, pages T132–133;
Spelling Workshop, page T137
✔ **TESTED SKILL**

Stone Soup, pages 58–59

One of the travelers states that meat would make the soup taste better. Villagers put meat and other food into the soup.

The villagers taste the soup and find it delicious. A man comments on how wise the travelers are to make soup from stones.

Meeting Individual Needs

Comprehension Support

Monitoring Reading Help children to complete the sequence chart started on page T120. Encourage them to use the chart to retell the story.

| Village people hide their food from the three travelers. | → | The travelers start a stone soup with a pot and stones. | → | Village people add vegetables and meat. | → | Everybody loves the stone soup. |

FIGURE 8.3, continued

Stone Soup, page 60

The villagers put the travelers up for the night. The next morning the villagers thank the travelers, and the travelers continue on their journey to the next village.

INFORMAL ASSESSMENT CHECKLIST

Learning Goal
Children use personal experience, prior knowledge, and higher-order thinking skills and strategies to construct meaning.

Performance Indicators
- ✓ Can children develop a sequence chart and use it to retell the events of "Stone Soup" in logical sequence?
- ✓ Do they understand how to read a play?
- ✓ Do they appreciate the humor in the play and the cleverness of the travelers' solution to their problem?

GUIDED READING: SUMMING UP

Comprehension/Critical Thinking
For Collection pages 50–60

Comprehension Check
1. How did the travelers trick the people of the village? *(By saying the stone soup needed flavor, they tricked the villagers into adding food to the soup pot.)*

Critical Thinking
2. What lesson do you think the villagers learned from the travelers? *(Possible answer: It's better to share.)*

FIGURE 8.3, continued

Response Options

In Response

Children can read page 61 and discuss, draw, or write about their "funny soup." Invite them to tell what they think the villagers would say about their soup.

Personal Response

Encourage children to tell what lessons they learned from "Stone Soup." Children can discuss their ideas or write about them in their personal journals.

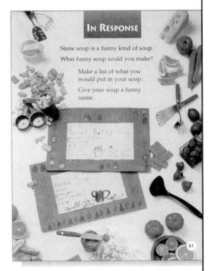

Stone Soup, page 61

Reader Response Groups

Children could meet in small groups to discuss "Stone Soup." Ask them to discuss the following questions or other ideas of interest:

- Which word do you think best describes the travelers: *wise* or *tricky*? Why do you think so?
- What else could the travelers have done to get food for themselves?

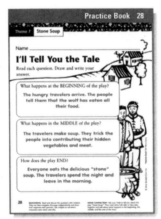

Optional Independent Practice

FIGURE 8.3, *continued*

Letter to the Villagers

Have children pretend that the travelers are writing a letter to the villagers. Partners or small groups can discuss what the travelers might like to write to the townspeople. Ask: *What might the travelers say about their stay in the village? What might they say about their adventures after they left?* Then children can work alone or in pairs to write letters.

Perform a Puppet Play

 If possible show children pictures or a set of Matryoshka (mah TRUSH ka) dolls, the Russian nesting dolls made of wood. Provide groups with the Matryoshka-shaped cutouts from pages 405–407 in the SourceBank. Have children use the cutouts to make stick puppets of each of the characters in "Stone Soup." Encourage each child to color a puppet, making his or her character distinct. Then groups can use the puppets for the dramatic retelling or rereading of the play.

Russian Village Pictures

Let children work in small groups to look over the illustrations in "Stone Soup" and brainstorm different things that they might see if they could visit a Russian village long ago. Then have children each create a picture of a Russian village.

Talking About Traveling

To help children connect the story to personal experience, ask them to tell about a trip they have taken or would like to take to a new place. Encourage them to discuss what is fun and what is difficult about traveling to a place where they don't know how to get around or they don't know anybody.

Children can perform a puppet show of "Stone Soup" with Matryoshka-shaped stick puppets.

ESL **English Language Support** See pages 135 and 137 for children who need additional help in reading and responding to the selection.

FIGURE 8.3, continued

| Comprehension |

Sequence

Skills Trace	Sequence
▶ Introduce	T128
Review	T172, 8:T176
Assess	T196
Reteach	T128

Blue numbers refer to other Themes.

Materials

- Collection pages 46–61
- Practice Book page 29
- Teaching Chart/ Transparency 124
- SourceBank pages 32, 535, 536

◻1 Teach

Teach from the Literature
Remind children that in "Stone Soup" events happen in a certain order—or sequence: some things happen at the beginning of the play, some in the middle, others at the end. Point out that paying attention to the order in which things happen in a play or a story can help them better understand and remember what they read.

Tell children that they can follow these steps to keep track of the order in which things happen:

1. Always remember what happens first and last in the story.
2. Look for picture clues to recall story order.
3. Make a sequence chart or a story map to record what happens at the beginning, middle, and end of a play or a story.

◻2 Practice

Make a Story Map Ask children to retell "Stone Soup," starting at the beginning of the play. Ask them to think of one or two sentences that tell about the beginning, the middle, and the end. Record their responses on a story map on the chalkboard. You may also want children to fill out one of the story map forms in the SourceBank.

Meeting Individual Needs

Comprehension Support

Auditory Activity Have groups of three children sit in a story circle and retell the story of "Stone Soup." Have the first "storyteller" tell what happens at the beginning, the second tell what happens in the middle, and the third tell what happens at the end. Children might enjoy recording their summaries and then listening to them.

Reteach

Hands-on Activity In small groups, have children reread a story that has a clear beginning, middle, and end, such as *Any Kind of Dog* or *The Paper Crane*. Children can discuss the story and record their story sequence on a SourceBank story map form.

Further Support SourceBank Reteaching page 32

FIGURE 8.3, continued

3 Apply

Display Teaching Chart 124 Tell children that the teaching chart tells about what happened when the travelers went to another town. Point out that the sentences are out of order.

Read the teaching chart aloud to children. Then ask them to help you number the sentences in the right order and read them aloud.

Have partners copy each sentence from the teaching chart onto strips of construction paper. Then have them mix the strips and put them in order.

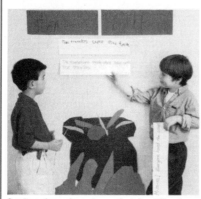

Creating and arranging sentence strips helps children learn about story sequence.

Have Children Make Sequence Charts Children can make charts to show things that they do during a school day. To start the activity, you might point out that what they do from the time they wake up until they go to bed has a sequence, or order, just as "Stone Soup" does. Suggest that children make a chart to show, in order, what they did yesterday or will do today.

I woke up and ate breakfast.

↓

I went to school and read three books.

↓

Then I went home and did my homework.

↓

After I ate dinner, I went to bed.

INFORMAL ASSESSMENT CHECKLIST

Learning Goal
Children use personal experience, prior knowledge, and higher-order thinking skills and strategies to construct meaning.

Performance Indicators
✓ Can children retell the important events of "Stone Soup" in logical sequence?
✓ Can they determine the logical sequence of events on Teaching Chart 124?

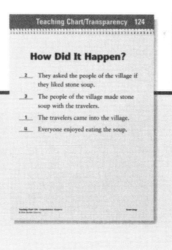

Teaching Chart/Transparency   124

How Did It Happen?

_2_ They asked the people of the village if they liked stone soup.

_3_ The people of the village made stone soup with the travelers.

_1_ The travelers came into the village.

_4_ Everyone enjoyed eating the soup.

Practice Book   29

Name _____

When Did It Happen?

To understand a story, think about the sequence, or what happens first, next, and last.

Read each group of sentences. Write first, next, or last to show the order in which each thing happened.

1. The people see the travelers.   **first**

2. The travelers make stone soup.   **last**

3. The people hide their food.   **next**

4. The people find food for the soup.   **next**

5. The people get a pot of water.   **first**

6. The people eat the soup.   **last**

Optional Independent Practice

FIGURE 8.3, continued

High Frequency Words

Skills Trace	High Frequency Words
▶ Introduce	T130
Assess	T196
Reteach	T130

Materials

- Collection, pages 46–61
- Teaching Chart/ Transparency 125
- Readable 61, *Once Upon a Time*
- Sourcebank pages 127, 223
- Practice Book page 30
- Display Word Cards

High Frequency Words

hide	they
stone	much
you're	went
good	

◼ Teach

Teach from the Literature As you reread "Stone Soup" with children, listen to hear if children can read high frequency words from this and earlier lessons on their own. Then tell children they are going to practice reading and writing some words from the play.

◼ Practice

Choose from these interactive activities.

Create a Class Story Show children the Display Word Cards or write the high frequency words on the chalkboard. Then read the words.

- Ask a volunteer to choose a word and use it in a sentence to begin a story. Have other children continue the story, using a new high frequency word. Write each sentence on the board and read it back to children.
- When the story is completed, have children read it chorally with you.

Playing bingo provides practice in reading high frequency words.

Play Word Bingo Make bingo cards filled with high frequency words from this and earlier lessons.

- Put an X in the middle of each card. Provide each group with a bag of SourceBank word cards that match the bingo word cards.
- Children can play bingo in small groups. One child can choose and read words from the bag, while other children mark matching words on their bingo cards. Supply enough cards to allow children to play several rounds.

Meeting Individual Needs

Book Concepts

Folk Tale Working in small groups, children can use *Once Upon a Time* as a model to retell and then write down a new version of a familiar folk tale. After retelling the story, group members can divide it up so that each child writes and illustrates one part. The completed stories can be placed in the reading center for everyone to read.

Home Connections

Reread the Readables Have children take home *Once Upon a Time* to share with family and friends. They can challenge family members to name all of the folk tales that appear in this story.

Reteach

Using Cueing Systems Record children's dictated sentences for the class story on strips. Shuffle the sentence strips. Ask children to put the sentences back in order. Encourage them to use what they know about letter sounds and context if they see words they don't know.

Further Support SourceBank Reteaching page 127

FIGURE 8.3, continued

❸ Apply with the Readable

Read Aloud Tell children that you are going to read a story about a young storyteller who tells her sister a funny tale. Encourage them to look at the cover and predict why the story is called *Once Upon a Time*. Have them listen carefully to find out whether the storyteller tells a story they already know.

Display Teaching Chart 125 Read aloud the story text selected for the chart to reinforce high frequency words. Then, using the overlay provided, have volunteers find and underline the words *hide, much, went,* and *good.*

Writing Options Use one or both of the following activities to provide writing practice.

- On the chalkboard, write two or three sentences containing high frequency words, such as *She made some _____ food* and *The girl and the wolf ran to _____* . Write *good* and *hide* below the sentences. Have children copy and complete each sentence with the correct high frequency word.
- Invite children to write a letter to the young storyteller in the Readable, using as many high frequency words as possible.

◀ **Readable Book 61**
Stage 4

Reading Options To prepare children for reading the story, make sure that they understand that the storyteller mixes up several stories to make a new one. Then they can read the story by themselves, with partners, or in supervised groups. They can

- identify the folk tales used to create *Once Upon a Time.*
- read the words on the back cover and use each one in a sentence.

To practice high frequency words from earlier lessons, children can also read the Readables *Freddy Frog's Note* (46) and *A Rainbow Somewhere* (49).

INFORMAL ASSESSMENT CHECKLIST

Learning Goal
Children use knowledge of story and sentence structure to achieve their purposes when reading, writing, listening, and speaking.

Performance Indicators
- ☑ Can children recognize high frequency words in "Stone Soup" and *Once Upon a Time*?
- ☑ Can they use high frequency words to complete written sentences and to write a letter to the storyteller of *Once Upon a Time*?

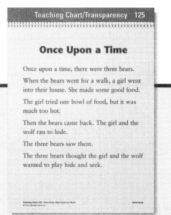

Teaching Chart/Transparency 125

Once Upon a Time

Once upon a time, there were three bears.

When the bears went for a walk, a girl went into their house. She made some good food.

The girl tried one bowl of food, but it was much too hot.

Then the bears came back. The girl and the wolf ran to hide.

The three bears saw them.

The three bears thought that the girl and the wolf wanted to play hide and seek.

Practice Book 30

Theme 7   Stone Soup

Name _____

Finish the Story
Read the words in the box. Read the story. Write the word from the box that completes each sentence.

stone	You're
hide	much
good	went

The animals wanted to play a ___good___ game.

They decided to play ___hide___ , a stone. They

closed their eyes while Crow ___went___ to hide it.

Then they all looked for the ___stone___ . When

Wolf found it, Crow cried, " ___You're___ it!"

The animals had so ___much___ fun.

Optional Independent Practice

FIGURE 8.3, continued

| Phonics Review |

Short and Long *a*

Skills Trace	Short and Long *a*
Introduce	6:T88
▶ Review	T94, T132, 8:T174
Assess	T196
Reteach	T132

Blue numbers refer to other Themes.

Materials

- Collection pages 48–61
- Teaching Chart/ Transparency 126
- Readable 62, *A Giant-Sized Day*
- Practice Book pages 31–32
- SourceBank pages 81, 248–250, 268, 277, 308, 369
- Display Picture Cards
- AstroWord: Short Vowels: *a, i*; Long Vowels: *a, i*

1 Review

Teach from the Literature Have children work in two groups. Ask one group to find three words on pages 50–51 with the short *a* vowel sound they hear in *at.* Ask another group to find three words on pages 52–53 with the long *a* vowel sound they hear in *cake.* Write column heads *Short a, a-e,* and *ay* on the board. List children's findings in the appropriate columns. Invite them to add other words to the chart.

Develop Phonemic Awareness Using Display or SourceBank picture cards, have children name the objects and say whether they hear the sound of short or long *a.*

Connect Sounds to Letters Create a long *a* wall chart with three columns labeled *a-e, ay,* and *ai.* Have children name the objects in the picture cards again. List the names in the appropriate columns. Discuss the different spelling patterns, and tell children these are all ways to write the long *a* vowel sound.

2 Practice

Choose from these interactive activities.

Have Children Write Rhymes In pairs, children can read the SourceBank word cards and write rhymes that use two or more of the words.

Have Children Play Hot Potato Have children sit in a circle. Toss a ball to one child, and say *short a.* The child who catches the ball says a short *a* word, then tosses the ball to another child, saying *long a* or *short a.* The child who catches the ball says a word that fits the category.

Children name long or short *a* words in a game of hot potato.

Meeting Individual Needs

Challenge

Extending Meaning Remind children that the villagers said that a wolf had stolen their food. Ask them to pretend that the wolf stole only foods with names with the short *a* sound they hear in *apple,* leaving foods with names that have the long *a* sound in *cake.* Using the pail shape from the SourceBank, children can write the names of foods with long *a.*

Reteach

Hands-on Activity Using pocket charts and letter cards from the SourceBank, children, in pairs, can make short and long *a* words. They can help each other with the different spelling patterns for long *a,* and list all the words they make.

Further Support SourceBank Reteaching page 81

FIGURE 8.3, *continued*

3 Apply with the Readable

◀ Readable Book 62
Stage 4

Read Aloud Tell children you will read a story about a giant. Have them listen to find out how the giant made a change.

Display Teaching Chart 126 Read the text on Chart 126 selected from the story to reinforce long and short *a*; then have children read it. Then they can

- find and frame words with short *a*.
- find and frame words with long *a*.

Writing Options The following activities reinforce children's recognition of short and long *a* words.

- Dictate two sentences for children to write with long and short *a* words, such as *Clad took his hat, and off he went. He tried to take a train to the beach.*
- Have children use long and short *a* words from the Readable to write and illustrate a "For Sale" sign of things for giants.
- Children can write a story about a very large or a very small character. Remind them to use a story map to record characters, setting, and events before they begin to write.

Reading Options Before children read the story, discuss the words in the story that have to do with water: *beach, waves, lake, pool, sailboat.* Then children can read the story alone, in pairs, or in small supervised groups. They can take turns

- reading and acting out the story.
- finding and reading the short *a* story words and then the long *a* words.

INFORMAL ASSESSMENT CHECKLIST

Learning Goal
Children integrate and apply a variety of cueing systems to construct meaning.

Performance Indicators
- ✓ Can children use letter-sound associations to hear, read, and write short and long *a* words?
- ✓ Can children categorize short and long *a* words?

 Children read and write short and long *a* words while completing a Take-home Book.

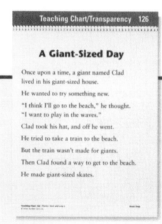

Teaching Chart/Transparency 126

A Giant-Sized Day

Once upon a time, a giant named Clad lived in his giant-sized house.

He wanted to try something new.

"I think I'll go to the beach," he thought.
"I want to play in the waves."

Clad took his hat, and off he went.

He tried to take a train to the beach.

But the train wasn't made for giants.

Then Clad found a way to get to the beach.

He made giant-sized skates.

Optional Independent Practice   Practice Book   31–32

FIGURE 8.3, continued

Writing Workshop

Writing How-to Steps

1 Teach from the Literature

Remind children that the travelers in "Stone Soup" made a good soup by tricking the people of the town.

Have children look through the play to find out how to make "stone" soup. Help children list steps, and write them on the board. If the steps are out of order, you can add numbers to show the correct order. Then read the steps aloud, adding order words, such as *first, next, then,* and *last.*

> First, put water and three big flat stones in a pot.
>
> Next, make a fire under the pot from sticks.
>
> Then cook the soup.
>
> Next, add green beans, a turnip, peas, beets, and meat.
>
> Last, cook the soup some more!

Explain that when writing a how-to list, it is important to

- tell the steps clearly.
- give the steps in order.
- use order words.

2 Practice/Apply

Help children brainstorm a list of things they know how to do and could explain easily to another person. Then have children work in pairs to choose one of their ideas and write their own how-to list.

Other Writing Options

Self-selected Writing Encourage children to use order words in their own writing when telling how to do or make something.

Writing Process Remind children that they can also use order words in their stories for the Writing Process on pages T192–193.

Real-world Literacy: Writing a Shopping List Point out that the travelers had a list in mind of things they needed for making soup. Have children think of their favorite kinds of sandwiches and make a list of the foods they need to prepare them.

Optional Independent Practice

FIGURE 8.3, continued

Grammar Workshop

Past and Present Tense

1 Teach from the Literature

Write these sentences about the travelers in "Stone Soup" on the chalkboard: *Today, the travelers make soup. Yesterday, the travelers made soup.*

Ask children to underline the action word in each sentence. Point out that

- the word *today* is a clue that the action is happening now, or in the present.
- the word *yesterday* is a clue that the action happened in the past.

Explain that some action words, such as *walk*, add *-ed* to show that something happened in the past, but other action words, such as *make*, change spelling to show the past. Create a chart with two columns labeled *Now* and *Past*. Begin filling in the chart with *make, made; eat, ate; run, ran; get, got*. Invite children to add to the chart other action words that change spelling.

Now	Past
make	made
eat	ate
run	ran
get	got
take	took

2 Practice/Apply

Have children write a sentence using a word from the *Now* column on the chart you have created. Then have them write another sentence using the form of the word from the *Past* column. Encourage children to read their sentences to partners.

Additional Resources

Daily Language Activities: page T203

SourceBank Reteach: See SourceBank page 155.

Optional Independent Practice

FIGURE 8.3, continued

Language Workshop

Vocabulary: Words for Cooking

1 Teach from the Literature

Ask children if they know different ways to cook an egg. List their suggestions on the chalkboard. (*fry, scramble, boil*) Then ask how to cook the following:

cake (*bake*)   steak (*grill*)   cocoa (*boil water*)

chicken (*fry, bake, grill*)   soup (*boil*)

Add these cooking words to the list.

2 Practice/Apply

Invite children to draw some foods that are cooked and to write under each food the word that tells how it is cooked in their drawings. Suggest that they share their drawings in small groups.

Optional Independent Practice

Speaking: Dramatizing

1 Teach from the Literature

Tell children that "Stone Soup" is written as a play, which is a story that can be acted out. Remind them that the narrator is the person who tells the story. Ask children to identify the other characters.

Read the lines of several characters. Point out that movements are often indicated in parentheses. Demonstrate how to

- read a part with expression and feeling.
- use facial expressions and body movements.

Have children suggest simple props and costumes that might be used to put on this play.

2 Practice/Apply

Invite small groups of children to act out one part of the play, for example, the part where the villagers find out that hungry travelers have come to town. Children can design simple props and costumes. Have groups practice their lines, and then perform them for another group or for the whole class.

Listening Center Children may enjoy recording a reading of "Stone Soup" and then listening to their performance.

 English Language Support See pages 135 and 138 for additional help with language skills related to the selection.

FIGURE 8.3, continued

Spelling Workshop

Long *a* Spelled *ay* and *ai*

MINI LESSON

1 Teach from the Literature

Write this sentence on the chalkboard: *You may wait in this room.* Read the sentence aloud, emphasizing the long *a* sound. Have children identify the words in which they hear the long *a* sound. (*may, wait*) Then ask a volunteer to underline the letters in each word that make this sound. (*ay, ai*)

Now write the Spelling Words on the chalkboard. Have volunteers underline the two letters in each word that make the long *a* sound. Then elicit from children that

- the long *a* sound can be spelled *ai* or *ay*.
- the long *a* sound is spelled *ay* when it comes at the end of a small word.

Remind children that the long *a* sound is sometimes spelled with the CVCe pattern.

2 Practice/Apply

Have children work with partners to write rhyming poems, using the Spelling Words and other words that rhyme with them.

Challenge Words: clay, drain

See page 59 of Spelling Source for optional independent practice.

Additional Resources

Daily Language Activities: page T203

Pre- and Posttests: page T207

Home Connections: See the Home Spelling Study List in the Spelling Source Teacher's Edition.

AstroWord: Long Vowels: *a, i*

Spelling Words

may*
day*
say
wait
pain
sail

*Word appears in the story.

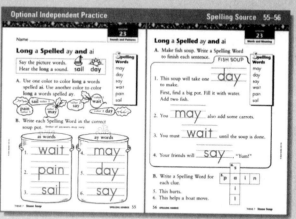

Cross-curricular Connections

SCIENCE

Supporting Science Goals:
Noting Characteristics Through Observation

Comparing Stones Provide an assortment of rocks and stones in as great a variety of shapes, sizes, colors, and textures as possible, or take children outside to collect stones and rocks. (You may want to suggest that children start a rock collection.) Have small groups of children draw the stones and describe them on a chart according to these characteristics: size, color, texture, and shine or luster.

Community Connection Invite a geologist from a local college or museum, a parent with a rock collection, or a representative of a local business to visit the class and show children several kinds of rocks.

After studying a variety of rocks and stones, children can record their characteristics on a chart.

MATHEMATICS

Supporting Math Goals: *Using Standard Measurements*

Making Stone Soup Children may enjoy making and eating their own version of "stone soup." Children can help with gathering, measuring, and preparing the ingredients, but only adults should use sharp cutting or peeling tools. To avoid burns, do not turn on the heat until all the ingredients are in the soup pot and everyone has had a chance to stir. (You may wish to cook the soup in the school kitchen.) In addition to the listed ingredients, you will need the following items:

- measuring cups (liquid and solid)
- measuring spoons
- a large soup pot
- long-handled wooden spoons
- an electric hot plate (or stove)
- bowls or cups and spoons

Stone Soup

1 c. chopped onion
1 c. cut green beans
8 c. water
8 bouillon cubes
2 c. sliced carrots
2 c. diced potatoes
1 tsp. salt
1 c. sliced celery
2 c. stewed tomatoes
2 c. canned corn
1 medium "stone" (scrubbed, unpeeled, whole potato)

Have children measure and add all ingredients to the soup pot. Don't forget the "stone"! Soup needs to be stirred exactly as many times as the number of cooks you have. Bring soup to a boil, cover the pot, and cook over low heat for about an hour, or until vegetables are soft. Allow to cool slightly before serving.

FIGURE 8.3, continued

MUSIC

Listening to *Peter and the Wolf* Play a recording of Russian composer Prokofiev's *Peter and the Wolf* for children. Tell them to listen for the repeated musical phrase that represents each character. To set the stage, read the story aloud. You might find these or other titles at the library:

- *Peter and the Wolf* retold by Samantha Easton, published by Andrews McNeel
- *Peter and the Wolf* by Selina Hastings, published by Holt
- *Peter and the Wolf* retold and illustrated by Michele Lemieux, published by Morrow

Children can draw pictures and write about their favorite parts of the story. You can add their completed work to the Story Tree bulletin board.

Children may enjoy listening and responding to the classic Russian folk tale *Peter and the Wolf.*

I liked when the bird flew in the foxs face and Peter hid.

My favrite part was wen the bird flew away from the wolf into the tree.

ART

Making Vegetable Prints Invite children to use some of the vegetables they read about in "Stone Soup" for making vegetable prints. If you choose to do the soup-making activity, you can set aside any bruised or wilted vegetables to use for printing. Cut the vegetables to expose the insides. Have children dip the cut side into a shallow dish of tempera which has been thinned with water and press the vegetable slice onto a sheet of construction paper. (You can have children use ink pads instead of paint.) Ask children to label each print with the name of the appropriate vegetable.

Vegetables not perfect enough for the soup pot can be put to good use by children when they make vegetable prints.

FIGURE 8.3, continued

■ A Critical View

Critics have attacked basal readers through the years. They have alleged basals to be inferior because of boring content, cultural bias, absence of literary merit, and unrealistic and repetitive language. Responding to these and other criticisms, authors and publishers have made significant changes in basals to reflect current reading research and teacher effectiveness studies (McCallum, 1988).

Other critics have attacked basal readers for the ways that teachers use them. These criticisms should not be aimed at the materials themselves, however. The practices criticized are neither suggested nor condoned by any basal program, even though certain critics contend that these practices are inevitable outcomes of using the basals. For instance, when using basals, teachers sometimes do the following:

- Have a group of students read every story in a round-robin manner.
- Use three groups within a classroom, and retain the same groups throughout the year.
- Make no provision for individual differences beyond the three-group pattern.
- Restrict the more capable readers to the basal material, forcing them to move at a pace far below their capacities.
- Prohibit students from selecting and reading other books in which they are interested.

Research by Durkin (1984) provides some insights into the use of basals in teaching reading. Durkin observed 16 teachers during their reading instruction to better determine how they used basal manuals. She observed first-, third-, and fifth-grade classes. Her findings are not very encouraging; however, if teachers become aware of them, perhaps it will help them improve the quality of basal reading instruction. Following is a summary and discussion of her findings.

Introduction and Presentation of New Vocabulary Words.   Most basal manuals suggest introducing new words in written context and illustrating them in familiar, written sentences. Few of the teachers followed this recommendation and rarely did they give any attention to teaching and practicing new vocabulary words.

Discussion and Presentation of Background Information.   Basal manuals often provide background information about concepts and themes found in stories that are intended to activate students' experiential and conceptual backgrounds. Durkin found that none of the teachers reviewed or developed background information for their students.

Presentation and Discussion of Prereading Questions.   Rarely did the observed teachers present and discuss questions before their students read a story from their basals. Most manuals present questions to ask students before they read a story for the first time to guide students' reading.

Silent Reading of the Story.   Durkin reported that silent reading was uncommon in the first grade. Although third- and fifth-grade teachers used silent reading more often, they typically ignored the recommendations found in the manuals. Basal manuals often recommend that teachers supervise students' silent reading by questioning them after they have read a few pages or discussing their reading immediately following silent reading of the whole story.

Meaningful Oral Reading or Rereading.   Basal manuals do not typically recommend oral reading or rereading of every story assigned to students; however, the observed teachers spent considerable time on oral reading.

Instruction.   Today, considerable emphasis is given to instructional procedures that foster comprehension and provide meaningful, supervised skill practice. All teachers, except one fifth-grade teacher, used the manual sections on practice assignments. The focus, however, was on completing written practice assignments rather than using many of the manuals' suggestions for instruction.

Practice Assignments.   Suggested assignments are often abundant in basal manuals, but manuals seldom suggest that teachers use every one of these. All but one of the observed teachers assigned all of the written practice activities found in the skill-development portions (workbook pages and worksheets). None of these teachers used the manual when giving assignments, and the teachers did not appear to make assignments in terms of students' needs. The teachers also failed to provide students with a purpose for reading, to review the format and directions, to complete practice examples, or to establish a relationship between the assignment and the ability to read.

Provisions for Individual Differences.   With most stories in the basal, manuals include provisions intended to help teachers differentiate their instruction and address the needs of individual students. Durkin found that one third-grade teacher used these recommendations with the whole class, and a first-grade teacher used some of them for her whole class. The other teachers did not use the recommendations in their teaching.

Durkin's findings are limited because they deal with a small number of teachers observed for a short time; however, these findings are no different from those reported in other classroom observation studies (Durkin, 1984). Teachers do not use the suggestions and recommendations in basal reader manuals for two common reasons: (1) they do not have the time to do everything the manual recommends, and (2) they often do not think the manual recommendations are important. Durkin thought teachers should connect these two concerns. That is, if teachers don't have the time to follow all of the recommendations, they should heed those that develop and enhance students' reading abilities. Durkin offers the following advice for using the basal manual to improve the quality of reading instruction:

> Giving more time to new vocabulary, background information, prereading questions, instruction on essential topics, and better but fewer assignments, and . . . spending less time on oral reading and comprehension questions is a

◀||| F L A S H B A C K

The hornbook was the earliest form of reading activity that children were to use by themselves. It received its name from the thin layer of horn that was placed over the text to prevent it from becoming dirty. Most hornbooks were in the shape of a paddle and measured about 2½ by 5 inches. The alphabet, Arabic numerals, and the Lord's Prayer were usually written or printed on a piece of paper. The paper was then pasted onto the paddle and covered with the thin layer of horn. Hornbooks were used in America into the nineteenth century.

From **McGuffey's First Eclectic Reader,**
Revised Edition. New York: American Book
Company, 1896.

Photo courtesy of The Horn Book, Inc.

From McGuffey's *Eclectic Reader*, published in the mid-1800s, children were taught to read and recite. The readers primarily used an alphabetic-phonetic approach along with a controlled vocabulary. Although the language of the beginning-level readers was choppy and uninteresting, the readers were extremely popular for many years. The story content often was intended to teach religious, moral, and patriotic values.

Dick, Jane, Sally, Spot, Father, Mother, and Puff are familiar to many of us as the characters of a popular reading series used in the mid-1900s. These readers were characterized by controlled vocabularies, near-total emphasis on a narrative style of writing, and stories dealing with middle-class white families living in single-family homes.

"Look here," said Father.
"Look at Mother and me.
Here we come."

Sally said, "Away we go!
Dick and Jane.
Father and Mother.
Tim and me."

"And Spot and Puff," said Dick.
"Away we go!"

From **Fun With Our Family** by Helen M. Robinson et al. Copyright © 1962 by Scott, Foresman and Company. Reprinted by permission.

UPDATE ⫸

Today's reading programs are characterized by the use of quality literature as the central component in developing competent readers. This is the case for reading programs utilizing the basal reader as the core, those programs embracing the whole-language philosophy, and literature-based reading programs. Various literacy works are the primary vehicle for developing attitudes, skills, strategies, and understanding in each phase of a complete reading program: developmental reading, application-transfer, independent or recreational reading, content reading, and functional reading. Also, the content of today's basal series represents the multiracial, multicultural, and multiethnic nature of our society.

possible change that is not likely to promote any more problems than were seen in the classroom. What the different allotment of time may promote, however, is better readers. (p. 744)

Bacharach and Alexander (1986) also found teachers to be selective in using the basal manual. As in the Durkin study, teachers did not give the prereading step the attention it should have in teaching a lesson. Teachers in this study viewed the vocabulary suggestions as most helpful, followed by comprehension instruction, skill instruction, and background and prereading questions. Least helpful were enrichment activities.

■ Important Considerations in Using a Basal

Basal manuals offer many suggestions for teaching reading, but teachers should not follow these suggestions blindly. Teachers should use their knowledge of students' needs and capabilities to determine which recommendations to use, which to modify, and which to ignore. Mason (1983) identified three important features that teachers should consider in evaluating and preparing lessons in manuals. First, a lesson may need to be reorganized to focus on the story's topic, illustrate its purpose or value, and relate to students' existing knowledge and to other texts. Second, the teacher should choose activities that relate to the workbooks and worksheets selectively; not all of them recommended in the manual need be assigned. The teacher can omit activities that are of questionable value, too lengthy, or unrelated to the lesson at hand, which allows for more teacher-directed instruction. Third, the teacher must develop alternatives for independent student work and practice. Independent activities such as library reading, research projects, and creative writing are essential to foster comprehension abilities and provide application of literacy in real-life situations.

A final important consideration is how much teacher time and effort are needed to learn how to effectively use any basal reader program. Tulley's (1991–1992) research on how first-year teachers employed a new basal program indicated that "(1) for many of these teachers at various grade levels and with differing amounts of experience, learning to use a new basal reading program was a relatively lengthy and difficult process, and that (2) loyalty to proven and effective instructional techniques and methods, coupled with the absence of any systematic training scheme, may lead teachers to depend upon self-designed and capricious approaches when learning to use a basal" (p. 20). Such findings underscore the importance of not only knowing the basal program but also continually monitoring one's application of the approach to ensure student learning.

■ Going Beyond the Basal

The overall goal of teaching literacy is to develop students who can (and do) read and write on their own for a variety of reasons. Teachers at every level must be sensitive to a range of instructional goals: mastery of basic skills, facility in using comprehension strategies, development of critical and creative responses to various forms of text, and growth of appreciation and enjoyment of language used in reading and writing. However, the transfer of reading skills and strategies to recreational reading is not automatic: Skills and strategies are mastered through wide reading of literature (Alex, 1988).

Although one may suspect that mastery of literacy skills automatically leads to increased recreational reading and learning, a study by Blair and Turner (1984) indicates otherwise. As part of a status study of reading interests and attitudes, they assessed the perceptions of middle-school students regarding how well basic reading instructional materials fostered recreational reading. Surprisingly, almost half of the students thought their regular reading materials neither helped them learn in other school subjects nor develop recreational reading habits.

The findings of this study strongly support the integration of literature into the regular basal program. A common strategy for elementary teachers using a basal is to encourage students to read library books related to a basal story or to bring in copies of the book excerpted in a basal for students to read. This practice integrates literature more fully into the basal reader program.

In addition to individual classroom strategies to implement a literature-based reading approach, the following are strategies for the school environment:

- reading and literature, including **silent sustained reading** (SSR), book fairs, and multimedia projects
- magazines, including opportunities to read a variety of magazines independently, group discussions of various stories, and student oral reports
- reading-related projects, including a literature emphasis based on writing (e.g., plays) and a semester project (e.g., on China or energy)
- careers, including extensive reading and writing about careers and assembly programs on various occupations with guest speakers

As the preceding discussion indicates, basal readers cannot be viewed as the complete reading program. No matter how comprehensive a basal program might appear to be, it must be combined with other materials for students to learn what they need to know. Clements (1991) agrees and suggests "that we go beyond the basal and the workbook to supplement reading programs with extensive reading, enrichment, and follow-up" (p. 59). Clements's undergraduate students compiled the following excellent listing of ways reading teachers can go beyond the basal:

storytelling	letters
menus	recipes
music	cereal boxes
games	read-along cassettes
projects	comic books
filmstrips	computers
plays	puppet shows
language experience	paired reading

Finally, an excellent source for not only a complete view of the basal but also for specific ways to supplement and extend the basal is the text *Improving Basal Reading Instruction* by Winograd, Wixson, and Lipson (1989).

Adjusting Instruction in Beginning Basal Anthologies

Many students with varying exceptionalities have difficulties in learning new words. Some students are extremely weak in the area of auditory discrimination of letter sounds and as such have difficulty in learning letter-sound correspondences (i.e., phonics). Without adjusting instruction for these students, success in beginning reading is threatened. If you desire to use a basal program and capitalize upon its built-in structure and specific skill and strategy development with students lacking some of the necessary readiness abilities to be successful in learning the alphabetic principle, a different approach to individual word learning in conjunction with using the regular basal program may prove to be successful.

A very popular, effective, and time-honored approach to use with students experiencing extreme difficulty in learning words through the usual auditory-visual (AV) method is the Fernald-Keller approach. Harris and Hodge (1995) define this approach as "a technique for learning to identify printed words also called VAKT because it involves looking at a word (visual) while saying it (auditory) and tracing it (kinesthetic, tactile)" (p. 83). This approach enables the reader to learn words through a combination of four senses: seeing the word, hearing the word said, tracing the word with a finger, (i.e., movement), and feeling the word being traced (i.e., touch). The procedure itself is based on a four-stage process (Fernald, 1943), bringing students to the point of identifying unknown words through visual analysis. No phonic analysis techniques are taught in this method, whose outline follows:

Stage 1:   The teacher writes a new word on paper and pronounces it for the student. The student then traces the word and pronounces the word by syllables until it can be written from memory. The word is then used in a short language experience story for practice.

Stage 2:   The student reaches this stage when words can be learned without tracing. The teacher still writes the word for the student. New words are used in experience stories and kept in a file for practice.

Stage 3:   The student has reached this stage when the word can be written by looking at it and having the teacher pronounce it. The teacher no longer writes the word for the student but does continue to pronounce it.

Stage 4:   The student should now be able to recognize new words by comparing them to similar words that have been learned. No longer must the

Instructional Procedures

The Language-experience Approach (LEA)

A valuable supplemental reading approach is the **language-experience approach** (LEA). Regardless of what other materials schools or other teachers may have adopted, most teachers of beginning literacy include teacher-written charts student write a word to remember it. Some students may need considerable teacher assistance to note the similarities between known and new words. The major focus of this stage is on visual analysis of words by syllables and reading in a variety of materials.

While this approach has proved to be successful on a one-to-one basis, disadvantages include the heavy time commitment and the approach's reliance on visual learning of new words that come from the student's experience. Dr. Louis Cooper of the University of Connecticut devised a modification of the Fernald-Keller method that can be successfully implemented by classroom teachers using a published basal program. The Cooper method (1964) recommends that words to be learned come from the first readers in the basal program, that book reading be introduced from the outset, and that the inclusion of both structural and phonic analyses eventually replace sight-word learning. An outline of the Cooper method is as follows:

1. Select the basal reader program.
2. Find the child's instructional level by means of an informal reading inventory.
   (**Note:** It is assumed here that if this procedure is indicated, the child's instructional level will not be more than primer level and probably will be lower.)
3. Assess the child's recognition of the total list of words in the first preprimer and make a list of those words that are not known. These become the words to be taught as the book is read.
4. Teach these words to the child, using the appropriate stage of Fernald-Keller and have the child read them in the contextual setting of the book.
5. Practice these words, both in context and isolation.
6. Repeat steps 3, 4, and 5 with the second preprimer, third preprimer, primer, and so on, moving from one stage to another as the child is able to do so.
7. Parallel the early stages with additional visual discrimination training and auditory discrimination training.
8. At some point in the sequence of stages, depending on the readiness of the child, introduce a systematic program of word-analysis skills, which will eventually replace all sight techniques.

The implementation of Cooper's method to word learning used in conjunction with the regular basal anthologies may be a viable alternative for teaching students with varying exceptionalities beginning reading in the regular classroom. Students are using the same materials as their classmates with the same advantages of reading high-quality literature with specific instruction and structured practice activities. Thus, the same materials are used, but instruction in word learning is **adjusted** to meet students' needs.

and stories in their literacy programs (Eichenberger & King, 1995). Using student experiences as the content for writing charts and stories is a long-standing practice. Throughout the years, modifications and extensions have placed renewed emphasis on this procedure (Combs, 1996). The LEA is used predominately with primary-grade children but is also adaptable for slower learners of all ages and for ESL students. Hall (1981) summarized the rationale and philosophy of the language-experience approach.

The language-experience approach for teaching literacy, Hall said, is based on the relationship of language to the learner's experiences as the core from which language communication radiates. Language-experience literacy is viewed as a communication process closely related to communication in speaking and listening. The approach uses students' oral language and experiences to create personal reading and writing sources. This approach integrates the teaching of literacy with all of the language arts; as students listen, speak, write, and read about their personal experiences and ideas, their speech determines the language patterns of their reading materials, and their experiences determine the content. The language-experience approach assumes that literacy has the most meaning to students when the materials being read are expressed in their language and are rooted in their experiences.

■ Features of the LEA

Although the language-experience approach has many variations, teachers should understand some basic features when using this approach. They include the following:

- a shared experience for the students
- shared talk about the experience
- decisions about the written product, including a group chart or story or individual student stories
- shared reading of the charts or stories by the students
- follow-up activities
- group-experience charts and stories

Group-experience charts and stories are means of capturing students' interest by tying their personal experiences to their literacy activities. The charts and stories, which tell about shared activities, are prepared cooperatively by the teacher and the class. They are often extensions of earlier and less difficult experiences, wherein the teacher wrote single words, short sentences, days of the week, names of the months, the seasons, and the dates of students' birthdays and holidays on the chalkboard. Group-experience charts and stories provide practice and application in a number of developmental areas closely related to literacy, including the following:

- using oral language in group planning prior to a trip and in recounting the experience after a trip
- giving and taking ideas as the experience is discussed
- sharpening sensory acuity, particularly visual and auditory, while on excursions
- developing and expanding print-related concepts, such as directionality (left to right), space between letters and words, punctuation, capital letters, and the relationships between oral and written language
- expanding concepts and vocabulary
- learning words as wholes in meaningful contexts, thus building a sight vocabulary based on one's language

- focusing on reading and writing as a process of constructing meaning
- reading and writing about one's own experiences

In preparing group-experience charts and stories, the teacher should plan a meaningful shared experience, such as taking a field trip, viewing a film or filmstrip, hearing a story, reacting to a picture, observing an experiment, or participating in a class or school activity. Let us assume that the teacher arranges a trip to a nearby farm. This teacher organizes the necessary transportation and visits the farm in advance to determine specifically what students will experience. As a result of the visit, this teacher identifies what students need to know to benefit from the experience. Several days of instruction help prepare students for their visit.

Following the trip to the farm, the teacher guides the students through a discussion and sharing of the highlights of their experiences. This discussion serves to get all of the students involved and attending to the task to follow—writing the experience chart. After each student's response, the teacher writes it on the chalkboard or on large poster paper. Students are encouraged to respond and to discuss their response. The group-composed chart follows:

Our Trip to the Farm

We went to Mr. Johnson's dairy farm.

We saw lots of cows.

We saw a machine that milks the cows.

The cows' heads are put in bars.

In Mr. Johnson's big barn, he milks five cows at once.

After the teacher and children read the completed chart, the teacher may ask a student to point out (1) the line that tells what kind of farm they visited, (2) the line that tells the name of the owner of the farm, (3) his or her favorite or most exciting event, and so forth.

The same chart may be used in other ways. The teacher may duplicate each line in the chart on a strip of heavy paper, hand a sentence to a student, and ask him or her to find this line on the chart. The teacher may print individual words on oaktag or cardboard, hold them up, and ask a student to point out that particular word on the chart. The teacher may prepare word cards for a particular line, hand them to a student in mixed order, and ask him or her to arrange them in proper order to correspond with the line on the chart. A group-experience chart can be used with a class as a whole and also with various groups of students. After its use with a unit, the teacher may refer to it when certain words used on the chart arise in other contexts and activities.

Individual Experience Stories.   Children enjoy talking about their experiences, particularly about incidents that involve them, their families, their pets, special events, and the like. One of the best ways to take advantage of such motivation is to write individual experience stories. These language productions are usually brief, ranging from one to several sentences about one incident. In the early stages of literacy, students usually dictate the stories and the teacher usually transcribes them. Because these brief stories relate to students' own experiences, they encourage involvement in literacy. The stories are always meaningful and should be written using words that parallel students' own language usage.

■ Expansions and Variations of the Language-experience Approach

In addition to the features and uses of LEA mentioned earlier, teachers can use this instructional approach in a variety of ways. Reimer (1983) suggests several ways to expand and vary the use of the LEA; these are presented in the following paragraphs.

Direct and Indirect Discourse. Use different-colored pens to identify different speakers when recording a group experience story. Students can identify who said what by noting the color of the writing. The teacher should use the same color consistently for each individual so that the class can associate that color with a particular student. As a variation, use a photograph of each student and attach a discourse balloon to help everyone understand who contributed what to a group story. Later, write these stories with the youngsters and replace the color or picture with the words, "May said," or "Benny said," to help students understand how these words function in direct discourse. Teach indirect discourse by removing the punctuation marks and introducing the word *that* (as in "Sue said *that* the horse is big.").

Various Forms of Writing. Use group LEA to introduce different forms of writing. Demonstrate a science experiment and have the group tell what happened, have students report a shared experience by responding to reporters' questions (who, what, where, when, why, and how), or have students learn about letter writing by composing a group letter.

Shape Stories. Guide children to write stories about an experience that is represented by a shape—a fish, clown, car, dog, and so on. As children dictate the story, write it on paper cut into that particular shape.

Written Dialogue. This procedure works well with many youngsters at all elementary levels. Rather than talking with students, exchange notes. These notes may range from extremely simple phrases ("Good job!") to paragraphs. Match the complexity of the notes to the students' abilities to read and respond in writing. This variation of LEA helps students to understand the relationships between oral and written language and realize that written language must make sense to the reader.

The concept of language experience has been extended far beyond the group chart and writing individual stories. Today, the term *language experience* applies to practically every type of self-expression through language and every experience that involves manipulation of language.

The role of teachers has undergone considerable change also. Teachers now assume responsibilities far beyond those of scribes who write down stories that students tell. Teachers still reinforce students' egos by writing personal stories, but by using additional language stimuli, they also help students expand their concepts and improve their language proficiency.

Language activities that promote both learning about language and using language as a tool for further learning are becoming major features of instruction (Dole, 1984). Students write poetry, read poetry, solve riddles, and make up some of their own. Working with homonyms, they learn that different spellings may have the same pronunciation. Working with homographs, students learn that words may be spelled the same but have different meanings and pronunciations. They learn about relationships through analogies, combining sentences, and arranging sentences into larger units. In working with language, students learn that a word may have dozens of meanings, that plurals take many forms, that new words are constantly added to our language, and that over time, the meanings of words change.

Language experience is, thus, experiencing language. The teacher's role is to help children understand that:

> Writing a word is an achievement
> Writing a story is a larger achievement
> Combining stories into a book is quite a production.
>
> Saying something one way is an achievement
> Saying it another way and noting what you did the second time permits you
>   to control language!
>
> When you can control language
> you can mold words like clay
>   mix words like paints
>   use words to draw pictures.

The next step is to let children try it. Let them tell or write the answer to the following question:

How many ways can a leaf fall?

> "Down" you say.
> Surely there's another way.
>   A leaf can
>   just fall—
>   fall gracefully
> glide—
>   glide like a glider
>   glide and swerve
>
> sail—
>   sail like a rudderless ship
>   sail like it had a mind of its own

dip—
> dip and glide
> dip and rise and bank gracefully to a landing

dance—
> complete its solo dance
> dance with the wind
> fall with no map to guide it—
> map its own course
> try many detours
> twist slowly in the wind.

How many ways can a leaf fall that we didn't write today?

"No other way," you say?
Don't you think leaves like to play?
> playfully! (of course)
>> If in a hurry?
> plummet
>> with memories of summer?
> reluctantly

Any procedure has both merits and limitations, and this is true of the language-experience approach to teaching reading. The major strengths of experience charts and stories have already been discussed. Relying too heavily on teacher-written materials may have drawbacks of its own, including the following:

- Difficulty in controlling the vocabulary—too many words may be introduced at one time.
- Not enough repetition of basic sight words to ensure mastery.
- When used exclusively as a method, too much of a burden on the teacher, demanding too much time and too high a level of training.
- Difficulty in adapting this type of instruction to the needs of all students.
- Encouragement of memorization rather than mastery of sight words.
- The strengths and weaknesses of the experience method are a factor of the teacher's application and are not inherent in the method itself. Under certain conditions, overemphasis, misuse, or lack of understanding may cancel out all the advantages of the method. The language-experience approach is vulnerable when used as the total reading program. Most teachers prefer to use the approach as a supplement to other materials and instructional procedures (see Figure 8.4).

Language-experience activities can enhance basal reading instruction and vice versa. Aspects of LEA can be used to do the following:

- Provide for both individual and group reading instruction.
- Allow for practice, transfer, and application of word-identification and comprehension skills and strategies in meaningful context.

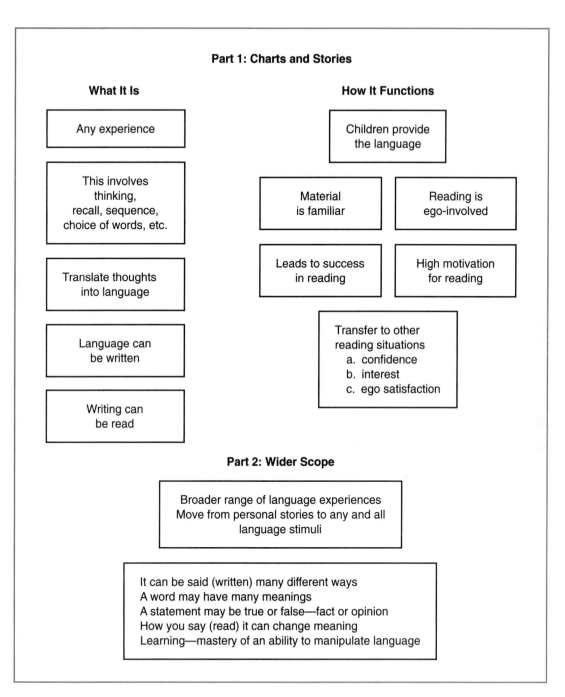

Part 1: Charts and Stories

What It Is

Any experience

This involves thinking, recall, sequence, choice of words, etc.

Translate thoughts into language

Language can be written

Writing can be read

How It Functions

Children provide the language

Material is familiar

Reading is ego-involved

Leads to success in reading

High motivation for reading

Transfer to other reading situations
a. confidence
b. interest
c. ego satisfaction

Part 2: Wider Scope

Broader range of language experiences
Move from personal stories to any and all language stimuli

It can be said (written) many different ways
A word may have many meanings
A statement may be true or false—fact or opinion
How you say (read) it can change meaning
Learning—mastery of an ability to manipulate language

FIGURE 8.4
The basic features of the language-experience approach

- Build on and emphasize students' life and language experiences.
- Emphasize the relationship between oral and written language to help students understand that reading and writing are constructing meaning.
- Engage students in meaningful instruction based on their own interests.
- Encourage vocabulary development by having students try new words and use these new words in meaningful context.
- Develop better writers and children who will experiment with writing. (Rupley & Blair, 1989)

As emphasized throughout this text, the processes of reading and writing development are complementary. LEA is a wonderful springboard for both processes. Karnowski (1989) proposes linking the process-writing approach and LEA by combining process-writing steps (i.e., prewriting discussion, actual writing, revising, and publishing) in a modified language-experience approach. Karnowski explains: "By using a modified LEA in which students decide what topics to explore, what ideas to include, and what modifications to make, young readers and writers begin to realize the work and the job of becoming published authors" (p. 465).

Use of Technology in Literacy Instruction

Every school district in our country is using computers in one way or another. Computers are also becoming more and more a part of literacy instruction in our classrooms. In many schools, students interact with computers in all phases of learning. In addition, students (i.e., "surfers") browse the Internet for information on a variety of subjects both at home and at school. Any display of literacy approaches, materials, and activities today includes myriad computer applications, so a key concern is how schools and teachers are using the computer's marvelous capabilities. Like other tools, computers can help teachers and students. The challenge is to harness the computer's power and versatility to provide interesting and meaningful learning.

The first thing teachers should realize is that computers cannot replace good teaching. Second, computers may or may not assist individual teachers in achieving their instructional goals. Third, computers can certainly supplement books but computers cannot replace them. The advantages to using the computer to aid in teaching literacy are many. Teachers must always consider the possible uses of technology in relation to students' learning needs. If computers are used properly, they have enormous potential to increase literacy levels. Conversely, if computers are not used in relation to student needs and offer little opportunity for students to interact meaningfully with various texts, literacy levels can adversely be affected. Among the advantages of using computer-based instruction in literacy instruction are the abilities to do the following:

increase the motivational levels of students

present information in a variety of formats

give immediate feedback

2. All reading instructional materials that follow the structures and patterns of English usage can be said to be linguistic.

3. The time it takes for teachers to integrate the features of the language-experience approach with basal readers is not worth the effort.

4. Teachers who do not use the basic recommendations of a basal manual are probably better than are teachers who use such recommendations blindly.

Field-Based Assignments

1. **Building Background Knowledge.** As you know, recent research on comprehension has highlighted the utmost importance of prior knowledge to understanding new ideas. Even with this strong finding, researchers such as Durkin have noted that few teachers do indeed develop prior knowledge in introducing a story even though teacher's manuals give explicit directions in this area. In your classroom, teach a story and concentrate on reviewing students' prior knowledge and developing background knowledge. Develop your prereading section in detail. Write down the specific questions you will ask your students that will review and highlight what students already know about the topic, what background experiences students may have relating to the story, and how you will help your students make connections regarding what they already know to new upcoming information in the story.

2. **Collaborative Basal Reader Evaluation.** Using your college's materials curriculum lab or public school resources, obtain a copy of a student reader, teacher's manual, and any other materials connected with the basal program used at the school in which you are completing your field experiences. Arrange yourselves in groups of four. Each of you are to choose two of the following eight topics common to most published reading programs:

   - Comprehension lessons on skills and strategies
   - Word-identification lessons on skills and strategies
   - Content reading/study skills and strategies
   - Reading and writing instruction
   - Vocabulary development
   - Testing materials
   - Workbook and practice materials
   - Directed reading lessons

   Prepare a written report on your two areas using the questions below as departure points (and others depending on your particular published program). Meet as a group and share your findings. If possible, share your group report with the entire class.

   How is your area covered and presented to students? (Provide a brief overview of essential components.)

   What specific types of materials and/or teaching strategies are utilized to fulfill your area? (Provide examples to show your classmates exactly how the area in questions is taught.)

In your opinion, does your area provide a balance between direct or explicit instruction and practice in authentic materials? (Provide an example supporting your opinion.)

Are there provisions made for students needing additional help? What are they?

Are there recommendations made that you feel are unimportant and should be omitted? What are they?

Are there recommendations made that you feel should be modified in some way to improve the instruction or process? What are they?

Portfolio Entry

Because children are different in a multitude of ways, there is no one miracle approach to the teaching of reading that is successful with all children. Given this reality, it is imperative for effective teachers of reading to know a variety of approaches. Recall the quote by Pescosolido in Chapter 2 regarding effective teaching: "Just being a 'nice' person doesn't a teacher of reading make, but a nice person doing some important things in terms of the reading process results in good teaching and good learning." Respond to the following two questions.

What does this quote mean to you in relation to the implementation of different approaches to literacy? What are the key areas of concern and emphasis a teacher should focus on regardless of the approach being used in the school or classroom?

Write a one-page typed entry in your portfolio responding to these two questions.

Bibliography

Aiex, N. K. (1988). ERIC/RCS: Literature-based reading instruction. *The Reading Teacher, 41,* 458–461.

Alvermann, D., Bridge, C. A., Schmidt, B. A., Searfoss, L., Winograd, P., & Paris, S. G. (1993). *Health Reading.* Lexington, MA: D. C. Heath and Co.

Anderson, R. C., Hiebert, E. H., Scott, J. A., & Wilkinson, I. A. G. (1985). *Becoming a nation of readers: The report of the Commission on Reading.* Washington, DC: The National Institute of Education.

Apple Early Language Connections (1992). Cupertino, CA: Apple Computer, Inc.

Bacharach, N., & Alexander, P. (1986). Basal reader manuals: What do teachers think of them and how do they use them? *Reading Psychology, 7,* 163–172.

Blair, T. R., & Turner, E. (1984). Skills instruction and independent learning. *Middle School Journal, 16,* 6–7.

Center for the Study of Reading. (1986). *A guide to selecting basal reading programs.* Urbana, IL: Center for the Study of Reading, University of Illinois.

Chu, M-L. L. (1995). Reader response to interactive computer books: Examining literary responses in a nontraditional reading setting. *Reading Research and Instruction, 34,* 352–366.

Clements, N. E. (1991). Maximizing time on task: Supplementing basals and workbooks. In R. A. Thompson (Ed.), *Classroom Reading Instruction.* Dubuque, IA: Kendall/Hunt.

Combs, M. (1996). *Developing competent readers and writers in the primary grades.* Upper Saddle River, NJ: Prentice Hall.

Cooper, J. L. (1964). An adaptation of the Fernald-Keller approach to teaching an initial reading vocabulary to children with severe reading disabilities. *The Australian Journal on the Education of Backward Children, 10,* 131–145.

Dole, J. A. (Spring 1984). Beginning reading: More than talk written down. *Reading Horizons, 24,* 161–166.

Durkin, D. (1984). Is there a match between what elementary teachers do and what the basal reader manuals recommend? *The Reading Teacher, 37,* 734–744.

Durkin, D. (1993). *Teaching them to read* (6th ed.). Boston: Allyn & Bacon.

Greenlinger-Harless, C. S. (1987). A new cross-referenced index to U.S. reading series, grades K–8. *The Reading Teacher, 41,* 293–303.

Eichenberger, C. J. & King, J. R. (1995). Two teacher roles in language: Scaffold-builder and gatekeeper. *Reading Research and Instruction, 35,* 64–84.

Hall, M. (1981). *Teaching reading as a language experience* (3rd ed.). Upper Saddle River, NJ: Merrill/Prentice Hall.

Harrison, N. F. (1987). *The relationship between opportunity to learn basic reading skills and student achievement via computer assisted instruction.* Doctoral dissertation, Texas A & M University, College Station.

Heinich, R., Molenda, M., Russell, J. D., & Smaldino, S. E. (1996). *Instructional media and technologies for learning.* Upper Saddle River, Prentice Hall.

Hoffman, J. V. & McCarthey, S. J. (1995). The new basals: How are they different? National Reading Research Center. *The Reading Teacher, 49,* 72–75.

Issak, T., & Joseph, J. (1989). Authoring software and teaching reading. *The Reading Teacher, 43,* 254–255.

Karnowski, L. (1989). Using LEA with process writing. *The Reading Teacher, 42,* 462–465.

Mason, J. M. (1983). An examination of reading instruction in third and fourth grades. *The Reading Teacher, 37,* 906–913.

McCallum, R. D. (1988). Don't throw the basals out with the bath water. *The Reading Teacher, 42,* 204–209.

Osborn, J. (1984). Workbooks that accompany basal programs. In G. G. Duffy, L. R. Roehler, & J. Mason (Eds.), *Comprehension instruction: Perspectives and suggestions* (pp. 163–186). New York: Longman.

Piernek, F. T. (1979). Using basal guidebooks—The ideal integrated lesson plan. *The Reading Teacher, 33,* 167–172.

Reimer, B. L. (1983). Recipes for language experience stories. *The Reading Teacher, 37,* 396–404.

Reutzel, D. R. (1985). Reconciling schema theory and the basal reading lesson. *The Reading Teacher, 39,* 194–197.

Richardson, J. (1984). *The three A's: Influencing teachers' awareness, attitudes, and anxieties about using computer assisted instruction for reading classes.* Richmond: Virginia Commonwealth University.

Rickleman, R. J., Henk, W. A., & McKenna, M. C. (1991). Computerized reading assessment: Its emerging potential. *The Reading Teacher, 44,* 692–693.

Rickleman, R. J., & Henk, W. A. (1990). Reading and technology in the future. *The Reading Teacher, 44,* 262–263.

Rupley, W. H., & Blair, T. R. (1989). *Reading diagnosis and remediation: Classroom and clinic* (3rd ed.). Upper Saddle River, NJ: Merrill/Prentice Hall.

Schaudt, B. A. (1987). Selected research on computer-assisted instruction. In M. J. Burger & R. J. Kansky (Eds.), *Technology in education: Implications and applications. College Station,* TX: Instructional Laboratory, College of Education, Texas A & M University.

Singer, H., Samuels, S. J., & Spiroff, J. (1973–1974). The effect of pictures and contextual conditions on learning responses to printed words. *Reading Research Quarterly, 9,* 355–367.

Stauffer, R., (1975). *Directing the reading-thinking process.* New York: Harper & Row.

Thompson, R. A. (Ed.) (1991). *Classroom reading instruction* (2nd ed.). Dubuque, IA: Kendall/Hunt Publishing Co.

Tulley, M. A. (1991–1992). Learning to teach with a new basal reading program. *Journal of Reading Education, 17,* 12–28.

Weisberg, R., & Balajthy, E., (1989). Reading diagnosis via the microcomputer. *The Reading Teacher, 42,* 636.

Wepner, S. B. (1991). Linking technology to genre—basal reading. *The Reading Teacher, 45,* 68–70.

Wiggins, R. A. (1994). Large group lesson/small group follow-up: Flexible grouping in a basal reading program. *The Reading Teacher, 47,* 450–460.

Winograd, P. N., Wixson, K. K., & Lipson, M. Y. (Eds.). (1989). *Improving Basal Reading Instruction.* New York: Teachers College Press.

Yeager, B. (n.d.). *Data management and decision making in the PLATO elementary reading project.* Urbana: University of Illinois.

CHAPTER 9

Literature-based Reading Instruction

Donna E. Norton

Chapter Outline

For the Reader

Our nation is currently emphasizing an increase in the use of literature in its reading programs. According to **Reading Today** (1988), the newspaper of the International Reading Association, "Everywhere you look, there seems to be a renewed interest in the use of children's literature in the school reading program. This trend is evident in increased coverage of the topic in conference presentations, journal articles, and books" (p. 1).

The same article identifies both concerns and realizations that encourage this emphasis. Many communities believe that students are neither learning to read adequately nor choosing to read independently. Of equal concern are the criticisms that many basal readers are limited in their scope and contain neither classic nor contemporary literature. On the other hand, literature-based reading programs appear to promote the fun and joy of reading, enrich students' lives, provide material that is inspiring, interesting, and informative, and increase reading ability.

In the literature-based view, reading is not the acquisition of a set of isolated skills. Instead, reading is the ability to read all types of literature with understanding, appreciation, and enjoyment. In this viewpoint, literature can be used to support the reading curriculum, to teach or reinforce reading skills, and to introduce students to a wide variety of good and enjoyable books. Students discover that reading is more than skill lessons, workbook pages, and short, disconnected stories. Through literature, students discover that reading can become a lifelong habit that brings both knowledge and enjoyment.

Key Ideas

- In the reading program, the use of literature should develop in students an understanding of literature and an appreciation for it.
- Teachers can develop reading capabilities through the use of literature.
- Literature-based reading programs include objectives related to understanding and appreciating the different literary genres and elements.
- Developing an understanding of and appreciation for literature requires that teachers help students recognize the literary elements and the ways that authors use those elements to create exciting and credible stories.
- Strategies for teaching reading through literature include using predictable books, analyzing plot structures, semantic mapping, and modeling.

Literature-based Reading Programs

Literature may support the basal reading curriculum or it may be the core of the total reading program. When teachers use literature to support the reading curriculum, they identify reading skills taught in the basal approach and assign literature selections that reinforce those skills. As a result, students see that the major goal of the reading program is to understand, appreciate, and enjoy, not merely to complete workbook pages.

The belief in the power of literature is reinforced by a study by Freppon (1990), who investigated students' feelings about the purposes and nature of reading. Findings indicated that students in literature-based programs view reading as language- and meaning-based. An appreciation of language and an emphasis on meaning are certainly two of the goals of any reading curriculum.

Programs in which teachers use literature as the core of the reading and language arts curriculum are multiplying rapidly (Norton, 1992, 1997). These programs frequently identify books according to core literature, extended literature, and recreational literature. **Core literature** includes books that should be taught in the classroom. With close reading and intensive consideration, they are likely to be important stimuli for writing and discussion. **Extended literature** includes works that teachers may assign to individual students or small groups of students as homework or supplemental classwork. Recreational-motivational literature includes works for students to select for individual, leisure-time reading from classrooms, schools, and community libraries. This literature-based curriculum uses the primary sources of the literature (as opposed to anthologies). This approach promotes literacy, developing an understanding of and appreciation for literature.

Hiebert and Colt (1989) identify the varied instructional formats that can be found in effective literacy programs that focus on children's literature. These formats range from teacher-led instruction using teacher-selected literature for teaching critical strategies to teacher- and student-led interaction using teacher- and student-selected materials to independent reading from student-selected literature.

According to Hiebert and Colt (1989), effective literature programs include a variety of these formats because

> When teachers focus only on independent reading of student-selected material, they fail to consider the guidance that students require for becoming expert readers. A focus on teacher-led instruction fails to develop the independent reading strategies that underlie lifelong reading. A total reading program should contain various combinations of teacher and student interaction and selection of literature so that children develop as thoughtful, proficient readers. (p. 19)

Whether a total literature approach or a support for the basal reading curriculum is used, teachers must be aware that use of literature in the reading curriculum should develop understanding of literature and an appreciation for it. To choose literature that motivates students to read and that stimulates an appreciation for literature requires knowledge about literature, awareness of students' interests, and knowledge about instructional approaches that stimulate interest and books, traditional literature, fantasy, poetry, contemporary realistic fiction, historical fiction, multicultural books, biography, and informational literature. The books discussed range from those for younger children to those for students through the middle school. Norton's *The Impact of Literature-Based Reading* (1992) suggests books and strategies that may be used with the books. *Children's Literature* (1993) by Huck, Hepler, and Hickman contains chapters on the major literature genres. Sutherland and Arbuthnot's *Children and Books* (1991) discusses the major authors who write in each of the genres.

Literature journals are fine sources for current books as well as for specialized lists. *Booklist, Horn Book, School Library Journal,* and *Publishers Weekly* include reviews. They star reviews of books that the editors believe are of exceptional quality. *Booklist* also publishes specialty lists of books. *School Library Journal* publishes a "best books" list for each year as well as lists of specific subjects. Other helpful journals include *The Reading Teacher, Language Arts,* and *The New Advocate.* "Children's Choices" is published each year in *The Reading Teacher.* The journal *Book Links,* a publication of the American Library Association, is also extremely helpful when selecting books that are related to specific type of literature, theme, or author.

Award-winning books and classics, whether they are read to or by students, are of special interest in reading programs. These books encourage students and teachers to explore and discuss selections considered the best in their fields. For example, the Caldecott Medal and Honor Awards, presented since 1938, are awarded annually to the illustrators of the most distinguished books published in the United States. The Newbery Medal and Honor Awards, presented since 1922, are awarded annually for the most distinguished contributions to children's literature published in the United States. The Children's Book Award, presented since 1975, is awarded by the International Reading Association to a children's author whose work shows unusual promise. These and additional awards are listed on pages A-3–A-10, Appendix B, in Norton's *Through the Eyes of A Child: An Introduction to Children's Literature* (1995).

Many of the older award-winning books are now considered classics. Many other books, however, were published before the awards were given. According to Rudman and Pearce (1988), **classics** are extraordinary books that last beyond their authors' lives and continue to delight and reach the minds and hearts of readers for many generations. The folktales of the Brothers Grimm and Charles Perrault, the picture books of Kate Greenaway *(A Apple Pie)* and Robert McCloskey (1941) *(Make Way for Ducklings),* the fantasies of A. A. Milne (1926) (the "Pooh" books) and E. B. White *(Charlotte's Web),* the poetry of David McCord *(One at a Time)* and Edward Lear *(Book of Nonsense),* the realistic fiction of Frances Hodgson Burnett *(The Secret Garden)* and Robert Louis Stevenson *(Treasure Island),* and the historical fiction of Esther Forbes *(Johnny Tremain)* and Laura Ingalls Wilder (1932) (the "Little House" series) deserve to be shared with all students. These books and other noteworthy classics have been identified by the Children's Literature Association as touchstones in children's literature. These books are considered so good that they should be used to evaluate all literature. A list of "Touchstone Books" is available from the Children's Literature Association, publisher of *Children's Literature Association Quarterly.* Breckenridge (1988) compiled a list of

The Caldecott Medal is awarded annually to the artist of the most distinguished American picture book of the year. The text also must be of a high quality and worthy of the pictures. The award is named after Randolph Caldecott, an English artist in the mid 1800s. Caldecott's picture books for children were beautifully illustrated nursery rhymes and old ballads.

A major topic of discussion at the 1921 American Library Association meeting was children's reading in the library, home, and school. Frederic C. Melcher, who was the founder of *Children's Book Week,* felt that librarians could encourage the writing of quality children's books. He proposed that a medal be awarded for the most distinguished children's book written by a citizen or resident of the United States. The proposal was overwhelmingly supported. Mr. Melcher suggested the award be named the "John Newbery Medal," in honor of the bookseller who was keenly aware of children's reading interests and sought to find authors to write quality children's books.

Awards for outstanding children's books are usually selected by a committee made up of adult members. As a result, many of the books that children would find interesting and fun to read may be omitted. Since 1975, however, *The Reading Teacher* has published annually "Children's Choices," a listing of books that children themselves like. The list is based on the responses of 10,000 children from five different regions of the United States.

1996 Award Winners

from The Mini Page by Betty Debnam © 1996 Universal Press Syndicate

"Oh, the Places You'll Go" is the theme of this year's Children's Book Week, Nov. 18-24. Visit some wonderful places in these 1996 award-winning books.

The John Newbery Medal is awarded each year to the author of the most outstanding children's book. There were four runners-up, or Honor Books.

The Newbery Medal went to Karen Cushman for "The Midwife's Apprentice." It tells the story of a homeless girl in the Middle Ages.

Newbery Honor Book winners

Carolyn Coman has worked as an editor for educational materials. She lives in Massachusetts.

Carolyn Coman

"What Jamie Saw" deals with the scary life of a family who are trying to escape an abusive man.

Christopher Paul Curtis worked for 13 years at an auto body plant before writing this, his first book.

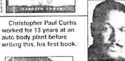
Christopher Curtis

In "The Watsons Go to Birmingham — 1963," a family heads to Alabama at a time of violence against civil rights workers. This was also a Coretta Scott King Honor Book.

Carol Fenner has been writing since she was about 5 years old.

Carol Fenner

In "Yolanda's Genius," a fifth-grade girl faces the difficult task of convincing people her little brother is a musical genius.

Jim Murphy has written more than 20 books. Many are nonfiction books with historical photos.

Jim Murphy

"The Great Fire" is a photo essay about the 1871 fire that burned much of Chicago.

The Randolph Caldecott Medal is awarded each year to the illustrator of the most outstanding children's picture book. Four Honor Book awards were also given.

The Caldecott Medal went to Peggy Rathmann for "Officer Buckle and Gloria." In it a policeman teaches kids about safety with a lot of help from his dog, Gloria.

Next week learn what it would be like to share Thanksgiving with the Pilgrims.

Caldecott Honor Book winners

Stephen T. Johnson studied art in Kansas and in France.

"Alphabet City" shows letters of the alphabet appearing in everyday scenes of the city.

Marjorie Priceman has illustrated several children's books. She lives in Pennsylvania.

Marjorie Priceman

"Zin! Zin! Zin! a Violin" by Lloyd Moss introduces us to the sounds of the instruments of the orchestra.

Brian Pinkney learned to paint by watching his illustrator father, Jerry Pinkney.

Brian Pinkney

"The Faithful Friend" by Robert D. San Souci tells of the self-sacrificing love between two friends. This was also a Coretta Scott King Honor Book.

Janet Stevens has been drawing since she was a child. She once designed fabric for Hawaiian shirts.

Janet Stevens

"Tops & Bottoms" is the tale of a lazy bear and a clever, hard-working rabbit.

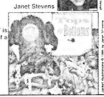

Source: From a poster of Newbery Award Medal Winners. Used by permission of Library Binding Service, Inc., 2134 East Grand Ave., Des Moines, Iowa 50305.

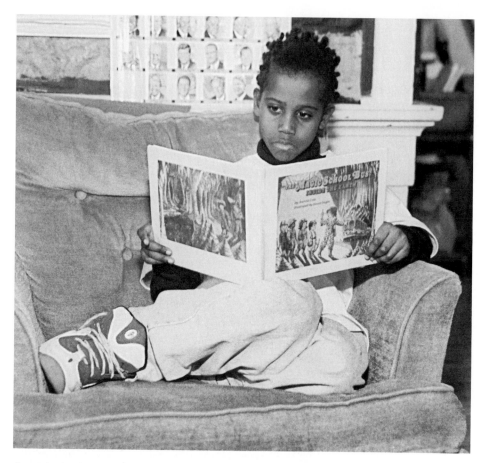

Award-winning books and classics encourage students and teachers to explore and discuss selections considered to be the best in their fields.

modern classics in 1988. These lists offer many good examples of children's literature. They include books that teachers and students should read, discuss, and evaluate.

■ Evaluation Criteria

The various book sources emphasize different and valuable aspects of evaluation. Teachers must be aware of how books are evaluated when they read book reviews and choose literature from those reviews. Older students may also use these different criteria when they discuss or write about books.

Kennemer (1984) identified three classifications of book reviews: (1) descriptive, (2) analytical, and (3) sociological. Descriptive reviews provide factual information about the story, plot, characters, theme, and illustrations. These reviews look at the who, what, where, and when of a story. Analytical reviews discuss, compare, and evaluate such literary elements as characterization, plot, setting, theme, and style. Analytical reviews may also discuss illustrations and relationships to other books. These analyses encourage their readers to see literature in new ways, to consider what makes the story believable or worthwhile, to note the techniques authors use, and to discover why they are successful or unsuccessful. Sociological reviews emphasize social context, concerning themselves with the characterizations of particular social or ethnic groups, the moral values, possible controversy, and potential popularity. They consider the social impact of the book. For example, a review might consider how the author depicts specific groups and what, if any, are the stereotypes.

Most of the textbooks in children's literature include review elements from all three types. There is, however, a greater emphasis on analytical reviews related to literary elements. Kennemer (1984) reported that the reviews in *Bulletin of the Center for Children's Books* are mostly descriptive. Reviews in *Booklist, The Horn Book, Kirkus Reviews,* and *The School Library Journal* chiefly analyze literary elements. *The School Library Journal* also emphasizes sociological analysis.

Reviews in content-area journals emphasize important elements in that specific content area. For example, in each April/May issue of *Social Education,* the book review subcommittee of the National Council for the Social Studies–Children's Book Council Joint Committee (1992) publishes a bibliography, "Notable Children's Trade Books in the Field of Social Studies." The books selected for this bibliography "(1) are written primarily for children in grades K–8; (2) emphasize human relations; (3) represent a diversity of groups and are sensitive to a broad range of cultural experiences; (4) present an original theme or a fresh slant on a traditional topic; (5) are easily readable and of high literary quality; and (6) have a pleasing format and, when appropriate, illustrations that enrich the text" (p. 253).

Reading and discussing the facts of literature are obviously easier than analyzing the literary or sociological aspects. A good literature program enables students to go beyond the factual level. Reading and discussing good children's literature increases one's awareness, enables one to discover the techniques an author uses to create a believable plot or memorable characterizations, and provides standards for comparison. Reading and discussing good literature help every student become a worthy critic, what Kingsbury (1984) defines as one "who offers us new perspectives on a text, who sees more in it than we saw, who motivates us to return to it for another reading" (p. 17).

This chapter refers to the literary elements that students should understand and appreciate. It briefly reviews the literary elements of plot, characterization, setting, theme, style, and point of view.

Plot.   The plot of a story is the plan of action or sequence of events. A plot must have a beginning, a middle, and an end. A good plot allows students to become involved in the action, feel the conflict developing, recognize the climax, and respond to a satisfactory ending. The plots in most books for younger children follow a chronological, or sequential, order of the character's life, whether the story occurs over a day, several days, or a longer period. Cumulative action, such as that found in "The House That Jack Built," is popular in books for younger students, as the actions and characters are mentioned again when new action or new characters are introduced. Books for older students sometimes use flashbacks in addition to chronological order.

Excitement in the plot occurs when characters experience struggles or overcome conflict. The major types of conflict found in children's literature include person against person, person against society, person against nature, and person against self. With believable conflict, the readers understand the conflicting circumstances. For example, in *Hatchet* (1987), Paulsen describes nature in such a way that readers visualize the power and the danger. We know that the main character is in a life-or-death struggle and that he must learn about nature if he is to survive alone in the Canadian wilderness.

Many books for more advanced readers develop person-against-self conflicts and person-against-society conflicts. In Curtis's *The Watsons Go to Birmingham—1963* (1995) the plot develops as the characters face person-against-society conflicts in Alabama and then face the conflicts within themselves.

Characterization. Believable characters, especially in books for older students, should be three dimensional—characters with pasts, futures, hopes, fears, parents, and siblings. Most memorable characters develop throughout the course of the story. To develop the many sides of a character, an author can reveal the character's strengths and weaknesses directly or by describing the character's thoughts, showing the character in action, and recording the character's dialogues. Characters such as Burnett's Mary Lennox in *The Secret Garden* (1911) are memorable because, like real people, they are neither all good nor all bad. Like real people, they must overcome believable problems as they progress through life.

Contemporary characters such as the heroine in Fenner's *Yolanda's Genius* (1995) frequently relate more closely to modern problems. The author develops vivid characterization for both a bright fifth grader and her slower younger brother, Andrew. The author develops a heroine whose actions show both her intelligence and her respect for her younger brother's musical ability. Her ability to retaliate against those who torment her brother leaves little doubt about her attitude.

Setting. Setting is where the story takes place. It identifies the time as past, present, or future. Whether the setting is developed through illustrations or text, it must provide details that reinforce the plot and characterization. Setting in historical fiction is especially important, because the details must be true to the time period. In science fiction and fantasy, the author must provide enough detail to make the readers believe in a world that is yet to materialize or in a place that is impossible from what we know of our world, as in Pullman's *The Golden Compass* (1966). As in Brown's *Shadow* (1982), the setting may create both an antagonist and a detailed fantasy world, and the setting may create the mood of a story. As in Sperry's *Call It Courage* (1940), setting may create the antagonist. As in Freedman's *Lincoln: A Photobiography* (1987) and Cushman's *The Midwife's Apprentice* (1995), setting may create the historical background. Finally, as in *The Secret Gar-*

den (1911), setting may create a symbolic location for human growth and healing as well as natural growth.

Theme.   **Theme** is the central idea that ties the plot, characterizations, and setting together into a meaningful whole. The theme is frequently the authors' purpose for writing the story, the message. Authors of books for younger children frequently state the theme, while authors of books for older students usually imply the theme through characterizations and conflict resolution. A memorable theme usually relates to the reader's needs. For example, Grifalconi's *Darkness and the Butterfly* (1987) develops two themes: (1) it is all right to experience fears and (2) we can and must overcome our fears. In *Walk Two Moons,* a book for older readers, Creech (1994) uses mysterious messages to formulate her themes.

Style.   **Style** is an author's choice and arrangement of words to create plot, characterizations, setting, and theme. The sounds may appeal to the senses. The word choices and sentence lengths may create a leisurely or frightening mood. Figurative language may allow us to visualize concepts in new ways. Symbolism, such as that found in Voigt's *Dicey's Song* (1982), may allow us to understand characterization and appreciate a well-crafted novel. Effective style is usually most noticeable when reading a book orally. For example, Alexander's often poetic style in *The Arkadians* (1995) enhances a fantasy formulated on Greek mythology.

Point of View.   Authors choose a viewpoint to use when they tell a story, including the details they describe and the judgments they make. Frye, Baker, and Perkins (1985) state, "The narrator, or teller of the story, may stand within the story or outside it, narrating as it occurs, shortly after, or much later, providing in each instance a different narrative perspective in space and time" (p. 302). Consequently, the same story would change drastically if told from another **point of view.** For example, Potter's *The Tale of Peter Rabbit* (1902) would certainly change if told from the viewpoint of Mr. McGregor.

Avi's *Nothing but the Truth: A Documentary Novel* (1991), a fictional novel written in documentary format, allows readers to interpret each of the incidents, draw their own conclusions about the truthfulness of the documents, and decide which characters are changed the most by the incidents and the conclusions. As a consequence, students may gain insights into how emotions define and distort the truth and how important understanding of point of view is when reading a book.

Authors may use first person, which allows them to speak through the "I" of one of the characters; an objective point of view, which lets actions speak for themselves; an omniscient point of view, which allows the author to tell the story in third person and be all-knowing about the characters; or a limited omniscient point of view, which allows the author to concentrate on one character but to still be all-knowing about other characters. First-person narratives are frequently used in books for younger students, such as in the various "Ramona" stories. Books for older students frequently use the omniscient or limited omniscient point of view. Whatever point of view is used, it should be consistent.

Developing Literary Enjoyment and Appreciation

One of the primary goals of any reading program is to develop readers who turn to literature for both pleasure and knowledge. Providing many opportunities for students to listen to, read, and discuss literature entices them to love and appreciate books. This section focuses on two activities that are beneficial to the reading teacher who is trying to increase enjoyment of reading: (1) oral reading to students and (2) recreational reading groups.

■ Oral Reading to Students

Reading to students develops understanding of various story structures, increases knowledge of language patterns, expands vocabularies, and introduces genres of literature that students might not read independently (see Chapters 3 and 4). Consequently, the book selected for reading aloud should be worthy of the time spent by both the reader and the listeners. Children's ages, attention spans, and levels of reading ability are important considerations. The books chosen should increase students' appreciation of outstanding literature. The numerous easy-to-read books should usually be left for younger students to read independently.

Reading aloud should not end in the lower elementary grades. Older students also benefit from being exposed to literature too difficult for them to read independently. Books such as Esther Forbes' *Johnny Tremain* (1943) and Kenneth Grahame's *The Wind in the Willows* (1908) should not be missed because the language is too difficult for students to read.

After selecting a book, the teacher should read it silently to understand the story, identify the sequence of events, recognize the mood, identify any concepts or vocabulary that may cause problems, decide how to introduce the story, and consider the appropriate type of discussion. Next, the teacher should read the book aloud to himself or herself in order to practice pronunciation, pacing, and voice characterization. Teachers should *never* read stories aloud to an audience before reading the stories themselves.

Lamme (1976) provides the following observations concerning effective oral reading to students:

1. Child involvement, including predicting what will happen next and filling in missing words, is the most influential factor during oral reading.
2. Eye contact between the reader and the audience is essential.
3. Adults who read with expression are more effective than those who use a monotonous tone.
4. Good oral readers put variety into their voices; pitch should be neither too high nor too low, and volume should be neither too loud nor too soft.
5. Readers who point to meaningful words or pictures in a book as they read are better than those who merely read the story and show the pictures.

6. Knowing the story, without needing to read the text verbatim, is more effective than straight reading.

7. Readers who select picture books large enough for the students to see and appealing enough to hold their interest or elicit their comments are most effective.

8. Grouping students so that all can see the pictures and hear the story is important.

9. Adults who highlight the words and language of the story by making the rhymes apparent, discussing unusual vocabulary words, and emphasizing any repetition are better readers.

It is impossible to have an effective oral reading experience without adequate preparation. Also notice that many factors, such as highlighting the language of the story and encouraging students to predict what will happen next, are related to important reading skills.

■ Recreational Reading Groups

Reading widely and frequently encourages literary appreciation and reinforces the development of reading skills. Reading activities based on literature help students synthesize information from several sources, clarify their developing literary skills, and share revelations about their discoveries. Uninterrupted sustained silent reading (USSR) and **recreational reading groups** encourage the reading of literature.

Recreational reading groups are especially appropriate for literature-based reading programs because they encourage discussion of books. The criteria of selection allow discussions that relate to specific objectives for the reading groups.

If students select their own materials, divide the class into about three groups, with a leader designated for each group. Have students bring their books to one of the three circles, read silently for about 30 minutes, and then tell something interesting about their books. During the first experience, it is advisable to form one group in which you model independent reading behavior and begin telling something about the book. Later, you may move from group to group. By placing competent readers next to less efficient readers, you encourage students to get help with unknown words. The reading groups may contain different students each time, or the groups may remain together until their books are finished.

If the groups are formed according to topic, literary genre, or characteristics of literature, leave them together until the subject has been thoroughly explored. Focus discussions on that element of the literature, the authors' development of the element, and what students liked or did not like about the authors' development. Focus groups should provide opportunities to reinforce specific reading skills or to explore topics of interest.

For example, form a group around personification. Choose literature from picture storybooks, poetry, and longer novels, depending on the students' interests and reading levels. Choices of literature may include picture storybooks, such as Anthony Browne's *Gorilla* (1983), Virginia Lee Burton's *The Little House* (1942), Emily Arnold McCully's *School* (1987) (a wordless book in which personification

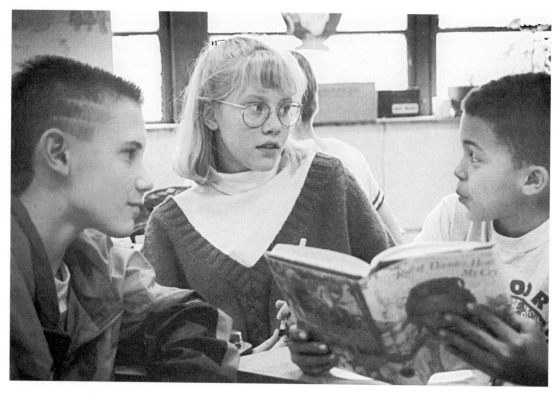

Recreational reading groups are especially appropriate for literature-based reading programs.

is interpreted through the illustrations), and Margery Williams' *The Velveteen Rabbit* (1958); poetry, such as Stephen Dunning's *Reflections on a Gift of Watermelon Pickle . . .* (1967), Jamake Highwater's *Moonsong Lullaby* (1981), and Henry Wadsworth Longfellow's *Hiawatha* (1893); and longer novels, such as W. J. Corbett's *The Song of Pentecost* (1983), Kenneth Grahame's *The Wind in the Willows* (1908), Brian Jacques' *Redwall* (1986), Robert Lawson's *Rabbit Hill* (1944), and E. B. White's *Charlotte's Web* (1952).

If personification is the focus, have students look for and discuss evidence of personification by identifying how the authors personify animals, nature, and objects; by discussing the meaning of personification; and by deciding on the appropriateness of the personified images for the story.

If symbolism is being studied, have students discuss the symbolism in books such as Frances Hodgson Burnett's *The Secret Garden* (1911), Sid Fleischman's *The Whipping Boy* (1986), Sharon Bell Mathis's *The Hundred Penny Box* (1975), and Cynthia Voigt's *Dicey's Song* (1982). Other effective literary topics include characterization, setting, conflict, theme, point of view, and style. Focus discussions on specific literary characteristics that are also important reading objectives. Focusing on specific genres of literature helps students broaden their reading interests and increase their understandings of the characteristics of folklore, fantasy, poetry, realistic fiction, historical fiction, biography, and nonfiction.

Topics for recreational reading groups are as varied as the students' interests and the available literature. Humorous literature, animal stories, space science, stories by specific authors, and stories about children who are the same ages as the class are just a few. Focus the reading and discussion on such topics as how the author develops humorous stories and the effectiveness of the techniques, and how the readers respond to the humor in the stories. Looking at the various books of one author or poet is interesting. Authors such as Maurice Sendak, Dr. Seuss, Russell Hoban, and Tomie de Paola have written numerous stories for younger students. Likewise, authors such as Betsy Byars, Beverly Cleary, Helen Creswell, and Marguerite Henry have written many stories for middle elementary students. Authors such as Lloyd Alexander, John Christopher, Susan Cooper, Jean Craighead George, Virginia Hamilton, Madeleine L'Engle, Scott O'Dell, Katherine Paterson, and Cynthia Voigt have written numerous stories for older elementary and middle school students. Ideas for lessons on these topics are found in Norton's *The Impact of Literature-Based Reading* (1992). Norton's *Through the Eyes of a Child: An Introduction to Children's Literature* (1995) and *Children's Literature Update* (1996) provide sources for identifying literature according to genre, literary elements, and authors.

Developing Reading Skills Through Literature

Literature and literature-related activities are important for improving and developing reading skills. Predictable books help students predict language and plot structures. Studying literature and developing semantic maps to accompany literature improve vocabulary.

Using Predictable Books

Books that encourage students to predict language and plot structures are recommended for teaching reading and language skills to younger students. Books with repetitive language and plot development may be used for readiness or beginning reading. Predictable books are frequently introduced for oral-language activities and then used for reading activities. Tompkins and Weber (1983) and McCracken and McCracken (1986) have developed guidelines for this sequence.

Tompkins and Weber describe the following five-step teaching strategy to direct students' attention to repetitive and predictable features of a book:

1. The teacher reads the title orally, shows the cover illustration, and asks students what they believe the story is about.
2. The teacher reads through the first set of repetitions, stopping where the second set of repetitions begins and asking students to predict what will happen next or what a character will say.

3. The teacher asks students to explain why they made their specific predictions.
4. The teacher reads the next set of repetitive patterns to allow students to confirm or reject their predictions.
5. The teacher continues reading the selection, repeating steps 2, 3, and 4.

For example, to use this technique with Mem Fox's cumulative tale *Hattie and the Fox* (1987), read the title, pointing to each word. Point to the cover illustration and ask students what they think the story will be about. Through discussion, encourage the students to predict that Hattie is a hen because a hen's picture is on the cover, that the story is about a fox and a hen because the word *fox* is in the title, and that the story includes a confrontation between the fox and the hen because we know from other stories that the fox and hen are usually enemies. Expand the predictions by recalling other stories that give hints to the possible characterizations of fox and hen, such as "The Cock and the Mouse and the Little Red Hen" (a folktale found in Anne Rockwell's *The Three Bears and 15 Other Stories*, 1975). To help confirm these initial predictions, turn to the title page within the text. On this page, a fox is lurking behind a tree.

During the second step, read the first three pages of the text. These pages introduce the main character, a big black hen named Hattie, the beginning of a cumulative description of the hidden fox, and the repetitive responses of the various farm animals. Read the beginning of the fourth page of the text, "And Hattie said, . . ." Stop here and ask students what they think Hattie will say. Tell the students to look at the illustrations because the illustrator is providing hints about what Hattie will say. Turn the page and ask the students to predict the responses of the goose, pig, sheep, horse, and cow.

During the third step, ask students to provide reasons for their predictions. They should notice that the illustrator helps with the predictions by showing only a hidden nose in the first series of illustrations and increasing the view to a nose and eyes in the second series. Likewise, if students have had frequent experiences with repetitive text, they will expect that the animals will use the same language during the second series.

Next, read the text to allow students to confirm or reject their predictions. Continue the process, as with each repetition Hattie sees a little more of the fox's body. Students enjoy this book, because they quickly catch on to the cumulative action and the repetitive responses of the animals. They easily predict the conclusion, in which the fox acts in a predictable manner and the animals change their complacent responses.

Hattie and the Fox is equally successful with the beginning reading approach recommended by McCracken and McCracken (1986). After reading a predictable book several times to students, they encourage students to join in the reading. They use pictures to help the students follow the sequence. Then, they introduce the students to the text by printing the repetitive portion on the chalkboard or word cards in a pocket chart. They point to the words as the students say the lines.

Next, the students match the words on the word chart or chalkboard with a second, identical set of word cards. If the words form a refrain, they either place the whole refrain on the chart while the students match the words by placing identical words on top of the cards, or they create the first line of the refrain while the students produce the next lines. They repeat this activity several times to provide many opportunities for students to read the text.

Finally, they place the story on phrase cards in the pocket chart, then have the children match the phrases to pictures that represent each phrase. They continue this type of activity as the students build and rebuild the entire story, providing many opportunities for individual and group reading practice.

Additional books that may be used for these activities, because they contain either predictable plots or repetitive language, include the following:

- Bryon Barton   *The Wee Little Woman*
- Arnica Esterl   *The Fine Round Cake*
- Nancy White Carlstrom *Baby-O*
- Arnold Lobel   *A Rose in My Garden* (cumulative illustrations reinforce this cumulative poem)
- Tracey Pearson   *Old MacDonald Had a Farm*
- Jonathan London   *Fireflies, Fireflies, Light My Way*
- John Ivimey   *The Complete Story of Three Blind Mice*

■ Increasing Vocabulary Knowledge Through Literature

Reading or listening to literature encourages vocabulary development and expands vocabulary comprehension. Through literature, students discover the impact of carefully selected words. Many of the vocabulary techniques developed elsewhere in this text are equally effective with literature.

Picture books that contain extensive details or that provide motivational excitement are excellent sources for oral or written vocabulary expansion. Students may examine pictures and describe objects, animals, colors, shapes, and actions. Two books by Chris Van Allsburg are very successful with students in first through fifth grades. *The Z Was Zapped* (1987) encourages interaction between the reader and the text by presenting the alphabet in the form of a 26-act play. In each act, a letter is treated to an action that begins with that specific sound.

For example, introducing the play, the letter *A* is bombarded with falling rock. The reader must look carefully at the page to develop a script to accompany the first act. Prediction enters into the discussion, because readers must turn the page before they discover that the author describes Act 1 as "The *A* was in an avalanche." The readers can then compare their titles with the one identified by the author and consider how to change their scripts and alter their vocabularies if they consider the author's title. They can ask, What words describe an avalanche? What words emphasize the causes of an avalanche? What words tell where an avalanche takes place? What words detail the consequences of an avalanche on an unsuspecting letter?

Van Allsburg's almost wordless book, *The Mysteries of Harris Burdick* (1984), presents 14 full-page illustrations, a title, and a one-line caption to accompany each illustration. In the introduction to the book, Van Allsburg asks readers to provide the missing stories. Teachers report that the illustrations contain enough elements of mystery and fantasy to motivate excellent oral and written stories.

Concept books enhance categorizing vocabulary according to specific functions. For example, Anne Rockwell's *First Comes Spring* (1985) may be used to categorize vocabulary related to clothes, work, play, and environmental characteristics that accompany each season of the year. Janet and Allan Ahlberg's *The Baby's Catalogue* (1982) may be used to classify vocabulary according to such categories as breakfast, toys, shopping, pets, gardens, and games. Gail Gibbons' *Trains* (1987) encourages expansion of specific vocabulary. Books such as Tana Hoban's *Shapes, Shapes, Shapes* (1986), *Circles, Triangles, and Squares* (1974), and *Round & Round & Round* (1983) stimulate identifying and categorizing vocabulary according to shapes. Hoban's *All About Where* (1991), Hutchins's *What Game Shall We Play?* (1990), and Noll's *Watch Where You Go* (1990) foster categorizing vocabulary according to spatial concepts such as *above, behind,* and *under.* Emberley's *Let's Go: A Book in Two Languages* (1993) may be used to categorize vocabulary in both English and Spanish around topics such as seasons, the zoo, and airports.

Older students benefit from responding to wordless books that have geographical, historical, or literary connections. For example, John Goodall's *The Story of a Main Street* (1987) and *The Story of an English Village* (1979) depict changes over time. Detailed illustrations in *The Story of a Main Street* trace the evolution of an English street from medieval, to Elizabethan, to Restoration, to Georgian, to Regency, to Victorian, to Edwardian, and to current times. Describing the architecture, costumes, customs, trade, or transportation, students may compare similarities and differences across periods as well as increase their technical vocabularies.

Mitsumasa Anno's detailed wordless books contain literary, historical, and geographical details. Some are in the correct time and place, while others are not; therefore, students must search the illustrations for literary, artistic, and historical details. The detailed drawings in *Anno's Britain* (1982), *Anno's Italy* (1980), *Anno's Flea Market* (1984), and *Anno's USA* (1982) encourage extensive vocabulary development; analysis of time and place; and application of literary, artistic, and historical knowledge.

Semantic mapping or webbing procedures, identified as effective for vocabulary development by Toms-Bronowski (1983) and Johnson and Pearson (1984), are especially effective when used with literature. Semantic mapping can help students identify words with similar meanings, expand a precise vocabulary, understand multiple meanings for words, develop concepts, and perceive relationships among words and ideas.

■ Semantic Mapping and Vocabulary Development

To use a semantic-mapping approach to increase vocabulary development, first read the literature selection and identify vocabulary words or concepts that are crucial to understanding that book. Next, draw a web on the board with the title of the book in the center of the web (see Figure 9.1). On the arms extending from the center, place the important words from the story. During a brainstorming session, have students add words, such as synonyms and definitions that expand their comprehension of the key words. Complete this activity as a prereading vo-

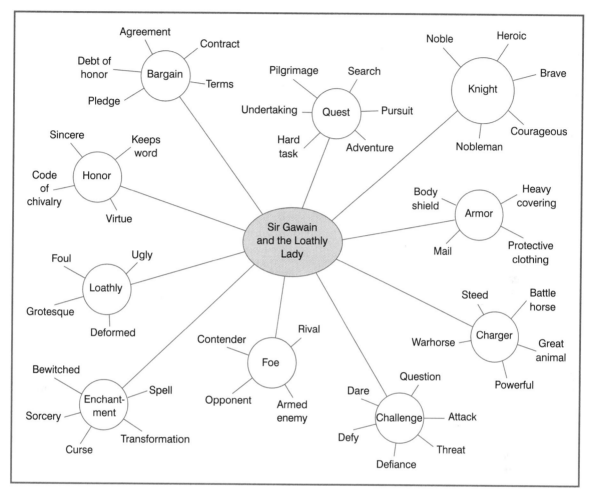

FIGURE 9.1
Vocabulary web for a literature selection

cabulary introduction, an exploration to discover students' previous knowledge, or an introduction to important information.

Use the same web to build students' understandings of each vocabulary word. Have them consider the meaning developed by the author, select the term that is closest to that developed in the story, add new words or even phrases gained from the story, and use the vocabulary word identified in the web to increase their story comprehension. Vocabulary webs are appropriate at any grade level and may accompany books either read by students or to them (see Chapter 6).

The following is an example of how to conduct this activity with upper elementary students reading a legend, Selina Hastings' *Sir Gawain and the Loathly Lady* (1981). On the chalkboard, draw a web similar to that shown in Figure 9.1. Place the title of the book in the center of the web. Extend the vocabulary words *knight, armour, charger, challenge, foe, enchantment, loathly, honor, bargain,* and *quest* from the center. During the prereading activity, introduce these vocabulary words and have students define them or identify synonyms. Next, have students read the literature. Finally, have them add vocabulary terms to the web and identify the best meanings for the vocabulary within the context of the literature.

Developing Understanding of Literary Elements

Reading literature with understanding and appreciation requires readers to recognize various literary elements and the ways that authors use those elements to create exciting and credible stories. This section describes some of the techniques teachers may use to develop understanding of the literary elements.

■ Semantic Mapping

Semantic mapping or webbing is effective for identifying the literary elements in a book and extending discussions around those literary elements. Prior to the webbing experience, introduce and discuss the literary elements of setting, characterization, conflict, plot, and theme by reading and discussing folktales with the students. Tales such as "The Three Little Pigs" and "Cinderella" are good for this introduction because the good and bad characters, the conflict, and the theme are easy to recognize.

For the first webbing activity around literary elements, demonstrate the technique to the entire group. On the board, draw a web around the title of the story, with the literary elements extending from the center. As you read the story, have students listen for the various categories. After you complete the story, lead a discussion encouraging students to fill in the various categories on the web or only one element. If necessary, reread sections to help students identify the specific element(s) and choose appropriate wording for the web.

After demonstrating this activity several times, let the students try the webbing approach with other types of literature or with more complex literature. Either read the literature to the students or have them read it themselves. Have students develop their own webs before you lead the discussion or have them develop the webs concurrently with the discussion. If students developed their own webs beforehand, have them add to the webs during the discussion to focus their attention on the task and involve them in the discussion.

The lesson plan shown in Figure 9.2 was developed for and taught in the upper elementary grades (Norton & Norton, 1994). The lesson plan demonstrates the development of a lesson for webbing literary elements using Avi's *The True Confessions of Charlotte Doyle* (1990) (see Figure 9.3).

Activities such as those outlined in the previous lesson plan encourage higher thought processes, analysis of text, synthesis of ideas, understanding of literary elements, and comprehension of story structures. The activities encourage interaction among the students and the text and among the students and the teacher. As students expand their ability to identify and analyze various literary characteristics, they may add new insights to the literature discussion. Additional

Purpose:	1. To develop an understanding of the integrated nature of literary elements in a book
	2. To develop a literary web that includes setting, characterization, conflicts, and themes
	3. To discuss the importance of each of the literary elements in a book
	4. To write journal entries that could be the background for the book
Materials:	Avi's *The True Confessions of Charlotte Doyle* (1990), 1991 Newbery Honor Award Winner
Grade level:	Upper elementary, middle school
Book summary:	*The True Confessions of Charlotte Doyle* is a historical fiction novel set in 1832 aboard the *Seahawk* as it sails from England to America. The only passenger on the ship, 13-year old Charlotte Doyle, is caught between the cruelty of the captain and the mutinous actions of the crew. Details develop the historical accuracy of the time period and a carefully constructed plot creates considerable action as the heroine faces and overcomes charges of murder on the high seas. The heroine shares with the readers the information that she would not have been able to recreate her story if she had not kept a detailed journal of her experiences.
Procedures:	1. Introduce the book by reading and discussing the introduction, "An Important Warning." Ask the students to think about what the author is revealing about the story and the character in the first paragraph: "Not every thirteen-year-old girl is accused of murder, brought to trial, and found guilty. But I was just such a girl, and my story is worth relating even if it did happen years ago. Be warned, however, this is no *Story of a Bad Boy*, no *What Katy Did*. If strong ideas and action offend you, read no more. Find another companion to share your idle hours. For my part I intend to tell the truth as I lived it" (p. 1). Also, ask the students to respond to the impact of this first paragraph on readers.
	To introduce the setting for the book, show and discuss pictures of smaller merchant sailing ships that would have crossed the Atlantic

FIGURE 9.2
Webbing literary elements
Source: From D. E. Norton and S. E. Norton, **Language Arts Activities for Children,** Third edition (Upper Saddle River, NJ: Merrill/Prentice Hall). Reprinted with permission of Prentice Hall.

in 1832. You can also discuss the author's references to the two books in the first paragraph. For example, *The Story of a Bad Boy* was written by Thomas Bailey Aldrich in 1870. The types of exploits described in the book are common for Victorian heroes during the late 1800s: boys practiced the "manly arts," formed clubs, and played pranks. These activities are very different from the exploits of Charlotte Doyle. Students can compare what they believe Charlotte's exploits will be with those of *The Story of a Bad Boy.*

2. Place a literary elements web on the board (see Figure 9.3). As you write *setting, characterization, conflicts,* and *themes* on the board, ask the students to consider what they might expect to find under each element in this book after they listen to and discuss the introduction. Ask the students to fill in the details on the web as they either listen to or read the book *The True Confessions of Charlotte Doyle.* After the web is completed, discuss the interactions and importance of each of the details under the literary elements. Figure 9.3 is a partial example of a resulting literary web.

3. After completing the web, ask students to consider the importance of the journal entries in the following quote: "Keeping that journal then is what enables me to relate now in perfect detail everything that transpired during that fateful voyage across the Atlantic Ocean in the summer of 1832" (p. 3). Ask the students to select one of the chapters in *The True Confessions of Charlotte Doyle* and to write the journal entry that motivated the writing of and provided the details for the incidents described in the chapter.

4. Another writing activity may be developed around point of view. Ask students to consider and discuss why they think Avi wrote this story from Charlotte Doyle's point of view. Ask them to look again at the web to identify each of the instances on the web in which the heroine's point of view is extremely important in developing the various literary elements. Then, ask the students to consider how the story might change if told through the point of view of Captain Jaggery, Zachariah, or one of the other crew members. They could also choose to write a response to Charlotte Doyle's journal from the point of view of her father.

FIGURE 9.2, *continued*

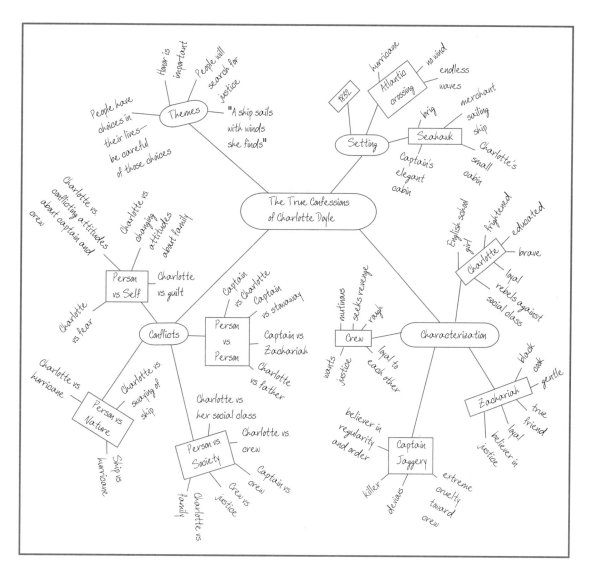

FIGURE 9.3
Literary elements web

literary webs are found in Norton's *Through the Eyes of a Child* (1995), *The Effective Teaching of Language Arts* (1997), and *The Impact of Literature-Based Reading* (1992).

■ Plot Structures

As noted, a story must have a beginning, a middle, and an end. Diagrams of plot structure help students understand plot development and the inherent conflicts. Two plot structures are especially important in children's literature: (1) those with external conflict and (2) those with person-versus-self conflict.

Most plots in stories for younger students follow a structure that introduces the characters and conflict at the beginning of the story, increases the conflict until a climax, identifies the turning point, and ends the conflict. This structure is usually found when the main character faces external forces. You can help your students recognize and understand this structure by diagramming the key incidents from such a story. Figure 9.4 diagrams a structure with such external conflict. Using this structure, Figure 9.5 diagrams the plot structure of *Sir Gawain and the Loathly Lady*.

In a second plot structure, the conflict is basically within the main character (see Figure 9.6). Cohen (1985) states that person-versus-self stories follow a structure that introduces the character and conflict, follows the conflict within the character, moves to a climax (the point at which the character realizes the problem and accepts it), and concludes when the character finally achieves peace. Figure 9.7 applies this person-versus-self structure to Marion Dane Bauer's *On My Honor* (1986), a contemporary realistic fiction story.

■ Modeling Literary Analysis

Modeling is one of the most important strategies to use when developing students' comprehension of literature (Dole, Duffy, Roehler, & Pearson, 1991). Researchers Roehler and Duffy (1984) and Gordon (1985) developed an instructional approach that places the teacher in an interactive role with the students (see Chapters 2 and 7). In this approach, the teacher analyzes literary concepts

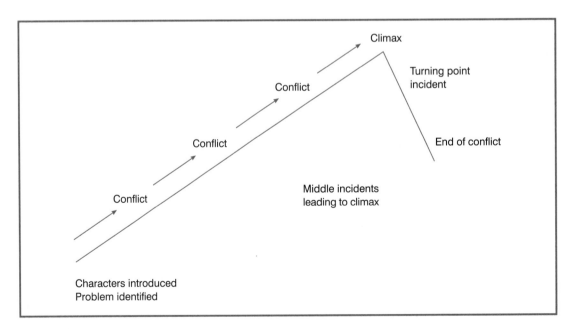

FIGURE 9.4
Plot structure for external conflict

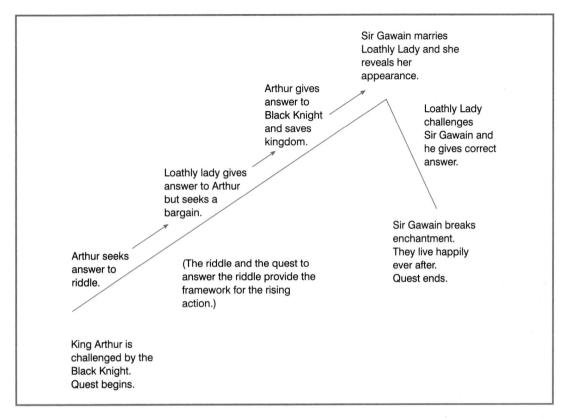

Sir Gawain marries Loathly Lady and she reveals her appearance.

Arthur gives answer to Black Knight and saves kingdom.

Loathly Lady challenges Sir Gawain and he gives correct answer.

Loathly lady gives answer to Arthur but seeks a bargain.

Sir Gawain breaks enchantment. They live happily ever after. Quest ends.

Arthur seeks answer to riddle.

(The riddle and the quest to answer the riddle provide the framework for the rising action.)

King Arthur is challenged by the Black Knight. Quest begins.

FIGURE 9.5
External conflict structure for _Sir Gawain_ _and the Loathly Lady_

before expecting the students to accomplish a similar task. The modeling helps students understand important cognitive processes. As the modeling progresses, the approach proceeds from total teacher modeling, to gradual student interaction, to total student analysis. This section considers how to use modeling when developing students' literary understanding.

Modeling is especially effective when developing understanding of literature, because the longer literature texts encourage a synthesis of ideas and provide more opportunity for teachers and students to draw evidence. The reasoning stage of literary analysis encourages teachers and students to think about some of the more difficult aspects of the literature and to draw on their previous experiences. Modeling is especially effective with complex tasks, such as inferring characterization, identifying theme, and speculating about allusions and symbolism.

Teachers who are developing and teaching modeling lessons should follow the recommendations for effective modeling identified by Dole and colleagues (1991):

1. Modeling that provides explicit, unambiguous information is more effective than modeling that provides vague or jumbled information.

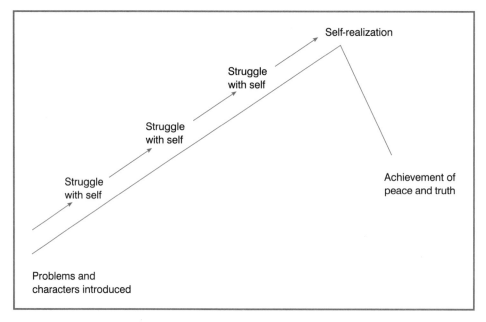

FIGURE 9.6
Plot structure for person-versus-self conflict

2. Modeling that demonstrates flexible adjustment to text cues is more effective than modeling that emphasizes rigid rules.

3. If teachers merely ask questions without explaining the reasoning employed to answer those questions, many students will have difficulty understanding how the questions were answered.

If students do not understand how the questions were answered, they will not gain control of the process associated with answering the questions. Consequently, the process suffers.

Gordon (1985) uses a five-step approach to help students understand important cognitive processes associated with comprehension of text. First, the teacher identifies the skill to be taught, analyzes the requirements for effective reasoning within that skill, identifies text samples that require the skill, and identifies questions to stimulate the students to use that skill or thought process. During this preparatory phase, the teacher also considers how to introduce the skill to students.

Second, the teacher completely models the strategy by reading the text, asking a question, answering the question, citing evidence that supports the answer, and then verbally following the reasoning process used to acquire the answer.

Third, the teacher involves the students in citing the evidence. During this step, the teacher reads the text, asks a question, and answers it. Then the teacher asks the students to cite evidence for the answer. Finally, the teacher leads a discussion that explores the reasoning. The strategy is more clear to students if they make notes concerning the various parts.

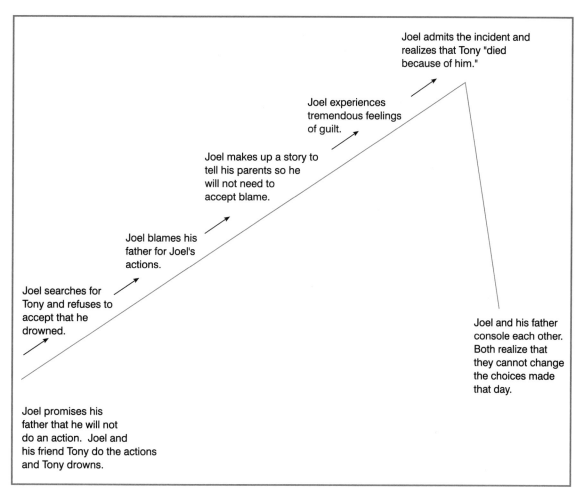

Joel admits the incident and realizes that Tony "died because of him."

Joel experiences tremendous feelings of guilt.

Joel makes up a story to tell his parents so he will not need to accept blame.

Joel blames his father for Joel's actions.

Joel searches for Tony and refuses to accept that he drowned.

Joel and his father console each other. Both realize that they cannot change the choices made that day.

Joel promises his father that he will not do an action. Joel and his friend Tony do the actions and Tony drowns.

FIGURE 9.7
Person-versus-self structure for On My Honor

Fourth, the teacher involves the students in answering the question. During this step, the teacher reads the text and asks a question; the students answer the question; the teacher cites the evidence; and then the teacher leads a discussion that explores the reasoning process.

Fifth, students have primary responsibility during most of the strategy. The teacher reads the text and asks a question, but the students answer the question, cite the evidence that supports the question, and explain the reasoning involved in reaching their answers.

This approach is especially effective with children's literature in which the author uses inferences to develop characterization; uses figurative language to create mood, suggest characterization, or enhance conflict; uses conflict and interactions among characters to develop theme; or uses historical settings to develop background, create an antagonist, or develop person versus society conflicts, because such literary concepts are difficult for students to understand. Books that contain these characteristics stimulate exciting discussions as students recognize the author's techniques and discover the impact of well-developed literature.

Teachers may model with picture storybooks that are completed in one lesson or with books that take several days to complete. Modeling is especially effective when the teacher identifies techniques used by an author and then demonstrates how to read and understand the techniques. Modeling may introduce a book that the students will read later. In this way, the modeling stimulates interest in the literature and encourages students to read with understanding and appreciation.

Consider how to use modeling to introduce the understanding of figurative language in Rudolf Frank's *No Hero for the Kaiser* (1986). In this historical fiction book for older students, Frank uses figurative language to depict the wartime setting, enhance characterization, clarify the conflict, and suggest theme.

In step 1, identify a skill, such as inferring the author's meaning from figurative language. Analyze the requirements for effective inferences, which follow:

- To identify nonliteral comparisons.
- To realize that figurative language is meant to clarify and enlighten by developing new relationships.
- To identify the similarities or differences between two things.
- To go beyond the information the author provides in the text.
- To use clues from the text to hypothesize about the relationships between figurative language and setting, characterization, conflict, and theme.
- To use background knowledge gained from other experiences.

Then identify text examples of figurative language. For example, similes appear on pages 2, 12, 44, and 46 of *No Hero for the Kaiser.* Many more similes are in the text, but these few should produce interesting modeling and discussions. Contrasts appear on pages 45, 46, and 65. Symbolism appears on pages 2 (plum tree), 18 (Wild Goat), and 59 (Lance Corporal Poodle). Allusions to Napoleon appear on pages 42 and 49–51. Allusions to a myth about the skull of an African sultan that supposedly influenced the beginning of World War I appear on pages 21 and 70–71. Note that students may have comprehension problems in these areas.

In step 2, introduce the text. Review the place by identifying Germany, Russia, and Poland on a map. Discuss these places, the students' knowledge of the historical time (1914–1918), the seasons, and the fact that war causes desolation and destruction. Review figurative language, such as similes, contrasts, symbolism, and allusions, using examples. For example, be sure that the students know that a simile is a direct comparison in which the author uses *like, as,* or *as if.*

Begin reading, stopping on page 2 to emphasize and discuss the meaning of the similes in this passage:

> The distant thud of cannon came closer, like a thunderstorm brewing. And as if the storm had already broken, women, boys, girls, and soldiers began to rush around in confusion; trumpets sounded, and suddenly the Russians had swept out of the village like the wind. Now they were firing down from the low hills

into the village. It sounded like the high-pitched whine of mosquitoes as they fly past your ear looking for a place to settle and bite: zzzzzz—a thin, sharp noise, full of malice. (p. 2)

Ask an inferential question or questions, such as "What is the author telling us about the setting in the Polish village?" "What is the author telling us about war?" "How does the author's use of simile increase your ability to visualize the setting and the war that will follow?" "Do you believe that these are good comparisons?" and "Why or why not?"

Answer the question or questions. Tell the students, "The town is, or will be, the setting for a noisy and destructive battle. Soldiers who once enjoyed the town are running to take their places on the battlefield. People in the town are also running. The author tells us that war is terrible and destructive. The author's use of similes helps us hear the battle, see the movement, and feel the danger. I believe that the similes are good comparisons."

Cite evidence for your answers. Say, for example, "The author describes the normal activity and appearance of the town and describes changes. The sound of cannon is compared to a thunderstorm. The rapidly advancing Russian soldiers are compared to wind sweeping through the town. The sound of bullets is compared to the whine of mosquitoes."

Explore your own reasoning process. For example, "The author describes the village and then shows what happens to it when two forces are about to fight. I know from my own experience that a thunderstorm and a cannon sound alike. I also know from my experience and from other reading that a thunderstorm can bring destruction in the form of lightning and high winds. I believe that this is a good comparison for an approaching battle. I can close my eyes and see and hear the battle.

"I also know from experience that when wind sweeps through the streets, it moves everything in front of it. I can close my eyes and see people rushing away from the army as it sweeps through town without thinking of the consequences of its actions. In this way, the army is also like the wind.

"I also know that bullets and mosquitoes sound somewhat alike. I know that mosquitoes have a nasty bite. When the author uses expressions such as "sly malice," I think that he is saying that the bullets are much worse than mosquitoes.

"The author also may be saying that mosquitoes and bullets are alike in another way. They both hit innocent victims. I believe from these comparisons that the author is telling us that war is terrible for all people, including innocent bystanders." Notice that this last statement may also encourage a discussion about what the students believe to be the theme of the book.

Continue the modeling approach, using other examples, until the students can provide evidence for their answers and can rationalize them. Encourage discussion and varied viewpoints. This approach helps students check their reasoning and does not suggest that there is only one correct answer. In fact, modeling lessons usually broaden rather than narrow the students' answers.

Asking students to jot down their answers, their evidence, and their reasoning before discussion encourages them to focus on the task, interact during the discussion, and develop their thought processes. Additional good subjects for modeling and discussion include the following:

- *Additional similes,* such as, "What does the author mean when he states, 'Like huge wolves the four cannons of the Seventh Battery went into the field'?" (from page 46).
- *Contrasts* of the peaceful and war meanings for words and phrases, such as *bullseye* (from page 45) and *in the fields* (from pages 45–46). Ask, "What is the author saying when he uses these comparisons?" and "How does the author use these comparisons to reinforce the antiwar theme of the book?" Encourage the students to cite evidence that supports their answers and to describe the reasoning they used to reach their answers.
- *Symbolism.* Model and discuss the significance of symbolism for things and names. Ask, for example, "What does the symbolism of the plum tree (on page 18) reveal about the author's attitude toward war?" "What does the author's symbolism of Wild Goat (on page 54) and White Raven (on page 18) reveal about the characterization of the two German officers?" and "What is the author telling us about war when he names the dog Lance Corporal Poodle on page 59?"
- *Allusions.* Model and discuss the author's choice of allusions to Napoleon (see pages 42 and 49–51), the skull of the African sultan (see pages 21 and 70–71), and the Flood (see page 56).

☑ Summary

Literature-based instructional programs, in which teachers use literature as the core of the reading curriculum, are increasing rapidly. In such programs, reading is considered the ability to read all types of literature with understanding, appreciation, and enjoyment. Creating students who both understand and appreciate literature has specific requirements.

Choosing literature that motivates students to read and stimulates an appreciation of literature requires knowledge about literature and an awareness of the students' interests. Likewise, teaching literature requires knowledge about literature and instructional approaches that encourage the broad development of reading skills. In addition to developing literary understanding and appreciation, literature-based programs encourage students to realize the importance of literature as a mirror of human experience, be able to gain insights from their involvement with literature, become aware of writers who represent diverse backgrounds and traditions, become familiar with past and present masterpieces of literature, develop effective ways of discussing and writing about various forms of literature, appreciate the rhythms and beauty of the language in literature, and develop lifelong reading habits.

As students expand their abilities to read literature for understanding, appreciation, and enjoyment, they are confronted with such terms as *plot, characterization, setting, theme, style,* and *point of view.* Literary enjoyment and appreciation are enhanced through oral reading to students and recreational reading groups. Reading skills are strengthened through literature using predictable books, increasing vocabulary knowledge, and developing understanding of literary elements.

Discussion strategies that encourage students to respond to and interact with literature are especially effective. This chapter develops several of these strategies, including semantic mapping of literary elements and vocabulary, plot structuring for conflicts outside or within a character, and modeling of the thought processes associated with analyzing literary elements.

☑ Your Point of View

Discussion Questions

1. Identify the reading objectives stated in a unit of a basal reading series. Develop a list of literature selections that would reinforce and strengthen those objectives. Share your rationales for choosing the books.
2. Assume that you will be teaching a literature-based program at a specific grade level. What are the literature selections that you consider important for that grade? Take into consideration the quality of the literature, the appropriateness of the literature for the grade level, and the reading objectives that you want to teach. Develop a core list of books. Give your reasons for selecting the books.
3. Choose an instructional approach, such as modeling, semantic mapping, or plot structuring. Develop a lesson plan that uses one of these strategies to increase understanding of literature.
4. Assume that you will be using recreational reading groups to enhance students' enjoyment of literature. Develop a list of books that follow a genre approach, an author approach, or a literary elements approach. Try one of the recreational reading groups in your college reading class. Analyze the responses of the class. What types of information did they share? Did you want to read any of the books discussed by other members of the group? Now, what do you believe are the strengths of recreational reading groups?

Take a Stand For or Against

1. Some reading authorities want literature to supplement the basal reading curriculum. In contrast, other reading authorities want literature to form the total reading curriculum. Consider the advantages and disadvantages of each approach. Share your responses with your class.
2. Several groups have identified the literature selections that should be the core of the school literature program. Read and analyze several of these lists, such as *Recommended Readings in Literature: Kindergarten Through Grade Eight* (1986) and "Education Secretary Bennett's Suggested Reading List for Elementary-School Pupils" (1988). What is your opinion of each list? Are there books that should be added or deleted? Is there a core of books that every educated person should read? Why or why not?

Bibliography

Ahlberg, J., and Ahlberg, A. (1982). *The baby's catalogue*. Boston: Little, Brown & Co.

Alexander, L. (1995). *The Arkadians*. New York: Dutton.

Allison, D. and Watson, J. A. (1994). The significance of adult storybook reading styles on the development of young children's emergent reading. *Reading Research and Instruction, 34,* 57–72.

Anno, M. (1980). *Anno's Italy*. Ontario, Canada: Collins.

Anno, M. (1982). *Anno's Britain*. New York: Philomel.

Anno, M. (1982). *Anno's USA*. New York: Philomel.

Anno, M. (1984). *Anno's flea market*. London: Bodlet Head.

Avi. (1991). *Nothing but the truth: A documentary novel*. New York: Orchard.

Avi. (1990). *The true confessions of Charlotte Doyle*. New York: Orchard.

Barton, B. (1995). *The wee little woman*. New York: HarperCollins.

Bauer, M. D. (1986). *On my honor*. New York: Clarion.

Book Review Subcommittee of the National Council for the Social Studies—Children's Book Council Joint Committee. (April/May 1992). *Social Education,* 253–264.

Breckenridge, K. (April 1988). Modern classics. *School Library Journal, 34,* 42–43.

Brown, M. (1982). *Shadow*. New York: Charles Scribner's Sons.

Browne, A. (1983). *Gorilla*. New York: Watts.

Burnett, F. H. (1911). *The secret garden*. New York: J. B. Lippincott Co.

Burton, V. L. (1942). *The little house*. Boston: Houghton Mifflin Co.

Cohen, C. L. (August 1985). The quest in children's literature. *School Library Journal, 31,* 28–29.

Corbett, W. J. (1983). *The song of Pentecost*. New York: E. P. Dutton.

Creech, S. (1994). *Walk two moons*. New York: HarperCollins.

Curtis, C. P. (1995). *The Watsons go to Birmingham—1963*. New York: Delacorte.

Cushman, K. (1995). *The midwife's apprentice*. New York: Clarion.

Dole, J., Duffy, G., Roehler, L., & Pearson, P. D. (1991). Moving from the old to the new: Research on reading comprehension instruction. *Review of Educational Research, 61,* 239–264.

Dunning, S., Lueders, E., & Smith, H. (Eds.) (1967). *Reflections on a gift of watermelon pickle. . .* New York: Lothrop, Lee & Shepard.

Early, M., & Ericson, B. (1988). The act of reading. In B. F. Nelms (Ed.), *Literature in the classroom: Readers, texts, and contexts*. Urbana, IL: National Council of Teachers of English, 31–44.

Education Secretary Bennett's suggested reading list for elementary-school pupils (September 1988). *The Chronicle of Higher Education,* B3.

Emberley, R. (1993). *Let's go: A book in two languages*. Boston: Little, Brown.

Feitelson, D., Rita, B., & Goldstein, Z. (1986). Effects of listening to series stories on first graders' comprehension and use of language. *Research in the Teaching of English, 20,* 339–355.

Fenner, C. (1995). *Yolonda's Genuis*. New York: McElderry.

Five, C. L. (1988). From workbook to workshop: Increasing children's involvement in the reading process. *The New Advocate, 1,* 92–102.

Fleischman, S. (1986). *The whipping boy*. New York: Greenwillow.

Forbes, E. (1943). *Johnny Tremain*. Boston: Houghton Mifflin Co.

Fox, M. (1987). *Hattie and the fox*. New York: Bradbury.

Fox, P. (1991). *Monkey island*. New York: Orchard.

Frank, R. (1986). *No hero for the Kaiser*. New York: Lothrop, Lee & Shepard.

Freedman, G. (1987). *Lincoln: A photobiography*. New York: Clarion.

Frye, N., Baker, S., & Perkins, G. (1985). *The Harper handbook of literature*. New York: Harper & Row.

Gardner, M. (1988). An educator's concerns about the California initiative. *The New Advocate, 1,* 250–253.

Gibbons, G. (1987). *Trains*. New York: Holiday.

Goodall, J. (1987). *The story of Main Street*. Upper Saddle River, NJ: Prentice Hall.

Gordon, C. (1985). Modeling inference awareness across the curriculum. *Journal of Reading, 28,* 444–447.

Grahame, K. (1908). *The wind in the willows.* New York: Charles Scribner's Sons.

Greenaway, K. (1979). *A apple pie.* Secaucus, NJ: Castle Books.

Grifalconi, A. (1987). *Darkness and the butterfly.* Boston: Little, Brown.

Hastings, S. (1981). *Sir Gawain and the loathly lady.* New York: Lothrop, Lee & Shepard.

Hiebert, A., & Colt, J. (1989). Patterns of literature-based reading instruction. *The Reading Teacher, 43,* 14–20.

Highwater, J. (1981). *Moonsong lullaby.* New York: Lothrop, Lee & Shepard.

Hoban, T. (1991). *All about where.* New York: Greenwillow.

Hoban, T. (1974). *Circles, triangles, and squares.* Upper Saddle River, NJ: Prentice Hall.

Hoban, T. (1983). *Round & round & round.* New York: Greenwillow.

Hoban, T. (1986). *Shapes, shapes, shapes.* New York: Greenwillow.

Huck, C., Hepler, S., & Hickman, J. (1993). *Children's literature.* Orlando: Harcourt Brace Jovanovich.

Hutchins, P. (1990). *What game shall we play?* New York: Greenwillow.

Illinois State Department of Education (1985). *State goals for learning and sample learning objectives: Language arts.*

International Relations Committee (May 1988). The U.S.A. through children's books. *Booklist,* 1532–1534.

Ivimey, J. (1987). *The complete story of three blind mice.* New York: Clarion.

Johnson, D., & Pearson, P. D. (1984). *Teaching reading vocabulary.* New York: Holt, Rinehart & Winston.

Kennemer, P. K. (1984). Reviews of fiction books: How they differ. *Top of the News, 40,* 419–421.

Kingsbury, M. (1984). Perspectives on criticism. *The Horn Book, 60,* 17–32.

Jacques, B. (1986). *Redwall.* New York: Philomel.

Lamme, L. (1976). Reading aloud to young children. *Language Arts, 53,* 886–888.

Lawson, R. (1944). *Rabbit hill.* New York: Viking Press.

Lobel, A. (1984). *A rose in my garden.* New York: Greenwillow.

London, J. (1996). *Fireflies, fireflies, light my way.* Illustrated by Linda Messier. New York: Viking.

Longfellow, H. W. (1893). *Hiawatha.* New York: E. P. Dutton.

Mathis, S. B. (1975). *The hundred penny box.* New York: Viking Press.

May, J. P. (1987). Creating a schoolwide literature program: A case study. *Children's Literature Association Quarterly, 12,* 135–137.

McCloskey, R. (1941). *Make way for ducklings.* New York: Viking Press.

McCracken, R., & McCracken, M. (1986). *Stories, songs, and poetry to teach reading and writing: Literacy through language.* Chicago: American Library Association.

McCully, E. A. (1987). *School.* New York: Harper & Row.

Meeks, M. (1983). *Achieving literacy: Longitudinal case studies of adolescents learning to read.* London: Routledge and Kegal Paul.

Milne, A. A. (1926). *Winnie-the-pooh.* New York: E. P. Dutton.

National Council of Teachers of English (1983). Forum: Essentials of English. *Language Arts, 60,* 244–248.

Noll, S. (1990). *Watch where you go.* New York: Greenwillow.

Norton, D. E. (1996). *Children's literature update.* Upper Saddle River, NJ: Merrill/Prentice Hall.

Norton, D. E. (1995). *Through the eyes of a child: An introduction to children's literature* 4th (ed.). Upper Saddle River, NJ: Prentice Hall.

Norton, D. E. (1997). *The effective teaching of language arts* (5th ed.). Upper Saddle River, NJ: Merrill/Prentice Hall.

Norton, D. E. (1992). *The impact of literature-based reading.* Upper Saddle River, NJ: Merrill/Prentice Hall.

Norton, D. E., & McNamara, J. (1987). *An evaluation of the BISD/TAMU multiethnic reading program.* College Station, TX: Texas A&M University, research report.

Norton, D. E. and Norton, S. E. (1994). *Language arts activities for Children,* (3rd ed.). Upper Saddle River, NJ: Merrill/Prentice Hall.

Paulsen, G. (1987). *Hatchet.* New York: Bradbury.

Phelan, C. (1988). Poetry for young children. *Booklist, 84,* 790–792.

Potter, B. (1902). *A tale of Peter Rabbit.* New York: Warne.

Pullman, P. (1996). *The golden compass.* New York: Knopf.

Roehler, L., & Duffy, G. (1984). Direct explanation of the comprehension process. In G.

Durry, L. Roehler, & J. Mason (Eds.), *Comprehension instruction.* New York: Longman.

Rockwell, A. (1975). *The three bears and 15 other stories.* New York: Crowell.

Rockwell, A. (1985). *First comes spring.* New York: Crowell.

Ruddell, R. (1992). A whole language and literature perspective: Creating a meaning-making instructional environment. *Language Arts, 69,* 612–620.

Sadoski, M., Wilson, V. & Norton, D. (1996). The relative contributions of research-based composition activities to writing improvement in grades 1–8. *Research in the teaching of English.*

Sawyer, W. (1987). Literature and literacy: A review of research. *Language Arts, 64,* 33–39.

Sperry, A. (1940). *Call it courage.* Upper Saddle River, NJ: Prentice Hall.

Sutherland, Z., & Arbuthnot, M. H. (1991). *Children and books.* New York: HarperCollins.

Taxel, J. (1988). Notes from the editor. *The New Advocate, 1,* 73–74.

Tompkins, G., & Weber, M. (1983). What will happen next? Using predictable books with young children. *The Reading Teacher, 36,* 498–502.

Toms-Bronowski, S. (1983). An investigation of the effectiveness of selected vocabulary teaching strategies with intermediate grade level students. *Dissertation Abstracts International.*

Van Allsburg, C. (1984). *The mysteries of Harris Burdick.* Boston: Houghton Mifflin Co.

Van Allsburg, C. (1987). *The z was zapped.* Boston: Houghton Mifflin Co.

Voigt, C. (1982). *Dicey's song.* New York: Atheneum.

White, E. B. (1952). *Charlotte's web.* New York: Harper & Row.

Wilder, L. I. (1932). *The little house in the big woods.* New York: Harper & Row.

Williams, M. (1958). *The velveteen rabbit.* Garden City, NJ: Doubleday & Co.

10

Content-area Reading

Chapter Outline

Major Goals and Trends in Content Reading
Content-oriented Literature
Integrating Writing in the Content Areas
Integrating Comprehension Strategies
Primary-grade Emphasis

Expository Text
Organizational Structures
Readability

Components of Content Reading
Vocabulary Development
Studying Strategies
Reading and Study Skills
Locational Skills
Critical-reading Skills

For the Reader

You might logically assume that concentration on providing excellent instruction in the various word-identification and comprehension skills and strategies will automatically produce mature, flexible readers. Such is not the case. Early in the reading program, children are expected to read content material successfully and to locate and synthesize information. Although you could make a case for more than one neglected area in a school's curriculum, the area of reading in content subjects is probably the most important. Think of your own background for a moment and answer the following questions:

Were you directly taught how to understand text written in an expository style?

Were you directly taught how to study in your content subjects (such as math, science, and social studies)?

Were you directly taught how to locate and synthesize information from an almanac, an encyclopedia, and an atlas?

Were you directly taught how to interpret various maps, graphs, charts, and diagrams?

Notice the key word **directly** in the preceding statements. Many content-reading strategies receive only passing mention in our schools. However, everyone needs direct/explicit planned instruction and practice to meet the challenge of content material and to read in order to learn throughout life.

In each For the Reader section of this text, we ask you to preview the chapter before plunging into reading. We are attempting to change your reading habits by ensuring that you take advantage of the organization of most textbooks. By now, you have probably realized the importance of previewing what you are about to read. This is but one aspect of content reading that we recommend you directly teach in your classes. This chapter presents content-area strategies along with recommended teaching procedures.

Key Ideas

- The ability to read well in a basal reader does not ensure the ability to read well in a subject area.
- Students must apply specific strategies and skills to comprehend expository text.
- How successfully a student reads content material depends on the text, the student, and the teacher.
- The major components of content reading include vocabulary development, studying strategies, reading and study skills, locational skills, and critical-reading skills.
- Teachers should strive to tailor their instruction in the content areas to the needs of their students.

Major Goals and Trends in Content Reading

The major goal of content-area reading instruction is to teach students the attitudes, skills, and strategies that will enable them to become independent learners. While this goal has always been of paramount importance, its fulfillment has not been achieved and it is a continuing concern for literacy educators (Kinney-Sedgwick & Yochum, 1996). With the new emphases on constructing meaning in text and integrating reading instruction with the other language arts across all curricular areas, the following are growing trends in the content-reading area: content-oriented literature, integrating writing in the content areas, integrating comprehension strategies, and primary-grade emphasis.

■ Content-oriented Literature

The world of literature serves many purposes, including that of a rich source of information on content-oriented themes. Students should be exposed not only to narrative literature but also to expository literature (Armbruster, 1991; Smith & Johnson, 1994). Whether the topic is history, different cultures, animals, science, environmental concerns, or mathematics, quality literature not only will help students understand content, but also will stimulate their interest and active engagement, promote reading as a lifelong activity, aid in developing reading fluency, and promote application of reading-comprehension strategies. Incorporating good expository literature, including picture books, into the content areas is an excellent means for reinforcing all of the language processes—reading, writing, listening, and speaking—across the curriculum (Farris & Fuhler, 1994). Choosing a number of expository books at various difficulty levels dealing with a particular topic is another way of meeting the varied needs of students in any classroom.

■ Integrating Writing in the Content Areas

As stressed throughout the text, reading comprehension improves when the writing and reading processes are combined. Reading and writing simultaneously interact to make content learning more enjoyable and understandable. French, Danielson, Conn, Gale, Lueck, and Manley (1989) state, "Reading and writing in the content areas relates prior knowledge, classroom interaction, cooperative learning, vocabulary instruction, and questioning techniques" (p. 266). Both basal and literature-based programs are beginning to capitalize on this supportive relationship.

Typically, content material is more difficult for students to comprehend, primarily because of its presentation of difficult concepts, the technical vocabulary, and the different text structures of expository writing. Combining various writing assignments—whether before, during, or after content-reading instruction—can help improve students' basic understanding of ideas, inferences to be drawn from the text, and creative reactions to topics under study. This trend also must be viewed and implemented from a developmental perspective, which occurs in content instruction throughout all grades.

Opening students to the world through good literature should be a goal of content reading instruction at every grade level.

■ Integrating Comprehension Strategies

With the explosion of knowledge on how readers actively and strategically interact with text, content-reading instruction now emphasizes the learning and application of this new knowledge. Intricately related to the last two trends, content reading is viewed more as a prime area for students to learn and apply various comprehension and studying strategies and reading-study skills. They need those same skills to become successful readers of expository text. In many cases, literature and writing assignments can be the vehicles to accomplish these worthwhile goals.

The regular reading program can teach many skills and strategies, but students must apply them to content subjects to comprehend content material. Reading-comprehension and studying strategies and specific reading-study skills also must be taught directly during the content instructional period. Most importantly, students need ample teacher assistance in terms of initial instruction, explanation, clarification, guidance, and ongoing instruction in content-area activities to become strategic, independent learners. Hadaway and Young (1994) recommended using various graphic aids such as timelines, maps, flowcharts, graphs, and Venn diagrams to help build and review background knowledge and teach difficult concepts. Students need to see content reading-study skills and strategies applied to everyday materials they encounter in their own lives (Richardson & Morgan, 1993).

◼ Primary-grade Emphasis

Traditionally, formal content-area reading instruction was limited mainly to the intermediate, middle, and high school levels. This was true despite the age-old adage that every teacher should be a reading teacher and despite the descriptions of a complete reading program as including broad areas of the instructional curriculum, an independent or recreational program, and skill and strategy development in the content areas at all grade levels. A much-needed emphasis is now occurring at the primary level. Olson and Gee (1991) reported on content instruction in the primary grades and the problems that students at this level experience with expository text. The authors surveyed primary-grade teachers regarding recommended content-reading practices and strategies. They reported that "70% of the teachers found content texts more difficult than stories" (p. 300). The six highest rated practices of the teachers were "previewing concepts and vocabulary, using concrete manipulatives to develop concepts, requiring retellings, developing summaries, visualizing information, and brainstorming" (p. 300). Based on these results and recent research, Olson and Gee (1991) recommended that primary teachers use the following instructional strategies in teaching content reading:

- semantic mapping
- K-W-L: What I know, What I want to learn, What I learned
- concrete manipulatives and experiences
- expository paragraph frames
- group summarizing
- visual imagery

This primary-grade emphasis on content-reading instruction again reflects the developmental nature of learning to read, as discussed in Chapter 1 along with Chall's Stages of Reading Development.

Expository Text

Content reading ability is the degree to which a student can adequately comprehend and retain content or expository text. An adequate instructional and independent reading program does not ensure successful readers in content material. Students frequently struggle with content materials. A lack of knowledge about **expository text** is a chief reason for this difficulty (Cheek, Flippo, & Lindsey, 1997). More specific reasons include a lack of direct instruction in studying strategies and research skills, the difficulty of many content materials in terms of vocabulary and concepts, and inadequate transfer of skills from the basic reading program to content areas. In essence, students' general reading ability often does not predict how well they will do in various content areas. Evidence of this is not new, although its ramifications for instruction are still under investigation (Readence, Bean, & Baldwin, 1995; Shores, 1943).

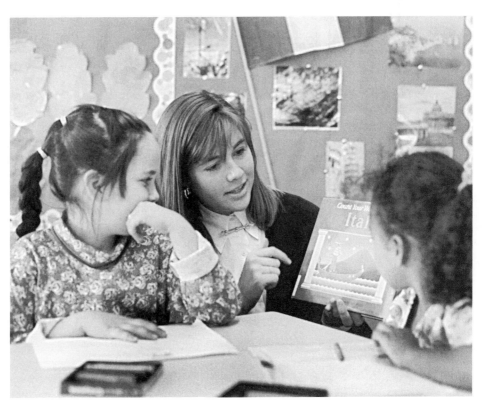

Success in the regular literacy program does not automatically spell success in reading for content. Success in understanding any new content requires teachers to teach students necessary strategies and skills.

■ Organizational Structures

Students are generally more familiar with narrative writing, because most basal reader stories follow this organizational structure. Yet, students increasingly are expected to read and understand material presented in content textbooks. Most content texts are written in an expository style. While narrative materials follow a traditional story structure (including setting, theme, plot, and resolution), expository writing is organized differently. This structure is more compact, detailed, and explanatory in nature.

Meyer and Freedle (1984) identify five common expository text structures: (1) description, (2) collection, (3) causation, (4) problem-solution, and (5) comparison. McGee and Richgels (1985) discuss the importance of understanding text structure by preparing a graphic organizer for a specific passage and writing with students a passage to mirror the graphic organizer. Figure 10.1 describes each type of structure identified by Meyer and Freedle, giving a sample passage and clue words.

STRUCTURE	DESCRIPTION*	SAMPLE PASSAGE	CLUE WORDS
Description	Specifies something about a topic or presents an attribute or setting for a topic.	The Summer Olympic Games are the biggest entertainment spectacles of modern times. Every four years they offer two weeks of non-stop pageantry and competition.	
Collection	A number of descriptions (specifics, attributes, or settings) presented together.	The Summer Olympics have so many different things to offer. First, there are many kinds of events: big shows like the opening and closing ceremonies, pure competitions like the races and games, and events that are partly artistic and partly competitive like the subjectively scored diving and gymnastics contests. There are old things and new things, like the classic track and field events staged in 1984 in the same stadium where they were held in 1932, and the almost bizarre sport of synchronized swimming, first presented in 1984.	*First, second, third, next, finally*
Causation	Elements grouped in time sequence (before and after) with a causative relationship (the earlier causes the later) specified.	There are several reasons why so many people attend the Olympic Games or watch them on television. The first Olympics were held in Greece more than 2,000 years ago. As a result of hearing the name "Olympics," seeing the torch other and flame, and being reminded in ways of the ancient games, people feel that they are	*so that, thus, because of, as a result of, since, and so, in order to*

*Descriptions adapted from Meyer and Freedle, 1984, pp. 121–24.

FIGURE 10.1

Expository text structures with sample passages and clue words
Source: From L. M. McGee and D. J. Richgels, "Teaching Expository Text Structure to Elementary Students," **The Reading Teacher, 38** (April 1985), pp. 741–742. Reprinted with permission of Lea M. McGee and the International Reading Association.

STRUCTURE	DESCRIPTION*	SAMPLE PASSAGE	CLUE WORDS
		escaping the ordinariness of daily life. People like to identify with someone else's individual sacrifice and accomplishment, and thus an athlete's or even a team's hard-earned, well-deserved victory becomes a nation's victory. There are national medal counts and people watch so that they can see how their country is doing. Since the Olympics are staged only every four years and maybe only in a particular country once in a lifetime, people flock to even obscure events in order to be able to say "I was there."	
Problem/ solution	Includes a causative relation (between a problem and its causes) and a solution set, one element of which can break the link between the problem and its antecedent cause.	One problem with the modern Olympics is that they have gotten so big and so expensive to operate. A city or country often loses a lot of money by staging the games. A stadium, pools, and playing fields are built for the many events and housing is built for the athletes, but it is all used for only two weeks. In 1984, Los Angeles solved these problems by charging companies for permission to be official sponsors and by using many buildings that were already there. Companies like McDonald's paid a lot of money to be part of the Olympics. The Coliseum, where the 1932 Games were held, was used again and many colleges and universities in the area became playing and living sites.	*a problem is, a solution is, have solved this problem by*

FIGURE 10.1, continued

STRUCTURE	DESCRIPTION*	SAMPLE PASSAGE	CLUE WORDS
Comparison	Contains no element of time sequence or causality; organizes elements on the basis of their similarities and differences.	The modern Summer Olympics are really very unlike the ancient Olympic Games. Individual, events are different. For example, there were no swimming races in the ancient Games, but there were chariot races. There were no women contestants and everyone competed in the nude. Of course the ancient and modern Olympics are also alike in many ways. Some events are the same, like the javelin and discus throws. Some people say that cheating, professionalism, and nationalism in the modern Games are a disgrace to the ancient Olympic tradition. But according to ancient Greek writers, there were many cases of cheating, nationalism, and professionalism in their Olympics too.	*different from, same as, alike similar to, resemble*

FIGURE 10.1, continued

As a teacher of reading, you must realize that your students will not be familiar with these expository text structures. As a result, they probably will have trouble learning material presented in content subjects. Recent research supports a long-held belief that how well a text is written and how successfully readers recognize writing patterns affect student understanding (McGee & Richgels, 1985).

■ Readability

A possible explanation for problems in content subjects is the increased difficulty of the materials to be read. **Readability** is the approximate difficulty level of written material. The concept of readability is important for all teachers. Teachers should strive to match a book's readability with the students' instructional level. Students tend to learn the most from material that is neither too easy nor too difficult. Readability depends on factors inherent in the text (e.g., sentence structure, organizational pattern, physical presentation of the material, and vocabulary), the reader (knowledge of text structures, interest in the subject, and prior knowledge of a topic), and the teacher (the presentation). To provide effective instruction, teachers must judge the readability level of material.

Many readability formulas are available to judge difficulty of traditional text factors. Fry's readability formula (see Figure 10.2) is based on word and sentence length and is quick to use. Remember, however, that any readability formula will yield only an approximate, not an exact, level of difficulty. Indeed, using different readability formulas on the same material can yield different results. Remember, too, that readability varies within a given text.

Teachers should use a combination of a formula, personal knowledge of their students, and an informal appraisal of text characteristics to assess the suitability of a particular text. Irwin and Davis (1980) recommend an informal method for estimating the appropriateness of a textbook. Their readability checklist rates understandability, learnability, reinforcement, and motivation. Zakaluk and Samuels (1988) recommend a broader method of predicting text difficulty, by collecting and assessing information about outside-the-head and inside-the-head factors. Outside-the-head factors include the traditional text factors of word difficulty, sentence length, and adjunct aids (such as study questions). Inside-the-head factors include facility in word recognition and knowledge of the topic.

In contrast to providing a designation of grade level for readability, the Cloze procedure for content material may indicate students' abilities to read a particular text. The Cloze procedure yields information indicating whether the material matches a student's instructional, independent, or frustration reading level. (See Chapter 11 for a description of the Cloze procedure.) This procedure can be used with a large group and can quickly indicate class and individual capabilities for reading a particular content text.

Because content textbooks pose a readability problem, teachers need to supplement their instruction with a variety of materials. Hadaway and Young (1994) concur, and they propose a multiple-perspective approach recommending that teachers consider using literature, magazines, newspapers, environmental print (such as brochures, advertisements, and junk mail), and informational picture books to supplement textbooks.

Components of Content Reading

Formal education has many goals, one of which is to help students become increasingly independent within the framework of the school setting. To achieve such independence, learners must master a number of related language skills. One important cluster of skills determines success in content reading. In schools dominated by basic skills, instruction often gives content skills mere lip service. Although current educational trends emphasize teaching basic skills and administering tests to show that a student is literate, teachers also need to emphasize skills that enable learners to acquire information on their own.

The major functions of teaching content reading fall into three interrelated categories: (1) specific skills and strategies needed to read a chapter in a content

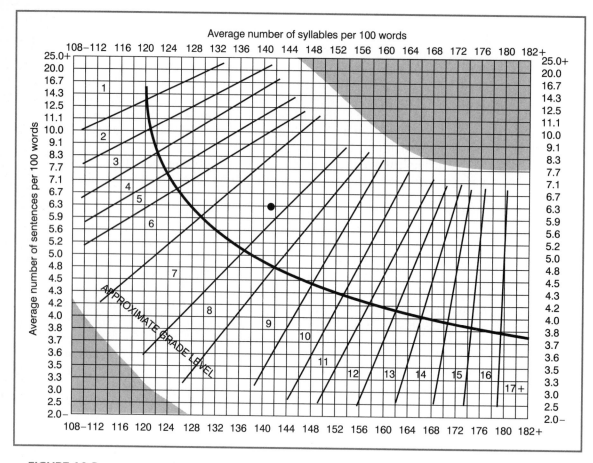

FIGURE 10.2
Graph for estimating readability—extended (Note: This "extended graph" does not outmode or render the earlier (1968) version inoperative or inaccurate; it is an extension.)
Source: By Edward Fry. Reprinted from **The Journal of Reading,** December 1977. Reproduction permitted. No copyright.

subject, (2) study skills instruction, and (3) skills and strategies required for collecting, organizing, and criticizing data. Within these categories, the following five major components of content reading interact: (1) vocabulary development, (2) studying strategies, (3) reading and study skills, (4) locational skills, and (5) critical-reading skills.

■ Vocabulary Development

Curriculum materials in content subjects confront readers with an ever-increasing number of unknown and relatively difficult words and concepts. Students must know many new, more-difficult connotations for familiar words and must under-

EXPANDED DIRECTIONS FOR WORKING READABILITY GRAPH

1. Randomly select three sample passages and count out exactly 100 words each, beginning with the beginning of a sentence. Do count proper nouns, initializations, and numerals.
2. Count the number of sentences in the hundred words, estimating length of the fraction of the last sentence to the nearest one tenth.
3. Count the total number of syllables in the 100-word passage. If you don't have a hand counter available, an easy way is to simply put a mark above every syllable in each word, then when you get to the end of the passage, count the number of marks and add to 100. Small calculators can also be used as counters by pushing numeral 1, then pushing the + sign for each word or syllable when counting.
4. Enter on the graph the *average* sentence length and *average* number of syllables; plot dot where the two lines intersect. Area where dot is plotted will give you the approximate grade level.
5. If a great deal of variability is found in syllable count or sentence count, putting more samples into the average is desirable.
6. A word is defined as a group of symbols with a space on either side; thus, *Joe, IRA, 1945,* and *&* are each one word.
7. A syllable is defined as a phonetic syllable. Generally, there are as many syllables as vowel sounds. For example, *stopped* is one syllable and *wanted* is two syllables. When counting syllables for numerals and initializations, count one syllable for each symbol. For example, *1945* is four syllables, *IRA* is three syllables, and *&* is one syllable.

FIGURE 10.2, continued

stand a large number of idiomatic and figurative expressions. The amount of required reading suddenly increases, and students must read and comprehend at a faster rate. They must also develop the flexibility to adjust their rate to both the difficulty level and the purpose.

Because of the rigid control of vocabulary in beginning reading materials, teachers frequently fail to arouse and maintain students' interest in content materials. Content textbooks introduce so many difficult words and concepts that many students are frustrated and lost. In addition, content vocabulary differs from vocabulary in regular reading lessons in important ways. Armbruster and Nagy (1992) report that unlike vocabulary in regular reading lessons, content vocabulary is absolutely crucial for comprehension, usually represents unfamiliar concepts, and is usually related to other content vocabulary in the same chapter.

Understanding the meaning of specialized content words and concepts requires planned, systematic instruction. Nagy (1988), summarizing recent research

Vocabulary development in the content areas needs to include interesting and varied practice.

on vocabulary development, concludes that effective vocabulary instruction to improve comprehension includes three properties: (1) integration (relating new words with known concepts and experiences), (2) repetition (sufficient practice to know words quickly while reading), and (3) meaningful use (interesting practice that results in the ability to use new words properly).

For integrating new words with known concepts and experiences in content reading, various visual aids (e.g., diagrams, flowcharts, outlines, maps, and time lines) are particularly useful. Semantic mapping (Johnson & Pearson, 1984) is a popular visual technique for showing how words relate to one another. To design a semantic map, lead a brainstorming session around a particular word or topic. After listing all the words that come to mind relating to the key word or topic on the board, group the words into meaningful categories. Finally, draw a semantic map and use it as a vehicle for discussion both before and after reading a portion of text. Figure 10.3 is a semantic map completed by sixth graders before reading a story about rattlesnakes (Heimlich & Pittleman, 1986).

Meaningful content-area reading requires students to understand new concepts continually, because this type of reading presents more difficulties per reading unit than does primary reading. One of the major problems in reading is the gap between students' store of meanings and the demands of the content reading

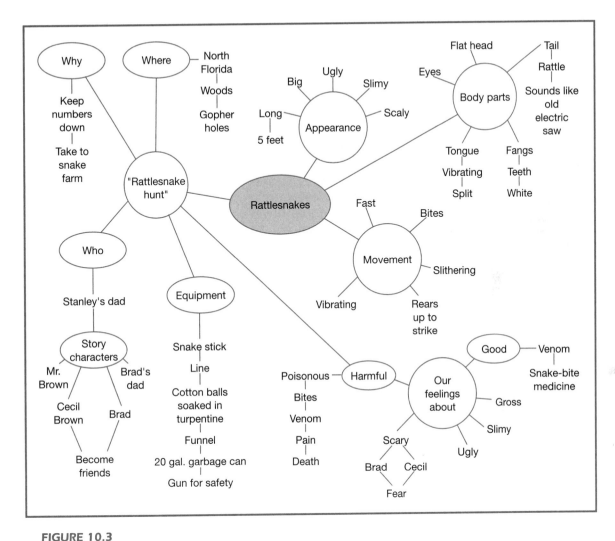

FIGURE 10.3
Group map for rattlesnakes
Source: From J. E. Heimlich and S. D. Pittleman, **Semantic Mapping:**
Classroom Applications (Neward, DE: International Reading
Association, 1986), p. 28. Reprinted with permission of Joan E. Heimlich
and the International Reading Association.

matter. In addition, content reading contains many idiomatic expressions, abstract and figurative terms, and new connotations for familiar words. In the primary grades, even though they occur less frequently, the teacher's editions accompanying basal reader series point out these expressions. Workbooks provide instruction supplementing the reader series.

The shift to separate textbooks in the content areas reduces the emphasis on helping students with meaning difficulties—just when they need the most help. Teachers find that many students do not understand concepts even after the material has been assigned and covered in class. The following are examples of difficult concepts from fourth- and fifth-grade geography, science, and mathematics books:

- The native city is backward and ugly.
- Now, as in ancient times, the Mediterranean is a great connecting highway.
- The people who lived in fixed settlements made far greater progress than the nomads.
- Gradually the continent was opened. Another jewel had been added to the British crown.
- Business and industry were paralyzed.
- A belt of irrigated land stretches almost all the way along the coast.
- The shrinking world and new inventions have made this possible.
- Almost every farmer grows some cash crops besides food for his family.
- Ornithologists have examined the crops of many birds to find out what kind of food they eat.
- We can use a ruler to subtract fractions.

Studying Strategies

Understanding expository text depends largely upon knowledge and application of comprehension strategies to fulfill one's purpose in reading. Good readers, who are aware of what they are doing during their reading, can apply specific strategies and can monitor their progress.

Metacognition. *The Literacy Dictionary* (Harris & Hodges, 1995) defines **metacognition** as "awareness and knowledge of one's mental processes such that one can monitor, regulate, and direct them to a desired goal" (p. 153). Metacognitive awareness applied specifically to reading is "knowing when what one is reading makes sense by monitoring and controlling one's own comprehension" (p. 153). Good readers generate and monitor purposeful reading of text. In fulfillment of this purposeful reading, metacognition involves not only appropriate reading strategies but also awareness and control of these strategies while reading. Jones (1986) summarized the basic elements of metacognition:

> Metacognition in reading to learn centers around the learner's knowledge about the strategic coordination of the four variables of text, task, strategies, and learner characteristics. Text knowledge has to do with the learner's understanding of the features that aid comprehension and retention of what is read such as text difficulty, familiarity with language and content, interest in content, and structure of the text. Task knowledge deals with the learner's awareness of purposes for reading and the requirements of the assignment. The learning activities that are used to deal with the task demands, and to store and retrieve information from the text are considered strategy knowledge. The self-knowledge a learner has about himself or herself regarding ability, motivation, interest, and many personal attributes and states is considered learner characteristics. (p. 2)

To comprehend content material, students must learn and strategically apply various studying strategies before, during, and after reading. Successful readers are strategic; that is, they know various reading strategies, consciously apply these reading strategies to the particular text at hand, and monitor their comprehension as they read. Conversely, poor readers are not strategic readers. Paris, Lipson, and Wilson (1994) state, "A large body of evidence reveals that poor readers do not skim, scan, reread, integrate information, plan ahead, take notes, make inferences, and so forth as often as skilled readers" (p. 795). Yet, students can become strategic readers through meaningful instruction and practice.

Before Reading, include the following strategies.

- Review prior knowledge on the topic.
- Relate the new chapter to previous chapters.
- Relate the new material to personal experiences.
- Discuss key vocabulary and concepts.
- Read the introduction to create a proper mind-set.
- Predict what will be included in the text.
- Establish an overall purpose for reading the text.
- Review the pattern of the text to be read.

Teachers can accomplish the preceding strategies in various ways, including the following:

- *Direct/explicit instruction and thinking aloud.* Walk the students through an appropriate strategy by explaining it point-by-point or by modeling it. Following the direct explanation or modeling, afford sufficient practice in the strategy.
- *The directed reading activity (DRA).* Apply this teaching strategy to all content reading, not just basal materials. The elements of the readiness step (motivation, vocabulary, background, and purpose setting) help students read and learn specific content.
- *The advance organizer.* Provide students with a short written summary and highlight new vocabulary and concepts, background information, and main ideas. Advance organizers help students establish a correct mind-set before reading and aid them in establishing purposes for reading.
- *The structured overview.* This is similar to the advance organizer. Present a structured overview containing the key ideas of the chapter and their relationships in a visual format (usually a flowchart or a hierarchy, spoke, or pie chart). Discuss the key vocabulary words in the chapter before students read silently.
- *The directed reading-thinking activity (DR-TA).* Similar in purpose to the directed reading activity, the **directed reading-thinking activity (DR-TA)** directs students' thinking about the text to be read (Haggard, 1988; Stauffer, 1975). In the first step of a DR-TA, introduce students to the material to be read and help them set their own purposes for reading by predicting what they think will be covered.
- *Semantic mapping.* This is a visual way to expand vocabulary knowledge and to show relationships among ideas (Heimlich & Pittleman, 1986). Used before reading, semantic mapping teaches new words and introduces relationships developed in the content chapter.

■ *The K-W-L teaching model (Ogle, 1986).* This dialogue between the teacher and students uses prior knowledge for comprehension. *K-W-L* stands for (1) assessing what I *know,* (2) determining what I *want* to learn, and (3) recalling what I *learned.* Following a discussion of each of the three steps and using a portion of text, have the students write their personal responses on a worksheet that highlights the three steps. Figure 10.4 provides an example of a K-W-L worksheet.

HURRICANES

K (Known)	W (Want to know)	L (Learned)
They are dangerous. They change directions. They bring rain and wind. You must get away from beaches. The eye is the center of the storm.	What is a category III storm? What is the difference between a tropical hurricane watch and a hurricane warning? What do you do during a hurricane if you are at home?	A category III storm has winds of 111–130 mph and a storm surge of 9–12 ft. A hurricane watch is an announcement for specific areas that hurricane conditions pose a threat to a coastal area. A hurricane warning is an announcement that winds of 74 mph or higher are expected in a specific coastal area within 24 hours. During a hurricane, stay indoors, stay away from windows and glass doors, and fill water containers with a week's supply of water.

Categories of Information

Types of hurricanes: _____

Terms to know: _____

Things to do: _____

_____

FIGURE 10.4
Sample K-W-L worksheet on hurricanes

Study skills and being able to read content text with a specific purpose were important in the early 1800s. The partial page shown is from Daniel Adams's *Geography of the World,* 1830. Students reading the text were directed to questions the teacher would ask by the use of a superior *q*. Students were directed to ask themselves questions for each of the *q* symbols and come up with the appropriate answers.

GEOGRAPHY.

☞ The " Interrogative system" of teaching, has now become very general in almost every branch of school education. The introduction may be traced to the Scholar's Arithmetic, in 1801, many years before the appearance of Goldsmith and of Guy in our country. A further improvement in this system is here attempted, and instead of printing the question at length, which necessarily swells the book, a character (ᶦ) is introduced, intimating both to the Instructer, and the pupil, that a question is required, and this character is invariably placed BEFORE the word or words intended to ask the question, and to which the answer, FOUND BY READING THE SENTENCE, is to be a direct reply. For example, take the first sentence ; the character is placed before the words "certain knowledge ;" the question then is, Had the ancients any certain knowledge of the figure of the earth ? The answer, from reading the sentence, is evident, No ; or, They had not. Where the construction of the sentence suggests no particular form to put the quest   What is said

THE WORLD.

THE ancients had no ᶦcertain knowledge of the figure of the earth. But later discoveries, both by astronomy and navigation, demonstrate the world we inhabit to be a large opaque globe or ball, nearly eight thousand ᶦmiles in diameter. In proof of this it is only necessary to notice, that various navigators have actually sailed around it. Of these, the ᶦfirst was Sir Francis Drake, who in 1580 completed the circumnavigation of the globe, after an absence of two years, ten months, and twenty days, from England, his native land.

U P D A T E IIII▶

The superior *q* was in vogue more than 260 years ago, and today, this whole area of promoting a self-questioning, self-monitoring attitude while one reads is once again in style. Today, the new cognitive view of reading stresses interactive reading through the development of strategies students use themselves to understand, reason, and reflect on ideas in the text. As students make sense of the text, one strategy emphasized today is student-generated questions. Teachers of reading need to teach students specific ways to generate their own questions before, during, and after reading. Examples of questioning strategies recommended today include QAR, K-W-L, and reciprocal teaching.

During Reading, include the following strategies.

- Turn bold-print headings into questions to guide reading.
- Answer bold-print questions before moving on to the next section.
- Reread parts of the text that cannot be remembered (indicated by not being able to answer bold-print questions).
- Find the author's pattern.

Teachers can accomplish the preceding reading strategies in various ways. These include the following:

- *Study guides.* Study guides provide students with chapter questions to answer while reading and purposes for reading. The questions asked should balance literal, interpretive, and critical comprehension.
- *Direct/explicit instruction and thinking aloud.* Show students how to turn bold-print heads into questions using reporters' questions *(who, what, where, when, why* and *how).* If students cannot recall an answer after reading a section, explain to them that they should reread the section to answer their purpose-setting questions.
- *The directed reading-thinking activity (DR-TA).* After students make predictions, ask them to read silently to prove or disprove their predictions.

After Reading, include the following strategies.

- Check comprehension by answering the end-of-chapter questions.
- Assess the information conveyed and predict what will happen next.
- Summarize key points.
- Look back or reread parts of the text to understand particular points.

Teachers can accomplish the preceding postreading strategies in various ways. These include the following:

- *Study guides.* Lead a discussion of questions in the study guide.
- *The directed reading activity (DRA).* Following silent reading, ask students to answer their purpose-setting questions. Ask a variety of comprehension questions at different levels of thinking. Directly teach a reading skill or study skill related to the chapter. Then, provide independent practice activities for the skill. Check students' comprehension of the ideas in the text.
- *The directed reading-thinking activity (DR-TA).* Following silent reading, ask students questions to check the accuracy of their predictions.
- *Semantic mapping.* Rework the map that you and the students devised before they read the chapter.
- *Reciprocal teaching.* Reciprocal teaching is a dialogue between the teacher and students concerning a portion of the text (Palincsar & Brown, 1986). In this dialogue, the teaching function gradually shifts to the students. Following silent reading, model four strategies: (1) summarize key points, (2) ask questions requiring different levels of thinking, (3) clarify answers to questions, and (4) predict what will be discussed in the next section of

the text. Gradually let students take over one or more of the strategies, continually facilitating the process by providing timely feedback.

- *The K-W-L teaching model.* Complete the last step of this model by asking students to write down what they learned and what they still need to know.
- *Cooperative grouping.* Design discussion or assignment groups, grouping students of different ability levels. Have each group complete the end-of-chapter activity together.

Writing to Learn. Reading and writing are interdependent. As we have emphasized, reading is best learned through integration with the other language arts. Just as reading and writing are complementary and effective in the regular reading program, the combination yields impressive results in the content areas (Myers, 1984; Tadlock, 1978). In the content areas, writing to learn should be an integral part of the instructional program. Combining reading and writing makes students more aware of text structure and helps them understand ideas better (Holbrook, 1987). Anderson (1984) states, "Writing . . . is a way to improve students' schemata, or structured knowledge of subjects encountered in the content areas . . . [and is] fundamental to comprehending, learning, and remembering concepts in stories and texts" (p. 243).

Writing should be an integral part of content-reading instruction beginning in kindergarten. Using shared experiences, student-dictated language-experience charts can be springboards for content learning and writing development. For example, students can summarize their understanding of content through writing (even invented spelling), illustrate their writing, and make individual or class books. Kinney (1985) recommends using the language-experience approach to teach first graders about text structure. The teacher leads the discussion on a topic and a particular type of organization—for example, comparing and contrasting pairs of objects such as a football and baseball—and the students dictate stories to make them aware of the text structure. The results of Kinney's study lend support to the use of the language-experience approach in the content areas.

Teachers can integrate writing into content instruction in a number of ways. It is probably best to think of creative ways to incorporate writing during the prereading or postreading phases of a lesson. During the prereading portion, instruct students to write about a particular topic after reviewing their prior knowledge or brainstorming about their past experiences. Following guided silent reading, have students write to fulfill a number of purposes: to summarize main ideas, to classify information, to compare and contrast, and to predict future consequences.

Holbrook (1987) reviewed and summarized a number of specific ways to integrate writing into the content areas, including those of Smith and Bean (1980) and of Myers (1984). Smith and Bean advocate the two-step method. After discussing a topic in the prereading step, have students write two paragraphs using information from the discussion. Following silent reading of the text, have the students revise their first draft and discuss their revisions. Myers recommends a variety of creative-writing assignments for social studies, including writing letters to the editor, assuming the role of a historical person, and interviewing and transcribing oral histories.

Different Approaches for Different Abilities. Invariably, classrooms use one content textbook for each subject and grade. This practice presents problems in accommodating differing student abilities. Because many students cannot read successfully in a particular text, teachers should understand the concept of readability and know how to measure a text's difficulty level. Teachers should teach and model reading and study skills to help students understand expository text. Finally, teachers should know various ways to tailor instruction to students who are unable to read a required text. Alternative instructional approaches that move away from reliance on a single text include providing different assignments, using multilevel content materials, providing meaningful oral reading, using educational media resources, conducting small-group instruction, assigning library books of various difficulty levels for a particular topic, and incorporating the arts in instruction.

SQ3R. In addition to individual studying strategies, many students profit from learning a specific approach to reading content chapters. Reading a content chapter resembles following a road map: Students must learn how to get from point A to point B in the shortest, most meaningful way. The best-known systematized procedure for reading content chapters is SQ3R.

This procedure applies many skills and strategies. In fact, many of the previously discussed studying strategies are part of SQ3R. Developed by Robinson (1961), **SQ3R** stands for "survey, question, read, recite, and review." Students need direct instruction and a great deal of practice in each step of the procedure.

Survey encourages students to get an overall picture of the chapter before reading it by looking at the title, introduction, main headings, illustrations, and end-of-chapter questions. *Question* helps students read with a purpose by turning each bold heading into questions. *Read* asks students to read each chapter section and to answer each purpose-setting question, keeping in mind the chapter organization and visual aids. *Recite* involves stopping periodically to answer the purpose-setting questions in one's own words. Students are encouraged to take notes during silent reading. *Review* instructs students to check their memory by reviewing their notes and reciting major points under each heading.

The steps we have asked you to follow so far in the text are a modification of this procedure. We recommend teaching the following method and practicing it with students.

1. Read the introduction.
2. Survey all visual aids in the chapter and read each bold heading.
3. Read the summary.
4. Study the questions at the end of the chapter.
5. Return to the beginning of the chapter and read.

Tadlock (1978) concurs that when teaching a study method such as SQ3R, teachers must also explain why and how the method will aid students' retention of content material. She states that each step in SQ3R "is designed to facilitate the processing of incoming information (print) so the reader can deal with more of it and deal with it more effectively" (p. 111).

■ Reading and Study Skills

Every instructional level presents its own challenges to teachers. The emphasis on separate textbooks in the various subject areas is a chief source of instructional problems. These books call for a high level of independent reading ability and special facility in a number of reading and study skills. Following is a listing of some of the major reading and **study skills** needed for comprehension in the various content subjects.

In math, the ability to

1. Use a slow and deliberate reading rate.
2. Master technical vocabulary and symbols.
3. Follow directions.

In social studies, the ability to

1. Follow ideas and events in sequence.
2. Read maps, tables, time lines, and graphs.
3. Outline main ideas.
4. Follow directions.
5. Master a specialized vocabulary.
6. Use reference materials.
7. Identify and use the author's organizational pattern.
8. Summarize key ideas.

In science, the ability to

1. Follow sequence.
2. Follow directions.
3. Classify details and main ideas.
4. Interpret graphic material visually.
5. Identify and use the author's organizational pattern.
6. Master a specialized vocabulary.
7. Summarize key ideas.

Teachers and other educators constantly stress teaching various facets of reading concurrently with subject matter. Even in departmentalized schools, with one teacher responsible for social studies, another for science, another for mathematics, and so forth, the importance of integrating reading and the content subjects emerges in the slogan "Every teacher is a teacher of reading."

New teaching materials are helping both teacher and students meet the demands of content reading. For example, new basal programs integrate content knowledge, strategies, and skills into their total program. New basal teacher's manuals include lesson suggestions for teachers as well as practice materials in a variety of forms, including both narrative and expository literature.

The nature of reading materials and the great difference in students' instructional needs make it logical and perhaps even essential to relate some reading instruction to social studies, science, literature, mathematics, and other subject areas. This very point was emphasized in *Becoming a Nation of Readers* (Anderson, Hiebert, Scott, & Wilkinson, 1985). The authors state, "The most logical place for instruction in most reading and thinking strategies is in social studies and science rather than in separate lessons about reading. The reason is that the strategies are useful mainly when the student is grappling with important but unfamiliar content" (p. 73).

Each reading skill applied in a content area should be taught in a systematic, direct fashion. Teachers must not assume that students already know and can apply various reading skills in content areas.

A major problem undermining mastery of reading and study skills is insufficient attention to these skills in both teaching and practice. To properly emphasize teaching of reading and study skills, teachers should use the direct/explicit instructional model and practice these skills primarily in the content areas. Instruction in connection with content subjects has many advantages, including a text organization, a functional setting, and motivation. Figure 10.5 presents a lesson on sequence of events using direct/explicit instruction.

Transfer.   Student difficulty in content materials may result from the absence of interesting, varied practice. Furthermore, students do not automatically transfer skills to content materials. For example, students taught how to interpret a diagram in science require additional practice in a variety of situations before they can transfer this skill to their reading of mathematics or social studies materials. Following are examples of ways to encourage transferring the skill of interpreting a diagram:

- Bring in supplemental materials containing diagrams of topics already studied. Ask students appropriate questions about each diagram, or allow individuals to assume the role of the teacher and explain the diagram to the rest of the class.
- Have students make their own diagram on a topic of their choice. Make certain each diagram is labeled properly. Ask students to construct a series of questions concerning their diagrams.

Teachers can use numerous kinds of meaningful practice to promote transfer of a particular skill. Teachers must be aware of this need and provide the necessary time and opportunity to ensure the transfer.

■ Locational Skills

To find answers in varied reading materials, students must understand and use all available aids. In other words, knowing how to use a book is a prerequisite for intelligent use of supplementary reading materials in the subject areas or in any unit of work. In the intermediate grades, study skills grow more important, reflecting the nature and variety of the materials used and the fact that supervision is not always readily available. Although development of study skills requires reading ability, this ability in itself does not ensure that students have mastered the study skills.

Strategies for Visually and Hearing Impaired Students

As you know, success in the regular reading program does not automatically spell success in reading in the content areas. This is true for all students. However, teachers must make adjustments for students with special needs in the content areas. The content subjects of mathematics, science, and social studies pose literacy difficulties especially for students with visual and hearing disabilities. When possible, pair impaired and non-impaired students to work together on an assignment. In addition to using the instructional techniques described in this chapter to meet students' needs, one must be conscious of the physical environment of the classroom itself. Seating special-needs students near the chalkboard, computer, overhead screen, or activity centers and near doors will provide for easy movement and help eliminate physical barriers for completing assignments. Audiotaping of content chapters is beneficial for students with visual impairments, as well as using the many visual formats discussed throughout this text, including pictures, videotapes, semantic maps, webs, K-W-L worksheets, time lines, graphs, diagrams, and charts. Also, captioned films and filmstrips aid students with hearing impairments. Multimedia CD-ROM computer programs are effective with all students, especially students with special needs. In addition, the use of the overhead projector can be beneficial for all students. Teachers can put outlines of chapters, write pre-, during-, and after-reading questions, and write page-by-page study guides on overhead transparencies. Use verbal directions and explanations for visually impaired students as you interact with the class. Realia, (i.e., actual objects) and hands-on activities are especially helpful. For example, in social studies, the use of braille globes, maps, and atlases and models of landforms to promote the use of the tactile mode of learning is effective for students with visual impairments. In introducing science vocabulary and concepts, use objects that students can hold and manipulate. In both science and mathematics, the use of manipulatives to reinforce concepts is effective. Your goal of improving all your students' literacy abilities is greatly enhanced when you are sensitive to the needs of exceptional students and adapt your instruction to meet student needs.

During the past few years, the availability of books, professional journals, and other printed matter has expanded tremendously. The past three decades have seen such a dramatic advance in knowledge that this period has been labeled the "knowledge explosion." Competency in any given field has taken on new meaning, and educational methods, of necessity, have changed radically to adapt to this new challenge.

No single textbook or even series of texts can completely cover a subject. The time lag between research, publication, and the adoption of textbooks causes inadequacies in even the most recent texts. To address this situation, good teachers have always provided supplementary reading materials. Today, however, providing a wide array of supplementary materials is not only desirable, but necessary. Thus, learners need study skills more now than ever, but the school's respect for these skills and its ability to teach them effectively have declined. The following discussion deals with instruction regarding locating information.

AREA OF NEEDED READING INSTRUCTION

Reinforcement of ability to arrange events and ideas into proper sequential order.

INTENDED LEARNING OUTCOME

Students will list events described in a newspaper article in sequential order.

PAST LEARNING

Students understand that being able to arrange events and ideas in sequential order closely relates to the ability to comprehend a story.

Students are aware that events occurring in sequential order can be related to each other to bring meaning to a story.

BUILDING BACKGROUND

Review the importance of sequencing events in a story. List two or three events on the chalkboard that are from a story with which students are familiar. Ask students to identify additional events by telling you what key words and phrases helped them know when things happened in the story. Call on various students to give their answers. Write the responses on the chalkboard and discuss common key words and phrases that students were able to recall. These responses might include the following:

then	last
now	event
today	after a while
first	the next day
second	only yesterday

Increase students' engagement and attention by telling them that these key words and phrases will help them complete the activity at the end of this lesson. Describe briefly what that activity will be and stress the idea that you know they will be successful with the task.

FIGURE 10.5
Direct/explicit instruction lesson
Source: Reprinted with the permission of Macmillan Publishing Company
from **Teaching Reading: Diagnosis, Direct Instruction,**
and Practice, Second Edition, by William H. Rupley and Timothy R.
Blair. Copyright © 1988 by Macmillian/Prentice Hall.

TEACHER-DIRECTED INSTRUCTION

Provide students with a written list of questions that they should focus on as they read the story you will provide. Display a newspaper article on the overhead projector and have students read it silently. After reading, engage students in a discussion by asking such questions as the following:

What is the first thing that happened in this story?

Which events in this news story are the important ones to list in order?

How could we summarize in sequential order the events that occurred?

Remind them that these questions focus on a sequence of events and set their purpose for reading. Discuss the students' responses, then write them in sentence form on the chalkboard and number them.

INDEPENDENT STUDENT PRACTICE

Allow each student to choose one of two or three newspaper articles that you have selected for this seat-work activity. Carefully select articles that emphasize sequential order. Instruct students to read the newspaper article and write in numerical order the major events as they happened.
After all the students have completed the activity, they can compare their lists.

ONGOING DIAGNOSIS

Evaluate students' ability to sequence events of the newspaper article. Discuss with students why they identified specific events for sequencing.

MODIFYING INSTRUCTION

This activity can be extended, using the same procedure, by providing students with two or more articles to sequence. Difficulty level depends on the selection of reading material. To maximize students' success, the material should clearly contain events that can be sequenced and the content of the articles should contain information with which students are familiar.

FIGURE 10.5, continued

Using Books.   In teaching any study skill, the teacher at each grade level must build on what students already know. To do this, first the teacher must determine each student's ability level. A good place to begin is with the textbook adopted for a given course. Teachers can assess their students' ability to understand the text and their knowledge of specific study skills and their application.

Exercises that foster such growth are easy to devise. The major concern is how to use exercise materials in relation to the goals to be achieved. Some important learnings deal with the mechanics of learning—how to use a card catalog, where to look in an encyclopedia, when an appendix or glossary might be useful, and what is likely to be found in an appendix or glossary.

Written exercises are often used to help students understand the function of an index, table of contents, or appendix. It is common to find students who can work out correct solutions to workbook problems consisting of sample lines from an index but who still do not know how to get help from a real index. One of the best ways to teach children how to use a book effectively is to design a learning situation around a textbook they will be using throughout the year. A social studies, health, or other text can provide ample opportunities for teaching the functions of the table of contents, charts, indexes, and appendices. The text the student is using will give him or her something concrete to return to when in doubt. Skills learned in using one text should transfer more readily to books in other areas, provided there is teacher direction and guidance.

Teachers frequently fail to detect student deficiencies in using a table of contents, index, glossary, and appendix, so they do not teach these skills. Too often, they assume that these basic skills have been taught or are being taught elsewhere. For example, as an outcome of an inservice program, one group of teachers agreed to build a one-page testing and teaching exercise consisting of 15 to 20 questions to measure students' skills in using the parts of a book. The exercise was to be specifically applicable to the textbook the students were using in one of their courses. Although students had used the books for nearly 3 months, few were able to complete the exercise perfectly. The teachers discovered glaring deficiencies and individual differences in students' ability to use these reader aids. In one class, students took from 6 to 22 minutes to do the "book-mining" exercise, with some students unable to complete the task.

Exercises such as that presented in Figure 10.6 may be used initially with an entire class and can serve as diagnostic instruments. Observant teachers will note which students have difficulty and what their problems are. Those findings should help them teach small groups and individual students the skills they need along with general concepts. This exercise was constructed for use with a sixth-grade social studies text.

The exercise shown in Figure 10.6 teaches a number of facts about the book. Question 1 takes the readers to the table of contents and requires them to associate their home state with part of a larger geographical region of the United States. Question 2 calls attention to a 16-page atlas; the next question focuses on a second, highly specialized table of contents dealing exclusively with maps.

Questions 4 through 8 deal with areas in which the index may be helpful. The reader must locate pictures using key words and must be prepared to look under different headings. Topics may be listed as subheads under a more general heading. Questions 9 through 11 deal with information about pronunciation and meanings of difficult words and emphasize that these aids are divided between the index and glossary.

Students sometimes fail to realize that most reference books and textbooks include a number of reader aids. Lack of familiarity with or inclination to use these aids inhibits students from optimizing their use of books. Although students need these skills, they do not always recognize their value.

One purpose may require students to skim the table of contents, while another demands that they read it critically. Comparing different books discloses that a table of contents may consist exclusively of chapter titles, similar to an outline composed of nothing but major topics. In some books, chapter titles precede a number of topics in their discussion order. Students may note that this is essentially a modified index containing only major headings in chronological order. In contrast, the index is in alphabetical order, dealing with narrower topics and cutting across chapters.

Every student should learn that (1) parts of the book are deliberately designed as aids, (2) these are valuable and are used profitably by efficient readers, and (3) the different parts of a book have definite purposes. Efficient readers decide instantly where to go for specific types of help. To do so, they must know what type of information each section contains, where the various aids are, and how to use each effectively. Once learned, this knowledge can be transferred and applied to any book. Figure 10.7 is an abbreviated treatment of what a reader might expect to gain from the aids found in most books.

Using the Library.   Effective use of library resources may well be one of the most underrated and undertaught skills in the entire school program. The library is where students read and receive guidance in both the use of books and research techniques. Students at all grade levels need the experience of frequent contact with a good school library.

Some teachers use the library effectively themselves but do not assume responsibility for teaching students to do so. On the other hand, a number of teachers make little personal use of library facilities.

At one school we visited, the librarian and principal believed that a substantial portion of the teaching staff seldom used the library for personal reasons. They also found that students seemed less inclined to turn to the library for these teachers' classes. The school incorporated a one-hour library unit into its total in-service program. Teachers were each relieved of their regularly scheduled duties to spend an hour in conference with the librarian. The librarian discussed and pointed out resources directly related to the teachers' various subjects, locating pamphlets, bound volumes, pertinent books, government documents, current magazines, and the like. The librarian also suggested ways to help the faculty members and students. The attitudes of a number of the teachers changed markedly after this experience. Some teachers visited the library more frequently, spent more time there, and checked out more materials. In addition, students in these teachers' courses began to use the library much more effectively.

It is generally conceded that teaching library usage is difficult in a classroom setting removed from the library materials themselves. However, students can

---

HOW TO USE A BOOK

1. The region in which we live is discussed under the heading _____

_____

2. The last 16 pages in the book are called an *atlas.* Looking at these

    pages, can you define *atlas?* _____

    _____

    _____

3. On what page can you find a listing of all maps, graphs, and diagrams

    found in the book? _____

4. Does the book contain a picture of Wonder Lake? How did you go about

    answering this question? _____

5. Is there a picture of the Grand Coulee Dam in the text? _____

    _____

6. Under what heading must you look to find it? _____

    _____

7. In the index, there is a main heading entitled "Exploration." What six

    subheadings are found under it? _____

    _____

    _____

FIGURE 10.6
A study skill assignment and diagnostic test

learn important points about the library prior to a library visit. Several teachers in one school built a model card catalog drawer using a box for 3-by-5-inch index cards and compiled approximately 100 author cards ranging from *A* through *Z.* The teachers used this model in various classrooms, particularly in working with individual students who were not yet competent in using the card catalog. Another useful teaching device was a library checklist that teachers and the librarian devised. The list consisted of 8 or 10 specific tasks for the students to perform with teacher direction. Examples included the following:

1. Find the book *King of the Wind* by Marguerite Henry.

2. **a.** Who is the author of the book *A Child's History of Art?* _____

_____

8. The book contains a double-page map called "Main Air Routes in the U.S." There is no "Main Air Routes" heading in the index. How can you find this map? _____

_____

_____

9. There are two sections of the book that provide the pronunciation of difficult words. These are _____ and _____ .

10. The pronunciation of the following words is provided in the _____ _____ . In the blank spaces, show the pronunciation and page number where the word is found.

Shoshone _____ Page _____

Comanche _____ Page _____

Fort Duquesne _____ Page _____

11. A particular page contains the definition of difficult words used throughout the book. That page is called the _____ .

FIGURE 10.6, continued

b. What is the call number of this book? _____

c. Fill out a library card for this book. _____

3. Where are the bound volumes of *My Weekly Reader* located? _____

_____

These items provided guided practice in using title and author cards, locating books and journals on the shelves, and filling out library request cards properly. Other tasks covered specific information about the library.

To use this checklist technique effectively, small groups or individual students go to the library at specific times. The librarian briefly demonstrates and explains how to use certain facilities in the library. Each student then receives a checklist of

AID	INFORMATION
Title Page	The main title and possibly a subtitle. (The latter may set forth the limitations and narrow the topic.) The name of the author and where the book was published.
Table of Contents	Chapter titles possibly followed by the major topics discussed in each chapter. Is the book divided into major parts (I, II, III)? What are these? The length of the chapters gives a hint to thoroughness of the treatment.
Preface	To whom does the author address the book? What is the author's stated purpose? What new features does the author stress? What unique features does the author believe are found in the book?
List of Illustrations	The title, item, and page where it can be found.
Index	The major topics in alphabetical order; minor topics under each heading; key phrases, cross-references, photographs, drawings, charts, and tables.
Glossary	Difficult or specialized terms are presented in alphabetical order with a definition.
Appendix	An organized body of facts related to the subject under consideration. For example, in a geography book the appendix may give the areas of states or nations, populations, state and national capitals, the extent of manufacturing, exports, imports, and mineral deposits.

FIGURE 10.7
Typical book aids for the reader

tasks, which the librarian reviews briefly to ensure that students understand them. Such tasks should vary according to grade level and individual student needs.

Using Reference Materials.   Using reference materials is an important study skill that generally is not thoroughly taught in our schools. Many students reach high school or even college with only a hazy idea of how to systematically search available materials. Although many students in the upper primary grades are ready for limited use of reference materials, teachers have a major responsibility to teach these skills in the intermediate grades.

The Encyclopedia.   The use of encyclopedias and other reference books should be deliberately and systematically taught. If such materials are in the classroom, different groups of students can learn their use at various times. Instruction should parallel points already covered; for example, topics are arranged in alphabetical order, books are numbered in a series, the alphabetical range covered is indicated on the cover, and cross listings and key words must be used.

Any given unit in any content area can provide the framework for teaching efficient use of the encyclopedia. Assume a health class is considering the topic The Adventure of Medicine. The teacher asks students to list all of the possible headings under which they might find information relating to the topic. The responses might range from one suggestion, "look under medicine," to a half-page of suggestions, including medicine, surgery, disease, medical research, drugs, germ theory, space medicine, and public health. Other headings might include particular diseases, such as cancer, tuberculosis, yellow fever, diabetes, or poliomyelitis, or the names of individuals who made significant medical discoveries, such as Walter Reed, Jonas Salk, and Louis Pasteur.

An encyclopedia is a book or series of books that contains a little information about a great number of topics. A user must know what heading, or topic, to look under for particular information. Usually, an encyclopedia contains hundreds of headings that tell the reader "see _____ ," which is another heading under which the topic is discussed. For instance:

baking soda; *see* soda

Old Faithful; *see* Wyoming, Yellowstone National Park

Lennon, John; *see* Beatles

knee jerk; *see* reflex action

toadstool; *see* mushroom

INSTRUCTIONAL ACTIVITY

Using the Encyclopedia.   Using the following drawing, have students write the number of the volumes that will likely contain the information called for in the following questions.

Vol. 1	Vol. 2	Vol. 3	Vol. 4	Vol. 5	Vol. 6	Vol. 7	Vol. 8	Vol. 9	Vol. 10	Vol. 11	Vol. 12	Vol. 13	Vol. 14	Vol. 15	Vol. 16
A	B	C	D-E	F	G	H	I-J	K-L	M	N	O-P	Q-R	S	T-U	V-Z

_____ 1. Is more money spent on newspaper advertising or television advertising?

_____ 2. Where would you find hitches, knots, and splices?

_____ 3. Where would you find timber wolves?

_____ 4. Is there a bird called a kite?

_____ 5. What is a spelling demon?

_____ 6. Where would you find data on animals that sleep through the winter?

_____ 7. What are the previous names of the city of Leningrad?

_____ 8. What is the habitat of the Eastern gray squirrel?

Maps. The ability to read maps is important in our highly mobile society. Students should have opportunities to develop this skill in various content areas. Formats for teaching map reading can involve the entire class as well as individual students, pairs, or teams of students pursuing given learning tasks.

INSTRUCTIONAL ACTIVITIES

Using Maps. Use a series of letters to represent the location of the major cities. Have students identify those cities. Draw a line connecting two cities (e.g., San Francisco and St. Louis). Have students estimate the number of miles or kilometers between them. Using numbers to represent various states, have students identify the selected states. Have them identify lakes, rivers, mountain ranges, national parks, time zones, and so on. Have students color or crosshatch a state or region that is a major producer of oil, wheat, coal, iron ore, or other resources. Assign students the following exercise based on the simple outline map of the continental United States.

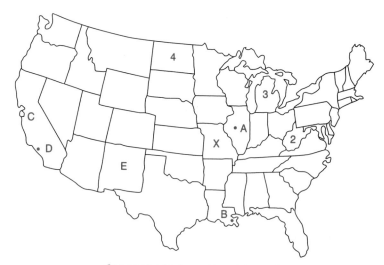

Can you locate the various states and
major cities on a map of the U.S ?

Can you locate the various states and major cities on a map of the U.S.?

1. The state of Missouri is represented by an X. Starting at the north and moving clockwise, name the states that border Missouri. _____

2. The number 2 indicates a state formed at the outbreak of the Civil War; this state is _____ .

3. The inland state marked 3 has more water boundary than land boundary. This state is _____ .

4. The number 4 is found in the state of _____ .

5. The state directly west of the state marked 4 is _____ .

6. Does Idaho border Canada? (Answer yes or no.) _____

7. Write the name for city A. It is a state capital and the burial place of Abraham Lincoln. _____

8. The letter B locates a city identified with the "birth of the Blues" and is the home of Dixieland jazz. _____

9. Two cities in California are marked C and D. C represents _____ ; D represents _____ .

10. Write the name of the southwestern state marked with an E. _____

Use the same type of activity in map study of foreign countries and regions, such as Central and South America, Europe, Africa, and Asia.

Map Reading.   Through the use of actual road maps, develop a number of map-reading activities. For one activity, plan a trip from Lisbon, Portugal, to Paris, France. Select the fastest route. Select the most scenic route. List, in order, the highways on which you will travel. Estimate the approximate distance to be traveled on each route. Plan side trips to historical sites or parks.

Maps often contain guides for finding places or cities (Heilman & Holmes, 1978). Example A tells us how to locate Detroit. Example B locates Austin, Texas.

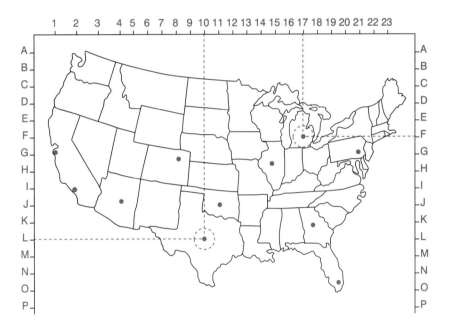

- Example A: Detroit, Michigan, is found by drawing a line down from 17 and a line over from F. The place where the two lines meet is the location of Detroit.
- Example B: Lines drawn down from 10 and over from L locate the capital city of Texas, which is Austin.

INSTRUCTIONAL ACTIVITIES

Find the City.   The problems that follow provide clues that will guide you to certain cities. You are to name these cities. Complete all the problems you can without using a map. Then use a map of the United States if needed. You need not draw lines on the map; use imaginary ones.

_____ H-15 The capital city of a midwestern state; Lincoln is buried there.

_____ I-1 Not a state capital, but the largest city in Southern California.

_____ J-11 A capital of a southwestern state (Will Rogers country).

_____ D-23 The capital of a state located in the northeast corner of the United States.

_____ K-17 The capital and largest industrial city of this southeastern state.

_____ C-7 Straight lines drawn from these points intersect in this state.

_____ G-21 A large city in eastern Pennsylvania (not the capital).

_____ J-4 The capital of a southwestern state.

_____ O-20 An Atlantic coastal city.

_____ G-8 The "mile-high city" and a state capital.

■ Critical-reading Skills

Locating information is an important part of the learning process, but it is only a small step toward the goal of assimilating material. The ability to locate information has little impact on personal or academic growth if one is unable to read critically the material located.

Teaching students how to read critically is undoubtedly the most difficult task attempted in our schools. A literate person not only possesses facts, but also can analyze information and think divergently. Analyzing and evaluating information presented in text are synonymous with critical reading. Critical-reading abilities involved in content reading include the following:

- ■ Knowing what the author has said.
- ■ Grasping the validity of statements and knowing when and how to verify them with other sources.
- ■ Differentiating between facts and opinions.
- ■ Noting when inferences are being drawn and drawing them when they are not stated.
- ■ Detecting author bias as well as inaccuracies that might not be traceable to bias.
- ■ Understanding your own biases as these relate to what is being read.
- ■ Taking into consideration an author's use of allusions, satire, humor, irony, and the like.
- ■ Developing some criteria for judging an author's competency in the area in which he or she writes.

Undoubtedly, this list could be extended. The abilities are developmental in nature, so they should be taught at all grade levels. These critical-reading abilities are not important by themselves but are a means to an end. Students need considerable meaningful practice to see how these skills apply to materials they encounter in their own lives. As in all content reading instruction, teachers need to review and reinforce reading abilities continually to ensure that students become independent learners. Students will face increasingly difficult reading tasks in the content areas, and their competency will need to grow if they are to learn. This need continues through high school and beyond. How many adults are immune to propaganda, know both sides of controversial issues, and do not let their emotions color their interpretations while reading?

Inability to discern what an author is saying may well be evidence of inability to read material critically, but paraphrasing, by itself, is not evidence of critical reading, either. Restating the gist of a passage but failing to detect author bias results in a transfer of author bias to the reader. Knowing what the author is saying without realizing that some statements contradict facts is not critical reading, nor is reciting strongly expressed opinions as if these were statements of fact. Interpreting and evaluating require applying various mechanical reading skills and higher-level abilities. Students need both teacher-directed instruction and systematic practice to develop effective work habits and study techniques (Stotsky, 1983).

Knowledge of Propaganda.   Resisting propaganda depends to a large degree on the reader's background or knowledge of the techniques people use to manipulate facts. Critical readers assume responsibility for questions. Although they respect language, they know that some people use it to control others' behavior. The purpose here is not to explain all of the various propaganda techniques used to obscure meaning or take the reader on a detour, but to provide examples to help students detect these devices.

INSTRUCTIONAL ACTIVITIES

Identifying Propaganda Techniques.   To introduce the concept of propaganda, list a number of popular propaganda techniques. Provide illustrations and discuss them with the class. Then guide students in writing examples. Discuss these examples and elaborate upon them in relation to the earlier discussion. Following are some propaganda techniques:

- Begging the issue or throwing up a smoke screen. Here, one does not discuss the real issue, but switches the discussion to other topics. For example, candidate A has charged that B has violated the law by not filing a statement of his campaign expenses. B replies, "A has accused me of not filing a statement of expenses. Why should he care? Is he a police officer? Have I ever lied to the voters? Who voted against raising taxes last year? I'll tell you who did—I did! And I'll tell you something else—A voted for the tax bill. I support every worthwhile charity in this community. I was born here, I went to school here! Can A make this statement?"
- Generalizing from too few cases.
- Ignoring the idea and attacking the person suggesting it.
- Using a false analogy.
- Appealing to authority.
- Relying on guilt by association.
- Using a faulty cause-and-effect relationship.
- Misusing figures or statistics.

Thinking Critically.   Prepare a number of propositions that might be an issue in any community. Follow each proposition with an imaginary statement that someone included in a letter to the editor. Have the students analyze and point out what the writer was up to. Following are several examples:

- **Proposition:** The city council should pass an ordinance requiring fluoridation of the city water supply in an effort to decrease tooth decay among children of the community.
  Letter to the Editor: "Of course some people favor fluoridation; they spend so much time in the Roaring Twenties Bar that they probably don't drink enough water to care how it tastes."

Letter No. 2: "The real issue is that fluoride is a poison. We shouldn't poison our fine water supply." (Beware of jumping to the conclusion: Fluoride is a poison. What is the missing detail?)

■ **Proposition:** The voters should approve a proposed school bond issue.
Letter to the Editor: "As Lincoln said, 'You can fool all of the people some of the time,' and this is one of those times! Our schools are as good as any in the country. The people pushing this school bond proposal want to raise your taxes. I say vote this bond issue down."

■ **Proposition:** We should adopt a city ordinance, proposed as a safety measure, that would prohibit the sale of fireworks.
Letter to the Editor: "The Fourth of July is one of our great holidays. This proposal is unpatriotic. It is a direct slap at free enterprise. A lot of American firms make fireworks. The next thing you know somebody will try to outlaw automobiles because people get hurt in accidents."

■ **Proposition:** The city should construct a swimming pool in the city park.
Letter to the Editor: "The people in this town do not want a municipal pool. It is obvious that if the people favored this harebrained idea, we would have had a pool by now!"

■ **Proposition:** We should extend the runways at our municipal airport so that jet planes can land here.
Letter to the Editor: "When we built the airport, the planners said the present layout would be adequate for at least 20 years. That was just 10 years ago. These people are experts, and we should listen to them."

Clues to Reading the News.   Teachers use newspapers and other mass media for teaching both critical analysis and the mechanical skills related to such analysis. The potential values of using such materials are numerous. There are also barriers to significant learning, including inadequate planning and the tendency to avoid discussion of controversial issues. Teachers should permit and encourage students to interpret and analyze advertisements, political cartoons, editorials, and syndicated columns. Develop clues to the news by direct instruction, focusing on discussing editorials, political cartoons, propaganda techniques, and current issues.

INSTRUCTIONAL ACTIVITIES

Analyzing Editorials.   In four or five metropolitan newspapers, compare editorials that deal with a particular current issue. Assuming that there are differences of opinion, what might account for these differences? What is the political orientation of the editor or publisher? Does a particular newspaper have a standing policy on certain issues (e.g., pro labor or management or foreign aid)?

Analyzing Political Cartoons.   Gather political cartoons that deal with the same topic from different papers and drawn by different artists. Direct students to analyze and verbalize what the cartoons are attempting to say. Student interpretations of any given stimulus will vary considerably. This will facilitate discussion and help students to see the importance of the reader's background, which includes bias, emotional attachments, and the like. Such factors always influence interpretation of a cartoon, editorial, feature article, or news story.

Analyzing Propaganda Techniques.   Prepare and duplicate an editorial that contains biased statements, factual errors, and various propaganda techniques. Give each student a copy of the material and direct edits or rewrites of the editorial. Next, have the class discuss the original materials and the substitutions, deletions, and corrections that they made. In many cases, students' reactions will be markedly different, particularly if the topic is chosen wisely. In the discussion, students will be exposed to a variety of viewpoints different from their own.

Studying Current Issues.   To study a current issue longitudinally, have students do the following:

1. Compare different newspaper and news magazine treatments of the problem.
2. Attempt to account for differences in the editorial points of view.
3. Study the interpretations of several columnists or news analysts.
4. Analyze the day-to-day statements of the decision makers or spokespersons attempting to mold public opinion. Based on the issue being studied, these might be legislative leaders, state department officials, labor leaders, candidates for high office, the President, or White House staff.

Distinguishing Between Fact and Opinion.   In content-area reading materials, students frequently must decide whether a statement is fact or opinion. Inexperienced readers develop habits that are not always helpful in this type of problem solving. One such habit is a tendency to accept what is written as factual. In addition, when a reader strongly agrees with a statement, he or she frequently accepts it as a fact. Finally, young readers may accept as fact a position that is developed logically or is repeated often enough. Thus, the statement "finding a four-leaf clover always brings good luck" may be doubted, but the statement "finding a four-leaf clover can bring good luck" may seem a bit more logical.

Probably the best way to help students learn how to differentiate fact from opinion is planned discussion of statements they encounter in textual material. This is difficult to do, however, when a teacher is limited to a particular textbook or certain materials. Another possibility is collecting statements of fact and opinion from various sources and discussing these. Obviously, all items may pertain to one subject area such as social studies, health, geography, or literature. On the other hand, exercises may deal with general statements or cut across various content areas.

INSTRUCTIONAL ACTIVITY

Fact Versus Opinion.   Have students read each statement carefully. If the sentence states a fact, have them write **F** on the line in front of the sentence. If the sentence states an opinion, have them write **O.**

_____ Democracy is the best form of government.
_____ Wild animals will not attack if you do not run.
_____ Pollution is the most serious problem in the world today.
_____ Rich people do not pay a fair share of taxes.
_____ Football is the roughest of all sports.
_____ Different brands of aspirin are essentially the same.
_____ Compact cars are not as safe as larger cars.
_____ The United States spends too much money on arms and weapons during peacetime.
_____ People will never be able to settle on the moon.
_____ In the United States, women live longer than men.

✔ Summary

Content reading presents many challenges to both students and teachers. To be successful in reading content materials, readers must know the characteristics and demands of expository text. To maximize student understanding, teachers must understand the concept of readability and factors that determine the difficulty of content material. To facilitate successful reading of expository text, teachers should actively teach and guide student involvement in (1) content reading vocabulary, (2) studying strategies to employ before, during, and after reading, (3) reading and study skills, (4) locational skills, and (5) critical-reading skills. Skills in these five areas should be taught in a direct fashion integrated into the curriculum. Following instruction, an abundance of varied and interesting practice will help ensure that students transfer these skills automatically to expository text.

✔ Your Point of View

Discussion Questions

1. Why is it possible that certain students may be proficient readers in science and also be incompetent readers in social studies?
2. The statement "Every teacher should be a teacher of reading" was first made more than 50 years ago. Why do you think it has not become a reality?
3. With regard to the studying strategies discussed in the chapter, how do teacher and student behaviors change before, during, and after reading strategies?

Take a Stand For or Against

1. Reading skills pertinent to specific content areas should be exclusively taught by content teachers.
2. The organizational structure of classrooms prohibits individualized instruction in the content areas.

Field-Based Assignments

1. Read the article by Hadaway and Young, "Content Literacy and Language Learning: Instructional Decisions," in *The Reading Teacher* (Volume 47, pp. 522–527, 1994). Design a Venn diagram, an H-map, or card sort for use in your classroom. Following your lesson, critique and reflect on its usefulness with one of your classmates.
2. Using the following questions, interview six students concerning their exposure to content reading instruction. Summarize your findings and share them with the class.

   Have you been taught

   ■ a study skill method for reading a content chapter in science or social studies?

- the different types of maps, charts, and graphs?
- how to use an index, atlas, and encyclopedia?
- how to outline a chapter?
- how to summarize a chapter?
- how to skim a chapter for main ideas?
- how to scan a chapter for a specific fact?

Portfolio Entry

Reflect on how you were taught social studies and science in your elementary school years. Compare your recollections with the way in which social studies and science are taught today and described in this chapter.

What are the similarities and differences? Is it easier to teach these content areas today? Why or why not? Write your findings and feelings for your portfolio.

Bibliography

Anderson, R. C. (1984). Role of the reader's schema in comprehension, learning, and memory. In R. C. Anderson, J. Osborn, & R. J. Tierney (Eds.), *Learning to read in American schools: Basal readers and content texts.* Hillsdale, NJ: Lawrence Erlbaum Associates, 243–257.

Anderson, R. C., Hiebert, E. H., Scott, J. A., & Wilkinson, I. (1985). *Becoming a nation of readers: The report of the Commission on Reading.* Washington, DC: National Institute of Education.

Armbruster, B. B. (1991). Using literature in the content areas. *The Reading Teacher, 45,* 324–325.

Armbruster, B. B., & Nagy, W. E. (1992). Vocabulary in content area lessons. *The Reading Teacher, 45,* 550–551.

Cheek, E. H., Flippo, R. F. & Lindsey, J. D. (1997). *Reading for success in elementary schools.* Dubuqe, IA: Brown & Benchmark.

Farris, P. J. & Fuhler, C. J. (1994). Developing social studies concepts through picture books. *The Reading Teacher, 47,* 380–387.

French, M. P., Danielson, K. E., Conn, M., Gale, W., Lueck, C., & Manley, M. (1989). In the classroom: Reading and writing in the content areas. *The Reading Teacher, 43,* 266–271.

Hadaway, N. L. & Young, T. A. (1994). Content literacy and language learning: Instructional decisions. *The Reading Teacher, 47,* 522–527.

Haggard, M. R. (1988). Developing critical thinking with the directed reading-thinking activity. *The Reading Teacher, 41,* 526–535.

Harris, T. L. & Hodges, R. E. (Eds.) 1995. *The literacy dictionary.* Newark, DE: International Reading Association.

Heimlich, J. E., & Pittleman, S. D. (1986). *Semantic mapping: Classroom applications.* Newark, DE: International Reading Association.

Holbrook, H. T. (1987). Writing to learn in the social studies ERIC/RCS. *The Reading Teacher, 41,* 216–219.

Irwin, J. W., & Davis, C. A. (1980). Assessing readability: The checklist approach. *Journal of Reading, 24,* 129–130.

Johnson, D. D., & Pearson, P. D. (1984). *Teaching reading vocabulary* (2nd ed.). New York: Holt, Rinehart & Winston.

Jones, M. P. (1986). *Effects of the reciprocal teaching method on third graders' decoding and comprehension abilities.* Doctoral dissertation, Texas A&M University, College Station.

Kinney, M. A. (1985). A language experience approach to teaching expository text structure. *The Reading Teacher, 38,* 854–856.

Kinney-Sedgwick, M., & Yochum, N. (1996). Content area literacy instruction: Viewpoints of elementary teachers and literacy professors. *Reading Research and Instruction, 35*(4) 298–315.

McGee, L. M., & Richgels, D. J. (1985). Teaching expository text structure to elementary students. *The Reading Teacher, 38,* 739–749.

Meyer, B. J. F., & Freedle, R. O. (1984). Effects of discourse type of recall. *American Educational Research Journal, 21,* 121–143.

Myers, J. W. (1984). *Writing to learn across the curriculum.* Bloomington, IN: Phi Delta Kappa.

Nagy, W. E. (1988). *Teaching vocabulary to improve reading comprehension.* Urbana, IL: ERIC Clearinghouse on Reading and Communication Skills and Newark, DE: International Reading Association.

Ogle, D. M. (1986). K-W-L: A teaching model that develops active reading of expository text. *The Reading Teacher, 39,* 564–570.

Olson, M. W., and Gee, T. C. (1991). Content reading instruction in the primary grades: Perceptions and strategies. *The Reading Teacher, 45,* 298–307.

Palincsar, A. S., & Brown, A. L. (1986). Interactive teaching to promote independent learning from text. *The Reading Teacher, 39,* 771–777.

Paris, S. G., Lipson, M. Y., & Wilson, K. K. (1994). Becoming a strategic reader. In R. B. Ruddell, M. R. Ruddell, & H. Singer (Eds.), *Theoretical models and process of reading* (4th ed.). (pp. 788–810). Newark, DE: International Association.

Pescosolido, J. R., Schell, L. M., & Laurent, M. J. (1967). *Reading approaches and rituals.* Dubuque, IA: Kendall/Hunt.

Readence, J. E., Bean, T. W., & Baldwin, R. S. (1995). *Content area reading: An integrated approach* (5th ed.). Dubuque, IA: Kendall/Hunt.

Richardson, J. S., & Morgan, R. F. (1993). *Reading to learn in the content areas* (2nd ed.). Belmont, CA: Wadsworth.

Robinson, F. P. (1961). *Effective study* (rev. ed.). New York: Harper & Row.

Shores, J. (1943). Skills related to the ability to read history and science. *Journal of Educational Research, 36,* 584–594.

Smith, C. C., & Bean, T. W. (1980). The guided writing procedure: Integrating content reading and writing improvement. *Reading World, 19,* 724–738.

Smith, J. L. & Johnson, H. (1994). Models for implementing literature in content studies. *The Reading Teacher, 48,* 198–209.

Stauffer, R. (1975). *Directing the reading-thinking process.* New York: Harper & Row.

Stotsky, S. (1983). Research on reading/writing relationships: A synthesis and suggested directions. *Language Arts, 60,* 627–642.

Tadlock, D. F. (1978). SQ3R—Why it works, based on an information processing theory of learning. *The Journal of Reading, 22,* 110–116.

Zakaluk, B. L., & Samuels, S. J. (1988). Toward a new approach to predicting text comprehensibility. In B. L. Zakaluk & S. J. Samuels (Eds.), *Readability: Its past, present, and future.* Newark, DE: International Reading Association.

CHAPTER 11

Literacy Assessment

Chapter Outline

Meeting Individual Needs
Differentiated Instruction
Forms of Assessment

Standardized Tests
Typical Features
Norm-referenced Tests
Criterion-referenced Tests
Diagnostic Tests
Cautions About Standardized Tests

Informal Assessment
Teacher Observation/Kid Watching
Assessment Materials That Accompany
    Published Reading Materials
Informal Reading Inventories
Cloze Procedure
Authentic Assessment/Performance-based
    Assessment
Anecdotal Records
Response Journals
Portfolios

For the Reader

Assessment is an important part of every school's curriculum and it must serve a justifiable purpose in order to merit so much attention. The only justifiable purpose for the use of literacy assessment is to obtain information about students' reading and writing abilities in order to design and improve the quality of literacy programs. In practice, however, some schools and teachers believe that testing programs per se have little educational value. Sometimes testing becomes an end in itself rather than a basis for instruction. In some communities, a metal filing cabinet with a folder for each student represents evidence of good teaching practices. This phenomenon suggests that some teachers have forgotten that assessment alone has no beneficial effect on students. Teachers using this method of assessment do not realize that the importance of assessment is to help design instruction based on students' literacy strengths and to improve their literacy weaknesses. As you read this chapter, focus on how to assess students' reading and writing and how to use this information in planning and evaluating your instruction.

Key Ideas

- Ongoing assessment of students' literacy development and teachers' instruction form the foundation for planning literacy instruction and determining its effectiveness.
- Students' reading and writing abilities can be assessed through the use of (1) norm-referenced tests, (2) criterion-referenced tests, (3) placement tests, (4) informal reading inventories (IRIs), (5) teacher-developed procedures, and (6) authentic assessment.
- Standardized reading tests only sample students' reading (and sometimes writing) behaviors and provide only a small piece of a much larger picture.
- Informal and teacher-developed procedures are more valuable because they use assessment strategies that are more in line with the current thinking about literacy learning.
- An effective reading teacher interacts with students as they engage in reading and writing to assess the processes the students employ.

Meeting Individual Needs

It is important to remember that assessment alone cannot change the profile of the learner, but it can have a direct affect on the method of instructional delivery. The *Standards for the Assessment of Reading and Writing* (1994) point out that the fundamental purpose of assessment is to improve teaching and learning. Ongoing assessment of students' reading and writing development forms the foundation for planning both reading and writing instruction and determining its effectiveness. Information about students' literacy strengths and weaknesses allows teachers to select instructional strategies and materials in relation to students' needs. The key here is not simply gathering information about students' reading and writing, but determining how to use the information to optimize growth for each student.

Differentiated Instruction

Students at any given grade level show great differences in their literacy skills and abilities. Some of them read and write at a level considerably below their grade-level placement, while others have advanced literacy capabilities. Figure 11.1 illustrates the overlap between grades and the range of abilities found at the primary level.

These facts, which apply to practically every classroom, emphasize the need for differentiated instruction. One criterion that distinguishes excellent literacy programs from others is the degree to which they accommodate individual needs. Teachers must be alert to differences among students in order to follow sound teaching principles. Only various means of assessment can help teachers determine needs and plan instruction for students whose needs vary considerably. Assessment should be ongoing, because students change rapidly. An assessment conducted in September may be followed by a student having a breakthrough in some vital skill or by a failure to understand some new step in reading and writing. In either case, the earlier assessment is obsolete.

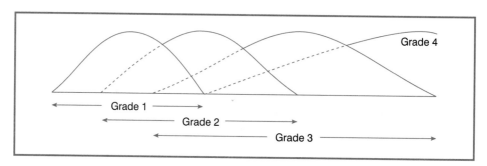

FIGURE 11.1
Graphic representation of reading abilities in the primary grades.
Note that the range of abilities increases at each succeeding
grade level.

Forms of Assessment

Assessment of literacy strengths and weaknesses can take a variety of forms, including standardized tests, informal tests, observation, portfolios, and interaction with learning tasks and activities. However, the most prevalent form of assessment stems from the daily instruction delivered in the classroom. During this informal on-the-spot assessment, the teacher reflects and evaluates how the lesson was received by the students and makes the appropriate adjustments for the next lesson. Although tests are designed for use at every grade level, no purpose would be served by a separate discussion of tests for each instructional level. The following discussion of assessment applies to the various levels of the elementary school.

Standardized Tests

Assessment comes in many different forms, has many different purposes, and is used at many different levels. Standardized tests are one of the most formal measures of assessment and serve several educational purposes, which may not always be clear to the classroom teacher.

Standardized tests sample students' reading in a controlled, systematic fashion. Procedures for administering, scoring, and interpreting each test are determined under controlled experimental conditions. These procedures are usually explained in a manual accompanying the test.

Essentially, schools use two types of commercially published standardized reading tests: (1) norm-referenced tests and (2) criterion-referenced tests. Both may feature similar types of test items, but each serves a different purpose and has a different interpretation. **Norm-referenced tests** are used to compare a student's performance with that of a representative sample (the norming group) of students. **Criterion-referenced tests** compare a student's performance with established benchmarks or criteria that have been identified as abilities that students are to achieve.

Commercially printed standardized tests fall into two classes: (1) those designed for group administration and (2) those designed to be administered individually. Both give credit for acceptable responses and determine the student's score by correct responses, lack of errors, and rate of reading.

Typical Features

Commercially published standardized tests usually provide a manual of directions for administering, scoring, and interpreting them. Information contained in the manual generally includes (1) an overview, (2) directions for administering, (3) directions for scoring, (4) a description of the types of scores, (5) procedures for using the results, and (6) information on development, national norms, reliability, validity, and other technical aspects.

Read the administrator's manual carefully to ensure that you understand fully each important aspect of administering, scoring, and interpreting the test.

Failure to administer the test according to the manual can seriously jeopardize the validity of the test results. A **valid** test is one that measures what it purports to measure. In addition to studying the manual carefully, it is a good idea to take the test yourself. This allows you to become familiar with what the students must do when taking the test. Furthermore, by giving close attention to individual test items, you can determine how well the test fits the class based on past reading instruction. If the items do not accurately reflect past reading instruction, then the test lacks content validity and the results have little value in decisions about students' reading and writing.

Most standardized tests have a template or scoring key to facilitate rapid, accurate hand-scoring of answer sheets. This can be very beneficial to the teacher who wants to use the results of the standardized test to help plan instruction for individual students. By scoring the test by hand, the teacher has useful information about the questions asked as well as the reading strengths and weaknesses of individual students. A large number of norm-referenced test publishers also provide computer scoring services for their test users.

Although computer scoring frees the teacher from spending time scoring each student's test, the teacher often must wait for the results. The teacher thus cannot immediately use the test results to plan and implement reading instruction.

Reliability. The consistency with which a test measures reading skills is referred to as its **reliability.** A reliable test provides a stable sample of students' reading performance. For example, if test X was administered to a student in September, you would expect that administering the test 2 or 3 weeks later would result in a similar score. If the student's score was 80 on the first administration and 15 on the second administration, however, then it is impossible to decide which score accurately reflects the student's reading ability. Such a test would be highly unreliable because it does not consistently sample students' reading skills.

Test reliability is generally reported in the administrator's manual and is expressed as a coefficient of reliability. Tests with reliability coefficients of .80 or above are considered highly reliable. Test X presented in the earlier example would have a low coefficient of reliability. Reliability is one important feature to consider when selecting or interpreting students' reading performance on standardized tests. If the test does not report reliability, you can assume that it has low reliability and should select another form of assessment to use. High reliability does not ensure, however, that a test is also valid.

Validity. As noted earlier, a valid test measures what it purports to measure. As with reliability, the administrator's manual also discusses the validity of a standardized test. Several different types of validity are important to consider in relation to the intended use of the test results, including content validity and criterion-related validity.

Content validity means that the test items are an accurate sampling of reading-instruction content and the behavioral changes under consideration. A test may be called a reading test, and the test items may be easily identified as measuring reading skills, but the test still may not have content validity. Content validity means that the test measures the same aspects of reading that students had an opportunity to learn in the instructional program. This is why it is extremely important for the teacher to examine the test beforehand in order to determine whether the test has content validity.

If the results from a test are used to predict future reading performance or estimate current performance in a reading task (i.e., mastery or lack of mastery in reading skill areas), then criterion-related validity is extremely important. Criterion-related validity is especially crucial in reading-readiness tests, which are used to predict the likelihood of success in beginning reading tasks. The administrator's manual for readiness tests specifies criterion-related validity as a coefficient of correlation between performance on the readiness test and other standardized tests measuring beginning reading ability. The higher the validity coefficient, the more accurately the readiness test predicts later reading performance.

■ Norm-referenced Tests

Norm-referenced tests compare the performance of an individual or individuals with the performance of a norming group. The norming group generally consists of a large sample of students who are representative of the national school population. These students take the test, and their performance determines the test's national norms. Following this, each student's raw score (total number of correct responses) on the test is compared to the norming data. It is important for teachers to examine the norming information in the administrator's manual to make sure the norming population is representative of the class being assessed.

Several types of norms compare an individual's relative standing to a defined variable. Norming information found in the administrator's manual is based on the test's national norms. Similar norms, however, can be developed locally for a school district, school, or individual classroom. Most standardized norm-referenced tests provide for the conversion of a student's raw score to a percentile rank, stanine, and grade-level equivalent.

Percentile Ranks.   Percentile ranks range from 1 to 99 and indicate the percentage of students in the norming group that scored at or below a given score. For example, if a raw score of 62 is equal to a percentile rank of 80, this means that the student did as well as or better than 80 percent of the individuals in the norming group. A percentile rank of 50 represents the median, or middle score, and indicates average performance.

Stanines.   Stanines also indicate a student's relative standing in comparison to other students in the norming group. As the term implies, stanines range from a low of 1 to a high of 9. Stanines 1 through 3 usually indicate below-average performance, 4 through 6 average performance, and 7 through 9 above-average performance. Stanines represent a range of scores rather than a specific score. For example, a raw score of 28 at the 77th percentile and a raw score of 31 at the 88th percentile could be equivalent to stanine 7. Stanines represent units that are approximately equal; a difference between stanines 5 and 7 is about the same as the

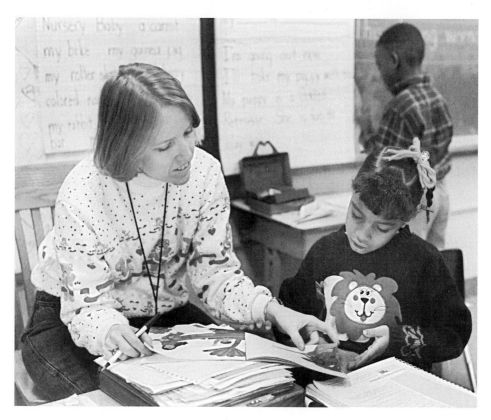

Ongoing assessment of students' reading and writing development form the foundation for effective instruction.

difference between stanines 3 and 5. Because of this, stanines can help in comparing a student's performance across various sections of a test and are better at determining student gains than percentiles are.

Grade-level Equivalents. Grade-level equivalents of raw scores on a norm-referenced test indicate a student's performance in relation to the average score for the grade level of the norming group. Grade-level scores are reported by school grade and tenths of the school year. A grade-level equivalent of 4.0 indicates that a student's raw score equals the score of the average fourth grader in the norming population.

A grade-level equivalent is not necessarily the same as the level at which a student should be reading. A fourth grader who scored a grade-level equivalent of 6.5 on a recently administered standardized test should not be given sixth-grade work. Instead, these results indicate that this fourth grader scored the same on the fourth-grade test as a sixth grader would have on the same test. Likewise, a fourth grader who received a grade equivalent of 2.5 probably should not be instructed at the second-grade level; instead, it should be noted that this fourth grader did as well on this test as a second grader taking the same test. In the former example, the grade equivalent suggests that this student is above average. In the latter example, the grade equivalent indicates that this student may be a low achiever for his or her grade. Grade-level equivalents can often be very confusing to both parents and students who do not understand the definition of these scores.

■ Criterion-referenced Tests

Criterion-referenced tests (CRTs) are designed to measure students' mastery of specific reading skills. Rather than comparing a student's performance to that of the norming group, CRTs view performance in relation to mastery level of one or more skills. These skills are usually stated as performance, or behavioral, objectives; for example, "The student will identify correctly the order of events found in short reading passages."

CRTs include several items for each reading benchmark or objective. A student's response to these items is evaluated in terms of the number of correct items for each benchmark or objective. Evaluation typically compares the student's performance to established criteria. For example, if 20 items test an objective, a student who scores 16 or more correct may have mastered the skill or demonstrated acquisition of the benchmark; 12 to 15 correct answers might indicate that review is needed; and fewer than 12 correct items could indicate a need for reteaching the skill. Some criterion-referenced tests use only one criterion of performance to indicate a level of competence: 15 out of 20 similar items correct may mean mastery, but fewer than 15 correct is lack of mastery. The criterion for mastery can be established by the teacher, the district, the state, or the testing company.

■ Diagnostic Tests

In addition to standardized achievement tests that contain reading subtests, standardized diagnostic reading tests are available for classroom use. These tests help teachers sample specific reading strengths and weaknesses in a variety of areas. Diagnostic tests often have more subtests than achievement tests do. They also test items related to specific reading behaviors. The number of subtests included on diagnostic reading tests varies; however, most of them have from 5 to 10.

Many standardized tests can provide information about students' reading. All norm-referenced achievement batteries designed to test elementary students contain reading subtests. These tests usually provide a vocabulary score, a comprehension score, and a total reading score (the average of vocabulary and comprehension). Many criterion-referenced reading tests include subtests that focus on specific aspects of word identification and comprehension. With so many different reading tests, it is no surprise that many measure virtually the same aspects of reading. Nevertheless, tests vary significantly in what they measure, their intended level of difficulty, the care that went into their construction, and their ease of administration. Each of these factors influences two important attributes of reading tests: (1) how consistently they measure reading skills and (2) how well they actually measure the skills that they supposedly measure.

■ Cautions About Standardized Tests

Standardized tests have been criticized because they do not reflect all of the skills and capabilities associated with literacy, are often assumed to accurately measure students' learning, and provide little information about students' problem-solving capabilities and learning processes (Winograd, Paris, & Bridge, 1991). Students bring much more to a reading task than a standardized test can sample. Nonetheless, many school districts and states still require the administration of standardized tests for reading and writing. Some states, such as Kentucky, have recently argued for authentic assessment, sampling both students' performance in important learning tasks (discussing books read) and students' products (writing samples).

Standardized tests sample only students' literacy in relation to the tasks (identifying words in context, selecting word definitions) and do not provide a broad view of how well an individual reads. Teachers should view results from standardized tests as only one part of a much larger picture of a student's literacy. Also, test results provide little meaningful information that teachers can use to improve the quality of their literacy instruction and better address the needs of individual students. The shortcomings of standardized tests were recently noted by Early (1992/1993): "The need to know how children are doing persists—with teachers, with parents, with the children themselves—but recently gained knowledge of the reading process convinces us that standardized tests fail to measure those processes accurately, wholly, or diagnostically" (p. 306). Even with these noted weaknesses, standardized tests continue to play a major role in our evaluation of our schools. As stated earlier, assessment is used at many different levels, and while the information provided on standardized tests may not be of particular importance to the classroom teacher or the students, it is of high value to school districts and state officials who are examining the success and failure rates of schools. Information gained at the state level can help teachers continue their professional development and increase funds to schools that are not reaching the same criteria that other schools are, though they are often within the same district.

Assessment that is more useful to teachers and students is informal assessment. Informal assessment is much more valuable in helping teachers determine students' literacy development and adjust literacy instruction accordingly.

Informal Assessment

Conventional literacy tests examine the products of a student's performance (such as instructional level, specific skill strengths and weaknesses, and national, state, or local ranking), not the processes a reader and writer employs. Yet certain strategic processes characterize effective reading and writing.

The discrepancy between our knowledge of effective reading and writing and the prevailing assessment procedures has prompted many experts to recommend changes in how we assess literacy. The *Standards for the Assessment of Reading and Writing* (1994) indicate that the most productive way to assess students' read-

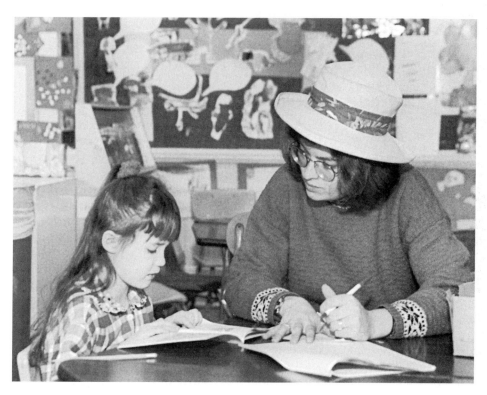

**Teacher and student interaction can provide a wealth
of assessment information.**

ing and writing processes is when teachers observe and interact with students as
they read authentic texts and write for genuine purposes. As teachers interact
with students, they evaluate the ways in which the students construct meaning,
and they are able to intervene in order to provide scaffolding support or suggestions when the students appear to have difficulty.

While our knowledge of various reading strategies has dramatically improved in the last 20 years, effective teachers have always known the value of simultaneous assessment and instruction. In interacting with students, effective
teachers assess each student's reading strategies. In doing so, they look at the student's use of prior knowledge, story structure, headings, self-questioning, and
purpose setting. They also look at how the student understands main ideas, summarizes key points, infers relationships, and rereads parts for clarification. This is
called process-oriented assessment.

Effective classroom reading teachers modify existing informal tests to accen-
tuate the processes of reading rather than the products. They may add expository
passages to the traditional narrative or expand the passage length to more realis-
tically assess a student's reading skills and abilities. Before reading, they may informally assess prior knowledge by asking questions and initiating a discussion
with the student. After reading, they may ask questions, encourage retellings, and

promote discussion to assess summarizing or inferencing abilities. Additionally, teachers may assess metacognition by asking students how they make sense of what they read.

■ Teacher Observation/Kid Watching

The most powerful assessment tool is keen teacher observation, which has also been referred to as kid watching. Effective kid watchers know what to look and listen for and then translate this information into instructional decisions to improve students' facility in interacting with text. Observations are often the first step in informal on-the-spot assessment. Teachers use observation to interpret whether students are listening and understanding what they are learning. They use observation to help detect distractions and avoid complications that could interrupt learning. Some teachers use checklists (see Figure 11.2) that serve as guides to help them focus on observing stimuli that will best enable them to make accurate assessments.

Walker (1996) addresses this quality of assessment during instruction to emphasize the reflective and self-monitoring attitude of effective teachers. Diagnostic teachers assess while they teach. They evaluate children's use of strategies in a specific context for varying reading purposes. Questions such as "Do students use both text-based (bottom-up) processing and reader-based (top-down) processing when they read?" and "When a reading task for the students is modified, do they gain more understanding and control of their reading process?" help diagnostic teachers think about what students already know and how they can guide students to a more integrated understanding of the reading process.

The power of watching kids is that it helps teachers to pinpoint students' strengths and weaknesses in a variety of literacy tasks and use such information to plan appropriate instruction. Standardized tests are limited in helping the teacher identify students' literacy strengths and weaknesses. Furthermore, standardized tests alone cannot accurately assess students' literacy and the effectiveness of literacy instruction. Effective teachers combine observation with a variety of informal assessment procedures. Informal assessment of students' literacy can include materials that accompany reading instructional materials, informal reading inventories, performance-based assessment, portfolios, observation, interviews, and interaction with students.

■ Assessment Materials That Accompany Published Reading Materials

A large number of published reading materials contain student assessment materials. The main purposes of these materials are to (1) facilitate assignment at the appropriate level of difficulty in the materials, (2) determine whether students have progressed in their reading development, and (3) identify some reading strengths and weaknesses. In comparison with norm-referenced standardized tests, assessment materials do not compare students' performance with that of students at a grade level in a wide geographic area.

Many assessment materials provide criteria, or benchmarks, to assist the teacher in identifying whether students have acquired various aspects of reading. Unlike standardized criterion-referenced tests, benchmarks are presented only to assist the teacher in evaluating students' performances. Placement tests can help you to make decisions about students' placement in a particular level of a literature series, but they also can help you to evaluate students' progress in the materials.

Assessment materials are content specific; that is, they assess students' progress in terms of the reading materials for which the assessments were developed. You should, however, evaluate and review them carefully to ensure that they closely match what is taught. Also, pay careful attention to the number of items and the descriptions of benchmarks to ensure that they adequately sample the area of reading identified. Some assessment materials that accompany reading materials are attempting to incorporate more of the features of reading reflecting current thinking. Figure 11.3 is an example of recent changes in placement tests accompanying literature-based reading series.

■ Informal Reading Inventories

One of the more helpful tools one can use in the classroom to assess students' reading strengths and weaknesses is the **informal reading inventory (IRI).** Essentially, IRIs take three forms: (1) commercially published, (2) accompanying reading series, and (3) teacher prepared. Regardless of the type of inventory you choose, its major purposes are to establish students' reading levels and to identify their reading strengths and weaknesses. The typical IRI consists of graded word lists, graded reading passages (often both narrative and expository), and comprehension questions.

Graded word lists consist of 10 to 20 words for each grade level represented in the IRI. Most commercially published and reading series IRIs have graded word lists for preprimer through sixth grade. A student's performance on the graded word list provides the teacher with information for placement in the graded passages, sight vocabulary strengths and weaknesses, and word-identification strategies used to decode and identify words presented in isolation.

Graded reading passages are series of passages, usually ranging in reading difficulty from preprimer or primer through eighth or ninth grade. Performance on the passages can provide insights about a reader's strategies in using context, attention to meaning, identification of unknown words, reading interests, and different levels of reading competence.

Comprehension questions consist of 5 to 10 questions for each graded reading passage. The questions typically cover vocabulary, main idea, inference, literal meaning, cause and effect, and sequence. The questions are intended to identify students' reading-comprehension competence. Some IRIs also have features to evaluate the children's retelling of the passages that they read.

Most commercial IRIs have at least two equivalent forms. Either form may be administered orally or silently. A student's performance on the oral administration of the IRI can identify his or her independent, instructional, frustration, and listening-capacity reading-competence levels. At the independent level, the student can read materials without any assistance. The instructional level is the

Name _____ Age _____ Grade _____ Date _____

School _____ Teacher _____

Examiner _____

I. *Word Analysis*
   A. Knows names of letters
      Needs work with: _____ Yes   No
   B. Attacks initial sound of words
      Deficiencies noted: _____ Yes   No
   C. Can substitute initial letter sounds
      Further drill needed: _____ Yes   No
   D. Can sound out initial blends and digraphs
      Deficiencies noted: _____ Yes   No
   E. If root word is known, can solve words
      formed by adding prefixes and suffixes _____ Yes   No

II. *Sight Words* (check if applicable)
   _____ Knows a word one time, misses it later
   _____ Guesses at unknown words
             _____ Errors frequently do not change intended meaning
             _____ Errors indicate not reading for meaning
   _____ Frequently adds words
             _____ Errors frequently do not change intended meaning
             _____ Errors indicate not reading for meaning
   _____ Omits words
             _____ Errors frequently do not change intended meaning
             _____ Errors indicate not reading for meaning

III. *Reading Habits Noted*
   _____ Reads word-by-word   _____ Loses place frequently
   _____ Phrasing inadequate   _____ Does not utilize punctuation
   _____ Poor intonation   _____ Lacks persistence

   Explain: _____

   _____

IV. *Sustained Reading* (basal, textbook, trade book)
    (Do quantitative and qualitative analysis using techniques presented earlier.)

	Grade Level	*Approx. Number of Running Words*	*Number of Errors*
1.			
2.			

Errors noted (example): Said *lied* for *lying; banged* for *bumped; stuck* for *start* (corrected)

Needed help with: *clown, stomach, curious, squeal*

Read with some hesitation, not smoothly, etc.

FIGURE 11.2
Reading observation checklist

	Excellent	Average	Below Average
V. *Comprehension*			
Recall of facts	————	————	————
Recognizes main ideas	————	————	————
Draws inferences	————	————	————
Maintains sequence of events	————	————	————
Understands humor	————	————	————
Interprets figurative expressions	————	————	————
VI. *Oral Reading Skills*			
Relates with audience	————	————	————
Enunciation	————	————	————
Adequate volume	————	————	————
Reads with intonation	————	————	————
Phrases for meaning	————	————	————
VII. *Behaviors Related to Reading*			
Attitude toward reading	————	————	————
Self-confidence	————	————	————
Background knowledge	————	————	————
Language facility	————	————	————
Originality of expression	————	————	————
Range of vocabulary	————	————	————
Stock of concepts	————	————	————
Variety of sentence patterns	————	————	————

VIII. *Other Comments* _____

_____

_____

_____

_____

_____

_____

_____

_____

_____

_____

_____

_____

FIGURE 11.2, continued

Understanding What I Read

Directions. Read the following questions about the selection you have just read. Select the answer or answers that are correct. There may be one, two, or three correct answers for each question. You may look back at the story to answer the questions.

THEME

1. What is this story mostly about?
   a. Texas cowhands name a horse Widow-Maker.
   b. Pecos Bill can do many things that other men cannot do.
   c. The wildest horse in the West is captured and tamed.
   d. There are many different tasks to do on a ranch.
   e. Cowhands are known to be jealous of each other.

1. _____

VOCABULARY

2. Why did the cowhands rename the horse Widow-Maker?
   a. The horse is wild enough to kill a man.
   b. Men would rather die than ride the horse.
   c. The horse is the color of a black widow spider.
   d. The horse can buck very hard.
   e. Pecos Bill's wife could not ride the horse.

2. _____

PROBLEM

3. What problems does Pecos Bill face in the beginning of the story?
   a. He must find a way to capture a wild horse.
   b. He must keep other cowhands off his horse.
   c. He must tame the horse but not break its spirit.
   d. He must find the right bit for the horse's mouth.
   e. He must stay on the horse until it tires.

3. _____

CHARACTER

4. How do we know that Pecos Bill was a kind person?
   a. He does not leave Old Satan on Pike's Peak.
   b. He wants to let Old Satan ride the horse.
   c. He does not want to break the spirit of the horse.
   d. He gives his friends a prize for renaming the horse.
   e. He pats the horse gently and talks to him.

4. _____

FIGURE 11.3
Example of assessment materials accompanying a literature-based reading series
Source: From William H. Rupley and John W. Logan, **Vistas in Reading Literature,** Silver Level (Evanston, IL: McDougall, Littell & Co., 1990), p. 31.

SETTING	5. In what location is this story set?	5. _____
	a. the North	
	b. the East	
	c. the West	
	d. Mexico	
	e. Texas	

SUPPORTING IDEA

6. Which of the following is NOT supported by information in the story?   6. _____
   a. Pecos Bill talks to the horse.
   b. The horse is easy to capture and tame.
   c. Pecos Bill sells the horse to his good friend.
   d. The horse agrees to let Pecos Bill ride him.
   e. The horse does not mind who rides him.

BACKGROUND KNOWLEDGE OF STORY TYPE

7. Which of the following are typical of folk tales?   7. _____
   a. The characters can be animals.
   b. The story is set in a distant time and place.
   c. The main character is a person who is alive today.
   d. The story teaches a lesson about life.
   e. The story takes place in outer space.

TEXT STRUCTURE

8. What information is given in the first paragraph?   8. _____
   a. The reason the writer wrote the story is given.
   b. The problem Pecos Bill will face is identified.
   c. The problem Pecos Bill faces is solved.
   d. The main characters are introduced.
   e. The reason for renaming a horse is told.

TEXT/LITERARY DEVICE

9. What does the writer say to make the horse seem human?   9. _____
   a. The horse wears fine, expensive clothing.
   b. The horse begs Pecos Bill to be his master.
   c. The horse asks the cowhands to give him a new name.
   d. The horse is honored to be Pecos Bill's horse.
   e. The horse refuses to eat his oats.

10. What do the words *horse, cowhands, lasso, Texas,* and *canyons* tell you about the story?   10. _____
    a. The story takes place on a ranch.
    b. The story is about life in New England.
    c. The story is about cowboys.
    d. The story could never have really happened.
    e. The story takes place in a large city.

FIGURE 11.3, continued

11. Which of the following experiences would help   11. _____
    you understand the story?
    a. Raising horses.
    b. Climbing a mountain.
    c. Reading stories about the old West.
    d. Reading other stories about Pecos Bill.
    e. Making promises to friends.

12. Which *one* of these strategies would best help   12. _____
    you find out how Pecos Bill feels when Old
    Satan rides his horse?
    a. Guess from what you remember reading.
    b. Reread the story, starting at the beginning.
    c. Reread the beginning and end.
    d. Search quickly for that information.
    e. Reread every other sentence.

13. In retelling this story, which of these facts would   13. _____
    be MOST important to include?
    a. Pecos Bill is a folk tale hero who is very brave.
    b. The horse's color is white.
    c. Only Pecos Bill can ride the wild horse.
    d. The horse is very difficult to capture and tame.
    e. Widow-Maker is the son of the White Mustang.

FIGURE 11.3, continued

teaching level at which students can read materials successfully with teacher guidance. At the frustration level, materials become too difficult and, as a result, frustrating for the students. The listening-capacity level indicates what students can understand when material is read aloud to them. It is identified by evaluating responses to the comprehension questions for grade-level passages that are read aloud to students.

Reading the passages aloud and responding to comprehension questions orally allows identification of instructional, independent, and frustration levels for both word recognition and comprehension. Silent reading of the passages identifies the same reading-competence levels, but only for comprehension.

Administration. Administering an informal reading inventory is easy. You should follow some basic guidelines, however, to ensure that the oral reading accurately samples a student's reading. The following paragraphs outline the procedures to follow when administering an IRI.

1. Prior to administering the IRI, become thoroughly familiar with the coding system used to record students' deviations from the text as they read passages orally. Figure 11.4 presents a coding system that you can use to note such deviations. It is strongly recommended that you

TYPE OF MISCUE	HOW TO MARK	EXAMPLE
Omission: Word, several words, or punctuation is omitted.	Circle (⬭) the word(s), part of word, or punctuation omitted.	The large (black) dog jumped (high) into the air and grabbed the ball.
Substitution: Real word is substituted for text word.	Draw a line through the word substituted and write the substituted word above the text word.	*huge* *leaped* The large black dog jumped high *bait* into the air and grabbed the ball.
Insertion: Word is inserted in the passage text.	Use a caret (∧) to indicate where word was inserted and write the word.	The large black dog jumped high *big* into the air and grabbed the ∧ball.
Unknown or Aided Words: Word or words are pronounced for the reader.	Place a letter "P" over the word pronounced for the reader.	*P* The large black dog jumped high into the air and grabbed the ball.
Transposition: Order of words in the text is transposed.	Use a curved mark (∿) over and under the words transposed.	The ⌒large⌣black⌒dog jumped high into the air and grabbed the ball.
Repetition: Phrase or several words are repeated. Count as one miscue.	Place an "R" with lines extending in both directions over the words repeated.	The large black dog jumped high ——R—— into the air and grabbed the ball.
Mispronunciation: Word is pronounced incorrectly.	Write the phonetic spelling above the word or use diacritical markings to indicate the pronunciation.	*largé* *jumpted* The large black dog jumped high into the air and grabbed the ball.
Self-correction: Miscue is self-corrected by the reader. Important to note, but do not count as a miscue.	Place a check mark (✓) above the miscue.	✓ *jumpted* ✓ The large black dog jumped high into the air and grabbed the ball.

FIGURE 11.4

Marking system for recording oral reading miscues

practice using the coding system and also tape-record the student's oral reading to ensure accurate coding of miscues. The importance of using the described coding system is that other teachers who examine your IRI will know what they are looking at.

2. To administer the IRI, select an area that is free of distractions. Establish a relaxed atmosphere to minimize student anxiety. Tell the student that the IRI is not a test and that he or she is going to read aloud some words and stories and answer some questions about each story. Also, it is extremely important to explain that you will be doing some writing as the student reads the story, because many students become highly anxious when the teacher begins to write. Introduce the student to the tape recorder and let the student record his or her name, the date, and something about himself or herself. Play back what is recorded to check for proper settings. This procedure usually eliminates the novelty of the tape recorder and prevents it from becoming a distraction.

3. Select the graded word list that is two levels below the student's current grade level (word lists for the student should be typed on separate note cards) and ask the student to read the list of words aloud. Some teachers use a flash and untimed measure to determine word-recognition automaticity as well as word-attack skills. Encourage the student to read each word, even if the student is not sure of a word's pronunciation. This provides some indication of the student's word-identification strategies. The teacher should write the word as the student phonetically pronounces it.

   If the student makes a miscue on this first word list, drop to an easier list until there are no miscues. Continue administering more difficult word lists and noting the student's miscues by using the coding system. Stop administering the word lists when the student's miscues reach the maximum number suggested in the teacher's manual. If you use teacher-prepared graded word lists, stop administering the lists when the student's miscues reach 30% or greater.

4. The highest graded word list on which the student makes no miscues is the entry level for the oral reading passages. For example, if a student read from graded word lists 1 through 6 and made no miscues on list 4 but missed several on list 5, then the teacher should begin administering the oral reading passage at level 4. Some teachers, in order to save time, place students in the oral reading passage at the highest place that the student scored 85% on the graded word lists. Before a student begins the oral reading passages, provide a reminder that he or she is going to be reading a story aloud and that after reading the story you will ask some questions about it. Some published IRIs have motivation or overview statements for each passage that you are to read to the student just before beginning oral reading of the passage. The manuals may encourage you to ask the student whether he or she is interested in the topic or whether the student knows anything about the topic to be read. These two simple questions may provide insight into the student's reading interests and background knowledge. As the student reads, record the miscues on the

teacher's corresponding passage. Because many students rapidly read the passage or make many mistakes, it is the recommendation of this text that the teacher use a tape recorder so he or she can go back and listen to the reading passage at a convenient time.

Once the student has read the passage, remove it and ask the student to provide you with a retelling of the story. This step provides the teacher with another measure of comprehension. During the retelling, the teacher judges the student's comprehension based on the retelling. After the student has completed the retelling, ask the student the comprehension questions that were not addressed during the retelling. If necessary, you may restate the questions. If the student responds to the questions correctly, indicate this with a check beside the question. If the student responds incorrectly or only partially, write the response beneath the appropriate question. The student need not respond to each question on the question sheet, but he or she should answer correctly to get credit.

5. Continue having the student read subsequent passages and answer comprehension questions until you identify a frustration level for either word recognition or comprehension, or both (see Figure 11.5).

6. To assess the student's silent reading capabilities, the teacher begins the silent reading passages at the highest instructional level that the child read during the oral reading. During this informal assessment, the student reads the passage silently and then responds to comprehension questions asked by the teacher. Many teachers time the student as he or she reads the passage to get information about the student's reading rate. It is important to use the silent reading assessment in order to accurately judge the student's reading comprehension. Comprehension difficulties that were noted during oral reading may not be noticed during silent reading because the student may not feel as pressured to decode accurately aloud to the teacher. Some manuals encourage teachers to assess silent reading first and then proceed to the oral reading of the same passage. This method provides the student with practice before reading the passage out loud.

7. To identify the student's capacity or potential reading level, have him or her begin reading at the level above the passage that produced frustration. Again, set purposes by telling the student to listen carefully as you read the story aloud and that he or she will answer some questions after hearing the story. Stop administering passages when the student answers less than 75% of the comprehension questions correctly. The highest level at which the student answered 75% of the questions correctly is the capacity level.

Interpretation.   Use both quantitative and qualitative analysis to interpret a student's performance on an IRI. Counting the number of scorable miscues in each passage and the number of incorrect comprehension questions for each passage and determining reading competence levels are the bases of a quantitative analysis. Figure 11.5 presents two sets of criteria for determining reading

Betts's Criteria   **Powell's Differentiated Criteria**

Reading Compency Level	Word Recognition	Comprehension	Word Recognition in terms of grade-level difficulty of passage being read:			Comprehension in terms of grade-level difficulty of passage being read:		
			PP–2	3–5	6+	PP–2	3–5	6+
Independent	1 miscue per 100 words (99% accuracy)	90% or greater accuracy	94% + accuracy	96% + accuracy	97% + accuracy	81% + accuracy	86% + accuracy	91% + accuracy
Instructional	5 miscues per 100 words (95% accuracy)	75%–89% accuracy	87–93% accuracy	92–95% accuracy	94–96% accuracy	55–80% accuracy	60–85% accuracy	65–90% accuracy
Frustration	10+ miscues per 100 words (less than 90% accuracy)	less than 50% accuracy	86% or less accuracy	91% or less accuracy	93% or less accuracy	54% or less accuracy	59% or less accuracy	64% or less accuracy
Capacity or Potential	at least 75% accuracy		at least 75% accuracy for all levels					

FIGURE 11.5
Criteria for determining reading competence levels from student performance on an IRI

competence levels. Betts's (1946) criteria for independent, instructional, and frustration levels apply to all passages, regardless of difficulty. Powell's (1976) criteria take into account the passage's level of difficulty and permit more miscues below the sixth-grade level.

When both criteria are applied to a student's performance in word recognition and comprehension, Betts's criteria usually place the student at a lower competency level. Remember that reading tasks should be at a level of difficulty that maximizes students' chances of success yet should not be so easy that students lose interest. Therefore, teachers could apply both sets of criteria to students' performance. If they yield a noticeable difference in competency levels, it might be best to assign students reading materials with a difficulty between the two competency levels rather than at either extreme. This increases the likelihood that the reading task is at an appropriate difficulty level. If a student's actual reading performance suggests that the task is either too easy or too difficult, however, then move the student up or down to the appropriate level.

Most published IRIs have forms for analyzing results (see Figure 11.6) and forms for summarizing students' performance (see Figure 11.7). A summary sheet enables you to identify reading levels and tally both oral reading miscues and comprehension difficulties. Also, such sheets consider the types of oral reading responses a student makes. Using only the initial-letter cues to recognize words, a student could pronounce every word beginning with *m* as *mom*. If a student frequently substitutes words, qualitative analysis could identify (1) graphic/sound similarities (i.e., did the substituted word have similar graphic and pronunciation features as the text word?), (2) meaning features (i.e., did the substituted word have a similar or identical meaning to the text word, e.g., *car* for *automobile*?), and (3) syntactic features (i.e., was the substituted word the same part of speech as the text word?). Qualitative analysis of miscues (see Figure 11.8) provides insights into the reading strategies that students use in their reading. Specific reading strengths and weaknesses become more evident as miscues are qualitatively analyzed for several orally read passages. Students' IRI performance can be qualitatively analyzed with all three types of informal reading inventories.

As teachers practice using informal reading inventories and make them a part of their ongoing assessment, they will become better at assessing their students' daily work. They will begin to qualitatively analyze student miscues in order to determine reading strengths and weaknesses. As teachers develop competency in analyzing students' daily work, they will become better equipped for developing instruction that is most appropriate for groups of individual student needs.

■ Cloze Procedure

The **Cloze procedure** is an informal diagnostic procedure that helps identify reading levels and provides information about a reader's ability to deal with the content and structure of the information presented—syntax, word meanings, and story grammar. A Cloze test is typically constructed by selecting a freestanding written passage approximately 250 to 300 words long and deleting every fifth word. The first and last sentences are left intact; the first deletion is the fifth word in the second sentence. Every fifth word after this is deleted throughout the

LEVEL 4, FORM C (144 WORDS, 12 SENTENCES)

Examiner's Introduction (Student Booklet, page 160):

If you ever had a pet that you loved, then you will understand how Jody felt about Gabilan in John Steinbeck's book, *The Red Pony*. Please read a retelling of one of the incidents from this book.

Note: Self-corrections (SC), hesitations (/), and inattention to punctuation (⌣ or X) are marked in the text portion but not counted as miscues. Code all miscues as change in meaning (CM) or no change in meaning (NCM).

TEXT	O	I	S	A	REP	REV
Jody was so/worried that he didn't even (care to)eat. He had stayed	CM					
in the barn all day to take care of his sick pony,/Gabilan. The pony's/				(NCM)	(NCM)	
condition was growing worse as his/breathing grew louder and harder. *cold*	CM		CM		(NCM)	
At nightfall Jody/brought a blanket from the house so he could sleep *horse SC*	CM				(NCM)	
near/Gabilan. In the middle of the night a wind whipped around the barn *wind SC*	CM					
and blew the door open						
At dawn Jody awakened to the banging of the barn door./Gabilan *day* *woke-up*		CM NCM			(NCM)	
was gone! In/alarm he ran from the barn following the pony's tracks.	CM					
Looking upward he saw buzzards, the birds of death, flying overhead.	(NCM)					
Jody stood still, then ran to the top of a small hill. In a clearing below.	CM CM					
he saw something that filled his heart with anger and hate. A buzzard/ *anjer*			CM		(NCM)	
was perched on his dying pony's head.						
TOTALS:						

Number of miscues = _18_   Number of self-corrections = _2_

FIGURE 11.6

An informal reading inventory (IRI) student-teacher response sheet
Source: Reprinted with permission from Mary Lynn Woods and Alden J. Moe, **Analytical Reading Inventory,** 4th ed. (Upper Saddle River, NJ: Merrill/Prentice Hall, 1995), pp. 40–41.

Retelling:

It's about a horse. Jody is real worried about the horse. It's sick. The wind blew the door open. It started banging.

Probe: Can you tell me more?

Resp: That night Jody stayed with the horse. The alarm went off and he saw something buzz around. The horse was gone.

Probe: Can you tell me more?

Resp: No response

Probe: In 1 or 2 sentences. . .

Resp: It's about a sick horse. The boy is worried.

Note: Indicate any probing with a "P."			
STORY ELEMENTS	**ALL**	**SOME**	**NONE**
Main character(s)	✓		
Character(s) described		✓	
Time of story	N/A		
Place	✓		
Problem	✓		
Plot details in sequence (includes turning point and resolution)		✓	
Summary		✓	

Examiner's Comments:
• retelling was incomplete, important concepts left out (pony's tracks and buzzards)

Comprehension Questions and Possible Answers:

(mi) ½ 1. In this passage, what was wrong with Jody's pony?
(Gabilan <u>was sick</u> and getting worse.)

(t) ½ 2. In this story, what is meant by the phrase, "pony's condition"?   (Gabilan's poor health) his cold

(ce) ok 3. Why did Jody take a blanket from the house?
(so he could sleep near Gabilan) He wanted to stay with his sick pony.

(f) ok 4. What awakened Jody at dawn?
(<u>the banging of the barn door</u>)

(t) ok 5. What is meant by the phrase, "dawn"?
(<u>at sunrise</u>, at the start of the day)

(ce) ✓ 6. Why was the barn door banging?
(In the middle of the night a wind whipped around the barn and blew the door open.) an alarm or something

(f) ✓ 7. What did Jody do to try to find his pony? He ran through the banging door.
(followed the pony's tracks)   Probe: How did Jody know where to look for his pony?   Resp: The door was open.
The horse was gone.

(inf) ✓ 8. What is said in this story that makes you think Jody thought his pony was dying?
(Looking upward he saw buzzards, the birds of death, flying overhead. Buzzards eat dead animals.) He ran out of the barn.
Probe: Do you remember anything that told you the pony was dying?   Resp: No response.

CASE STUDY

STUDENT RECORD SUMMARY SHEET

Student _John Stone_   Grade _4_   Sex _M_   Age _9-10_

School _Merrill Elementary_   Administered by _M L Woods_   Date _1/18/95_

Grade	Word Lists	Graded Passages			Estimated Levels			
	% of words correct	WR Form _C_	Comp. Form _C_	Listen. Form _C_	Narrative			
								Grade
Primer	100%				Independent			2
1	100%				Instructional			3
2	100%	−3 Instr (high)	−0 Ind		Frustration			4
					Listening			5
3	95%	−11 Instr	−3 Instr		Expository at Grade Level			
4	75%	−18 Frust	−4 Frust			Science		Social Studies
5				Instr (low)	WR	Comp.	WR	Comp.
6								
7					−42	−5½	Incomplete	
8					Frust.	•	Frust.	
9								

Checklist of Reading Strengths and Difficulties
(+ = strength, O = difficulty)

Oral Reading

+ self-corrections (lower levels)
O word by word
+ sentence punctuation
O omissions
+ insertions
O substitutions
O aided words
O repetitions
+ reversals

Word Recognition

+ single consonants
+ consonant clusters
O long vowels
O short vowels   medial portion
O vowel digraphs
O diphthongs
+ use of context (lower levels)
+ basic sight   only
O grade level sight

Retelling

Narrative
+ main characters
___ time
+ place
+ plot sequence (lower levels)
+ summary   only

Expository
___ enumeration
___ time order
___ compare/contrast   needs more reading experience
___ cause/effect
___ problem/solution
___ summary

Comp. Ques.

+ main idea
O factual
+ terminology
O cause/effect
O inferential
O conclusions

FIGURE 11.7

An informal reading inventory (IRI) student record summary sheet
Source: Reprinted with permission from Mary Lynn Woods and Alden J. Moe, **Analytical Reading Inventory,** 4th ed. (Upper Saddle River, NJ: Merrill/Prentice Hall, 1995), p. 33.

DESCRIPTION OF READING BEHAVIORS

NARRATIVE PASSAGES, FORM C

Level 2 (independent)

<u>Word Recognition:</u> When John read Level 2, he was searching for meaning as he read. For example, he self-corrected many of the miscues *(nose* to *noise; scar* to *scared)*, showing that he was using context clues to select the correct word. Even though the miscue count was 3, the miscue was of the same word *(Sheep* for *Shep);* thus the word recognition score was high instructional or independent.

The reading was filled with hesitations making for choppy, word-by-word reading. Despite this difficulty, John energetically persisted through to the end of the passage.

<u>Comprehension:</u> The retelling was very thorough and reflected all the story elements. John used completed sentences and retold the story in language that was close to the author's meaning.

<u>Emotional Status:</u> John was confident and relaxed.

Level 3 (instructional)

<u>Word Recognition:</u> John made some self-corrections but not as many as he did in Level 2. He made some word substitutions that were appropriate choices within the context *(banging* for *pounding, said* for *declared),* which shows that he continues to search for meaning as he reads. At first he miscued the word *belong (be in),* but later he correctly pronounced the word, which verifies his ability to search for meaning. Predominantly, he attended to the initial single consonants or blends, and then thought about the meaning to make a word choice. Omissions and substitutions comprised the majority of the miscues. He failed to correct some miscues, (e.g., *Triggers* for *Tigers; soon* for *suddenly).*

<u>Comprehension:</u> Despite the fact that the number of miscues increased, John still retold much of the story; however, some important information was omitted (e.g., the boy was new to the neighborhood). His failure to correct the word *Tigers* caused him to miss an important concept in the story (the connection between the yellow and black paint and the name of the club). The responses to some of the comprehension questions were not as complete. The comprehension score turned out to be instruction, but the number of word recognition miscues significantly affected the meaning of the passage.

<u>Emotional Status:</u> John's reading became choppier, and he made a number of repetitions. He did not have the same confidence as he did reading Level 2. Still, he persisted with determination.

FIGURE 11.8
Description of reading behaviors for a student's reading
of narrative and expository passages from an IRI
Source: Reprinted with permission from Mary Lynn Woods and Alden J.
Moe, **Analytical Reading Inventory,** 4th ed. (Upper Saddle River, NJ:
Merrill/Prentice Hall, 1995), pp. 55–56.

Level 4 (frustration)

Word Recognition: The number of miscues increased to 18. The reading became even less fluent, and many more repetitions were made. Omissions (whole word and word endings) and substitutions comprised the majority of miscues. Only 2 self-corrections were made, indicating that John was less able to use context clues than he had been at Levels 2 and 3 because the miscues were in fact changing the meaning of the text. The strategy of using the initial single consonants and blends continued to be reliant.

Comprehension: John's retelling was scanty and less specific. Despite the fact that he retold information in sequence, many important concepts were omitted (e.g., Jody followed the pony's tracks; the buzzards indicated the pony was nearly dead). He continued to use complete sentences, but the miscues had severely affected the meaning of the passage, and therefore he often gave misinformation. The restating of the main idea was incomplete. When answering the comprehension questions, he had difficulty recalling some of the factual information and missed a cause-and-effect and an inference question.

Emotional Status: Despite the numerous miscues in the oral passage at Level 4. John did persevere to the finish. He did not look like or sound like a confident reader, however. He showed physical signs of stress and sometimes appeared confused. He was reluctant to take any risks as he did at Level 3 (e.g., meaningful word substitutions) and he made few self-corrections.

Level 5, Listening Level (instructional, low)

Comprehension: John's retelling was very scanty with few details included. His summary of the main idea was still okay, but so many details were missing that he could not comprehend key concepts (e.g., she's the only woman licensed to drive Top Fuel cars). He missed 3½ comprehension questions. Considering both the retelling and the comprehension questions, the reading level is low instructional, almost frustration. John's background vocabulary seems strong (e.g., *determination*).

Emotional Status: John seemed anxious. The enthusiasm he showed at Levels 2 and 3 was gone. I was concerned that he was tiring, so I stopped the evaluation, intending to give the expository passages at another time.

Silent Reading, Form B, Level 4 (frustration)

John read through the text very rapidly. It appeared that he was just glancing at the words rather than carefully analyzing the text. The retelling was scanty, and the responses to the comprehension questions were mostly incorrect. Questions 7 and 8 were not asked.

FIGURE 11.8, *continued*

EXPOSITORY PASSAGES, FORMS S AND SS

Science, Level 4 (frustration)

Word Recognition: The miscues (42) continued in the same pattern as in narrative Level 4. There was only 1 self-correction. The number of repetitions and hesitations increased. Omissions (whole word and word endings) and substitutions comprised the majority of miscues. John continued to rely on the use of initial consonants and blends as a key strategy in recognizing words. Toward the end he was so tired and frustrated that he asked for assistance.

Comprehension: The retelling was scanty with only 2 details (parts of the comet: head and tail), and 5½ comprehension questions were missed.

Emotional Status: Even though this was the first reading of the second diagnostic session, John's anxiety was worse when reading expository text than for the longer session with the narrative text. He wiggled in his chair, and I could see other signs of stress such as tense facial expressions and tenseness in his hands.

Social Studies, Level 4 (frustration)

Word Recognition: John was unable to complete the reading of this passage. He made 15 miscues in the first paragraph and asked for help with so many words that I felt it was best to stop the session.

Comprehension: It seemed to me that his inexperience with expository text interfered with his ability to sustain the energy it takes to read. I didn't ask for a retelling or any responses to comprehension questions.

Emotional Status: He showed obvious signs of frustration. He simply had no stamina for reading the text.

FIGURE 11.8, continued

passage. Each deleted word is replaced with a line of uniform length, as illustrated in the following example:

Jake saw the two horses just south of the timber ridge over by Clear Lake. He and Rusty had _____ hunting these Mustangs for _____ last two days. Yesterday _____ horse ran away and _____ gone for several hours. _____ time that Jake lost _____ searching for the runaway _____ had made him think they would not _____ the wild horses. (The deleted words are **been, the, Rusty's, was, The, while, horse, seriously,** and **catch.**)

The words deleted from a passage may be any part of speech. The basic rule is to delete the fifth word regardless of its function in the sentence.

Administering and scoring a Cloze test for determining reading levels are simple, straightforward procedures. Instruct students to read the passage and write in the blank the word that was deleted. Then score each of the responses as either correct or incorrect. Only the exact word is considered a correct response.

Determine the percentage of correct responses by dividing the total correct replacements by the number of deleted words (e.g., 30 words correctly replaced divided by 50 words deleted would be a 60% correct replacement). Compare the percentage of correct word placement with this scale: 61% or more correct replacements for the independent reading level, 41% to 60% correct for the instructional level, and less than 40% correct for the frustration level (Rankin & Culhane, 1969).

Determining reading levels using the criterion of exact word replacement is intended to help you decide whether students can handle the content and language structure of various reading materials, such as science, social studies, and math texts. You can better understand a reader's use of syntax, semantics, and reasoning by qualitatively looking at incorrect word choices. If incorrect choices are syntactically correct (the same part of speech), the student may be analyzing words preceding and following the deletion in an attempt to supply a meaningful response. Semantically correct word choices may indicate that the reader understood the meaning but chose a different word from the author's. If the words are both syntactically and semantically correct, then the reader is revealing meaning and applying a knowledge of language.

Cloze testing is an informal assessment strategy that is neither time-consuming nor difficult. Interpreting the responses may prove more valuable in securing information about a student's reading level than simply identifying the level. Many teachers use the Cloze procedure as a prereading activity in order to determine the students' background knowledge for the content. If the majority of the students perform at the instructional level, the teacher may decide to spend time developing students' prior knowledge before actually beginning the unit, or the teacher may decide to bring in additional resources about the subject at varying readability levels.

Just as with all forms of informal assessment, the teacher may decide to modify the Cloze procedure to make it more appropriate for diverse learners. A fifth-word deletion may be too difficult for some students, so you may wish to delete every eighth or tenth word.

A modification of the Cloze procedure is the maze procedure. Rather than supplying the deleted word, the student selects a word from a vertical array. The Cloze procedure is essentially a recall task, whereas the maze procedure is a recognition task. Selective identification of words allows you to determine a student's attention to context and understanding of language. Obviously, in using this or any idea incorporated into informal assessment, you must fit the levels of the students involved. Following is an example of the maze procedure.

> paddled
> The boy swam his boat across the large lake,
>   leaned
>
> swimming
> searching for a good fishing spot. He saw a small
> moved
>
>   water.
> cove with tree limbs hanging over the ice.
>   case.

◀ |||| F L A S H B A C K

Teachers of literacy have long realized the value of gathering informal assessment information on individual students. Such information is needed to adequately plan an instructional program that meets each student's needs.

Photo courtesy of Anne M. Hyland, Bexley, Ohio Schools; photographer, Arthur Burt, Inc.

U P D A T E |||| ▶

In addition to the teacher's gathering informal assessment information on individual students for planning instruction, students are also becoming active participants in the assessment process. Portfolios are expandable folders for each student that can include a variety of literacy learning indicators. For example, students often select their best works to include in their portfolios. Actively involving students in the assessment process makes them more aware of their own learning and causes them to reflect on their own learning in positive ways.

■ Authentic Assessment/Performance-based Assessment

Observing, interacting, and interviewing are authentic or performance-based assessment procedures that provide information beyond basic skills development. Whether you use the term **authentic assessment,** *alternative assessment,* or *performance-based assessment,* you are still using a form of assessment that no longer views assessment as the endpoint to learning. Instead, assessment is viewed as an integral part of teaching (Reichel, 1994). Authentic forms of assessment enable the teacher to gather information specific to instruction and to students' progress while they are engaged in meaningful reading and writing tasks. Assessing for instruction provides teachers with the opportunity to gain useful information about students' world knowledge; attitudes towards reading, writing, and content area; and strategies used to gain meaning from text.

One of the simplest and most-used authentic assessment procedures might consist of having a student read aloud a short selection from a book to determine whether he or she can identify the words and construct meaning for that particular book. Such an informal assessment procedure can yield important information about the student's word-recognition strategies and comprehension. In addition, such interaction focuses on real literature that engages the student over longer passages of sustained reading than standardized tests generally contain.

Another form of authentic assessment is interviewing. Interviewing students about their reading and writing can provide teachers with valuable insights and help students become more aware of their own literacy interests, reading and writing strategies, and progress (McKenna & Kear, 1990). Examples of questions that teachers can use when interviewing students include the following:

1. What do you think makes a good reader? What do you think makes a good writer? (These questions indicate how the student conceptualizes reading and writing.)
2. If you were to read a story about (any chosen topic), what kinds of information do you think you would find in the story?
3. When you come to a word you don't know, how do you figure it out? Show me in a story how you would figure out a word you did not know.
4. Let's look at the list of books that you have read. Which ones were your favorites? Which books did you find hard to read? Which book(s) would you like to read again and again? Why?
5. What do you enjoy most about writing? What do you not enjoy about writing? What makes writing fun or easy for you?
6. What makes understanding some stories easy for you?
7. If you have to read a science book to discuss in class, what do you think this means? Tell me how you would read a science book so we can later talk about it.
8. What do you like to write about the most? Why?
9. What does the title of a story or book tell you?
10. If we had a new student entering our class who did not know what it meant to read, how would you describe reading to him or her?

Insights for both the teacher and students can be gained from such interviews about perceptions of reading and writing, strategies used for both reading and writing, and growth and development in literacy.

It has also been determined by teachers that asking students about their writing and reading miscues can shed some light on the thought processes used by the students. Asking a child why he or she pronounced a word a certain way forces the child to analyze his or her own miscues. Audio-taping students while they read orally and having them go back and critically listen to themselves read while the teacher leads them in discussion about their reading performance is also a beneficial interviewing technique.

Besides interviewing your students orally, using an interest inventory or a reading experiences inventory can provide additional information. Figure 11.9 is an example of a reading experiences inventory that teachers can use to gain insights about students. Students' responses to the questions provide information about their interests, attitudes, reading habits, and perceptions.

■ Anecdotal Records

Observation checklists can be helpful when teachers are focusing on features of reading and writing for a number of students. **Anecdotal records,** however, provide more detail, allow for variations among students, and recognize the range in literacy capabilities within a classroom. As noted by Rhodes and Nathenson-Mejia (1992), "What is focused on and recorded depends upon the teacher, the student, and the context, not on predetermined items on a checklist" (pp. 502–503).

Guidelines for writing anecdotal records (Rhodes & Nathenson-Mejia, 1992) include the following steps: (1) describe the event or product rather than just recording the general impression, (2) focus on rich descriptions rather than evaluations, and (3) relate the anecdote to information known about the child. The following example illustrates these features:

> Showed Mary how to skip a word that she didn't know in her reading as a way to figure out its meaning. She was reading a book about experiments for children and didn't know the meaning of **absorbed.**

> She grasped the idea quickly and read two sentences beyond the word and noted excitedly that the word must mean the liquid went from the glass up to the petals of the flower. Encouraged her to do this with other words that she might not know the meaning of.

Anecdotal records can be used effectively with individual students as well as with small groups. Teachers can identify students for whom anecdotal information would be beneficial. For example, anecdotal records might help in trying to determine what is contributing to a student's disruptive behavior at the writing center, or why Jason is unwilling to edit his writing, or how well Mary is using context to figure out the meaning of unknown words.

Analysis of anecdotal records often reveals patterns of both difficulty and success for students. Teachers using anecdotal records for assessment have noted

Reading Experiences Inventory

Beginning of the School Year

Read each question or statement below. Circle the letter of each item that best describes you as a reader. You may circle more than one letter. You may write your own response where a line is provided.

1. Which sentence below explains how you feel about reading?
   a. I like to read at home and at school.
   b. I like to read at home, but I do not like to read at school.
   c. I do not like to read and would rather do other things for fun.
   d. I would like reading more if I could become a better reader.

2. I like to read when . . .
   a. I am alone in a quiet place.
   b. I can talk with the other students about what I read.
   c. I know my teacher will help me with my reading.
   d. I can talk with my teacher about what I read.
   e. _____

3. It helps me with my reading when . . .
   a. I read with an older student who is a better reader.
   b. I read aloud with another student or in a reading group.
   c. I work with students who are in different reading groups.
   d. I work alone and think about what I read
   e. _____

4. It helps me with my reading when . . .
   a. my teacher gives me questions before I read to think about as I read.
   b. my teacher helps me understand the directions for my work.
   c. my teacher lets me work alone and think about what I read.
   d. my teacher directs discussion about what I have read.
   e. _____

5. How often do you read at home for enjoyment?
   a. never
   b. up to 30 minutes a week
   c. 30 to 60 minutes a week
   d. more than an hour a week

FIGURE 11.9

Example of a reading experiences inventory

Source: Reprinted with permission from William H. Rupley and John W. Logan, **Vistas in Reading Literature** (Evanston, IL: McDougall, Littell & Co., 1990), pp. 1–2.

6. Which sentence below *best describes* what you do at home?
   a. I spend more time reading than I do watching television.
   b. I spend more time watching television than I do reading.
   c. I spend about the same amount of time watching television and reading.
   d. _____

7. Below are listed several types of literature. Circle the letters of ones you most like to read or have read to you.
   a. stories about animals.
   b. science fiction
   c. mysteries
   d. sports stories
   e. stories about faraway places
   f. plays
   g. poems
   h. stories about boys and girls my own age
   i. folk tales and fairy tales
   j. stories about real events in the past
   k. biographies
   l. fables
   m. myths and legends
   n. humorous stories
   o. adventure stories
   p. science and nature articles
   q. books of facts and records

8. On another piece of paper, complete the sentences below.
   a. If I read the newspaper, the sections I usually read are . . .
   b. My favorite book is . . .
   c. The best books I have read in the past year include . . .
   d. Topics I like to read about include . . .
   e. The number of books I read outside of school each month is about . . .
   f. Some magazines I like to read are . . .
   g. A reading goal I would like to set for myself this year is . . .

FIGURE 11.9, *continued*

INCLUSION STRATEGIES

Meeting Students' Literacy Needs

Assessment is an essential component of every classroom literacy program. The value of assessment is increasing as we include children with special needs in regular classrooms. Effective teachers of reading employ a variety of informal assessment procedures, as evidenced by the following description of Joan Thrumond's assessment of Brett's delayed literacy acquisition.

Mrs. Thrumond used a variety of informal assessment procedures with Brett. She administered an IRI, observed literacy behavior in a variety of contexts, and focused on construction of meaning. Mrs. Thrumond's qualitative analysis of Brett's miscues resulted in the following:

> Brett relies heavily on a limited sight vocabulary to recognize words. He guessed at many words using the initial letter as a cue to identification. He recognized few words on sight and would not attempt to identify words that did not offer him initial-letter cues (this could account for the large number of teacher-pronounced words on the IRI). It appears that Brett has minimal strategies for recognizing and identifying words. He does not appear concerned with whether or not his guesses make sense in the context of the sentence or the text. There were no regressions or self-corrections noted in his reading.

Brett had minimal success in both answering comprehension questions and retelling the stories he had read. This came as no surprise to Joan, however; she had anticipated that Brett would construct little meaning from what he read. He appeared to have no idea that we read to get meaning. When he was asked to describe reading, Brett used examples that related to identifying words, completing school-related tasks, and performing a difficult task.

Synthesizing assessment information gained from the IRI (word recognition, comprehension, and strategies), observation, and the interview, Mrs. Thrumond felt that Brett

why certain organizational schemes (e.g., paired reading, interest groups, peer editing) were successful or unsuccessful, how students used or failed to use strategies for reading informational text, how certain instructional features (e.g., time allotted for an activity, modeling, scaffolding, feedback) enhanced and facilitated students' learning, and how much growth students have experienced over a period of time. One of the most important features of anecdotal records is that their use makes teachers more aware of their interaction with their students and the effects of their instruction on students' learning.

■ Response Journals

Although all forms of student writing can be used in assessment, response journals are of important value because they integrate reading and writing. **Response journals** (discussed in Chapter 3) are written responses, between the inventories, observation records, and conference notes (Tierney, Carter, & Desai, 1991).

Portfolios are expandable file folders, binders, or boxes created and decorated by each student that include a variety of indicators of learning to help students, teachers, administrators, and parents understand literacy growth and development. These selected collections of student work and records of performance collected across diverse contexts over time demonstrate the advancement of student learning (Wolf & Runyan, 1996). For portfolios to be useful, they should be kept in an easily accessible place for students and teachers, and both students and teachers should contribute to them regularly and use the contents for planning subsequent learning (Valencia, 1990).

What should be included in a student's portfolio? Any item that the student deems important and shows development and growth of the student's learning over time should be included in the portfolio. A portfolio is a repository of a student's thoughts, ideas, and language-related growth and materials. Because many portfolios are working portfolios, students often include original pieces, thoughts, and inspirations. These pieces should reflect a student's work and growth in the creation process. The best portfolio pieces represent the integration among all learning and are constantly evolving to illustrate life-long learning.

How often should portfolios be used? Portfolios are used on a daily basis and become the focal point for student and teacher interactions and discussion. Students should have access to their portfolios at all times and should be encouraged to assess their working portfolios on the basis of need. Because student-teacher discussion is a key element in the success of the portfolio assessment, teachers should regularly talk with students about their developing processes as language users. Teachers and students should also discuss student attitudes and interests related to reading, writing, and thinking through the use of their portfolios.

According to Wolf and Siu-Runyan (1996), portfolios should meet the following criteria:

1. Portfolios should be selective. They should include a selection of information gathered for specific purposes. These purposes can include self-assessment, documentation of student learning, guidance for teacher instruction, and communication among parents, teachers, and students. Portfolios also can be used to provide administrators and policy makers with information about the school district's instructional program.
2. Portfolios should be a collection of students' work and progress. The essential element of all portfolios is the students' work. This can include student writing, reading journals, collaborative projects, and artistic creations.

3. Portfolios should contain diverse information. When students' portfolios include diverse information, the teacher is able to see each students' full range of talents and interests.

4. Portfolios should show development over time. One of the differences between standardized tests and portfolios is that standardized tests provide the teacher only with black-and-white snapshots of students' performance, while portfolios are more like color movies that show events over time.

5. Portfolios should be reflective. Student portfolio reflection allows students to assess their own learning experiences and become more evaluative of their work. Reflections in portfolios often take the form of written comments focusing on the quality of the work and the revision processes that were used in improving the portfolio piece. Reflection can be in the form of drawings and graphs as well as other types of student and teacher reflection.

6. Portfolios should be collaborative. Because learning is not viewed as a solitary process, portfolios should include the interactions of others. The interaction of one's peers, parents, and teachers should play a significant factor in the portfolio process. When students discuss their ideas with others, they deepen their ability to reflect on their own work from more than one perspective.

7. The goal of portfolios is to advance student learning. The advancement of student learning must be the overall objective of portfolio development.

The form of a portfolio can vary greatly, depending upon its purpose. Wolf and Siu-Runyan (1996) identified three distinct portfolio models. These three models are the ownership portfolio, the feedback portfolio, and the accountability portfolio. Ownership portfolios contain samples of student's work and self-assessment. Students choose which examples of their work to add to their portfolios. Often, the teacher may wish to help students select the examples by discussing with each child the features of the selection and reasons for including it in the portfolio. The major advantage of having students select their own examples for ownership portfolios is that it actively involves them in the process and makes them more aware of their own learning. The teacher can use students' portfolios to engage them in discussions about why they included a particular sample, how they have grown in their learning, what they liked and disliked in books they read, the quality of their writing, and their use of reading and writing strategies. Ownership portfolios provide students with the opportunity to take an active and responsible role in their own learning.

The feedback portfolio, coconstructed by the student and the teacher, includes comprehensive collections of student work and teacher records. These portfolios not only include student work and reflection, but also include anecdotal records about student learning, observations, interviews, response journal entries, activity work, and responses to discussion, as well as peer and parent feedback. These portfolios provide students, parents, and teachers with information about students' learning strengths and weaknesses (Holmes & Morrison, 1995). They are extremely useful in assisting teachers in designing effective instruction based around student learning styles and needs as well as assessing students' learning growth. This type of portfolio is also valuable in communicating with parents about their child's use of effective learning strategies.

An accountability portfolio includes selective collections of student work, teacher records, and standardized assessments selected by both student and teacher according to structured guidelines. Accountability portfolios are used primarily to evaluate student achievement for accountability and for program evaluation.

Portfolios can be extremely useful in instructional decisions because they provide a broad sampling of students' literacy development over extended periods, in a variety of tasks, and in different contexts. These features are important for several reasons. First, multiple samples of students' reading and writing help better explain individual students' learning of these complex processes. Second, by collecting current information about their students, teachers can better understand how their students regularly perform classroom tasks (Winograd & Jones, 1992).

A discussion of some of the basic assessment purposes (Defina, 1992; Engel, 1995) of portfolios follows. Teachers need to determine which of the basic purposes are appropriate for their students and their instructional goals.

- *Monitoring students' growth over time.* Contents of students' portfolios will provide information about how much they have learned in specific areas, such as descriptive writing, use of reading strategies, and so forth.
- *Examining students' understandings about process.* Students going back to learning activities and products will help provide the teacher with insights into their understanding that a completed product (a piece of writing) requires careful deliberation, revision, and rethinking.
- *Creating opportunities for students' self-evaluation.* Portfolio contents readily identify students' literacy strengths and weaknesses, which helps teachers address individual student needs.
- *Observing growth of culturally and linguistically diverse students.* Diverse students' performance on standardized tests typically does not accurately reflect their literacy capabilities. Portfolios do, however, allow teachers to determine better students' growth and development in relation to literacy tasks occurring in the classroom.
- *Observing students' language development.* Because portfolios contain samples that represent students' actual language use, they can help teachers evaluate students' language comprehension and development.
- *Evaluating and developing a literacy curriculum.* Teachers can revise the curriculum based on students' learning in relation to what they know, what they have learned, and what they need to know.
- *Determining the effectiveness of literacy instruction.* The teacher can analyze items in portfolios to determine what is effective with individual students, groups of students, and the class.

Although portfolio assessment can be extremely beneficial for both teachers and students, some obstacles hinder its successful use in an elementary school. Portfolios will work successfully only if they have (1) schoolwide support, particularly from the principal, (2) no competition from other forms of assessment, such as skills tests, which can result in teachers becoming frustrated, (3) self-reliance on the part of the teacher, and (4) valid teacher judgments (Dewitz, Carr, Palm, & Spencer, 1992).

☑ Summary

Students' literacy abilities, interests, and development in any given classroom reflect a wide range. Assessment is necessary to differentiate instruction, which, in turn, is essential for a sound literacy program. In effective literacy instruction, ongoing assessment provides the blueprint for instruction.

Formal assessment generally involves the use of standardized tests. Unfortunately, many of the standardized tests do not accurately reflect all of our knowledge about the reading and writing processes. Assessment of students' learning should include a combination of procedures that reflect what we know about literacy and the use of literacy skills in meaningful reading and writing situations.

Meaningful assessment is ongoing and includes a variety of informal procedures, such as anecdotal records, informal reading inventories, portfolios, and teacher observation. Any time students engage in a literacy activity or event—reading, writing, and editing, to name a few—they provide the teacher with clues about their instructional needs and literacy growth.

☑ Your Point of View

Discussion Questions

1. You have just gotten your first teaching position. You are teaching fourth grade and it is the third week of school. You suspect that Dee cannot read the social studies text that has been adopted for class use. You wish to verify or refute this suspicion. What assessment procedures would you use? How would you interpret the assessment information?

2. A new student has enrolled in your classroom and you want to plan her reading instruction. What assessment procedures would you use if no information is available from her former school?

Take a Stand For or Against

1. Informal assessment procedures can yield as much information about an individual student's reading as can standardized tests.

2. Authentic assessment is better than any type of assessment strategies or procedures that a teacher could use.

Field-Based Assignments

1. Administer an informal reading inventory to a child in the classroom in which you are working. Conduct a qualitative analysis of the child's performance on the IRI. Interview the child using the questions suggested in this chapter. Record the child's responses and discuss them with him. Compare the results of your IRI analysis with the child's performance in class.
2. Request to look at several teachers' examples of how they use portfolio assessment in their literacy program. Using the information about different types of portfolio entries presented in the chapter, identify the types being used by these teachers. Discuss with one or two children the entries they chose to include in their portfolios and why they selected those pieces.

Portfolio Entry

Draw a chart of how you would begin assessment in your own classroom and what steps would emanate from that beginning. Reflect on what you would do, what information you would gain for instructional planning, and your rationale for using different types of literacy assessment.

Bibliography

Benson, T. R. (1995). Portfolio-based assessment: Tips for a successful start. *Dimensions of Early Childhood, 23,* 21–23.

Betts, E. A. (1946). *Foundations of reading instruction.* New York: American Book Co.

Defina, A. A. (1992). *Portfolio assessment.* New York: Scholastic Professional Books.

Dewitz, P., Carr, E. M., Palm, K. N., & Spencer, M. (1992). The validity and utility of portfolio assessment. In C. Kinzer & D. Leu (Eds.), *Literacy research, theory, and practice: Views from many perspectives* (pp. 153–159). Chicago: National Reading Conference.

Early, M. (1992/93). What ever happened to . . . ? *The Reading Teacher, 46,* 302–309.

Engle, B. S. (1994). Portfolio assessment and the new paradigm: New instruments and new places. *Educational Forum, 59,* 22–27.

International Reading Association and National Council of Teachers of English. (1994). *Standards for the assessment of reading and writing.* Author.

McKenna, M., & Kear, D. (1990). Measuring attitude toward reading: A new tool for teachers. *The Reading Teacher, 43,* 626–639.

Powell, W. R. (1976). Informal reading inventories: Points of view. Speech presented at the annual meeting of the College Reading Association, Miami.

Rankin, E., & Culhane, J. (1969). Comparable Cloze and multiple choice comprehension test scores. *Journal of Reading, 13,* 193–198.

Reichel, A. G. (1994). Performance assessment: Five practical approaches. *Science and Children, 22,* 21–25.

Rhodes, L. K., & Nathenson-Mejia, S. (1992).

Anecdotal records: A powerful tool for ongoing literacy assessment. *The Reading Teacher, 45,* 502–511.

Santa, C. M. (1995). Assessment: Students lead their own parent conferences. *Teaching PreK–8, 25,* 92–94.

Tierney, R., Carter, M., & Desai, L. (1991). *Portfolio assessment in reading-writing classrooms.* Norwood, MA: Christopher-Gordon.

Valencia, S. (1990). A portfolio approach to classroom reading assessment: The whys, whats, and hows. *The Reading Teacher, 43,* 338–341.

Walker, B. J. (1996). *Diagnostic teaching of reading: Techniques for instruction and assessment* (3rd ed.). Upper Saddle River, NJ: Merrill/Prentice Hall.

Winograd, P., Paris, S., & Bridge, C. (1991). Improving the assessment of literacy. *The Reading Teacher, 45,* 108–117.

Winograd, P., & Jones, D. L. (1992). The use of portfolios in performance assessment. In J. Craig (Ed.), *New directions for education reform: Performance assessment* (pp. 37–50). Western Kentucky University.

Wolf, K., & Siu-Runyan, Y. (1996). Portfolio purposes and possibilities. *Journal of Adolescent and Adult Literacy, 40,* 30–37.

Wollman-Bonilla, J. (1991). *Response journals.* New York: Scholastic Professional Books.

Woods, M. L., & Moe, A. J. (1995). Analytical reading inventory (5th ed.). Upper Saddle River, NJ: Merrill/Prentice Hall.

12

Classroom Management and Organization

Chapter Outline

For the Reader

Do you recall your first experience with a large group of students in a classroom? If you have not yet started to teach, do you worry about how you will handle a large group of children? In either case, you can contemplate some of the demands and constraints of a classroom. Your perceived notions of assessment teaching—pretesting, setting objectives, teaching, allowing for student practice, using a variety of materials, reinforcing abilities in a variety of situations, and posttesting—must operate in the context of a class of 20 to 35 children.

As you know, students within any group differ in a variety of ways. Within the context of the classroom, you must strive to accommodate these individual differences. Effective reading teachers understand the organizational conditions found in their teaching situations and use various grouping procedures to maximize student learning.

This chapter discusses the various options teachers have in teaching a large group of children. Current research suggests a strong relationship between classroom management and student achievement; therefore, meeting the demands of the classroom setting will provide rewards for both you and your students.

Key Ideas

- Effective classroom management and organization correlate with increased student achievement.
- Teachers of reading must be adept at planning and organizing their classrooms.
- Effective teachers are successful managers; they are aware of the total classroom environment and practice preventative measures to maintain a good learning environment.
- Small-group instruction promotes more interaction, discussion, and learning than does whole-class instruction.
- Cooperative grouping promotes peer tutoring, encouragement, and achievement.
- An individualized reading approach uses the principles of seeking, self-selection, and self-pacing.
- Implementing effective reading instruction in a class requires careful planning of materials, instruction, and time to meet the needs of individual students.

The Importance of Classroom Management

A history of U.S. education dealing primarily with classroom practices would be, in essence, a history of the attempts to deal with student differences. All of the principles, techniques, approaches, materials, and assessment tools of effective teachers contribute to the instruction of students. The plural *students* is key in the previous sentence; effective teaching of reading includes organizing and maintaining a classroom environment for 20 to 35 students that maximizes their learning. Effective classroom management and organization correlate with increased student achievement. In reviewing the data from California's Beginning Teacher Evaluation Study in the late 1970s, Guthrie (1980) stated:

> Classroom teachers contribute to reading achievement by optimizing the scheduled time for reading and related activities, selecting materials that insure learning, minimizing the interruption of student attention, and assessing the amount of learning as a guide to assigning new materials. When these conditions are met, time in school has a handsome payoff. (p. 502)

The preceding quote underscores the interdependence of instructional and managerial concerns. A teacher can employ the best reading techniques and materials but be unsuccessful as a result of poor classroom management. The reverse can also happen; a teacher may implement management techniques for conditions conducive to learning but not provide differentiated instruction. Often, new teachers are judged by their ability to manage a classroom effectively. In addition, studies of new and experienced teachers indicate that classroom management is one of the most difficult and stressful elements in teaching (Lasley, 1987).

Preventative Classroom Management

The literature on teacher effectiveness indicates that effective classrooms are well managed and feature large amounts of quality time, that is, periods when students are actively engaged with the teacher or materials (Edwards, 1997; Blair, 1988). Poor management of students, reading groups, and activities usually translates into little quality engaged time. Effective classroom managers devote considerable time to **preventative classroom management.** As Good and Brophy (1987) succinctly state, "The key to success lies in the things the teacher does ahead of time to create a good learning environment and a low potential for trouble" (p. 177).

Effective classroom managers (1) prepare and plan, (2) manage group instruction, and (3) monitor student progress. At the beginning of the school year, successful teachers devote the time and energy necessary for getting to know their students, setting instructional goals, and making sure that the students know what is expected of them. Successful teachers also plan their lessons in advance, break their lessons down into small, concise parts for presentation, and

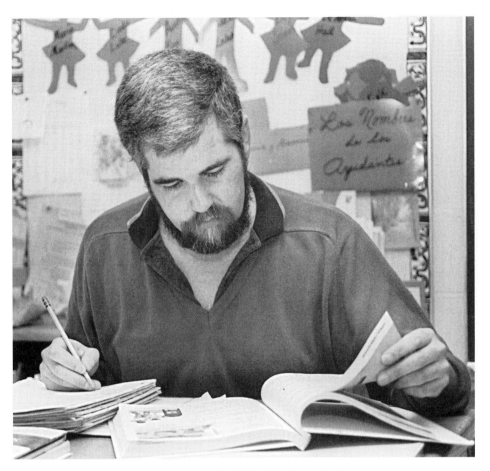

Preventative classroom management includes having all plans and materials ready to use well in advance of the actual lesson.

plan a variety of activities to keep students engaged in learning. Effective teachers invest time and energy into planning. As a result, they have fewer disruptions and are more productive during the reading class.

Grouping students by itself does not automatically boost student achievement. The quality of student and teacher interaction during grouping is the key. The successful teacher manages group instruction by maintaining quality learning time.

Kounin (1970) identified group management techniques of effective teachers. His findings relate to both planning the groups of students and actually conducting group discussion. Blair (1988) reported on the six qualities of successful managers that Kounin identified:

1. With-it-ness is a teacher's ability to be continuously aware of what's going on in the classroom and to communicate this awareness to students.

2. Overlapping is a teacher's ability to do more than one thing at a time in the classroom without getting frustrated.
3. Smoothness of transition is the ability to go from one activity to another or one part of a lesson to another without wasted time and/or undue delay.
4. Momentum is the teacher's ability to pace lessons.
5. Group alerting is the teacher's ability to keep students' attention during lessons.
6. Accountability is the teacher's ability to know how well students are learning. (pp. 35–36)

Monitoring students during group work entails (1) interacting directly with students or checking on student progress during seatwork and (2) using physical proximity or task-related comments to ensure that the students are working productively. Monitoring students helps you realize how well your students are understanding the activity; it also serves to maintain student engagement. Monitoring can help prevent, or at least minimize, potential management problems.

Following are practical suggestions by Blair (1988) to implement the preventative classroom management areas. Consider the following suggestions in your preparation before the school year begins:

- Collect as much assessment data on students as possible.
- Decide on classroom behavior rules and procedures that are not negotiable with students. These rules may concern tardiness, dismissal, hall passes, makeup work, homework, and so forth.
- Decide how you will explain classroom behavior standards, your expectations concerning assignments, and classroom procedures.
- Organize and arrange instructional materials for easy access or distribution.
- Plan the seating arrangement to ensure a smooth transition of movement from one activity to another. When teaching, you should be able to see the whole class.
- List your rules and procedures on the chalkboard or on a bulletin board. Communicate to students the consequences of improper behavior. (p. 34)

Consider the following suggestions in your preparation to teach a lesson:

- Have all materials ready to use well in advance of the actual lesson.
- Decide on how and when you and the students will use the materials.
- Know when you will distribute materials.
- Highlight times when students will be moving around the room, planning ahead for smooth transitions.
- Plan how you will handle seatwork assignments—including giving directions, collecting finished products, and providing activities for students who finish early—and how you will monitor the students' attention to assignments. (p. 35)

Consider the following suggestions while teaching a lesson:

- Be sensitive to the timing of your explanation. Notice cues from students that indicate interest or lack of interest.
- Do not dwell too long on a topic or a response, but do not leave a question hanging.

■ Anticipate problems and handle any misbehavior as quickly and positively as possible.

■ Move around the room. (p. 36)

Consider the following suggestions in monitoring student progress:

■ Have students show their work to you.

■ Have students demonstrate any particular skill or knowledge.

■ Ask students directly how they are proceeding.

■ Provide meaningful praise.

■ Monitor seatwork by walking around the room and stopping to work with individuals.

■ Give explicit directions for seatwork assignments. Go over the first two or three examples of any assignment to be certain that students understand the task.

■ Be sensitive to signs of confusion, such as unnecessary movement or talking, puzzlement, or an incorrect response to an easy question. (p. 37)

Grouping for Instruction

Grouping students to achieve instructional goals facilitates literacy learning. Grouping for instruction was formerly done more for administrative convenience than anything else. Research supports the use of grouping to increase direct instruction and the amount of engaged time in the classroom. Yet, grouping per se is ineffective if it fails to account for individual needs. The effective teacher uses flexible grouping plans, depending upon the instructional goal. The key is how well various grouping procedures permit the teacher to teach what students need to know.

Teachers must plan and organize their classrooms according to the particular learning goals they have established for their students. Teachers can choose from three basic grouping procedures: (1) whole groups, (2) small groups, and (3) individual learning. At various times, every classroom should incorporate all types of groups.

■ Large Groups

Large-group or whole-class instruction is appropriate at times in any classroom. When all children need to learn certain skills, large-group instruction is a more efficient use of both teacher and student time. This grouping is appropriate for storytelling, working on art activities related to a story, and teaching various study skills (such as SQ3R; skimming; scanning; reading maps, graphs, diagrams, and charts; using reference books; and using the library effectively).

■ Small Groups

Small-group instruction is certainly not new. However, various forms of small-group instruction are becoming more and more popular in today's classrooms. Under the umbrella of small groups, skill or special-needs groups, paired or partner groups, interest groups, research groups, and cooperative learning groups are being practiced and studied in classrooms across the country. With learning to read and write an active process in which students need numerous opportunities to construct meanings, more learning results from more classroom interaction than passively listening to a teacher in a large-group setting or reading a book alone. Furthermore, because students are different in so many ways, whole-class grouping does not provide for adapting a lesson's objective to each student's learning needs, nor does it provide the corrective feedback that comes from personalized instruction in small groups. Researchers at the National Reading Research Center (Alvermann et al., 1996) reported that middle and high school students preferred small-group to whole-class discussions. Students felt they had more opportunities to talk and were more willing to take risks and share their ideas in small-group discussions. Newmann (1992) points out the advantages of small groups:

- With appropriate tasks and enough flexibility in use of time and resources, small groups afford all students the opportunity to work with knowledge actively—through writing, talking, and dramatization.
- Small groups increase opportunities for feedback on individual work from peers and from the teacher, who can circulate throughout the class and give sustained attention to specific groups and students.
- Small groups offer a motivational boost, because they situate learning in a social setting that many students find more satisfying than working alone.
- In addition to cognitive objectives, small groups offer opportunities to pursue affective and social goals such as building student respect for individual and cultural diversity and developing cooperative social skills. (p. 2)

■ Paired/Peer Groups

Pairing two students together to read a story or learn and practice a reading skill or strategy has long been an effective classroom arrangement. Students of similar ability or students of differing abilities can be paired together. In a study by Benton, Belk, and Holifield (1994), high-achieving students were paired with low-achieving students in the fourth grade for all reading activities. Results indicated that the paired reading arrangement motivated children to read more. It was further observed that all the students enjoyed the sharing of a good story with a partner.

Leal (1993) reported on the benefits of peer-group discussions of all types of text. Nine groups of six students in grades 1, 3, and 5 were read a storybook, an informational book, and an informational storybook. Three benefits identified from the collaborative talks about the three types of text were (1) students' assuming responsibility for the discussion, sharing their background of experiences with other students, (2) the opportunities for peer tutoring and collaboration, and (3) the opportunity for a genuine audience of one's peers for discussion topics. In commenting on the positive outcomes of the collaborative talks, Leal states, "When children are provided opportunities to share their own ideas with peers, many good things can happen" (pp. 114–115).

■ Skill Groups

This type of grouping should depend on assessment of students' specific strengths and weaknesses. Such grouping brings together a small number of students for a specific purpose. Once the skill is mastered, the group is disbanded. Skill groups formed on the basis of students' needs include those for specific word-skill instruction (e.g., sounds represented by consonants) and those for specific comprehension instruction (e.g., inferring character traits).

■ Interest Groups

Groups also may be formed based on a common interest. If group members are on different instructional reading levels, cooperation among members can increase motivation and self-satisfaction. Many activities lend themselves to interest grouping. Students who read books by the same author can research that author's life or style of writing, compare stories, or complete artwork related to his books. Students who are interested in a particular subject can come together and read various books on their instructional level and prepare a group report. Others can listen to a recorded story or watch a filmstrip about a particular topic together.

■ Research Groups

Grouping students together to research a particular topic is similar to interest grouping. With research grouping, students collect, organize, and synthesize information from a variety of sources and produce a final product (e.g., an oral report, a written report, an art activity, or a play). Topics may include, for example, life in the local community 50 years ago, how electric lights work, exploration and settlement of the West, the growth and change of the South, John F. Kennedy, the Supreme Court, Albert Einstein, hurricanes and tornadoes, how our circulatory system works, or the United Nations.

■ Cooperative Groups

Cooperative learning is rapidly becoming one of the most popular teaching techniques throughout the country. Cooperative learning involves placing students in small groups to work together in completing learning assignments. Cooperative grouping is enormously popular, and justifiably so. Research on teaching and learning supports the use of cooperative learning (Putnam, 1997). With the great range of differences in today's classrooms, **cooperative grouping** places students into small, heterogeneous groups. This type of grouping mixes ability levels of students. Combining a fast, moderate, and slow reader encourages peer tutoring. These groups have the potential to increase students' academic engaged time and achievement by promoting active learning, with students talking and working together rather than passively listening. Being active in the learning process and having the support of peers, students have opportunities to explain what they are learning, apply and strengthen their critical-thinking and problem-solving skills, discuss the pros and cons of an idea, receive help in learning the

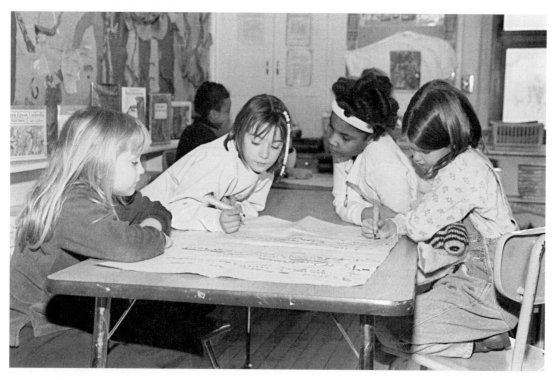

Cooperative learning groups promote active learning with students talking and working together.

lesson objective, and give support to other members of the group. The major requirement of cooperative groups is that individual members have a vested interest in ensuring that other members learn. In contrast to traditional groups that pit one student against another, cooperative learning fosters combining energies of students toward a common goal. Skill, interest, and research groups can be arranged to promote cooperative learning. Johnson and Johnson (1990) completed extensive research on the use of cooperative groups in elementary and secondary classrooms. Their research has supported the overall finding that students working together with other students will generate positive effects. The authors summarize the positive benefits of cooperative learning as follows:

> Cooperative learning experiences, compared with competitive and individualistic ones, promote higher achievement, greater motivation, more positive interpersonal relations among students (regardless of differences in ability, ethnic background, handicap, or sex), more positive attitudes toward the subject area and teacher, greater self-esteem and psychological health, more accurate perspective taking, and greater social skills. Employability and career success largely depend on a person's ability to work cooperatively with others. (p. 4)

In addition, Johnson and Johnson feel that cooperation among students positively affects critical thinking and metacognition. In cooperative groups, students have multiple opportunities to orally summarize, explain, teach, and elaborate on ideas and receive feedback from their peers to improve their reasoning (Johnson & Johnson, 1989).

Although no one set of guidelines ensures successful implementation of cooperative grouping, the following steps can help teachers initiate cooperative groups:

1. Specify the instructional objectives.
2. Provide an explicit or direct explanation of the lesson objective with guided practice to the whole class.
3. Select the group size most appropriate for the lesson.
4. Assign students to heterogeneous groups.
5. Arrange the classroom so that group members are close together and the groups are as far apart as possible.
6. Provide appropriate materials.
7. Explain the task and the cooperative goal structure.
8. Observe student-student interaction.
9. Intervene as a consultant to help the group solve its problems in working together effectively and to help the group learn the interpersonal and group skills necessary for cooperating, or check that all members are learning the material.
10. Evaluate the group products, using a criterion-referenced evaluation system.

An interesting spin-off involving literature-based reading, interest groups, and cooperative learning groups is the use of literature study groups (Keegan & Shrake, 1991). Heterogeneous groups meet three times during the week to discuss a particular novel that each group selected to read. Students interact with each other on various levels and complete different tasks, including writing their reactions to the novel in literature logs. The group's discussion is taped and the teacher critiques it and provides valuable feedback. Citing students' resulting enthusiasm and excitement for reading, Keegan and Shrake (1991) "are convinced that literature study groups offer a framework for allowing children opportunities to discover what they know, to extend their thinking, and to develop strategies that will make them lifelong readers" (p. 547).

Cooperative learning is the basis for a highly effective elementary school literacy program entitled "Roots and Wings" (Slavin, Madden, Dolan, & Wasik, 1994), a part of the overall program called "Success For All," which is a delivery program with a focus on prevention and early intervention. Currently in place at elementary schools in areas with high rates of poverty in 200 schools and 59 districts nationwide, this literacy program integrates reading with writing and is based on cooperative learning groups. "Roots and Wings" promotes a balanced approach to reading development combining various approaches and integrating phonics and meaning-centered reading of whole stories. In describing the cooperative aspects of the program, Slavin et al. (1994) note that children "are placed in cooperative learning groups, where they read to one another and work together to find the main elements of stories. They learn to support one another's reading and to challenge one another to explain and justify their understanding" (p. 12).

Evaluations of this program have found positive effects on reading achievement, especially reading comprehension.

■ Ability Groups

Grouping students on the basis of previous learning in order to satisfy instructional needs is a long-standing practice in our schools. Ability grouping is an accurate description when it refers to present rather than potential achievement. It was (and still is) sometimes used to imply intellectual capacity, however. When this occurs, the grouping suggests a final judgment rather than an initial step in ongoing diagnosis.

Certain other widespread but indefensible practices have resulted in criticism of ability grouping. Once groups are established, often their composition changes very little. Also, student mobility among groups does not follow any performance criteria. Often, the high, medium, and low groups all inexplicably follow the same procedures—all read, or attempt to read, the same book(s) and attempt to cover the same amount of material. Without differentiation of instruction, the grouping is assumed to be a ritual unrelated to instructional strategy. Special care must be exercised in using ability and cooperative groupings. Although ability grouping helpfully narrows the range of ability a teacher has to deal with in a class, the possible negative effects often outweigh this initial potential advantage. Other negative practices sometimes associated with ability grouping include the teacher's inadvertently treating groups differently according to whether they are labelled of high, middle, or low ability; that is, the teacher may give more time, attention, smiles, physical contact, comprehension instruction, and wait-time, as well as higher-cognitive-level questions to high-ability groups. Research by Allington (1983, 1994) also indicates that students in low-ability groups often receive less beneficial instruction than students in other groups. He notes that children with reading difficulties actually read less than advanced students and have fewer opportunities to be engaged with real stories. If grouping by ability is used, it is wise to employ other types of grouping as well. It is crucial that teachers be aware of the possible negative effects of ability grouping and guard against them to ensure each student a quality education.

It is realistic to assume that grouping is inherently neither good nor bad. Practices within any type of grouping may either enhance student growth or become meaningless and even harmful educational rituals. Grouping students on the basis of instructional needs can, however, provide the framework for an alert teacher to develop meaningful, differentiated instruction. Grouping can narrow the range of differences and reading problems that face a teacher during a given instructional period. As a result, teachers can focus on particular short-term goals for specific students.

Practical considerations should always influence group management. Attempting to work with five or six groups, for example, may result in instructional time blocks that are too small to be effective. Two groups may produce too heterogeneous a collection of students in both groups. Such problems emphasize that grouping practices should be flexible.

In *Becoming a Nation of Readers* (1985), Anderson, Hiebert, Scott, and Wilkinson concluded that "grouping by ability may slow the progress of low-ability stu-

INCLUSION STRATEGIES

Teaming with the *Special Education Teacher* to Achieve the Correct Balance

Professionals in every field work together. Effective literacy teachers realize that they are members of a team, acknowledge the expertise of other professionals, and seek their advice or help when necessary. It is common today for regular classroom teachers and special education teachers to collaboratively plan for the education of students with special needs. Classroom teachers realize that they will not be able to solve all problems by themselves. While the same principles of effective instruction apply to all students, both teachers need to pool their resources together in designing and devising accommodations for students with special needs. It may be helpful to return to Chapter 1 and review the major content strands of an elementary school reading curriculum of word recognition, word meaning, comprehension, reading study skills, recreational reading, and literature and the major program areas of a complete reading program of developmental reading, application-transfer, recreational reading, content reading, and functional reading. With respect to these areas, how can you as a classroom teacher ensure that all your students will receive the best instruction possible? What must you do in order to deliver a balanced literacy program to all students? Effective teachers believe that all their students will be successful in reading, assume personal responsibility for the progress of their students, and believe in their ability to provide instruction to meet the varied needs of all their students. Yet you must realize that no simple recipe is available for effective instruction in all situations with all students. Effective teachers work together with the special education teachers to combine different grouping and management plans, teaching strategies, and approaches to literacy to meet the needs of all students. In discussing the importance of the teaming process, noted special-education experts Ysseldyke and Algozzine (1995) report that, by doing the following, teachers can accommodate diversity in the classroom:

- varying the amounts of instruction on the basis of individual student capabilities.
- using modified instructional approaches, materials, and procedures to enable students to master content at paces suited to their individual capabilities and interests.
- monitoring pupil progress and providing students with immediate feedback. Instruction is then adapted on the basis of student performance.
- teaching students to monitor their own performance and identify modifications they need in order to make satisfactory progress.
- providing students with opportunities to make choices and decisions about their learning objectives.
- using peer teaching, in which students assist one another in mastering subject matter content. (p. 116)

dents" (p. 92). To improve the instruction provided to low-ability groups, the authors suggest "switching group assignments periodically, using criteria other than ability for group assignment, and maybe, increasing the time devoted to the whole classroom" (p. 92).

The basal reader is a systematic, coordinated, sequential anthology of stories and related materials designed to teach reading. The effective implementation of the basal reader approach relies heavily on grouping students by ability. Although ability grouping narrows the range of ability a teacher has to deal with in a class, the possible negative effects often outweigh this initial potential advantage. In response to the possible negative effects of the basal and as a way to keep and to enhance the basal as the main program, Wiggins (1994) proposed an adaptation of the traditional grouping by ability using the basal reader. Wiggins's flexible "Large Group Instruction/Small Group Follow-up" approach to using basal materials included presenting a main lesson to the whole class followed by small-group instruction based on need. Students were placed in the same basal reader and instruction was adjusted to meet student needs. While initial findings were positive, it is important to note that this arrangement did not include students reading below grade level. However, the potential of this innovative practice in providing for a balanced reading program is promising. Highlighting the advantages of this **flexible grouping** plan, Wiggins stated:

> This type of organization for instruction frees the teacher to circulate throughout the room providing more student-teacher interaction. This should contribute to more effective classroom management, an increased use of classroom learning centers, more independent reading and, ultimately, a greater sense of responsibility and independence on the part of the students. Most important, this arrangement puts the responsibility for instructional decision making back into the hands of the classroom teacher. (p. 456)

Organizing a Class for Instruction

Implementing reading instruction in a class requires careful orchestration of time, materials, and instruction to satisfy the needs of individual children. Based on assessment data, teachers must make several decisions regarding student instructional levels, their specific skill development needs, materials to use, and types of grouping to improve learning. A visitor to a typical classroom will readily see that a reading class can be organized many ways. No one way is the only correct one. The guiding principle in deciding how to organize reading instruction should be how best to accommodate students' needs in reading.

Effective teachers use different types of groups at different times to achieve desired results. Flexibility in using groups is a key, because students are different and their needs continually change. They need a careful blend of teacher-directed and independent activities for their reading ability to improve. Figures 12.1 and 12.2 suggest possible ways to organize a class for reading instruction using a basal reader approach and two or three reading groups. Although many other combinations are possible, these figures should help you visualize the decisions a teacher must make when organizing instruction. Each day's reading lesson includes both teacher-directed and independent activities. The schedules offer one possible way to distribute components of the directed reading activity (DRA) throughout a week. The organization gives students a balance of instructional and independent activities.

Regardless of group membership, differences among students always exist. Therefore, teachers need to plan time for special-needs grouping. Teachers can use this time to provide instruction to students lacking in particular skills (e.g.,

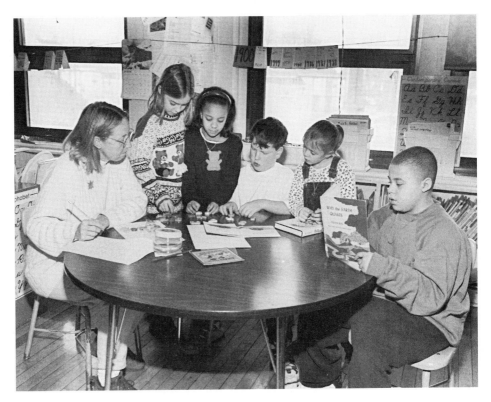

Integrated units can and should include many hands-on experiences.

In developing an integrated unit, teachers may discover that the first important task is finding materials at various levels. The references available vary from school to school. Basal readers at all levels can serve for such a unit, as can subject-matter texts. Functional resources can provide materials on many topics, and the school and public libraries can be sources of books on special topics.

The teacher can devise a unit for any subject area. It can span a few days, during which students attempt to find the answer to a particular question, or it may extend over several weeks and end in some type of class project. The product might be a play, a school program, or a science fair with many individual and committee projects. Although the unit approach is not new, it is consistent with the aims of modern curriculum planning. Unit study can help avoid the tendency toward fragmentation of the curriculum into isolated, seemingly unrelated parts.

Units lend themselves to two types of major emphasis. The first builds students' experiences around a specific topic, such as How We Get Our Food. Experiences might include visits to various types of farms, a cannery, a cold storage plant, a meat packing plant, a dairy, and a bakery. Students may plant and care for a garden or window box. The second major emphasis is broad reading. The early elementary grades will probably emphasize the experience approach, while the intermediate grades will shift to reading. These two methods are extremely compatible; when combined properly, they undoubtedly make for a better total learning situation.

Advantages.   The potential advantages of the integrated-unit approach are numerous. Actual benefits of its use vary according to such factors as the teacher's skill, the students' reading ability and work habits, and the amount of supplementary reading material available. Following are some of the more frequently mentioned advantages of the integrated-unit approach:

- The unit serves as the framework for shaping learning experiences into larger, more meaningful wholes. The unit permits more than the superficial study of a topic and encourages application of skills in broadly varied reading.
- Units can be used in any curricular area.
- Students learn that reading is the key to learning about all subjects and not just an operation performed in the basal reader and accompanying workbooks.
- The unit approach can and should include a great variety of experiences related to reading, such as excursions, field trips, and small-group participation, in working on various facets of the topic.
- Units structure the learning situation to make reading more varied, more meaningful, and more interesting.
- Units permit readers of widely different abilities to work on different facets of the same project. Reading materials at many levels of difficulty can be used, and students need not be directly compared as readers.
- The unit approach gives teachers flexibility and freedom to work with an individual or group engaged in some reading activity at its own level. The reader with problems and the accelerated reader can work independently and successfully on something that is challenging.
- Units aid independent reading and help foster independence in research reading.

A unit on weather for a fifth-grade class may be used as an illustration. The teacher arouses the interest of the class through an assignment to watch weather reports on television, to find interesting pictures of weather stations, and to discuss in class stories dealing with weather. Out of this grows the decision to have a study unit on weather. Under the teacher's direction, students work cooperatively in identifying objectives, finding questions to be answered, and working on individual projects within the unit's limits.

Objectives of the unit on weather include the following:

- To learn ways in which weather helps or harms people.
- To learn what causes various types of weather and changes of seasons.
- To learn the causes and effects of rainfall, temperature, and fog.
- To become familiar with the instruments used in measuring or predicting weather changes.

Questions to be answered include the following:

- How is a thermometer constructed and how does it work?
- What is fog?
- What causes hail?
- What is lightning? Why is it followed by thunder?
- Why do we have seasons such as winter and summer?
- Why are some parts of Earth always hot and others always cold?
- Why is there very little rainfall in one part of a country and a great deal in another part?
- Why is it important for people to be able to predict the weather?
- What is a barometer? How does it work?
- What is humidity?

Activities or projects, both individual and group, include the following:

- Keeping a daily record of temperature. Recording temperatures registered in cities in different parts of the country.
- Preparing charts and graphs illustrating some aspect of weather, including average rainfall for different states and countries, the relationship between rainfall and the type of crops raised in a particular area, and the effect of rainfall on population density.
- Preparing maps showing occurrences of tornadoes, hurricanes, and floods during the past decade.
- Explaining and demonstrating a thermometer and barometer.
- Researching the work of the U.S. Weather Bureau in predicting weather.
- Studying the effects of weather on human dress, shelter, and diet.
- Measuring rainfall during a rain.
- Obtaining pictures illustrating any facet or effect of weather, such as floods, erosion, storms on land and sea, barren deserts, and permanent snow.

For the culminating activity, the class decides to have a weather fair. They display all individual and group projects, including posters, graphs, charts, picture series, student-made instruments for measuring weather, and written projects. Parents are invited to visit the class on a particular afternoon, and other classes in the school see the displays at certain times that day. Students explain their projects and derive a great deal of satisfaction from this culminating activity.

This well-planned unit provides a variety of purposeful learning experiences. The teacher structures activities so that all facets of the curriculum receive attention.

Mathematics.   In the intermediate grades, a lack of understanding of the problems to be solved is more of a stumbling block in mathematics than is a lack of computational skills. Failure to read problems critically results in hazy understanding. In unit work, math problems emerge from the learner's immediate experiences. Problems such as finding the average rainfall, average temperature, or total foodstuffs raised are related to larger goals and become meaningful. The need for accurate measurement becomes apparent in building a barometer or measuring rainfall.

Health.   One particular topic, how weather affects our health, almost becomes a unit within a unit. The entire class participates, with students writing a brief account of anything they find in their reading that pertains to the topic. The teacher has a few references for students who need help in finding material. The health lesson also becomes a lesson in communication skills as students work on their written assignments. Students also practice their oral language skills as they report their findings to the class.

Social Studies.   The discussion on health leads into social studies topics. A discussion of diet in relation to health leads to questions and discussion of how weather affects diet or production of foodstuffs. A discussion of the economic value of climate logically follows. The class discusses climate's relationship to certain natural resources, such as forestry, deposits of coal, and petroleum. The relationships among rainfall, temperature, winds, forests, and the types of crops are discussed. Methods of cultivation and crop rotation are studied in relation to land erosion.

Science.   This unit essentially is a science unit. It emphasizes how scientists predict and track the weather and the scientific instruments they use in the process. Studying the thermometer and barometer raises many scientific principles and questions, such as the principles of expansion, gravity, and pressure, and the questions of whether mercury is a metal, why it is used in the instruments, and how heat causes a thermometer to work.

Spelling.   Students learn many words incidentally as they print them on their posters or charts. The teacher assigns new words as part of the unit (such as *weather, thermometer, mercury, rainfall, temperature, erosion,* and *bureau*).

Reading.   Reading provides the vehicle for all of the other curricular activities. The unit stresses that students are getting information for health, geography, and science. The reading is purposeful. Neither the reading nor the teaching of it is the compulsive let's-get-this-workbook-page-finished approach. The teacher keeps in mind the principles of teaching reading, being particularly careful to provide a variety of supplementary materials at many grade levels.

Using the integrated unit method in no way restricts the teacher in developing students' reading skills. In fact, once the teacher has completed preliminary planning, he or she has as much time and opportunity to help individual students or small groups as with conventional lessons.

Most unit work introduces a heavy vocabulary load, so the class must spend time on vocabulary development. As different students read and ask for help with unknown words, the teacher can prepare several lists of new words to be studied during the course of the unit. One such list might be taken from the more difficult sources and used exclusively with the advanced reading group. Vocabulary exercises for average readers and those experiencing problems can include easier words. Many new and unknown words can help in teaching phonic analysis and stressing the importance of contextual clues in solving meaning difficulties.

Individualized Reading

A movement? A method? A classroom organization? A philosophy of instruction? The term **individualized reading** has different meanings for different users, but it has enjoyed wide acceptance and use in our schools for many years. Paradoxically, its greatest potential strengths and weaknesses stem from the same factors. It has no concise definition, and no blueprint exists for making it work. Its success depends upon creative responses. However, its drawback is its inability to prevent teachers from developing nonproductive rituals.

Background

During the 1950s, frustration with the status quo in reading instruction reached a new high, and the climate for change seemed particularly good. The new emphasis on gearing reading instruction to individual students' needs and interests came to be known as individualized reading. Proponents of this reform movement had great enthusiasm, which was essential for change. They attacked two educational practices in particular: the use of basal readers and ability grouping.

Critics found certain indefensible practices in the use of basals and groupings. Some teachers relied on basal texts to the exclusion of other materials. When this occurred, reading and learning to read were easily reduced to deadly routines. Some students who had the ability to move through basals fairly rapidly were kept with the group, severely limiting their advancement. These students were asked to complete tasks such as workbook exercises that added nothing to their growth in reading. Students at the other end of the achievement continuum were kept reading the same primer and first-grade basals for 2 or more years even though they did not make any progress.

The other area of concern, the practice of dividing a class into three groups, was made to look like a ritual that ignored individual differences and needs. Some teachers had students read round-robin, embarrassing poorer readers and providing unacceptable models of oral reading for the remainder of the group. Classes probably never enjoyed stories read under such adverse conditions. These practices were not inherent in the use of basals or grouping. Rather, they developed as a result of teachers and school systems.

Practices

Individualized reading rejects the lockstep instruction that tends to become standardized within the framework of the graded system and traditional graded materials. The success or failure of an individualized program rests almost exclusively with the teacher, which is one of the reasons why individualized reading is so difficult to define.

◀||| F L A S H B A C K

Individualized reading is an approach based on the concepts of seeking, self-selection, and self-pacing. Willard C. Olson, who proposed these concepts in the early 1950s, believed that youngsters, moving at their own pace, grow best when surrounded by a large selection of books from which to choose. This approach stresses that each child differs with respect to learning style, learning rate, and interests.

Photo courtesy of Mrs. Willard C. Olson.

U P D A T E |||▶

With a greater emphasis on literature in modern reading programs, Olson's original views on individualization are at the heart of everyday reading in today's American classrooms. Literature-driven programs have resulted in more instructional time being allocated to a variety of authentic reading situations. Realizing that comprehension is best fostered within the context of literature, that students will be achieving at different levels of ability, and that students in our classrooms are increasingly diverse, teachers are creating more situations involving literature in classrooms. Hand-in-hand with this literature emphasis goes the importance of effective classroom management techniques. With greater time being devoted to a variety of authentic reading situations, teachers of reading need to be able to create, manage, and maintain an environment conducive to learning.

Over the years, a number of practices have become associated with individualized reading. These include students' self-selection of materials, self-pacing in reading, individual student conferences with the teacher, and emphasis on record keeping by the teacher, student, or both. One other notable characteristic is the need for a wide variety of reading material in each classroom. This becomes mandatory if students are to select books that they are interested in and can read.

Seeking, Self-selection and Self-pacing. Willard C. Olson's writing (1949, 1959) is frequently cited as the basis for the emphasis on seeking, self-selection, and self-pacing. Although these concepts are not new to education, the individualized reading movement has given them a new emphasis in reading instruction. The principle underlying the advocacy of self-selection is psychologically sound. Because individual differences among students in a given classroom are tremendous, the teacher cannot assume that one basal series or a single text will address all their needs.

The success of self-selection depends on several factors. First, students must have some interests they wish to explore further. This helps motivate them in the reading situation. Second, the available materials must fit their interests and ability to read independently. When these conditions are met, students should seek out the materials fitting their needs, interests, and reading levels. If they select wisely, their reading ability should grow.

Carried to extremes, this idea of individualized reading minimizes the teacher's role in guiding students to materials, so that self-selection almost becomes a fetish. Teachers should not assume that students, when permitted to do so, will select materials they can read. While that may be true in a number of cases, it is not an inevitable law of child behavior.

Students' self-selection is often limited by the fact that teachers have previously chosen the 100 or 200 books found in the classroom from among thousands available. Individualized reading and self-selection do not preclude teachers from recommending books or guiding students toward certain materials, but this type of guidance does call for a high level of teacher competency. The teacher must know students' interests, their reading abilities, and the difficulty level of materials if their suggestions are to help students grow.

Economy in the teacher-learning situation must also be considered. If, after a period of seeking, students have not made a selection and settled down to reading, they may not yet be ready for self-selection. Thus, with many students, self-selection can safely be tempered with guidance.

Teacher-Student Conferences. The teacher-student conference is one of the major features of individualized reading. It is also potentially one of its great strengths. The conference is a brief session in which teachers give their undivided attention to one student. The primary goal of the conference is to assure children that they have an appreciative audience.

The chief value of the conference is that it involves students in the reading process. For the conference to be most effective, however, teachers must be more than listeners. In addition to being appreciative audiences, teachers must assume some responsibility for helping students develop values and self-understanding, goals often best achieved through judicious questioning. The conference provides a means by which teachers can learn important facts about students' psychological needs and how they fulfill these needs. Discussing reading with a respectful adult helps give students insights into their own problems and discover how others have handled such difficulties.

The conference serves as a catalyst for teacher-student rapport. For some students, the teacher's positive response to their reading is a stronger motivation than the act of reading itself. A skillful, sympathetic teacher can provide this extrinsic reward while slowly moving the student toward accepting reading as its own reward.

Preparing for the conference is essential, but one should avoid a standardized format. Veatch (1963) recommends factors that teachers should consider in setting up conferences:

- As a general rule, students should inform the teacher when they feel ready to participate in the conference.
- The teacher should be familiar with the book or story that a student plans to discuss.
- The teacher should inform students when or in what order they will be scheduled for the conference.
- All other students in the class should be engaged in some other meaningful activity. One suggestion is to have them selecting and reading books independently.
- The teacher must be prepared to ask questions that stimulate thought instead of asking only for factual information.
- The class and teacher should work out some system for students to receive help pronouncing unknown words during their independent reading.

Frequency, length, and format of conferences were the basis for many questions from teachers in the early days of the individualized reading movement. Today, we understand that practices in these areas must vary from classroom to classroom. No single proposal regarding format, frequency, or length of conferences is the best for all situations. A logical schedule for a classroom of 24 students may be unworkable with a class of 35. Furthermore, the length and frequency of the conference should vary with different grade levels and different ability levels within a grade. The student who has read a story consisting of only several hundred words will probably not take as much time with the teacher as the one who read *Charlotte's Web*. All conferences, therefore, need not use the same procedures nor last the same amount of time.

In the case of a reader who needs little encouragement to read, a brief exchange between the teacher and student may suffice on some occasions. A word of praise, a question about whether there are still a number of books in the classroom that the student wishes to read, and an offer of help when needed may be adequate. Because the sharing conference is primarily a confidence-building experience, some students obviously will need more attention than others. Some continually avoid a conference because they consider reading a threat rather than a pleasure. These students need constant encouragement and praise for their accomplishments.

Record Keeping.   Record keeping received considerable attention in the early descriptions of individualized reading. This activity generally had little or nothing to do with actual diagnosis of reading needs. Rather, records seemed to emphasize the number of books read and to offer proof that the system was working. In some cases, this feature became dominant, with students reading primarily to add titles to their lists. Also, it tended to invite comparisons of achievement, the opposite intention of individualized reading. Over the years, attention to this activity has diminished.

Problems

The idea of students reading independently, selecting what they wish to read, and reading at their own pace strikes some critics as quite idealistic. To keep this philosophy from becoming unrealistic, teachers must expend a great deal of effort in classroom management. Over the years, teachers have voiced a number of concerns, including the following:

- What types of materials are needed?
- How does one initiate an individualized program?
- When and how is ongoing diagnosis achieved?
- How is provision made for teaching the necessary reading skills?
- When the teacher is involved in teacher-student conferences, what are the other students doing? How do these students get "instant help" for their reading problems?

How the teacher handles these and other issues determines the success or failure of an individualized program.

Materials.   A reading program embracing self-selection and self-pacing and tailored to individual students' interests cannot function in a learning environment that does not include a wide selection of reading materials. This is not a special problem limited to individualized reading. Every classroom and school should meet this requirement, regardless of the methodological approach or program.

Although it is difficult to say how many books are adequate, a minimum figure frequently mentioned is approximately 100 different trade book titles per classroom. These 100 books also should be changed throughout the year. Factors to consider include grade level, students' interests and abilities, class size, whether books can be rotated with other classrooms, whether the school supports a central library, and whether the same materials are used extensively in other subject areas, such as social studies and science, in preparing units. Trade books are not the only source of materials, although they are likely to be the major source. Classrooms should contain magazines, newspapers, various reading kits, *My Weekly Reader, Reader's Digest* (skill-builder materials), and other reading materials students might choose. Reading materials should cover many areas, such as biography, science, sports, exploration, hobbies, fairy tales, medicine, space, poetry, humor, adventure, myth, and travel.

Starting a Program.   All elementary teachers are likely to be doing some things that fit logically under the heading of individualization. Any of the formal aspects of individualized reading, such as self-selection or individual conferences, can be used with one student, a small group, or an entire class. Obviously, the latter approach presents the most problems; therefore, perhaps you should start with one of the alternatives.

Prior to any conference, assemble a number of books on a reading table. Include a number of new books and books that you think will appeal to the student or students involved. Begin by calling together five or six students. Explain that they will be selecting their own books to read at their desks during the reading period. At the end of the group conference, tell the group members that after selecting the books they wish to read, they are to go to their desks and read their selections silently. Also tell students that they may keep the books at their desks until they are finished.

Within a day or two, have students meet again in the individualized group. Explain that each student is to schedule a conference with you to tell you something about the book and to read a part of the book to you that was particularly interesting. Individuals are to tell you when they are ready for a conference.

Providing for Assessment.   Individualized reading is an approach that by its very nature calls for considerable assessment if students are to progress smoothly in reading. Some may not be able to achieve in an individualized setting without ongoing assessment. No assessment techniques are associated exclusively with individualized reading. Yet, by its very nature, individualized reading lends itself to performance-based or authentic assessment procedures. Anecdotal records, collecting samples of work, conferencing, and portfolios are examples of ways to monitor students' growth in literacy.

Teaching Reading Skills and Strategies.   The early individualized movement was in part a reaction against reading instruction that stressed skills at the expense of the total reading process. In some classrooms, all students received the same instruction, worked on the same skill-building exercises, and read the same materials. When these practices were prevalent, one could argue that instruction was predetermined rather than based on students' needs and abilities. Such uniform practices inevitably caused some students to become bored with reading instruction.

Unfortunately, the attack on uniform skills instruction for all spread to the teaching of skills themselves. Actually, skills teaching was not explicitly rejected, but this facet of individualized reading instruction was neglected. In recent years, most proponents of individualized reading have accepted the importance of direct instruction on skills and strategies. How and when the program incorporates this instruction remain open to question, however. Two common responses are to (1) teach some skills and strategies in the teacher-student conference and (2) teach other skills and strategies as students need them.

The first answer represents an inefficient procedure, unless the student participating in the conference is the only one in the class who can profit from the instruction. Any reading skill that can justifiably be taught to the entire class should be taught to everyone. Students who learned with the first presentation should be doing something else when the teacher makes subsequent presentations to students who did not learn.

The basic validity of the second response (teach skills and strategies when they are needed) cannot be faulted, but it can be both vague and difficult to implement when each student in the class is reading a different book. Differentiating skills instruction need not assume that no two students or groups can profit from the same instruction. This extreme position is simply the opposite of the idea that all students in a class can profit from the same amount of time spent with the same book. Diagnosis is the best way to identify what is appropriate instruction.

Basic skills can include dozens of abilities. The major concerns for the elementary teacher include word identification, knowledge of word meanings, and application of reading skills in meaningful context.

Meaningful Class Activities.   Individualized reading calls for a high degree of planning and subtle directing. The following brief listing of activities is only illustrative. The tasks are not identified by grade level, because many may be adapted to various levels. The listing includes class, group, and individual activities covering skill development, recreational reading, reading in curricular areas, and creative activities.

1. Self-selection of books or other reading materials. This may include browsing and sampling. Selection is followed by independent reading of materials.

2. Conducting library research for an individual or group report. Such an activity may relate to a unit in some other subject.

3. Planning creative writing experiences to include original stories, poems, letters to a classmate who is in the hospital or who has moved away, invitations to parents to visit school, or a riddle composition to be read to the class during a period set aside for such activities.

4. Preparing artwork such as
   a. drawing or pasting pictures in a picture dictionary.
   b. drawing a picture to accompany a student-dictated, teacher-written story.
   c. preparing posters or book covers to illustrate the key point in a book or story the student has read.

5. Using workbook pages or teacher-prepared seatwork guides to develop particular skills such as
   a. a dictionary exercise that follows an introduction of a skill, for example, alphabetizing by initial letter or by two or more letters, use of guide words, pronunciation guides, or syllabication.
   b. word-analysis skills, for example, associating sounds with graphic symbols, noting compound words, abbreviations, and the like.
   c. study skills involving effective use of parts of a book, such as the index, table of contents, glossary, or appendix.
   d. study skills involving effective use of the library card catalog or reference materials.

The use of research groups in individualized reading programs is an excellent means to integrate literacy skills and strategies in the content areas.

6. Using an appropriate filmstrip with the entire class, a smaller group, or two students.

7. Teaching and testing word meanings.
   a. Workbook pages or teacher-prepared seatwork.
   b. Vocabulary building cards or notebooks in which students write one or more common meanings for new or unknown words that they come across in their reading.
   c. Activities in which students write as many sentences as possible, using a different connotation for words listed by the teacher, for example, *light*—light in weight, light in color, light the fire, light on his feet, her eyes lighted up, and lighthearted.

8. Making a tape recording of a story. A group of four to six students may each read the part of one character. Students may do practice reading and actual recording in the rear of the classroom or in any available space in the building.

9. Testing or assessment activities. The entire class or any size of group may take a standardized test (or reading subtest), tests that accompany

basal series, *My Weekly Reader* tests, or informal, teacher-made tests. These should be scored and studied for assessment information.

■ Applications

It is important to remember that the basal reading approach, not individualized reading, is the most prevalent method of instruction in our schools. However, the basic tenets of individualized reading—seeking, self-selection, and self-pacing—form a basis for any successful reading program. Every reading program should be individualized in the sense that it addresses students' individual needs.

Grouping students to achieve instructional goals is part of individualizing instruction. As discussed, grouping students for particular purposes can result in improved achievement scores. This is the essence of individualized instruction. It is particularly satisfying to note that instruction can be individualized in many ways, depending on the teacher, the program, and the students.

Effective teachers use assessment procedures and teacher-student conferences. Using individual teacher-student conferences in every reading program is perhaps the greatest contribution of individualized reading. With conferences, teachers can personalize their teaching, diagnose student strengths and weaknesses, teach necessary skills, and prescribe individual assignments.

Teachers at every grade level, in all reading programs, should promote independent reading habits. Student self-selection and self-pacing can be integrated with the basal reading program, giving teachers and students some measure of flexibility but still retaining the structure inherent in the basal system. Students can have some freedom in choosing particular stories, and the teacher can assign workbook and reinforcement activities to fit individual needs.

Moreover, the essential elements of individualized reading closely resemble the literature-based reading program (see Chapter 9). This literary approach uses various types of literature to teach reading skills and stimulate reading as a leisure-time activity. An experimental study by Eldredge and Butterfield (1986) supported the effectiveness of a literature program incorporating many of the qualities of individualized reading. The authors concluded that a literature program is a viable alternative to traditional reading instruction. Indeed, all teachers should embody the basic tenets of individualized reading in their own teaching, regardless of grade level or reading approach.

☑ Summary

Effective reading teachers are proficient in providing and maintaining conditions conducive to learning. These teachers practice preventative managerial strategies to reduce the likelihood of trouble and to maintain student engagement in reading activities.

Key elements of classroom management include planning reading activities, managing group instruction, and monitoring student progress. Students can be grouped several ways. Options of maximizing student involvement include flexible use of the whole group, small groups, and individual learning. Small groups can be arranged according to ability, skill, need, interest, or a research topic. Peer, or paired, grouping also is effective.

Cooperative learning groups benefit all students and promote active learning. Alternative approaches to classroom management include the ungraded school, integrated-unit teaching, and individualized reading. Grouping itself is not the most important factor in learning, however. The real concerns are accommodating individual differences and increasing the degree of students' time engaged in selected tasks.

Your Point of View

Discussion Questions

1. Is it possible to overemphasize a concern for classroom management?
2. What are the disadvantages of cooperative grouping?
3. What are the major advantages and disadvantages of the unit approach? The ungraded school? Individualized reading?
4. A major feature of individualized reading is the student-teacher conference. What are some important features to consider before, during, and after such a conference?

Take a Stand For or Against

1. Being proficient in classroom management is not as important in kindergarten and grade 1 as it is in grade 6.
2. Teachers tend to view their students in terms of their placement level.
3. Ability grouping reduces the opportunities for students to learn from one another.
4. The present structure of the classroom environment prohibits cooperative learning groups.

Field-Based Assignments

1. Interview your supervising teacher regarding classroom management and discipline during the reading period. Use the following questions as a starting point and discuss the responses with your teacher. Share your findings with a small group of your peers and classmates.

   What are the four or five most common management or discipline problems you experience in the reading class?

   What do you usually do to resolve these problems?

   How can I prepare to be an effective classroom manager in teaching reading?

2. One major problem teachers have is maintaining student engagement in reading and writing activities while working with another group of students. Inter-

view as many teachers and administrators as you can regarding possible solutions to this perennial dilemma. Share your findings with other members of the class in a collaborative group, discuss your findings together, and present a group summary of what teachers do to resolve this issue to the whole class.

Portfolio Entry

The advantages and disadvantages of grouping students for instruction were discussed in this chapter. Research has indicated that in many instances, students having difficulties in learning to read are simply not involved in the learning process as much as other students are. These students are called on less oven, receive less praise, and receive less actual instruction from the teacher. Obviously, students falling behind in reading need more instruction, more praise, and involvement in the reading class. As a prospective teacher, it is important that you are aware of your expectations and provide ways to ensure that all students are receiving instructional programs that meet their needs. What can you do as a beginning teacher to ensure that all your students (even those who are falling behind in reading) receive a top-notch education in your class? Write a response in your portfolio to this question listing specific things you intend to do in your classroom that will ensure that **all** students will have your attention and be totally involved in the teaching-learning process.

Bibliography

Allington, R. L. (1983). The reading instruction provided to readers of differing reading abilities. *Elementary School Journal, 82,* 548–559.

Alvernmann, D. E., Weaver, D., Hinchman, K. A., Moore, D. W., Phelps, S. F., Thrash, E. C., & Zalewski, P. (1996). *Middle- and high-school students' perceptions of how they experience text-based discussions: A multicase study.* No. 36. Athens, GA: National Reading Research Center, University of Georgia.

Anderson, R. C., Hiebert, E. H., Scott, J. A., & Wilkinson, I. A. G. (1985). *Becoming a nation of readers: The report of the Commission on Reading.* Washington, DC: The National Institute of Education.

Benton, G., Belk, J., & Holifield, S. (1994). Increased student motivation through paired reading. *Balanced Reading Instruction, 1,* 16–20.

Blair, T. R. (1988). *Emerging patterns of teaching: From methods to field experiences.* Upper Saddle River, NJ: Merrill/Prentice Hall.

Edwards, C. H. (1997). *Classroom discipline and management* (2nd ed.). Englewood Cliffs, NJ: Prentice Hall.

Eldredge, J. L., & Butterfield, D. (1986). Alternatives to traditional reading instruction. *The Reading Teacher, 40,* 32–37.

Evertson, C. M., Emmer, E. T., Clements, B. S., & Worsham, M. E. (1997). *Classroom management for elementary teachers* (4th ed.). Needham Heights, MA: Allyn & Bacon.

Good, T. L., & Brophy, J. E. (1987). *Looking in classrooms* (4th ed.). New York: Harper & Row.

Guthrie, J. T. (1980). Time in reading programs. *The Reading Teacher, 33,* 500–502.

Johnson, D. W., & Johnson, R. T. (1990). Cooperative learning and achievement. In Shlomo Sharan (Ed.), *Cooperative learning: Theory and research.* (pp. 22–37). New York: Praeger.

Johnson, D. W., & Johnson, R. T. (1989). *Collaboration and cognition.* Minneapolis, MN: Cooperative Learning Center, University of Minnesota.

Johnson, D. W., & Johnson, R. T. (1988). *Cooperative classrooms, cooperative schools.* Minneapolis, MN: Cooperative Learning Center, University of Minnesota.

Keegan, S., & Shrake, K. (1991). Literature study groups: An alternative to ability grouping. *The Reading Teacher, 44,* 542–547.

Kounin, J. S. (1970). *Discipline and group management in classrooms.* New York: Holt, Rinehart, & Winston.

Lasley, T. J. (1987). Classroom Management. *The Educational Forum, 51,* 285–298.

Leal, D. J. (1993). The power of literary peer-group discussions: How children collaboratively negotiate meaning. *The Reading Teacher, 47,* 114–120.

Newman, F. M. (1992). *Issues in restructuring schools: Making small groups productive.* Madison, WI: Center on Organization and Restructuring of Schools, School of Education, Wisconsin Center for Education Research, University of Wisconsin–Madison.

Olson, W. (1949). *Child development.* Boston: D. C. Heath Co.

Olson, W. (1959). Seeking, self-selection, and pacing in the use of books by children. In J. Veatch (Ed.), *Individualizing your reading program.* New York: G. P. Putnam's Sons.

Putnam, J. (1997). *Cooperative learning in diverse classrooms.* Upper Saddle River, NJ: Prentice Hall.

Slavin, R. E., Madden, N. A., Dolan, L. J., & Wasik, B. A. (1994). Roots and wings: Inspiring academic excellence. *Educational Leadership,* 10–14.

Veatch, J. (1963). Self-selection and the individual conference in reading instruction. In *Improving reading instruction. Joint Proceedings of Reading Conference and Summer Workshop (Vol. 1).* State College, PA: Pennsylvania State University, 19–29.

Wiggins, R. A. (1994). Large group lesson/small group follow-up: Flexible grouping in a basal reading program. *The Reading Teacher, 47,* 450–460.

Ysseldyke, J. E., & Algozzine, B. (1995). *Special education: A practical approach for teachers.* Boston: Houghton-Mifflin.

CHAPTER 13

Focus on All Learners

Viola E. Florez
William Dee Nichols

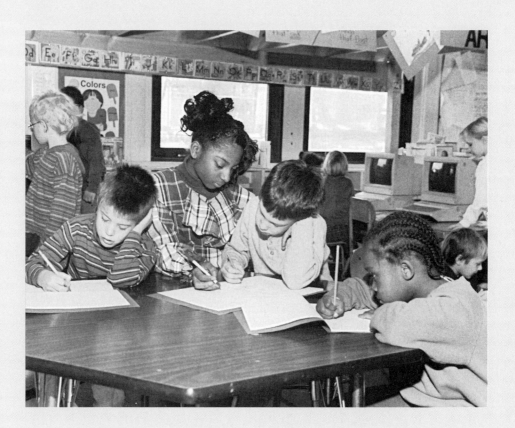

Chapter Outline

For the Reader

Every classroom is composed of individuals of varying intellectual ability, social or cultural background, language ability, and physical attributes. Today, more than ever, all teachers should be prepared to deal effectively with diversity. Since the evolution of P.L. 94-142 into the Individuals with Disabilities Act (IDEA), the focus has switched off of the disability and onto the individual. More and more students who were once enrolled in special education classes are now included in the regular classroom. This chapter focuses attention on culturally and linguistically diverse students as well as special-needs students. Although such students are certainly receiving considerable attention in professional journals, newspapers, magazines, and school programs, it is important to remember that all children have specific needs and that literacy instruction should consider these needs. This separate chapter on the topic of diverse learners highlights this important aspect of teaching reading in today's schools and focuses its attention on the classroom teacher rather than specialty teachers.

Key Ideas

- Student differences must be a primary consideration in effective literacy instruction.
- Culturally and linguistically diverse and special-needs students require an education based on their educational needs rather than on clinical or diagnostic labels.
- Teachers must be knowledgeable of and sensitive to the dialects and languages of the students they instruct.
- P.L. 94-142, the Individuals with Disabilities Education Act, mandates a free and appropriate education for all special-needs children and encourages the teacher to consider the individual rather than the disability.
  An individualized education plan (IEP) must be developed and maintained for all students with learning disabilities.

Accepting Differences

Proper acknowledgement of students' differences requires the teacher to adjust each student's educational program appropriately. All teachers encounter students who are different intellectually, psychologically, culturally, or physically. Knowledge of each student's background and learner characteristics is necessary for effective instruction. Teachers must remember that all students are individuals who require educational modifications based on their needs. The diagnostic teaching procedures previously recommended for regular classroom instruction also apply to culturally and linguistically diverse, disabled, and gifted students. Teachers must understand cultural diversity, however, to diagnose accurately a student's strengths and weaknesses.

Cultural and Linguistic Diversity

In Chapter 3 we discussed the term **culturally and linguistically diverse,** which refers to students whose culture and language or dialect differ from those of the school. The term refers to individuals from diverse ethnic and racial backgrounds, including Native American, Mexican American, Puerto Rican, Asian, and African American (Norton, 1995; Wood, 1993). Difficulty in learning to read and write has been a major educational problem for some students from these groups. Even though America is often referred to as a "melting pot," today, as we become more aware of the importance of cultural identity, it may be better to view America as a quilt—one that allows its cultural pieces to remain intact (rather than being melted down). When students of various cultures are allowed to maintain their cultural identities, learning and literacy problems could become a thing of the past for culturally and linguistically diverse groups.

Chapter 3 included instructional recommendations and guidelines for working with culturally and linguistically diverse students. These guidelines and recommendations can apply to all students, but they are crucial when teaching linguistically and culturally diverse students. Knowledge and application of these guidelines within the instructional approaches and strategies presented in this chapter can better serve the literacy needs of culturally and linguistically diverse students. An important instructional feature is the interrelatedness of the language arts (speaking, listening, reading, and writing) coupled with children's literature. Literature provides students with additional vocabulary and ideas to enhance their knowledge base of English (Bieger, 1996; Morrow, 1992; Norton, 1995).

Early Reading Approaches for Culturally and Linguistically Diverse Students

When culturally and linguistically diverse children enter school, a major problem is likely to be a lack of school-related experiences. The school is structured to provide learning experiences that may be largely foreign to some of these children.

Two potential solutions are obvious: (1) providing experiences the children need to cope with the tasks that they face in school and (2) altering the curriculum to accommodate their needs. Teachers need to take care when altering the curriculum not to stereotype and create a segregated curriculum that weakens the educational program (Guild, 1994).

Although culturally and linguistically diverse students are on the same continuum as other children, they often have experiences that are different from the mainstream. For example, insufficient emergent literacy experiences and exposure to literature from their own culture or from traditional American literature may inhibit their early success in early literacy instruction. Culturally and linguistically diverse students may have such diverse emergent literacy experiences that traditional early literacy programs do not adequately prepare them for beginning reading instruction (Stahl, 1990). Sometimes even well-structured early reading activities fail with these students because they need additional or different activities. These students demand a rethinking of early reading activities to use their strengths and concentrate on eliminating their weaknesses. Banks (1994) suggests that instead of adding units or special topics to the curriculum or discussing the different cultural heroes, teachers need to transform their curriculum so students interact with content from a variety of cultural perspectives.

The early reading and writing approaches discussed in this section attempt to redefine early literacy activities in terms of the needs of culturally and linguistically diverse learners. Their philosophy and techniques differ, but all share the goal of maximizing the probability of success in reading and writing development.

■ Academic Early Reading Intervention

Perhaps the most radical procedures for helping culturally and linguistically diverse students get off to a successful start in literacy instruction are found in academic early reading programs. Some of these programs concentrate on the direct/explicit teaching of specific language and reading skills. This is a teaching strategy in which the teacher presents stimuli designed to elicit specific language responses. Integrating specific language activities that encourage student involvement is critical for early intervention of language development, especially for students who have limited opportunities to experience literacy outside of the classroom. A wide range of literature-based activities (see The Basal Reader Approach and The Literature-based Reading Approach sections in this chapter) combined with such a program can enrich students' early reading experiences. Figure 13.1 illustrates some of the goals and direct/explicit instruction techniques for teaching specific language skills. These skill activities should not be considered the sole focus of this program. Skills can be taught throughout the school day by engaging students in meaningful language that focuses on acquisition of each goal. For example, if the teacher asks, "Where are the scissors?" students should be encouraged to respond in a manner that describes where the scissors are ("The scissors are on the big table").

A beginning reading program can serve as an extension of the language development program. It can be designed to help students become familiar with letter names, associate pictures visually with their naming words, recognize

GOAL 1: To move from one-word responses to complete affirmative and negative statements in reply to questions.

Teacher	Student
"What is this?"	"Dog."
"Say it all."	"This is a dog."
"Is this a dog?"	"Yes."
"Say it all."	"Yes, this is a dog."
"Is this a dog?"	"No."
"Say it all."	"No, this is not a dog."

GOAL 2: To respond with both affirmative and negative statements when told to "tell about something."

Teacher	Student
"Tell me about this ball."	"It is round."
	"It is blue."
	"It is not big."
	"It is not square."

GOAL 3: To develop the ability to handle polar opposites for at least four concept pairs.

Teacher	Student
"If this is not up, what is it?"	"Down."
"Say it all."	"It is down."
"If this is not big, what is it?"	"It is little."

GOAL 4: To use the prepositions *on*, *in*, *under*, *over*, and *between* in statements describing arrangements.

Teacher	Student
"Where is the turkey?"	"The turkey is *on* the table."

FIGURE 13.1
A procedure for teaching specific language skills

"Where is the long line?"   "The long line is over the short line."

"Where is the number 2?"   "The number 2 is *between* the numbers 1 and 3."

1 2 3

GOAL 5: To name positives and negatives for at least four classes.

Teacher	*Student*
"Tell me something that is clothing."	"A hat is clothing."
	"A chair is not clothing."
"Tell me something that is food."	"An apple is food."
	"A pencil is not food."

GOAL 6: To perform simple "if-then" deductions.

Teacher	*Student*
"If the circle is big, what else do you know about it?"	"It is blue."

Teacher	*Student*
"If the circle is little, what else do you know about it?"	"It is black."

GOAL 7: To use *not* in deductions.

Teacher	*Student*
"If the circle is blue, what else do you know about it?"	"It is not little."
"If the circle is black, what else do you know about it?"	"It is not big."

FIGURE 13.1, continued

INCLUSION STRATEGIES

The Beginning Reading Program

Many educators feel that bilingual or bicultural students who also have **limited-English proficiency (LEP)** need to understand and speak English before they can begin to read it (Brisbois, 1995). Other educators feel that it is not necessary for LEP students to master the oral language before they are introduced to the written form (Fitzgerald, 1993; Gonzales, 1994). Even though the research seems to be divided on whether students need to proficiently speak the English language before they can read it, the majority of the research seems to be in agreement that **English-as-a-second-language** (ESL) students will learn to read better if the initial reading instruction is in their native language (Allen, 1994; Schifini, 1994). Gonzales (1994) and Brisbois (1995) determined that students can learn to read in their native language and English at the same time if teachers use strategies that are mutually reinforcing and provide adequate vocabulary instruction in both languages. Some strategies that have been successful for developing reading skills for LEP students are discussed in the following sections.

and produce rhyming words, and learn and use a limited number of sight words. Cognitive embedded tasks can help relate these activities to real-life experiences.

In the alphabet-learning phase of the program, children familiarize themselves with the letter names of the alphabet through identity and position statements. The child is taught first to spell words by letter sounds* (*cat*—kuh ah tuh) and is then presented clusters of words that follow the same spelling pattern (such as *cat, fat, hat,* and *bat*). As students become more aware of the patterns found in word families, they develop a metacognitive awareness of orthographic features of words that enables them to increase their word-recognition skills. Word meanings are reinforced by *yes-no* questions of lexical terms.

Brisbois (1995) discusses the importance of vocabulary instruction and word-recognition instruction in the second language. Word recognition begins with the production of isolated words in the clarification of meaning as related to the learner. A word is printed on the chalkboard and the rule "This is a word" is taught and followed by the identity statement "This is the word *man.*" Students are then encouraged to respond with complete identity statements in answering questions such as "Is this the word *dog?*" "No, that is not the word *dog.* That is the word *man.*" Gestures illustrate action words. Students are invited to suggest other words they wish to learn. If no one volunteers, the teacher supplies another word. Students should be encouraged to use instrumental language with other children. By providing directions to their peers they will be expanding their own language (Pinnell, 1996).

Word-placement exercises teach visual discrimination of word forms and word meanings. The teacher labels objects with five-by-eight-inch cards and identifies them: "This card has a word on it. This is the word *toy.*" Five or more words are identified in this way, and the teacher places one word card on the proper object. Students are asked, "This is the word what?" *(desk)* "So where does it belong?" *(on the desk)*. Each child has a turn at naming and placing a word. The class then identifies these words on the chalkboard. The rule "If all the letters are the same, the words are the same" is taught.

Word-identification exercises help students develop a small sight vocabulary useful for developing simple sentences. Students learn to recognize their own names, then they receive instruction in recognizing other children's names. They also learn names of body parts this way. New sets of words (such as *is not* and *big*) are added to construct sentences: "Joe is not big." Meaning is stressed in sentence reading by having students answer questions about their reading. "Is Joe big?" "No, Joe is not big." "Is Joe little?" "Yes, Joe is little." After students master the basic tasks, they learn to read from teacher-prepared booklets.

Approaches to Teaching Reading and Writing to Culturally and Linguistically Diverse Students

Several approaches can provide reading instruction to students who speak a nonstandard dialect or a primary language other than English. Teachers must have an awareness of the students' cultural background and the linguistic features of their language. They must realize that a multicultural education is based upon the "fundamental belief that all people should be respected regardless of age, race, gender, economic class, religion, or physical or mental ability" (Bieger, 1996, p. 308). One way to demonstrate respect is to use the student's own language and cultural experiences to facilitate reading.

The Language-experience Approach

A frequently used approach for introducing and teaching literacy to linguistically diverse students is the language-experience approach (LEA). The language-experience approach has several advantages (Lewis, 1990). First, by using the student's oral language, the reading material reflects the student's syntax and sentence structures, eliminating much of the comprehension difficulty caused by using other beginning reading materials. Another advantage is vocabulary usage. Words used in constructing the reading materials come from the student's language and experiential background. These words reflect meaningful content for the student, facilitating the student's construction of meaning. The student's own oral vocabulary is often larger than his or her sight vocabulary, which allows the student to read words that he or she ordinarily would not recognize in traditional reading approaches. Students who have experienced difficulty in the past in traditional reading approaches experience success at reading stories created from their own language and experiences. This newfound success in reading is often extremely motivational to the beginning reader and produces a positive attitude towards reading. An additional advantage is the incorporation of writing in the creating of individual- and group-experience stories.

While using the LEA, it is important to use the student's own language. Attempts to correct grammatical miscues and dialectical differences defeats the purpose of the language-experience approach. In order for the student to benefit from the LEA, it must be consistent with the student's spoken language. As the teacher makes authentic assessment of the student's instruction, he or she may want to focus on syntactic miscues as a reading skill for future lessons. These skills may be taught in the context of the LEA, but the purpose of the LEA is to teach the student to read; in order to do this, the story must be transcribed in the student's authentic form.

The advantages of the language-experience approach multiply when an individual story is dictated. However, when a group story is dictated, the vocabulary and syntax both may exceed an individual student's abilities. Teachers, therefore, should encourage group discussion to help linguistically diverse students construct meaning for group-dictated stories.

Teachers may wish either to incorporate the language-experience approach into their reading programs or to use it as the primary instructional program. Because of the flexibility of the LEA, it can easily be combined with other approaches. Another possibility is to begin reading instruction with the language-experience approach and then gradually introduce a literature-based approach. Stahl (1990) states that there is research evidence to support the use of an LEA and the whole-language approach for students who do not yet understand the purpose of reading or who lack exposure to printed literature. Stahl states that for beginning readers in kindergarten, the use of an LEA approach can have positive gains; however, as students progress through the phases of reading development, he feels that a larger emphasis needs to be placed on direct instruction in the areas of decoding, which are typically found in basal reader programs.

An instructional aide or parent volunteer can facilitate implementation of the LEA. An aide or volunteer can record and copy stories, make word cards and follow-up practice materials, read and reread stories with students, create an LEA classroom library, and follow up with practice activities for students who otherwise might not succeed in reading.

■ An Integrated Language Approach Based on the Whole-language Philosophy

Many schools are adopting an integrated language approach that uses the whole-language philosophy to teach reading and language development to culturally diverse students. The major features of this approach reflect important theories stressing natural acquisition of second languages and building on each student's linguistic strengths. Integrated language instruction incorporates literature to develop and enhance students' knowledge base. The approach also integrates language with all other aspects of language teaching, such as content-area instruction in science or social studies.

In a whole-language-based classroom, students engage in reading for enjoyment and to gather information. Teachers are available to give students the help they need at a particular time, but the guidance the teacher provides enables students to become problem solvers and to seek other resources to help solve problems. This is an important goal of the whole-language reading experience. In addition, the mentoring of students to read and locate information and how to use the information they obtain is an important feature of this approach. Students sharing their work with others and communicating their accomplishments orally or in written form are major goals of a whole-language-based classroom. Workbooks and graded readers are not often used in the whole-language classroom, because the idea is that students learn from relevant, meaningful instructional materials. Students have the opportunity to learn all of the necessary reading skills, but the reading materials are student-centered and the teacher functions as the facilitator of learning.

Literature-based instruction for culturally and linguistically diverse students can feature stories from various cultures and languages displayed around the classroom; writings of students covering the walls like ribboned wallpaper; portfolios showing drafts of creative writing pieces, such as journals of all kinds, letters, and poetry; and field notes of student activities. Heidger (1991) states that it is extremely important to the bilingual education program that the instruction be authentic. ESL students should be able to use literature that reflects their language and culture. Bieger (1996) encourages teachers to develop lessons using traditional literature to help provide a multicultural education to all students. Because myths, legends, and folktales reflect the values of people from around the world, these forms of literature are encouraged for teachers to use when working with culturally and linguistically diverse learners. Integrated language instruction values all languages, and students become literate in their own language and ultimately in English. Students accomplish this using real books in real writing and learning situations (Flores, Cousin, & Diaz, 1991; Heidger, 1991).

Because children develop language naturally, teachers must create classrooms where students can interact with others and experiment with language. Similarly, second-language learners need to construct their own meanings rather than memorize text or reiterate others' thoughts. Bilingual and English language programs should use a wide variety of instructional activities designed to encourage student interaction. These can be literature-based activities that focus on developing various language and literacy skills: reading, writing, listening, and speaking. Using thematic units to teach language is an excellent way to introduce meaning that interconnects with students' lives. These units may incorporate stories that include everyday language events. Developing language through stories in the primary language and in the students' second language is important to cognitive development. Using literature to help students become literate and educated in their own language while adding another language builds students' self-concepts and encourages a positive attitude toward learning. An acceptance of each student's culture and language is a major principle of second-language teaching. The whole-language approach fosters this idea by promoting real, meaningful language instruction.

Teaching language to bilingual and second-language learners suggests that students naturally construct new meanings from whole to part of the whole. The parts—for example, the specific skills of reading and writing—must be broken down by the learner, not the teacher, and learned as needed within the context of real books and stories and writing activities (Poplin, 1992). The whole-language orientation in a bilingual classroom should emphasize early literacy teaching of skills as a whole and within context, such as literature stories to promote meaningful literacy. Emphasizing teaching language with meaning will prevent instruction in isolated skills. Skill instruction separate from the primary literacy activities can be irrelevant and not make any sense to the student. Teachers must integrate language with real situations to stimulate a positive language-learning attitude.

Stressing meaning within context and students' experiences facilitates reading comprehension. The process of learning to read involves a whole approach to literacy, which stresses the reciprocal, interactive aspects of the four language arts: reading, writing, listening, and speaking (Williams & Snipper, 1991). Engaging all of the modes of language as they interact in learning settings helps students acquire language skills. Teachers must understand all of the factors that influence students' work in teaching reading and writing to second-language learners. The match between what is being taught and what is being comprehended is especially critical for the second-language learner. When students are working in their primary language, a mismatch is unlikely to occur, but occasionally it does. When that happens, the student will attempt to understand meaning in various ways. Because the mental mismatch often reflects a student's cultural or linguistic background, integrating literature to supplement instruction is often recommended. The reader must make a connection between what he or she knows and what is being read or heard to comprehend it.

Predictable reading materials offer another way to develop bilingual language literacy skills. Patterned books have stories with predictable features such as rhyming and repeated phrases or refrains that promote language development (Norton, 1995). Patterned books frequently contain pictures that may facilitate story comprehension. The predictable patterns immediately involve beginning second-language readers in a literacy event in their first or second language. Books with patterned structure can provide modeling as a reading strategy, challenge students' current level of linguistic competence, and provide assistance in comprehending difficult concepts. Comprehension through the repetition of a simple sentence pattern can motivate second-language learners to continue trying to learn to read. The process is important for developmental purposes and teaches students to use contextual and syntactic features of the text to identify the repeated words or phrases. A popular patterned book is Bill Martin's *Brown Bear, Brown Bear, What Do You See?* (1970). The fully illustrated story repeats simple patterns that second-language learners can use to begin the reading process. Students become familiar with the story and language patterns and soon begin to create their own text with their own illustrations. In the early stages of second-language acquisition, the use of the first and second language is critical for conceptual development. Later, as the second-language proficiency develops, the student will focus on learning English. Patterned books' most important function is to offer immediate access to meaningful, enjoyable literacy experiences that facilitate lifelong reading.

The language-experience approach should be a major component of an integrated language approach for teaching reading and writing to linguistically di-

Stressing meaning within context and students' experiences enhances their comprehension.

verse students. In addition to the LEA, teachers should use materials from a variety of sources. The following materials have been recommended for whole-language-focused programs in Spanish language classrooms: (1) poetry and stories from Spanish language basal readers, (2) Spanish language trade books, (3) Spanish language resource books, (4) Spanish language newspapers, newsletters, comics, and magazines, (5) Spanish language publications from government and health agencies, (6) telephone books, cookbooks, and television guides in Spanish, (7) books and stories written in Spanish by members of the Hispanic community, and (8) stories written by the students themselves. In addition to these sources, Freeman (1988) has compiled a list of sources for alternatives to Spanish-language basals. This list is presented in Figure 13.2. In a recent article, Godina (1996) discusses the cognitive dissonance that many Mexican American students feel. In order for bicultural students to see a connection between

Bibliographies

Dale, Doris Cruger, *Bilingual Books in Spanish and English for Children.* Littleton, CO: Libraries Unlimited, 1985. 163 pp. ISBN 0-87287-477-X.

Schon, Isabel, *A Hispanic Heritage: A Guide to Juvenile Books about Hispanic People and Cultures.* Metuchen, NJ: Scarecrow Press, 1980. 178 pp. ISBN 0-8108-1290-8.

Schon, Isabel. *Books in Spanish for Children and Young Adults: An Annotated Guide, Series II.* Metuchen, NJ: Scarecrow Press, 1983. 174 pp. ISBN 0-8108-1620-2.

Schon, Isabel, *Books in Spanish for Children and Young Adults: An Annotated Guide, Series III.* Metuchen, NJ: Scarecrow Press, 1985, 208 pp. ISBN 0-8108-1807-8.

Schon, Isabel. *Books in Spanish for Children and Young Adults: An Annotated Guide, Series IV.* Metuchen, NJ: Scarecrow Press, 1987. 301 pp. ISBN 0-8108-2004-8.

Schon, Isabel, *A Hispanic Heritage, Series II: A Guide to Juvenile Books about Hispanic People and Cultures.* Metuchen, NJ: Scarecrow Press, 1985. 164 pp. ISBN 0-8108-1727-6.

Schon, Isabel. *Basic Collection of Children's Books in Spanish.* Metuchen, NJ: Scarecrow Press, 1986. 240 pp. ISBN 0-8108-1904-X.

Catalogues

Children's Press
Libros en español para niños
1224 West Van Buren Street
Chicago, IL 60607
1-800-621-1115

Hispanic Books Distributors, Inc.
1665 W. Grant Rd.
Tucson, AZ 85745
602-882-9484

DLM Teaching Resources
55 W. 13th Street
New York, NY 10011
212-627-0099

Gessler Publishing Co.
900 Broadway
New York, NY 10003
212-673-3113

Scholastic
Spanish Big Books, Book Collections,
 Wordless Big Books
PO Box 7520
Jefferson City, MO 65102
1-800-325-6149

Lectorum Publications, Inc.
137 West 14th Street
New York, NY 10011
212-929-3833

Claudia's Caravan
Multicultural Multilingual Materials
PO Box 1582
Alameda, CA 94501
510-521-7871

Newsletters

Scholastic Language Newsletters
¿Qué Tal?; El Sol; Hoy Dia
Scholastic Inc.
PO Box 644
Lyndhurst, NJ 07071-9985

El Informador
Fiesta Publishing Co.
PO Box 9609
San Diego, CA 92019

La Luz
Alan Company
230 South Berniston
Clayton, MI 63105

FIGURE 13.2
Sources for culturally and linguistically based Spanish reading materials
Source: From "Do Spanish methods and materials reflect current understanding of the reading process?" Yvonne S. Freeman, **The Reading Teacher,** March 1988, p. 660. Reprinted with permission of Yvonne S. Freeman and the International Reading Association.

what they learn at school and their daily life encounters, schools must include a larger multicultural selection of literature in their curriculums.

Whole-language-based teaching encourages production of student-generated stories (Freppon, 1995). The stories help develop students' self-concept simply by the creation of their own works. The language-experience approach and a process approach to writing offer students an excellent way of developing skills that integrate cooperation—fostering story writing and peer interaction strategies for language and content learning (Godina, 1996). Promoting story writing by second-language learners will create a literate classroom with students enthusiastic about reading and writing. Allowing students to read and write every day about their own experiences enhances literacy skills and the desire to learn. Positive literacy experiences involving reading promote students who learn to enjoy reading and begin to seek out more information to accomplish classroom tasks in the early grades.

■ The Literature-based Reading Approach: Integrating Multiethnic Literature

Banks (1994) emphasizes the importance of our becoming a more diverse nation that is accepting and tolerant of others. In order for our country to develop an understanding and tolerance of others, we will have to become educated about other people's cultural heritages. One of the easiest ways to accomplish this task is to incorporate multiethnic literature into our schools.

An important aspect of a literature-based reading program is the use of multiethnic literature to enhance reading. Multiethnic literature helps students discover the intricacies of a language, as well as its people's history and culture (Bieger, 1996; Godina, 1996; Norton, 1995). In addition, when students read literature, they encounter a multitude of characters who are both similar to and different from themselves (Norton, 1995). Each character of a story is driven by certain emotions and must deal with the problems and joys of life in various ways. How the heroes and heroines react and cope provides students with insights and information well beyond their own personal experiences.

Integrating multiethnic literature into a school curriculum for second-language learners helps students realize that all ethnic groups have roots in the past and a strong heritage that is a part of their culture (Bieger, 1996). Knowing about others from a similar culture develops a sense of pride that builds a positive self-concept for students. They may discover by reading that others from their own culture made significant contributions to society. Students encountering multiethnic literature as a part of their reading curriculum benefit academically and learn the social values and behaviors of people in society (Bieger, 1996; Godina, 1996).

Existing reading programs can easily integrate multiethnic literature for explicit reading instruction. Teachers can share stories both orally and in written form, and instruction can coordinate language arts exercises such as vocabulary, comprehension, writing, and language development in both the first and second languages. Using literature such as the story "Bums in the Attic," from *The House on Mango Street* by Sandra Cisneros, is an excellent way of increasing cultural awareness, building vocabulary and language, developing comprehension skills, and providing writing opportunities. The language used in the story provides the opportunity for creating a lesson on figurative language, such as similes and idioms. Also, the story's symbolism uses concrete or familiar objects and images to represent abstract and unfamiliar ideas, such as "people who live on hills sleep so close to the stars they forget those of us who live too much on Earth." Idioms such as "stuck up" are often difficult for second-language learners to learn and understand. Stories that integrate context with idiomatic expressions help students understand meaning. The story just described has many aspects of language teaching that enhances the development of language and stimulates interest in reading.

The introduction of activities to expand vocabulary and conceptual knowledge can be supplemented by using literature as a means of bridging reading and language development for second-language learners (Freeman & Freeman, 1993). Class discussions, role play, and brainstorming are all activities in which students can participate, increase their background knowledge, and enrich their reading abilities. Vocabulary webs provide another rich source of language development. A literature web provides students with a way of organizing their thoughts and generating new ideas and vocabulary as related to the story. Numerous activities expose students to the different linguistic and cultural components of various stories. Teachers and students can build a classroom library of literature resources to teach reading while increasing students' level of cultural awareness and expanding their social and emotional awareness by exposure to new and different styles of living and thinking.

Banks (1989) discusses four levels that are used to integrate ethnic content into the curriculum. He cautions teachers that the lowest levels of integration are the "contributions approach" and the "ethnic additive approach." Teachers who use only the contributions approach have their students read only about the contributions of ethnic groups such as ethnic holidays, heroes, and customs. The ethnic additive approach does add content, concepts, and themes that reflect diverse cultures, but it does not integrate these into the existing curriculum. Instead, it may become a unit that is taught for a month out of the year and then forgotten. Banks encourages teachers to use the two highest levels of multicultural integration (the "transformation approach" and the "social action approach") when designing the curriculum. Teachers who use the transformation approach completely reconstruct the curriculum in order to allow students to view concerns, themes, problems, and concepts from the perspective of multiethnic groups. This is not a unit that lasts a month, but instead is a commitment to multiculturalism throughout the whole year. The highest form of cultural integration is the social action approach. In this approach, teachers select literature that allows students to identify social problems and concerns and to read about how the main characters made decisions and took action to solve the problems. Through the modeling of the characters' actions, students learn how to identify and resolve problems related to cultural differences.

■ The Oral Reading Approach

A reading approach developed for linguistically diverse students that is popular in New Zealand and the South Pacific stresses high interest in reading through the use of short stories with natural language and some vocabulary control for

Integrating multiethnic literature into a school curriculum helps students realize that all ethnic groups have roots in the past and a strong heritage that is part of their culture.

repetition. Norton (1995) believes that books that include repetitive language are excellent for oral reading. The teacher reads the story to the group, then the teacher and students chorally reread the story in unison. They discuss the story and read it once again. In this approach, the teacher selects individual words and phrases and emphasizes choral reading (all or several students reading in unison). Research has noted significant results in comprehension and word recognition for students with limited English proficiency who were taught with this method.

Choral reading has also been used successfully in promoting language learning for linguistically diverse students. The benefits of using choral reading to enhance children's acquisition of a second language are that it (1) creates a low-anxiety environment, (2) provides repeated practice, (3) is based on comprehensible input, and (4) incorporates drama (McCauley & McCauley, 1992).

Implementing choral reading for second-language learners begins with identifying poems and adapting them for students. Poems should cover familiar topics that students can relate to. For second-language learners, the poems should contain a lot of action and allow lines to be added to help clarify vocabulary and emphasize meaning.

After the poem has been selected and adapted, McCauley and McCauley (1992) suggest the following general procedure:

1. Give a quick, interesting introduction. Focus on getting students involved in talking about the poem.
2. Read the poem aloud to students. Use expression, sound effects, and movements that the poem could represent.
3. Make copies of the poem available to the students.
4. Read the poem again to the students as they follow along.
5. Read the poem with the students slowly at first, and gradually increase the speed of reading. Appropriate movements and sound effects also should be included.
6. Give lines to the students when they feel comfortable with the words and movements. Students who want solo lines may be given them.
7. Practice reading the poem with assigned parts.
8. Recognize a job well done with applause, verbal praise, or both.

An example (McCauley & McCauley, 1992) of how movement and drama are added to "Jack and Jill" is presented next. This acting-out part of choral reading is very important for second-language learners, because it aids in construction of meaning and helps text become more meaningful for them.

(Boys, as they stand)	Jack
(Girls, as they stand)	and Jill
(All, walking)	went up the hill to fetch a pail of water
(Boys)	Jack fell down and broke his crown
	Ouch! (Hold head)
(Girls)	And Jill came tumbling after.
	(Lean toward boys, hand gesture—i.e., hand on side of cheek—as if worried about Jack's fate, and say) Are you all right, Jack?
(Boys)	(While rubbing head) Yeah.
(Girls)	(While wiping forehead in relief) Whew!

Choral reading can be done with the whole class and ensures success for linguistically diverse students. It promotes positive attitudes toward both second-language acquisition and reading.

■ The Basal Reader Approach

Basal reading programs are still used throughout the United States, and teachers of linguistically diverse students often choose to use them to teach reading. However, teachers should be aware of special considerations when using basal readers as the main method for teaching reading, especially to linguistically diverse students. Among these considerations are (1) special attention to developing background concepts and vocabulary in depth before reading, (2) skillful questioning during silent reading to identify and clear up misunderstandings and to enhance the students' comprehension, and (3) specific emphasis on listening to the language rather than on oral reading. These three considerations are important to all reading approaches and should be considered when developing any reading plan. Linguistically diverse students often worry about having to read orally, so they may not concentrate on the language they hear, particularly in group situations. Keeping in mind the special instructional considerations, teachers may find that linguistically diverse students can progress with their classmates in a basal reading program.

Today, many of the basal series have integrated a literature approach to teaching reading and have become more sensitive to teaching reading skills in the context of the literature (Elderedge, Reutzel, & Hollingsworth, 1996). They have also shifted their design to include more shared reading approaches, rather than just directed reading approaches (Hoffman et al., 1993). However, an alternative to using only a basal reader program for instruction is to use basal readers and literature together in teaching literacy. Some individuals (Delpit, 1991) have indicated that culturally and linguistically diverse students may need a bridge from the basal series to a more process-focused literature-based program. Combining features of direct/explicit instruction with literature of the home culture of students from diverse backgrounds may benefit students.

Morrow (1992) conducted research in second-grade classrooms on how an integrated basal and literature-based reading program affected the literacy achievement of culturally diverse children. The features of her integrated program included the following:

1. Literacy centers within each classroom that provided students with access to a variety of books and literacy materials. Included in the centers were multiple genres of children's literature, comfortable seating, and manipulatives (felt stories, roll movies, and taped stories).

2. Teacher-guided activities that helped students understand what they could do and should do. Included in the activities were teachers' use of modeling and scaffolding, the use of the directed reading-thinking activity (DRTA), and retellings using both books and props (felt stories, puppets, and roll movies).

3. Independent reading and writing periods were used to allow students to choose between working alone or with others, and to select from a

variety of activities ranging from retelling to dramatizing stories. The basal reader portion of the literacy instruction was continued with the inclusion of the literature-based reading instruction.

Morrow's study showed that students from diverse backgrounds had improved literacy achievement. Concerns about whether students from diverse backgrounds would benefit from integrating the basal reader approach with a literature-based approach were unfounded. Components of the program that might account for its success were teachers demonstrating, facilitating, and participating in literature activities with high expectations for their students. In addition, the program featured literature that reflected the various cultural backgrounds found in the classrooms.

■ The Dialect Approach

The **dialect approach** teaches reading using materials written in the student's dialect. Research has not supported the use of reading materials written in the African American dialect, however.

Reading taught using standard materials takes dialectal and cultural differences among students into account. Currently, the best approach appears to be a conventional one, with enlightened teachers who are sensitive to students' motivations, values, backgrounds, and aspirations and who have a knowledge of the features of nonstandard dialects.

■ The Dual-language Reading Approach

Many bilingual programs provide reading instruction in the students' primary language as well as in standard English (e.g., Spanish and English). Gonzales (1994) found this to be an effective approach to reading instruction. Many of the bilingual programs in the southwestern United States teach reading with Spanish basal programs.

Research (Weber, 1991) indicates that some instructional practices in and beliefs about teaching reading may be counterproductive to reading and language development of linguistically diverse students. Many programs use only phonics to teach reading to students with limited English proficiency (as demonstrated by many Spanish basal reading programs). Teachers of linguistically diverse students often think that a phonics approach is the only way to teach reading to second-language learners. One need only observe readers both inside and outside a classroom to confirm that this is not so. If children's concept knowledge in their first language is limited, this inhibits their realization that print represents meaningful language (Neuman & Koskinen, 1992). Instruction that focuses only on decoding words in English limits students' opportunities to realize that reading conveys meaning.

Second-language learners benefit from reading programs that incorporate a range of contexts, both social and functional, in which reading begins and develops. Adapting several reading approaches can help linguistically diverse students become effective, efficient users of written English.

The **dual-language reading approach** makes use of native language and literacy skills to strengthen the reading process of speakers whose English is limited. Primary language reading materials, trade books, basal texts, and other instructional materials help strengthen bilingual reading programs. In addition, reading activities develop cognitive structures, vocabulary, comprehension strategies, and higher cognitive levels. This focus is important for a smooth transition from first-language to second-language reading.

Expanding and Developing Meaning Vocabulary

Linguistically diverse students need to develop a large base of immediately recognizable words for fluent reading (Brisbois, 1995). They come to school already knowing words related to logos, advertisements, and print in their environment. They see print everywhere—at home, on television, while shopping, and along highways, to mention a few—that can serve as a foundation for developing language-experience stories, writing stories, and learning other words.

Another approach that enables linguistically diverse students to acquire vocabulary in the second language is simply through the process of reading. This would suggest that a literature-based approach, an integrated language approach, or features of either combined with a basal reader approach would be more successful in expanding vocabulary than would learning words in isolation.

Teachers can choose words from the students' language-experience stories, discussions of stories read, writing activities, and environmental print. Words selected for the students should be familiar ones. Choral reading, which was presented earlier, can also enhance and expand second-language learners' vocabulary (Sampson, Allen, & Sampson, 1991). Students are more likely to recognize a word in print when they can recognize either how the word functions or what it represents.

Special Students

Addressing individual student needs in reading instruction has always been an enormous task. Providing appropriate instruction for individuals within a large group demands many long hours of planning and hard work by teachers. Today, with the implementation of the Individuals with Disabilities Act (IDEA), teachers are adapting their classrooms to accommodate individual needs and to provide appropriate education for special students.

Special students are those who have special needs. Included among this group are physically disabled, emotionally disabled, learning disabled, and gifted students. Special students may or may not have learning difficulties; however, they often require special teaching. Such teaching is intended to ensure that special students are successful learners.

■ Mainstreaming

In 1975, P.L. 94-142 (the Education for all Handicapped Children Act) was passed. This was one of the most significant developments in U.S. education. This law affected the placement of students with disabilities into the public schools. It allowed for students with disabilities to be mainstreamed into regular classrooms. Children with disabilities must be placed in the "least restrictive environment," which is interpreted, in many cases, to be the same environment as that for regular students. This trend to educate children with disabilities in the closest possible proximity to the regular classroom in which the child can succeed is often referred to as **mainstreaming.** Lewis and Doorlag (1991) define mainstreaming as the

> inclusion of special students in the general educational process. Students are considered mainstreamed if they spend any part of the school day with regular class peers. In a typical mainstreaming program, special students in regular classrooms participate in instructional and social activities side by side with their classmates. Often they receive additional instruction outside the regular classroom from a special educator such as a resource teacher. (pp. 3–4)

A critical concern for a classroom teacher is, Who is going to be placed in my classroom? P.L. 94-142 defines disabled students as those who are mentally retarded, hard of hearing, deaf, speech impaired, other health impaired, deaf-blind, multihandicapped, seriously emotionally disturbed, orthopedically impaired, visually impaired, or having specific learning disabilities, who because of those impairments need special education and related services (Sec. 121 a. 530-121 a. 534). Given these components, how might a mainstreamed classroom operate? Johnson (1987) provides the following description:

> Exceptional students spend most of the day in regular classrooms, leaving occasionally to go to a resource room or resource center for educational assessments, individual tutoring, or small group instruction, or to pick up and deliver assignments prepared by the resource teacher but completed in the regular classroom. The resource teacher and the regular classroom teacher, working as a team, may schedule a student to use the resource center for a few minutes or several hours, depending on the student's learning needs. The regular classroom teacher and the resource teacher share responsibility for the learning and socialization of the exceptional students, and both take an active instructional role. The exceptional students spend more than half the day in regular classes. While the regular classroom teacher is responsible for grades and report cards, she will usually consult with the resource teacher in giving exceptional students grades. (p. 425)

In 1990, P.L. 94-142 was ammended to allow for provisions and changes to the terminology of the act, which caused the new act, the Individuals with Disabilities Act, to reflect a more sensitive approach to the individual, rather than highlighting the disability (First & Curcio, 1993).

As part of the concern for the individual, mainstreaming in general has been examined. Students who have typically been mainstreamed into regular classrooms are often involved in many pull-out programs such as Chapter I. This frag-

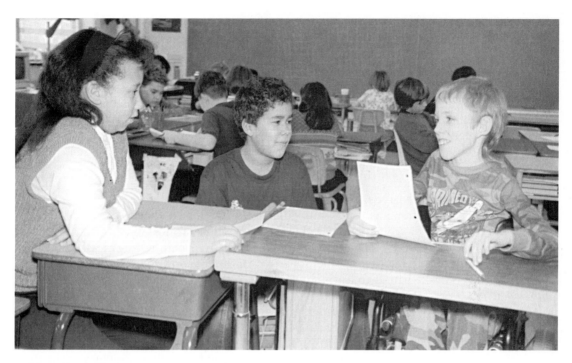

Addressing individual student needs in literacy has always been an important consideration.

mentation of the school day has caused some concern for the individual and raised the question, Is this the best instructional setting for the special-needs child? Educators have turned to inclusion for the answer to this question. **Inclusion** means that special-needs students are assigned to regular classrooms for the full instructional day and are allowed to participate in all school activities and functions. This type of inclusive atmosphere requires adequate support systems. Classrooms must be made physically accessible to accommodate all special-needs students. In addition to the physical setting, provisions need to be made for additional personnel, staff development, and technical assistance. This may mean that in addition to the regular classroom teacher, a special-education teacher will be made available to co-teach the entire class. It is important that the special-education teacher be involved in the instruction of the whole class so that students do not become overly aware of students with special needs (Friend & Cook, 1992).

For inclusion to work, teachers need to create a classroom atmosphere in which differences are addressed up front and accepted by everyone in the class. The students in the class are as much responsible for the success of inclusion as are the classroom and special-education teacher. One way to ensure student involvement in the inclusion process is to use cooperative groups as an instructional strategy. By allowing students to work cooperatively in groups, all students share in the contributions to the learning process and develop a positive attitude toward individual differences.

The success of students placed in the least restrictive environment depends upon the cooperation of teachers, administrators, specialized personnel, and parents. In essence, however, individual teachers' ability to accommodate all students in the regular classroom determines the success or failure of such efforts. Implications for reading teachers are clear—they must employ a variety of instructional and organizational techniques to suit a wide range of student abilities and encourage the constructive interaction of special students with regular students. Teachers should use the following guidelines, adapted from Mohr (1995), when teaching literacy to special students who exhibit learning difficulties:

1. Observe the student in authentic settings. Assess the student's learning strengths, styles, and differences, and the conditions of any disability or differences that may interfere with learning.
2. Teach to a student's strengths while remediating weaknesses and developing compensation skills. Do not allow the disability to become a barrier to learning.
3. Restructure a task when a student cannot master it. Change the way the task is presented or change the method of response.
4. Check understanding of the content material or directions by following up with a specific question. Avoid asking, "Do you understand?"
5. Repeat or rephrase what is being said in the classroom by varying the vocabulary and the mode of presentation or method of instruction.
6. Give both oral and written directions and provide both visual and auditory cues for directions and instructions.
7. Be aware of auditory and visual distractions in the classroom. Even subtle ones can be very distracting to some students, such as sitting near the window or a pencil sharpener.
8. Provide help through peer teaching or the buddy system. Provide reinforcement for newly learned or previously learned skills by allowing the student with differences to become a peer tutor to another student who is just beginning to learn a skill.
9. Include all students in classroom activities and projects. Minimize the differences and maximize the similarities during classroom participation.
10. Match a student's learning style with appropriate selection of methods and materials. Use learning styles and strengths of all learners in the classroom as tools for planning instruction.
11. Evaluate students by their individual performance without lowering the standards for the class. Investigate evaluation alternatives to ensure success and not failure.
12. Manage behavior positively, consistently, and assertively. Set limits, structure consequences, and follow through! The use of logical consequences, natural reinforcers, contingency contracting, praise, encouragement, and recognition will help structure success for all students. Some students with disabilities and learning differences may need differential discipline considerations.

The preceding guidelines suggest that most children with learning difficulties are not in need of specialized techniques, but simply good instruction. Indeed, the similarities between special children and so-called normal children are greater than the differences. Labeling children (emotionally disturbed, mentally retarded, learning disabled, and so forth) tells teachers next to nothing about how to develop an appropriate instructional program. A positive aspect of the Individuals with Disabilities Act (IDEA) is that it shifts the focus away from use of labels (which are usually negative and counterproductive) and toward consideration of students' educational needs.

No mystique should surround teaching of special children. These students, like all students, require instruction that emphasizes present achievement level, determination of student strengths and weaknesses, and appropriate approaches and materials. Many students carrying a label have been misdiagnosed and misplaced for years in school systems. Instruction should be based on student needs, not labels. Teachers can avoid the negative effects of labeling students by simply viewing these children as different. After all, nothing is more basic in teaching than learning how to deal with differences in individual students. Next time you come across a label, such as *dyslexic,* instead of saying "Oh no, how can I work with someone who is dyslexic?" try saying "Dyslexic—so what! What do I need to do to help this child learn to his or her fullest potential?"

■ The Individualized Education Plan (IEP)

The vehicle for providing the most appropriate educational program for many special students is an individualized education plan (IEP). An **IEP** is a written plan for each special child, detailing his or her educational program. In accordance with the Individuals with Disabilities Act (IDEA), the IEP must include the following:

- ■ The student's present achievement level, including the student's strengths, weaknesses, and learning styles.
- ■ A statement of annual goals.
- ■ A listing of long-range and short-term instructional objectives that include the materials, strategies, and assessment measures to indicate mastery of the objectives.
- ■ A statement detailing specific special educational services to be provided to the student and the extent to which the student will participate in the regular classroom.
- ■ The classroom accommodations that need to be made in order to provide general teaching techniques and subject matter modifications to enable the child to learn to his or her potential.
- ■ Identification of the person(s) (or agents) responsible for teaching each objective.
- ■ Project data for the beginning of program services and the anticipated duration of the services.

The IEP is an educational program that the multidisciplinary team, which includes the school, teachers, children, and parents, develop jointly (see Figure 13.3). Because many children with disabilities spend part or most of the day in

INDIVIDUALIZED EDUCATION PLAN (IEP)

Identification Information

Name James S.

School C. L. Bishop

Birthdate 9/2/84 Grade 2nd

Parents' Names H. R. and Betty S.

Address 1029 Langley Avenue

Lawrence, KS 66044

Phone: Home 841-0920 Office 869-4098

Continuum of Services

	Hours Per Week	Dates
Regular class	23	9/28/91-6/2/91
Resource teacher in regular classroom		
Resource room	5	9/29/91-6/2/92
Reading specialist		
Speech/language therapist		
Counselor		
Special class		
Transition class		
Others:		
Counseling	2	9/30/91-5/29/92

Yearly Class Schedule

Time	Subject	Teacher
9:00	Language Arts	Miller
10:45	Math	Miller
11:30	Social Studies	Miller
12:00	Lunch	
1:00	Science	Miller
2:00	Resource Reading	Houston

Testing Information

Test Name	Date Admin.	Interpretation
Stanford-Binet	9/13/88	low average range
Key Math	9/15/88	functioning on 1.8 level
Zaner-Bloser	9/22/88	scored "low for grade" difficulty copying
Slingerland	9/20/88	near & far points
Physical exam	8/15/88	mild paralysis left hand seizure prone
Disability Area		Physical Disability

Checklist

9-2   Referral by Mrs. Jenkins

9-8   Parents informed of rights; permission obtained for evaluation

9-21 Evaluation compiled

9-24 Parents contacted

9-26 IEP committee meeting held

9-26 IEP completed

9-26 Parent consent notification

9-27 Placement made

Committee Members

Teacher
Lew Ashley

Other LEA representative
Lois Seibler

Parents
Mrs. Betty S

Date IEP initially approved

Health Information

Vision: Normal

Hearing: Normal

Physical: Normal

Other: Medication-tegratol

FIGURE 13.3
Individualized education plan

Source: Reprinted with the permission of Merrill, an imprint of Prentice Hall from **Developing and Implementing Individualized Education Programs,** Third Edition, by Bonnie B. Strickland and Ann P. Turnbull. Copyright © 1990 by Merrill/Prentice Hall.

INDIVIDUAL EDUCATION PLAN (IEP)

Student's Name __James S.__   Subject Area __Handwriting__   Teacher __Houston/Miller__

Level of Performance __recognizes all manuscript letters; exhibits__
__proper sitting & writing position; can write 7–10 letters per__
__minute; makes frequent erasures; handwriting is often__
__illegible, slow, and laborious.__

Annual Goals __Print legibly all letters of alphabet (upper- and__
__lower-case); write numerals 1–10 with no erasures; write 35__
__letters per minute with 4 or less erasures.__

	September	October	November	December	January
Objectives	referral/evaluation, IEP development	1. Following a model, writes legibly letters: Aa, Cc, Dd, Ee, Gg, Oo 2. Following a model, writes legibly numbers 1–5 3. Following a model, writes legibly his first name 4. Writes legibly 10 letters per minute with 50% or less erasures	1. Following a model, writes legibly letters: Bb, Pp, Qq, Uu, Mm, Nn, Hh 2. Writes legibly numerals 1–5–no model 3. Writes legibly first name–no model 4. Writes legibly 13 letters per minute with 45% or less erasures	1. Following a model, writes legibly letters: Ll, Tt, Ff, Kk, Ii, Jj 2. Writes legibly numerals 6–10 with a model 3. Writes legibly last name with a model 4. Writes legibly 14 letters per minute with 40% or less erasures	1. Following a model, writes entire alphabet legibly 2. Writes legibly numerals 6–10–no model 3. Writes legibly first and last name–no model 4. Writes legibly 19 letters per minute with 35% or less erasures
Special Materials		"Beginning to Learn Fine Motor Skills" by Thurstone & Lillie			
Evaluation Agent		1,4–Houston 2,3–Miller			
		Informal assessment 80% accuracy of objectives 1–3 on 3 consecutive days			

FIGURE 13.3, continued

INDIVIDUAL EDUCATION PLAN (IEP)

Student's Name ___James S.___   Subject Area ___Handwriting___   Teacher ___Houston/Miller___

Level of Performance ___recognizes all manuscript letters; exhibits proper sitting & writing position; can write 7–10 letters per minute, makes erasures 50%–60% of time; handwriting is often illegible___

Annual Goals ___Print legibly all letters of alphabet (upper and lower-case); write numerals 1–10 with no erasures; write 35 letters per minute with 10% or less erasures___

	February	March	April	May	June
Objectives	1. Following a model, writes the entire alphabet legibly 2. Writes legibly numerals 1–10 in math lesson with 4 or less erasures 3. Writes legibly first and last names on all class assignments 4. Writes legibly 23 letters per minute with 30% or less erasures	1. Writes legibly Aa, Cc, Dd, Ee, Gg, Oo, Bb, Pp from dictation 2. Writes legibly numerals 1–10 in math lessons with 2 or less erasures 3. Writes 28 letters per minute with 20% or less erasures	1. Writes legibly Qq, Uu, Mm, Nn, Hh, Ll, Tt from dictation 2. Writes legibly numerals 1–10 in math lessons with 1 or less erasures 3. Writes 30 letters per minute with 20% or less erasures	1. Writes entire alphabet from dictation 2. Writes legibly numerals 1–10 with no erasures 3. Writes 35 letters per minute with 10% or less erasures	

Special Materials

"Beginning to Learn Fine Motor Skills" by Thurstone & Lillie

Evaluation Agent

1, 4–Houston
2, 3–Miller

1, 3–Houston
2–Miller

Evaluation

Informal assessment 80% accuracy of objectives 1–3 on 3 consecutive days

Informal assessment 80% accuracy of objectives 1–2 on 3 consecutive days

Informal assessment 80% accuracy of objectives 1–2 on 3 consecutive days

FIGURE 13.3, continued

◀IIII FLASHBACK

Special education has undergone a varied and at times rapid transformation relative to service delivery. Maria Montessori (1870–1952), a noted Italian developmentalist and physician, was perhaps the first to introduce innovative and effective instructional strategies for exceptional and disadvantaged children. Her methods and instructional philosophy clearly influenced the development of early childhood programs for exceptional children in the United States. The practices of heterogeneous grouping, experiential education, and structured learning environments support the basis of inclusive schooling for all children.

UPI/Bettman Newsphotos.

UPDATE IIII▶

Inclusion, an evolutionary concept, is based upon the concept that separate is not equal and that given appropriate services, the integration of youth serves both an educational and legal mandate. Each decade since the 1950's has offered an ever-increasing normalized learning environment for children with disabilities. To identify one or two individuals who best represent inclusion would certainly be misguided. From early normalization, through deinstitutionalization, least restrictive environment, mainstreaming, and the regular education initiative, the inclusive movement is clearly a paradigm shift that is shared and nurtured by many. The 1990's will undoubtedly be noted for its emphasis on inclusive schooling and the rights of all children to be educated together. Our recollection of Montessori not only underscores the importance of her numerous contributions, but perhaps more importantly stresses the need to integrate socialization skills with the academic needs for all children.

Note: Contributed by Dr. Michael W. Churton, Professor of Special Education, University of South Florida, Tampa, Florida.

the regular classroom, the classroom teacher must be involved in developing the IEP. As shown in Figure 13.3, the basic ingredients of an IEP are not new—they are essentially those of a good teaching plan (pretest objectives, teaching to those objectives, and the posttest). It is important to avoid thinking of inclusion (or least restrictive environment) as separate or different from the basic principles associated with any good learning environment. The principles of a quality learning environment include all aspects of an IEP, and thus the process of equal education for all children. Although many problems remain unsettled regarding the implementation of P.L. 94-142, cooperative interaction among teachers, students, parents, specialized personnel, and administrators in placing every individual in a setting in which he or she may succeed will yield benefits for all students.

■ Attention-deficit Hyperactivity Disorder (ADHD)

In today's classrooms, many children are described as having difficulty staying on task and maintaining attention. Teachers often use the label *attention-deficit hyperactivity disorder* (ADHD) to describe this behavior. While some teachers may describe their whole class as being ADHD, Neuwirth (1994) and the ERIC Digest (1996) state that only 3 to 5% of our school-age population is affected by attention-deficit hyperactivity disorder, which amounts to about one student per class. This disorder is the most frequently occuring disorder affecting our school-age children. According to Fowler (1994) **attention-deficit hyperactivity disorder** is a syndrome in which the learner is characterized by having serious and persistent difficulties in the following three areas:

1. attention span
2. impulse control
3. hyperactivity

Students with ADHD in the past were often referred to as having hyperkinesis, a minimal brain disorder, hyperactivity, or a learning disability. Even though ADHD may be a relatively new term, the disorder has been found in the medical literature for over 100 years (Fowler, 1994). The American Psychiatric Association (1994) has stated that in order for a child to be diagnosed with attention-deficit hyperactivity disorder, he or she must display for 6 months or more at least 8 of the following 14 characteristics prior to the age of 7:

1. Fidgets, squirms, or seems restless.
2. Has difficulty remaining seated.
3. Is easily distracted.
4. Has difficulty awaiting turn.
5. Blurts out answers.
6. Has difficulty following instructions.
7. Has difficulty sustaining attention.
8. Shifts from one uncompleted task to another.
9. Has difficulty playing quietly.
10. Talks excessively.
11. Interrupts or intrudes on others.

12. Does not seem to listen.

13. Often loses things necessary for tasks.

14. Frequently engages in dangerous actions.

Obviously, children displaying these characteristics may demonstrate difficulties in the areas of learning to read and write. To help treat this condition, doctors often prescribe stimulants such as Ritalin to help reduce hyperactivity and improve the student's ability to focus, work, and learn (Neuwirth, 1994). According to Neuwirth (1994) the use of medication has sparked quite a debate. Many critics feel that medication is often prescribed unnecessarily and that some students on medication often experience weight loss, grow at slower rates, and have difficulty with their sleep patterns. On the other hand, many children with ADHD have been helped tremendously by proper medication. If doctors carefully monitor a child's height, weight, and overall development, the use of medication to help control ADHD appears to be extremely beneficial to the student, and the positive results far outweigh the potential side effects.

While the use of medication is one way to help manage the behavior of the ADHD child, teachers can also provide behavioral support by following these recommendations, presented in *The Diagnostic and Statistical Manual of Mental Disorders* (1994):

1. Seat students with ADHD near the teacher's desk, but include them as part of the regular class seating.

2. Place ADHD students up front with their backs to the rest of the class to keep other students out of view.

3. Surround students with ADHD with good role models, preferably students whom they view as significant others. Encourage peer tutoring and cooperative/collaborative learning.

4. Avoid distracting stimuli. Try not to place students with ADHD near air conditioners, high-traffic areas, heaters, doors, or windows.

5. Children with ADHD do not handle change well, so avoid transitions, physical relocation (monitor them closely on field trips), changes in schedule, and disruptions.

6. Be creative! Produce a stimuli-reduced study area. Let all students have access to this area so the student with ADHD will not feel different.

7. Encourage parents to set up appropriate study space at home, with set times and routines established for study, parental review of completed homework, and periodic notebook and or bookbag organization.

In addition to these environmental features, teachers can also help ADHD students by doing the following:

1. Maintain eye contact during verbal instruction.

2. Make directions clear and concise and be consistent with daily instructions.

3. Simplify complex directions and avoid multiple commands.

4. Make sure students comprehend the instructions before beginning the task.

5. Repeat instructions in a calm, positive manner if needed.

6. Help the students feel comfortable with seeking assistance (most children with ADHD will not ask for help).
7. Gradually reduce scaffolding, but keep in mind that these students may need more scaffolding for a longer period of time than the average child.
8. Require a daily assignment notebook if necessary.

Teachers who are willing to modify their instruction to meet the needs of the ADHD child will help these students realize their potential and allow them to experience success that may have seemed unattainable in the past.

■ Gifted Students

A renewed thrust in the public schools is the development of programs for **gifted students.** In 1972, U.S. Commissioner of Education Sidney Marland defined the gifted and talented as "those identified by professionally qualified persons who by virtue of outstanding abilities are capable of high performance. These are children who require differentiated educational programs and/or services beyond those normally provided by the regular school program in order to realize their contribution to self and society" (p. 16). The U.S. Office of Education identified six areas of giftedness: (1) general intellectual ability, (2) specific academic aptitude, (3) creativity, (4) leadership ability, (5) ability in the visual or performing arts, and (6) psychomotor ability. Gifted students may demonstrate capability of exceptional performance in only one or two areas.

With specific reference to reading abilities, Shaughnessy, Siegel, and Stanley (1994) and Dooley (1993) noted that gifted students' cognitive skills are advanced beyond the activities and materials normally provided for students at their age and grade level. Common reading capabilities and behaviors of gifted students include the following:

1. A rich, well-developed vocabulary and interest in words.
2. Early reading ability prior to entering school.
3. An advanced linguistic ability in sentence construction, expression of ideas, and listening vocabulary.
4. An interest in library books and reading in a variety of topic areas.
5. An early interest in learning to write and in writing creative stories.
6. Frequent use of information sources, such as the dictionary, encyclopedia, and information texts, to explore ideas and areas of interest.
7. An enhanced ability in the area of critical thinking.
8. An inquisitive nature.
9. Comprehension abilities at early grade levels that exceed the literal level and demonstrate an understanding of the relationship of ideas.
10. Well-developed reading skills and abilities by the end of first grade.

Identifying gifted children and designing a curriculum to accommodate their learning needs should be accomplished through a variety of formal and informal assessment procedures. Standardized achievement tests, intelligence tests, creativity measures, actual student performance in the reading program, peer nomination procedures, and parent and teacher observations are avenues to employ for this purpose. Also, giftedness is not reserved for any one group or class of children. Teachers should not be preoccupied with ethnicity or social characteristics when identifying the gifted and talented.

For too long, gifted children were expected to be silent and follow along with the regular curriculum designed for less-able students. Many reading program administrators are realizing that gifted children have unique needs, as do all students, and require differentiated instructional programs. Gifted readers are not all the same; each has unique strengths and weaknesses. As such, gifted readers need the same diagnostically based instruction afforded all learners (Shaughnessy et al., 1994). Indeed, many gifted children are "disabled" readers when their performance is compared to their potential. Gifted children require an instructional program that reflects their needs.

There are several avenues available to meet gifted readers' needs in the classroom. One way to enhance the gifted student's reading performance is to make use of curriculum compacting (Dooley, 1993). Curriculum compacting assures student mastery of basic skills at a proficient rate to make time for enrichment and acceleration. To make use of curriculum compacting, the teacher must develop an assessment measure that will allow him or her to identify those skills and content areas that the student has already mastered for the next reading unit. Once the skills and content have been identified as already mastered, the teacher does not have to provide instructional activities in those areas. This allows the teacher to concentrate on undeveloped skills and content and provide additional enrichment activities without losing any instructional time. This form of instruction allows the gifted student to progress through reading materials at an appropriate pace (Dooley, 1993).

Another instructional approach suggested for the gifted child by Dooley (1993) is referred to as *content modification.* Content modification allows the gifted reader to read more-complex and in-depth selections. The selections that the gifted student reads can be related to the same theme, topic, or genre of the regular classroom instruction. For example, if students are studying World War II, all students might be encouraged to read *The Diary of Anne Frank* during reading instruction. In addition to *The Diary of Anne Frank,* the gifted child might also read *Zlata's Diary* so that he or she could make connections between the way Jewish people of Nazi Germany suffered and the way the Bosnians of Sarajevo suffered. This type of content modification allows gifted students more control over their academic content.

In addition to content modification, Dooley (1993) also suggests process modification. Process modification is implemented through activities and questions that require higher-level thought used in critical and creative reading comprehension. Process modification that requires students to become critical readers allows students to make judgements about the authenticity, accuracy, and validity of what they read. One way to help all students become more creative and critical readers is by effective questioning strategies and the use of reading guides.

Although research supports compacting the curriculum, content modification, and process modification, many teachers do not use these approaches. One underlying reason for this lack of implementation is classroom management. If each gifted child is instructed at his or her instructional level, how does the classroom teacher organize and plan for a high percentage of academically engaged time for all students? Dooley (1993) responds to this question by arguing that curriculum compacting should be done to assess every child, and that by determining the needs of students, it actually frees up time for enrichment activities. She feels that much of the instructional time in the classroom is wasted because many of the students have already mastered the skills and content being taught. She also feels that by taking advantage of content and process modifications, the teacher is not adding more work to the instructional day but actually enhancing the content being taught.

Whereas the reading curriculum goals are the same for gifted readers as for all readers, many educators (Lewis & Doorlag, 1991) think that the reading program should be differentiated in terms of content covered, methods taught, and pacing of instruction for gifted readers. A wide variety of literature should be used to tap gifted students' abilities and interests.

A greater emphasis on thinking and reasoning skills is recommended for teaching gifted readers. Integrating language arts with the development of critical thinking can also be accomplished by teaching writing as a thinking process (Jampole, Konopak, Readence, & Moser, 1991). Developing writing skills as a logical thinking process enables gifted students to refine, synthesize, and elaborate upon their understanding of a particular topic.

Gifted students learn material faster than other learners and thus require fewer drill exercises. Yet the overriding concern for gifted readers is that they too need instruction in various reading skills and strategies (Dooley, 1993). Providing such differentiated instruction requires diagnosis of students' strengths and weaknesses. It appears that the most essential point for teachers to keep in mind while developing their instructional plan is to consider the individual's learning style. To provide the ultimate lesson for the gifted student, the teacher must consider the learner's abilities, needs, and interests. Once again, this should not be considered an extra burden to the teacher. Instead, it should be considered part of the daily instructional practice that the teacher uses with all students. Further information on reading programs for gifted students can be obtained by contacting the Council for Exceptional Children and the ERIC Clearinghouse on Handicapped and Gifted Children.

☑ Summary

The ability to deal effectively with student differences is crucial to teaching reading. Teachers must address the needs of culturally and linguistically diverse and special-needs students in the regular classroom. The ability of teachers to handle differences effectively translates into instructional practices that provide for each student's self-respect and that lead all students to feel secure in the classroom.

Creating opportunities for success for students with limited proficiency in English requires an understanding of nonstandard dialects, characteristics of foreign languages spoken by the students in the classroom, and students' cultural values. Although speaking a nonstandard dialect or a primary language other than English can present problems in learning to read, a sensitive and knowledgeable teacher minimizes these problems.

Teachers can adapt reading instruction to the needs of speakers whose English proficiency is limited. The language-experience approach, whole-language-based approach, oral reading approach, basal reader approach, dialect approach, and dual-language reading approach can be useful in addressing the needs of culturally and linguistically diverse students.

Special-needs students are increasingly taught in the least restrictive environment, which often means the normal classroom. Mainstreaming and inclusion provide the most appropriate education for each student in the least restrictive setting, considering the educational needs of students rather than their clinical labels. A key ingredient of the legislative mandate for mainstreaming is the development of an individualized education plan (IEP) for each student with disabilities. The regular classroom teacher's total involvement in the team process is the key to successful implementation of the IEP. A special student needs the same individual approach to learning that every student needs.

ADHD is one of the most common mental disorders among children, and on the average, at least one child in every classroom in the United States needs help with this disorder. While at times this disorder can be frustrating and disruptive to the classroom teacher, there are effective environmental and instructional strategies that the teacher can take advantage of to ensure a successful learning climate for the child with attention-deficit hyperactivity disorder.

Gifted students also require instruction matched to their needs. In the past, gifted students were usually not identified and their instructional needs were ignored. Today's schools are recognizing their special needs, and teachers are differentiating their reading instruction to meet these needs.

 ## Your Point of View

Discussion Questions

1. Brainstorm: List ways teachers can help limited-English-speaking students feel more secure in the classroom environment.
2. Inclusion of special needs children into the regular classroom should produce a better learning environment for all students. However, inclusion can also make matters worse instead of making them better. What are possible reasons for this occurrence?

Take a Stand For or Against

1. Of all the factors that influence academic achievement in the school, the dialects or language behaviors of the culturally and linguistically diverse students are the most important.
2. An IEP should be required for all students.

Field-Based Assignments

1. Good teachers are constantly making adaptations to their lessons to meet individual students' learning styles and needs. Good teachers realize that the content must be taught, but they find ways to teach the content and still provide instruction that is at a level at which each child will be successful yet challenged at the same time. While you are working in the classroom, keep a reflectional journal on how the classroom teacher made modifications to work with students of diverse needs. Work with the teacher as he or she develops lesson plans and ask the teacher to think aloud while planning lessons that will be used with diverse learners.

2. When you have the opportunity to observe teachers providing instruction for diverse learners, take time to notice the way they use the classroom environment to provide effective instruction. See if the classroom teacher is taking advantage of collaborative instruction, environmental print, learning centers, and seating arrangements that would be beneficial to students with diverse learning styles and needs. If you do not notice the teacher taking advantage of environmental features while working with diverse learners, develop a plan that would make better use of the classroom environment to provide effective instruction for special-needs students.

Portfolio Entry

Working with diverse learners can be challenging and rewarding at the same time. Create a list that addresses concerns you have about working with diverse learners. Be sure to utilize the information discussed in the text as well as outside references while composing your list. After you have compiled your list of concerns, develop a plan that will enable you to overcome your concerns and provide you with the joyous rewards of working with diverse learners.

Bibliography

Allen, V. (1994). Selecting materials for the reading instruction of ESL children. In K. Spangenburg & R. Pritchard, (Eds.), *Kids come in all languages: Reading instruction for ESL students* (pp. 108–131). Newark, DE: International Reading Association.

American Psychiatric Association. (1994). *Diagnostic and statistical manual of mental disorders* (4th ed.) (DSM-III-R). Washington, DC: Author.

Banks, J. A. (1989). Integrating the curriculum with ethnic content: Approaches and guidelines. In J. A. Banks & C. A. McGee Banks (Eds.), *Multicultural education: Issues and perspectives* (pp. 189–207). Boston: Allyn & Bacon.

Banks, J. A. (1994). Transforming the mainstream curriculum. *Educational Leadership, 51*, 4–8.

Bieger, E. M. (1996). Promoting multicultural education through a literature-based approach. *The Reading Teacher, 49*, 308–312.

Brisbois, J. E. (1995). Connections between first- and second-language learners. *Journal of Reading Behavior, 27*, 565–584.

Delpit, L. D. (1991). A conversation with Lisa Delpit. *Language Arts, 68*, 541–547.

Dooley, C. (1993). The challenge: Meeting the needs of gifted readers. *The Reading Teacher, 46*, 546–551.

Elderedge, J. L., Reutzel, D. R., & Hollingsworth, P. M. (1996). Comparing the effectiveness of two oral reading practices: Round-robin reading and the shared book experiences. *Journal of Literacy Research, 28*, 201–225.

Filipovic, Z. (1994). *Zlata's Diary.* New York: Penguin Books.

First, P., & Curcio, J. (1993). *Individuals with disabilities: Implementing the newest laws.* Newburg Park, CA: Corwin Press, Inc.

Fitzgerald, J. (1993). Literacy and students who are learning English as a second language. *The Reading Teacher, 46*, 638–647.

Flores, B., Cousin, P. T., & Diaz, E. (1991). Transforming myths about learning, language, and culture. *Language Arts, 68*, 369–79.

Fowler, M. (1994). *Attention-deficit/Hyperactivity disorder.* National Information Center for Children and Youth with Disabilities, Washington, DC. (ERIC Accession No. ED 378729)

Frank, A. (1958). *Anne Frank: The Diary of a Young Girl.* New York: Doubleday & Co.

Freeman, D. E., & Freeman, A. W. (1993). Strategies for promoting the primary languages of all students. *The Reading Teacher, 46*, 552–559.

Freeman, Y. S. (1988). Do Spanish methods and materials reflect current understanding of the reading process? *The Reading Teacher, 7*, 654–663.

Freppon, P. A. (1995). Low-income children's literacy interpretations in a skills-based and a whole-language classroom. *Journal of Reading Behavior, 27*, 505–533.

Friend, M., & Cook, L. (1992). The new mainstreaming. *Instructor, 101*, 30–34.

Godina, H. (1996). The canonical debate—implementing multicultural literature and perspectives. *Journal of Adolescent & Adult Literacy, 39*, 544–549.

Gonzales, P. (1994). Second language literacy. *Illinois Reading Council Journal, 22*, 13–16.

Guild, P. (1994). The culture/learning style connection. *Educational Leadership, 51*, 16–21.

Heidger, B. (1991). No need to panic. In K. Goodman, L. Bridges, & Y. Goodman (Eds.), *The Whole Language Catalog.* Santa Rosa, CA: American School Publishers.

Hoffman, J. V., McCarthey, S. J., Abbot, J., Christian, C., Corman, L., Curry, C., Dressman, M., Elliot, B., Matherne, D., & Stahle, D. (1993). So what's new in the new basals? A focus on first grade. *Journal of Reading Behavior, 26*, 47–73.

Jampole, E. S., Konopak, B. C., Readence, J. E., & Moser, B. E. (1991). Using mental imagery to enhance gifted elementary students' creative writing. *Reading Psychology, 12*, 183–198.

Johnson, D. W. (1987). *Educational psychology.* Upper Saddle River, NJ: Prentice Hall.

Lewis, P. (1990). Language experience approach for ESL students. *Adult Learning, 1*, 27.

Lewis, R. B., & Doorlag, D. H. (1991). Teaching special students in the mainstream (3rd ed.). Upper Saddle River, NJ: Merrill/Prentice Hall.

Marland, S. P. (1972). Our gifted and talented children: A priceless natural resource. *Intellect, 101*, 16–19.

Martin, B. (1970). *Brown Bear, Brown Bear, What do you see?* New York: Holt, Rinehart and Winston, Inc.

McCauley, J. K., & McCauley, D. S. (1992). Using choral reading to promote language learning for ESL students. *The Reading Teacher, 45*, 526–535.

Mohr, L. L. (1995). *Teaching diverse learners in inclusive settings: Steps for adapting instruction.* Paper presented at the Council for Exceptional Children Annual Convention, Indianapolis, Indiana.

Morrow, L. M. (1992). The impact of a literature-based program on literacy achievement, use of literature, and attitudes of children from minority backgrounds. *Reading Research Quarterly, 27*, 250–275.

Neuman, S. B., & Koskinen, P. (1992). Captioned television as comprehensible input: Effects of incidental word learning from context for language minority students. *Reading Research Quarterly, 27*, 94–106.

Neuwirth, S. (1994). Attention-deficit hyperactivity disorder: Decade of the brain.

Handicapped and Gifted Children. National Institute of Mental Health, Washington, DC. ERIC Clearinghouse, ED 386011

Norton, D. (1995). *Through the eyes of a child: An introduction to children's literature* (4th ed.). Upper Saddle River, NJ: Merrill/Prentice Hall.

Poplin, C. E. (1992). Making our whole-language bilingual classrooms also liberatory. In J. V. Tinajero & A. F. Ada (Eds.), *The power of two languages: Literacy and biliteracy for Spanish-speaking students* (pp. 58–61). New York: Mcgraw-Hill.

Sampson, M. R., Allen, R. V., & Sampson, M. B. (1991). *Pathways to literacy.* Chicago: Holt, Rinehart, & Winston.

Schifini, A. (1994). Language, literacy, and content instruction: Strategies for teachers. In K. Spangenburg & R. Pritchard, (Eds.), *Kids come in all languages: Reading instruction for ESL students* (pp. 158–179). Newark, DE: International Reading Association.

Shaughnessy, M. F., Siegel, J., & Stanley, N. V. (1994). Gifted and reading. *Handicapped and Gifted Children.* (ERIC Accession No. ED 368145). NM: U.S. Information Analyses.

Stahl, S. A. (1990). Riding the pendulum: A rejoinder to Schickedanz and McGee and Lomax. *Review of Educational Research, 60,* 141–151.

Weber, R. M. (1991). Linguistic diversity and reading in American society. In R. Barr, M. L. Kamil, P. Mosenthal, & P. D. Pearson (Eds.), *Handbook of reading research (Vol. II)* (pp. 97–119). New York: Longman.

Williams, J. D., & Snipper, C. G. (1991). Literacy and Bilingualism. White Plains, NY: Longman.

Wood, J. (1993). *Mainstreaming* (2nd ed.). Upper Saddle River, NJ: Merrill/Prentice Hall.

Glossary

academic engaged time (time on task) classroom time in which students are actually attending to the valued learning.

academic learning time (ALT) classroom time in which students are actually attending to the work at hand with a high success rate (80% or above).

affixes prefixes, suffixes, and inflectional endings.

analytic phonics a phonic approach using letter-sound relationships by referring to words already known to identify a new phonic element.

assessment procedures used by teachers to identify students' literacy strengths and weaknesses in planning and executing instruction to meet the students' needs.

auditory discrimination the ability to recognize the differences in speech sounds within words.

automaticity the ability to decode words with minimal effort.

balanced literacy program the use of a variety of teaching approaches, strategies, and materials to teach students what they need to know.

basal reader "a collection of student texts and workbooks, teacher's manuals, and supplemental materials for developing reading and sometimes writing instruction used chiefly in the elementary and middle school grades" (Harris & Hodges, 1995).

big books books with large pictures and print that children in group settings can easily see. The stories often use predictable, repetitive language and pictures.

classics extraordinary books that last beyond their authors' lives and continue to attract readers.

computer-assisted instruction (CAI) instruction that interacts with a microcomputer.

content reading ability the degree to which a student can adequately comprehend and retain content or expository information.

contextual analysis a word-identification strategy that helps students figure out the meanings of words by how they are used in the context of sentences or passages.

contextualized language use keeping language in context, such as reading and writing full texts rather than excerpts.

contextual knowledge word knowledge derived from context.

core literature books that should be taught in the classroom through close reading and intensive consideration. These books can serve as important stimuli for writing and discussion.

culturally and linguistically diverse learners students whose culture as well as language or dialect differ from those of the school.

decontextualized language use the basis for literacy, requiring developing language awareness.

definitional knowledge word knowledge based upon a definition from a dictionary or glossary.

dialects the ways people speak in different parts of the country or in specific cultures.

directed reading activity (DRA) an organized, sequenced strategy for teaching a reading selection. Typical steps include motivation, vocabulary, silent reading, comprehension checking, purposeful oral reading, skill development, and enrichment activities.

directed reading-thinking activity (DR-TA) an organized, sequenced strategy for teaching a reading selection that focuses on reading as a thinking process. Three overall steps include readiness and prediction, active reading, and reaction (Stauffer, 1975).

direct/explicit instruction systematic teaching in which the teacher models and demonstrates learning and gradually turns the responsibility for learning over to the student. This teaching method emphasizes students' understanding of the "when" and "why" of utilizing various capabilities and strategies.

emergent literacy children's reading and writing behaviors that occur before and develop into conventional literacy.

environmental print print in the environment, such as store names, menus, and signs, that has meaning to children.

experiential and conceptual backgrounds readers' experiences that are both concrete and abstract (knowledge), as well as their reasoning abilities in using this knowledge. This is also known as background knowledge.

expository text the text structure found in content books, including (1) description, (2) collection, (3) causation, (4) problem-solution, and (5) comparison.

extended literature works that teachers may assign to individuals or small groups as homework or supplemental class work.

functions of written language to inform, entertain, and direct.

grapheme-phoneme relationships the relationships between written letters and letter combinations and the sounds they represent.

homonyms words that sound alike but are spelled differently.

inferential questions questions that combine background knowledge and text information to make predictions about story content.

interactive instruction imparting new information to students through meaningful teacher-student interactions and guiding student learning.

interactive theory of reading the theory that readers use information from the text, their experiential and conceptual backgrounds, and the context in which reading occurs to arrive at meaning.

language-experience approach (LEA) the approach for teaching reading that is built on children's experiences. Children dictate their experiences and the teacher writes them down or the children write their own stories as the basis for instruction.

literacy the ability to read and write proficiently.

literal questions questions based on information explicitly stated in the text.

literature-based reading program a program that emphasizes the ability to read all types of literature with understanding, appreciation, and enjoyment.

meaning vocabulary words whose meanings and concepts are represented by words already understood.

mediated instruction intervention or guidance that another person (such as a peer, parent, or teacher) provides in the teaching-learning process.

metacognition awareness and control of one's cognitive functioning while reading.

modeling demonstration of strategies and behaviors to enhance their conceptualization.

opportunity to learn allotment of time and exposure to instruction.

oral language the language abilities of speaking and listening.

paired reading one student reads aloud as another follows along in the text.

phonemic awareness understanding that spoken words are represented by units of sounds or can be separated into speech sounds.

phonics the teaching of reading in a manner that stresses symbol-sound relationships.

point of view the viewpoint that authors choose when they tell a story, including the details they describe and the judgements they make.

polysemous words words having different meanings (such as *air* in *air* ball and "to *air* one's views").

predictable books books in which students can grasp easily what the author is going to say next. Such books use much repetition of content, language, and illustrations.

readability the approximate difficulty level of written material.

readers' theater a performance of literature (e.g., a story, poetry, a play, or a picture book) that is read aloud in an interpretative manner.

reading the active process of constructing meaning from written text in relation to the experiences and knowledge of the reader.

reading log a short-term writing activity that supports student discussion or reflection on ideas found in literature that they have read.

recreational reading groups students grouped on the basis of their interests to discuss the same book, books by the same author, or books with similar characteristics.

response journals written letters or dialogues that students share with each other and/or their teacher on a regular basis.

scaffolds "forms of support provided by the teacher (or another student) to help students bridge the gap between current abilities and the intended goal (Rosenshine & Meister, 1992).

schema the background knowledge structure for an idea, object, or word meaning.

schemata the meaningful organization of knowledge based on one's experiences. We have schemata for places, events, and roles.

schema theory of reading the theory that reading involves many different levels of analysis at the same time but at different levels.

semantic clues a contextual-analysis strategy using the meanings of known words in a sentence or passage to identify an unknown word.

semantics the meaning features of language.

shared reading students see the text as it is read aloud to them—usually from big books—and are invited to read aloud.

sight vocabulary words that a reader knows and comprehends instantly.

skill learning that is specific in nature and amenable to behavioral objectives.

slots attributes of a schema that must be recognized for a reader to activate that schema.

SQ3R a systematized study procedure for reading content chapters. *SQ3R* stands for "survey, question, read, recite, and review."

sustained silent reading (SSR) a scheduled period of silent reading in the classroom. During this time, both teacher and students may read a book or any form of print without interruption.

story schema readers' mental representation of story parts and their relationships. Story schema is also referred to as story grammar and story structure.

strategic learning learning that is less specific than skill learning and represents higher-level cognitive thinking that is used in interacting with text information.

structural analysis a word-identification strategy that focuses on visual or structural patterns and meanings that change as a result of adding inflectional endings, prefixes, and suffixes and combining root words.

study skills a general term for those techniques and strategies that help a person read or listen for specific purposes with the intent to remember; commonly, following directions, locating, selecting, organizing, and retaining information, interpreting typographic and graphic aids, and reading flexibility.

style an author's choice and arrangement of words to create plot, characterizations, and setting together in a meaningful whole.

syllabication the division of a word into its basic units of pronunciation.

syntactic clues a contextual-analysis strategy using the knowledge of word order in a language to identify an unknown word.

syntax the word order or grammar of a language.

synthetic phonics a phonic approach beginning with instruction on individual sounds.

thematic units integrating content (e.g., of science, math, and social studies) and using literacy to facilitate children's learning of important concepts and ideas.

theme the central idea that ties the plot, characterizations, and setting together in a meaningful whole.

visual discrimination the ability to note visual similarities and differences, particularly in letters and words (e.g., the difference between *b* and *g* and the difference between *bat* and *bit*).

whole language a style of reading instruction based on the idea that students learn best when literacy is naturally connected to their oral language.

whole-word approach a word-identification strategy that focuses on learning words as wholes rather than by any form of analysis.

word identification the process of arriving at the pronunciation of a word, given the printed letter representations (also known as decoding).

Index